'A Mersshy Contree Called Holdernesse'

Excavations on the Route of a National Grid Pipeline in Holderness, East Yorkshire

Rural Life in the Claylands to the East of the Yorkshire Wolds, from the Mesolithic to the Iron Age and Roman Periods, and beyond

Edited by

Gavin Glover

Paul Flintoft

Richard Moore

with contributions by:

Hugo Anderson-Whymark (flint), Kevin Leahy (metal, glass, worked bone),
Terry Manby (earlier prehistoric pottery), Chris Cumberpatch (hand-made pottery),
Rob Ixer (petrography), Derek Pitman and Roger Doonan (suface residues: ceramics and slag),
Ruth Leary (Roman pottery), Felicity Wild (samian ware), Kay Hartley (mortaria),
Jane Young with Peter Didsbury (post-Roman pottery), Ruth Shaffrey (worked stone),
Lisa Wastling (fired clay), Jennifer Jones (surface residues: fired clay),
Katie Keefe and Malin Holst (human bone), Jennifer Wood (animal bone),
Don O'Meara (plant macrofossils), Tudur Burke Davies (pollen) and Matt Law (molluscs)

Illustrations by:

Jacqueline Churchill, Dave Watt and Susan Freebrey

ARCHAEOPRESS ARCHAEOLOGY

ARCHAEOPRESS PUBLISHING LTD
Gordon House
276 Banbury Road
Oxford OX2 7ED

www.archaeopress.com

ISBN 978 1 78491 313 7
ISBN 978 1 78491 314 4 (e-Pdf)

Cover: Excavation of ring gullies at Burton Constable (© Adam Stanford, www.aerial-cam.co.uk)

Printed in England by Oxuniprint, Oxford
This book is available direct from Archaeopress or from our website www.archaeopress.com

Contents

iv

List of Figures

List of Tables

Acknowledgements

The work described in this volume was commissioned by Murphy Pipelines on behalf of National Grid. We would especially like to thank Peter Johnson, the Project Manager for National Grid, Maurice Corridan of Murphy Pipelines, and all of the engineering staff and construction crews for their help and cooperation. The archaeological advisers for National Grid, Derek Cater and Jim Bonnor of Groundwork Archaeology, were unfailingly willing to offer their help and advice. Dave Evans of Humber Archaeology Partnership has been supportive throughout and we are grateful for his valuable advice. Thanks also to Victoria Brown for supplying information from the Humber Sites and Monuments Record and Andy Hammon, the regional science advisor for English Heritage.

The professional co-operation of commercial competitors is a welcome aspect of archaeology and for sharing information about their ongoing projects we should like to thank: Steven Rowland of Oxford Archaeology North, Jane Richardson of Archaeological Services WYAS, Ken Steedman of Humber Field Archaeology, Mark Allen of Allen Archaeology and Kirsten Holland of WYG Environment Planning Transport. Conversations with Robert Van der Noort and Peter Halkon, among others, were helpful and thought-provoking. We should also like to thank Thomas Whitbread, of North Pennines Archaeology and Jacqui Huntley of English Heritage for their advice on the environmental analysis, and David Knight of Trent and Peak Archaeology, for his views on the decorated hand-made pottery.

For Network Archaeology, the executive manager was Claire Lingard. Fieldwork was managed by Tom Wilson and directed by Gerry Martin in 2007, and by Paul Flintoft in 2008. The excavation team comprised: Aaron Chapman, Andy Lane, Andy Pascoe, Bryan Murray, Dan Ferguson, Fred Garrett, George Luke, Gwynfor Maurice, Jane Roberts, Jeff Lowrey, Mariusz Gorniak, Natasha Gaddas, Patrick Daniel, Rob Barnett, Sarah Mounce, Afon Bognor, Alan Wright, Alex Beeby, Bartoz Cicy, Ben Curtis, Bob Hamilton, Brian Pugh, Caoimhin O'Coileain, Cath Smyth, Damian Podlinski, David Marcus, Dennis Morgan, Derek Moscrop, Diana Quinn, Fay Slater, Fraser Stewart, Geoff Marshall, Geoff Snowdon, George Gandham, Hayley Saul, Imogen Smythson, Jason Hall, Jay Wood, Jeffery Nichols, Joe Warham, John Foulkes, John Moreno, John Ward, Johnny Onraet, Jonathan Potter, Katia Wisniewska, Kirsty Bone, Kirsty Tuthill, Krzysztof Gawrys, Lawrence Coalter, Les Bognor, Lindsay Powell, Lucy Loughman, Marcus Headifen, Mareck Lemiesz, Maria Salis, Mark Dennett, Mark Rafferty, Mathilde Jourdan, Mats Nelson, Matt Gault, Matthew Weightman, Mick Coates, Mike Tunnicliffe, Monika Kaminska, Nathan Thomas, Neville Steed, Pat Kent, Peter Cicy, Richard Falon, Richard Fenlan, Sara Gramazio, Sean Jackson, Sean Johnson, Slawomir Konieczka, Steve Porter, Stuart Randall, Yvonne Heath, Zoe Cameron and Zoe Hamilton. We also wish to thank Dave Bunn of Pre-Construct Geophysics for magnetometer and magnetic susceptibility surveys, Mike McKenzie, Guy Handley and Chris Baron for surveying and Adam Stanford of Aerial-Cam for mast-elevated aerial photography.

Janey Brant and Mike Wood coordinated finds processing and cataloguing, with the help of Caroline Kemp, Gordon Shaw and Stuart Shaw. Natasha Gaddas, Mariusz Gorniak and Aaron Chapman assisted with post-excavation work. Logistical and administrative support was provided by Kealey Manvell, Lisa Bea and Kelly Greenhough. Report illustrations are by Jacqueline Churchill, Dave Watt and Susan Freebrey. Claire Lingard and Patrick Daniel reviewed the draft text and provided perceptive and valuable comments.

In addition to the authors of the specialist analyses in Sections 4 and 5, assessments were carried out by: James Rackham; Alan Vince and Kate Steane; Trish Shaw; John Carrott, Helen Ranner and Alexandra Schmidl; Rod Mackenzie; Paul Courtney; Rachel Tyson; Susie White; Janey Brant; and Anwen Caffell.

Post-excavation work was carried out by the authors. Since the preparation of the draft text, Gavin Glover has joined Allen Archaeology as Project Manager and Paul Flintoft is currently a Project Officer with Trent and Peak Archaeology. Dick Moore co-ordinated the post-excavation work and, as compiler and editor, bears responsibility for any errors or omissions that remain in this volume.

Summary

Twenty archaeological sites, excavated on the route of a pipeline across Holderness, East Yorkshire, included an early Mesolithic flint-working area near Sproatley. *In situ* deposits of this age are nationally rare, and the findings are a significant addition to our understanding of the post-glacial development of the region. Possible Bronze Age round barrows and an Iron Age square barrow were also identified at this site. Elsewhere on the route, diagnostic Mesolithic, Neolithic and Bronze Age flints, as well as Bronze Age pottery, provide evidence of human activity during these periods.

Iron Age remains were found at all of the excavations, fourteen of which had ring gullies, interpreted as evidence for roundhouse structures. The frequency with which these settlements occurred is an indication of population density of this region in the later Iron Age and the large assemblage of hand-made pottery recovered provides a rich resource for future study. Activity at several of these sites persisted at least into the second or early third centuries AD, while the largest excavation site, at Burton Constable, was largely abandoned but then re-occupied in the later third century AD.

The pottery from the ring gullies was all in native hand-made wares, although there were quantities of later wares in other features on many of these sites. Roundhouses therefore seem to have fallen out of use by the later first century AD, when the earliest wheel-thrown wares appear. This would imply that the cultural changes associated with the transition from Iron Age to the Roman period occurred, in this region, at an early date.

Pottery and other artefacts dating from the late first or early second century AD from a site at Scorborough Hill, near Weeton, is of particular interest, as the nature of these finds strongly suggests that the site had an association with the Roman military.

Excavations at a cropmark complex, identified with the manorial site of Lund Garth, near Preston village, confirmed the presence of medieval settlement remains as well as activity in the Anglo-Scandinavian period. Enclosures dated to the early medieval period were also excavated close to the village of Winestead.

Section 1: Introduction

The Easington to Ganstead pipeline was constructed, in the summer of 2008, to supply natural gas from undersea pipelines coming ashore at Easington Terminal on the east coast of England (NGR: 540020 419590) to the National Transmission System, operated by National Grid. The 32km pipeline connects the terminal to a gas valve compound to the north of Ganstead, beyond the north-eastern suburbs of Kingston upon Hull (NGR: 516310 436840). The route lies wholly within the East Riding of Yorkshire (Fig.

1). Construction of the pipeline formed one element of a project to build a trans-Pennine pipeline, spanning almost the whole width of the country, to a compressor station near the village of Nether Kellet, 4.5km inland from the west coast at Carnforth (NGR: 351870 467410). Accounts of the archaeology of the western parts of this route have been published (Casswell and Daniel 2010, Gregory *et al.* 2013), and publication of the remaining section is in preparation (Daniel *et al.*, forthcoming).

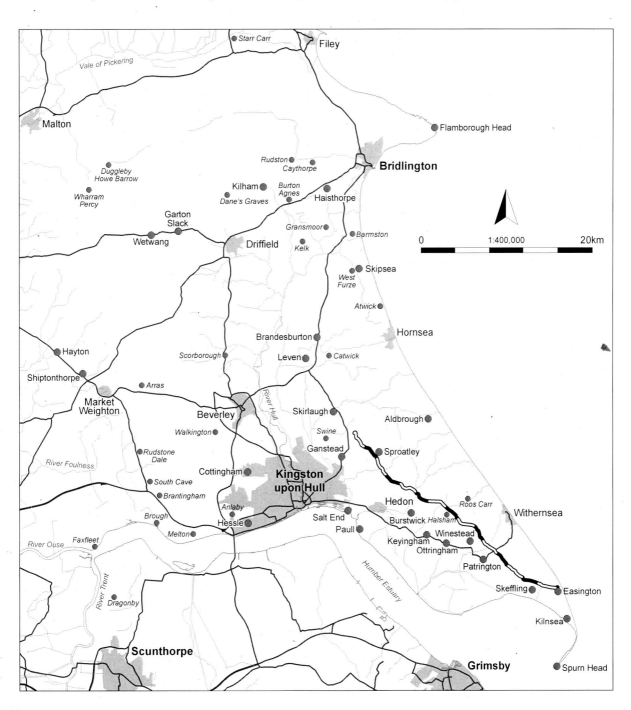

FIG. 1: THE ROUTE OF THE EASINGTON TO GANSTEAD PIPELINE, IN RELATION TO OTHER SITES MENTIONED IN THE TEXT

The impact on the archaeology of the area was considered by National Grid throughout the design and construction of the pipeline. At an early stage, archaeological information from readily available sources was used in the selection of a broad corridor between the two end-points of the pipeline that was considered to be environmentally and archaeologically least damaging. A full archaeological desk-based assessment (DBA) of the proposed corridor was then carried out (Holgate and Ralph 2006). The results of the DBA were incorporated into the cultural heritage section of an environmental impact assessment and were taken into account in the detailed planning of the final route.

Archaeological field surveys were carried out while the detailed route was being finalised: fieldwalking in all of the arable fields along the route and a reconnaissance survey noting visible indications of archaeological remains (Wilson 2006, 2007; Flintoft 2008). Datable finds were mainly post-medieval and modern, but included small but significant amounts of Iron Age, Roman and medieval material. Geophysical surveys of the whole pipeline route were also undertaken: fluxgate gradiometry of contiguous 30m-square grids along the proposed pipe centreline, and paired magnetic susceptibility readings taken at 20m intervals (Bunn 2007, 2008). These highlighted four areas of extensive magnetic anomalies, thought to indicate former settlement areas, as well as ten other areas of potential archaeological significance.

Collated evidence from these earlier stages of work was used to inform decisions on further mitigation, which included minor modification to the pipeline route and targeted evaluation trenching. Evaluation trenching was carried out in thirty-nine of the fields crossed by the pipeline route: a total of 187 trenches, generally 30m long and 2m wide. Where access to the land was available, this was carried out in the spring and summer of 2007, but elsewhere trenching was not possible until early 2008, immediately prior to construction (Savage 2011). Twelve of the evaluation areas proved to be of sufficient archaeological significance to justify further investigation. In each case, a larger area was opened, generally covering the whole of the width that would be affected by construction work and encompassing the extent of the exposed archaeological features along the length of the pipeline. A further eight areas with significant remains were identified as a result of continuous monitoring of ground-disturbing construction work, and open-area excavation was also carried out at these sites.

Section 1 of this volume provides a brief introduction to the pipeline and its physical, environmental and archaeological setting in southern Holderness. Section 2 introduces and describes the findings from each one, concentrating on the features that help to elucidate the form, function and chronological development of the site.

Specialist analyses of the artefacts and of the environmental evidence recovered in the course of the fieldwork are provided in Sections 3 and 4. To keep the volume to a manageable size, the specialist reports have been edited, to varying degrees: the guiding principle has been to include the specialist discussions and conclusions along with sufficient weight of supporting data to allow judgements about the basis of those conclusions. Excisions include the full primary data sets and details of findings which were negative or of little significance. These are included in the site archive, deposited with East Riding of Yorkshire Museums Service (Accession no. ERYMS 2006/48).

The broad themes that have emerged from analysis of the results are discussed in Section 5, while Section 6 briefly summarises the overall conclusions.

The landscape of Holderness

Holderness is flat or gently rolling, and rarely exceeds 20m above Ordnance Datum (OD). The region is bounded on two sides by saltwater: the rapidly eroding North Sea coast forming its eastern boundary and a wide meander of the Humber estuary defining its southern limit, with the thin crooked finger of Spurn Point separating the two. The floodplain of the Hull valley marks the western limit of Holderness, although the low, flat countryside thereabouts provides little indication of where one starts and the other begins. The northern edge of the Holderness is more clearly discernible, marked as it is by the chalk uplands of the Yorkshire Wolds.

The region is overwhelmingly rural and agricultural, the landscape mostly made up of large fields bounded by hedgerows and deep, steep-sided drainage ditches. Tree cover is sparse, so that the land feels open and exposed. Settlement is mostly confined to small dispersed villages and scattered farms, linked by minor roads. The few large modern developments are largely limited to windfarms and gas distribution works.

Geology

The region is underlain by Upper Cretaceous chalk of the Flamborough Chalk formation. The chalk rises to the west and north to form the sweeping ridge of the Yorkshire Wolds, which reach elevations of around 200m OD. The Wolds separate the Holderness plain from the Vale of Pickering to the north and the Vale of York to the west (Fig. 2). Beneath the base of the east-facing dip slope of the Wolds, the top of the chalk drops abruptly, forming a buried cliff along a line from the Humber at Hessle and passing to the west of Cottingham, Beverley and Driffield (Kent *et al.* 1980, 122). This cliff marks the

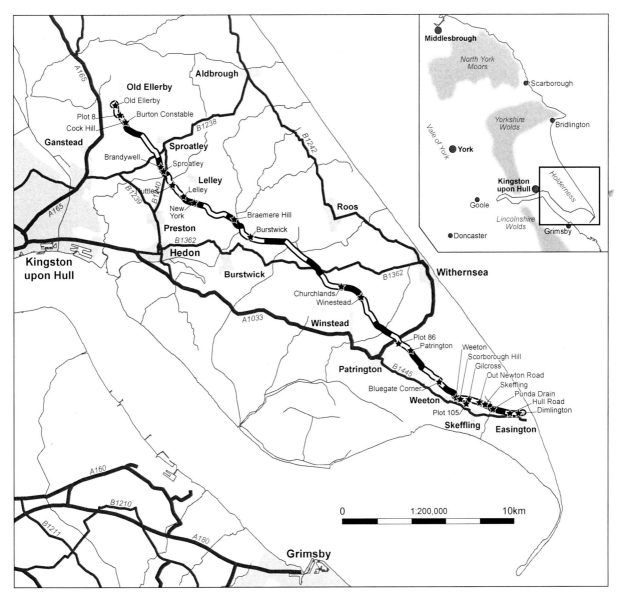

FIG. 2: THE PIPELINE ROUTE IN ITS SOUTH HOLDERNESS SETTING

position of the coastline at a time before the Devensian ice age, around 120,000 years ago, when the greater part of Holderness lay beneath the North Sea.

The Devensian glaciation saw ice sheets extend from Scotland and North Wales to completely cover the region, reaching their maximum extent around 18,500 years ago, the period of the Dimlington Stadial. As the ice retreated, around 13,000 years ago, a dramatically altered landscape was left, the ice and subsequent meltwaters having deposited an average of 20 to 30m of sediment, burying the pre-glacial cliff line and covering the chalk with tills or boulder clays, interspersed with localised deposits of sands and gravels.

In south-east Holderness, the sands and gravels can reach a thickness of up to 30m (Ellis 1995, 9) and various deposits have been commercially quarried, especially

the Kelsey Hill Gravels, near Keyingham and Paull, and Hornsea Gravels occurring further north, notably around Brandseburton, Leven and Sproatley (Catt 2007, 191). Alluvial lake deposits form a further widespread element of the drift geology, occurring in numerous extinct meres that formed in undulations in the post-glacial surface of the till. These silty deposits are often interleaved with layers of peat. The wide tract of flat land along the north shore of the Humber, much of it reclaimed marshland, is covered by varying thicknesses of estuarine alluvium.

Soils overlying areas of till are generally clay-rich, and suffer, in the absence of artificial drainage, at least seasonal waterlogging (SSEW 1983). Peaty soils are present in small pockets along valley floors, while coarse loamy soils overlying the patches glacial sands and gravels in valley bottoms are affected by ground-water but are freer draining than the surrounding clay-rich

3

areas. More than eighty per cent of the agricultural land in Holderness is arable, with grassland accounting for a further twelve per cent (Middleton 1995, 25), mostly in more poorly drained areas. Woodland covers a very small part of the total area. Stretches of open water are limited to Hornsea Mere and a small number of disused gravel pits, particularly around Brandesburton, Burstwick and Keyingham.

The post-glacial landscape

Holderness is today a coastal region, but has not always been so; the retreating Devensian ice sheets exposed a very different landscape. Sufficient water remained locked in the diminishing ice to reduce sea level to as much as 100m below modern levels leaving the bed of the southern North Sea exposed as dry land. Archaeological evidence for this was first explored by Clement Reid in his seminal 1913 publication *Submerged Forests*. Bone from terrestrial animals and occasional man-made artefacts were recovered from time to time during dredging, fishing or mineral prospection; the most celebrated was a bone 'harpoon' or notched point brought to the surface by the trawler *Colinda* in 1931. But in recent years, the realisation that high-quality remote sensing data, collected in the course of petroleum exploration, offered an opportunity to explore the landscape of this huge area has ignited great interest. Analysis of this data, coupled with systematic logging of finds from trawlers and dredgers, is revealing a complex and archaeologically diverse landscape (Gaffney *et al.* 2007).

No longer seen as merely a low-lying land-bridge, connecting Britain to the Continent, a picture is emerging of a wide plain, dubbed Doggerland after the Dogger Bank fishing grounds, by Bryony Coles. This would have encompassed the whole of the North Sea basin south of a line from Shetland to the Jutland peninsula, supporting a high level of exploitation and habitation (Coles 1998, 59). The area now constituting Holderness would have formed the foothills of highlands fringing the western edge of this plain. The Humber, at this time, would have been a fast-flowing river, in a deeper valley, part of a river system draining a prominent ridge extending eastwards from Flamborough Head, and the region extending to the north-east from the present-day area of the Wash (Gaffney *et al.* 2009, 98). The streams flowing southwards into the Humber would have been energetic enough to rapidly erode the glacial till, creating a valley relief far more pronounced than that today.

As sea levels rose, the North Sea gradually extended southwards, reaching the latitude of southern Holderness some time after 10,000 BC (Jelgersma 1979). The flow of the Humber and its tributaries gradually slowed, allowing alluvial silts to accumulate in valleys which had hitherto been actively eroding. This slowing of the natural drainage led to the formation of numerous meres in the valley bottoms and between the irregular low hills and ridges of the till landscape (Dinnin 1995, 9-16).

The broad pattern of the post-glacial landscape is preserved in the natural drainage of Southern Holderness with watercourses flowing towards the south and west, discharging into the Humber, directly or by way of the River Hull, rather than to the sea. The fine detail of the natural hydrology is lost within the extensive system of agricultural drainage but the original overall pattern is still traceable in the courses of the Burstwick, Keyingham, Patrington and Winestead Drains, each draining a wide basin of very low-lying land. The vulnerability of these shallow valleys to flooding was starkly demonstrated in the summer of 2007, when the first season of the archaeological excavation described in this volume had to be suspended for several weeks while flood waters receded.

Coastal erosion and land reclamation

The North Sea coastline of Holderness is one of the most rapidly eroding in Europe with up to 150m of land lost since the production of the first edition Ordnance Survey maps in the 1850s (Brigham, Buglass and George 2008, 18). Estimates and measurement of the rate of erosion have a long history (summarised in Quinn *et al.* 2009, 170) and show that there is considerable variability over small distances: an average of 2.3m of land lost per year at Easington Dunes compared with 0.91m south of nearby Seaside Road, for instance (ERY 2004). Extrapolation back in time is inherently uncertain as erosion is episodic, influenced by factors such as changing sea level and currents, storms and tidal surges, as well as the construction of coastal defences and changes in land use. Estimates in the archaeological literature include: 10km of land lost eastwards of Easington since the Neolithic period (Evans and Steedman 2001, 69), and as much as 4km (Sheppard 1912, 43), or up to 2km, lost since the Roman period (Brigham, Buglass and George 2008, 23). Thirty or more villages between Bridlington and the Humber have been lost since the medieval period (*ibid.* 19), including Dimlington, Tumarr and Northorp, close to the easten end of the pipeline. Most, if not all of these settlements, were victims of coastal erosion, rather than the factors that led to desertion of many inland villages during the Middle Ages.

A very different picture emerges along the banks of the Humber, where the modern Holderness shoreline is largely a result of land reclamation. Piecemeal embankment in the tenth to twelfth centuries eventually resulted in banked areas linking up to create a wide strip of agricultural land along the foreshore. Although much was temporarily lost in the thirteenth to fifteenth centuries to storms and erosion (Sheppard 1966, 3-6), the overall effect can be seen, for instance, at Ottringham, once a coastal village but now over 6km inland. The shoreline prior to reclamation would have followed a course not far south of the present day A1033 and B1445 roads between Hedon and Skeffling. The use of waterways through the marshes continued to be more efficient, in many cases, than overland transport and the inclusion of towpaths in dyke-making agreements shows that this was often a major consideration when planning the construction of new channels.

The draining of meres and wetlands in the valley bottoms has also dramatically altered the character of the region. Medieval documents show that fisheries and rights of turbary and wild-fowling were valuable assets and there was considerable litigation over common rights of summer pasturage in marshland areas. Land in valley bottoms was often rated more highly than the higher and drier arable lands, as were villages holding a high proportion of carrland. Meres continued to be fished in twelfth- and thirteenth-century Holderness and historical references and place name evidence show at least seventy meres still survived in the early medieval period (Dinnin 1995, 27, citing Sheppard 1956). Most, however, had been drained for pasture by the end of the medieval period and by the early eighteenth century Hornsea, Skipsea and Pidsea Meres were the only major stretches of open water surviving. Today, only Hornsea Mere is left.

Archaeological and historical background

Interest in the archaeology, ancient history and antiquities of Holderness can be traced back at least as far as the later sixteenth century, with William Camden's efforts 'to restore antiquity to Britaine, and Britaine to its antiquity'. He believed that the Holderness settlements of Patrington and Kilnsea could be identified with Roman settlements of Praetorium and Occellum Promontorium mentioned in Ptolemy's *Geographia* (Camden 1701, 739-742). This interest in finding the locations of places mentioned in Classical texts is echoed by the works of a number of writers, whose accounts and descriptions of Holderness span the eighteenth and nineteenth centuries (Defoe 1727, Oliver 1829, Poulsen 1841 and Knox 1855, for example). These early accounts are discursive and broad ranging, but have value today for details of antiquities uncovered during ploughing, construction work or digging of drains.

George Oliver's history of Beverley provided an account of the excavations of square barrows around the Wolds hamlet of Arras by Rev. E. W. Stillingfleet, in 1815-1817, the cemetery that subsequently became the type site for Iron Age barrow cemeteries in East Yorkshire. While isolated examples of Iron Age square barrows have been identified and investigated in other parts of the country, large cemeteries are found, in Britain, only in and around the Yorkshire Wolds.

Albert Denison Conyngham, later Lord Londesborough and the founding president of the British Archaeological Association, provided considerable impetus to the study of the archaeology of the region in the 1840s (Mortimer 1905, 271-297). This tradition was continued by J. R. Mortimer, who carried out numerous excavations from the 1860s until the early years of the twentieth century, the most celebrated perhaps being Duggleby Howe barrow (Kinnes *et al.* 1983). Mortimer and his rival, Canon Greenwell, and their contemporaries, investigated numerous barrows in the Wolds and on the western fringes of Holderness near Beverley and Driffield, including the Iron Age square barrow cemeteries at Danes Graves and Scorborough (north-west of Beverley, not to be confused with Scorborough Hill of this report). An enduring attraction was the occasional occurance of spectacular chariot burials within square barrow cemeteries, the body accompanied by a rich artefactual assemblage as well as a chariot or cart.

The discovery and recognition of the significance of the Roos Carr figures (Poulson 1841, 99-101) dates from the first half of the nineteenth century. These figurines, carved in yew wood with quartzite eyes, and set within a serpent-headed boat, were remarkably well preserved in waterlogged sediments. Recent radiocarbon determination has provided a date of 770 to 406 cal BC (Osgood 1998).

In the latter part of the nineteenth century, Thomas Boynton, a drainage engineer working in the Skipsea area, excavated a number of wetland sites, with guidance from Reginald Smith of the British Museum. These were originally interpreted as prehistoric lake dwellings (Smith 1911) but small-scale rescue excavations in advance of gravel extraction, by the Continuing Education Department at Leeds University in the 1950s, prompted their re-evaluation (Copley 1953); they are now considered to include a late Neolithic or early Bronze Age trackway at West Furze, a Bronze Age settlement at Barmston, an Iron Age settlement at Gransmoor and Iron Age enclosures at Kelk (Fletcher and Van de Noort 2007).

In southern Holderness, excavations undertaken by H. B. Hewetson in the 1890s investigated the site of a Bronze Age barrow at Easington. This site was re-excavated by Rod Mackey in the 1960s and Rod Mackey and Kate Dennett in 1996-97 because of the imminent threat of coastal erosion (Mackey 1998; Evans and Steedman 2001, 69). Nineteenth-century drainage works in Holderness also produced the most extensive range of Bronze Age artefacts from Yorkshire (Manby 1980, 358-62), the quantity and quality allowing the development of chronologies based on metalwork typologies. Two Bronze Age hoards are recorded from close to the pipeline route, at Sproatley and Skirlaugh (Manby *et al.* 2003, 80).

Chance finds of artefacts by amateur collectors and enthusiasts continued to be the main contributions to archaeological knowledge into the early twentieth century. The Mesolithic notched bone points found at Skipsea Withow, near Hornsea caused considerable academic and popular excitement during the 1920s and 30s and set in motion a prolonged and rather acrimonious debate, entertainingly summarised by Sitch and Jacobi (1999), between archaeologist Leslie Armstrong, who believed them to be genuine, and Thomas Sheppard, director of Hull Museums, who considered them fakes.

Through much of the twentieth century, archaeological interest in East Yorkshire remained firmly focused on the Wolds. The close, though not exact, parallels between the square barrow cemeteries in East Yorkshire and those in the Seine valley and Champagne regions of northern France have been central to debate on the mechanisms of cultural transmission in Iron Age Europe (Stead 1981). The chariot or cart burials of East Yorkshire recall the more numerous examples from the French cemeteries: 140 or more at Somme-Bionne (Cunliffe 2005, 214-215). Though different in detail, the similarities are sufficient to imply cultural affinities between the two regions.

Aerial photography added greatly to the number of square barrow cemeteries recorded in the East Riding and well over three hundred are now known (Stoetz 1997, 34). The majority are small, with no more than ten barrows, but there are over twenty examples that have fifty or more, including Arras, Burton Fleming, Wetwang and Garton Slack (Dent 1983), Danes Graves, Rudston and Scorborough (Stead 1986, 1991). These cemeteries are most densely concentrated on the eastern slope of the Wolds, but there are also clusters around Malton, in the Vale of Pickering, and examples to the west of the Wolds, as at Mirebrook Lane, South Cave (Brigham, Buglass and Steedman 2008, 18). In northern Holderness, a small group of square-barrow cemeteries cluster around the area to the south of Bridlington.

The predominantly clay soils of southern Holderness are less conducive to cropmark formation, but some isolated square barrows have been identified from aerial photographs, taken in years when conditions are particularly good (Brigham, Buglass and Steedman 2008). Chariot burials are represented in Holderness only by one example, at Hornsea, described by William Morfitt in 1904 as including spearheads of iron and bronze, iron wheels and horse trappings; it is not, however, well documented. There are continuing difficultes in dating Iron Age sites, but burial in square barrows seems to have first been used in the late fifth or early fourth century BC and to have ceased by the first century BC (Cunliffe 2005, 546-551).

The accumulation of information on the ways of death of the Iron Age population prompted interest and speculation about their less visible ways of life. Excavations in advance of gravel extraction at Wetwang and Garton Slack in the late 1970s revealed both the extent of the cemetery and also the remains of an adjoining settlement of up to eighty roundhouses and other structures (Dent 1983). Subsequently, the Yorkshire Settlements Project (Rigby 2004) undertaken by the British Museum, carried out research excavations at a dozen settlement sites identified by aerial photography. The primary aim of this study was to provide material for refining the dating of the Iron Age, and geophysical surveys were used in order to target large pits likely to be rich in artefacts. Most of the selected sites were on the lower slopes of the northern Wolds. It is still, however, probably true to say that the relationship between the cemeteries and their associated settlements or the wider landscape 'has yet to be seriously addressed' (Mackey 2003).

The last couple of decades of the twentieth century saw archaeological input into development projects becoming routine, encouraged by the strengthening of planning guidance and regulations on environmental impact assessment, and by the desire of large developers to follow best practice. The development of the gas supply industry, together with other infrastructure projects such as the construction of the A165 Leven to Brandesburton bypass (Steedman 1993), have increasingly served to highlight the archaeology of the Holderness claylands. Aside from the pipeline that forms the subject of this volume, other recent developments within the gas and petrochemical industry that have prompted excavations include: BP Teesside to Salt End ethylene pipeline; Salt End to Aldbrough electricity cable and Sproatley to Aldbrough gas pipeline (Savage 2014), Langeled natural gas terminal at Easington (Richardson 2011), Aldbrough gas storage facility (Bradley and Steedman 2014), Ganstead to Asselby gas pipeline (Daniel et al., forthcoming) and Easington to Paull gas pipeline (Rowland and Wegiel 2012).

As a result of such work, the contribution of Holderness has become as integral to the understanding of the archaeology of Yorkshire as that of neighbouring regions, despite the lack of research excavations of the type seen in the Wolds and beyond: at Shiptonthorpe (Millett 2006) and Hayton, at sites in the Foulness Valley (Halkon and Millett 1999), and at Star Carr and elsewhere in the Vale of Pickering. The Holderness area has also been well served by landscape studies: the Humber Wetlands Project (Van de Noort and Ellis 1995), the Rapid Coastal Zone Assessment Survey (Brigham, Buglass and George 2008) and the Resource Assessment of Aggregate-Producing Landscapes (Brigham, Buglass and Steedman 2008).

Section 2: The Excavation areas

The twenty excavation areas are described below, ordered geographically from north-west to south-east, and referenced by names taken from nearby villages, farms or landscape features. For the twelve sites located by evaluation trenching, the topsoil and, where present, any masking subsoil layers were removed by machine under the direction of an experienced archaeologist. In the case of the smaller sites revealed by monitoring of construction work, the area of the visible archaeology was barricaded to exclude construction traffic and, where necessary, cleaned by carefully supervised machining to remove any remaining overburden. In all cases, the exposed features were then surveyed with differential global positioning system (dGPS) survey equipment. Features and deposits were hand excavated, and all excavated interventions planned and drawn in section. Bulk soil samples were taken from deposits deemed to have potential for the retrieval of environmental micro-fossils: primary or secondary fills of features, waterlogged deposits; and any deposits in which significantly raised levels of faunal or macro-environmental remains were observed or suspected.

In the descriptions, the phrase 'hand-made pottery' should be understood to refer to late prehistoric or Roman pottery in the Iron Age tradition, as distinct from wheel-thrown wares. The period divisions commonly adopted in archaeological literature have been retained, although their limitations for describing the often gradual nature of changes in human action are acknowledged. It should

Name	Description	Civil Parish	NGR	
Old Ellerby	Late Iron Age ring gullies, Roman enclosure ditches and a Roman cremation	Ellerby	516499	436813
Burton Constable	Iron Age ring gullies and associated settlement features, field systems, a single human burial	Ellerby	517017	435860
Brandywell	Iron Age ring gullies, and settlement features; Roman field systems; three human burials	Sproatley	519056	433328
Sproatley	An in situ Mesolithic flint scatter; a separate disturbed scatter containing Mesolithic to Bronze Age artefacts; two possible Bronze Age barrows; a possible Iron Age square barrow; and Iron Age to early Roman boundary ditches	Sproatley	519174	433140
Nuttles	Iron Age settlement and Roman field systems	Burstwick	519707	432349
Lelley	Late Iron Age ring gullies, settlement features and human burial; Anglo-Saxon activity; medieval field systems and enclosures and possible building and oven, associated with nearby manorial complex	Burstwick	520340	431681
New York	Iron Age ring gullies and Iron Age or Roman ditch systems	Burstwick	520949	431348
Braemere Hill	Late Iron Age or early Roman ring gully; ditch with waste from salt-making	Burstwick	523158 523234	430459 430409
Burstwick	Iron Age ring gullies; possible enclosure ditches	Burstwick	524200	429400
Churchlands	Iron Age ring gully, boundary ditch and settlement features; medieval or post-medieval pits; residual Mesolithic and Bronze Age flint, and Bronze Age pottery	Halsham	529440	426616
Winestead	Ditched enclosures of possible Anglo-Saxon date	Rimswell	530564	426025
Patrington	Iron Age ring gullies and Iron Age and Roman ditch systems	Patrington	533400	423050
Bluegate Corner	Late Iron Age or Roman ring gullies and Roman ditch system	Welwick	535117 535173	421282 421190
Weeton	Parallel Iron Age boundary ditches and curvilinear gully	Welwick	536113	420408
Scorborough Hill	Artefact-rich early Roman pit; Iron Age and Roman ditches	Skeffling	536289	420374
Gilcross	Bronze Age pits and Iron Age ring gullies and ditches; a human burial	Skeffling	536858	420331
Out Newton Road	Corner of a large Iron Age enclosure, with a single large pit	Skeffling	537455	420134
Skeffling	Remnant Mesolithic soil layer, Iron Age pits, evidence of possible Bronze Age burnt mound	Skeffling	537755	420030
Hull Road	Late Iron Age settlement and ditches	Easington	539271	419542
Dimlington Road	Iron Age ring gullies, ditch systems; distinctive shallow stone-filled pits	Easington	539582 539779	419521 419525

TABLE 1: SUMMARY OF THE EXCAVATION AREAS

be noted that 'Roman' and 'Anglo-Saxon' are intended as period labels. Where necessary, 'Romano-British' has been used the culture which developed during the Roman period, and 'Anglian' or 'Anglo-Scandinavian' for identifiably distinct cultural styles within the Anglo-Saxon period.

Old Ellerby

Late Iron Age ring gullies, Roman enclosure ditches and a Roman cremation

The Old Ellerby site (Fig. 3) was on land sloping gently down to the west, towards the Hull valley. The top of the archaeological deposits was at a height 16.30m OD at the north end of the site, dropping to 15.50m at the south-west corner of the excavation area.

A number of possible archaeological sites in the vicinity can be seen as indistinct cropmarks on aerial photographs. These include a group of ring ditches and possible boundary ditches between 120m and 220m to the north-east and circular features 500m to the north and 650m to the west. The geophysical survey revealed a prominent annular magnetic anomaly, and a scatter of hand-made pottery was retrieved during fieldwalking in the same area (Flintoft 2008). The presence of archaeological features was confirmed by evaluation trenching before the site was opened for area excavation (Fig. 4).

A small number of struck flints, residual within later features, testify to a very limited early presence at the site, but the earliest substantial features were the ring gullies dating from some time in the Iron Age. The site at the time is probably best characterised as a small farmstead although, in common with many of the other sites along the pipeline route, the environmental samples provide little evidence for the nature of the agricultural economy.

Iron Age settlement

Two penannular gullies are interpreted as drainage gullies that would have surrounded Iron Age roundhouses. The interpretation of ring gullies, for the pipeline as a whole, is considered in Section 5 (page 253 below).

Structure 2 (Fig. 5)

A large ring gully, **3020**, in the centre of the excavation area corresponded to the magnetic anomaly observed in the geophysical survey, and proved to be up to 1m wide and 0.40m deep. The circuit was interrupted on the eastern side by an entrance at least 5m wide, but was otherwise complete. It enclosed a slightly oval area, with a diameter ranging from 12.90 to 14.10m. Total excavation of the fills yielded over 27kg of hand-made pottery, including parts of several near complete vessels. Three sherds from wheel-thrown vessels, ascribed to cut

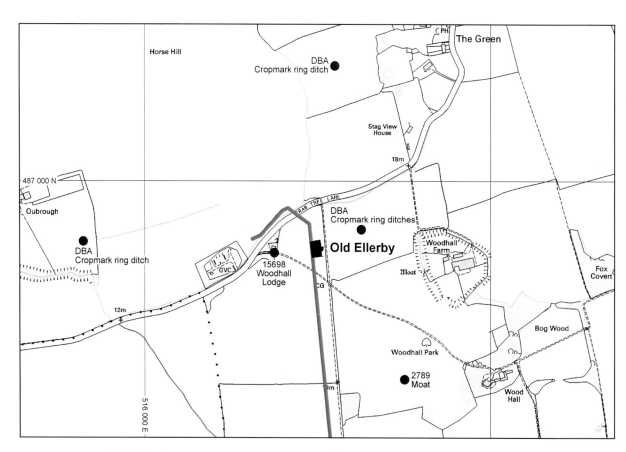

FIG. 3: OLD ELLERBY: LOCATION. CONTAINS OS DATA © CROWN COPYRIGHT [1:10 000 MAPPING]

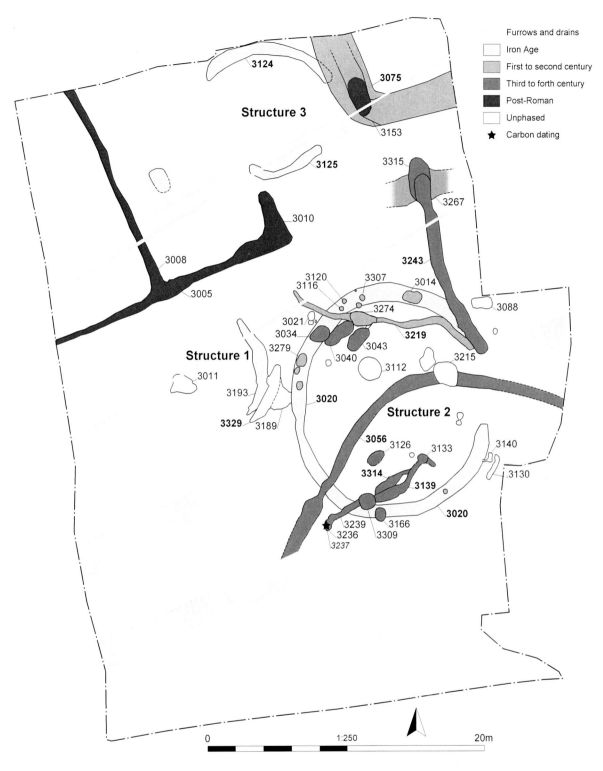

Furrows and drains

☐ Iron Age
▨ First to second century
▨ Third to forth century
■ Post-Roman
☐ Unphased
★ Carbon dating

FIG. 4: OLD ELLERBY: PLAN OF FEATURES

3255, were almost certainly intrusive from feature **3239**. The distribution of the pottery showed a very strong bias towards the eastern side, with a high proportion of the total assemblage being recovered from the southern terminal and from the easternmost intervention in the northern side (Cumberpatch, this volume, page 127). A cattle tooth from intervention **3249** returned a radiocarbon date of 180 to 1 cal BC (SUERC-38657).

Structure 3 (Fig. 6)

Towards the northern limit of the site, two curvilinear lengths of gully, **3124** and **3125**, together partially enclosed an area 8.20m in diameter. These steep-sided gullies were, on average, 0.70m wide and as deep as they were wide. A large assemblage of pottery recovered from the fills was exclusively of hand-made wares. A

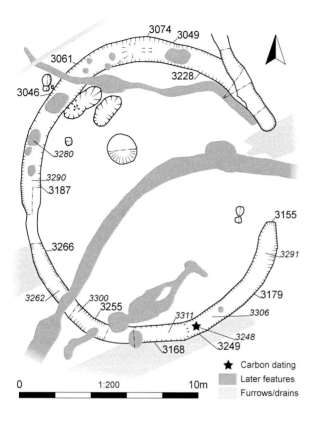

FIG. 5: OLD ELLERBY: STRUCTURE 2

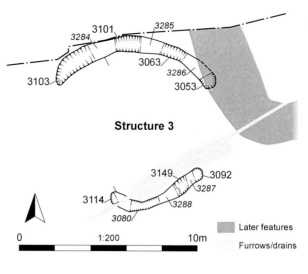

Structure 3

FIG. 6: OLD ELLERBY: STRUCTURE 3

particular concentration of pottery in the eastern terminal of ditch **3124** included eight largely complete, though broken, vessels.

Structure 1

A heavily truncated 7m length of curvilinear gully, **3193**, was tentatively identified as a small surviving portion of a third ring gully. No finds were recovered, and its relationship with pit **3189**, occupying the space between Structures 1 and 3, had been obscured by a later feature, **3329**. To the west, pit **3011** near to the centre of curvature of gully **3193**, contained hand-made pottery, along with undiagnostic struck flint.

First- to second-century ditches (Fig. 4)

The ring gullies had been infilled before the time when wheel-thrown pottery became readily available in the area. Nevertheless, activity on the site continued into the later first and second centuries AD. Ditch **3075**, towards the north-eastern corner of the site, was up to 3m wide and had an average depth of 0.40m. It turned through a right angle, extending beyond the limits of excavation to the north and east. The western side of the ditch appeared to encroach into the upper fill of Structure 3 although this relationship was not completely clear. The pottery from the ditch consists almost entirely of hand-made wares although there is a single sherd that may be an abraded piece of second-century samian ware. The ditch

could have been a recut of, or an extension to, an earlier feature, **3153**, the heavily truncated terminal of which partially survived beneath ditch **3075**.

Near the eastern edge of excavation, feature **3267** was obscured on the surface by furrows and drains but did not continue into the excavated intervention to the west, indicating that it terminated to the south of the corner of ditch **3075**. In its excavated section, it could be seen to be 2.10m wide and 1.10m deep. A far richer pottery assemblage than that from ditch **3075** indicates that there was considerable activity in the immediate area during the period that the ditch was infilling. Both hand-made and wheel-thrown wares are represented; the fifty-three wheel-thrown sherds include vessels from the late first century to the late second century, the majority belonging to the later period. The range of wares might suggest that the feature was open for an extended period. A residual late Neolithic or early Bronze Age flint knife (Fig. 84.36) was also recovered from the feature.

Gully **3219**, cut through the northern part of Structure 2, was generally well defined, with a steep-sided profile, although its sinuous course suggests that it may have incorporated, for some of its length, an animal burrow or similar natural feature. The gully was 0.40m wide, on average, and up to 0.45m deep, the depth diminishing towards either end. Wheel-thrown sherds among the pottery assemblage suggested a late second- to third-century date. The clusters of small pits or postholes in the same region of the site, cutting into the fills of Structure 2, were generally undated.

There is no positive evidence of domestic occupation at this time, and the installation of ditches, possibly elements of a system of enclosures, might suggest that the area was given over solely to agriculture. However, the quantity of finds, though fewer than those of Iron Age date, indicates a degree of material prosperity. A fragment of a samian vessel, for instance, shows that imported wares were available. This vessel, depicting the goddess Venus (Fig. 104.1), was probably made in central Gaul, between AD 150 and 180 (Wild, this volume, page 190).

Third- to fourth-century ditches, pits and cremation burial

There was a second peak of activity in the fourth century AD. The pattern of land division had been reordered by this time, and possibly included one or more large enclosures with rounded corners. This phase of activity also included pits and small linear features, none of which could be interpreted as structural remains; there must, however, have been an area of occupation nearby. There was evidence of small-scale metal working.

Curvilinear ditch **3056** cutting the south-western side of Structure 2, was up to 0.40m deep; Crambeck and Huntcliff wares among the pottery assemblage show that its infilling was not completed until the second half of the fourth century. The shape of the ditch in plan suggests that it formed the rounded north or north-western corner of a large enclosure extending to the south-east, although the feature became increasing shallow before being lost to furrows; nor could it be distinguished in the geophysical survey results. A second ditch, with similar dimensions, **3243**, had truncated the northern terminal of Structure 2, terminating to the north in the fills of a pit, **3315**, cut into the top of ditch **3267**. The range of pottery recovered from the fills of ditch **3243** was very similar to that from ditch **3056**.

Two small and very irregular linear features, **3139** and **3314**, to the south of ditch **3056**, also produced pottery with a similar date range. Ditch **3139** probably continued south-westward as feature **3239**. A small pit, **3236**, cut into the top of feature **3239** yielded 390g of burnt bone, the remains of a human cremation. The majority of the identifiable elements were long bone and lower limb fragments. Radiocarbon determination on a sample of charcoal from the same deposit returned a calibrated date of AD 170 to 390 (SUERC-36186), confirming the later Roman date implied by the stratigraphy.

The pottery assemblage from pit **3043**, in the northern part of the area enclosed by the Structure 2 ring gully, also suggests a late fourth-century date but its near neighbour to the west, pit **3040**, was probably infilled earlier in the century. Other pits in the vicinity of the ring gully, though less well dated, probably belong with the same phase of land use. These include pit **3274**, cutting gully **3219**, and pit **3126**, as well as features **3279**, **3034** and **3014**. A smaller pit, **3021**, just beyond the ring gully and close to pit **3034**, may have been part of the same group, although the only artefact recovered from it was a Mesolithic flint (Fig. 82.17). Pits **3133**, **3215** and **3309**

were stratigraphically later than ditches **3056** and **3139**, but again are likely to belong to the same broad phase.

Finds from pit **3014** included a button loop fastener (SF 1101, Fig. 85.1). A tiny fragment of fired clay from this pit joined with a large fragment, recovered from the machined surface, of a mould for casting non-ferrous metal. A third fragment (Fig. 107.1, 2 and 3), though superficially similar, lacked significant metal residues (Jones, this volume, page 223), and was probably from an object with a different function.

Post-Roman agriculture

The site seems to have been abandoned after the fourth century AD. Layer **3091**, the probable remnants of an old ploughsoil partly covering the north side Structure 2 yielded a considerable number of finds displaced from Iron Age or Roman contexts; these include a large whetstone (SF 1102: Fig. 106.1), found above ditch **3243**, as well as two sherds of late second- or possibly third-century samian ware and the fragments of the metal-casting mould joining with the piece from pit **3014**.

There is with no further evidence of activity until the twelfth- and thirteenth-century pottery, recovered from ditches **3005** and **3008** in the north-eastern quarter of the site. The similar orientations shared by these two features, the second-century ditches, the medieval furrows and modern field drains probably reflect the local drainage conditions rather than implying unbroken maintenance of the pattern of land division from the Roman period onwards. The more recent history of the site has been greatly influenced by its place in the managed landscape of the Burton Constable estate. Wood Hall Farm, 370m to the west, is the site of a late medieval moat (SMR MHU 2786) and the present Wood Hall (SMR MHU 7021), 350m further south, may have had a precursor in another nearby moated site (SMR MHU 2789).

Burton Constable

Iron Age ring gullies and associated settlement features, Roman ditch systems, a single human burial

The Burton Constable excavation area (Figs. 7, 8) lay within a wide area of relatively high ground along the eastern edge of the Hull valley. The top of the archaeological deposits rose from a height of 16.5m OD, at the edge of the substantial drain forming the southern boundary of the field, to a very slight ridge 17.2m OD 40m to the north-west. Thereafter, the level was relatively consistent, at around 17.0m, to the north-eastern limit of the excavation.

The geophysical survey of the pipeline route included a possible alternative route immediately to the east, but both this and the original route showed a similar complexity of linear and curvilinear anomalies, and the

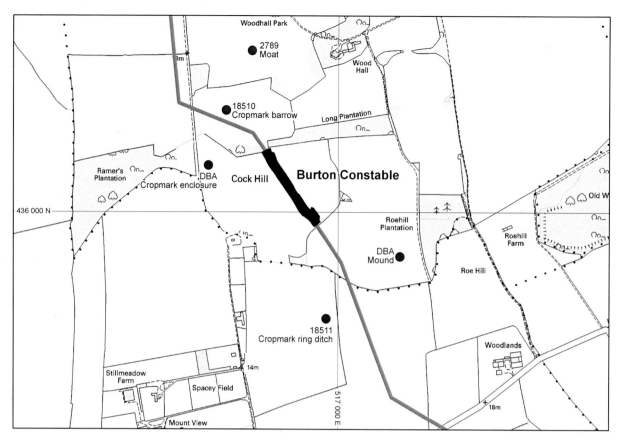

FIG. 7: BURTON CONSTABLE: LOCATION. CONTAINS OS DATA © CROWN COPYRIGHT [1:10 000 MAPPING]

re-route was not implemented. Trial trenching, carried out shortly before the start of construction, confirmed the presence of archaeological features. An earlier pipeline had disturbed the area south of the drainage ditch at the southern end of the excavation area, but beyond this, a small excavation (Flintoft and Glover 2010, 'Cock Hill') revealed several poorly dated linear and discrete features.

Earlier prehistoric

The drainage ditch at the southern boundary of the excavation area almost certainly had its origins in a natural watercourse. As a source of water for people and stock, a stream such as this would have been a prime area for hunting and could have been used as a routeway through the landscape. Possible evidence of Bronze Age activity in the area around the site is provided by two cropmarks which may represent round barrows: one approximately 250m to the south of the excavation area (SMR MHU 18511) and the other 400m to the north-west (SMR MHU 18510). If the attribution as barrows is correct, their presence would imply that the area had been cleared of woodland by the time of their construction, as such monuments were generally sited so at to be visible from a distance.

A number of pits in the southern corner of the site remained undated, but it is possible that some of these features were contemporary with elements of the

assemblage of 117 pieces of struck flint. However, no features or deposits could be positively assigned a pre-Iron Age date. Flints included a serrated flake of probable Mesolithic date, possibly used for processing plant fibres, perhaps for textiles or cord. An end scraper from the same broad period is likely to be have been used in the processing or working of animal hides. Broadly Neolithic or Bronze Age flintwork was more plentiful, strongly suggesting an increase in the amount of activity in these periods.

Iron Age, pre-dating settlement

At the southern end of the excavation area, Iron Age features were cut through a 7m-wide deposit of colluvial material, **118979** (Fig. 9). This layer produced hand-made pottery, as well as a small number of worked flints and a fragment of a pyramidal loomweight (Fig. 107.4). A second loomweight fragment (Fig. 107.5) and a large piece of a rotary quern (Fig. 106.2) were recovered from subsoil layer **118518,** overlying the colluvium. The flints may be an indication that the colluvium began to accumulate during the Neolithic or Bronze Age, perhaps a result of increased slope erosion caused by tree clearance in the immediate area.

Several poorly defined features, indicated by concentrations of pottery and charcoal, were cut into the lower layers

a)

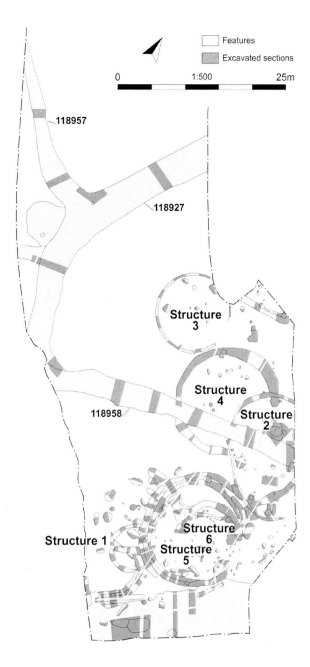

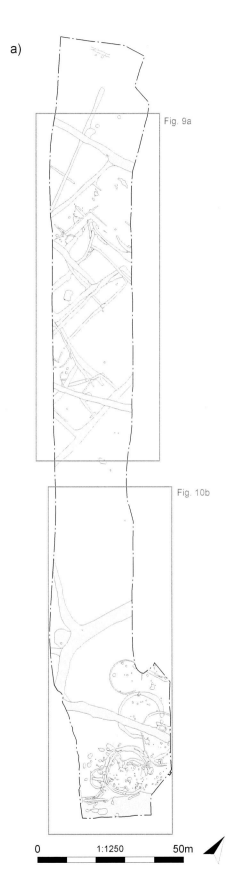

FIG. 9: BURTON CONSTABLE: SOUTHERN AREA OF THE SITE

FIG. 8: BURTON CONSTABLE: ALL FEATURES

of colluvium and backfilled with similar material. By contrast, pit **9476** in the same area was clearly visible in plan as its fill was markedly darker. The pottery from this pit included twenty-six body sherds from a single vessel. A large, rectangular steep-sided pit, **118198**, to its east was only clearly defined at depth, and the relationship between these two pits was unclear. Finds from pit **118198** included an unusual small thumb-pot, and a fragment of cattle metatarsal with a drilled hole.

An example of a lid-seated jar, for which an earlier Iron Age date has been suggested, was recovered from the fill of ditch **118954**, just beyond the northern extent of the colluvial layer and close to the eastern limit of excavation.

There were further sherds from similar vessels, otherwise very scarce along the pipeline route, in the fills of the Structure 5 ring gully and in pit **9665**.

The Iron Age settlement

Structure 1 and associated features (Figs. 10, 11)

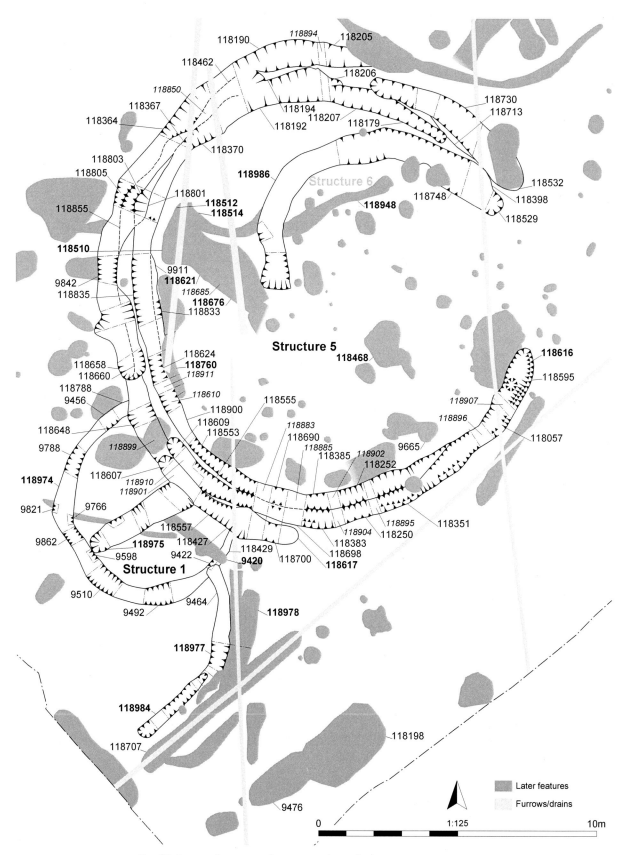

FIG. 10: BURTON CONSTABLE: STRUCTURES 1 AND 5, WITH ASSOCIATED FEATURES

FIG. 11: BURTON CONSTABLE, STRUCTURE 5, DURING EXCAVATION (PHOTO © ADAM STANFORD)

Ring gully **118974** formed a semi-circle with an internal diameter of 5.8m. It is likely to have originally been penannular, the eastern half having been lost to later truncation. The gully contained 171 sherds of hand-made pottery, along with a single sherd, small enough to be credibly intrusive, from a wheel-thrown Roman vessel. A calibrated radiocarbon date of 86 BC to AD 71 (SUERC-38659) was returned from a cattle bone from the ring gully. The upper surface of the internal area enclosed by the gully formed a distinct layer, **118980**, around 0.5 to 0.8m thick and similar in appearance to the colluvium. This layer yielded 385 sherds of pottery, all of typical hand-made wares.

A collection of short ditches to the south were cut into the colluvium, one of which, **118977**, truncated ring gully **118974**. Finds from this ditch included a highly polished fragment of worked bone (SF 1207, Fig. 88.2). The line of ditch **118977** was continued by a deeper steep-sided linear feature, **118984**. Among sixty sherds of pottery from this feature, a sherd from a globular jar could be fairly confidently dated to the range 100 BC to AD 100, and a flint tempered sherd is possibly of early or middle Iron Age date. In the same area, ditch **118978**, running for a short distance from the western edge of excavation before terminating, produced a fragment of a crucible, probably used for smelting bronze. Sixty-eight sherds of pottery and a possible blank for a barbed and tanged flint arrowhead (Fig. 81.27) were retrieved from the same feature.

Structure 4 (Figs 12b, 13)

Around 25m due north of Structure 1, a heavily truncated penannular gully, **118056**, enclosed an area 13.2m in diameter. A clearly defined terminal marked the north side of an east-facing gap, but the corresponding southern terminal had been lost to a later ditch. The ring gully was a substantial feature, up to 2.60m wide and 0.75m deep and produced over 500 sherds of pottery, including three fragments of a distinctive, barrel-shaped jar, comparable to examples dating from 900 to 400 BC, and three sherds from shallow bowls of possible early to middle Iron Age date. It also contained a fragment of the upper stone from a rotary quern (SF 1216). A radiocarbon date of 400 to 200 cal BC (SUERC-36190) from a charcoal sample recovered from the gully is consistent with a middle Iron Age origin, though there is a possibility that the charcoal derived from old wood or was residual.

Of particular note were five fragments of daub, recovered from the southernmost part of gully **118056**, four of which show very clear impressions of rope, around 18mm in diameter (Fig. 107.7-10). In the best example, individual fibres of the rope can be distinguished. Parallels for rope-impressed daub from Iron Age sites are proving difficult to find; these examples are highly unusual, if not unique. The remaining piece of daub from this context has finger-tip impressions.

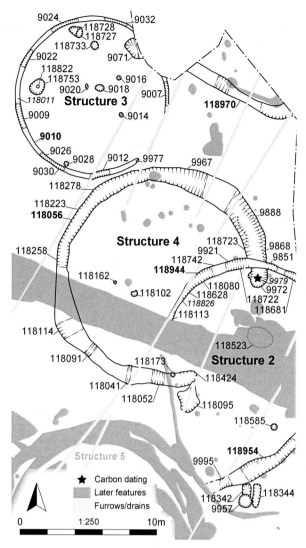

FIG. 12: BURTON CONSTABLE: STRUCTURES 3, 4 AND 2 WITH ASSOCIATED FEATURES

A number of pits in the area enclosed by gully **118056** may have held timber uprights, either structural members or internal features. Dating evidence from these pits was limited to a single sherd of hand-made pottery recovered from pit **118102** and three more from pit **118162**. A dump of possible domestic refuse, rich in charcoal and burnt clay and including sixty sherds of pottery, was found in irregular pit **118095** just outside the enclosed area. Its proximity to the entrance of Structure 4 might suggest an association, although there was no stratigraphic link to support this conjecture. There was a group of large intercutting pits beyond the entrance, the largest of which, **118523**, produced 390 sherds of hand-made pottery.

Structure 2 (Fig. 12c)

A heavily truncated, curved gully, **118944**, cut the Structure 4 ring gully just to the north of its terminal and most likely marks the location of a further circular structure. Little more than a quarter of a circle, with an

internal radius of approximately 5.6m, survived within the limit of the excavation. A small assemblage of hand-made pottery was recovered from its fills.

Running into the edge of excavation a short distance to the south-east, ditch **118954** produced a group of 201 sherds, including a distinctive lid-seated rim and a collared rim with internal finger prints. A fragment from an object made from the lower leg bone of a horse (SF 1210, Fig. 90.1) found in the same feature may have been part of a weaving tool. Two elongated pits or short lengths of ditch, **118344** and **118342**, and a 1.2m-deep vertical-sided pit, **9957**, adjacent to ditch **118954** and possibly broadly contemporary with it; each produced small assemblages of pottery.

Structure 3 (Fig. 12a)

A third penannular ring gully, **9010**, enclosed an area 10.6m in diameter. A break in the gully circuit suggests that the structure had a 3.5m-wide east-facing entrance, although damage by a modern field drain only allows for an approximate width to be given. The surviving gully was very shallow, with a maximum depth of 0.07m, but it produced fifty-one sherds of hand-made pottery, almost all from the gully terminals: thirty-two on the southern side and fifteen on the disturbed northern side. The composition of the botanical assemblage from bulk samples of the fills provided a very tentative suggestion of the presence of turfs, used, perhaps, in the construction of the structure enclosed by the gully, or for fuel (O'Meara, this volume, page 239). A tiny, irregular cylindrical bead made from opaque mid-blue glass (SF 3411) was also recovered from the sample. No more than 2.5mm across, and with a 0.8mm hole, this bead is of a kind that typically date to the fourth century AD, but may occur in both earlier and later contexts (Guido 1978, 94-96).

A clearly defined post-pipe was visible within posthole **118753**, one of the features within the area enclosed by the ring gully, indicating that it had held a fairly substantial timber. Post-packing of heat-reddened cobbles in pit **118733** suggests that a second post stood at this location. There was no indication that these cobbles had been burnt or scorched *in situ*. Ditch terminal **118972** was probably a continuation of ditch **118970** to the east, the two features together producing ninety sherds of pottery. Postholes and small pits in the same area of the site, to the east of Structure 3, were undated.

Structure 5 (Figs. 10, 11)

Structure 5 lay to the south of Structure 4 and truncated the eastern edge Structure 1. With an internal diameter of up to 13.5m, Structure 5 was the largest of this group of penannular gullies. It had an east-facing entrance around 5.5m wide. A number of recuts showed that the gully

FIG. 13: BURTON CONSTABLE: STRUCTURES

had been regularly maintained: in the clearest excavated section four superimposed cuts could be discerned. However these recuts could not be traced around the whole circuit of the gully and appeared to be local reinstatements of short sections of the feature rather than its complete renewal.

A total of 1986 sherds of pottery were recovered from the various gully cuts, all but four of which were hand-made wares. Datable pieces include three rim sherds from a deep-collared jar probably from the early or middle Iron Age, a wedge-rim from a globular jar from the same fill dating from 100BC to 100AD, a round lug handle from a jar dating to 400BC to AD100, and a clubbed rim of middle to late Iron Age date from a calcite-gritted jar with prominent fingertip impressions. The wheel-thrown sherds, of which three could be dated to the first century, came from upper fill of the gully. Their presence suggests that the ring gully may have survived as a negative feature into the early Roman period, perhaps simply as a slight dip formed as the earlier fills consolidated. But otherwise the pottery assemblage strongly suggests that the feature had infilled almost completely prior to significant Roman influence in the area. A cattle vertebra from the southern side of the gully gave a calibrated radiocarbon date of 86 BC to AD 71 (SUERC-38658).

Three crucible sherds, several pieces of bronze-working debris as well as green, powdery copper corrosion deposits (SF1227), spheroidal hammer slag and hammerscale were also recovered from the various interventions through the ring gully, along with two pieces of fuel ash slag and hearth lining. These finds indicate that iron-smithing and non-ferrous craft working took place either within Structure 5 or close to it, though the quantities imply that this was on a very small scale. An intervention in the northern side of the ring gully produced a fragment of daub bearing parallel rod impressions (Fig. 107.6): this intervention was less than 3m from the section of the Structure 4 ring gully that produced the rope-impressed daub.

A number of other features may have been related to Structure 5. A short length of ditch, or elongated pit, **118975**, abutted the ring gullies although its stratigraphic relationship with them was not well defined. It had a flat base and steep sides, and contained 53 fragments of pottery, including a sherd of Scored ware, dated to around 300BC to AD100. A sherd in a fine grey fabric showed signs of intense heating and may have derived from a crucible, a further indication of metal working in the immediate vicinity.

A large group of small pits, ninety-eight in total, were recorded within the area defined by the ring gully and to the north-east and south-west. At least some of these features are likely to have held timber uprights, either elements of Structure 5 or its internal fixtures. Stock may have been housed under the same roof as the human inhabitants, especially in winter in order to conserve heat and if this was the case, the internal features could also have supported tethering posts, stalls or mangers, in addition to more normal domestic fixtures, such as furniture items, looms or partition walls. The features outside the ring gully could have held the posts of fences or animal pens.

A lack of stratigraphic relationships among these small features and the poor chronological resolution provided by the pottery assemblage preclude a more detailed interpretation, and the association of particular pits with particular structures would be very tenuous. Pit **9617**, one of a group of well defined but fairly shallow and poorly dated pits to the west of the ring gully, contained a sandstone cobble that had functioned as a rubbing stone, a worn face and evidence of pecking (SF 1228) suggesting, perhaps, a use in polishing stone or metal.

Possible structural remains: Structure 6 (Fig. 10)

Curvilinear gully **118986**, within the circuit of Structure 5, bore some resemblance to the other ring gullies, but was irregular and indistinct in places. If the remains of a structure, it would represent the latest in this group. There were several other irregular ditches within the interior space of Structure 5, possibly the result of later disturbance, and gully **118986** could instead have belonged with these. A tiny scrap of Roman pottery was recovered from the gully, along with 130 sherds of hand-made pottery.

The Iron Age settlement: discussion

Possible early or middle Iron Age forms among the pottery assemblage indicate that there might have been activity at the site during these periods, but the bulk of the hand-made pottery cannot be closely dated, and it has not been possible to positively identify a distinct early or middle Iron Age phase within these features. Nevertheless, the complexity of archaeological remains and the quantities of pottery from successive stratigraphic phases would indicate an extended period of occupation. The size and nature of the pottery assemblages from the ring gullies supports the supposition that these surrounded domestic structures. The structures were clearly not all contemporary and the spacing suggests that no more than two were in use at any one time.

There is a strong likelihood that remains of further structures lie beyond the limit of excavation, as the geophysical survey of the alternative route to the east displayed magnetic anomalies comparable to those from the excavated area. The Burton Constable settlement was possibly no more than a relatively prosperous unenclosed farmstead, consisting of a handful of roundhouses and ancillary buildings, or it may have been something rather larger, extending along

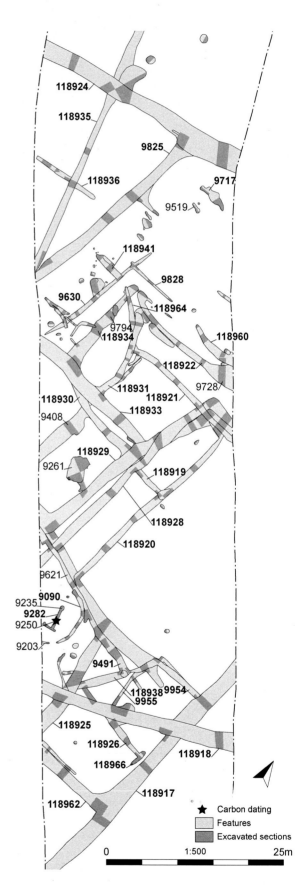

FIG 14: BURTON CONSTABLE, NORTH AREAS OF THE SITE

the stream bank. The buildings appear to have been rebuilt on a number of occasions, creating a complex sequence of remains and indicating the probable survival of the settlement through several generations.

Small-scale metal working was undertaken within the settlement, though not necessarily within the confines of the excavation area. Otherwise the economic focus would have been primarily agricultural. There was some evidence for grain production and processing, but it is likely that the settlement had a strong pastoral element: producing meat, predominantly from sheep and cattle, and maximising secondary products such as wool and milk. Cattle would also have been used as draught animals. The stream at the south end of the site would have provided a ready source of water but may have been substantial enough to allow the movement of boats, providing communication to the Humber and beyond.

Roman enclosures (Figs. 14, 15)

Very little pottery from the site could be dated to the early years of the Roman period, and the settlement at the southern end of the site had long been abandoned by the time that a system of enclosures was established to the north, in the later third century. Stratigraphic relationships

between features were often unclear, and correlation of sequences of recuts in adjacent excavated interventions was rarely possible with any degree of confidence. Some fairly closely datable vessels within the wheel-thrown pottery assemblages offer only very limited help in untangling the sequence of features, as in many instances a single context contained a range of types.

This pattern of small contiguous enclosures seems to have developed over a relatively short period of time. Reordering of enclosure boundaries, often on only slightly different alignments, is largely unexplained but is a relatively common phenomenon on Roman sites across the country. It may be a reflection of seasonality or a manifestation of tenure rights, with short periods of abandonment necessitating the often wholesale re-establishment of enclosures on a very similar pattern to their predecessors. Morphological parallels to this system of enclosures can be found in cropmark features around Leven and Routh *(Brigham, Buglass and Steedman 2008, Map 9)* and Halsham *(ibid.* Map 35).

The ditches forming Enclosures 1 to 3 (Fig. 15) are probably the earliest components of this system. A single Huntcliff sherd, of later fourth-century date, recorded from Enclosure 2 close to the intersection with ditch

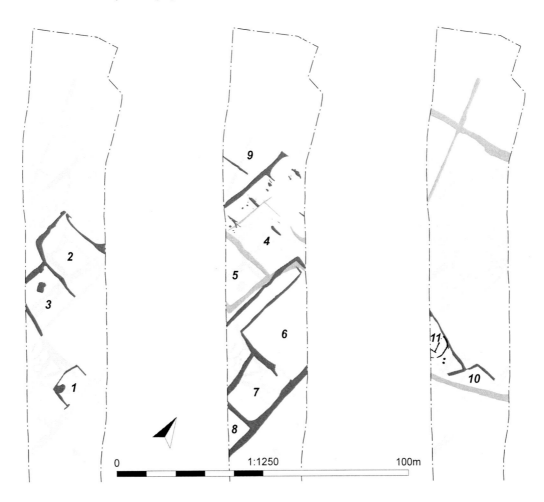

FIG. 15: BURTON CONSTABLE: ENCLOSURE SYSTEM

118931 may have been intrusive, as the rest of the pottery from these features is consistent with a late third-century date. The upper fill of ditch **9955** provided evidence for cereal processing, with over fifty charred grains being recovered from a processed bulk soil sample. Enclosures 4 and 5 seem to have been a direct replacement for 2 and 3, and were perhaps short-lived, the pottery assemblage suggesting that they had been abandoned by the mid-fourth century. Short and shallow lengths of ditch within Enclosure 4 suggest subsequent sub-division.

Enclosures 6, 7 and 8 appear to have been broadly contemporary with one another and with Enclosures 4 and 5, replacing the earlier Enclosure 1 to the east of the main north-to-south axis of the system. Enclosure 9 represents a possible elaboration of the system to the west, its northern limit removed by the later ditch **118924**. The stratigraphy indicated that the ditches forming Enclosures 10 and 11 were the latest elements of the eastern side of the system, although the small quantity of pottery from them was all in hand-made wares.

Other finds from this system of enclosures included a fragment of iron bar, possibly a scrap off-cut, from ditch **9955** of Enclosure 1, and a piece of a jet bracelet (SF 1213: Fig. 87.1) from Enclosure 2 ditch **118934**. Jet was commonly used for jewellery in the Roman period, particularly near its source in the Whitby area (Allason-Jones 2002, 125-132). A feldspathic sandstone pebble possibly used as a hone (SF 1201), fuel ash and iron-working slag, and a number of fragments of hearth lining, were also recovered from the same ditch fill.

As it crossed diagonally to the principal axis of the enclosures, the pipeline offered only a restricted view of the overall pattern and it is not possible to say what proportion of the complete system was sampled by the excavation area. The enclosures almost certainly continued beyond the western edge of excavation and probably also to the east; the whole system may have formed an elaborated double row of enclosures, bounded by ditches **9825** in the west and **118917** in the east.

Several internal features provide hints to possible functions of the enclosures: they include a small keyhole-shaped oven or furnace, **9519**. Pit **9261**, within the Enclosure 3, may have acted as a watering hole or animal wallow, possibly indicating the use of the enclosure as a livestock pen. The enclosure ditches and associated features together produced 1555 sherds of pottery, weighing 18.87kg, of which 61 per cent by count and 70 per cent by weight was wheel-thrown. While this is less than 15 per cent of the weight of pottery from Iron Age contexts in the southern half of the excavation area, it still indicates considerable activity, especially when the relative proportions of the features excavated are taken into account. Though the quantities of pottery strongly support the supposition that the enclosures were close to a contemporary settlement, none of the recorded features could be positively interpreted as structural remains.

Inhumation 9796

An oval grave, **9794**, within Enclosure 4 and cutting the western side of Enclosure 2 (Fig. 14), contained the moderately well preserved remains of an adult male human, **9796** (Fig. 16). Dental attrition indicates an age at death between 36 and 45 years. He was a muscular individual, but displayed a number of pathological symptoms: he had probably suffered from brucellosis, rarely recorded in skeletons from archaeological sites, and also had inflammatory lesions on the lower legs and in the upper jaw, degenerative disease in the elbow and chronic sinusitis. Vitamin B12 deficiency or infection in childhood had resulted in lesions in his eye sockets. He had lost several teeth during his lifetime and suffered from dental plaque and periodontal disease.

Possible grain dryer

A shallow L-shaped ditch, **9282**, within Enclosure 11 (Fig. 14), contained frequent charcoal inclusions within its fill, along with small amounts of burnt clay. A bulk sample of the fill produced forty-eight charred grains of unprocessed naked wheat and barley in roughly equal quantities, the largest assemblage of cereal grains from the site, along with a small assemblage of chaff. No pottery was recovered but a charcoal sample gave a calibrated radiocarbon date of AD 80 to 250 (SUERC-36191).

An oval pit had been cut into each end of the ditch, apparently after it had been filled in. Three further pits nearby may be related to the ditch, though a sherd of thirteenth- to sixteenth-century pottery, possibly intrusive, was recovered from the upper fill of one of them. The presence of cereal grains and chaff within the L-shaped ditch raises the possibility that the feature functioned as a grain dryer or a malting kiln, features commonly recorded on Roman rural sites, but the shallowness of the surviving features means that this interpretation is speculative.

Curvilinear gully **9090** cut through part of the Enclosure 11 boundary, implying a date no earlier than the late third century, and a sherd of late third or early fourth-century pottery from its fill lends weight to this dating. Other finds included a residual Neolithic or Bronze Age flint (Fig. 83.29). Its position suggests that it may have been contemporary with the L-shaped ditch, but this would require assumptions about the residuality of the radiocarbon sample from that feature. If the two features were contemporary, gully **9090** may have provided drainage or served as a bedding trench for a wind break or the walls of a more substantial structure.

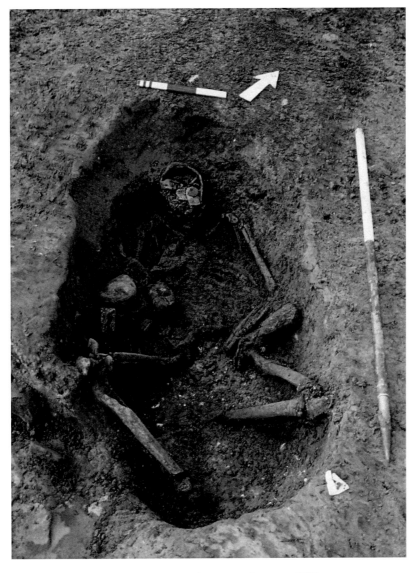

FIG. 16: BURTON CONSTABLE, SKELETON 9796

Substantial ditches

Three ditches at the southern end of the site (Fig. 9) were considerably larger than the enclosure ditches to the north. Despite their scale, very few finds were recovered from ditches **118957** and **118927**. Analysis of bulk soil samples taken from ditch **118927** indicated that it contained standing water, unsurprising given its depth of up to 1.70m, the poorly draining clay-rich drift deposits it had been cut into, and the low-lying situation of the site.

Although otherwise similar to the other two ditches, the most southerly of the group, **118958**, produced a large quantity of pottery, over a thousand sherds in total. This very diverse assemblage was concentrated in those parts of the ditch that cut through the Iron Age features towards the eastern side of the excavation area. The possibility that this ditch was roughly contemporary with Structure 5 cannot be entirely dismissed, if it assumed that the small

quantity of Roman pottery from its fill was intrusive, but it is more likely that the earlier material was residual, notwithstanding its large quantity. If this was the case, the state of preservation shows that the pottery must have slumped from features in the side of the ditch, and been rapidly buried in wet silts, soon after the ditch was first dug. As with ditch **118927**, the mollusc assemblage from the ditch indicated that this was a watery environment, making slumping and silting entirely plausible.

In the central area of the site (Fig. 14), ditch **118918** cut across Enclosures 7, 10 and 11 but again produced few finds; ditch **118924**, at the northern end of the site, likewise produced few finds. It seems likely that these ditches were a contemporary group post-dating the abandonment of the earlier enclosures. Ditch **118935** may also relate to this period of development, although it appeared to cut through ditch **118924**. These ditches may reflect a change in approach to persistent drainage problems as much as an attempt to draw major boundaries in the landscape. The wholesale reordering of the land division that they demonstrate may reflect a deliberate break with the earlier boundary system, but a later development undertaken without any knowledge of the earlier enclosure system seems more likely. This could date from the late fourth or early fifth centuries, but the re-establishment of agriculture some time after the Roman period is also a possibility.

Later activity

Among the unstratified finds from the site was a London issue silver groat of Richard II (North 1963, 1321a) dated to 1377 to 1399. At the northern end of the excavation area, a 0.70m-long and up to 0.54m-wide fragment of the jaw-bone of a Greenland right whale (*Balaena mysticetus*: identification by Richard Sabin, Natural History Museum) was found buried upright in the ground. This is almost certainly the remains of one of a number of whalebone arches that were erected on the Burton Constable estate between the second half of the eighteenth and the early twentieth centuries (Credland 1995, 106). The Constable family of Burton Constable had a long association with whaling, both commercially and as hereditary Lords Paramount of the Seigniory of Holderness, with rights to receive fishes royal stranded on the Holderness coast.

Brandywell

Iron Age ring gullies, and settlement features; Roman ditch systems; three human burials

The Brandywell excavation area was separated from the Sproatley site (see following section) by a 12m-wide baulk encompassing the hedgeline of the modern field boundary (Fig. 17). The land here slopes gently down to the south, the top of the archaeological deposits varying from 11.7m to 10.3m OD. The geophysical survey revealed an extensive area of complex magnetic anomalies. Evaluation trenching subsequently confirmed the presence of archaeological features.

Mesolithic, Neolithic and Bronze Age activity

The second largest assemblage of worked flint from the pipeline route, 130 pieces in total, was recovered from this site. Both Mesolithic (Fig. 82.19 and 20) and Neolithic or Bronze Age components (Fig. 84.37) are present in roughly equal quantities, and the assemblage can be considered as an extension of that from the Sproatley site, discussed below.

Iron Age ring gullies

The remains of a series of roundhouses, comprising ring gullies, and associated pits and postholes, were recorded

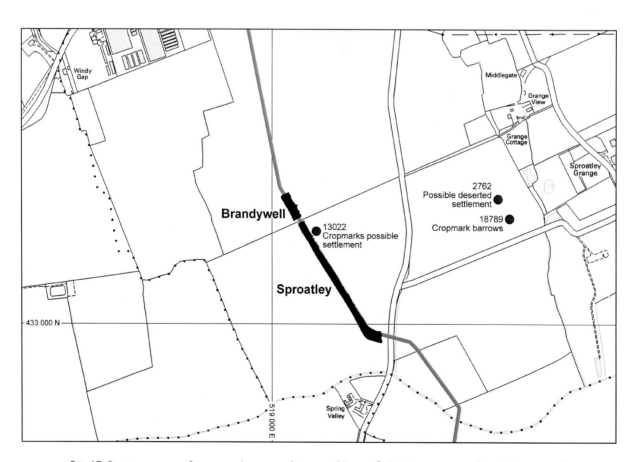

FIG. 17: BRANDYWELL AND SPROATLEY: LOCATION. CONTAINS OS DATA © CROWN COPYRIGHT [1:10 000 MAPPING]

(Fig. 18). Stratigraphic evidence suggests a sequence of structures, rather than a contemporary group. Identification of the total number of possible buildings is made difficult by the fragmentary nature and proximity of the surviving gullies. At least some of the gullies and pits may have arisen as repairs or alterations to a single structure, while it is clear that others must relate to entirely new buildings. A sequence of three structures is perhaps most likely.

Structure 1 (Fig. 19)

Ring gullies **25243** and **25238**, surviving as partial arcs, were concentric and have been regarded as elements of a single structure, although it may be the case that one of them was a replacement for the other, perhaps indicating later enlargement of the original structure. A line of postholes approximately 0.5m inside the inner gully are also considered to have belonged to the same structure. Although well defined features, with remains of post-packing in their fills, these postholes seem too insubstantial to have held structural timbers supporting a roof: uprights for a wattle and daub wall may be a more plausible interpretation. A charred seed from the fill of the southernmost member of the group, **25199**, returned a calibrated radiocarbon date of 174 BC to AD 1 (SUERC-38660).

A further curvilinear ditch, **25239**, truncating one of the postholes, is possibly the result of an alteration or re-build of the external wall after these posts had been removed; finds from it included a fragment of a fired clay rod (Fig. 107.14).

Structure 2

The fragmentary remains of two parts of a possible ring gully, **25129** and **25137**, may have marked the location of a further roundhouse with an east-facing entrance. Pottery recovered from the gullies was all hand-made but included a small number of decorated sherds. There is no stratigraphic relationship between the two roundhouses, although their proximity suggests that they are unlikely to have been contemporary. Evidence of domestic activity is provided by a fragment of a pyramidal loomweight and upper and lower quern stones (SFs 287, 288, Fig. 106.3) as well as a fired clay bar or slab fragment (Fig.

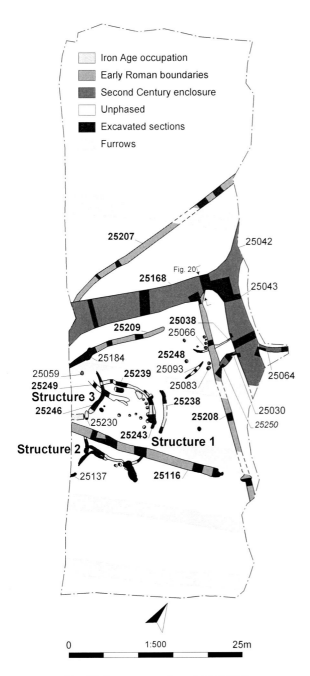

FIG. 18: BRANDYWELL: PLAN OF FEATURES

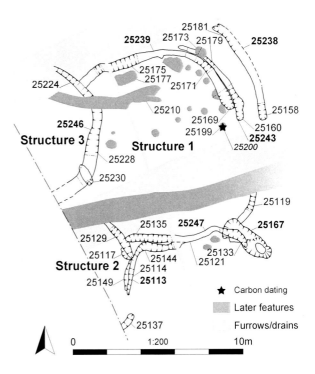

FIG. 19: BRANDYWELL: STRUCTURES

107.13). The quern stones were non-matching: the lower from a beehive quern, the upper probably from a typically Roman disc quern.

Structure 3

Ring gully **25246** truncated the wall line of Structure 1, clearly indicating that it belonged to a later construction. Pit **25230** was identified when the ring gully was partly excavated and the relationship between the two features had been lost, but it was almost certainly a later feature. It produced a sherd of wheel-thrown pottery with close parallels from late Iron Age or very early Roman contexts on sites in north Lincolnshire and the Trent valley. Similar pottery was also found in a shallow gully, **25249**, which cut through ring gully **25246**.

Further gullies

Several shallow gullies and a small number of pits in the immediate vicinity of the ring gullies may have represented the remains of further structures, although this is far from certain. The small pottery assemblages from these features consist solely of hand-made wares. Horncore fragments from two of the features have cut marks, throwing light on the craft working undertaken by inhabitants of the site.

Early Roman field boundaries (Fig. 18)

The abandonment of the roundhouses appears to have been quickly followed by the establishment of a series of linear boundaries, ditches **25207**, **25208**, **25209** and **25116** seeming to radiate from a point to the west of the excavation area. The Roman wheel-thrown components of their pottery assemblages suggested that they infilled during the mid-first to early second century AD. Some of the pottery forms, including rusticated jars and ring and dot beakers, are commonly linked with the movement of the Roman military, although not necessarily implying a military presence in the immediate area, while carinated bowls of a north Lincolnshire form attest to trade or movement of people across the Humber estuary at this time. Other finds included a possible fragment from a copper alloy bracelet (SF 285, Fig. 85.8) from an upper fill of ditch **25116**, and a pyramidal loomweight or thatch-weight from the same ditch (Fig. 107.15).

The animal bone assemblage indicates the presence of sheep, pigs, horses and cattle, its composition possibly indicating that this was a producer, rather than a consumer, site. The bones of younger animals within the cattle assemblage may be a pointer to at least a limited dairy economy.

Second-century enclosure ditch

The boundaries established in the early Roman period seem to have been short-lived, with at least two, and possibly all, filled in by the time that a substantial ditch, **25168**, was dug. This ditch, up to 4m wide and 1.30m deep, appeared to form the north eastern corner of an enclosed area; the south-western side of which would have been beyond the limit of excavation. It is possible that the modern hedgeline beyond the southern limit of excavation sites coincides with the south-eastern edge of the enclosure, maintaining an element of the boundary within the modern landscape. The northerly offshoot from the outer side of the corner, **25042**, perhaps bounded a second linked enclosure. Two shallow drainage gullies, **25030** and **25064**, fell out of use before the main ditch silted up.

The wheel-thrown wares recovered from the enclosure ditch are similar in date to those from the stratigraphically earlier ditches, with no pottery definitely post-dating the second century AD. The bone assemblage was also similar in composition apart from a lack of horse remains, unlikely to be significant within the small overall assemblage. Disarticulated human bones included a fibula shaft with a healed transverse fracture and two vertebral fragments with signs of a degenerative joint disease.

This enclosure was one of the few features on the pipeline of sufficient scale for a defensive function to have been feasible, but drainage is perhaps more likely. Environmental evidence shows that the ditch contained standing water, the fills being sufficiently waterlogged to preserve a good pollen sequence. The analysed samples imply that the area surrounding the site was an open landscape used for both pastoral and arable agriculture (Burke Davies, this volume, page 244). A peak in wetland taxa from the upper fills of the ditch indicates increased rainfall during their deposition coinciding with decreased arable production. A large increase in willow from the middle fills of the ditch may indicate a period of scrubland regeneration. The mollusc assemblage suggests that there was rank vegetation on the margins of the ditch, with short, possibly closely grazed, grassland beyond.

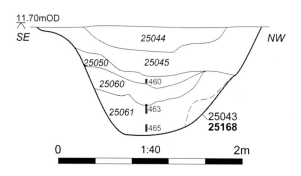

FIG. 20: DITCH 25043, NORTH-EAST FACING SECTION SHOWING LOCATION OF POLLEN SAMPLES

Just to the west of ditch **25168**, and broadly contemporary with it, a regular oval pit, **25250**, produced thirty-five sherds of pottery dating to the first half of the second century AD, as well as fragments of fired clay (Fig. 107.12).

Possible rectangular structure

A group of nine postholes, **25248**, of varying depths, may represent the location of a small rectangular, post-built structure. The postholes covered an area approximately 4m by 3m and shared the alignment of the second-century enclosure ditch, perhaps suggesting that all were contemporary. The pottery assemblage from the postholes was small and lacks diagnostic pieces.

The skeleton of a human neonate found within one of this group of postholes, **25066**, is moderately well preserved and 20 per cent complete. An age estimate of 40 weeks *in utero* implies that death occurred around the time of birth. The backfill of the feature also contained a few disarticulated human bones belonging to an infant or young juvenile. The burial of neonates and infants around or under buildings is a common feature of rural settlement sites of the Roman period. Feature **25083** contained the substantial remains of an articulated calf skeleton.

Early second century burials

Grave **25184**, containing the skeleton of a mature male, had been dug into one of the infilled field boundaries, indicating a date in the Roman period, or later, although the pottery assemblage from the grave fill was wholly hand-made. The skeleton is well preserved and 90 per cent complete (Fig. 21). Destructive lesions on the vertebrae suggest that the individual had suffered from tuberculosis. DNA analysis, carried out as part of the Biomolecular Archaeology of Ancient Tuberculosis in Britain and Europe project at Durham and Manchester Universities, was consistent with this diagnosis but did not positively confirm it (Keefe and Holst, this volume, page 226). The individual had also suffered a degenerative joint disease in

FIG. 21: SKELETON 25183

25

FIG. 22: SKELETON 25218

his left hip and probably inflammation of the shins. Both of his first metatarsals have evidence of bunions, and his eye orbit and teeth show indications of childhood stress.

Grave **25059**, around 2.5m to the south, contained the skeleton of a child aged three to four years old (Fig. 22). The child had probably suffered from actinomycosis, a rare gastrointestinal bacterial infection, and had two teeth with caries. The body had been laid in the grave wearing a necklace of eighteen glass beads (Figs. 88, 89); two cast bronze rings (Fig. 85.9 and 10) also accompanied the skeleton. The glass beads, all in good condition, were annular, with one exception, and undecorated, and may be placed in Guido's Group 6, (Guido, 1979 139-64), a type that was in use over a long period of time, occurring in contexts pre-dating the Roman conquest through to the end of the fourth century. The exception (Fig. 88.12) is a 'melon bead' (Guido 1979, 100), a type that is generally disappears, in British contexts, in the course of the second century (Leahy, this volume, page 98).

Abandonment

By the end of the second century, the settlement probably lay abandoned. This may be a consequence of a general decline in the local population, or the result of a wider reorganisation of the landscape. There was no further evidence for activity until the medieval or early post-medieval period, when ridge and furrow cultivation was established.

Sproatley

An in situ Mesolithic flint scatter; a separate disturbed scatter containing Mesolithic to Bronze Age artefacts; two possible Bronze Age barrows; a possible Iron Age square barrow; and Iron Age to early Roman boundary ditches

The archaeological potential of the location of the Sproatley site (Fig. 17) was known from cropmarks and the site was recorded as a possible Roman or earlier settlement (SMR MHU13022). Two possible round barrows, approximately 200m to the east, were also recorded (SMR MHU 18789). As there was a suggestion that the land could be used for future gravel extraction, various alternative routes for the pipeline were investigated, and the pre-construction geophysical survey was extended to cover the width of the field. This revealed a large-scale pattern of linear features, as well as possible settlement, and funerary and boundary features (Fig. 28). Fifteen evaluation trenches along the chosen route of the pipeline showed that a subsoil layer, up to 0.3m thick in places, sealed the underlying archaeological deposits. The whole working width was then stripped of topsoil and, subsequently, of the subsoil layer.

The site slopes gently down to the south-east, towards the Nuttles and Sproatley drains. The top of the archaeological deposits was at 11.5m OD at the north-western end of the excavation area, descending to 7.8m OD at the south-eastern end.

Mesolithic occupation

Mesolithic activity was represented by a flint-working area at the northern end of the site (Fig. 23), which, although having suffered disturbance, was still largely *in situ*. A separate deposit to the south contained a smaller flint assemblage, and had been disturbed and displaced from its original place of deposition. A number of Mesolithic flint tools were also recovered from the fills of later features.

The in situ scatter

Seventy-five per cent of the flintwork recovered from the site came from the northern flint scatter. It is estimated that this comprised over 30,000 pieces of flint, with the assemblage dominated by chips of less than 7mm in size. The deposit was sampled in a chequer-board pattern of one metre squares, a grid 15m by 10m covering the scatter (Fig. 23). Alternate squares were excavated with the entirety of the excavated material retained. Additional squares of particular interest were also targeted, so that a total of 53.2 per cent of the gridded area was excavated. The retained deposits were sub-sampled and sieved for environmental remains and the remainder washed through a 7mm mesh for retrieval of finds.

Analysis of the flintwork from the scatter concentrated on the fresh and slightly edge-damaged flints, excluding chips. In the main, diagnostic flints within the assemblage were typologically dated to the Mesolithic, a date supported by radiocarbon determinations on three hazelnut shells recovered from the layer, which returned calibrated dates of 8350 to 7750; 8600 to 8000; and 8610 to 8320 cal BC (SUERC-24872, -25015 and -24894). The fresh condition of the Mesolithic flints and the occurrence of joining flint fragments suggest that the disturbance from the small later features, described below, had only limited effects on the integrity of the scatter.

The distribution of charcoal recovered from the environmental samples showed three distinct areas of concentration. This may be an indication of the location of three distinct camp fires or hearths. Given their

proximity these are unlikely to have been contemporary and probably represent a sequence of fires in this general location. The densities of flints, hazelnuts and animal bone show a complementary pattern, lower where charcoal concentrations are higher (Fig. 26). This would fit with an interpretation of activity being carried out around the fires. This activity clearly included flint knapping, which was probably focused on the maintenance of tool kits, utilising both locally available flint and prepared cores imported to the site. The small assemblage of animal bone from the scatter included a fragment of an aurochs-sized cattle radius.

The disturbed scatter and other Mesolithic finds

To the south-east of the *in situ* scatter, a large linear feature, **26573**, interpreted as a former stream channel, produced a smaller assemblage of Mesolithic flints. This suggests that the stream was silting up during the Mesolithic period or that the Mesolithic deposits eroded into the stream. Layers of alluvium accumulating after the watercourse had completely silted, covering the area overlying the channel and extending to either side, show that the area was still prone to flooding after the watercourse ceased to be active. Debitage within these deposits is probably of early Neolithic date, reflecting continued, small-scale activity nearby.

Distinct darker layers overlay these alluvial deposits, and were excavated using a similar grid-based method as for the *in situ* scatter. Small numbers of Mesolithic, Bronze Age and Iron Age flints were recovered, along with fragments of ten Beaker pottery vessels (Manby, this volume; Table 14). Two hazelnut shells provided radiocarbon dates of 3700 to 3620 and 1300 to 1050 cal BC (SUERC-24896 and -24895). This range of dating evidence indicates a degree of disturbance and reworking, although the presence of unabraded flint fragments suggests that the flints had not moved very far from their original place of deposition. The location alongside a silted-up palaeochannel suggests that the deposits had been reworked as the banks of the channel eroded.

A Mesolithic base camp?

The deposit containing the larger northern flint scatter is likely to have been a remnant of the Mesolithic ground surface, protected from later plough disturbance within a slight natural hollow. If so, the flint scatter would have originally extended over a wider area, the surviving deposit representing only a fraction of the material that was originally present. The assemblage of flint recovered is not large in comparison with the scatter at Brigham, where over four thousand artefacts were recovered (Manby 1966), but is comparable to the 785 pieces collected, though without the use of sieving, at Stone Carr (Chapman *et al.* 2000). It is certainly the largest assemblage known from the southern part of Holderness.

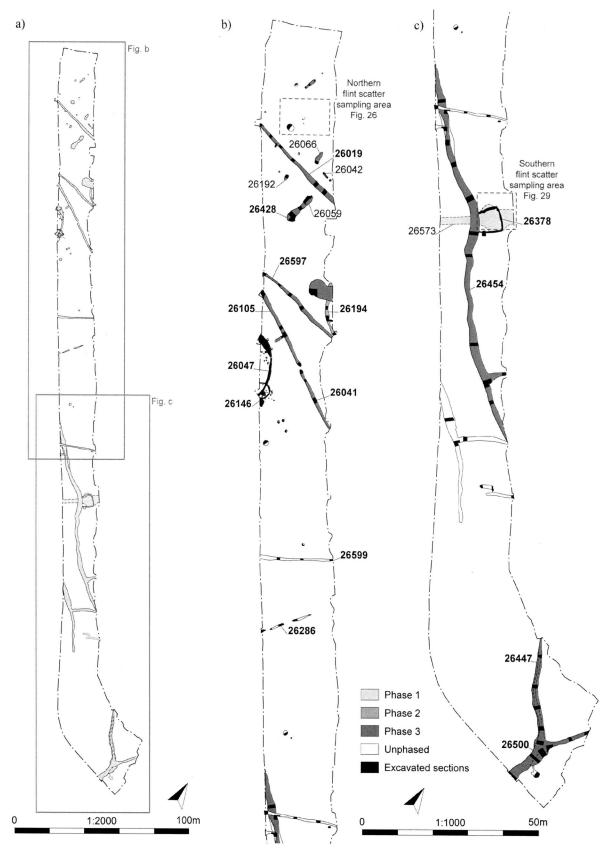

FIG. 23: SPROATLEY: PLAN OF FEATURES

FIG. 24: SPROATLEY: SAMPLE GRID

The size of the assemblage probably points to use as a settlement site, perhaps a winter base camp (Whymark-Anderson, this volume, page 78). The flint assemblage is not of sufficient size to suggest long-term permanent occupation or even regular episodic visits over an extended period, but is perhaps more likely to indicate either a single extended stay or a series of occasional short-term camps. The location may have been a natural clearing. The silted-up palaeochannel, if it was an active watercourse at the time, would have provided a source of water, and potential areas for hunting. This stream could also have been used as routeway and navigational marker through a landscape that was probably already heavily wooded. Itinerant groups could have ranged widely, from the Wolds to the Humber and Doggerland plains, the return to a familiar base camp allowing social interaction between groups.

Neolithic and Bronze Age activity

The earlier Mesolithic activity did not appear to continue into the later years of the period and by this time the use of the site may have been restricted to very occasional mobile groups passing through the area. Evidence for Neolithic activity is limited to a handful of diagnostic flints: a scalene micro-triangle recovered from the disturbed scatter; possible Neolithic debitage and a core from silting and alluvial deposits associated with the palaeochannel; and an intrusive find of a later Neolithic chisel arrowhead (Fig. 83.26) from the *in situ* Mesolithic flint scatter.

Later features cut into the in situ scatter

Five small pits, **26537**, **26538**, **26539**, **26541** and **26554**, measuring between 0.2m and 0.45m across and up to 0.15m deep, with similar irregularly tapering profiles, were cut through the deposits containing the Mesolithic flints. Radiocarbon determinations on charcoal fragments from the fills of pits **26539** and **26554** produced calibrated dates of 2470 to 2244 BC and 2470 to 2296 BC (SUERC-38661 and -38662) respectively. A larger feature, **26572**, a short distance to the south-west, contained a fragment of late eighteenth- or early nineteenth-century pearlware in one of its fills an is probably best interpreted as an animal burrow or a very disturbed pit. The localised disturbance to the Mesolithic deposits represented by this group of features would account for the small number of later finds from the scatter, including one Neolithic and two early Bronze Age arrowheads, as well as a small number of charred grains and seeds, indicating agriculture post-dating the Mesolithic activity (Rackham 2010).

Bronze Age finds were slightly more plentiful. Six pieces of Beaker pottery, weighing 26g were recovered as intrusive elements from the *in situ* scatter and 45 small fragments, weighing 24g in total, were recovered from the reworked scatter, the majority of which were abraded. Two early Bronze Age, Sutton type, barbed and tanged arrowheads were also found as intrusive finds within the *in situ* scatter, the only diagnostically Bronze Age pieces of flintwork recovered from the site.

Laboratory reference	Square	¹⁴C date	δ13C	Calibrated date	Sample type
Northern scatter					
SUERC-24894 (GU-19145)	94	9250 ± 40	-25.1 ‰	8610 (95.4%) 8320 cal BC	Hazel nut
SUERC-24872 (GU-19149)	121	8955 ± 95	*	8350 (95.4%) 7750 cal BC	Hazel nut
SUERC-25015 (GU-19150)	117	9100 ± 80	*	8600 (95.4%) 8000 cal BC	Hazel nut
Southern scatter					
SUERC-24895 (GU-19640)	216	2960 ± 30	-24.1 ‰	1300 (95.4%) 1050 cal BC	Hazel nut
SUERC-24896 (GU-19641)	214	4840 ± 35	-22.3 ‰	3700 60.2%) 3620 cal BC; 3590 (35.2%) 3520 cal BC	Hazel nut
Pits in northern scatter	**Context**				
SUERC-38661 (GU26358)	26553	3885 ± 30	-24.4 ‰	2470 BC (95.1%) 2286 BC; 2247 BC (0.3%) 2244 BC	Charcoal
SUERC-38662 (GU26359)	26557	3900 ± 30	-26.6 ‰	2470 BC (95.4%) 2296 BC	Charcoal
Possible square barrow					
SUERC-36192 (GU-24869)	26359	2755 ± 30	-28.3 ‰	980 BC (95.4%) 820 BC	Charcoal

TABLE 2: RADIOCARBON DATES FROM SPROATLEY

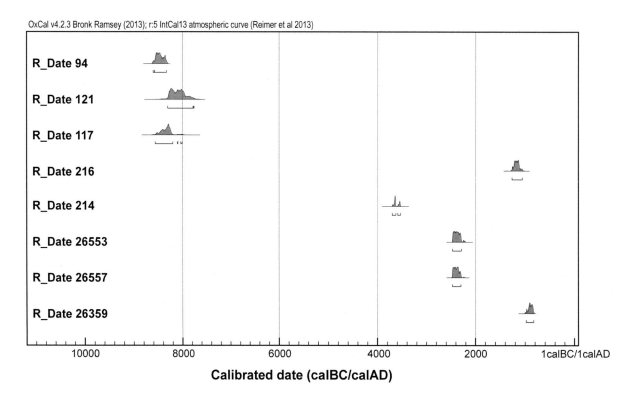

Fig. 25: Radiocarbon dates from Sproatley

Subsequently, a fieldwalking survey has been carried out in the area to the north of the site (Merrony 2007) and has found numerous flints, including two arrowheads.

Possible Bronze Age round barrows

Curvilinear ditch **26047**, visible along the western edge of the site forming an arc with a radius of around 13m (Fig. 27), coincided with a circular anomaly detected during the geophysical survey (Fig. 28). The ditch was up to 2.0m wide and had a maximum depth of 1.28m, although its base was highly irregular, the depth varying along the length of the feature. Although distinctly darker, the fill was similar in composition to the underlying drift deposits and largely devoid of finds. A piece of undiagnostic worked flint was recovered, along with a second flint from a possible posthole in its base. In the absence of datable finds or of material suitable for scientific dating the interpretation of the feature as the perimeter ditch of a Bronze Age barrow has to remain provisional.

An arc of a second ditch, **26194**, a short distance to the north-east of ring ditch **26047**, was also visible as a circular anomaly on the geophysical survey, with a radius of 14m. Only around one fifth of the full circuit

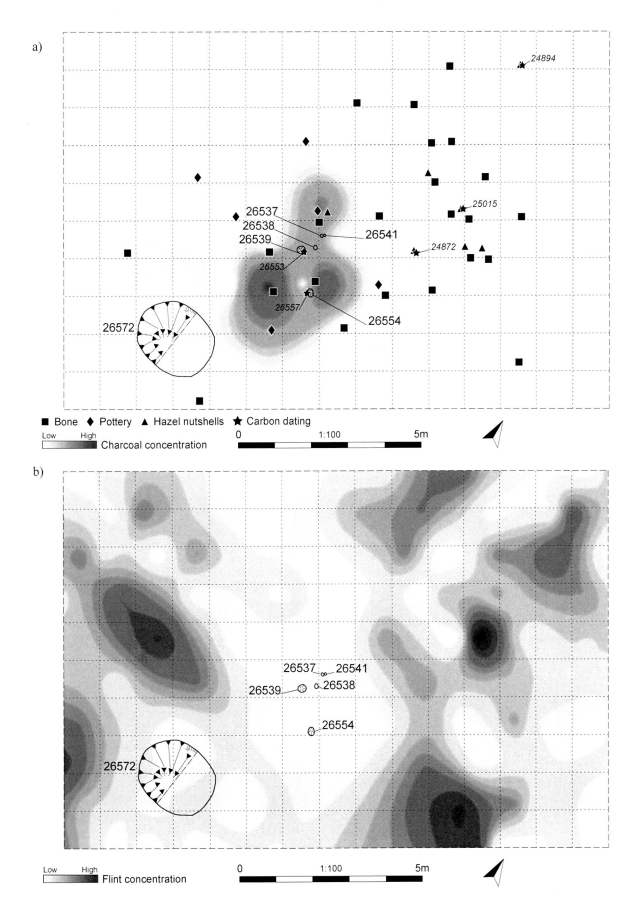

FIG. 26: SPROATLEY, NORTHERN FLINT SCATTER, SHOWING A) DISTRIBUTION OF CHARCOAL, POTTERY, BONE AND CHARRED HAZELNUT SHELLS; AND B) DISTRIBUTION OF FLINT DEBITAGE

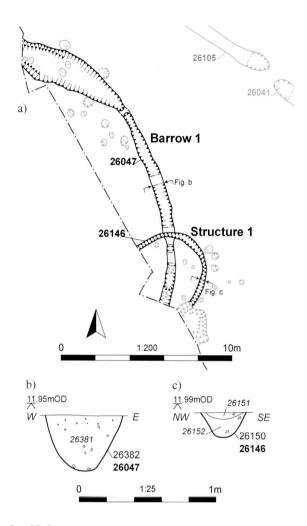

FIG. 27: SPROATLEY, PLAN SHOWING BARROW 1 AND STRUCTURE 1

As they provided no datable material, the interpretation of the two ring ditches as barrows is therefore based on their dimensions and morphological similarity to better preserved, and fully exposed, examples elsewhere. They are much larger than the annular or curvilinear ditches, interpreted as ring gullies of Iron Age roundhouses, recorded elsewhere along the pipeline route. Beyond Holderness some larger roundhouse ring gullies are recorded, such those at Aldclune in Perthshire and Ballacagen Lowgh on the Isle of Man (Pope 2003, 99-100), but neither of these examples exceeded 20m in diameter and the great majority of roundhouses in northern England are less than 15m in diameter (*ibid.* 100).

As well as the third similar monument seen on the geophysical survey results, there are cropmarks of two further round barrows at Sproatley Grange approximately 500m to the north-east of the Sproatley excavation area (SMR MHU18789). If these interpretations are correct, then the Sproatley and Sproatley Grange barrows may be a part of an extensive funerary landscape on the edges of the valley now occupied by the Nuttles and Sproatley Drains. If the barrows were intended to be visible from a distance, their occurrence would imply that the area was not densely wooded at the time they were constructed.

Iron Age remains

Structure 1 (Fig. 27)

Ring gully **26146**, extending beyond the western limit of excavation, truncated ring ditch **26047**. The visible portion of the feature formed a semi-circle with a diameter of 4.5m. If this ring gully surrounded a circular structure, it would perhaps have been too small for habitation, and the single small sherd of hand-made pottery recovered from the gully is much less than might be expected from a domestic feature. An agricultural function, such as a drainage gully around hay-rick, may be a plausible alternative. A group of undated pits clustered to the south-east may have been related to the ring gully, but are not readily interpretable.

Possible Iron Age square barrow (Fig. 29)

Three sides of a possible sub-square enclosure, **26378**, were cut into the disturbed flint scatter, the fourth side possibly having been removed by a later boundary ditch. The ditch was up to 0.70m wide and 0.22m deep with a steep-sided flat-bottomed profile. Assuming that a fourth side had been removed by the later ditch, the feature would have originally have enclosed an area of 6.20m by 5.80m. A possible recut, **26390**, was confined solely to the north-western side of the enclosure. No features were revealed within the enclosed area.

was exposed. At 1.1m wide and 0.35m deep, this was smaller than ditch **26047** and also more regular, with a gently sloping symmetrical profile. The fills and general appearance of the two features were, however, very similar and both are likely to have originated as the same kind of monument.

Horizontal truncation may have reduced the depth of both ring ditches to some extent, but the survival nearby of the *in situ* Mesolithic flint scatter suggests that the destructive effects of ploughing in this area were not great and it is more likely that they would never have been much of much greater depth than that excavated. This has implications for estimates of the size of any mounds within the ditched areas, as the amount of material won from the digging of the ditches would have been small; no signs of the remains of any mounds were evident, and the ring ditches may have been more akin to mortuary enclosures. Although the geophysical survey suggested that a third feature, approximately 22m in diameter, might have been present, extending some way into the eastern side of the excavation area, no corresponding ditch was found during the excavation.

FIG. 28: SPROATLEY: FEATURES OVERLAID ON GEOPHYSICS RESULTS

The only artefact recovered from the ditch was a large fragment of pottery (SF 562) which displayed the full profile of a shapeless jar (Cumberpatch 2009a) lying on its side in the south-eastern corner. A small piece of charcoal from a bulk sample of the fill returned a radiocarbon date of 980 to 820 cal BC (SUERC-36192), considerably earlier than the likely production date of the pottery vessel (Cumberpatch, pers. comm.), suggesting that the charcoal sample, used in the absence of any more suitable sample for dating, could have been residual or from old wood.

Grave **26353**, cutting the south-eastern side of the possible square barrow, was 1.4m long and 1.25m wide at its slightly wider southern end. Bone preservation was poor, the few surviving degraded fragments, **26354**, providing little information. Three bronze finger rings within the fills of the grave (SFs 565, 566 and 567; Fig. 85.16 and 12) are likely to have belonged to the interred individual, and fragments of an iron object (SF 564, Fig. 86.3), parts of a ring or curved bar, were also found.

Graves were commonly dug into square barrow ditches, although normally along the line of the ditch, as, for instance, at Nosterfield Quarry in North Yorkshire

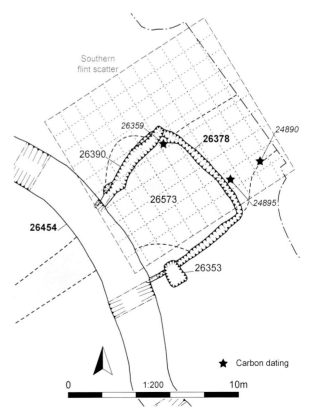

FIG. 29: SPROATLEY: POSSIBLE SQUARE BARROW

(Dickson and Hopkinson 2011, 151), rather than across it. It has been suggested that the positioning of such satellite burials may have had some significance to the community using the cemetery, relationships in death perhaps reflecting relationships in life (Giles 2012, 76-80). The square form of feature **26378**, its likely Iron Age date and the subsequent funerary use, all lend weight to the interpretation as a square barrow, the primary burial of which had been lost to later ploughing.

The presence of at least one possible Iron Age square barrow would indicate that the site continued its funerary usage beyond the Bronze Age. Although there is nothing to suggest that the presence of the earlier round barrows played any role in the location of the Iron Age barrow, and their propinquity could be merely accidental, it is quite possible that the Iron Age population would have had an awareness of the earlier use of the site and therefore considered it an appropriate place to lay their dead to rest. There are plentiful examples of the enduring use of burial places (for instance, Fenton-Thomas 2011, 373, 383, 389).

Trapezoidal enclosures (Figs. 23, 28)

The extensive linear anomalies visible on the geophysical survey seemingly radiated from a focus to the west of the northern end of the excavation area. These anomalies proved to be substantial ditches where they were exposed. Ditches **26500**, **26447** and **26454** could be seen on the geophysical survey to be a single feature recrossing the excavation area, while ditches **26286**, **26105**, **26041** and **26019** are different elements of the overall pattern. This must have been a planned landscape or an evolving system, where the ditches respected each other, and they are therefore, almost certainly, broadly contemporary.

In total, eight small sherds of Iron Age pottery were recovered from ditch **26454,** with two large sherds from its southward continuation, ditch **26447**. Seven small sherds of a samian dish of probable Antonine date were recovered from the primary fill of intervention **26401** through ditch **26454**, implying that the ditch was maintained well into the second century. It is nevertheless notable that this vessel was the only find of clearly Roman date from any of the elements of this ditch system, especially when contrasted with the relatively well dated linear features on the nearby Brandywell site.

The sub-division of the Iron Age or early Roman landscape has been revealed widely in Holderness and beyond, but the radiating boundary ditches, seen here and at Brandywell, appeared to be otherwise unique along the pipeline route. It should, however, be noted that the pattern here was only clear because of the extended geophysical surveys; their apparent uniqueness could simply be because of the unusually large extent of the surveyed area. The trapezoidal enclosures formed by

the ditches had maximum dimensions of at least 130m by 90m, and infilling with smaller features, pits and lesser boundaries between the major boundary ditches, is suggested by the geophysical survey and to a degree by the excavated evidence of a small number of pits and linear features. The radiating ditches ran down towards the Sproatley and Nuttles drains and their function was, perhaps, intimately linked to the valley wetlands. They could, for instance, have funnelled livestock, returning from grazing on the marshes, towards a farmstead at the apex of the system, or simply had a drainage function in an arable agricultural regime.

Bone at the site was poorly preserved and only nineteen fragments were recovered from features belonging to this phase of activity. Environmental evidence similarly provided few clues to the economy of the site. The bone assemblage was better preserved at the Brandywell site, and the conclusions from that site can perhaps be taken to apply to Sproatley as well: that these were largely sites producing, rather than consuming, animal products. An interpretation of the trapezoidal enclosures as stock management features therefore seems reasonable.

Early Roman pits (Fig. 23)

Roman features were confined to the northern part of the excavation area and can perhaps be regarded as an extension of the neighbouring Brandywell site. The wheel-thrown pottery from elongated 0.80m-dccp pit **26428**, and from pit **26059**, which truncated it, suggests that they both infilled during the second half of the second century or first half of the third century. This would have been contemporary with the latest phase of Roman activity at Brandywell. Sampling the fills from these two pits produced over five hundred charred cereal grains: mostly wheat, with both naked bread wheat and spelt varieties identified. There was also a significant proportion of oats. The relative richness of these samples was in marked contrast to the samples from other features across the site, which were almost totally lacking in any organic remains. An absence of evidence of scorching in the surrounding deposits suggests that these grains were not charred *in situ*, but were deposited within the pits as burnt refuse. They provide evidence that cereals were being processed on site, the contrast with the earlier periods reinforcing the impression that the pre-Roman economy was largely pastoral.

Four other small irregular pits nearby, pits **26022**, **26042**, **26066** and **26192**, are likely to have been the product of the same phase of activity, but produced only small quantities of hand-made sherds. A relatively large proportion of the hand-made pottery from the site, 56.5 per cent by sherd count and 32.0 per cent by weight, derived from remnant spreads of subsoil in this part of the site, indicating some loss of evidence for Iron Age or early Roman activity to later ploughing. Unstratified wheel-thrown pottery included mid-first- to early second-century wares.

Medieval and post-medieval agriculture

The site is close to the watercourses now marked by the Wyton, Nuttles and Sproatley Drains and is relatively low lying; in periods of adverse climatic conditions it would have been marginal land, prone to flooding. This is illustrated by the deep clay-rich subsoil layer, probably formed from the incorporation of flood deposits into reworked soils. The widespread medieval and later drainage of marginal land in Holderness would have made the area more attractive for farming and by the late medieval or earlier post-medieval period the site had been given over to strip fields. A possible field boundary, **26599**, and a series of furrows along with a number of shallow pits probably date from this time. The geophysical survey suggests that north-east to south-west oriented furrows extend across much of the wider area around the excavation.

Nuttles

Iron Age ring gully and Roman field systems

The Nuttles site was targeted for evaluation trenching, as the geophysical survey had detected a number of anomalies. Excavation of five trenches confirmed the presence of archaeological features and a controlled topsoil strip was then carried out (Fig. 30).

Ten residual flints, including an end scraper, provide evidence of activity pre-dating the Iron Age, the flake morphology indicating a late Neolithic or Bronze Age date.

Iron Age ring gully (Figs. 31, 32)

A small settlement was established, probably during the later Iron Age, with a single penannular gully, surviving as two segments, **31514** and **31522**, enclosing an area 9m in diameter. The gully was a fairly well defined feature, up to 1.40m wide and 0.50m deep. Both arcs of the gully produced assemblages of hand-made pottery, the largest quantity from the terminal, **31085**, of the southern arc, **31522**. A charred wheat grain from the fill of intervention **31022** in the northern arc of the gully gave a radiocarbon date of 348 to 52 cal BC (SUERC-38666). Joining sherds from three vessels were noted between the fill of the southern terminal and one of the fills of a very shallow curvilinear gully immediately to the south, **31519**.

Ditch **31518**, extending from the southern terminal of the ring gully, and the branch off it, **31101**, appeared to mark the position of small, broadly contemporary, enclosures, but the full extent of these shallow features did not survive. A cluster of six pits within the area defined by the ring gully may have been contemporary with it, perhaps representing internal features of the structure enclosed by the ring gully, or the settings of posts used during its construction. Two nearby pits, **31015** and **31502**, may also date to the same phase of use. Both produced quantities of burnt bone and posthole **31059** also yielded four sherds of pottery.

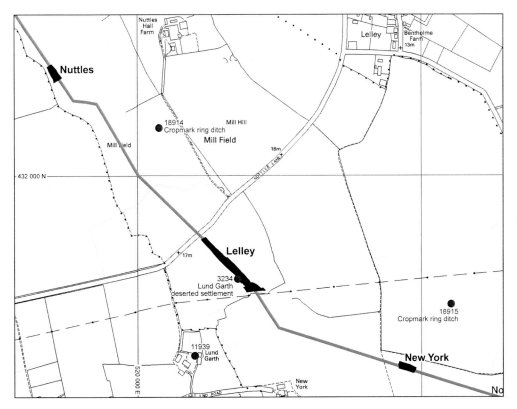

FIG. 30: NUTTLES, LELLEY AND NEW YORK: LOCATION. CONTAINS OS DATA © CROWN COPYRIGHT [1:10 000 MAPPING]

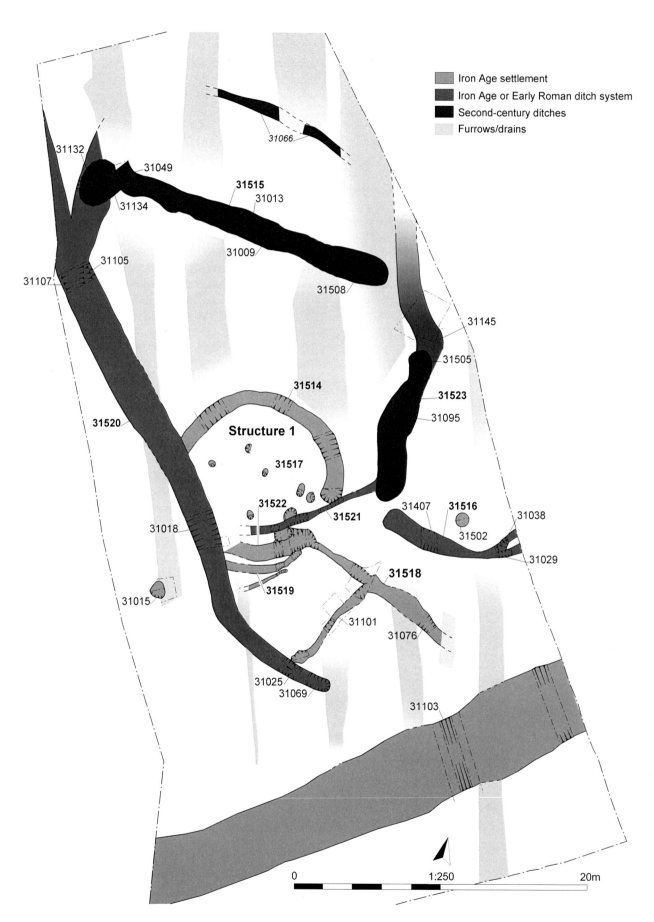

Iron Age settlement
Iron Age or Early Roman ditch system
Second-century ditches
Furrows/drains

31132
31049
31134
31105
31107
31066
31515
31013
31009
31508
31145
31505
31523
31095
31514
Structure 1
31517
31520
31522
31521
31516
31407
31502
31038
31018
31029
31015
31518
31519
31101
31076
31025
31069
31103

0   1:250   20m

Fig. 31 Nuttles: All features

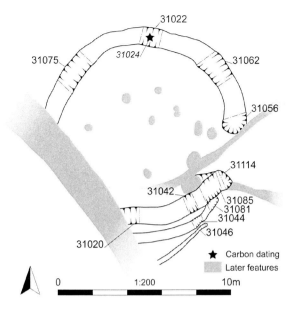

FIG. 32: NUTTLES: STRUCTURE 1

Late Iron Age or early Roman ditches

At some point during the late Iron Age, the structure fell into disuse, and a system of ditches was established. The absence of wheel-thrown pottery within deposits associated with this phase suggests that this change took place before Roman influence was well established. Ditch **31521**, a small feature extending south-westwards across the southern side of the ring gully, produced no dating evidence. Its western end was truncated by a slightly irregular ditch, **31520**, which had also removed the south-western side of the ring gully. Up to 0.75m deep, this ditch became increasingly shallow to the south, before terminating.

Second century AD ditch system (Fig. 31)

The ditch system was subsequently re-organised and elaborated during the later first or second centuries. Lying to the north of the penannular gully, ditch **31515** was 0.80m deep and had a shallow recut, **31009**, visible in one excavated section. Wheel-thrown wares were present in all of the fills of this ditch. One of the hand-made vessels is of particular interest: a shallow bowl with an inturned rim (Fig. 96.94) that may represent an unusual case of local potters copying wheel-thrown forms. The western end of ditch **31515** was in a confused area of the site, with a possible recut or large pit visible in section at the point where it cut ditch **31132**. At its eastern end, it terminated around one metre short of the point where it would have intersected ditch **31145**, perhaps implying contemporaneity between these two features.

The features along the eastern side of the site were recorded as a sinuous ditch with several recuts, but might be better interpreted as a line of intercutting pits.

Feature **31145** produced over fifty sherds of first- to second-century pottery, and a sherd from a reeded-rim mortarium, of late third- to fourth-century type, which probably derived from the furrow overlying the poorly defined western side of the feature. Feature **31523**, stratigraphically later than feature **31145**, contained similar wares to ditch **31515**, dated to the later first and second centuries.

At the southern limit of the site, a large ditch **31103**, nearly 2m deep, had no surviving stratigraphic relationships to the other features but the composition of the pottery assemblage from its fills was broadly comparable to that from ditch **31515** and it is likely that it was backfilling at the same time. Three small amorphous lumps of pale green mineral (SF 323), recovered from fill **31104**, may have been debris from metal working.

The considerable quantity of second-century pottery from the site, which included broken but substantially complete vessels, is certainly more than would be expected from simple field boundary or drainage ditches and indicates that there was a continuation of occupation, if not on the site itself, then very close by. The absence of later pottery, with the exception of the single late third- to fourth-century mortarium sherd, suggests that nearby occupation had ceased by the end of the second century. Thereafter, the site may have continued to be used as open pasture, such a use leaving few archaeological traces. Five furrows crossed the excavation area, traces of medieval or early post-medieval ridge and furrow agriculture.

Lelley

Late Iron Age ring gullies, settlement features and human burial; Anglo-Saxon activity; medieval enclosures and possible building and oven associated with manorial site

The pipeline crossed a complex area of cropmarks, identified with the medieval manorial site of Lund Garth (SMR MHU3234) and extending to the east beyond the pipeline working width. The name of the medieval site is preserved in Lund Garth Farm (SMR MHU11939), 300m to the south-west of the excavation area (Fig. 30). Cropmarks of possible ring ditches are recorded 500m to the north (SMR MHU18914) and 730m to the east (SMR MHU18915).

Nineteen sherds of medieval pottery were found during fieldwalking, all of them from a 60m-long stretch in the centre of the field. This area corresponded to dense anomalies detected by the geophysical survey. In an attempt to find a less archaeologically damaging alternative route for the pipeline, the magnetometry survey was extended by 60m to the north-east (Fig. 38). This revealed a system of rectilinear enclosures continuing across a wide area to the east of the pipeline route. Earlier phases of activity extending to the north-west were uncovered by evaluation trenching, which also confirmed the presence of the medieval ditched enclosures. The subsequently opened excavation area crossed a slight ridge, roughly corresponding to the north-western limit of the ditched enclosures and forming the highest ground in the immediate locality. The top of the archaeological deposits dropped from 16.9m OD on this ridge to 14.4m OD at the south-eastern limit of excavation.

Twenty-nine struck flints were recovered from the site, the majority probably of later Neolithic and Bronze Age date, providing the earliest evidence for activity at the site.

Late Iron Age settlement

The excavated Iron Age features were not identifiable from the geophysical survey, so it is not possible to say whether the settlement continues in the dense pattern of magnetic anomalies to the east of the site. This phase of use is consistent with a pattern of dispersed farmsteads in the landscape, each with no more than a few roundhouses and associated buildings.

Structure 1 (Fig. 34)

Ring gully **35593**, on the north-western side of the site, enclosed an area varying in diameter from 9.8m to 10.5m, and had a clearly defined east-facing entrance. A second, north-facing break in the ring was the result of truncation by ploughing. A large assemblage of hand-made pottery was recovered from the fills of the gully: nearly 38kg in total. A single medieval sherd is presumed to be intrusive or misascribed. The distribution of the pottery within the gully indicated a clear preference for deposition of finds in the southern half: eighty per cent of the sherds were deposited towards or at the southern terminal, with a lesser concentration directly opposite the entrance at the back of the ring gully.

Structure 2 (Fig. 35)

The heavily truncated remains of a second ring gully, **35601**, to the south-east of Structure 1, enclosed an area 5m in diameter. Two possible terminals, one rather better defined than the other, could have formed a south-west facing entrance. A second break in the gully suggested a possible south-east-facing entrance, but the gully was very shallow and a later ditch had truncated most of this part of the feature. Eighty-eight sherds of hand-made pottery were recovered from the gully but, unlike Structure 1, there was no clear indication of any pattern in the distribution of sherds.

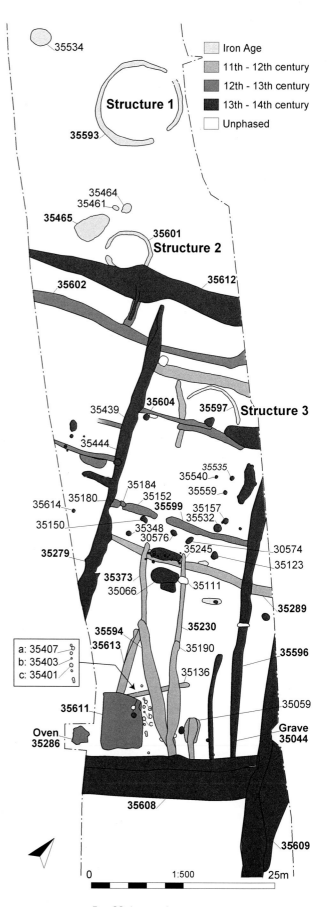

FIG. 33: LELLEY: ALL FEATURES

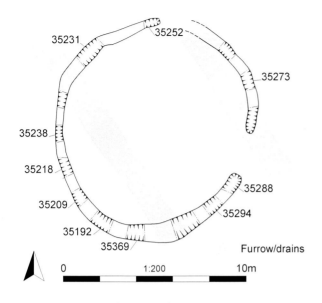

FIG. 34: LELLEY: STRUCTURE 1

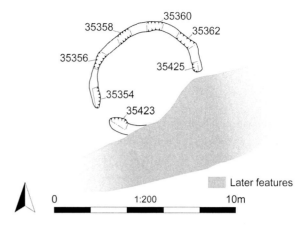

Later features

FIG. 35: LELLEY: STRUCTURE 2

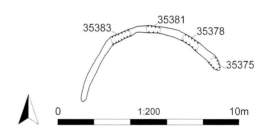

FIG. 36: LELLEY: STRUCTURE 3

Structure 3 (Fig. 36)

A curvilinear feature, **35597**, to the south-east of Structure 2, described a large proportion of a semicircle and may have been the heavily truncated remains of a further ring gully. If circular, it would have enclosed an area around 7.5m in diameter. It produced 242 hand-made pottery sherds.

Pits (Fig. 33)

To the west of Structure 1, pit **35534** had a fill rich in charcoal and heat-reddened clay and produced a small assemblage of hand-made pottery. Closer to Structure 2, pits **35464** and **35461**, produced forty-nine and eleven sherds respectively. A shallow undated feature with an irregular profile, **35465**, just to the west of Structure 2, was sealed beneath a spread layer, **35507**, rich in charcoal and burnt bone fragments. The upper surface of this layer had been prominently marked by plough-scores, made before the accumulation of the subsoil layer that covered the site. At least three crushed pottery vessels, along with other pottery sherds, were visible in the surface of this layer. The bulk of the 219 sherds from the layer were typical of Iron Age tradition wares, and are likely to have been associated with the nearby structure, but sherds from an Anglo-Saxon vessel were also recovered.

Iron Age activity towards the south end of the site

Although the overwhelming bulk of the Iron Age finds came from the north-western half of the site, a number of later features towards the other end of the excavation area contained small quantities of sherds, suggesting that there may have been another focus of activity to the north of ditch **35608**. No features in this part of the site could be positively ascribed to a pre-medieval period, but stratigraphically early features lacking other dating evidence, such as ditches **35289** and **35136**, could have been contemporary with the Iron Age settlement.

Burial

The moderately well preserved but fragmentary skeleton of a late term human foetus was found within a very shallow pit or grave, **35044**, a short distance to the north of ditch **35608**. The grave had been disturbed, in part, by ploughing, but some of the damage to the surviving long bones may also have resulted from truncation by an early medieval ditch cut through the grave. This stratigraphic relationship indicates that the burial pre-dates the establishment of at least some elements of the early medieval enclosures (see below), but it is otherwise undated.

Roman artefacts

There was a marked discontinuity following the abandonment of the Iron Age roundhouses with Roman artefacts limited to four pieces of pottery, including a possible Nene Valley beaker sherd from posthole **35401**, and samian and Crambeck grey ware sherds, and several large pieces of tile, including three pieces of *tegula* and two of *imbrex*. The tile was collected during initial topsoil removal: two different fabrics are represented, which have the same range of inclusions and other traits as can be seen in material from the Washingborough tilery, immediately to the east of Lincoln (Darling and Wood 1976). Tiles from this area were traded by boat down the Witham to its mouth, near Boston (Vince and Irving 2011), and they have also been noted at sites in the Lindsey Marshes (Vince 2006 and Vince and Steane 2006). These examples from Lelley, however, are the first to be identified north of the Humber.

Early medieval activity

In addition to the remains of several Iron Age vessels, the charcoal-rich deposit, **35507**, overlying pit **35465** to the west of Structure 2, also included eight sherds from a single jar in an organic-tempered fabric, probably dating to between the fifth and eight centuries AD. Pottery from this period is rare in Holderness. Its presence shows that there was some ongoing activity on the site, prefiguring that of the tenth century.

The establishment of the ditched enclosures

The central part of the excavation area was dominated by a series of ditches, forming a rectilinear system of small enclosures. The chronology of these ditches is complex, but it is possible that the rudiments of the system were in place as early as the tenth century, as the various fills yielded forty-eight Anglo-Scandinavian sherds representing up to thirty-two vessels. The features were bounded by ditches **35612** to the north and **35608** to the south. The line of these two boundaries must have been established very early but they were long-lived features, maintained and recut so that their fills contained finds from a range of dates.

The stratigraphic relationships of the fills of the elements of the ditch system, reflecting the sequence of abandonment and infilling of the ditches, show that those running longitudinally along the excavation area survived longer than those crossing transversely. Indeed, some of the transverse ditches produced little or no dating evidence and may have been backfilled before the intensification of activity early in the medieval period. This is particularly true of ditch **35289** which produced no pottery that could be dated beyond the Iron Age. The bulk of the Anglo-Scandinavian sherds were retrieved from features immediately to the north of ditch **35608**, especially from the smaller and slightly sinuous ditches in this part of the site, principally features **35230**, **35373** and **35594**. A U-shaped spur (SF 262, Fig. 86.7) was recovered from ditch **35230**.

Oven (Fig. 37)

On the south-west side of the site and extending beyond the original edge of excavation, a feature interpreted as an oven probably dated from the late eleventh or twelfth century. A sub-circular layer of cobbles, **35436**, set in an irregular levelling layer of clay, **35476**, was overlain by smaller cobbles, **35286**, in a clay matrix **35371**, scorched red in places as a result of exposure to high temperatures. A freestanding clay kerb or wall, **35437**, surviving in places to a height of 0.08m, partially constrained the cobble layers; it was probably originally penannular, having been lost to the south, but opening to the north, where the cobbles extended beyond its surviving limits. The clay kerb incorporated a large fragment of a disc-shaped rotary quern (SF 279). A layer of scorched compacted clay which sealed the cobbles could have been the remains of the collapsed superstructure, of which the kerb is the surviving *in situ* remnant.

Below the levelling layer, three pits were recorded in section, one of which, **35529**, tentatively interpreted as a fire-pit from an earlier phase of the oven, produced quantities of charred cereal grains. Oats, wheat and barley were present at relatively high densities. A distinct dark grey layer of clay, **35505**, extending beyond the edge of excavation and underlying the levelling layers, produced a sherd of Anglo-Scandinavian pottery, providing a mid-tenth- to late eleventh-century *terminus post quem* for the oven. This layer also contained four fragments of burnt daub with distinct wattle impressions (Fig. 107.16 and 17).

Large rectangular feature

The construction of an oven strongly suggests that there was occupation nearby, the rectangular feature immediately to its east being a possible, if not entirely convincing, candidate for its location. This feature, **35611**, had a flat base and a maximum depth of 0.20m, and cut ditches **35613** and **35136**, associated with the earliest development of the field system. A small assemblage of pottery recovered from the feature included two sherds of East Yorkshire quartz and chalk tempered ware, probably of twelfth- to mid-thirteenth-century date as well as earlier Torksey and Yorkshire gritty wares. Bulk samples from the various excavated fills of the feature contained over 160 charred grains, from which club wheat, barley and oats could be positively identified, as well as peas and hazelnut shell. Oyster shells were also noted.

A line of shallow postholes just beyond the north-eastern edge of the rectangular feature seemed to form a coherent group, all of similar shape, dimensions and profile. A single sherd of Roman pottery, from a colour-coated beaker, dated to the late second century AD, was recovered from one posthole **35401**; seven small crumbs of pottery from posthole **35407** were probably residual Iron Age material. The disposition of these features suggests that they were associated with the rectangular feature: if that was so, a fragment of clay pipe, of Yorkshire bulbous bowl type and dated to 1660 to 1700 (White 2009) from feature **35403** must have been intrusive.

FIG. 37: LELLEY, OVEN

The rectangular form and flat base of feature **35611** is very reminiscent of a sunken-featured building, although a twelfth-century date would be very late for what is a typical Anglo-Saxon form of structure. The general paucity of cultural material from it would argue against a domestic function. It is perhaps more likely that it was the site of an agricultural structure, such as a small barn. Though its contemporaneity with the oven cannot be unequivocally demonstrated, it is quite possible that these two distinctive features had related functions.

Medieval development of the ditched enclosures

The development of the ditch system continued on the same broad orientation established in the early medieval period, the ditches mostly being open to receive finds in the twelfth and thirteenth centuries, when activity at the site, at least as measured by the quantity of ceramics deposited, was at its zenith. The geophysical survey evidence (Fig. 38) indicates that the linear features visible in the excavation area continued to the east, forming at least three more contiguous enclosed areas.

Several of the smaller ditches fell out of use and the transverse ditches, **35604** and **35599** along with its continuation **35152**, produced no finds that could be confidently dated beyond the thirteenth century. Pit **35184**, cut into the westward continuation of ditch **35599**

but probably of the same general period, contained a fragment of a heavily worn and fire-affected disc-shaped quern stone (SF 265, Fig. 106.4). The longitudinal ditches, **35279** and **35596** in particular, continued to be maintained and recut.

The greatest concentration of finds during this period was further to the north than in the tenth and eleventh centuries. The most likely locus for this occupation was the remnants of a crushed chalk surface in the centre of the excavation area, **35366** and **35130**. These two chalk spreads, the group of thirteen small postholes cutting into them or in close proximity, and the five large postholes, **35348**, **35150**, **35576**, **35574** and **35123**, on the north side of the spread, may have been the remains of the floor surface and posts of a possible domestic or agricultural structure. Further to the north, a loose group of pits, including features **35540**, **35555**, **35157**, **35532** and, **35559**, seem to have been from the same phase of activity. Pit **35157** contained an iron horseshoe nail (Fig. 86.6), its occurrence in a dated context providing a useful confirmation of the thirteenth-century date (Clarke 1995, 87) for this type of nail. Though the evidence for the chalk surface and associated postholes being the remains of a structure is not entirely compelling, the site produced more than 2000 sherds of medieval pottery weighing over 25kg in total, an assemblage which would imply that there was settlement close by, if not actually on the site.

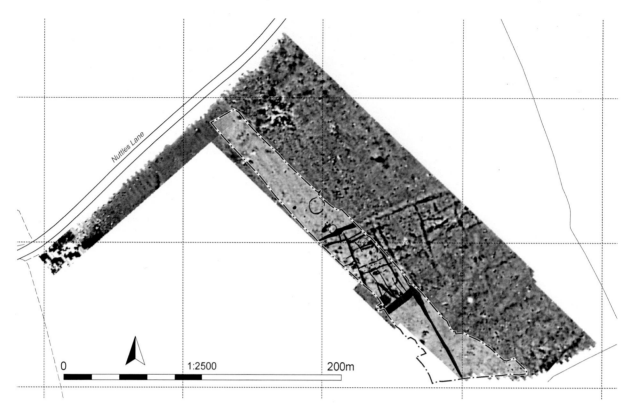

FIG. 38: LELLEY, SITE PLAN OVERLAIN ON GEOPHYSICAL SURVEY RESULTS

A large sub-oval pit, **35066**, that truncated the crushed chalk surface must have been dug after the structure had fallen out of use. An assemblage of over 250 pottery sherds, which included sherds dated to the early to mid-thirteenth century, was recovered from the pit, the largest assemblage from any of the medieval features. It also produced the remains of a C-shaped iron object (SF 260, Fig. 86.4), probably half of a double looped buckle frame. A fragment of a D-shaped copper alloy buckle (SF 37, Fig. 85.12) was recovered from the subsoil from an evaluation trench in the same part of the site.

Thirteenth- to fourteenth-century pottery fabrics were markedly scarcer than twelfth- to thirteenth-century wares, though still widely distributed in the fills of the larger ditches and many of the pits in the central part of the excavation area. Ditch **35609** may have been recut and extended south-eastwards at this time, after the similarly large ditch, **35608**, along the southern boundary of the site, had finally infilled. An upper fill of ditch **35608** produced an iron knife blade (SF 261, Fig. 86.5), while ditch **35609** yielded a large fragment of quern (SF 264), including part of the grinding surface. The mollusc shell assemblages from ditch **35609** indicated that it had held standing water.

Nine fragments of roof tile from later medieval features (Vince and Steane 2009) are not closely datable, as no suspension nibs are present, but their similarity of visual appearance and manufacturing technique to tiles recovered from Hull (Armstrong and Armstrong 1987) and Beverley (Armstrong 1991 and Armstrong 1992) are consistent with a mid-twelfth- to fifteenth-century date. This suggests that there may have been a tile-roofed building close by in the later medieval period. However, there seems to have been an abrupt cessation of activity thereafter, with very little, other than unstratified finds, post-dating the fourteenth century. One of the more notable finds, recovered from the subsoil in an evaluation trench to the south-east of ditch **35608**, was an architectural fragment: a section of a miniature column of millstone grit (Fig. 106.5).

Discussion: Lund Garth

The excavation results provided confirmation of the medieval date of the previously known cropmark site and increases confidence in its identification with the historic Lund Garth. The morphology of the excavated remains and their continuation seen in the geophysical survey results, with at least three contiguous ditched enclosures, suggests that the site consisted of a short row of settlement compounds. The documentary evidence for the history of the manor prior to the sixteenth century is scant (Allison 1984, 193) and by the time that it emerges clearly into the historical record, the remains revealed in the excavation had been long abandoned. It is likely that the focus of settlement had, by then, moved elsewhere, possibly to the area now occupied by Lund Garth Farm, 300m to the south.

Both the excavation results and the geophysical evidence suggest that the northern edge of the ditch system respected the line of a low, natural ridge which ran across the site, utilising it as a natural boundary, with a different land-use to the north of it. The First Edition Ordnance Survey map of 1858 shows a road or trackway following this line, running from Lund Garth Farm to join the Preston to Lelley Road, although no evidence of this track was found during the excavation.

New York

Iron Age ring gullies and Iron Age or Roman ditch systems

The New York excavation area (Fig. 30) was located almost centrally within an area of locally high ground, at around 18.0m OD. This gave the site an open aspect, with long views to the west, north and east.

Strong geophysical anomalies were evaluated and were found to correspond to changes in the drift geology. Two features were recorded at this stage (Savage 2011). Ditch **3619**, located 25m to the west of the eventual excavation area produced twenty pieces of pottery, including sherds from a carinated bowl of the late first to second century and a jar with tall everted rim, probably of similar date. Ditch **3612**, located 9m to the east of the excavation area, was a later feature, but produced only a small quantity of hand-made pottery. The full extent of the remains at the site only became apparent during monitoring of topsoil stripping. Heavily truncated features were visible (Fig. 39) and full area excavation was carried out.

Late Iron Age settlement

Four stratigraphically early curvilinear gullies were recorded, all heavily truncated by later features. These have been tentatively interpreted as ring gullies associated with roundhouses.

Structure 1 (Fig. 40)

Gully **120021**, near the western limit of the excavation area, survived to a depth of 0.26m. The well defined eastern terminal may have marked one side of a south-east facing entrance, but no sign of its counterpart survived. The upper fill of the gully was charcoal-rich silt incorporating occupation debris, including animal bone and pottery. Small quantities of iron-working waste and slag from this fill provide evidence for nearby metal working, although probably only on a very small scale. Charred oat and barley grains provide an indication of crop utilisation. The pottery consisted of only a small assemblage of body sherds.

Structures 2 and 3 (Fig. 41)

In an area of complex stratigraphy in the centre of the excavation area, the overlapping arcs of two curvilinear gullies could have been the remains of ring gullies, but neither arc was of constant radius; their interpretation as structural remains is, at best, open to question. Structure 2, the earlier and shallower gully, produced seven sherds of pottery from one of its fills; Structure 3, the later gully, was up to 0.50m deep, and produced a similar quantity of pottery.

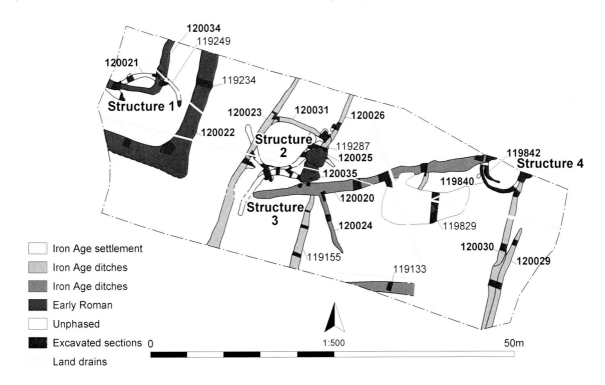

FIG. 39: NEW YORK: PLAN OF ALL FEATURES

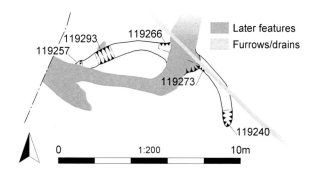

FIG. 40: NEW YORK: STRUCTURE 1

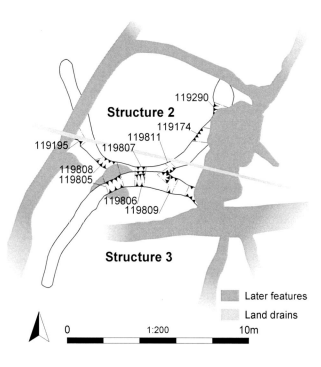

FIG. 41: NEW YORK: STRUCTURES 2 AND 3

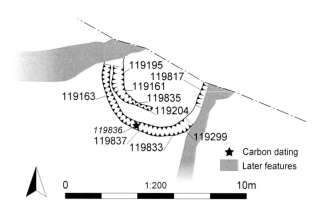

FIG. 42: NEW YORK: STRUCTURE 4

Structure 4 (Fig. 42)

A small, but clearly defined, gully, **119840**, formed a fairly regular semi-circle, running into the northern limit of excavation. Fifteen sherds of pottery, including one large rim sherd, were recovered from its various fills. A charred cereal grain from the fill of intervention **119837** returned a radiocarbon date of 201 to 46 cal BC (SUERC-38667). A fragment of a second gully, **119842**, set within the internal space of gully **119840**, may have been a remnant of a different phase of building or, just possibly, a feature within the same overall structure. Gully **119842** was insubstantial, tapering out to the east.

Late Iron Age ditch systems

The linear features post-dated the possible settlement features but were similarly devoid of any pottery or other artefacts of diagnostically Roman date, and are likely to have been abandoned before Roman material culture had spread through the region. The ditches in the central area of the site collectively formed an extended 'H' shape in plan and formed a coherent, and probably broadly contemporary, group. The western side of the group, **120023**, truncated Structure 2, while the eastern side, **120026**, cut the fills of a large irregular pit **119287** and was itself truncated by a later feature, **120025**. At the point where it intersected ditch **120031**, ditch **120026** produced a group of pottery sherds from which two vessels (SF 1383 and 1384) stand out, being largely complete and in a distinct fabric tempered by prominent angular rock fragments. It is of note that the hand-made pottery from the ditches, in general, is in a far better condition than the pottery from the fills of the ring gullies: it is therefore unlikely to be residual from the earlier settlement phase but originating rather from contemporary activity. Ditch **120026** also produced a fine-grained sandstone pebble with a hollow in each face, showing signs of percussion wear (SF 1382, Fig. 106.6).

Towards the eastern limit of excavation, ditch **120030**, recut on at least one occasion, was roughly parallel to ditch **120026**. It produced rims and bases of a number of pottery vessels. Though not diagnostic, they included one distinctive example (Fig. 97.122; context **119814**) from the intersection with the Structure 4 ring gully.

Reorganised field system

Ditch **120024**, in the centre of the site, produced ninety-three sherds of pottery, with over 96 per cent by weight of the total feature assemblage from one localised area within the fills. Decorated pieces included a rim with shallow impressed finger marks and a sherd with stamped decoration (Fig. 97.119). The same context included part of a pottery disc and a substantial group of crucible fragments, including rims and spouts.

Two possible crucible fragments were also retrieved from ditch **120020** where it truncated the Structure 4 ring gully. Otherwise the ceramic assemblage from this feature consisted of abraded body sherds and flakes. Five fragments of undiagnostic slag and a small number of fragments of burnt or vitrified clay were also recovered. Because their fills were similar, the relationship between these two ditches was not entirely clear, but ditch **120020** was recorded as the later. To the south, ditch **119133** was roughly parallel to ditch **120020** and may represent additional elements of the field system but it was poorly defined and could not be fully characterised during the excavation. Ditch **117024**, crossing the pipeline route 180m to the west, perhaps also formed part of the same system of land division.

Despite the lack of any evidence of structures from the later phases, the increase in the quantity of finds when compared with the earlier phase would suggest, if not intensification of occupation, then at least its continuation.

Early Roman enclosure and pits

The two parallel right-angled ditches in the north-west corner of the excavation area both produced wheel-thrown Roman pottery among larger quantities of handmade wares, indicating a likely mid-first- to second-century date for these features. Where the smaller ditch, **120034**, intersected the line of the Structure 1 ring gully it cut through a 0.35m-deep pit, **119249**, that had truncated the ring gully at this point. The fill of this pit was comparatively rich in charcoal and contained twelve fragments of heavy, dense non-metallic slag and a fragment of vitrified clay. The most distinctive vessel within the small assemblage of pottery from this pit was a jar with a base perforated like a modern flower pot (Fig. 97.118). The outer ditch of the pair, **120022**, was much larger: over 2m wide and 1.15m deep. A small assemblage of pottery from its fills included a footstand sherd with two rivet holes, from a samian bowl or dish dated to the late second or third century.

The proximity and similarity in form of these two ditches makes it almost certain that they were contemporary, possibly forming the south-east corner of a rectangular enclosure. Their westward extent was not ascertained as they became increasing difficult to discern on the surface and the discovery of the site at a late stage in the construction programme imposed limits of both duration and spatial extent on the excavation. Ditch **3619**, recorded in the evaluation, might have formed the western side of this enclosure implying that the area enclosed was at least 25m wide. There is a possibility that a significant site immediately to the north of the pipeline may be enclosed by these features.

In addition to the enclosure ditches, three pits could be dated to the same broad phase. Pit **119829**, in the eastern

half of the site, produced Roman grey ware pottery, similar to that from ditch **120034**. The later of two large features in the central area of the site, pit **120035**, contained wheel-thrown pottery, of Roman date but otherwise undiagnostic. Pit **120025** was stratigraphically earlier but was sufficiently similar to pit **120035** to suggest that it could have derived from the same phase. An irregular lump of copper alloy (SF 1361) from the upper fill of pit **120025** is probably a piece of casting spillage, providing further evidence of metal working on the site.

Later agriculture

After the third century AD the site probably reverted to open pasture. By contrast with many of the excavated sites along the pipeline route, there was no evidence for ridge and furrow agriculture, the area having been within the deer park (SMR MHU6610) of the North Park estate, centred on a moated site 850m to the east (Scheduled Monument 21199). Ceramic land-drains, on at least six different orientations, had caused considerable recent disturbance.

Braemere Hill

Late Iron Age or early Roman ring gully; ditch with waste from salt-making

The Braemere Hill site was low-lying, 5.4 to 5.7m OD, and more than 500m away from any ground above 10m OD. The land sloped down to the south-east, towards Burstwick Drain (Fig. 43). The name 'Braemere', occurring locally both as Braemere Hill and Braemere Drain, suggests there was once a mere in the vicinity but no other evidence has been found for this.

Several cropmark sites are recorded from this area: Bronze Age sites include two possible round barrows (SMR MHU18924) 900m to the east, two more (SMR MHU19314 and MHU19315) 600m and 900m away to the south-west, and a further example (SMR MHU19317) approximately 1km to the south. Two features 800m to the south-west (SMR MHU19316) and one 300m to the north-east (SMR MHU2854) have been identified as possible Iron Age square barrows.

Evaluation trenching was targeted on several strong magnetic anomalies, most of which proved to be caused by the patchy presence of alluvium, but a fairly substantial ditch was noted in one of the trenches and an excavation area (Area 1, Fig. 44) was opened to investigate this feature. During construction of the pipeline, a ring gully was identified 80m to the south-east and excavated as Area 2.

Twenty-five residual pieces of struck flint recovered represent artefacts dating from the Mesolithic through to the Neolithic or early Bronze Age. The presence of this

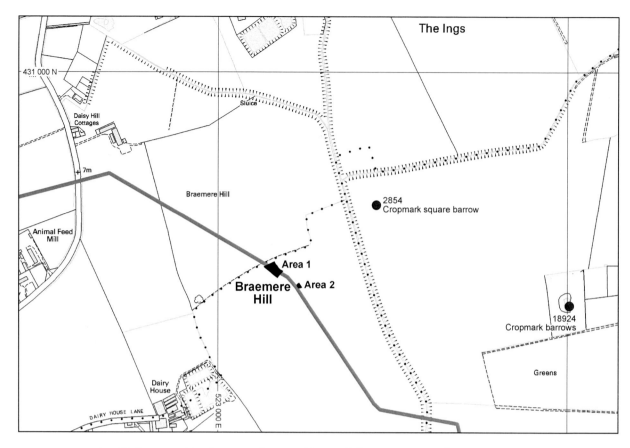

FIG. 43: BRAEMERE HILL: LOCATION. CONTAINS OS DATA © CROWN COPYRIGHT [1:10 000 MAPPING]

flintwork accords with the results from fieldwalking for the Humber Wetland Project, which identified a number of flint find spots in the Burstwick valley (Van de Noort and Ellis 1995).

Late Iron Age ditch

Ditch **4736** was at least 12m long; it had a rounded terminal at its south-eastern end, and continued beyond the north-western limit of excavation. A large pit, **4737**, lay some 3.30m to the south east of the terminal, possibly continuing the boundary line marked by the ditch. An assemblage of eighty-six sherds of hand-made pottery, weighing 1670g, were recovered from the ditch, with the pit producing a further nine sherds. There was no sign of the ditch continuing beyond the small drain that separated the modern field from its neighbour to the north-west.

Ditch **4736** and pit **4737** collectively produced 226 pieces of fired clay, a large majority of which are briquetage: the debris from salt-making (Fig. 107.18-28). Of the identifiable pieces, nearly all were from containers. Pieces of structural briquetage, the supports for evaporation vessels used during the heating and crystallisation of brine, were not identified and it is therefore unlikely that salt was being made at the site itself. Salt was transported considerable distances in

briquetage containers (Lane and Morris 2001, 398-401) but it is unlikely that the presence of this quantity of briquetage in a rural location would have any other explanation than proximity to a production site. The briquetage adds to a growing body of evidence in recent years for an Iron Age salt-making industry on the north side of the Humber Estuary, a counterpart to the extensive salterns on the Lincolnshire coast (e.g. Kirkham 2001).

Structure 1 (Fig. 45)

Ring gully **119101** enclosed an area 9.7m in diameter. Three interruptions in the circuit of the gully were visible: the western interruption possibly being the result of damage from later ploughing, but the other two, to the east and south-west, were more likely to have been entrances. The pottery assemblage largely consisted of hand-made wares but included the rim and upper body of a large vertical rimmed jar, probably dating from the early Roman period, from AD 70 to 120. By contrast, a charred wheat grain from the gully was radiocarbon dated to 367 to 181 cal BC (SUERC-38668). Many of the sherds within the assemblage were abraded, perhaps suggesting that their original point of deposition was not within the structure. It is therefore unclear as to whether the structure was contemporary with the ditch **4736**.

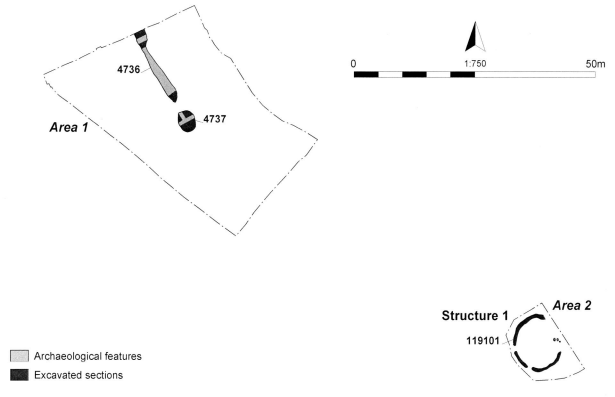

FIG. 44: BRAEMERE HILL: PLAN OF SITE

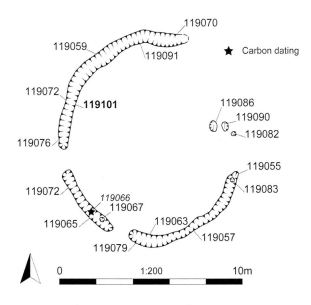

FIG. 45: BRAEMERE HILL: STRUCTURE 1

Three pits or postholes, **119082**, **119086** and **119090**, were revealed close to the eastern limit of the area defined by the ring gully. A small quantity of hand-made pottery was recovered from pit **119090**. The closeness of the pits to one of the interruptions to the ring gully suggests that they could have formed elements of an entrance feature. An east-facing entrance would be broadly consistent with the entrance orientation of the other circular structures on the pipeline route.

The remains at Braemere Hill stood out as being the lowest-lying of the ring gully sites along the pipeline route, and would have been at some risk of flooding. The structure enclosed by the ring gully may have been a temporary dwelling or refuge used during the drier summer months, rather than being permanently occupied.

Burstwick

Iron Age ring gullies; possible enclosure ditches

The Burstwick site was located in an area of locally high ground, the land dropping below the 5m contour towards the Halsham Drain to the east and the Burstwick Drain to the west. Two further slight rises in the generally flat landscape, Hinderset Hill and Rea Hill, lie 500m and 900m to the south and south-east respectively (Fig. 46). Following evaluation trenching of a rectilinear pattern of geophysical anomalies, a controlled topsoil strip revealed the remains of a ring gully and its subsequent replacement, along with two rectilinear ditched enclosures. A large pit at the corner of one of the enclosures and a number of smaller pits and postholes were also noted (Fig. 47).

The excavation contributes to the context of several undated sites recorded in the vicinity, mainly from analysis of cropmarks visible on aerial photographs. These include an enclosure and other possible ditches 550m to the east, with a second enclosure 700m distant

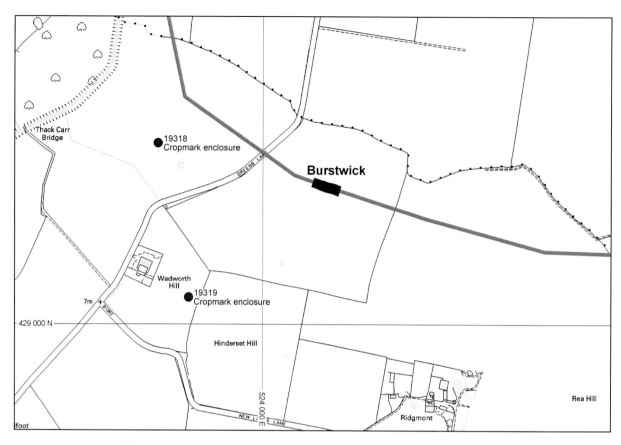

FIG. 46: BURSTWICK: LOCATION. CONTAINS OS DATA © CROWN COPYRIGHT [1:10 000 MAPPING]

in the same direction. Further enclosures are known 500m to the north-east and a similar distance to the north. A square enclosure (SMR MHU19319) and an oval enclosure (SMR MHU19318) are located 480m to the south-west and 470m to the west of the site respectively.

Of thirty-six pieces of worked flint recovered, several were in a fresh condition, including two flakes from the same core, from pit **51048**. This area of ground, raised slightly above the very low-lying surrounding land, was clearly utilised, in a limited way, during the Neolithic or Bronze Age.

Ring gullies

Ring gully **51145** was only partly visible within the excavation area. It was up to 0.35m deep and produced 182 sherds of hand-made pottery. It had been recut with a larger radius. The recut gully, **51148**, displaced slightly to the west, was shallower and had a noticeably darker fill. It produced, in total, 206 sherds of hand-made pottery with similar, predominantly rock tempered, fabric types, as the original gully.

The curvilinear feature to the north-east, **51106**, had a fairly well defined 0.22m-deep terminal, but became vanishingly thin to the north. Possibly the remains of a smaller ring gully, with a radius of less than 3m, it

produced four sherds of pottery and two irregular lumps of fired clay.

First enclosure ditch (Fig. 47)

The dating evidence does not provide sufficient resolution to be able to say if the ring gully is contemporary with ditch **51149** but its position within the angle of the ditch might indicate that this was so. This ditch was a substantial feature, 2m wide and up to 0.90m deep, with a fairly sharp V-shaped profile. It was filled by clean silty deposits interleaved with darker layers with more organic content, suggesting it infilled over a period of time, occasionally holding standing water. Compared with the ring gully, the fills were relatively poor in finds, with only twenty-two sherds of pottery from the four excavated interventions. This contrast might seem surprising, but a high proportion of the pottery from the ring gullies was deposited as substantially complete vessels, rather than accreting as the result of general activity in the area. The fill of ditch **51149** was noticeably cleaner towards the west, becoming very similar in appearance to the natural subsoil, so that its edges in the westernmost intervention were very difficult to define. Assuming that the entrance to the roundhouse was at the east or south-east side, as seems likely by analogy with similar features elsewhere, this part of the enclosure ditch would have been behind the roundhouse, where a reduced level of activity might, perhaps, be expected.

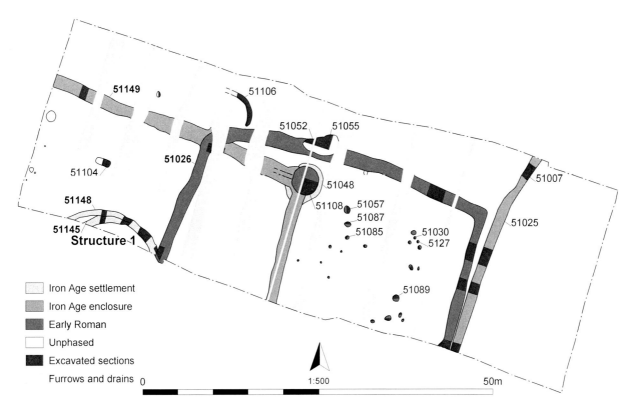

Iron Age settlement
Iron Age enclosure
Early Roman
Unphased
Excavated sections
Furrows and drains

51149 51106 51052 51055 51026 51104 51148 51145 Structure 1 51048 51108 51057 51087 51085 51030 5127 51007 51025 51089

0   1:500   50m

FIG. 47: BURSTWICK: PLAN OF ALL FEATURES

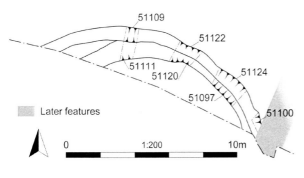

51109 51122 51111 51120 51124 51097 51100

Later features

0   1:200   10m

FIG. 48: BURSTWICK: STRUCTURE 1

The relationship of the corner of the enclosure ditch to the large pit, **51048**, at the same location was not entirely clear. The initial cut of the pit may have been contemporary with the ditch, as a local deepening of its base, perhaps to act as a soakaway or waterhole. Alternatively, the pit could have been a pre-existing feature used as marker when the ditch was laid out.

Second enclosure ditch

Following the disuse and infilling of the original enclosure, a second enclosure of broadly similar dimensions was established. It was defined by ditch **51026**, which overlapped the first enclosure and also cut the eastern side of ring gully **51145**. Eight interventions through ditch **51026** together produced 148 sherds of pottery. Tip lines in several of the sections through the

ditch suggest that it was backfilled by dumping from within the enclosures.

Pit **51048** was probably dug, or recut, during this phase. Though likely to have been intended originally as a water-management feature, the pit was later used for dumping of domestic detritus. Over two hundred sherds of pottery were recovered, differing from the material from the ring gully in both fineness of fabric and frequency of flint inclusions. Four flint flakes and a piece of irregular waste were all in a fresh condition, with two of the flakes probably coming from the same core, raising the possibility that these may have been examples of Iron Age flint-working. The three uppermost fills within the pit were considered to belong to a recut, **51108**. Two of these contexts contained pottery, seventy-two sherds in total. One of the environmental samples from the pit produced a comparatively rich botanical assemblage with species typical of waste ground, possibly near a waterlogged area, although aquatic species that would specifically indicate the presence of standing water within the feature were absent.

Discrete features enclosed by ditch 51026

The similarity of ditch **51026** to the earlier enclosure suggests that it was a direct replacement for it. If so it poses the question of what it was enclosing. One possibility is that the discrete features within the enclosure represent a post-built structure. There were twenty of these features recorded within the eastern half of the enclosed area, six of which contained pottery. The occurrence of these features within this one area might suggest that they and the enclosure were broadly contemporary; but they could equally have been contemporary with, and external to, the earlier enclosure or merely an accidental juxtaposition of disparate features.

Features **51057**, **51087** and **51085** formed a regularly spaced row, although their appearances were very different. The most northerly, **51057**, contained evidence of burning in the upper layer of fill: burnt stones, fired clay and charcoal as well as forty-six pottery sherds, again mostly burnt. The middle feature, **51087**, had a similar broad profile but a much cleaner fill, while the southernmost of the group, **51085**, was steep-sided with a probable post-pipe, from which twenty-three sherds of pottery were recovered. The other three features containing pottery, **51030**, **5127** and **51089**, formed a rough alignment towards the eastern arm of the enclosure, but are not convincing as a coherent group of postholes.

Other features

The eastern end of the site was defined by ditch **51025**. The pottery assemblage from this ditch included eight abraded sherds from a flat-rim dish, probably dating to the second century AD. Together with two grey ware sherds from the same context, these were the only Roman finds from the excavation area. Ditch **51025** probably post-dated enclosure ditch **51026**, but the relationship between the two features had been obscured by a land drain.

Pit **51104** was a shallow, rectangular, flat-bottomed feature with burnt clay and heat-affected stones in its fill, along with thirteen sherds of pottery. This stone-filled pit stands comparison with similar enigmatic features found at the Dimlington Road site (below, page 76).

The site was crossed by furrows from medieval ridge and furrow ploughing. Their similar alignment to the enclosure ditches reflect the natural drainage of the land, with the modern ceramic field drains also following the same alignment, but the site provides an example of where the general orientation of the landscape has been maintained from the Iron Age to the present day.

Churchlands

Iron Age ring gully, boundary ditch and settlement features; medieval or post-medieval pits; residual Mesolithic and Bronze Age flint, and Bronze Age pottery

The Churchlands site is close to the centre of a large area of relatively high ground at 20.0 to 20.5m OD (Fig. 49). Cropmark sites recorded in the area suggest

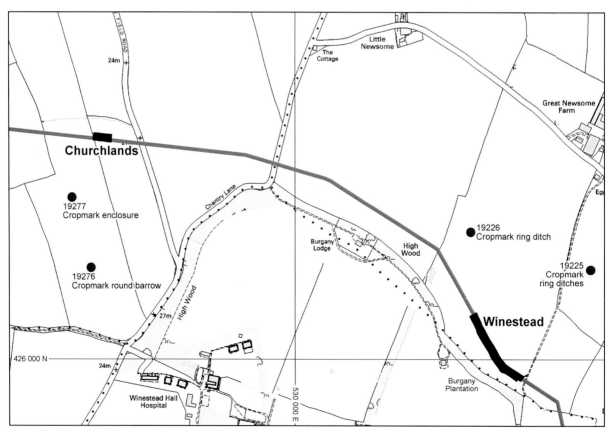

FIG. 49: CHURCHLANDS AND WINESTEAD: LOCATION. CONTAINS OS DATA © CROWN COPYRIGHT [1:10 000 MAPPING]

that this area of slightly higher ground may have been a favoured location for prehistoric funerary monuments: they include a possible Neolithic long barrow (SMR MHU19284) 1.7km to the north of the excavation site and a possible Bronze Age round barrow (SMR MHU19276) 350m to the south, with further possible round barrows or ring ditches to the north-west (SMR MHU 19290, MHU 19282 and MHU 19294) and to the south (SMR MHU19230 and MHU19292). Three possible square barrows (SMR MHU19291) have been noted 2km to the north-west and Iron Age occupation is recorded at Weldon's Plantation, near Winestead, almost 3km to the south-east (SMR MHU9794, Smith 1995). Undated cropmarks include an enclosure and ditches (SMR MHU19277) 180m to the south-west and rectangular enclosures (SMR MHU19274) 440m to the north.

The geophysical survey of the site covered an extended area to the south, proposed, but in the event not used, as a possible pipe storage area. Two areas of magnetic anomalies were noted within this extended area but nothing of significance, except for ridge and furrow agriculture, was seen within the regular working width. Archaeological features were, however, revealed during monitoring of topsoil stripping.

Mesolithic activity

Sixty-six pieces of residual worked flint include Mesolithic blades and bladelets, one of which may be serrated, as well as Neolithic or early Bronze Age pieces.

The relative elevation of the land hereabouts may have made it attractive to passing groups of Mesolithic hunter-gatherers. Scrapers within the assemblage suggest that animal skins were being processed, while the serrated flake most likely indicates the preparation of plant fibres for textiles or rope.

Bronze Age activity

The Neolithic or early Bronze Age component of the flintwork includes an awl or piercer (SF 1420, Fig. 84.31) and indicates continued sporadic use of the site. Clearer evidence of Bronze Age activity is provided by an assemblage of Biconical Urn sherds, four of which derived from a large irregular pit, **119406** (Fig. 50), which also produced a sherd of Roman pottery, and the remainder from a thin subsoil layer, interpreted as a buried medieval ploughsoil.

The insertion of Biconical Urns containing cremations into round barrows, as secondary burials, is a well attested phenomenon in the south of England, and the presence of Biconical Urn sherds at the Churchlands site may result from the disturbance of Bronze Age funerary remains. Aerial photographs indicate that there are round barrows in the general area, including the example 350m to the south (SMR MHU 19276). However, Biconical Urn sherds have also been recorded in occupation contexts at Rudston (Manby 1980, 324) and near Caythorpe (Abramson 1996, 13) and the sherds at Churchlands are perhaps as likely to represent local Bronze Age occupation as funerary activity.

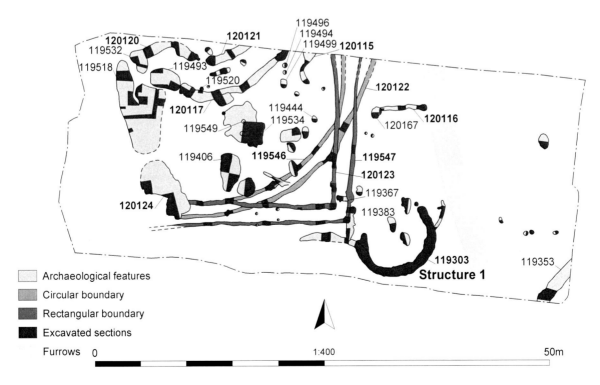

FIG. 50: CHURCHLANDS: PLAN OF ALL FEATURES

If the tentative identification of a Bronze Age cylindrical loomweight (Fig. 107.30) from pit **119499** is correct, it would lend support to this having been a site of Bronze Age occupation. A sherd of Scored ware from the same feature could date from the mid-third century BC through to the early to mid-first century AD. Bronze Age remains, lacking surviving evidence of their date or function, may have been present among the undated features: postholes or small pits, **119494** and **119496**, to the north of pit **119499**, are possible examples.

Late Iron Age settlement

There is no evidence of late Bronze Age or early Iron Age activity at the site, a hiatus that continued until the construction of a structure, possibly in the mid- or late Iron Age.

Structure 1 (Fig. 51)

Ring gully **119303** produced sixteen sherds of hand-made pottery. The low average sherd weight, 2.5g, and low sherd count, in comparison with those from the other ring gullies along the pipeline route, may point to a non-domestic function. The gully possibly had a north-west-facing entrance; this also suggests a different function, as domestic structures typically had entrances to the east or south-east. The sampled fills of the ring gully were largely sterile, producing only a single goosefoot seed and possible chickweed fragment, and so provide little insight on the patterns of past activity here; if the ring gully surrounded a structure with a non-domestic function, such as a shelter for agricultural or craft activities, or for animals, no evidence of such use survived.

Shallow pits and curvilinear gullies in the immediate vicinity may also have been associated with the ring gully, but their function is likewise unclear. The upper

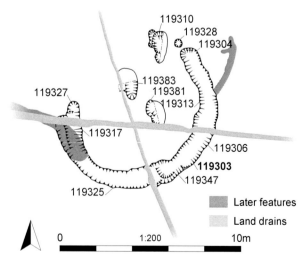

FIG. 51: CHURCHLANDS: STRUCTURE 1

fill of a deep, steep-sided pit, **119518**, at the western side of the excavation area, produced a fragment of daub with a finger impression (Fig. 107.29). The pit also contained nine sherds of pottery including the base and lower walls of a large jar.

Curvilinear and rectilinear double-ditched enclosures (Fig. 50)

Two concentric curvilinear ditches, **120122** and **119546**, approximately 0.9m apart, in the central area of the site had radii of around 16m. They were similar in size and form, measuring approximately 0.45m wide on average and 0.30m deep, although the inner ditch was consistently deeper by around 0.05m. Both had similar sandy clay fills. No finds were recovered from either ditch but their common alignment implies that they were contemporary. The ditches appear to form part of an enclosure, ploughed out to the west. Had a bank, hedgerow or some other feature been erected or placed in the gap between the two ditches, it had left no trace.

Two parallel linear ditches, **120123** and **119547**, appear to have been direct replacements for the curvilinear ditches **120122** and **119546**. The spacing, approximately 1.7m, was slightly greater than that between the curvilinear ditches but the ditches themselves were broadly similar in their dimensions to their curvilinear predecessors and were almost certainly constructed during the same broad phase of land use and had very similar functions. The twelve interventions excavated through the two ditches, yielded, in total, eight sherds of hand-made pottery, and five pieces of worked flint. A fragment of clay pipe stem, dated to the second half of the seventeenth century (White 2009), and ascribed to the outer ditch, **119547**, was probably from the fill of an unrecognised intrusive feature.

The rectilinear ditches appear to form the south-western corner of a double-ditched enclosure. The pottery evidence suggests an Iron Age date but no direct parallels from the period have been found, especially as the rectilinear enclosure appears to have replaced the very similar circular or curvilinear example. Both of these ditches ran out to the west, at around the same point, implying that the contemporary ground surface had been subsequently truncated.

Other Iron Age features

Numerous small pits and short lengths of irregular ditch were revealed in the northern half of the site. Small assemblages of hand-made pottery were recovered from ditches **120115**, **120117** and **120120**, and from features **119367**, **119444** and **119549**. The function of these features was not clear although some may have resulted from localised clay extraction. Few of these features were intercutting, suggesting that most or all of them were broadly contemporary and, perhaps, excavated for a similar purpose. This phase of activity had largely ceased prior to significant Roman influence in the area. No features of demonstrably Roman date were recorded, and the only two sherds of wheel-thrown Roman pottery recovered from stratified contexts were residual in post-medieval features.

Post-medieval extraction pits

Extensive evidence of ridge and furrow agriculture detected by the geophysical survey indicates that the general area was being used for arable cultivation at least by the post-medieval period. Clay extraction was probably intermittently undertaken into the eighteenth century. A number of large irregular pits, stratigraphically later than the Iron Age features, produced few finds, although pit **120124** contained two medieval pottery sherds, of late thirteenth- to fifteenth-century date and a sherd of sixteenth- to eighteenth-century glazed red earthenware. Pit **119532** produced a small assemblage of pottery finds, mostly hand-made but including an abraded base sherd from a later Roman vessel.

Winestead

Ditched enclosures, possibly of Anglo-Saxon date

The excavation area at Winestead was located in the centre of a broad area of relatively high land, with the top of the archaeological deposits varying in height between 23.75m and 25.65m OD (Fig. 49). The geophysical survey revealed a rectilinear pattern of ditch-like and pit-like anomalies. Six evaluation trenches confirmed the presence of significant archaeological remains and area excavation followed.

The area has few known sites, although possible Bronze Age barrows are recorded 400m to the south-east (SMR MHU19224) and just over 1km to the east (SMR MHU19276), as well as two undated circular cropmarks 225m to the north (SMR MHU19226) and 350m to the north-east (SMR MHU19225).

Enclosure boundaries and associated ditches (Fig. 52)

Linear and curvilinear ditches, forming a system of small enclosures or plots, extended over the site. The ditches seem to have been developed and maintained, probably over a number of years, with regular recutting and repositioning. The ditches yielded a small assemblage of pottery; fifteen hand-made and sixteen wheel-thrown sherds. There was little pattern to their distribution. Several of the wheel-thrown sherds could be dated to the late third- or fourth-century. Hand-made sherds included a fragment from an everted rim vessel, and almost the whole of the body of a thick-walled shapeless jar from ditch **73091**. Ditches **73094**, **73097** and **73137** also produced small quantities of daub fragments. Bulk samples from ditches **73097** and **73137** produced relatively large assemblages of charred cereal grains, including oat, hulled barley and naked hexaploid bread wheat.

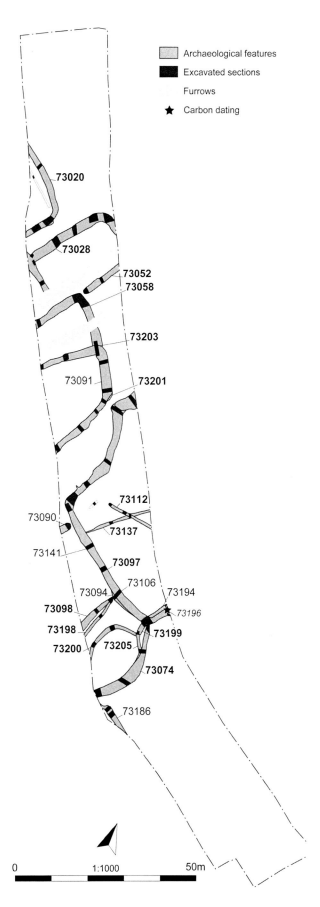

FIG. 52: WINESTEAD: PLAN OF ALL FEATURES

The bread wheat is of a form typical of a later period than the Iron Age or Roman dates suggested by the small quantities of pottery from the site, and a radiocarbon date of 660 to 830 cal AD (SUERC-36193) was obtained from one of the charred grains. The size and uniform composition of the assemblages makes it unlikely that the grain was intrusive or residual, and the radiocarbon result is therefore likely to be a good indicator of the date during which the ditch was infilling. The ditches respected one another to form a coherent system of roughly rectangular enclosures implying that they are all broadly contemporary. The balance of evidence is therefore thought to favour an Anglo-Saxon date for this system of enclosures.

If this is correct, the small assemblages of hand-made and Roman pottery, along with two flint flakes that were also recovered from the site, would have been chance inclusions within later features. Although these pieces are generally not abraded, the sherds, in general, are small, and an explanation relying on residuality would perhaps raise difficulties only in the case of the thick-walled jar from ditch **37091**. Although this vessel was thought most likely to date from the Iron Age, the lack of variation of locally produced hand-made ceramics from later prehistoric times through to the Anglo-Saxon period means that the possibility of a later date cannot be precluded. While the pottery assemblage indicates that there was some activity here during the late third or fourth century AD, and possibly also in the Iron Age, the small quantities involved suggest that this material did not originate from contemporary settlements in the immediate vicinity.

The enclosure system may have been linked to crop production, as the environmental evidence shows that oats, barley and bread wheat were all being grown or processed. The absence of other domestic debris could be taken as an indication that the site lay at some distance from any settlement and that its focus was solely agricultural, but Anglo-Saxon rural domestic sites often produce little artefactual evidence.

Patrington

Iron Age ring gullies and Iron Age and Roman ditches

The excavation area at Patrington was on relatively high ground, at 14.5m to 16m OD, the land falling away towards the Winestead valley to the north-west (Fig. 53). A circular cropmark, 500m to the north-east, is thought more likely to be a post-medieval landscape feature (DBA:DY, Holgate and Ralph 2006) than a prehistoric ring gully. There are cropmark enclosures identified to the south of Holmpton Road, which forms the boundary of the field within which the site was located, though some at least are thought to result from post-medieval field boundaries. Two possible linear features were

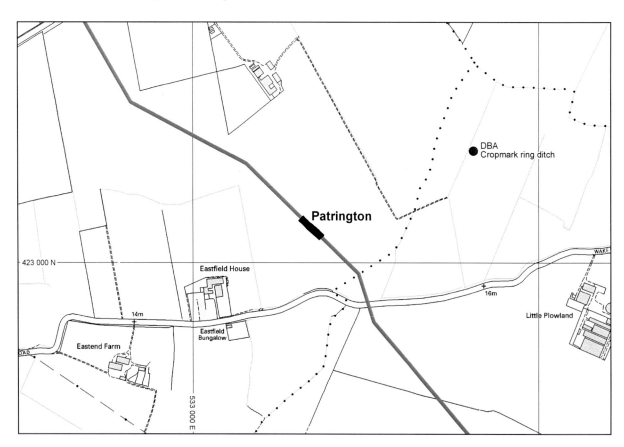

FIG. 53: PATRINGTON: LOCATION. CONTAINS OS DATA © CROWN COPYRIGHT [1:10 000 MAPPING]

identified among the magnetic anomalies revealed by the geophysical survey; subsequent evaluation trenching confirmed the presence of archaeological features.

Iron Age ditch (Fig. 54)

Five flint flakes, their relatively squat proportions suggesting a broad Neolithic or Bronze Age date, provide evidence of earlier activity, but the stratigraphically earliest cut feature was a boundary or enclosure, ditch **88171**, up to 2.5m wide and almost 1m deep. Excluding two fills that were contaminated by material from ditch **88174**, it produced 273 sherds of hand-made pottery. The size of the ditch, coupled with its rounded northern terminal, suggest that it may have formed part of an enclosure or major boundary, with an entrance close to the northern limit of excavation. A group of 110 sherds of pottery recovered from a continuation of the same ditch, beyond the limit of excavation, were included in the analysis as context **88167**.

Iron Age settlement (Fig. 55)

Following the infilling of ditch **88171**, a roundhouse was constructed and replaced on at least two occasions, shifting position each time. This would indicate a degree of longevity of the settlement, probably extending through a number of generations. The settlement is best interpreted as a small farmstead, probably relatively isolated. It seems unlikely that a roundhouse would have been deliberately constructed over the visible course of an earlier ditch, which would imply that all trace of ditch **88171** had been lost prior to the establishment of the settlement.

Structure 1

Ring gully **88169** cut through the fills of ditch **88171**. The gully enclosed an area 9.5m in diameter and had two well defined terminals marking an east-facing entrance. A second, south-facing, break in the gully circuit was more likely the result of truncation than deliberate design. An assemblage of hand-made pottery was recovered from the ring gully, 174 sherds in total, along with a single small piece of white ware probably dating to the first or second century AD. A charred grain from the fill was radiocarbon dated to 380 to 190 BC (SUERC-36194).

Structure 2

After the Structure 1 ring gully had fallen out of use, a second ring gully, **88170**, was cut through it. The ring gully enclosed an area 9.7m in diameter and had a fairly well defined south-east facing entrance. The west side of the gully circuit was vanishingly shallow, the break on that side almost certainly the result of later ploughing. Thirty-six sherds of hand-made pottery were recovered from the gully. The postholes within the enclosed area

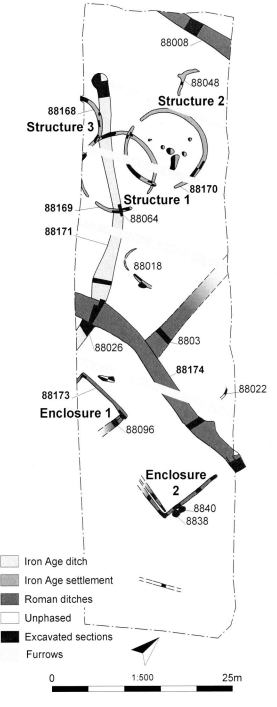

FIG. 54: PATRINGTON: PLAN OF ALL FEATURES

may have held timber uprights or internal features, but they were undated and may not be contemporary with the structure.

Structure 3

An arc of a further ring gully, **88168**, cut through both the earlier enclosure ditch and the circuit of Structure 1. An east-facing entrance was clearly defined and the feature was of similar dimensions to Structures 1 and 2. The ring gully produced forty-four sherds of hand-made pottery.

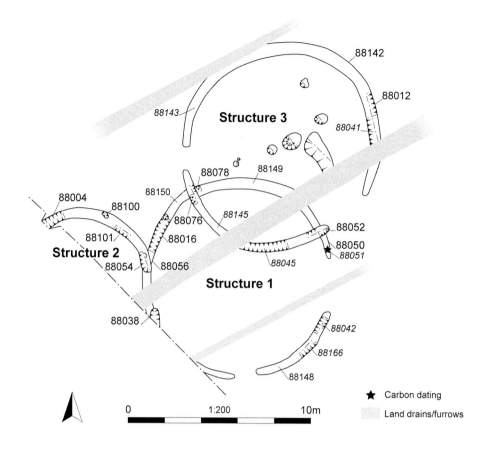

FIG. 55: PATRINGTON: STRUCTURES 1 TO 3

Further possible structures

The heavily truncated remains of another potential ring gully, **88018**, in the centre of the site, produced a single hand-made pottery sherd. Too little survived of a curved gully further to the east, **88022**, for confident interpretation as part of a ring gully; the same could be said of an undated irregular gully, **88048**, towards the northern end of the site.

Roman enclosure ditches

If the sherd of white ware from Structure 1 is accepted as intrusive, there is no evidence that the settlement survived into the early Roman period, and it appears to have already been abandoned by the time that the ditch system, with widely spaced boundaries sub-divided with smaller ditches, was first established. The larger ditches would undoubtedly have improved the drainage of the area, and this may have been their primary function, perhaps indicating an increased emphasis on arable agriculture in the local economy by this period. The smaller pottery assemblage from the Roman period suggests that settlement had moved away from the immediate vicinity by this time. Maintenance of the enclosures probably ceased during the late third or fourth century.

Ditch **88174**, extending across the centre of the excavation area, had a stony upper fill, initially interpreted as a trackway. Over 3m wide in places and up to 1.2m deep, with moderately steep sides and a slightly rounded, narrow base, it produced an assemblage of pottery that shows that it was infilling in the mid-third century, though a small number of second-century sherds might suggest that it had been open for some time. A similar sized ditch, **8803**, extending northwards, had a very clear recut and seems also to have been maintained for an extended period. The line of ditch **8803** continued northwards, where it was recorded as ditch **119562**. The twenty-six sherds of pottery recovered from the various fills of this ditch were all hand-made, suggesting that it belonged to an earlier phase of land use than ditch **88174**.

The geophysical results (Fig. 56) seem to show ditch **8803** continuing to the south of ditch **88174**, although this was not recorded during the excavation, and also confirm that the line of the ditch continued, after a break, beyond the north-eastern limit of excavation. The break suggests that there was an access across the ditch. The course of ditch **88008**, at the northern end of the excavation area, can also be followed westward in the geophysical survey results before it is lost in the anomalies produced by ridge and furrow agriculture.

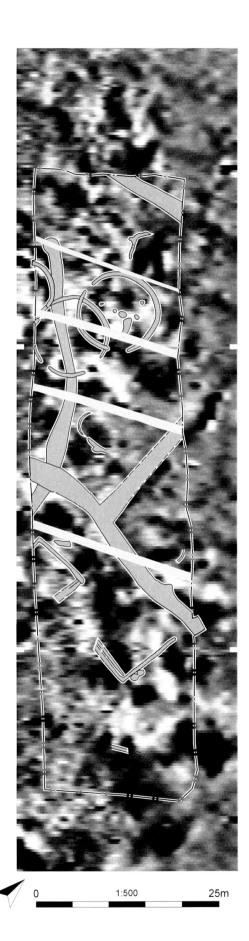

Enclosures 1 and 2

A series of shallow ditches, **88173**, formed part of a small rectilinear enclosure approximately 7m wide to the south of ditch **88174**. Very little datable material was recovered from these ditches, although two pieces of mid-second- to mid-third-century pottery suggest broad contemporaneity with the more substantial enclosure ditches to the north. If, as the geophysical survey suggests, a southern extension to the substantial ditch **8803** had existed then dating evidence suggests that Enclosure 1 was probably constructed over it. Enclosure 2 was undated. These features may have been all that remained of a more extensive network of small enclosures hereabouts. Two small intercutting pits, **8838** and **8840**, lay immediately to the east, the later pit containing a fragment of a rotary quern (SF 30) as well as three sherds of Roman pottery, dated to the late second or third century.

Bluegate Corner

Late Iron Age or Roman ring gullies and Roman ditch system

The remains at Bluegate Corner were at the southern edge of a large area of relatively high ground, with the top of the archaeological deposits varying between 17.20m OD to the north and 13.70m OD at the south (Fig. 57). To the south and east, the ground fell away towards the Humber estuary.

Cropmarks show a square enclosure and ditch (SMR MHU19401) 130m to the south and a possible Iron Age occupation site (SMR MHU 7649) 650m to the north-east, near to Lowclose Plantation. Iron Age and Roman pottery (SMR MHU 7637) has been found a similar distance to the north-west. A series of undated enclosures show as cropmarks (SMR MHU 21730) to the north-east, and there are further undated features to the north (SMR MHU 21731), as well as extinct field boundaries close to the site, all probably of post-medieval date (Holgate and Ralph 2006), and areas of former ridge and furrow in nearby fields.

Fieldwalking produced a small assemblage of finds, including two fairly large sherds of hand-made pottery, but the nearby geophysical anomalies were not thought to represent significant archaeological remains. The small excavation areas were identified and excavated during monitoring of the construction topsoil strip.

A small assemblage of flintwork includes seven flakes and a thumbnail scraper from one of the recuts of ditch **120665**. The scraper (Fig. 82.32) dates from the late Neolithic or early Bronze Age, and the whole assemblage could be of broadly similar date.

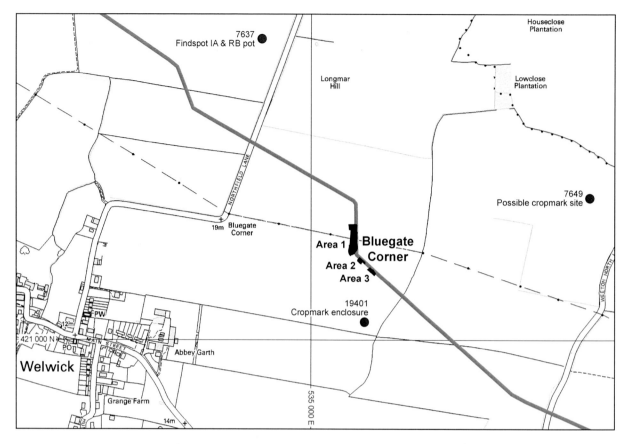

FIG. 57: BLUEGATE CORNER: LOCATION. CONTAINS OS DATA © CROWN COPYRIGHT [1:10 000 MAPPING]

Iron Age settlement

Structure 1 and pits (Fig. 59)

A steep-sided pit, **119883**, produced a single flint flake and a piece of fired clay. It had been heavily truncated by ring gully **119903**, which enclosed a slightly irregular area, 6m in diameter. A break in the western side of the circuit, defined by two distinct terminals, was only 0.15m wide: too narrow to represent an entrance. Thirty hand-made pottery sherds were recovered from the gully, along with a jet or shale disc, possibly a gaming counter (SF 1533), from the upper fill of one of the terminals.

A small number of charred grains were present in the environmental samples from the gully, along with small amounts of vitrified material and spheroidal hammer slag, an indication that iron smithing had taken place fairly close by while the gully was still open (Shaw and O'Meara 2010). A radiocarbon determination on one of the charred grains returned a date of 336 to 74 cal BC (SUERC-38669).

The two undated pits within the area enclosed by the gully may have been the positions of timber uprights of a structure. The larger and more central of the two pits contained a substantial amount of charcoal within its fill but the absence of scorching around the pit suggests that this entered the pit as burnt material rather than being the result of burning *in situ*.

The ground plan of Structure 1 perhaps indicates that it was constructed after the establishment of the adjacent enclosure, the irregular shape reflecting an attempt to avoid either the ditch itself or an upcast bank on the northern side of the ditch. The reason behind the pressing need to construct the ring gully so close to the enclosure ditch is not apparent.

Structure 2 (Fig. 60)

A shallow ring gully, **119967**, enclosed an area 7m in diameter. Though cut by a furrow, indications of a south-east facing entrance remained. The distribution of the one hundred and fifty-eight sherds of hand-made pottery recovered from the gully was heavily biased in favour of the surviving terminal, which contained 61 per cent by weight of the assemblage. The quantity of pottery, from what was a shallow and heavily truncated feature, is consistent with the ring gully having enclosed a domestic structure.

Boundary and enclosure ditches

The two ring gullies were probably abandoned prior to the Roman period. Late first- to second-century wares, though present only in small quantities, indicate some level of activity at the site during the earlier part of the Roman period; this may have included the maintenance of

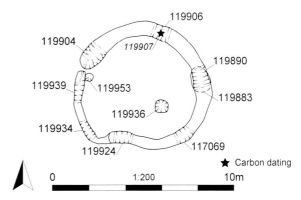

FIG. 59: BLUEGATE CORNER: STRUCTURE 1

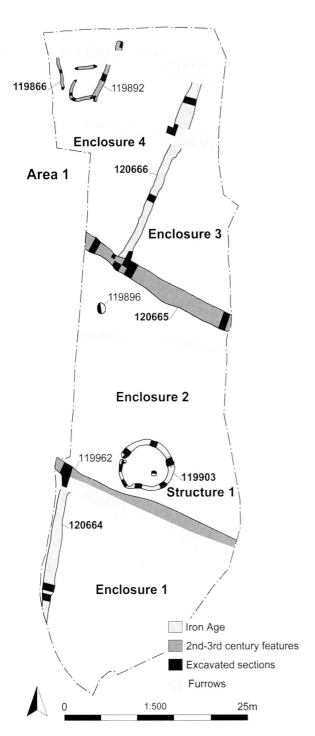

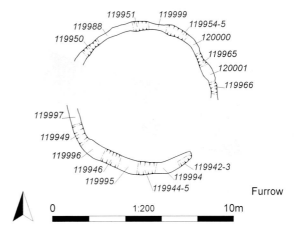

FIG. 60: BLUEGATE CORNER: STRUCTURE 2

at least one and possibly two boundary ditches originally established in the Iron Age. The ditches possibly formed part of a group of enclosures extending beyond the limit of excavation. The ditches defining Enclosure 1 produced twenty-three hand-made sherds together with two wheel-thrown sherds dating to the mid-second to mid-third centuries. The wheel-thrown sherds were both recovered from the same fill, which had been heavily truncated by a furrow, and it is quite possible that these sherds were intrusive. Ditch **119962**, which formed the northern boundary of the enclosure, survived after ditch **120664** had been allowed to silt up, but was undated and the longevity of the boundary is uncertain. Enclosure 2 (Fig. 58) had a maximum width of 25m and was defined by ditches up to 2.1m wide and 1m deep. The ditches would have served to aid drainage of the heavy soils as well as possibly marking boundaries.

Maintenance and recutting of ditches

The ditches which defined Enclosures 3 and 4 had been recut in part. Hand-made pottery was found throughout their fills, and was the only pottery recovered from ditch **120666**, which did not show any recuts in a generally

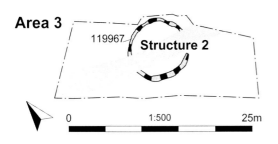

FIG. 58: BLUEGATE CORNER: PLAN OF ALL FEATURES

clean silty fill. In contrast, ditch **120665** continued to be maintained and produced a large assemblage of wheel-thrown pottery dating from the late first to fourth centuries, with third-century wares predominating. Over 300 sherds from this period were recovered. A series of irregular, largely curvilinear ditches at the northern end of Area 1 produced a small assemblage of second- to third-century wheel-thrown pottery in addition to handmade wares.

The increase in the amount of pottery from the third century is so marked that it suggests the establishment of a settlement nearby. If this was the case, there is little to indicate that it continued beyond the early years of the fourth century.

Subsequent activity

Traces of ridge and furrow show that the site was being used for agriculture, in the medieval or early post-medieval periods. The only feature noted in Area 2, ditch **119910**, corresponds to a field boundary shown on the 1854 Ordnance Survey map. Although it produced late first- to second-century pottery, it was on a different alignment to the other linear features on the site, and it is more probable that the pottery was residual rather than an indication that this was a long-lived boundary surviving from that time.

Weeton

Parallel Iron Age ditches and curvilinear gully

From the excavation area (Fig. 61) on the western side of Weeton Beck, the land rises gently to the north, while the present-day shoreline of the Humber is 1.8km to the south. The top of the archaeological features varied from 7.6m OD at the north-west end of the site to 6.8m OD at the south-east.

Trench evaluation, in deteriorating weather, showed that possible field boundaries or trackways, showing as linear geophysical anomalies, were of limited extent; the features were not defined and excavated until monitoring of topsoil stripping during construction.

Iron Age boundaries and arc-shaped gully (Fig. 62)

Parallel ditches **120164** and **120223** were similar in depth, at 0.71m and 0.85m, though differing considerably in width. The terminus at the southern end of ditch **120223** had been recut on at least one occasion. Both ditches produced assemblages of hand-made pottery, with forty-one sherds recovered from ditch **120223**, over twice as many as from its larger counterpart. It also produced a hand-squeezed briquetage support for a salt evaporation container

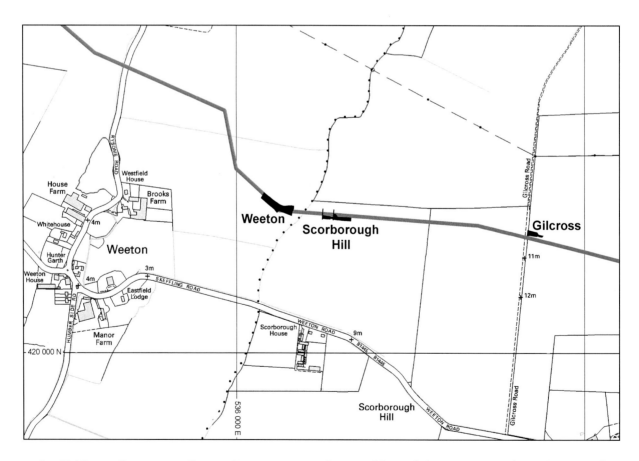

FIG. 61: Weeton, Scorborough Hill and Gilcross: location. Contains OS data © Crown copyright [1:10 000 mapping]

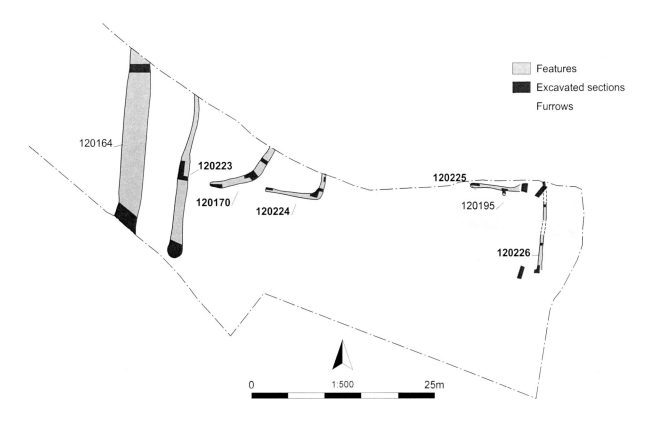

Features
Excavated sections
Furrows

120164
120223
120170
120224
120225
120195
120226

0   1:500   25m

FIG. 62: WEETON: PLAN OF ALL FEATURES

(Fig. 107:31). The two ditches may have formed part of a repositioned boundary or, if truly contemporary, drainage ditches marking the edges of a track or droveway. The geophysical survey for the Easington to Paull pipeline to the south (Bunn 2007, 2008) shows a number of possible enclosures and trackways, within a wider area interpreted as a focus of Iron Age and Roman activity.

Curvilinear gully **120170** produced eighty-four sherds of hand-made pottery, along with a stone implement formed from a quartzite cobble with depressions on opposing faces (SF 1601, Fig. 106.7). The gully can be seen in the geophysical survey results to continue beyond the limit of the excavation for a short distance before its line is obscured by other anomalies. The relatively large pottery assemblage recovered from this small feature suggests that it may have been the vestiges of a roundhouse ring gully.

Roman activity

Four hand-made pottery sherds and a wheel-thrown sherd dating to, at the earliest, the second century AD were recovered from L-shaped gully **120224**, to the east of gully **120170**. Gully **120226**, close to the eastern limit of the site, produced two hand-made and two wheel-thrown sherds, the latter probably dating to the third or fourth century AD.

Scorborough Hill

Artefact-rich early Roman pit; Iron Age and Roman ditches

The Scorborough Hill excavation area (Fig. 61) lay to the east of Weeton Beck, on land sloping gently down to the south, towards the reclaimed land bordering the Humber estuary. To the north, the ground rose steadily to a substantial area of relatively high land. The top of the archaeological deposits varied from 7.1m to 8.2m OD. With the exception of the site at Weeton (above), 90m to the east, few sites, monuments or findspots of Iron Age or Roman date are known from the immediate vicinity, though an Iron Age founder's hoard from Rysome Garth (SMR MHU7520), 1.7km to the north, has been recorded as well as a possible Iron Age settlement (SMR MHU7649) close to Lowclose Plantation, 1.5km to the north-west.

Fieldwalking ahead of construction recovered a Roman glass bangle (Figs 88.19, 89) typical of Kilbride-Jones' (1937-38, 382-4 Type 3C: opaque white bangles decorated with blue 'scrolls' dated to the later first to early to mid-second century AD; R. Tyson in Wilson 2006). Two very marked linear geophysical anomalies around 90m apart were evaluated by trenching. Two parallel ditches, **10412** and **10415**, were recorded corresponding to the eastern anomaly, but the other linear anomaly proved to be more complex, and an extended area was opened and excavated.

Mesolithic activity

Thirteen pieces of worked flint were recovered from the site, including three blades consistent with a Mesolithic date. The site would have overlooked a much more steeply sloping Humber valley at this time and could have been utilised by groups of hunters seeking animals watering in the forerunner of Weeton Beck, or foraging groups exploiting the resources of the coast and shoreline.

Early ditches

The common alignment of ditch **12103** and ditch segments **10430** and **12023** suggests that they were remains of a single ditched boundary, recut on several occasions (Fig. 63). The most complete element, **12103**, was 2.5m wide and 0.90m deep and appeared to terminate at its western end, part of the terminus having been removed by pit **12081**. A possible earlier terminus, **12070**, could be seen adjacent to the northern edge of excavation. Pottery from these features was sparse in comparison with subsequent phases, although small quantities of hand-made wares were recovered from each of the interventions. Diagnostic Roman pottery was limited to ditch **10430**, from five vessels which, together, suggest a mid-first- to early second-century date. Two joining fragments of structural briquetage (Fig. 107.35) were also found.

There are few finds from the earliest features, and little to suggest any settlement in the immediate vicinity in the late Iron Age, but the recutting and maintenance of the ditches implies the expenditure of effort over a period of time, and this must have been more than a marginal area.

Late first-century pit (Figs. 64, 65)

A significant change at the site occurred in the late first century. Some of the earlier ditches had been abandoned by this time, and were truncated when pit **12081** was dug. The finds assemblage from this pit is very different to that from any of the other sites along the pipeline route, the product of a richer and more sophisticated material culture.

The pit was 13.9m long and 4.3m wide, with a base that sloped down from the western end, initially fairly flat-bottomed but increasingly developing a ditch-like V-shaped profile. The pottery recovered from the fills of the pit includes both hand-made and Roman wheel-thrown sherds in fairly large quantities. Two sherds of medieval pottery assigned to one of the upper fills probably derived from the furrows or land drains which crossed the area. The wheel-thrown pottery assemblage, over 240 sherds weighing 3.2kg, is of particular interest for its early date and unusual composition, with a number of non-local pieces and exotic wares.

Six excavated sections through the pit showed it to have at least three distinct fills: one or more dark silty basal fills being generally sealed by a paler orange-brown silty clay layer, capped by a dark upper fill. Some gradation in dating could be discerned within the wheel-thrown pottery assemblages, those from the earlier fills tending towards a mid- to late first-century date, while the earlier part of the second century might be more appropriate for the later fills. Fragments of a substantially complete Kilbride Jones (1938) Type 2 glass bangle (SF 101, Fig. 88.21) along with a fragment of a second bangle of the same type (SF 104, Fig. 88.20) were found (P. Courtney, in Flintoft and Glover, 2010). In Price's (1988, 342-

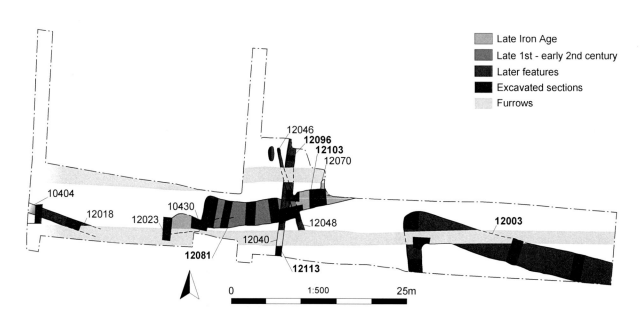

FIG. 63: SCORBOROUGH HILL: PLAN OF ALL FEATURES

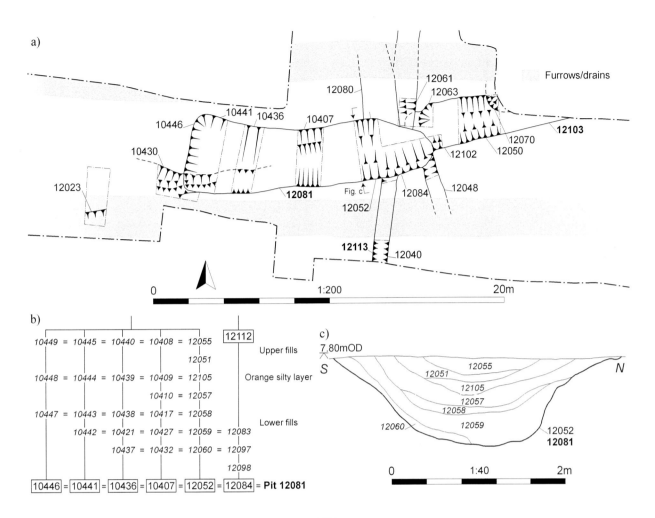

FIG. 64: SCORBOROUGH HILL, PIT 12081, PLAN AND REPRESENTATIVE SECTION

FIG. 65: SCORBOROUGH HILL, PIT 12081, EAST-FACING SECTION (PHOTO)

3) elaboration of the Kilbride-Jones classification the former is Type 2 Ai and the latter Type 2 Ci. She noted (*ibid.* 353-4) around 100 similar examples from Yorkshire and suggested that such bangles were an important chronological marker for late first- and possibly early second-century native settlement. An association with Roman military sites suggests a military role in their production or distribution (see also Maciness 1989). The bangle recovered during the fieldwalking survey (Fig. 88.19) was found within 15m of pit **12081**.

The bangles were found in association with a substantially complete, though broken, flat pottery dish. Burnt animal bone fragments were recovered alongside, along with numerous fragments of a burnt pottery vessel (SF 100). Human bone was also recovered from the same context: four fragments from a tibia shaft, which showed evidence of a healed break.

The paler clay layer had notably fewer artefacts than the darker layers below and above. It did, however, produce a small assemblage of briquetage, from salt-making, including a possible pedestal base and spacer clip (Fig. 107.33 and 34). Finds from the upper fill of the pit included a bezel from a copper alloy finger ring, (SF 103, Fig. 85.4) with second-century parallels, and a claw-shaped fitting (SF 201, Fig. 85.5), probably from a three-piece bit. The same context also produced two fragments of ferrous metal knife blades, one 58.7mm long, 11.0mm wide and 3.5mm thick and the other 32.5mm long, 11.4mm long and 5.5mm thick.

The function of pit **12081** is obscure. None of the fills of the feature appeared to have been deposited in standing water, so an interpretation as a watering hole or drainage sump is unlikely. Its positioning suggests that it may have reinforced the line of the earlier boundary, or deliberately blocked an access through the boundary. The pit and the other archaeological features were on the southern edge of the working width of the pipeline, suggesting that the source of these dumped artefacts was further south.

The pit had been cut by at least two linear features, but these were poorly defined, in part because of the difficult weather conditions when they were examined. A small quantity of pottery from ditch **12113** included a sherd of samian ware dated to the second half of the second century.

Ditch 12003

Ditch **12003**, up to 3.6m wide and 1.1m deep, extended into the eastern half of the site and turned to form the north-western corner of a possible enclosure, which would have been at least 21m wide. The acute angle of this corner might imply that the ditch was respecting pre-existing elements of the landscape. The fairly large pottery assemblage recovered from its various fills seems to date from firmly within the second century, slightly later than that from pit **12081**. This would suggest that ditch **12003** ceased to be maintained around the time that the final backfilling of the pit was complete, or shortly thereafter. A briquetage pedestal (Fig. 107.32) was also recovered from ditch **12003**.

At the western limit of the excavation, ditch **10404**, continuing eastward as ditch **12018**, was on a similar alignment to the northern arm of ditch **12003** and may have formed part of a contemporary system of land division. This smaller ditch also appears to have infilled during the second century. There was no further evidence of activity until the medieval or early post-medieval period, when ridge and furrow cultivation was carried out within the open fields of Skeffling village.

Scorborough Hill: discussion

This was certainly something more than a simple rural site. The assemblage of the pottery recovered from the pit, together with that from ditch **12003**, implies that an individual with a fairly direct link to the Roman culture of continental Europe was present in the area. In the late first century, that would almost certainly be a military figure, and the nature of the pottery assemblage and the distinctiveness of the other finds, especially the glass bangles, is typical of other similarly dated sites with a strong military character.

Scorborough Hill is around 40km from the nearest well attested Roman military site, the fort at Brough, though there may have been a more local military presence at Easington (Sheppard 1922, 208-209), lost to erosion of the sea cliffs. A possible explanation of the site invokes the settlement of an army veteran, perhaps with origins in Gaul, as a source of these artefacts, though their acquisition by a native leader, by plunder, trade or in the course of diplomatic contact could provide other convincing narratives.

The geophysical survey carried out in advance of the Easington to Paull pipeline (Bunn 2007; 2008), covering a wide area to the south of the Scorborough Hill excavation area (Fig. 66), shows several busy areas of archaeology. Around 20m beyond the edge of the pipeline easement to the south of ditch **12003** there is an anomaly which could possibly represent the remains of a structure: two apparently curving wings, marked by parallel paired anomalies, joined by a single linear anomaly to enclose a roughly square central space. Further afield, a square feature and two ring gullies, 200m to the south-east, show very clearly among a group of sinuously bounded enclosures; evaluation trenching on the Easington to Paull route confirmed the presence of these features, and showed them to contain hand-made pottery (Allen 2008, 7).

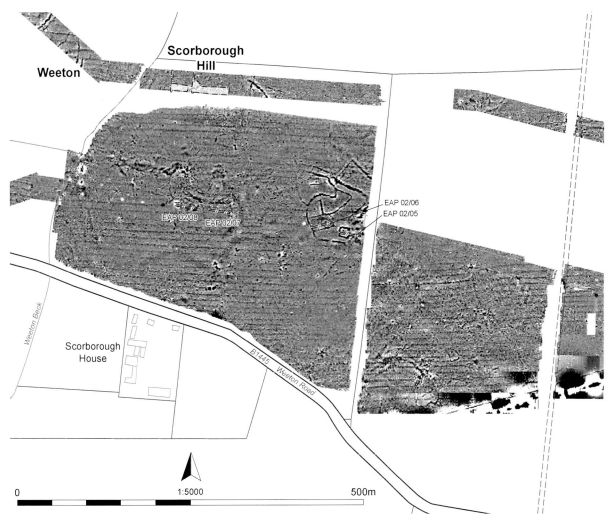

FIG. 66 GEOPHYSICAL SURVEY IN THE SCORBOROUGH HILL AREA

The Easington to Paull evaluation provided 'the first evidence for production of Roman ceramic building material in Holderness' (Tibbles 2008) in the form of several misfired tiles, a distorted and cracked *tegula* and fragments of kiln furniture, within a feature showing *in situ* burning. The site could have produced tiles either for export along or across the Humber, or for local use. By contrast, the Scorborough Hill site produced only a single piece of Roman tile, from ditch **10415**.

In addition to the archaeological features, the geophysical survey showed palaeochannels in the south-western part of the field, tracing the former courses of the outfall of Weeton Beck through the undrained marshes. Before the construction of the sea banks, it is likely that the Scorborough Hill excavation area and the cropmark sites were on the first dry land encountered when travelling up the creeks through the salt-marshes bordering the estuary, and may be the remains from settlements trading across the Humber and into the North Sea.

Gilcross

Bronze Age pits and Iron Age ring gullies and ditches, and a human burial

The Gilcross excavation area (Fig. 61) was on the level ground of a low headland, defined by the valleys of Weeton Beck and Punda Drain to the west and east. The top of the archaeological deposits was around 12.5m OD. To the north, the land rises to over 20m OD at Gilcross Hill and Crowhill, 800m and 1.2km away respectively.

The archaeological features, which were confined to a small area on the north edge of the working width (Fig. 67), were located during monitoring of the topsoil stripping.

Two intercutting Bronze Age pits

A pair of intercutting shallow features were excavated, 40m to the west of the main excavation area, beyond the field boundary to the west (NGR: 536800 420035).

65

The later feature, **117574**, was 1.50m by 1.15m, and 0.35m deep with a charcoal-rich upper fill containing a small concentration of heat-cracked stones. Its lower fill produced sherds from a Bronze Age beaker, with a probable date from 2050 to 1700 BC.

Late Iron Age field system

Within the excavation area, there was no evidence of activity pre-dating the Iron Age apart from two residual flint flakes. Ditch **121102**, in the central area of the site, and ditch **121006**, probably a continuation of the same feature to the south, had both been heavily truncated by later features. Feature **121049**, towards the western limit of the site, may have been an elongated pit or the largely ploughed out remains of a ditch. Pottery sherds recovered from ditch **121102** and feature **121049** suggest a late Iron Age date for the features, which may have formed part of a contemporary field system.

Late Iron Age settlement (Fig. 68)

Three intercutting ring gullies, partially visible within the excavation area, probably surrounded a large roundhouse rebuilt on two occasions, with a slightly displaced footprint. Several small pits are also likely to have originated in this phase of occupation. Although the geophysical survey carried out on the Easington to Paull pipeline route shows that there was a system of enclosures in the southern part of the same field, there is no evidence that the Gilcross settlement was enclosed.

Structures 1 to 3

Judging by the portion visible within the excavation area, the curvilinear gully comprising features **121089** and **121104** would have enclosed an area 19m in diameter. The eastern arc of the gully showed a distinct upper fill rich in charcoal, ash and burnt bone. These deposits were considered, during excavation, to be

possible cremations, but none of the bone could be positively identified as human, and dumping of burnt domestic waste is a more likely explanation. Structure 1 was cut by a second curvilinear gully, **121101**, which would have enclosed an area measuring 17m in diameter. Two curvilinear features, **121103** and **121078**, were probably the remains of a third ring gully, cutting the circuits of Structures 1 and 2; it would have enclosed an area approximately 15m in diameter. A single sixteenth-century Cistercian ware sherd was recovered from gully **121101**, at the point where Structure 2 was cut by a later furrow, but otherwise the pottery assemblages from the three structures are similar, consisting entirely of hand-made wares.

Pits 121011, 121012 and 121058

There were two pits within the area enclosed by Structure 1, their locations suggesting that they were related to the structures. Pit **121011**, which was also internal to Structure 2, was 0.43m deep and produced an assemblage of hand-made pottery. Similar pottery was also recovered from the upper and lower fills of the 0.30m deep pit **121012**. The upper fill of this pit was notable for a concentration of fire-cracked stones. The pit also produced a fragment of a briquetage container (Fig. 107.36). A third pit, **121058**, truncated by the eastern extent of the Structure 3 ring gully, produced a small assemblage of hand-made pottery.

Pit 121040 and burial 121051 (Fig. 67)

An irregular 0.55m-deep pit, **121040**, towards the western limit of the site contained the remains of a skeleton, **121051**, within its south-eastern quarter. The moderately well preserved skeleton, lying in a supine position with legs partly flexed, was of a young to middle aged adult, probable female. She had *cribra orbitalia* lesions in her eye orbits, indicating childhood stress, probably caused by infection or Vitamin B12 deficiency. She also had

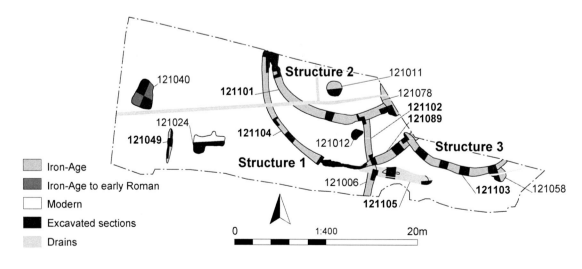

FIG. 67: GILCROSS: PLAN OF ALL FEATURES

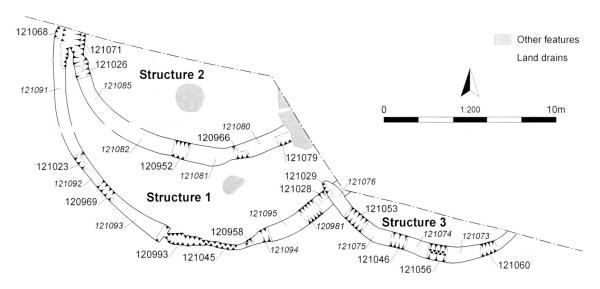

FIG. 68: GILCROSS: STRUCTURES 1 TO 3

mild degenerative disease in the joint between the lower jaw and skull. Her dental health was poor for her age, with widespread mineralised plaque formation, a dental cavity, *ante mortem* tooth loss and slight to moderate periodontal disease.

Late Iron Age fine ware sherds with burnished surfaces recovered from beneath the skeleton resemble sherds within the pottery assemblage from the Scorborough Hill site, which might imply that the burial dated from the early Roman period, rather later than the settlement features. Fragments of used crucibles were recovered from the fill of the same part of the pit and from the lower fill, **121041**, visible in the base of the north-western quarter. This context also produced a possible non-ferrous metal-casting mould (Fig. 107.39). Unused crucible fragments and two slab-like pieces of structural briquetage were also recovered (Fig. 107.37 and 38). Metal finds included two fragments of a spring from a brooch (SF 1662, Fig. 85.14) and an enamel-inlaid bar-toggle (SF 1663, Fig. 85.15). Both of these were found above the skeleton: 0.48m higher in the case of the brooch spring and 0.15m for the toggle, so it is unlikely that they were dress fittings being worn when the body was interred. The metal-work finds would be consistent with a peri- or post-conquest dating for the infilling of the pit.

There are contrasting ways to interpret this feature. The eccentric position of the skeleton towards the edge of the pit suggests that the body may have been dumped rather than having been respectfully placed in what would have been a very oversized grave. A mixed deposit, incorporating fragments of metal casting waste, broken dress fittings, salt-making waste, pottery and other miscellaneous rubbish then accumulated in the pit. The events that led to this undignified end are beyond recovery, but the pathological indications of malnutrition would indicate that the individual was of low status.

Or perhaps that she had an over-rich diet. A person of standing, she was buried in a large grave, allowing room for elaborate burial rites involving deposition of objects symbolising seemingly miraculous transformations: sea water into salt, clay into ceramic, dirt into jewellery, scrap into molten metal, the living into the dead.

Medieval and post-medieval agriculture

Although the metal finds suggest a general Roman date for the infilling of pit **121040**, there was no diagnostic Roman pottery and the settlement features seem to have been abandoned before Roman material culture become prevalent in the area. The nearby sites on the Easington to Paull pipeline route and from Scorborough Hill, demonstrate that the widespread Iron Age activity in the general area continued into the Roman period, but by this time, the Gilcross settlement had reverted to agricultural use, which has left no archaeological features, deposits or finds.

Feature **121105**, indistinct in places, in the eastern half of the site, was probably the remains of a furrow or old field boundary. The geophysical survey data suggests that east-to-west oriented furrows extended across much of the surrounding area, aligned with the modern field boundaries. A notable find, from the subsoil surface, was a seventeenth- to early nineteenth-century musket gunflint (Fig. 84.40). Pit **121024**, with regular vertical-sides, contained twentieth-century finds.

Out Newton Road

Corner of a large Iron Age enclosure, with a single large pit

The Out Newton Road excavation area was located 750m to the north of Skeffling village, on the western side of the shallow valley where the Fosse and Punda Drains

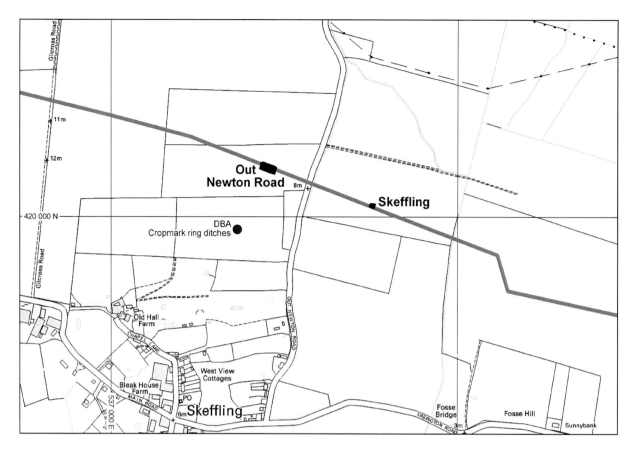

FIG. 69: OUT NEWTON ROAD AND SKEFFLING: LOCATION. CONTAINS OS DATA © CROWN COPYRIGHT [1:10 000 MAPPING]

now run (Fig. 69). The top of the archaeological deposits varied between 8.4m and 9.3m OD, with the land rising gently to the west. The shoreline of the Humber, 1.8km to the south, would have been much closer prior to the medieval and post-medieval embankment and drainage works.

The DBA identified two possible ring ditches, visible on aerial photographs, approximately 180m to the south-west of the site, and a possible enclosure, 340m to the west. The geophysical survey revealed a substantial curvilinear ditch-like anomaly, with at least one internal pit. The presence of the ditch and pit were confirmed during evaluation trenching, but the initial interpretation of the feature as a Bronze Age round barrow was shown to be wrong. The only evidence of activity pre-dating the Iron Age was twenty-six residual struck flints, of probable Neolithic or Bronze Age origin. Mostly broad flakes, these also include a core used for flake production.

Iron Age enclosure

The prominent geophysical anomaly corresponded to a substantial curvilinear ditch, **13070**, extending into the excavation area and forming a roughly semi-circular arc, 23m in diameter (Figs. 69, 70). The ditch was up to 6.4m wide and 1.4m deep with relatively steep sides, the outer side rather steeper than the inner side. The flattish base was at least 1m wide.

The primary fills of the ditch did not produce any finds and most likely derive from rapid erosion of the sides following the initial excavation of the feature. Subsequent fills had similar compositions and were not always readily distinguishable from one another, suggesting that the ditch infilled by gradual silting. A possible turf line was intermittently visible within the ditch, indicating that silting stopped or slowed when the ditch was approximately half filled, for long enough to allow grass growth. A small quantity of hand-made pottery was recovered from the earlier fills, the lack of wheel-thrown forms a strong indication that this earlier phase of silting occurred prior to the penetration of Roman material culture into the area. A jet ring, probably worn as a pendant (SF 280, Fig. 87.3), was also recovered.

The geophysical survey undertaken prior to the construction of the Easington to Paull pipeline (Bunn 2007; 2008) showed that the excavated portion of the ditch aligned with an enclosure ditch around a small area of settlement (Fig. 72); this settlement was subsequently excavated (site SPE4, Rowland and Wegiel 2012, 59-68). A radiocarbon date of 390 to 200 cal BC from a sample from the primary fill of the ditch on the Easington to Paull route (*ibid.* 60) is a possible indication of when the ditch was originally excavated. The ditch ceased to be maintained during the Iron Age and silted up, to the point where the sides had stabilised, remaining for some

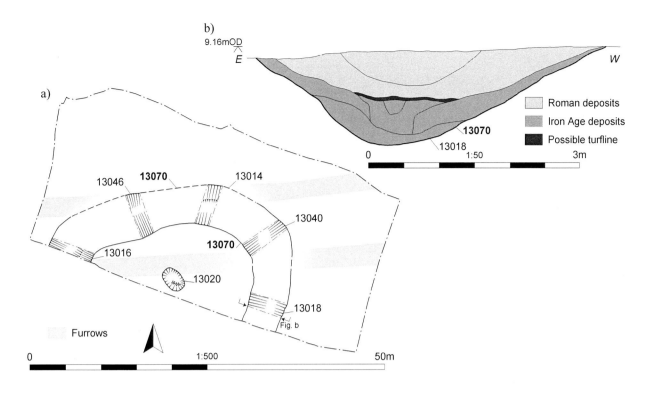

FIG. 70: OUT NEWTON ROAD: PLAN OF FEATURES

FIG. 71: OUT NEWTON ROAD (PHOTO © ADAM STANFORD)

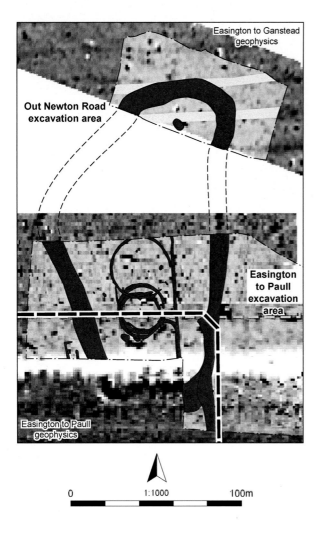

FIG. 72: OUT NEWTON ROAD: SITE OVERLAID ONTO GEOPHYSICS

time as a negative landscape feature. Few artefacts were recovered from fills associated with this initial silting, perhaps suggesting that settlement had ceased by this time, or that the main focus of settlement was some distance away.

Out Newton Road stands out from the rest of the Iron Age excavation sites as the only one that could reasonably be described as an enclosed settlement. This is discussed below, in relation to the form of the settlement sites. Judging from the geophysical surveys, the enclosure was an irregular pentagon with maximum internal dimensions of around 50m east-to-west and 80m north-to-south. It would have enclosed an area of rather less than a third of a hectare. The size of the ditch suggests that it may have been dug for defence. Although there was no appreciable difference between the fills on the inner and outer sides that might have indicated erosion or slumping of a bank back into the ditch, there would be an expectation that a defensive ditch would have had a bank on the inner edge, which may have considerably reduced the usable internal space.

Large Iron Age pit

Pit **13020** was 0.45m deep and had a thin layer of silt intermittently present in the base of the feature, above which the main fill was a dark, charcoal-rich, silty clay, merging towards the top into a slightly paler upper fill. Small quantities of charred chaff and cereal, including two oat grains, were recovered from environmental samples, along with a single tiny fish bone, a unique find from sites along the pipeline route (Shaw and O'Meara 2010). The small pottery assemblage from the pit comprised only hand-made wares.

The central location of the pit within the semi-circular loop of the ditch and the similarity of the pottery from the two features strongly suggest that they were broadly contemporary, and that the enclosure had deliberately included the pit, implying that the function of the pit was integral to that of the enclosure as a whole. An interpretation as a watering hole might be appropriate.

Early Roman infilling of enclosure ditch

The ditch was finally infilled no earlier than the mid-second century. The later fills, in the upper half of the feature above the possible turf-line, were, in the main, darker with higher proportions of coarse silt or sand than the lower fills. The large pottery assemblage from these fills included two sherds of Roman grey ware; one from a wide-mouthed jar of probable mid-second- to mid-third-century date and the other probably dating from the second century or later. A fragment of a copper alloy ring (SF 281, Fig. 85.6) was also recovered. The upper fill of intervention **13014** produced a small amount of cremated human bone, 1.9g in total. A small glass bead, recovered as an unstratified surface find (Fig. 89.22), had probably been displaced from its original context in the upper fills of the ditch.

The discernable change in composition suggests that rather different formation processes produced the earlier and later fills. The later backfilling may represent deliberate levelling, although the silty nature of the fills suggest that changes in the local environment were at work, such as increased woodland clearance or a change in the agricultural regime in the neighbourhood of the site. Ploughing of grassland, for instance, could have led to renewed silting. However, the mollusc assemblages from the upper ditch fills indicate a short grassland environment, probably exposed to seasonal flooding, which would suggest that the area was still being used primarily as pasture.

Medieval and post-medieval agriculture

Following the backfilling of the enclosure ditch, there is no evidence of further activity until the medieval or early post-medieval period, when furrows extended across the site. Finds included a residual sherd from the body of a hand-made pottery vessel, recovered from furrow **13011**, which is in an unusual fabric containing dense angular rock fragments and sparse quartz. The geophysical survey shows that these furrows are the remains of a wide area of ridge and furrow agriculture.

Skeffling

Remnant Mesolithic soil layer, Iron Age pits, evidence of possible Bronze Age burnt mound

The site was located on an east-facing slope leading down to the Fosse and Punda Drains (Fig. 69), at between 4.75m OD and 4.60m OD. No significant archaeological features were noted in the pre-construction surveys, but a cluster of pits and an old soil horizon were uncovered and investigated during monitoring of topsoil stripping.

Mesolithic land surface

A layer of dark grey silty clay, **120308**, surviving to a depth of up to 0.23m, produced twenty-two struck flints and one piece of burnt, unworked flint. A slight hollow in the surface of the brownish red silty clay drift deposits seems to have allowed this layer, probably a patch of old land surface, to survive the plough. At least seven of the struck flints are products of blade production. Three of the blades are complete, their narrow proportions suggesting a Mesolithic provenance. This small concentration of flints might indicate use of the area as a camp or tool production site. Results from the Humber Wetlands Project indicate that Mesolithic activity in Holderness is closely associated with watercourses and meres (Van de Noort and Ellis 1995, 359), and the location of the Skeffling site, close to a watercourse, surviving as the Fosse and Punda Drains, fits this general pattern.

Pits

Four sub-oval pits, **120301**, **120307**, **120309** and **120312**, were all similar in appearance: clearly defined, with near vertical sides and flattish bases, and around 0.30m to 0.35m deep (Fig. 73). The proximity of the pits to one another and their similarity of form implies that they were broadly contemporary, deriving from the same phase of land use. Hand-made pottery was recovered from the fills of pits **120301** and **120312**. Twenty-four of the thirty sherds recovered from pit **120301** appear to be from the same vessel, with a flat-topped plain rim, in a coarse fabric tempered with abundant angular rock fragments up to 10mm across. The vessel was decorated externally with shallow impressed lines (Cumberpatch 2009a). Pit **120312** produced a sherd in a similar fabric.

Fire-cracked stones were revealed in the fills of pits **120301**, **120307** and **120312** and high concentrations of charcoal were present in pits **120301** and **120307**.

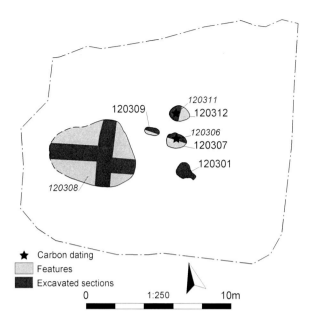

FIG. 73: SKEFFLING: PLAN OF FEATURES

There was no evidence, however, of *in situ* burning. Samples of the charcoal from pits **120307** and **120312** were radiocarbon dated to 1750 to 1490 and 1760 to 1610 cal BC, respectively (SUERC-36200 and -36196). However, pottery recovered from two of the four pits is not substantially different to the hand-made pottery found elsewhere on the pipeline, and is most likely to be of Iron Age date.

The heat-cracked stones in the fills of three of the pits are reminiscent of the stones found in burnt mounds. Increasingly recognised, characterised and documented, burnt mounds are enigmatic features, very commonly found adjacent to rivers or streams (Topping 2011). The location of the Skeffling site, close to the watercourse now formalised as the Punda Drain, would be entirely typical. The remains of a burnt mound in the vicinity would also account for the increased presence of residual charcoal within the pit fill, and the radiocarbon dates from the two samples would sit comfortably within the broad date range typical of burnt mounds.

An extensive area of Iron Age activity was investigated in advance of construction of the Easington to Paull pipeline (Allen 2008), of which the Out Newton Road site, 300m to the west, was an outlying part. The pits may have been associated with this activity, although their function is not clear. Their regular shape implies a degree of care was taken in digging them and they are unlikely to have been simple quarry pits. An interpretation as large postholes is tenable although their oval shape and irregular arrangement makes this explanation less likely. Pits at the Iron Age settlement at Ledston, West Yorkshire (Roberts 2005) could provide a possible parallel.

Hull Road

Iron Age ring gully and ditches

The Hull Road excavation area lay on slightly sloping ground, with the top of the archaeological features at 12.90m OD at the western end to 12.50m OD at the east. Further to the south-east, the land continues to fall away towards the former Kilnsea Fleet watercourse, and to the north, it rises towards the higher ground that forms the sea cliffs north of Easington (Fig. 74). An undated linear cropmark is recorded to the north of the site (MHU 18782), but neither the field surveys nor the geophysical survey suggested the presence of any significant remains. The site was discovered during monitoring of topsoil stripping during construction.

Iron Age settlement and land division (Fig. 75)

The earliest cut features, defining the north-western corner of a heavily truncated enclosure, were gullies **120722** and **120760**, the latter probably continuing to the south-east as gully **120727**. Eighty-four sherds of hand-made pottery were recovered from gully **120760**, all from a single small area. To the north, a fourth gully, **120736** was of similar appearance and most likely contemporary, suggesting that it may have formed the limit of a further enclosure to the north.

Structure 1 (Fig. 76)

A single ring gully comprising two curvilinear segments, **120712** and **120761**, enclosed an area 8.5m in diameter. Sixty-five sherds of hand-made pottery were recovered, with roughly equal amounts from the two surviving sections. The assemblage, though not large, represents a high density, as the ring gully was very shallow, little more than a few centimetres deep in places. A sample of charcoal from the gully gave a radiocarbon date of 410 to 200 cal BC (SUERC-36201). The break in the western side of the circuit is likely to have been the result of truncation by ploughing, but the south-east facing break was probably a true entrance. Two small postholes, **120744** and **120746**, may have held uprights of a structure relating to the entrance.

This small settlement site formed part of an extensive pattern of exploitation of the local area, which included the nearby Dimlington Road site (below), the settlement excavated ahead of the construction of the Langeled Receiving Facility beyond (Richardson 2011), and the sites close to the eastern end of the Easington to Paull pipeline (SPE1 and 2, Rowland and Wegiel 2012, 44-51). Undated cropmark sites recorded in the same area, such as the linear cropmark to the north (SMR MHU18782), may have been components of the same landscape.

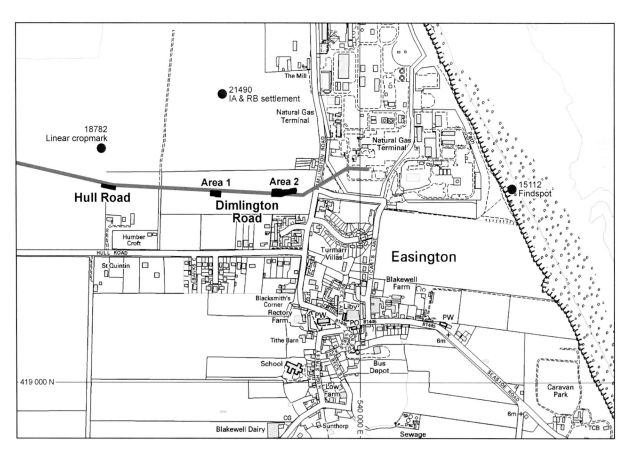

FIG. 74: HULL ROAD AND DIMLINGTON ROAD: LOCATION CONTAINS OS DATA © CROWN COPYRIGHT [1:10 000 MAPPING]

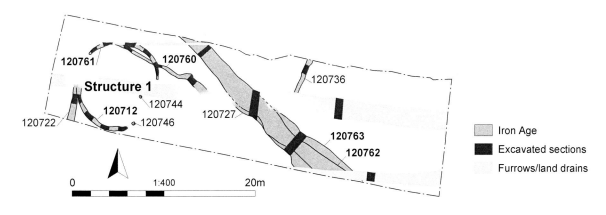

FIG. 75: HULL ROAD: PLAN OF ALL FEATURES

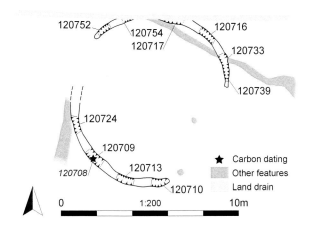

FIG. 76: HULL ROAD: STRUCTURE 1

Ditch 120763 (Fig. 75)

Ditch **120763**, recut by ditch **120762**, was up to 2.66m wide and 0.85m deep, and produced twelve sherds of hand-made pottery. This ditch probably formed part of a boundary or enclosure, its size possibly indicating control of livestock or drainage. While there is no evidence to indicate whether the ditch and Structure 1 were contemporary; the relative scarcity of pottery from the ditch might suggest that they were not. This recut ditch could be seen continuing to the south-east on the Easington to Paull pipeline (Roland and Wegiel 2012, 50).

Later activity

There was no evidence of activity between the end of the Iron Age and the medieval period or later, when ridge and furrow cultivation was established, the site being within the West Field, shown on the 1771 inclosure map of Easington (ERY Archives, ref. DDCC/32/42).

Dimlington Road

Iron Age ring gullies, ditch systems; distinctive shallow stone-filled pits

The Dimlington Road excavation areas were on land rising to the east, towards the sea cliffs (Fig. 74), with the higher land extending northwards along the coastline. Two areas were excavated, located 145m apart, the top of the archaeological deposits being around 11m OD in the western area and 12.5m OD in the larger eastern area.

Excavations undertaken ahead of construction of the Langeled Receiving Facilities 250m to the north revealed remains dating from the Bronze Age to medieval periods including burials, cremations, trackways, enclosures and evidence of Iron Age settlement (Richardson 2011). Finds of Romano-British pottery (SMR MHU 15112) have been recorded at Easington cliff 650m to the east, along with evidence of Bronze Age to Iron Age occupation. The Kilnsea and Easington areas have also produced considerable quantities of unprovenanced finds of the Roman period since the nineteenth century (Brigham and Jobling 2011) including a small bronze figure depicting the Roman god Mercury, and the remains interpreted by Sheppard (1922, 208-209) as the site of a 'small though not unimportant station', now lost to coastal erosion. The figure of Mercury would indicate the local presence of Roman personnel or the assimilation of Roman deities into indigenous belief systems.

The geophysical survey showed numerous magnetic anomalies but these were not clearly defined and lacked any coherent patterns. However, archaeological features were discovered at both areas in the course of monitoring of topsoil stripping (Fig. 77).

Mesolithic to Bronze Age activity

The earliest evidence for activity at the site consists of fifty-three pieces of worked flint. Diagnostic Mesolithic

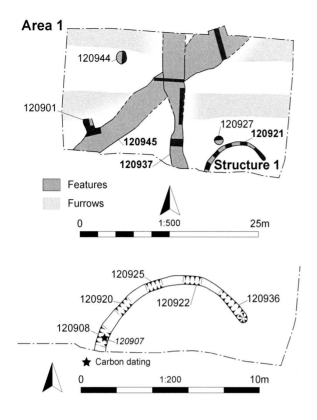

Area 1

120944

120901

120927
120921
120945
120937
Structure 1

Features
Furrows

0   1:500   25m

120925
120920   120922   120936
120908
120907

★ Carbon dating

0   1:200   10m

FIG. 77: DIMLINGTON ROAD: PLAN OF ALL FEATURES

pieces were recovered from three intercutting pits, **120592, 120594, 120596,** at the eastern end of the eastern excavation area. These flints were in a fresh condition and are unlikely to have moved far from where they were originally deposited. There were also Mesolithic flints in unstratified contexts in the same area of the site. The Neolithic and early Bronze Age component of the flint assemblage, again mostly retrieved from the eastern area of excavation, comprised a small number of flakes, a core and three scrapers. Pottery from the latest of the intercutting pits, **120592,** included thirty-nine sherds that may derive from Bronze Age Bucket Urns. The other

pottery from the feature was non-diagnostic but was similar to the hand-made pottery from other Iron Age contexts from the pipeline.

These finds show the site has been used, at least sporadically, from the early post-glacial period. The possible Bucket Urn sherds, in particular, may relate to the siting of Bronze Age funerary monuments along the ridge of relatively high coastal land.

Iron Age settlement

Structure 1 (Fig. 78)

Ring gully **120921** was partly visible in the western area; the remainder extended beyond the limit of excavation, but was subsequently excavated on the route of the Easington to Paull pipeline (Rowland and Wegiel 2012, 45). The ring gully enclosed an area 8m in diameter, and had an east-facing entrance. Two sherds of hand-made pottery were recovered from the gully and a calibrated radiocarbon date of 50 BC to AD 80 (SUERC-36202) was obtained from a charred grain from the fill of its western side. A second ring gully, centred 16m to the west and visible on the Easington to Paull site had been truncated by ditch **120945** within the Dimlington Road excavation area. Pit **120927** may have been associated with the ring gully but it did not produce any finds. Pit, **120944,** to the north-west, produced three hand-made pottery sherds.

Structure 2, Eastern area (Fig. 78)

Three fragments, **120456, 120543,** and **120627,** were possibly the heavily truncatied remains of a single ring gully, 13.5m in diameter. A break in the western side of the ring could have been an entrance, but the gully was no more than 0.08m deep at this point, so truncation by ploughing is a possibility. Eight sherds of hand-made pottery were recovered from the northern arc of the gully.

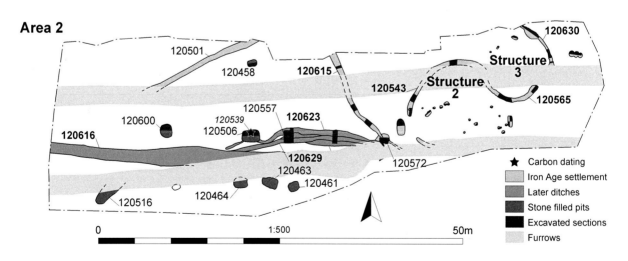

Area 2

120501
120458   120615
120543   **Structure 2**   **Structure 3**   120630
120557   **120623**
120600   *120539*   120565
120506
120616
120629
120463   120572
120464   120461
120516

★ Carbon dating
Iron Age settlement
Later ditches
Stone filled pits
Excavated sections
Furrows

0   1:500   50m

FIG. 78: DIMLINGTON ROAD: STRUCTURE 1

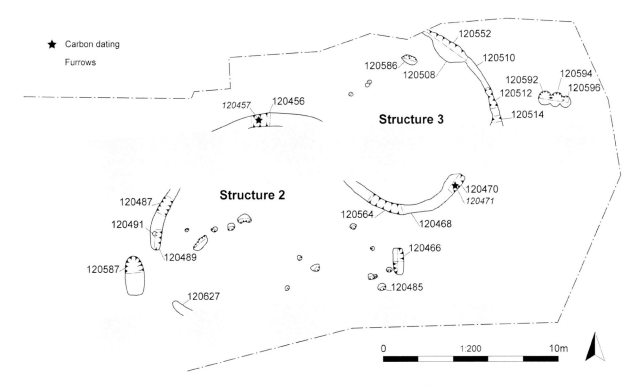

FIG. 79: DIMLINGTON ROAD: STRUCTURES 2 AND 3

A calibrated date of AD 530 to 650 (SUERC-36203) from a sample of charcoal from the fill throws some doubt on the interpretation as an Iron Age ring feature but there is a possibility that the charcoal sample was intrusive. The same could also be true for the two joining fragments of bone or antler (SF 1626, Fig. 88.4) recovered from the same context and best seen as being parts of the side plates for a double-sided comb, for which an early medieval date seems likely.

No obvious patterns are discernible in the thirteen minor features within the area enclosed by Structure 2. Pit **120485** produced a single sherd of hand-made pottery, the only find from this group of features. Elongated, sub-rectangular pits lay either side of the ring gully: two sherds of hand-made pottery were recovered from pit **120466**, while the thirty-two sherds from pit **120587**, the majority from its upper fill, was the second largest assemblage from any of the features on this site. Dumped burnt material and several fragments of large mammal bone suggest that the final use of this pit was the disposal of domestic rubbish.

Structure 3, Eastern area (Fig. 79)

A further possible ring gully was represented by two curvilinear features, **120565** and **120630**, immediately to the north-east of Structure 2. These gullies enclosed an area 9m in diameter, possibly with a south-east facing entrance disrupted by a later furrow. Four sherds of pottery were recovered, all from the southern terminal. A charred cereal grain from the same context gave a

radiocarbon date of 1490 to 1310 (SUERC-36204) cal BC. This suggests the possibility that the gully pre-dates the Iron Age, especially as the flint assemblage indicates Neolithic or Bronze activity in the immediate area, but a more likely explanation is that the charred grain was residual.

The interpretation of Structures 2 and 3 as roundhouse ring gullies is less secure than many of the other examples along the pipeline route. As interpolated, they deviated considerably from circularity, and it is questionable whether the two arcs of Structure 3, in particular, belong to the same phase of construction.

Linear features (Fig. 77)

Ditches **120501** and **120615** had similar dimensions and profiles, and would have intersected beyond the northern limit of excavation, perhaps forming the corner of an enclosure. Their alignments differed from those of the later linear features, and were more similar to that of the earlier substantial ditch, **120945**, crossing the western excavation area. The different scale of the ditches in the two areas may reflect a greater need for the drainage in the lower lying western area. A series of shallow intercutting ditches in the eastern area, **120629**, **120623**, **120531**, **120557** and possibly **120516**, appeared to represent the recutting of a single feature, although at least some of the components of this complex may have simply been natural runnels. No finds were recovered from any of these features; their relationship with ditch **120615** had been removed by a deep furrow.

75

Both ditch **120616**, which cut through the shallow intercutting ditches in the eastern area, and ditch **120937**, which ran across the western area cutting ditch **120945**, were substantial features, up to 0.60m deep. Their orientation, roughly at right angles to one another, suggests the possibility that they formed elements of a reorganised and realigned system of land division. Nine hand-made sherds from these ditches indicate that the realignment was probably carried out prior the Roman period. An eastward continuation of ditch **120616** was recorded as ditch **2250** during topsoil stripping of the access area on the western side of the road crossing. It produced a bone pin made from a pig fibula (SF 1000, Fig. 90.3), in addition to a small assemblage of hand-made pottery.

In the absence of secure stratigraphic phasing, it is not certain whether the linear ditches were contemporary with the ring gullies. Nevertheless, it is likely that they were located fairly close to a settlement, forming a system of fields extending over a fairly wide area and possibly encompassing both excavation areas. The reordering of boundaries that occurred later, but probably still within the Iron Age, could have been as a result of changes in land tenure, or a response to a need for improved drainage, perhaps as a result of environmental changes. By the early Roman period the ditches had ceased to be maintained.

Roman pit

A short length of ditch or an elongated pit, **120901**, cut into the earlier of the large ditches in the western area, produced six sherds from a Roman grey ware vessel along with a similar number of hand-made sherds.

Stone-filled pits

Five very shallow, regular, flat-bottomed pits, **120506**, **120461**, **120458** and **120463**, **120464** towards the western side of the eastern excavation area all had charcoal-rich fills containing an abundance of cobbles. The stones, typically fist-sized, showed little sign of being affected by heat, but pits **120506** and **120463**, in particular, showed noticeable reddening of the underlying natural deposits indicating at least some *in situ* heating. Pit **120600**, in the same area, with similar dimensions and charcoal-rich fill but lacking cobbles, may have been another example of the same kind of pit. Feature **120516** also had a charcoal-rich fill although its orientation suggested that it might have been a terminal of ditch **120531** or **120623** isolated by the deep furrow running across the excavation area. Pit **120572**, belonging to an earlier phase of activity and severely truncated by other features, could also have had the same function as the other members of this group.

Pit **120506**, the best preserved of the stone-filled pits, cut ditch **120623**. Two sherds of hand-made pottery were

Fig. 80: Dimlington Road, stone filled pit 120506

recovered from its upper fill, **120539**. A radiocarbon date of AD cal 420 to 557 (SUERC-38670) for a fragment of large mammal long bone from the same fill raises the possibility that these puzzling features originated in the Anglo-Saxon period, but in the absence of further dating evidence this cannot be more than conjecture. Whatever their date, these distinctive features clearly shared a specific purpose: perhaps salt-making, drying or malting grain, cooking, or the smoking of fish or other foodstuffs.

Two shallow pits recorded in the road-crossing area to the east, also contained burnt material within their fills, but were different in appearance to the stone-filled pits and from each other. A 2m-diameter pit, **2254**, cutting ditch **2250** (NGR: 539855 419520), produced a small assemblage of hand-made pottery. A smaller oval pit, **2247**, near the northern limit of excavation (NGR: 539853 419538), produced no finds.

Other sites

In addition to the excavation areas described above, archaeological features, most poorly dated, were excavated and recorded in twenty-nine other locations during the pipeline project. Details are given in the assessment report (Flintoft and Glover 2010) but several features and finds warrant mention here.

To the north of the Burton Constable excavation area (NGR: 516677 436865), a small shallow feature, **117007**, contained 130.2g of cremated human bone. The majority of the identifiable pieces were long bone fragments, with around 10 per cent of skull fragments. There was no sign of an urn or other container, nor any other associated finds. It is of note that the feature was less than 20m south of the location of a possible barrow recorded from cropmarks (SMR MHU 18510).

Near Daisy Hill, north of Burstwick village (NGR: 521940 430760), a very shallow gully, **117026**, aligned roughly north-to-south and visible for just over 5m, had a fill rich in charcoal and animal bone, and contained pottery sherds including a sherd of mortarium, in a fabric very close to Crambeck 'parchment' though more likely to be fineware made at a local workshop. It can be dated to AD 370 to 400 or later. Gully **117028**, on a roughly perpendicular alignment 180m to the south-east (NGR: 522105 430575), had similar dimensions and a fill similarly rich in burnt animal bone. The presence of these two features might be an indication of a heavily truncated system of late Roman land division in this area.

South of Southside Road in Halsham (NGR: 528630 426790), a shallow ditch, **117053**, produced fifty-one sherds of a single vessel of an unknown but probable Saxo-Norman ware type that may be related to a newly defined reduced gritty ware found in Ripon, Wetherby (Young and Didsbury, forthcoming) and York (Mainman 1997, 132-134). The handled vessel, most probably a pitcher, had a wide everted rim with incised lines.

The ditch also produced offcuts of lead sheet. North of Halsham, just west of the access road to Hill Top Farm (NGR: 528134 427581), an unstratified find of a bone thread-picker-cum-beater with the pointed end now missing (SF 1001, Fig. 90.5), can be paralleled by thread-pickers found on early medieval sites.

During the evaluation, the remains of a medieval trackway were investigated on the eastern side of Hollym Road, north-east of Patrington (Savage 2011). Finds from the site included two iron studs (SF 8, SF 9, Fig. 86.1 and 2) of a kind generally said to have been used in the construction and decoration of heavy doors (Rees *et. al* 2008, 330, Fig. 180). A copper alloy belt plate (SF 5, Fig. 85.2), and buckle fragment (SF 6, Fig. 85.3) were recovered from the silting layer over the trackway.

Section 3: The Artefacts

Lithics

Hugo Anderson-Whymark

Introduction

During the various stages of fieldwork, 2781 pieces of struck flint were recovered along with 5 pieces of struck chert, 579 pieces (1.481kg) of burnt unworked flint and one hammerstone (869g). Lithics were recovered from fifty-nine of the ninety fields along the route, although the majority of these yielded only small artefact assemblages. The 2036 lithics, excluding chips, from the Sproatley site amounted to 73 per cent of the entire assemblage. These figures exclude approximately 40,000 pieces of micro-debitage measuring less than 10mm by 10mm from Sproatley.

The assemblage provides evidence for several millennia of activity on Holderness. The lithics from Sproatley predominately date from the early Mesolithic. Small, broadly contemporary groups of artefacts were identified at various other sites along the route of the pipeline. Small numbers of late Mesolithic, Neolithic and Bronze Age lithics were recovered; two post-medieval gun-flints were also found. Full details of the assemblages from each site are included in the project archive.

Methodology

The flint assemblage was recorded using standard morphological and typological descriptions. Retouched artefacts are classified using standard morphological descriptions (Bamford 1985, 72-77; Healy 1988, 48-49; Bradley 1999, 211-227; Butler 2005). Core typology follows Bradley (1999, 212), rather than the commonly adopted classification of Clark (Clark *et al.* 1960) as the former is more informative for reduction strategies. Additional information was recorded on the condition of the artefacts, including burning, breakage, degree of edge-damage and degree of cortication. Unworked burnt flint was quantified by weight and number.

A blade is defined as a flake with at length to breadth ratio of 2:1 or higher and a bladelet as a small blade less than 40mm in length; blade-like flakes are those that exhibit traits of true blades, such as parallel sides, but do not achieve blade proportions. Chips are flakes with a maximum dimension less than 10mm. For the Sproatley site, chips from the sieved residues were typically quantified by weight. The total number of chips has been extrapolated from the numeric quantification of 4083 chips that weighed 288g.

Metrical and technological attribute analysis was undertaken on 284 complete and 221 broken fresh or slight edge-damaged flakes from Sproatley to clarify dating and reduction strategies. The attributes of the 221 broken flakes revealed no significant differences to the sample of complete flakes. Technological attributes recorded include butt type (after Inizan *et al.* 1992), extent of dorsal cortex, termination type, flake type (after Harding 1990), hammer mode (Onhuma and Bergman 1982) and the presence or absence of platform edge-abrasion and dorsal blade scars. Metrical attributes were recorded following Saville (1980).

Raw material

Flint is readily available from surface outcrops of Lower and Upper Chalk flint on the Yorkshire Wolds to the west and north (Kent *et al.* 1980) and from the surface tills of Holderness, which contain significant quantities, some comparable to raw materials from the Wolds, but most distinctly different. Flint from the Lower Chalk is slightly translucent, whitish-grey and occurs in nodular form while flint from the Upper Chalk is opaque white with large interconnecting cherty inclusions and occurs in tabular form (Head 1995, 312-313). In the till, flint occurs as angular nodules created by frost-induced thermal fracture. The surfaces of these nodules are frequently iron-stained or corticated white and any cortex is usually heavily abraded, thin and pitted. The flint has also frequently been leached and stained various colours (see Shepherd 1972). The leaching and staining of flints is a localised phenomena and considerable variation has been demonstrated in the Holderness Tills.

The lithics recovered from the project appear to have been predominately manufactured from raw materials readily available from the extensive beach deposits present along the coastline. This material is generally of good quality for flaking, thermal fractures permitting. The only potentially imported flints are five flakes manufactured from an opaque greyish-white flint comparable to material from the Yorkshire Wolds, although pieces of this flint are also available from the tills.

A small number of artefacts were manufactured from raw materials that could be classified into one of the three main types of Holderness till flint identified by Ruth Head (1995, 312-3); the majority were not classifiable. The most common flint was light to mid- brown with few inclusions and of reasonably quality for flaking. The raw material exploited in the Mesolithic was of higher quality than that employed for later flake-based assemblages, but this probably results from the selection of better quality nodules rather than the exploitation of different sources. A flint recovered from Halsham Carrs during topsoil stripping (NGR: 527000 428500) exhibited a chattered surface typical of beach-pebble flint.

Four flakes and one end scraper were manufactured from chert. The four flakes were coarse-grained light greyish-white translucent chert. Notably, three of these flakes were recovered from Sproatley, in the northern flint scatter, and the fourth from the fill of ring gully intervention **25181** at Brandywell, suggesting that this chert was probably exploited in the Mesolithic. An end scraper recovered from Halsham Carrs during fieldwalking (NGR: 527130 428360) was manufactured from coarse textured, mid-orange brown chert.

The Mesolithic assemblage

Mesolithic flintwork was recorded from sixteen fields, distributed along the entire length of the pipeline. The majority of these fields yielded small assemblages

of between one and twenty flints, but a substantial assemblage of several hundred artefacts and numerous chips was recovered from the northern flint scatter at Sproatley (Scatter 1), which covered an area of 10m by 15m. The landscape surrounding Scatter 1 yielded a background of residual artefacts, recovered from a reworked scatter (Scatter 2) and the fills of later archaeological features. In total, this site yielded 2036 lithics with a maximum dimension over 10mm, and an estimated figure of 39,788 chips. There are 671 artefacts in a fresh or slightly edge-damage condition. The majority of these artefacts date from the Mesolithic, although a small number of Neolithic and Bronze Age artefacts were also recovered.

Condition

The lithics exhibit exceptionally varied surface conditions: many were comparable to flints in the local gravel making artefact identification a challenging and onerous task. Some flints are free from surface

| Category type | Degree of edge-damage | | | | | |
	Fresh	Slight	Moderate	Heavy	Rolled	Total
Flake	136	303	844	21	451	1755
Blade	29	13	4			46
Bladelet	32	21	2			55
Blade-like	24	14	4	1		43
Irregular waste	22	16	28		7	73
Micro burin	2	1				3
Burin spall	1					1
Rejuvenation flake other	3	1				4
Thinning flake	1					1
Single platform blade core	2					2
Bipolar blade core	1					1
Tested nodule/bashed lump	5	5	2			12
Single platform flake core	1					1
Multiplatform flake core	7	1				8
Core on a flake	1					1
Unclassifiable core	1	1				2
Microlith	6	1				7
Burin		1				1
Laurel leaf	1					1
Chisel arrowhead		1				1
Barbed and tanged arrowhead	1	1				2
End scraper	5	1				6
Side scraper	1					1
Scraper on a non-flake blank					1	1
Other scraper		1				1
Awl		1				1
Notch	1					1
Retouched flake	3	2				5
Grand total	**286**	**385**	**884**	**22**	**459**	**2036**

TABLE 3: THE FLINT ASSEMBLAGE FROM SPROATLEY, EXCLUDING CHIPS, BY ARTEFACT CATEGORY AND THE DEGREE OF EDGE DAMAGE

cortication, while others exhibit a light, moderate or heavy white cortication. A number of flints are iron-stained orange to dark red.

The degree of edge-damage present on the lithics is also highly variable and the assemblage contains 906 flints in moderate to heavily edge-damaged condition and 459 rolled flints (Table 3). The latter are mostly small cortical flakes, and only a small number of edge-damaged or rolled blades, bladelets and blade-like flakes and one scraper were recorded. It is proposed that the majority of the edge-damaged and rolled artefacts resulted from natural processes, such as the detachment of small flakes in a high energy fluvial environment. Although a small number of man-made flints are certainly present in this group, all moderate to heavily edge-damaged and rolled flakes have been excluded from any further analysis in order to establish a coherent dataset and focus the analysis on the largely *in situ* assemblage.

Excavation methodology for Scatters 1 and 2

The artefacts in the two flint scatters were initially three-dimensionally recorded, but it became apparent that there was very little vertical stratification within the scatters. In a revised excavation strategy, the deposits were excavated in 1m squares, and the soil retained for later bulk sieving off site. A 10m by 15m area (150m²) of Scatter 1 and a 9m by 10m area (90m²) of Scatter 2 were excavated.

In order to assess the potential of the excavated deposits, initial samples of 1299 litres of soil from Scatter 1 and 1539 litres of soil from Scatter 2 were processed. This exercise recovered 518 flints with maximum dimensions over 10mm, 588 chips from the >7mm residues and an estimated 24,545 chips from the 7mm to 2mm residues. Excluding chips, the 7mm mesh recovered 90.7 per cent of the flintwork including small diagnostic artefacts, such as two microliths and a micro-burin. The 2mm mesh retrieved a small number of flakes and blades, too small to be retained in the 7mm mesh. These included a small scalene micro-triangle and a burin spall. In light of these results, it was decided to process 50 per cent of the deposits from each scatter, with the samples taken from alternate metre squares on a chequerboard pattern. The residues from these additional squares were sorted to 7mm, but the smaller 7mm to 2mm residues were not sorted, as it was judged that the disproportionate amount of time required in the initial assessment exercise had not produced a significant amount of extra information.

In Scatter 1, seventy-five square metres of deposits were sampled, totalling 7880 litres of soil, including 270 litres that were sieved during the excavation. An additional 4.75m² (650 litres) of deposits from squares of interest increased the total sample to 53.2 per cent of the total deposit. In Scatter 2, 46m² (3160 litres) was processed,

representing around 50 per cent of the excavated grid. Scatter 1 yielded an average density of 58.6 flints in fresh and slightly edge-damaged condition per cubic metre of soil and Scatter 2 yielded a lower density of 28.5 flints per cubic metre of soil.

The lithic assemblage

The assemblage of fresh or slightly edge-damaged lithics is summarised in Table 4. Three Neolithic/early Bronze Age arrowheads in Scatter 1 and a small group of early Neolithic knapping debitage and a laurel leaf in Scatter 2 are also included as it is not possible to segregate this material with absolute confidence.

Unretouched flakes and blades: The Mesolithic assemblage is dominated by flake debitage and a large number of chips measuring less than 10mm. A sample of 284 complete flakes and blades over 10mm in size from Scatter 1 and 2 were measured and examined for technological attributes in order to characterise the debitage and clarify reduction techniques (Tables 5-12). Two distinct flake products are present in the assemblage: the first technique produced narrow and thin flakes and blades, while the second produced small flakes of broad proportions typically less than 20mm in length.

The flake assemblage over 20mm includes a significant proportion of blades (31.4%) and provides good evidence for controlled reduction, including the use of platform-edge abrasion (33.1% of flakes). Small blades were the desired product of the industry and the average blade measured 32.6mm long by 11.4mm wide; the longest measuring 69mm. The presence of a few preparation flakes indicates that some cores were being prepared at this location; however, the proportion is relatively low (8.1%) indicating that prepared cores were also probably imported to the site from elsewhere. The preparation of cores was a comparatively simple process and focused on establishing a unifacial crest, to initiate blade production, and a plain platform, from which flakes were struck. Cortex was present on a large number of the flakes (55.6%) and was clearly not systematically removed before reduction. Moreover, 27 per cent of blades are side trimming flakes, indicating that cortex was commonly present on the sides of blade cores. Both hard and soft hammer percussion was employed but the majority of blades were detached using a soft hammer percussor, such as antler (Table 10).

In contrast to the larger flakes, flakes measuring less than 20mm are typically of squat proportions (Table 11), with only 8.7 per cent of flakes achieving blade proportions (Table 9). These small flakes were, however, removed with same degree of care as the larger flakes, as demonstrated by the presence of platform-edge abrasion on 19.1 per cent of the flakes and the frequent occurrence of linear and punctiform butts (9.6 and 17.4 per cent

Category type	Scatter 1	Scatter 2	Others	Total
Flake	331	57	51	439
Blade	33	2	7	42
Bladelet	42	7	4	53
Blade-like	26	5	7	38
Irregular waste	31	5	2	38
Micro burin	2	1		3
Burin spall		1		1
Crested blade	2			2
Rejuvenation flake other	2			2
Thinning flake	1			1
Single platform blade core	2			2
Bipolar (opposed platform) blade core	1			1
Tested nodule/bashed lump	4	3	3	10
Single platform flake core		1		1
Multiplatform flake core	2	3	3	8
Core on a flake	1			1
Unclassifiable/fragmentary core	1		1	2
Microlith	6	1		7
Burin	1			1
Laurel leaf		1		1
Chisel arrowhead	1			1
Barbed and tanged arrowhead	2			2
End scraper	4	1	1	6
Side scraper	1			1
Other scraper	1			1
Awl			1	1
Notch		1		1
Retouched flake	3	1	1	5
Grand total	**500**	**90**	**81**	**671**
Burnt unworked flint: No/Wt (g)	460/980	22/49	21/123	503/1152
Burnt flints: No. (%)	21 (4.2)	3 (3.3)	4 (4.9)	28 (4.2)
Broken flints: No. (%)	213 (42.6)	21 (23.3)	20 (24.7)	254 (37.9)
Retouched flints: No. (%)	19 (3.8)	5 (5.6)	3 (3.7)	27 (4)

TABLE 4: FRESH AND SLIGHTLY EDGE-DAMAGED FLINTS FROM SPROATLEY, EXCLUDING CHIPS, BY ARTEFACT CATEGORY AND SCATTER

Flake type	Flake size (max. dimension)				Total	Total %	Blades only	
	<20mm		>20mm					
	No.	%	No.	%			No.	%
Preparation flake	12	10.4	14	8.3	26	9.2	1	1.6
Side trimming flake	15	13.0	34	20.1	49	17.3	17	27.0
Distal trimming flake	3	2.6	20	11.8	23	8.1	5	7.9
Miscellaneous trimming flake	27	23.5	27	16.0	54	19.0	4	6.3
Non cortical 'blank'	58	50.4	70	41.4	128	45.1	31	49.2
Rejuvenation			3	1.8	3	1.1		
Thinning flake			1	0.6	1	0.4		
Total	**115**	**100.0**	**169**	**100.0**	**284**	**100.0**	**63**	**100**

TABLE 5: TECHNOLOGICAL ATTRIBUTES OF COMPLETE FLAKES, SPROATLEY: FLAKE TYPE

Butt category	Flake size (max. dimension)				Total.	Total %	Blades only	
	<20mm		>20mm					
	No.	%	No.	%			No.	%
Cortical	19	16.5	22	13.0	41	14.4	2	3.2
Plain	40	34.8	75	44.4	115	40.5	22	34.9
>1 Removal	4	3.5	11	6.5	15	5.3	2	3.2
Faceted		0.0	1	0.6	1	0.4		
Linear	11	9.6	13	7.7	24	8.5	8	12.7
Punctiform	21	18.3	30	17.8	51	18.0	20	31.7
Other	20	17.4	17	10.1	37	13.0	9	14.3
Total	**115**	**100.0**	**169**	**100.0**	**284**	**100.0**	**63**	**100**

TABLE 6: TECHNOLOGICAL ATTRIBUTES OF COMPLETE FLAKES, SPROATLEY: BUTT TYPE

Extent of cortex on dorsal surface	Flake size (max. dimension)				Total	Total %	Blades only	
	<20mm		>20mm					
	No.	%	No.	%			No.	%
0%	58	50.4%	75	44.4%	133	46.8%	37	58.7%
1-25%	32	27.8%	43	25.4%	75	26.4%	9	14.3%
26-50%	6	5.2%	25	14.8%	31	10.9%	12	19.0%
51-75%	7	6.1%	12	7.1%	19	6.7%	3	4.8%
76-99%	4	3.5%	7	4.1%	11	3.9%	1	1.6%
100%	8	7.0%	7	4.1%	15	5.3%	1	1.6%
Total	**115**	**100.0%**	**169**	**100.0%**	**284**	**100.0%**	**63**	**100%**

TABLE 7: TECHNOLOGICAL ATTRIBUTES OF COMPLETE FLAKES, SPROATLEY: EXTENT OF CORTEX ON THE DORSAL SURFACE

Termination type	Flake size (max. dimension)				Total	Total %	Blades only	
	<20mm		>20mm					
	No.	%	No.	%			No.	%
Hinge	13	11.3	18	10.7	31	10.9	6	9.5
Step	9	7.8	10	5.9	19	6.7	1	1.6
Plunging	8	7.0	19	11.2	27	9.5	6	9.5
Feather	85	73.9	122	72.2	207	72.9	50	79.4
Total	**115**	**100.0**	**169**	**100.0**	**284**	**100.0**	**63**	**100**

TABLE 8: TECHNOLOGICAL ATTRIBUTES OF COMPLETE FLAKES, SPROATLEY: TERMINATION TYPE

Flake size	Number (%) with L:B ratio >2:1	Number (%) with platform edge abrasion	Number (%) with dorsal blade scars
Max. dimension <20mm	10 (8.7)	22 (19.1)	5 (4.3)
Max. dimension >20mm	53 (31.4)	56 (33.1)	41 (24.3)
Combined	63 (22.2)	78 (27.5)	46 (16.2)
Blades only		33 (52.4)	36 (57.1)

TABLE 9: TECHNOLOGICAL ATTRIBUTES OF COMPLETE FLAKES, SPROATLEY: PROPORTION OF BLADES, OCCURRENCE OF PLATFORM-EDGE ABRASION AND DORSAL BLADE SCARS

Hammer mode	Flake Size (max. dimension)				Total	Total %	Blades only	
	<20mm		>20mm					
	No.	%	No.	%			No.	%
Soft	10	8.7	48	28.4	58	20.4	29	47.6
Hard	11	9.6	50	29.6	61	21.5	7	11.1
Indeterminate	94	81.8	71	42.0	163	58.1	27	41.3
Total	115	100.0	169	100.0	284	100.0	63	

TABLE 10: TECHNOLOGICAL ATTRIBUTES OF COMPLETE FLAKES, SPROATLEY: HAMMER MODE

Length to breadth value	Max dim. <20mm		Max. dim. >20mm		Combined	
	No	%	No.	%	No.	%
<0.6	3	2.6	6	3.6	9	3.2
0.6-1.0	62	53.9	47	27.8	109	38.4
1.1-1.5	28	24.3	32	18.9	60	21.1
1.6-2.0	13	11.3	35	20.7	48	16.9
2.1-2.5	4	3.5	15	8.9	19	6.7
2.6-3.0	3	2.6	14	8.3	17	6.0
3.1-3.5			10	5.9	10	3.5
3.6-4.0	1	0.9	2	1.2	3	1.1
4.1-4.5			3	1.8	3	1.1
4.6-5.0			1	0.6	1	0.4
5.1-5.5			3	1.8	3	1.1
5.6-6.0	1	0.9	1	0.6	2	0.7

TABLE 11: COMPARISON OF LENGTH/BREADTH INDEX VALUES FOR UNRETOUCHED FLAKES, SPROATLEY

	Length	Breadth	Thickness
Average dimension	32.6mm	11.4mm	4.1mm
Minimum size	15mm	3mm	1mm
Maximum size	69mm	24mm	17mm
Standard deviation	13.2mm	5.1mm	3mm

TABLE 12: SUMMARY OF COMPLETE BLADE SIZES, SPROATLEY

of flakes, respectively). These shared technological attributes indicate that the small flakes and the larger blade-oriented flakes are the product of the same industry. There is no evidence that the small squat flakes were being modified into specific tool types, so the reason for their production is unclear. One possible explanation for these small squat flakes is that they resulted from the *ad hoc* working of small but readily available local raw materials.

Cores: Fifteen cores and ten tested nodules are present. The tested nodules reflect attempts to work local gravel pebbles and the majority of these examples were abandoned due to thermal flaws; the tested nodules weighed between 5g and 42g. Only three cores were oriented to blade production: a bipolar core weighing 51g (Fig. 81.2) and two single platform blade cores, weighing

24g and 41g (Fig. 81.3 and 4). The single platform cores were abandoned after the removal of only a few blades while the bi-polar core was abandoned because of a flaw in the core face. The final removal on the latter core was 36mm long. Notably, all three of these cores have cortex on their back surface and they would have produced a good proportion of blades with cortex along one edge. Blade production on one of the single platform cores was initiated by the removal of a uni-facial crest, but the distal end of the crest survives on the core; the use of this technique on other cores is attested to be the presence of two uni-facial crested blades in the assemblage (e.g. Fig. 81.6). The technology of these cores therefore compares well to the traits observed on the blades in the assemblage. The flake cores recovered from Sproatley include a few probable Mesolithic examples that yielded small squat flakes (e.g. Fig. 81.1) but several others have been attributed a Neolithic or Bronze Age date. The latter include five multi-platform flake cores, a single platform flake core and a core on a flake. The flake cores weighed between 11g and 81g.

Tools: A limited range of retouched tools are present, accounting for 4 per cent of the total assemblage. Scrapers are the most common tool type with eight examples, followed by microliths (7) and edge-retouched flakes (5); single examples of an awl, a notch and a burin were recovered.

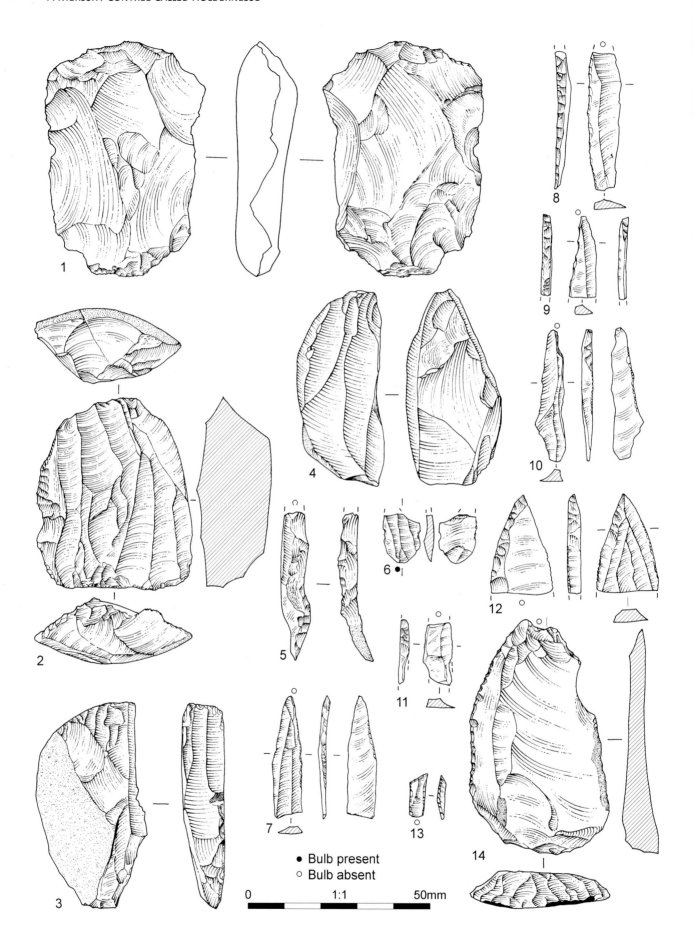

● Bulb present
○ Bulb absent

0   1:1   50mm

FIG. 81: FLINT: ILLUSTRATIONS 1 TO 14

Illustrated flint 1

Mesolithic lithics, nos 1-17

1. FLAKE CORE: WT 49G; SPROATLEY, SCATTER 1, LAYER *26020*, SAMPLE 710, SPIT 1. EARLY MESOLITHIC

2. BI-POLAR BLADE CORE: WT 51G; FLAT CORTEX BACK; EVIDENCE OF LATERAL CRESTING AND TABLET REJUVENATION; ABANDONED DUE TO THERMAL FLAW IN FACE. SPROATLEY, SCATTER 1, LAYER *26222*, SAMPLE 1001, SQ. 104. EARLY MESOLITHIC

3. MINIMALLY WORKED SINGLE-PLATFORM BLADE CORE: WT 24G; EVIDENCE OF UNI-FACIAL CRESTING; ABANDONED DUE STEP FRACTURES ON CORE FACE. SPROATLEY, SCATTER 1, LAYER *26222*, SAMPLE 1073, SQ. 116, SPIT 1. EARLY MESOLITHIC

4. SINGLE-PLATFORM BLADE CORE: WT 42G; SPROATLEY, SCATTER 1, LAYER *26222*, SAMPLE 1073, SQ. 116, SPIT 1. EARLY MESOLITHIC

5. PLUNGING UNI-FACIAL CRESTED BLADE, BROKEN AT PROXIMAL END: SPROATLEY, SCATTER 1, LAYER *26222*, SAMPLE 1067, SQ. 110, SPIT 2. EARLY MESOLITHIC

6. PROXIMAL MICRO-BURIN, NOTCHED ON THE RIGHT HAND SIDE ON VENTRAL SURFACE: SPROATLEY, SCATTER 1, LAYER *26020*, SQ. 34. EARLY MESOLITHIC

7. EDGE-BLUNTED POINT WITH SLIGHT BREAK AT DISTAL END: SPROATLEY, SCATTER 1, LAYER *26222*, SF 531. EARLY MESOLITHIC

8. EDGE-BLUNTED POINT WITH SLIGHT BREAK AT PROXIMAL END: SPROATLEY, SCATTER 1, LAYER *26020*, SQ. 39. EARLY MESOLITHIC

9. EDGE-BLUNTED POINT WITH BREAK AT DISTAL END: SPROATLEY, SCATTER 1, LAYER *26020*, SAMPLE 741, SPIT 1, SQ. 55. EARLY MESOLITHIC

10. EDGE-BLUNTED POINT: SPROATLEY, SCATTER 1, LAYER *26222*, SAMPLE 1073, SPIT 1, SQ. 116. EARLY MESOLITHIC

11. MEDIAL FRAGMENT OF A BURNT AND BROKEN MICROLITH, PROBABLY AN EDGE-BLUNTED POINT: SPROATLEY, SCATTER 1, LAYER *26222*, SAMPLE 1067, SPIT 2, SQ. 110. EARLY MESOLITHIC

12. MICROLITH/SERRATED FLAKE WITH PROXIMAL BREAK, DISTAL END RETOUCHED TO A POINT WITH SEMI-ABRUPT RETOUCH ALONG THE VENTRAL SURFACE ON THE RIGHT HAND SIDE AND SEMI ABRUPT RETOUCH ON THE DORSAL SURFACE AT THE DISTAL LEFT HAND SIDE; MEDIAL LEFT HAND SIDE HAS FINE SERRATION: SPROATLEY, SCATTER 1, LAYER *26020*, SQ. 44, SF 527. EARLY MESOLITHIC

13. SCALENE MICRO-TRIANGLE OF JACOBI (1978) TYPE 7A²: SPROATLEY, SCATTER 2, LAYER *26002*, SAMPLE 1155, SQ. 204. LATE MESOLITHIC

14. END SCRAPER MANUFACTURED ON A PLUNGING FLAKE; DISTAL EDGE AND RIGHT HAND SIDE EXHIBIT ROUNDED USE-WEAR: SPROATLEY, SCATTER 1, LAYER *26020*, SF 512. EARLY MESOLITHIC

Scrapers comprise six end scrapers, one side scraper and a possible scraper manufactured on a piece thermally fractured flint. The scrapers from Scatter 1 include one example manufactured on a blade-like flake and a second on a flake with blade scars on its dorsal surface (Figs. 81, 82.14 and 15). Scrapers are not intrinsically datable, but the technological attributes of the flakes on which they were manufactured indicate these scrapers date from the Mesolithic.

Six microliths were recovered from Scatter 1 and one microlith from Scatter 2. The microliths from Scatter 1 comprise four edge blunted points (Fig. 81.7 to 10), one burnt and broken medial fragment that was probably part an edge-blunted point (Fig. 81.11) and a broken obliquely blunted flake with a serrated edge (Fig. 81.12). The microliths from Scatter 1 all exhibit long truncations and are comparable to forms identified at Deepcar, Yorkshire (Radley and Mellars 1964). The microlith from Scatter 2 is an 11mm by 5mm scalene micro-triangle of Jacobi's (1978) type 7a² (Fig. 81.13). In addition two micro-burins were recovered from Scatter 1 (see Fig. 81.6) and one from Scatter 2.

Five edge-retouched flakes were recovered: four of these pieces represent small fragments of flakes or blades with slight edge retouch and the other is a complete blade with slight abrupt edge-retouch along one side.

One flake exhibited a series of burin removals simply struck from the edge of the flake. One burin spall was recovered. A 56mm-long plunging blade exhibits a small notch in the proximal end (Fig. 82.16). A large thermally fractured flake with a broad point enhanced by retouch is of uncertain date.

Burnt unworked flint: In total, 503 pieces of burnt unworked flint weighing 1152g were recovered. The assemblage is dominated by light burnt and reddened pieces, but with a few heavily burnt white calcined flints. The majority, 460 pieces weighing 980g, were recovered from Scatter 1 and are therefore likely to relate to the Mesolithic activity in this area.

Artefact distribution

The bulk of the Sproatley assemblage was recovered from Scatter 1. This lithic scatter is likely to have once been considerably larger before plough truncation. The recovery of a light scattering of Mesolithic flints across the northern end of the Sproatley excavation area and into Brandywell provides an indication of the original extent of the Mesolithic site.

The preservation of Scatter 1 within a palaeosol raises the possibility that the lithic assemblage is *in situ*. The extent to which the flint scatter has been disturbed within the soil horizon, by vertical movement, soil processes

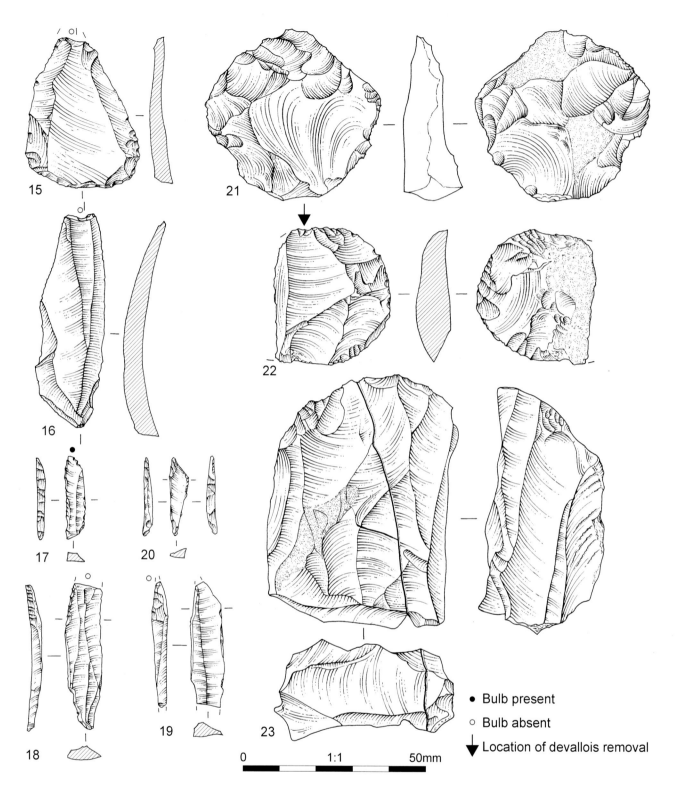

FIG. 82: FLINT: ILLUSTRATIONS 15 TO 23

and human, plant and animal activity is, however, open to question. The distribution and condition of the Mesolithic artefacts provide the best guide to establishing the integrity of this deposit, and those within Scatter 1 are predominately in fresh condition and lack the edge-damage typically present on artefacts recovered from re-worked deposits. The condition of the artefacts is therefore entirely consistent with *in situ* preservation. Moreover, the struck and burnt flint exhibits distinct concentrations within the palaeosol, and two conjoining fragments of a blade were recovered from a single square. In light of these points, it seems reasonable to conclude that later disturbance to Scatter 1 was limited in extent and effect, and that the artefact distribution patterns are likely to reflect Mesolithic rather than later activity.

Illustrated flint 2

Mesolithic, lithics (nos 18-20)

15. END SCRAPER: SPROATLEY, SCATTER 1, LAYER *26020*, SPIT 1, SQ. 32, SF 526. EARLY MESOLITHIC

16. PLUNGING BLADE WITH A PROXIMAL NOTCH AND EXTENSIVE USE-WEAR ALONG BOTH SIDES: SPROATLEY, SCATTER 1, LAYER *26524*, SQ. 262. EARLY MESOLITHIC

17. BACKED BLADELET: OLD ELLERBY, FILL *3022* OF PIT 3021. MESOLITHIC

18. OBLIQUELY BLUNTED POINT WITH RECENT PROXIMAL AND DISTAL BREAKS: SURFACE FIND 4121067, NGR: 527229 428267. EARLY MESOLITHIC

19. OBLIQUELY BLUNTED POINT WITH SLIGHT PROXIMAL AND DISTAL BREAKS: BRANDYWELL, FILL *25096* OF CUT 25095, DITCH 25208. EARLY MESOLITHIC

20. SCALENE TRIANGLE, COMPARABLE TO JACOBI (1978) 7A: BRANDYWELL, FILL *25159* OF CUT 25258, GROUP 25238. LATE MESOLITHIC

Neolithic and early Bronze Age lithics (nos. 21-23

21. DISCOIDAL CORE OF DIMLINGTON TYPE FLINT: WT 31G; SURFACE FIND SOUTH-WEST DAISY HILL COTTAGES, NGR: 522700 430700. LATER NEOLITHIC/EARLY BRONZE AGE?

22. LEVALLOIS-STYLE DISCOIDAL CORE, BROKEN: SURFACE FIND 4109011, NGR: 527612 428066. LATE NEOLITHIC

23. FLAKE REFITTED TO AN OPPOSED PLATFORM FLAKE AND BLADE CORE: COMBINED WT 128G; MISSING ATTEMPTED TABLET REJUVENATION FLAKE STRUCK AFTER THE REMOVAL OF REFITTED FLAKE: SPROATLEY, LAYER *26592*. EARLY NEOLITHIC?

For the most part, the struck flint was distributed widely across the 10m by 15m excavation area as a comparatively low density scatter (Fig. 26b). However, a dense concentration of artefacts was centred between 3m and 4m from the north-eastern edge of the sampling grid and a similar distance from the north-western edge, where a single square yielded 43 artefacts. These comprise 38 flakes and blades, two single platform blade cores (Fig. 82.3 and 4), a core face rejuvenation flake, an edge blunted point (Fig. 81.10) and a micro-burin. This assemblage provides evidence for the manufacture of flakes, blades and a microlith and, although no refits were found, this concentration may therefore have resulted from a single comparatively brief event, focused on the knapping of flints for tool maintenance. It is also possible that the concentration represents the maintenance of a composite tool with the manufacture of a microlith, potentially to replace the broken example that was found. The lithics from the wider scatter further demonstrate that such tasks were repeatedly undertaken in this area, although the broad distribution precludes the identification of individual events.

The burnt unworked flint exhibits a different pattern, with a moderate concentration in the central southern area of the scatter. This concentration correlates with the densest distribution of charcoal (Fig. 26a) and it may reflect the presence of fires or a dump of material from one or more fires.

The Mesolithic assemblage from Brandywell

Brandywell yielded 130 lithic artefacts; approximately half were the products of a blade-oriented industry of Mesolithic date. The blade-oriented assemblage comprises a number of flakes, blades, bladelets, blade-like flakes, two blade cores, a tested nodule, two microliths and possibly an end scraper. The blades are comparatively small, with several around 40mm in length, and the longest measuring 52mm. Dorsal blade-scars were frequently observed, demonstrating that the blades were removed from cores specifically directed to the production of narrow blanks. The cores include one with removals from a single platform and a second with opposing removals. These cores were both abandoned at 34g in weight, with final removals measuring 35mm and 32mm, respectively. They exhibit plain platforms in one case regenerated by the removal of a platform tablet. The use of this rejuvenation technique is further confirmed by the presence of a platform tablet in the assemblage.

The recovery of a crested blade indicates that blade production was initiated or rejuvenated by the removal of a crest. A tested nodule, weighing 24g, exhibits the scars of two bladelet removals without any preparation: this represents an opportunistic attempt to work the local raw material. The retouched component of the assemblage comprises a scalene triangle manufactured in a distinctive translucent orange flint (Fig. 82.20) that is most comparable to Jacobi's type $7a^2$ (1978), an obliquely blunted point with a slightly broken tip and base (Fig. 82.19) and a fine end scraper that exhibits semi-abrupt retouch. The date of the scalene triangle is open to question, but the obliquely blunted point and the majority of the flake debitage is comparable to, and probably contemporary with, the nearby early Mesolithic Sproatley Scatter 1.

Mesolithic lithics from other sites

Small Mesolithic assemblages were retrieved from several of the excavation areas with Churchlands, Dimlington Road, Burton Constable, Skeffling and Scorborough Hill producing between five and twenty flints each, with a single find of a backed bladelet from Old Ellerby (Fig. 82.17). The assemblages from Burton Constable and Dimlington Road each include a micro-burin, resulting from the production of a microlith. Tools include an end scraper/serrated flake combination-tool from Burton Constable and an end scraper, edge-retouched flake and serrated blade from Chuchlands.

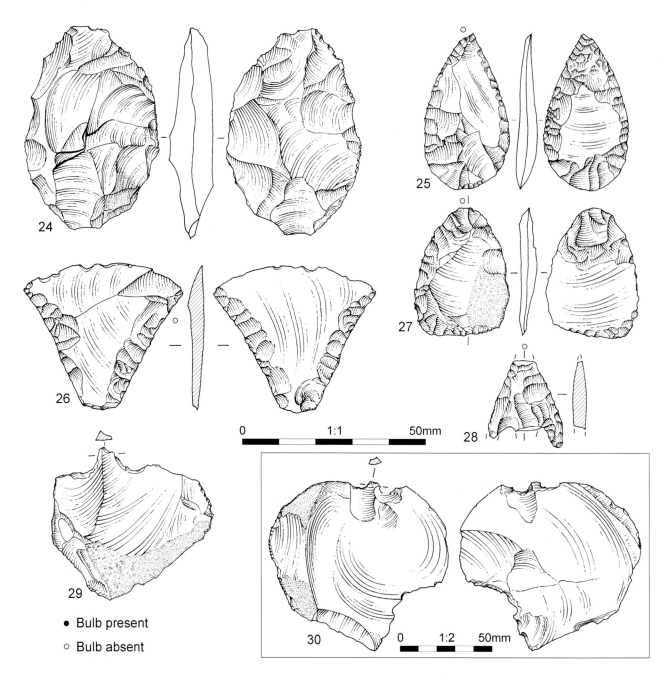

FIG. 83: FLINT: ILLUSTRATIONS 24 TO 30

• Bulb present

○ Bulb absent

Apart from the excavation areas, small groups or isolated Mesolithic flints were recovered as surface or topsoil finds from eight fields along the pipeline route. The majority of these assemblages consist of a limited number of flakes or blades, but a single-platform core, from the North Park area (NGR: 521400 431200), is an indicator of the production of blades. Crested blades were recovered from the North Park and Thack Carrs (NGR: 523700 429900) areas. Tools recovered comprise an early Mesolithic obliquely blunted point from Halsham Carrs (NGR: 527130 428360; Fig. 82.18) and an end scraper from Manor Farm, Thirtleby (NGR: 517700 435200).

Discussion of the Mesolithic flintwork

The Mesolithic flintwork adds significantly to our understanding of hunter gatherer activity in the local lowland landscapes of Holderness. Prior to the Humber Wetlands Survey (Van de Noort and Ellis 1995) few Mesolithic flints were known from the region and the entire lithic collection housed in the local museum and Archaeology Unit comprised only 148 pieces from all periods (Head 1995, 311). The Humber Wetlands Survey recovered a further 2254 flints, but the majority of these artefacts were of Neolithic date and only seven sites yielded Mesolithic or Mesolithic/Neolithic flintwork (Halsham-65, Halsham-45, Aldbrough-11,

Illustrated flint 3

Neolithic and early Bronze Age lithics (nos. 24-30)

24. LAUREL LEAF POINT, CRUDELY FLAKED: SPROATLEY, LAYER *26591*. EARLY NEOLITHIC?

25. LEAF-SHAPED ARROWHEAD EXHIBITING VERY REGULAR PRESSURE FLAKING, RETOUCH IT NOT ENTIRELY INVASIVE: SURFACE FIND, WEST OF PUNDA DRAIN, NGR: 538200 419800, CONTEXT *121166*. POSSIBLY EARLY NEOLITHIC, BUT FLAKING AND ORIENTATION OF BLANK MAY IMPLY A LATE NEOLITHIC/EARLY BRONZE AGE DATE

26. CHISEL ARROWHEAD: SPROATLEY, SCATTER 1, LAYER *26020*, SQ. 44. MIDDLE NEOLITHIC

27. BLANK FOR BARBED AND TANGED ARROWHEAD: BURTON CONSTABLE, FILL *9469* OF DITCH *9468*. LATE NEOLITHIC/ EARLY BRONZE AGE

28. BARBED AND TANGED ARROWHEAD, COMPARABLE TO SUTTON'S TYPE 'C' (GREEN 1980): SPROATLEY, SCATTER 1, LAYER *26222*, SPIT 2, SQ. 121. LATE NEOLITHIC/EARLY BRONZE AGE

29. SPURRED PIECE ON IRREGULAR WASTE: BURTON CONSTABLE, FILL *9244* OF DITCH *9090*. NEOLITHIC OR BRONZE AGE

30. SPURRED PIECE ON A THERMALLY FRACTURED FLAKE; ADDITIONAL CONCAVE EDGE-RETOUCH: SURFACE FIND WEST OF SPROATLEY VILLAGE, NGR: 518500 434430, CONTEXT *11961/*. NEOLITHIC OR BRONZE AGE

Aldbrough-28, Skipsea-21, Skipsea-25 and Skipsea-40). Moreover, diagnostic Mesolithic artefacts were limited to two backed bladelets (Skipsea-21 and Halsham-34) and a truncated blade (Halsham-65; *ibid.* 316).

The current project therefore adds a significant number of sites, including diagnostic artefacts, and the most substantial assemblage from Scatter 1 at Sproatley is associated with radiocarbon dates and limited faunal and environmental remains. Scatter 1 was potentially once part of a far larger scatter, but what remains provides some insight into the range of activities undertaken and the character of the site. The six microliths recovered directly from Scatter 1 are all edge-blunted forms comparable to examples recovered from Deepcar (Radley and Mellars 1964). Michael Reynier has demonstrated that Deepcar-type microliths occur within a distinct horizon of the early Mesolithic dating from around 9400 to 8700 BP (Reynier 1998). The three radiocarbon dates obtained on from Scatter 1 all fall within this period. Deepcar type sites are well represented in Yorkshire, although this is the first example from Holderness, and, as with this site, the majority are found in lowland locations below 100m OD (Spikins 1999, 11).

The range of artefacts present in Scatter 1 indicates that a broad variety of activities were undertaken. The knapping of local raw materials and imported cores into flakes and blades was a prominent activity, and the manufacture of tools including microliths and burins is indicated by the presence of micro-burins and a burin spall. It is, however, notable that more microliths were recovered than micro-burins, potentially indicating that more tools were being used and discarded at this location than were being manufactured. The range of retouched tools is comparatively limited and dominated by roughly equal numbers of scrapers and microliths. In Mellars' (1976) terms this is a balanced assemblage and in general these sites are considered to represent aggregation and occupation in the winter season.

The assemblage of several hundred artefacts from the Sproatley and Brandywell excavation areas is distinctly different to the other Mesolithic assemblages from the pipeline route. None of the other assemblages exceed twenty flints from a single field. Only six fields produced isolated Mesolithic finds; this rarity, in comparison with the late Neolithic/early Bronze Age flintwork (below), is significant as it may indicate that the small artefact clusters are more than just stray finds and that these locations may represent distinct scatters that result from a period of occupation or the performance of a specific task. The microlith from Halsham Carrs may reflect hunting or the maintenance of related toolkits, while the scrapers could represent locations with a focus on the processing or working of animal hides. Serrated flakes at Burton Constable and Churchlands perhaps indicate that the tasks performed also included the processing of plant materials into fibres for cordage or textiles (Hurcombe 2007). Notably, the range of tools in the small assemblages is comparable to that from Scatter 1, but the proportions of these tool types differ. In contrast to Scatter 1, the small scatters yielded more scrapers than microliths and more serrated flakes were found. This may indicate differences in the activities undertaken at these locations, but this pattern should be treated with caution as the sieving of Scatter 1 may have enhanced the recovery of small tools, such as microliths.

Whatever the precise character of these small sites, the limited number of artefacts indicates that each results from a brief period of activity. In terms of modelling this pattern, we may envisage Sproatley and Brandywell as the location of a base camp, while the other sites are short term and possibly task specific. The pattern may be seasonal: a population aggregation at a base camp in the winter and population dispersal in the summer months, or the presence of a central base camp from which small groups radiate to undertake specific tasks and activities throughout the year.

In contrast to the early Mesolithic, the later Mesolithic is poorly represented and only one scalene micro-triangle from Sproatley Scatter 2 can be directly attributed to this period. The reason for the decline in activity is unclear, but wider environmental changes, for example the loss of land to rising sea level and the inundation of Doggerland, may have marginalised Holderness.

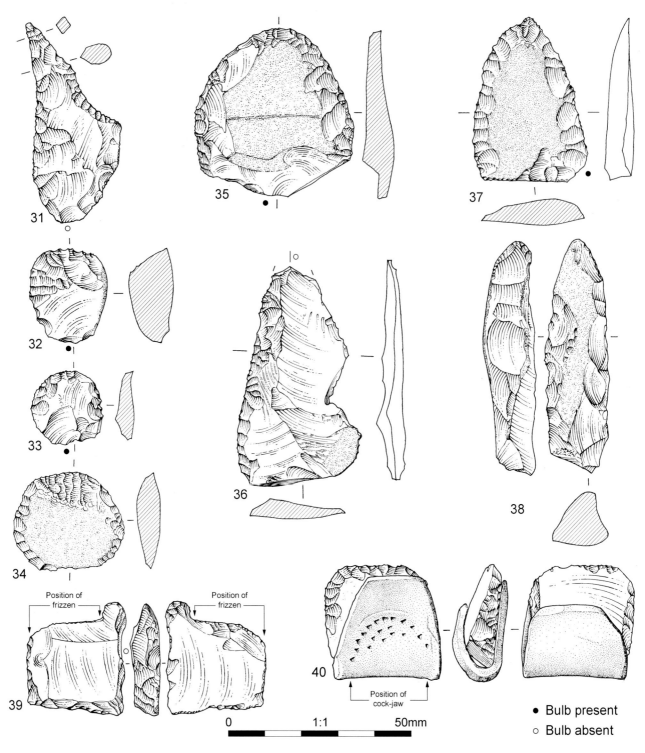

FIG. 84: FLINT: ILLUSTRATIONS 31 TO 40

Earlier Neolithic

The evidence for earlier Neolithic activity is comparatively sparse and a laurel leaf from Sproatley (Fig. 83.24) and a leaf-shaped arrowhead found during topsoil stripping near Fosse Hill (NGR: 538366 419747; Fig. 83.25) are the only diagnostic artefacts recovered. Small assemblages of potentially contemporary debitage were recovered from the same fields but not from secure archaeological contexts.

However, the debitage from Sproatley on the edge of Scatter 2 is in fresh condition and refits were located between a trimming flake and a core (Fig. 82.23), and between two flakes. The radiocarbon date of 3700 to 3520 cal BC from Scatter 2 is broadly consistent with the lithic technology, although the charcoal was not directly associated with the flints. Further afield, Old Ellerby and the adjacent field to the south yielded a small number of blades and blade-like flakes that are broadly dated to the Mesolithic/early Neolithic.

Illustrated flint 4

Neolithic and early Bronze Age lithics (nos. 31-38)

31. AWL/PIERCER MANUFACTURED ON A FLAKE: CHURCHLANDS, SUBSOIL *119301*, SF 1420. NEOLITHIC OR EARLY BRONZE AGE

32. THUMBNAIL SCRAPER EXHIBITING FINE INVASIVE PRESSURE FLAKED RETOUCH AND A SLIGHTLY DENTICULATED DISTAL END: BLUEGATE CORNER, FILL *119991* OF POST-MED FEATURE 119910. LATE NEOLITHIC/EARLY BRONZE AGE

33. 'D'-SHAPED THUMBNAIL SCRAPER: TOPSOIL FIND, NORTH OF MANOR FARM, THIRTLEBY, NGR: 517800 436160. LATE NEOLITHIC/EARLY BRONZE AGE

34. DISC SCRAPER MANUFACTURED ON A THERMAL FLAKE EXHIBITING FINE SEMI-ABRUPT PRESSURE-FLAKED RETOUCH: SURFACE FIND FIELD TO WEST OF BURTON CONSTABLE EXCAVATION, NGR 516650 436250: LATE NEOLITHIC/EARLY BRONZE AGE

35. END AND SIDE SCRAPER MANUFACTURED ON A HARD HAMMER FLAKE: DIMLINGTON RD. LAYER *2245*. NEOLITHIC OR EARLY BRONZE AGE

36. KNIFE MANUFACTURE ON A THIN, HINGED, BLADE-LIKE FLAKE; THE RIGHT-HAND SIDE EXHIBITS LOW ANGLE TO SEMI-ABRUPT PRESSURE FLAKING: OLD ELLERBY, FILL *3268* OF DITCH 3267. LATE NEOLITHIC/EARLY BRONZE AGE

37. KNIFE MANUFACTURED ON A HARD HAMMER CORTICAL FLAKE; REGULAR SLIGHTLY CONVEX SEMI-ABRUPT EDGE RETOUCH ALONG LEFT AND RIGHT HAND SIDES THAT CONVERGE TO FORM A POINTED DISTAL END: BRANDYWELL, CONTEXT *25131*. LATE NEOLITHIC/EARLY BRONZE AGE?

38. ROD-SHAPED FABRICATOR (STRIKE-A-LIGHT); CRUDELY MANUFACTURED WITH A TRIANGULAR CROSS-SECTION, EXTENSIVE USE-WEAR ALONG ALL SIDES TOWARDS POINTED END, SURFACE FIND. NEOLITHIC OR EARLY BRONZE AGE

Post-medieval flints (nos. 39-40)

39. PLATFORM GUN-FLINT FOR A MUSKET; DEMI-CONES ON BOTH SIDES INDICATE PRODUCTION BY PERCUSSION AGAINST STAKE; EXTENSIVE USE-WEAR INDICATES FLINT WAS MOUNTED OFF CENTRE TO THE FRIZZEN, TOPSOIL FIND, NORTH OF RIDGMONT, NEAR BURSTWICK, NGR: 524700 429200. *c.*1780/90 ONWARDS

40. WEDGE-SHAPED GUN-FLINT FOR A MUSKET WITH LEAD MOUNT FOR FIXING IN THE COCK-JAW; IMPRESSION OF COCK-JAW APPARENT ON SURFACE OF LEAD, INDICATES SURFACE UPPERMOST IN COCK JAW: GILCROSS, SURFACE FIND. *c.*1630 TO EARLY NINETEENTH CENTURY

The limited evidence for earlier Neolithic activity would seem to indicate that the clay till geologies of Holderness were less favoured than the chalk landscape of the Yorkshire Wolds. Alternatively, the earlier Neolithic activity in Holderness may have been focused on the wetlands and meres present along the coast of Holderness, for example at Skipsea (Van de Noort and Ellis 1995), rather than the inland landscape bisected by the pipeline route.

Later Neolithic/early Bronze Age

In contrast to the earlier Neolithic, later Neolithic and early Bronze Age flintwork is widely distributed along the pipeline route, but no substantial scatters and few potentially *in situ* context groups were observed. A fine later Neolithic chisel arrowhead (Fig. 83.27) and two Sutton type early Bronze Age barbed and tanged arrowheads (Fig. 83.28) were recovered from Sproatley, Scatter 1, but these were isolated finds. Other diagnostic artefacts include thumbnail scrapers (Figs. 84.32-34) and scale-flaked knives (Fig. 84.35) and scrapers. In addition, flat flake cores, including discoidal examples (Fig. 82.21 and 22) broadly date from this period. The diagnostic artefacts were frequently recovered as isolated finds and only Old Ellerby and the area to the west of Hill Top Farm, Halsham (NGR: 527900 477800) yielded more than a few flakes.

Other Neolithic and Bronze Age flintwork

Broad flake debitage was recovered from numerous locations, along with less diagnostic tool types such as scrapers and piercers (Figs. 83, 84.29 to 31). Thirty-one fields yielded less than five flints and a further eight yielded fewer than ten. Of the excavation sites, Lelley, Braemere Hill, Burstwick Churchlands, Out Newton Road and Dimlington Road all produced between ten and fifty flints and Burton Constable, Brandywell and Sproatley more than fifty. This debitage is problematic to date and, while a few earlier Neolithic flakes may be included in the total, most of these flints can be assigned a broad late Neolithic or Bronze Age date. This flintwork was recovered from topsoil or the fills of later archaeological features, with no significant artefact groups from potentially contemporary depositional contexts. The sites yielding the largest number of flints clearly represent the focus of later prehistoric activity, but, in the absence of diagnostic artefacts and *in situ* groups, it is not possible to be specific about the activities undertaken.

Post-medieval lithics

A musket-sized wedge-shaped gun flint in a lead mount, recovered from Gilcross (Fig. 84.40), is of a style manufactured from around 1630 to the early years of the nineteenth century at centres in Wiltshire, Hampshire, Kent and East Anglia (de Lotbiniere 1977; 1984a; 1984b). The mark of the cock jaw on the lead mounting indicates that the flat dorsal surface was mounted uppermost in the jaw. A second gun-flint, from the field to the east of the Burstwick site (NGR: 524700 422300), is a platform-type of musket size that was manufactured in England, probably Suffolk, from around 1780 to 90 onwards (*ibid.* Fig. 84.39). The wear on the blade edge of the flint indicates that it was mounted off-centre in relation to the frizzen.

Metal-work and other small finds

Kevin Leahy

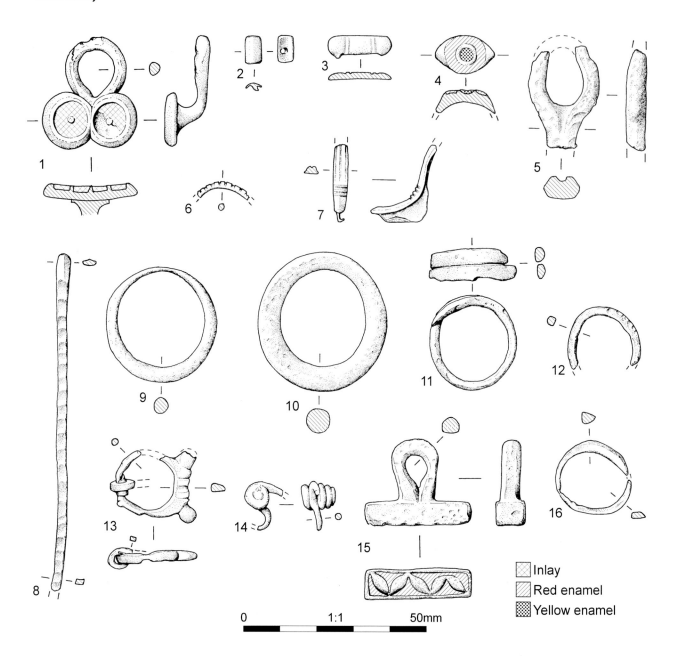

FIG. 85: COPPER ALLOY OBJECTS

Illustrated copper alloy objects

1. FILL *3016* OF PIT 3014, OLD ELLERBY SF 1101; BRONZE BUTTON LOOP FASTENER; BUTTON OF TWO DISCS, EACH WITH CENTRAL RECESS CONTAINING INLAY SECURED BY RIVET. NATURE OF INLAY UNKNOWN. LOOP TEAR-SHAPED AND INTEGRAL WITH BUTTON, TO WHICH LINKED THROUGH RAISED BOSS. GOOD CONDITION BUT SOME BRONZE DISEASE. L: 29.8MM; W: 26.1MM; HT: 11.0MM; THICKNESS OF BUTTON: 3.9MM; WT: 6.85G

THIS PIECE BELONGS TO WILD'S TYPE I, DATED TO 50 BC TO AD 50 (WILD, 1970, 137-55). GOOD PARALLELS FROM

HEADBOURNE WORTHY, HAMPSHIRE (PAS HAMP-2250) AND BROMPTON, NORTH YORKSHIRE (PAS NCL-9C9AB2)

2. EARLY POST-MEDIEVAL SILTING OVER TRACKWAY *8536*, HOLLYM ROAD EVAL, SF 5; RECTANGULAR BRONZE PLATE WITH CONCAVE/CONVEX SECTION, THROUGH WHICH IS A RIVET, 1.4MM DIAM. BY 1.0MM LONG; NOW BENT; PROBABLY A BELT PLATE. CORRODED AND DIRTY. L: 7.4MM; W: 5.0MM; TH: 1.0MM; WT: 0.16G

COMPARES TO FINDS FROM LONDON IN CONTEXTS DATING TO THIRTEENTH TO FOURTEENTH CENTURY (EGAN AND PRITCHARD, 1991, 211-13, FIG. 133)

3. EARLY POST-MEDIEVAL SILTING OVER TRACKWAY *8536*, HOLLYM ROAD EVAL. SF 6; FLAT-SECTIONED BRONZE BAR, STUB AT EACH END, SEPARATED FROM BAR BY TRANSVERSE GROOVE AND MOULDING. GOOD CONDITION BUT DIRTY. L: 17.4MM; W: 5.5MM; TH: 1.8MM; WT: 0.78G

PROB. FRAGMENT OF A TYPE OF BUCKLE IN USE, IN LONDON, FROM THE LATER THIRTEENTH TO THE FIFTEENTH CENTURY (EGAN AND PRICHARD 1991, 72-4, FIG. 44)

4. FILL *10445* OF EARLY ROMAN PIT 12081, SCORBOROUGH HILL, SF 103; BEZEL FROM BRONZE FINGER RING, OVAL AND INLAID WITH A RING OF RED CHAMPLEVÉ ENAMEL SURROUNDING YELLOW DOT. BEZEL NARROWS TO FORM THE HOOP OF THE RING. POOR CONDITION, CORRODED, DIRTY AND INCOMPLETE. L: 16.7MM; W: 10.2MM; TH: 3.2MM; WT: 2.16G.

THIS RING IS OF A TYPE WHICH HAS BEEN DATED TO THE SECOND CENTURY AD. ENAMEL DECORATED FINGER RINGS ARE WIDESPREAD IN BRITAIN WITH A CONCENTRATION ACROSS NOTTINGHAMSHIRE AND WEST YORKSHIRE. A GOOD PARALLEL IS AN EXAMPLE FROM DEVIZES, WILTSHIRE (PAS WILT-E6FC32)

5. FILL *12051* OF EARLY ROMAN PIT 12081, SCORBOROUGH HILL, SF 201; BRONZE FITTING, POSSIBLY PART OF THREE LINK BIT; CLAW-SHAPED BUT ARMS PROBABLY ORIGINALLY CLOSED, NOW WORN AND BROKEN; 3.0MM WIDE GROOVE DOWN ITS LENGTH. GENERAL SECTION OF THE OBJECT IS TRAPEZOID GIVING IT FLAT BACK. POOR CONDITION, CORRODED. L: 27.4MM, W: 19.9MM, TH: 6.4MM; WT. 7.90G. THE CLAW-SHAPED FITTING IS WORN AND BROKEN BUT ARMS WERE PROBABLY ORIGINALLY CLOSED. THE CLAWS SPRING FROM A TRAPEZOID-SECTIONED PROJECTION, NOW TRUNCATED. A 3MM-WIDE GROOVE RUNS DOWN THE LENGTH OF THE PIECE.

THIS FRAGMENT PROBABLY REPRESENTS PART OF A LATE IRON AGE THREE LINK BRIDLE BIT, ITS SIZE, FORM, AND DEGREE OF WEAR IN KEEPING WITH THIS INTERPRETATION. A GOOD PARALLEL FOR THIS PIECE IS A FRAGMENT FROM QUEEN MARY'S CAIRN, EAST KILBRIDE (MCGREGOR 1976, NO 9) WHICH, ALTHOUGH INCOMPLETE, APPEARS TO HAVE HAD ITS LOOP ON A STEM, AS REPRESENTED ON THIS FIND. THESE BITS ARE FOUND IN FIRST-CENTURY CONTEXTS DATED BY ASSOCIATED ROMAN MATERIAL BUT THIS IS LIKELY TO REPRESENT THE FINAL, DATED HORIZON IN WHAT WAS A LONG SEQUENCE WITH EXAMPLES IN THE 'ARRAS CULTURE' GRAVES OF EAST YORKSHIRE (STEAD, 1979, 47-50).

6. UPPER EARLY ROMAN FILL 13052 OF ENCLOSURE DITCH 13070, OUT NEWTON ROAD, SF 281; FRAGMENT OF 1.8MM DIAM. BRONZE WIRE FORMING PART OF A *c*.20.0MM DIAM. RING, ONE SIDE NOTCHED AT 1.5MM INTERVALS. ONE END BROKEN, OTHER SQ. CUT. GOOD CONDITION. L: 14.7MM; WT: 0.21G

7. SUBSOIL *25003* SW CORNER OF EXCAVATION, BRANDYWELL, SF 289; BRONZE FRAGMENT FROM FOOT OF BROOCH, CONSISTING OF PART OF BOW AND CATCH PLATE; SINGLE TRANSVERSE GROOVE AT BASE OF BOW; FOOT TRIANGULAR IN SECTION WITH RIDGE DOWN LENGTH. CATCH

PLATE TURNED TO HOLD PIN. GOOD CONDITION. L: 25.0MM; W: 12.1MM; TH: 4.9MM; WT: 1.55G

8. FILL *25107* OF DITCH 25116, BRANDYWELL, SF 285. BRONZE STRIP, POSSIBLE BRACELET FRAGMENT, 2.5 BY 1.8MM SECTION AT ONE END, OTHER SPLAYED TO 4.0 BY 2.0MM. STRIATIONS DOWN LENGTH OF BOTH FACES: ONE FACE BEARS SERIES OF TRANSVERSE HAMMER MARKS AT APPROX 4.0MM INTERVALS. SLIGHT S-SHAPED CURVE. GOOD CONDITION BUT BROKEN AT ONE END. L: 89.2MM; WT: 2.64G

NO DIRECT PARALLEL HAS BEEN FOUND: HAMMERED DECORATION OCCURS ON ROMAN BRACELETS BUT IT WOULD BE UNSAFE TO QUOTE DATED PARALLELS FOR SUCH SIMPLE, AND CRUDELY EXECUTED, DECORATION.

9. BURIAL *25218*, BRANDYWELL; CAST BRONZE RING, SECTION 4.5MM DIAM. TAPERING 1.2MM. SURFACE POOR AND CORRODED. OUTSIDE DIAM: 31.2MM; INSIDE DIAM CONSTANT AT 24.0MM; WT: 6.81G

10. BURIAL *25218*, BRANDYWELL; CAST BRONZE RING, ROUND SECTION, 7.0MM DIAM. TAPERING 4.6MM. SURFACE POOR AND CORRODED. OUTSIDE DIAM: 36.1MM; WT: 21.12G

RINGS 9 AND 10 ARE BOTH PLAIN AND ASYMMETRIC. THEIR EXTERNAL DIAMETERS SUGGEST THAT THEY WERE HAIR RINGS. BOTH ARE OF ROUND SECTION, TAPERING FROM 4.5MM TO 1.2MM AND 7.0MM TO 4.6MM RESPECTIVELY. THIS ASYMMETRY IS NOT DUE TO WEAR AS THE INSIDE DIAMETER IS CONSTANT. SIMILAR RINGS FOUND AT CAMERTON, SOMERSET WERE LIKELY TO HAVE BEEN DEPOSITED IN THE MID-FIRST CENTURY AD (JACKSON 1990, 49, PL. 14, CAT. 150-157). A RING FROM WONSTON, HAMPSHIRE (PAS HAMP-FCFA25), ALTHOUGH SMALLER AND DECORATED SHOWS A SIMILAR ASYMMETRY. A PARALLEL MAY ALSO BE DRAWN WITH THE ASYMMETRICAL JET OBJECT FROM OUT NEWTON ROAD (SF 280)

11. UPPER FILL *26354* OF GRAVE 26353, SPROATLEY, SF 565; SPIRAL TWISTED BRONZE FINGER RING, ENDS OVERLAPPING BY ONE THIRD OF THE DIAM. SECTION OVAL 4.2 BY 2.4MM. POOR CONDITION, CORRODED, SOME LOSS OF SURFACE. DIAM: 25.0MM; WT: 3.72G

THE FORM OCCURS IN IRON AGE CONTEXTS, AS AT MEARE, SOMERSET (COLES 1987, 70, FIG 3.12, E77, E88), THROUGH TO THE EARLY ANGLO-SAXON PERIOD (MCGREGOR AND BOLICK, 1993, ITEMS 27.4-27.16)

12. MIDDLE FILL *26377* OF GRAVE 26353, SPROATLEY, SF 567; FRAGMENTS OF RING MADE FROM BRONZE WIRE, MUCH DETAIL OBSCURED BY CORROSION BUT APPEARS TO HAVE HAD SQ. SECTION 2.8 BY 2.4MM WITH CHAMFERED CORNERS. POOR CONDITION, CORRODED, IN TWO NON-JOINING FRAGMENTS. OUTSIDE DIAM: 20.3MM; WT: 1.04G

13. SUBSOIL *3506*, EVAL TR 51 LELLEY, SF 37; FRAGMENT OF D-SHAPED BRONZE BUCKLE, BAR SLIGHTLY OFF-SET AND ENCIRCLED BY STRIP OF SHEET METAL FOLDED AROUND IT. FACE OF BUCKLE DECORATED WITH TWO PROTRUDING KNOBS AND CENTRAL PIN NOTCH FLANKED BY TWO NARROW GROOVES. PIN BROKEN BUT WAS OF WRAP AROUND TYPE

WITH A 2.5 BY 1.5MM SECTION. DIRTY, CORRODED AND BROKEN. L: 24.2MM; W: 19.0MM; TH: 3.2MM; WT: 2.40G

THIS IS OF A TYPE TYPICAL OF THE THIRTEENTH OR FOURTEENTH CENTURY, WITH A DIRECT PARALLEL FROM LONDON BEING FOUND IN A CONTEXT DATED BY CERAMICS TO 1350-1400 (EGAN AND PRITCHARD, 1991, 74, NO. 299)

14. UPPER FILL *121043* OF BURIAL PIT 121040, GILCROSS SF 1662; TWO FRAGMENTS OF 1.9MM DIAM. BRONZE WIRE REPRESENTING PART OF A COILED SPRING PROBABLY FROM BROOCH, FOUR COILS ORIGINALLY PRESENT. BROKEN BUT GOOD CONDITION. FRAG. A: 13.0 BY 9.0 BY 4.5MM; WT: 0.65G; FRAG B: DIAM. 8.0MM; L: 5.7MM; WT: 0.64G

15. UPPER FILL *121043* OF BURIAL PIT 121040, GILCROSS SF 1663; BRONZE TOGGLE CONSISTING OF A RECTANGULAR BLOCK 29.8 BY 8.5 BY 7.0MM, THE LOWER FACE S INLAID WITH RED CHAMPLEVÉ ENAMEL, IN CELLS BETWEEN FIVE COUNTER-ANGLED LEAF-LIKE MOTIFS. ON TOP OF THE BAR THE LOWER PART OF PEAR-SHAPED LOOP IS MARKED BY NOTCHES ON BOTH FACES. GOOD CONDITION. L: 29.8MM; W: 22.9MM; TH: 8.3MM; WT: 15.10G

NO DIRECT PARALLEL HAS BEEN FOUND BUT THE FORM MAY BE COMPARED TO AN UNDATED TOGGLE FROM EASTBURN, EAST YORKSHIRE, WHICH ALSO BORE TRACES OF ENAMEL (STEAD, 1979, 86, FIG 34, 6). SIMILAR OBJECTS WERE FOUND IN LATE IRON AGE CONTEXTS AT MEARE (COLES 1987, 70, FIG 3.12, E76). IN SOME RESPECTS THIS OBJECT APPEARS TO BE LINKED TO THE IRON AGE AND ROMAN 'BUTTON AND LOOP FASTENERS' (WILD, 1970 137-55) ITS GEOMETRIC CHAMPLEVÉ ENAMEL DECORATION PERHAPS FITTING BETTER INTO A POST-CONQUEST MILIEU

16. UPPER FILL *26354* OF GRAVE 26353, SPROATLEY, SF 566; BRONZE FINGER RING, SECTION D-SHAPED, OUTER EDGE CURVED, BREAK IN HOOP NOW MISALIGNED AND CORRODED. BROKEN, DETAILS HIDDEN BY CORROSION

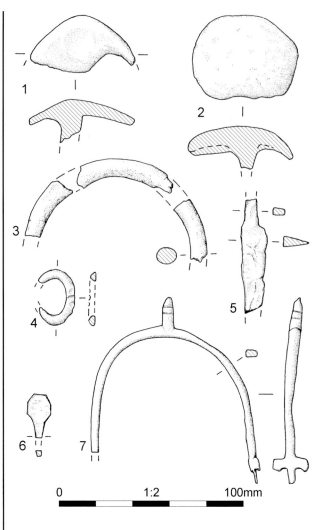

FIG. 86: IRON OBJECTS

Illustrated iron objects

1. LATE MEDIEVAL TRACKWAY SURFACE *8529*, HOLLYM RD EVAL. SF 8; STUD, DOMED SQUARE HEAD 44.6 BY 49.5MM, UNDERSIDE CONCAVE. 19.6 BY 10.4MM, BROKEN IN ANTIQUITY; SURVIVING SHAFT 14.0MM. CORRODED, RECORDED FROM X-RAY. WT: 49.64G

2. LATE MEDIEVAL TRACKWAY SURFACE *8529*, HOLLYM RD EVAL. SF 9; IRON STUD, DOMED SQUARE HEAD 54.2 BY 43.5MM, ROUNDED CORNERS, UNDERSIDE CONCAVE. SHAFT SQUARE SECTION 18.0 BY 11.4MM, BROKEN: SURVIVING LENGTH OF 15.0MM. CORRODED, RECORDED FROM X-RAY. WT: 97.40G

NAILS WITH MASSIVE HEADS, LIKE THE TWO ABOVE, ARE COMMON FINDS AND ARE GENERALLY SAID TO HAVE BEEN USED IN THE CONSTRUCTION AND DECORATION OF HEAVY DOORS (REES ET. AL 2008, 330, FIG. 180)

3. FILL *25354* OF GRAVE 26353, SPROATLEY, SF 564 RING, FRAGMENTS, OUTER RADIUS APPROX 51.0MM, CIRCULAR SECTION 10.6MM DIAM. CORRODED, COVERED WITH CONCRETIONS, BROKEN IN ANTIQUITY INTO THREE PIECES. TOTAL LENGTH OF FRAGS: 121.4MM; WT: 53.13G

4. UPPER FILL *35063* OF PIT 35066, LELLEY, SF 260; C-SHAPED OBJECT PROBABLY HALF OF DOUBLE LOOPED BUCKLE FRAME. FLATTENED D-SHAPED SECTION. PIN NOTCH IN MIDDLE OF FRONT EDGE WITH FACET EITHER SIDE. CORRODED BUT GOOD CONDITION, RECORDED FROM X RAY. L: 20.8MM; W: 29.6MM; TH: 3.7MM; WT: 3.33G. A FOURTEENTH-CENTURY DATE WOULD SEEM APPROPRIATE (*CF.* EGAN AND PRITCHARD, 1991, 82-87)

5. UPPER FILL *35067* OF DITCH 35608 LELLEY, SF 261; BLADE FROM IRON WHITTLE-TANGED KNIFE, END OF BLADE AND TANG MISSING. SINGLE EDGED BLADE STEPPED BOTH ABOVE AND BELOW THE TANG. BLADE TAPERS FROM 14.4MM TO 9.6MM AT THE BREAK. TANG 15.4MM LONG, 6.7 BY 5.0MM SECTION. GOOD CONDITION BUT CORRODED WITH SOME EXFOLIATION. L: 59.0MM; WT: 12.50G

THIS BLADE IS INCOMPLETE BUT ITS FORM MAY BE BEST PARALLELED BY KNIVES OF EARLY- TO MID-THIRTEENTH-CENTURY DATE (COWGILL ET. AL. 1987, 80, FIGS. 54-55)

6. Fill *35153* of pit 35157, Lelley; Iron horseshoe nail, trapezoid head, 12.8 to 8.4 by 14.7mm; Th: 4.1mm. Shaft section square 4.2 by 3.5mm, tip missing. Corroded, otherwise good condition. L: 23.3mm; Wt: 2.45g

7. Fill *35212* of ditch 35230, Lelley, SF 262; Iron spur, original section of arms cannot be determined, now measures 6.6mm diam. One terminal survives, other truncated in antiquity leaving a square cut. Surviving arm terminates in two rounded lobes above and below. Between the lobes is a small spike-like projection. Corroded but good condition except for some exfoliation. L: 98.2mm; W: 91.0mm; Terminal 21.0mm across; Wt: 31.54g

Ellis (2002) saw examples such as this, with straight horizontal sides and smaller goads, as being characteristic of the of the tenth and eleventh centuries

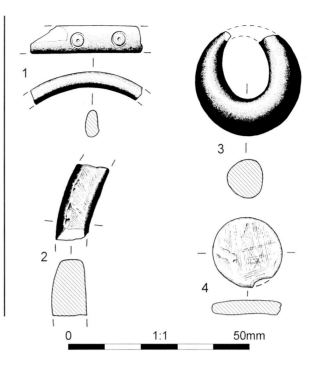

Fig. 87: Jet and shale objects

Illustrated jet and shale objects

1. Fill *9882* of ditch 118934, Burton Const. SF 1213; Frag. jet bracelet, section 7.7 by 4.3mm, orig. outside radius 28mm. Outer edge: two incised, 4.5mm diameter, ringed dots, at 11.8mm centres. Round inner edge: step cut around one third through ring, prob. marks removal of core at end of turning. Gd, stable cond. L: 31.1mm; Wt: 0.94g

Compares to finds from South Shields fort (Allason-Jones and Miket, 1984, 313, 7.114 and 7.115). Similar bracelet, in shale, in deposit dated late second or third cent. at Winchester (Rees et. al 2008, 52, fig 26: 204)

2. Unstrat. subsoil surface *12001*, Scorborough Hill, SF 200; Frag. jet bracelet, outer edge curved, highly polished. Top and inner face rough, appear orig. tooling marks. Both ends and bottom face broken. Section, as survives, tapering 9.9mm to 5.9mm, depth 14.7mm. Curvature suggests *c.*40mm radius. Gd cond. but with some craze cracking on polished outer face. L 23.0mm; Wt: 2.69g

Large bracelets, like this, known from Roman contexts, for inst. frag. from Winterton, Lincs. (Stead 1976, 202, fig. 103: 41)

3. Lower late Iron Age fill *13053*, enclosure ditch 13070, Out Newton Road, SF 280; Penannular jet ring or amulet, D-shaped section 10.3 by 9.8mm, straight inner edge. Likely orig. annular but central hole worn through; wear conc. on one part of circumf. Gd cond. but some craze cracking. Diam. (outside) 30.0mm; Wt. 3.98g

May be compared to example from York, described as 'hair-ring' (Allason-Jones, 1996, 46: 283), similar ring from Coventina's Well, Carrawburgh showed wear pattern suggesting use as pendant (Allason-Jones and McKay 1985, no. 101). Parallels ring from South Shields, clearly a pendant (Allason-Jones and Miket 1984, 235: 7.212). Similar 'hair-rings' are known from Iron Age (Coles, 1987, 132, Fig. 3.56, K).

4. Upper fill *119905*, ring gully term. 119903, Bluegate Corner; SF 1533; Jet or shale disc, poss. gaming counter, one face rough, other covered fine scratches. Tooling marks not present around edges of disc, but circular shape and scratches suggest it has been worked to shape seen. Gd cond. Diam: 19.6mm; Th: 4.1mm; Wt: 1.18g.

Roman counters and gaming pieces are well known (Crummy 1983), but commonly of bone. Also differs in absence of chucking point in centre and not lathe turned. Likely, made locally using local material; similar to counters from pottery sherds. Larger but gen. similar jet counter found at South Shields fort (Allason-Jones and Miket 1984, 326: 7.153)

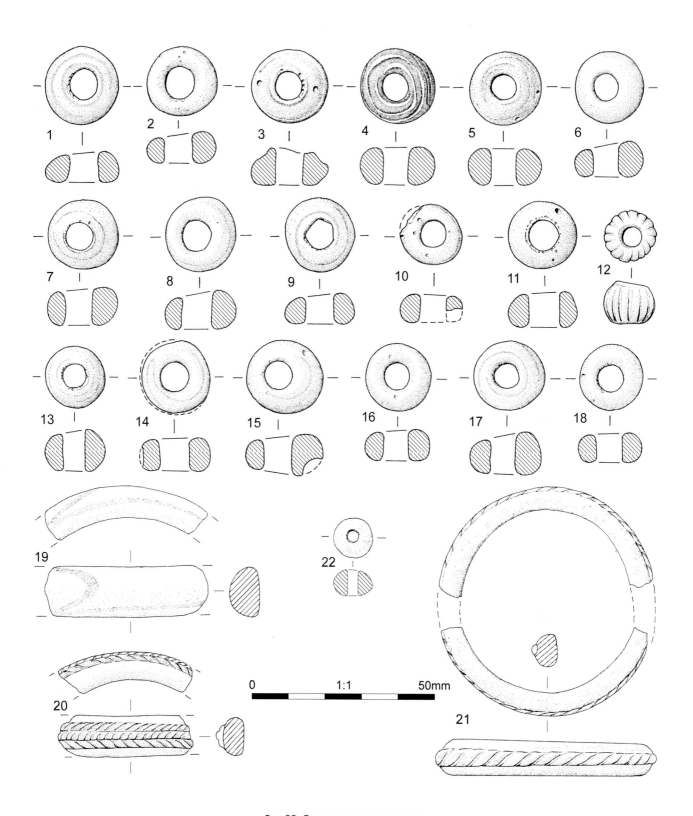

FIG. 88: GLASS BEADS AND BANGLES

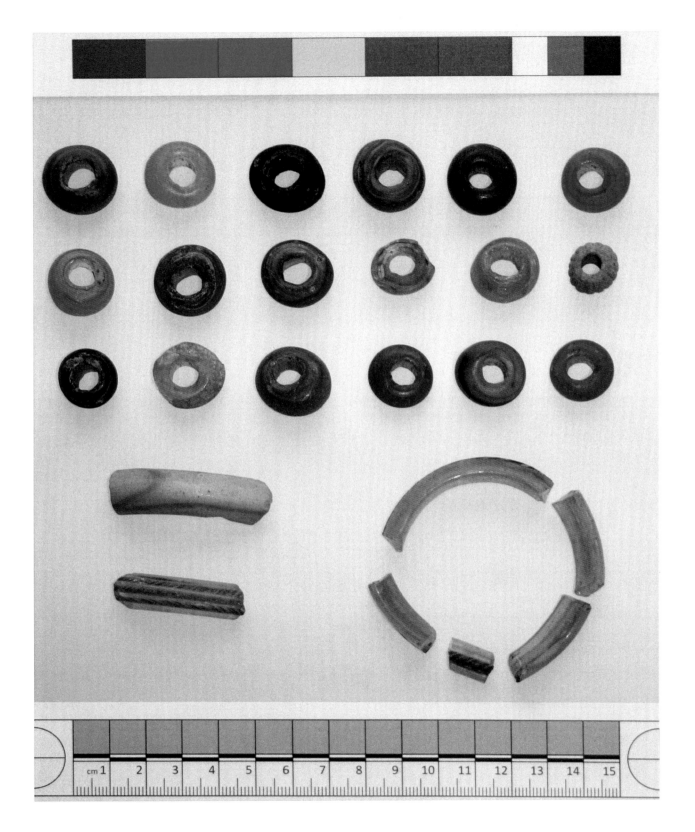

FIG. 89 GLASS BEADS AND BANGLES

Illustrated glass beads and bangles

Beads from Burial 25218

THE ANNULAR AND UNDECORATED BEADS FROM BURIAL 25218 MAY BE PLACED IN GUIDO'S GROUP 6, (GUIDO, 1978, 139-64). THEY ARE A TYPE THAT WAS IN USE OVER A LONG PERIOD OF TIME, OCCURRING IN CONTEXTS PRE-DATING THE ROMAN CONQUEST THROUGH TO THE END OF THE FOURTH CENTURY. ALL ARE IN GOOD CONDITION

1. TRANSLUCENT; PALE GREEN WITH LIGHT BROWN WHIRLS; SOME BUBBLES AND FLOW LINES. OUTSIDE DIAM: 20.2MM; INSIDE DIAM: 8.0MM; TH: 9.6MM MAXIMUM; WT: 4.14G

2. TRANSLUCENT; PALE BLUE; SOME BUBBLES. OUTSIDE DIAM: 19.5MM; INSIDE DIAM: 8.1MM; TH: 9.2MM MAXIMUM; WT: 4.03G

3. COLLAR AROUND THE HOLE ON ONE SIDE; ALMOST OPAQUE; DARK GREEN; BUBBLES. OUTSIDE DIAM: 21.0MM; INSIDE DIAM: 7.6MM; TH: 10.0MM MAXIMUM; WT: 4.25G

4. SEMI-TRANSLUCENT; MARBLED LIGHT AND DARK GREEN WITH SOME BROWN; BUBBLES. STAB MARK (5.7 X 2.4MM TO 2.5MM DEEP) ON ONE SIDE. OUTSIDE DIAM: 21.0MM; INSIDE DIAM: 7.7MM; TH: 10.2MM MAXIMUM; WT: 4.93G

5. TRANSLUCENT; MARBLED GREENS BANDED WITH GREY; BUBBLES. OUTSIDE DIAM: 20.2MM; INSIDE DIAM: 6.6MM; TH: 9.8MM MAXIMUM; WT: 4.96G

6. TRANSLUCENT; PALE BLUE; BUBBLES. OUTSIDE DIAM: 19.0MM; INSIDE DIAM: 6.9MM; TH: 9.5MM MAXIMUM; WT: 3.75G

7. TRANSLUCENT; PALE GREEN; BUBBLES AND SOME WHIRL LINES. OUTSIDE DIAM: 19.3MM; INSIDE DIAM: 7.4MM; TH: 10.4MM MAXIMUM; WT: 4.25G

8. TRANSLUCENT; MID-GREEN WITH BROWN WHIRL LINES; BUBBLES. OUTSIDE DIAM: 20.7MM; INSIDE DIAM: 7.7MM; TH: 10.4MM MAXIMUM; WT: 4.88G

9. TRANSLUCENT; PALE GREEN WITH MID-GREEN WHIRL LINES; BUBBLES. OUTSIDE DIAM: 20.0MM; INSIDE DIAM: 7.4MM; TH: 9.0MM MAXIMUM; WT: 3.98G

10. TRANSLUCENT; PALE GREEN; BUBBLES, SOME LARGE RESULTING IN BREAK. OUTSIDE DIAM: 17.4MM; INSIDE DIAM: 7.2MM; TH: 7.3MM MAXIMUM; WT: 2.00G

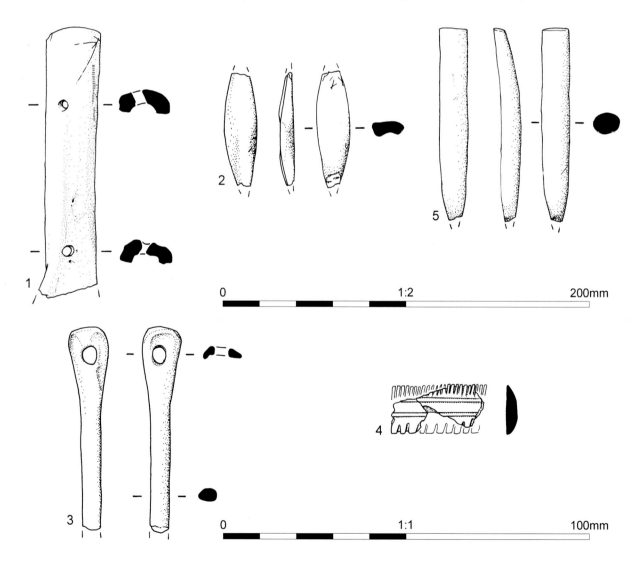

FIG. 90: WORKED BONE OBJECTS

11. TRANSLUCENT; PALE GREEN; BUBBLES AND SOME FLOW LINES. OUTSIDE DIAM: 19.5MM; INSIDE DIAM: 7.6MM; TH: 9.7MM MAXIMUM; WT: 3.86G

12. GLASS FRIT/FAIENCE; LIGHT BLUE; OPAQUE WITH ROUGH, PITTED, SURFACE; VERTICAL INCISED LINES ON SIDES SET AT 2.5MM INTERVALS. OUTSIDE DIAM: 14.8MM; INSIDE DIAM: 6.5MM; TH: 11.6MM MAXIMUM; WT: 1.79G

THIS BEAD IS OF A TYPE GENERALLY KNOWN AS A 'MELON BEAD'. GUIDO (1978, 100) WAS DISMISSIVE OF THE TYPE AS SHE CONSIDERED THAT THEY WERE NOT CHRONOLOGICALLY SENSITIVE, BUT SUGGESTED THAT THEY WERE NOT PRESENT IN BRITAIN PRIOR TO THE ROMAN CONQUEST, ALTHOUGH IN USE IN BOTH IRELAND AND ON THE CONTINENT. BRITISH EXAMPLES COME FROM FLAVIAN AND ANTONINE CONTEXTS, DISAPPEARING FROM THE RECORD IN THE COURSE OF THE SECOND CENTURY. THE TYPE REAPPEARS IN THE POST-ROMAN PERIOD, ALTHOUGH IT HAS BEEN ARGUED THAT THESE ARE RE-USED ROMAN BEADS

13. TRANSLUCENT; MID-BROWN; FLOW LINES AND BUBBLES. OUTSIDE DIAM: 16.8MM; INSIDE DIAM: 6.5MM; TH: 11.6MM; WT: 3.40G

14. TRANSLUCENT; VERY PALE BLUE/GREEN WITH PALE BLUE FLOW LINES; BUBBLES. SOME DAMAGE AND BREAKING DOWN OF SURFACE. OUTSIDE DIAM: 19.5MM; INSIDE DIAM: 7.3MM; TH: 9.0MM MAXIMUM; WT: 3.98G

15. SEMI-OPAQUE; GREEN/GREY WITH BROWN FLOW LINES; BUBBLES, SOME LARGE RESULTING IN BREAK. OUTSIDE DIAM: 21.4MM; INSIDE DIAM: 7.4MM; TH: 10.9MM MAXIMUM; WT: 4.89G

16. TRANSLUCENT; BROWN; BUBBLES. OUTSIDE DIAM: 18.2MM; INSIDE DIAM: 6.5MM; TH: 8.6MM MAXIMUM; WT: 3.39G

17. TRANSLUCENT; PALE GREEN; BUBBLES AND FLOW LINES. OUTSIDE DIAM: 19.4MM; INSIDE DIAM: 6.7MM; TH: 11.8MM MAXIMUM; WT: 4.83G

18. TRANSLUCENT; MID-BLUE; BUBBLES. OUTSIDE DIAM: 17.7MM; INSIDE DIAM: 6.8MM; TH: 8.0MM; WT: 3.10G

Other glass finds

19. SURFACE FIND; SCORBOROUGH HILL; GLASS BANGLE, OPAQUE WHITE GLASS, DECORATED WITH LOOP AND LINE OF BLUE GLASS, MARVERED FLUSH WITH SURFACE. D-SHAPED SECTION; INTERNAL DIAM. *c.*62MM

20. SF 104; FILL *10437* OF PIT 12081, SCORBOROUGH HILL; GLASS BANGLE, PALE BLUE-GREEN GLASS; THREE CABLES, EACH COMPOSED OF ALTERNATE TWISTED STRANDS OF BLUE AND WHITE GLASS; DIAM .*c.*70MM

21. SF 101; FILL *10413* OF PIT 12081, SCORBOROUGH HILL; GLASS BANGLE, BLUE-GREEN GLASS WITH A SINGLE TWISTED APPLIED CABLE IN DARK BLUE AND WHITE GLASS. FIVE FRAGS, NEARLY COMPLETE, THOUGH ONLY ONE JOIN FITS EXACTLY; DIAM. *c.*60MM

22. CONTEXT *13069*, UNSTRATIFIED SURFACE FIND, OUT NEWTON RD; ANNULAR-GLASS BEAD, DEEP BLUE ROMAN TO EARLY SAXON (GUIDO 1999, 48), DIAM. 10MM, HT 7MM

Illustrated worked bone

1. FILL *9661*, DITCH 118954, BURTON CONST. SF 1210. MADE FROM SPLIT SHAFT OF HORSE METAPODIAL. ONE END DAMAGED, OTHER SHAPED TO ASYMMETRIC CURVING LINE WITH UNDERCUT BEVEL, FINE SAW OR TOOL MARKS. OUTER FACE OF BONE COVERED WITH TOOLING MARKS: LONGITUDINAL SCRATCHES, LINES OF SMALL TRANSVERSE 'CHATTERING' MARKS OF SCRAPER OR KNIFE. GD COND. BUT BROKEN, TWO PARTS. L: 144.5MM; W: 28.9MM; TH: 11.6MM; WT: 39.62G. HIGH DEGREE OF POLISH ON SURFACE SUGGESTS CONSIDERABLE USE BUT FUNCTION, DATE UNKNOWN. RESEMBLES ONE SIDE OF H-SHAPED ANTLER OBJ., DESCRIBED AS SLOTTED WEAVING TOOL, FROM IRON AGE CONTEXT AT MEARE, SOMERSET (COLES 1987, 104, FIG 3.33 NO H131)

2. FILL *9589*, DITCH 118977, BURTON CONST. SF 1207. HIGHLY POLISHED SPLINTER FROM SHAFT OF LARGE MAMMAL LONG BONE, BROKEN BOTH ENDS. BACK FLAT, SIDES ANGLED; OTHER FACE CONCAVE INT. OF BONE. GD COND. L: 60.6MM; W: 17.8MM; TH: 7.7MM; WT: 5.86G

3. FILL *2252*, DITCH 2250, DIMLINGTON RD. SF 1000. PIG FIBULA PIN, SHANK SECTION OVAL, 5.5 BY 3.8MM, BROKEN: 3 PIECES, TRUNCATED. FLATTENED END SHAPED AND SQUARE CUT, 4.0MM DIAM. HOLE. HIGHLY POLISHED OVERALL; GD COND. L: 54.1MM; W (HEAD): 10.8MM; WT: 1.30G. PIG FIBULA PINS ARE WELL-KNOWN, IN USE FROM IRON AGE TO VIKING PERIOD (MCGREGOR, 1985, 120-10). SIMILAR PIN FROM LURK LANE, BEVERLEY IN CONTEXT DATED TO LATE NINTH-EARLY TENTH CENTURY (ARMSTRONG ET AL, 1991, 190, FIG 127, NO. 1100), BUT THIS OBJ. UNDATABLE

4. FILL *120457*, RING GULLY 120456, DIMLINGTON RD, SF 1626. TWO JOINING FRAGMENTS OF DECORATED BONE OR ANTLER COMB: FLATTENED D-SECTION, WITH TWO PAIRS OF FINELY INCISED LONGITUDINAL LINES. EDGES MARKED BY ROWS OF TRANSVERSE NOTCHES, WITH PITCH OF 4 PER CM, ON ONE SIDE AND 10 PER CM ON THE OTHER. GD COND. BUT BROKEN, INCOMPLETE. L: 24.9MM; W: 11.8MM; TH: 2.7MM; WT: 0.51G. DOUBLE-SIDED BONE OR ANTLER COMBS WERE MADE BETWEEN THE THIRD AND THIRTEENTH CENTURY (MCGREGOR 1985, 92). AN EARLY MEDIEVAL DATE SEEMS LIKELY FOR THIS FIND

5. UNSTRATIFIED (NGR: 528134 427581); BONE OR ANTLER, PROBABLE THREAD-PICKER CUM BEATER; FLATTENED OVAL SECTION 15.6 BY 11.2MM, SLIGHTLY CURVED ALONG LENGTH. ONE END ORIG. POINTED; OTHER SQUARE-CUT, TERMINATING IN BEVELLED PANEL, 15.4 BY 6.3MM. HIGHLY POLISHED; NO SIGN TOOLING MARKS. GD COND. TRUNCATED. L: 102.0MM; WT: 20.83G. CAN BE PARALLELED BY THREAD-PICKERS ON EARLY MED. SITES SUCH AS WINCHESTER (BIDDLE 1990, 229- 231, FIG 47) AND BEVERLEY (ARMSTRONG ET ALL 1991, 193, FIG 129 NO 1134-38). THREAD PICKERS WITH ONE END POINTED AND OTHER SPATULATE WERE USED ON TWO-BEAM LOOM WHICH CAME INTO COMMON USE IN ENGLAND IN EARLY TENTH CENTURY (LEAHY 2003 72-4, FIG 35)

Pre-Iron Age pottery

T. Manby

Analysis of 603g of fragments recorded vessel features: rims, bases and decoration, fabric and wall thickness; also sherd size and condition such as abrasion and post-depositional changes. Recording was based on the guidelines of the Prehistoric Ceramic Research Group (1992). In describing the fragmentary pottery, the designations used are 'sherd': any piece in excess of 25mm square; 'small sherd': any piece between 10 and 25mm square; 'flake': an angular piece split off vertically from the sherd wall; and 'crumb': a featureless piece less than 10mm square. Wall thickness is recorded within a tolerance of 1mm. Representation of temper contribution is estimated as 'rare': less than 5 per cent; 'sparse': 5 to 10 per cent; and 'common': 10 to 20 per cent. The maximum size of temper particles was measured to within 1mm using an electronic calliper. Within each context, the pieces considered to derive from an individual vessel have been assigned a catalogue number and separately bagged.

The lowlands of Holderness, in contrast to the upland Yorkshire Wolds to the west, have produced only a limited quantities of Neolithic and Bronze Age ceramic material; surface-recovered flint, stone and bronze artefacts are the principal evidence for occupation (Manby et al 2003, 78-80). For southern Holderness there have been comb-decorated Beaker sherds collected in the former gravel diggings at Burstwick (Hull and Yorkshire Museums). Excavated sites of a particular geographical significance are centred on Easington Warren: a barrow overlying a Middle Neolithic structure and extensive occupational assemblage, including plain Beaker pottery, and a burial (Evans and Steedman 2001, 69-75). An adjacent henge monument had an associated Collared Urn. Middle Bronze Age Bucket Urns previously came from this area (Wenham 1960, 310-313, fig. 9B). Further occupational activity area in the same area has recently been excavated (Manby 2013).

Brandywell

A single decorated wall sherd, weighing 14g, from fill **25195** of pit **25158** (Fig. 91.1) is problematic in cultural attribution and dating. Certainly from an overhanging rim bowl or jar, comparison may be made with the heavy rim Middle Neolithic Towthorpe Style bowls, where incised decoration is occasionally present (Manby 1988, 48-52, fig. 4.5).

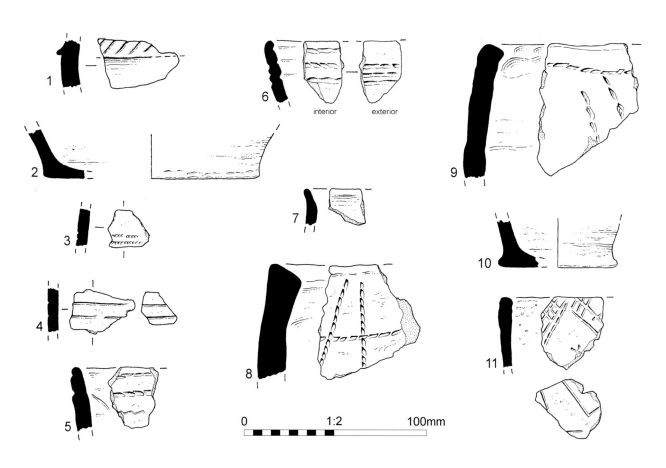

interior   exterior

0   1:2   100mm

FIG 91: EARLY PREHISTORIC POTTERY

Sproatley

A total of 71 pieces weighing 244g derived from both the northern (Fig. 91.2-4) and southern (Fig. 91.7) flint scatters, and as residual finds in an early Roman context (Fig. 91, 5-6). A Beaker attribution for this assemblage (Table 13) is based on fabric character and decoration that is confined to the Basic European Motif No. 1 of closely spaced horizontal lines. In a very fragmentary assemblage, there are no partial or reconstructable profiles; sherd size does not exceed 5cm across, and there is a high proportion of crumbs (Table 14). All of the sherds are in a compact buff to brown fabric, with a fine sand temper with rare angular quartz and grog. Rims are simple and out-splaying, bases are flat with none showing any out splaying wall to the body; wall thicknesses are generally 6 to 10mm, rarely up to 12mm.

This assemblage provides few specific characteristics. Decoration consists of the most basic motif: closely spaced horizontal lines, variously by point incision,

Illustrated earlier prehistoric pottery

1. HARD COMPACT GREY, REMAINS OF ORANGE EXT. SURFACE; FINE SAND TEMPER; SOME LIGHT BROWN ENCRUSTATION ON INT. EXTENDING TO BROKEN EDGES: POSS. MINERAL 'PAN'. FILL 25195, PIT 25158, BRANDYWELL

2. SPLAYED WALL PROFILE; PLAIN; DIAM. 11.5CM. LAYER 26020, NORTHERN FLINT SCATTER, SPROATLEY

3. TWO HORIZONTAL FINE TOOTHED COMB LINES: 6 TEETH TO 1CM. LAYER 26020, NORTHERN FLINT SCATTER, SPROATLEY

4. THREE COMB LINES, 6MM SPACING. LAYER 26020, NORTHERN FLINT SCATTER, SPROATLEY

5. EXTERIOR: HORIZONTAL THICK CORD LINES: 2 TURNS TO 1CM. UPPER FILL OF PIT 26192, SPROATLEY

6. ROUNDED LIP; HORIZONTAL CORD LINES ON INT. AND EXT. UPPER FILL OF PIT 26192, SPROATLEY

7. OUT-CURVING PROFILE, SIMPLE ROUNDED LIP. UPPER FILL 26524 OF PALAEOCHANNEL, SPROATLEY

8. RIM FRAGMENTS, REJOINED; LARGE DIAMETER RIM WITH FLAT INT. BEVEL. FILL OF PIT 119406, CHURCHLANDS

9. THREE REJOINING FRAGS; INT. BEVELLED LIP, SLIGHT INT. EXPANDED; IMPRESSED 'FALSE CORD' FROM STROKES OF SHARP POINT; HEAVY GREY FABRIC, BROWN EXT. HACKLY FRACTURE; PROFUSE SAND, SOME ANG. IGNEOUS ROCK TEMPER <10MM. FILL OF IRREG. PIT 119406, CHURCHLANDS

10. BASE ANGLE SEGMENT; MOULDED FOOT; ROUGH BROWN EXT., GREY INT.; IGNEOUS TEMPER; IRON AGE. FILL OF IRREG. PIT 119406, CHURCHLANDS

11. SIMPLE FLAT LIP, JOINED WALL SHERD; DARK GREY FABRIC, ERODED BROWN EXT. SURFACES; FINE SAND, TEMPERING, GROG AND SCARCE ANGULAR SANDSTONE <5MM; SLIGHTLY WEATHERED EDGES. PRIMARY FILL OF PIT 119574, GILCROSS

rectangular toothed comb and twisted cord impressed techniques; these have a recurring usage among pottery of the All-Over-Cord (AOC) decorated Beaker Group (Clarke 1970, 52-56; Case 2001, 367; Needham 2005, 183-188). Such an attribution is supported by the single distinguishing rim sherd that has a zone of horizontal cord lines inside the lip (Fig. 91.6). This can be paralleled among eastern Yorkshire Beakers from Kettlethorpe, South Cave (Bartlett 1963, 21, fig. 3) and Barnby Howes (Ashbee and ApSimon 1956, 25, fig. 8.1); also among Beakers in assemblages across the wider geographical distribution (Clarke 1970, No. 980, 1663, 1788, 1789, 1527, 1659). However, such an interior zone of thick cord lines is also a feature of the Goodmanham Barrow 99 Beaker, which has comb impressed spined herringbone motif on its neck exterior (Clarke 1970, No. 1311, fig. 303).

A predominance of horizontal line decoration in the three techniques of cord, incision and comb is characteristic of the fragmentary All-Over Cord/Comb/Incised Beaker assemblages of the Scottish sand dune sites such as Archerfield, Brackmont Mill, Luce Bay and Hedderwick (Gibson 1982, 98, 114, 192, 170); also at Ross Links, Northumberland (Tait 1965, 15) and, for Lincolnshire, among some sherd assemblages collected from Risby and Crosby Warrens (Riley 1957, 50, fig. 6. 19-29 and unpublished Scunthorpe Museum). In Stuart Needham's chronological scheme for the Bronze Age, AOC Beakers have early dating within Period 1: 2500-2300 cal BC (Needham 1996, 124-127), recently revised for a Chalcolithic Period *c.* 2450/2400- 2200/2150 cal. BC. (Needham 2012, 3-11).

Churchlands

Four pieces from fill **119413** of pit **119406**, weighing 73g in total were examined (Fig. 91.8-10), together with a mixed sherd assemblage of twenty-seven pieces, weighing 428g, from subsoil layer **119301**. The condition of the latter group varies considerably from sharp-edged unabraded to very worn, surface-eroded and rounded-edged pieces, with sizes ranging from 58 by 74mm to flakes and crumbs. Several fabrics, based on temper variations, were present. Biconical Urn fragments were identified in both groups.

These Biconical Urn fragments are of a particular significance as this style is relatively scarce compared with other Bronze Age pottery types; across Yorkshire and the East Midlands; and not previously recorded in Holderness. Their biconical profile is divided by the raised moulded shoulder angle, the inward sloping neck is decorated with a limited geometric motif range executed in coarse twisted cord or by point incision, and the rim and shoulder can have finger tip or nail impressions. Treatment of the body is confined to vertical finger stippling or furrowing. The fabric is coarse and heavy,

Context	Scatter	Sq or cut	Pieces	Wt/g	Sherds	Small sh.	Flakes	Crumbs	Rims	Bases	Decoration or notes
26020	1		3	11	1			2		1	SF 501
26020	1		1	23	1					1	SF 514
26020	1	27	1	10	1						Comb lines
26020	1	79	6	25	2	1	2	1		1	Comb lines
26067		26066	1	1		1	1				Weathered
26193		26192	3	50	2	1			1		Cord line
26193		26192	4	18	2	2			1		Incised lines
26240		26192	2	7		2				2	Incised lines
26524	2	228	2	?	2						
26524	2	258	5	10	1		1	3			Plain
26524	2	238	1	6	1						Plain
26524	2	286	4	6	1		3		1		Plain
26525	2	246	1	2		1					Plain
26525	2	216	20	36	2	1	4	12			Weathered
26525	2	220	4	8	2		2				Incised line
26525	2	232	5	1			5				-
26525	2	230	3	13	2	1					Plain
26525	2	242	2	5		2					Plain
Totals			71	244g.	22	12	13	23	3	5	

NB: Rejoined pieces counted as a single sherd, modifying count

TABLE 13: SUMMARY OF BEAKER SHERDS FROM SPROATLEY

Context	<1 cm.	1- 2.5 cm.	2.5-3 cm	3-4.5 cm.	4.5-5 cm	>5 cm.
26020	3	4	2	3	1	1
26193	1	1		2		
26524	3	4	2	1		
26525	17	5	1			
Totals	24	14	5	6	1	1	51

TABLE 14: SPROATLEY BEAKER POTTERY, SUMMARY OF FRAGMENT SIZES

and crushed stone tempering is a characteristic. The urn class can be described as Northern Biconical Urn as a distinction from other regional developments, such as Wessex Biconical (ApSimon 1972, 141-143).

Nineteenth-century excavations recovered individual Biconical Urns containing cremated bones that had been inserted into earlier round barrows on the Yorkshire Wolds and North York Moors (ApSimon 1972, 151-152 and 157). A more recent find from eastern Yorkshire, since ApSimon's review, is the fragmented urn with traces of burnt human bone likely derived from an eroded secondary burial in pre-Roman silting of the ring ditch around Walkington, Barrow 1 (Bartlett and Mackey 1973, 34, fig.14.36). The Rudston Wold occupation area also provides wider ceramic and lithic associations (Manby 1980, 324, fig. 8) and a nearby pit group on the Caythorpe Gas Pipeline provided a radiocarbon date in a 1400-995 cal BC range (Abramson 1996, 13 and 41-43).

South of the Humber, in the East Midlands, there are comparable Biconical Urns from modern excavated barrow and cemetery sites, with associated high quality radiocarbon dates; notable the penannular-ditched Stainsby barrow on the Lincolnshire Wolds (May 1976, 77, fig. 43) and, in Leicestershire, the Cossington Barrow (Thomas 2008, 30-34, fig. 33-34) and the Eye Kettleby enclosure cemeteries complex (Finn 2012, 44-68). Narrower dating ranges are provided from cremated bone for the Stainsby urn burials, of 1740-1500 cal BC (pers. comm. J. A. Sheridan) and for Cossington of 1750-1520 cal BC (Thomas 2008, 96). The extensive burial series at Eye Kettleby from clusters of Biconical Urns and Bucket Urns provide a potential stylistic progression from the later Early Bronze Age into the Middle Bronze Age (Woodward and Marsden 2012). The Biconical Urns, classed as Group 3A fall within a 1610-1500 cal BC range, or later Early Bronze Age to the beginning of the Middle Bronze Age (Woodward 2012, 75-76) and in a Midlands regional ceramic sequence that has some contemporary multi-ribbed Cordoned Urns in this and other regional cemeteries. In Stuart Needham's Bronze Age periodisation scheme (1996, 132-134), the Biconical Urns fall within his Bronze Age Period 4 (1700-1500 cal BC), with possible continuation into Period 5 (1500-1150 cal BC).

Pit 119574, Gilcross

Three pieces from the primary fill of pit **119574** weigh 20g in total. They include a rim sherd with a simple flat lip (Fig. 91.11) and a wall sherd. The sherds derive from a beaker with the highly characteristic floating motif of David Clarke's (1970, 234-238) Final Southern British Beaker or S4, decoration, executed either by comb- or point-incision on vessels of slack profile, and on some forms of handled Beakers; this style motif has an eastern distribution from the English Channel coastlands northwards to Yorkshire, and becoming scarce in Northumberland and into eastern Scotland (*ibid.* Map. 9). In eastern Yorkshire, individual Beakers with floating lattice-infilled motifs have both burial associations, such as Folkton Barrow 242 (*ibid.* No. 1280, Fig 979), and midden derived fragmentary assemblages in barrow structures at Walkington Barrow 1 (Bartlett and Mackey 1973, 32, Fig 13.27-29), and Gallows Hill, Kilham (Clarke 1970, No. 1339). In recent typo-chronological schemes, slack-profiled Beaker with floating motif decoration date are in the final period of Beaker development (*ibid.* 241-243; Lanting and van der Waals 1972, 26; Case 2001, 374) dated to Early Bronze Age Period 3 (2050-1700 cal BC: Needham 1996, 125 and 134).

Later prehistoric hand-made pottery

C.G. Cumberpatch

The excavations produced, in total, 27,487 sherds of hand-made pottery. Since earliest days of archaeological research in England, the later prehistoric archaeology of East Yorkshire has received a good deal of attention and the data available is considerable. Holderness has seen less work than other parts of the region (Hyland 2009) and the extent of socio-cultural variation between geographical zones within eastern Yorkshire is unclear, the issue having rarely been tackled since Evans' (1995) survey. Some of the data presented below seems to be at odds with Rigby's conclusions based on her survey of the material from the northern part of eastern Yorkshire but how far these are matters of detail and how far they represent significant variations in practice and *habitus* is unclear, even after the analysis of the material presented in this report.

In spite of a considerable amount of work on eastern Yorkshire pottery assemblages, the material has resisted the construction of chrono-typologies, such as those for Lincolnshire. A number of problems inherent in dealing with pottery assemblages stood out and structured the approach taken here:

- The absence of a reliable chrono-typological framework for the period between the early/ middle Iron Age and the period of Roman occupation, reflecting the lack of definable change in the typology and style of the pottery over a very long period. This would seem to reflect a distinctive form of organisation of production which saw regularity in style over a discrete area and stability in style. Strongly held and shared cultural preferences for the shape and size of pots seem to have persisted, even while production appears to have been organised at the household level.

- The contrast with the very limited quantity of hand-made pottery found from sites in the neighbouring areas of South and West Yorkshire which were virtually aceramic in the later prehistoric period and, on rural sites at least, into the Roman period.

- A very limited degree of exchange with the inhabitants of Lincolnshire, at least as represented by the occurrence of Lincolnshire vessels north of the Humber and of Yorkshire vessels south of the Humber (Elsdon 1997, May 1996).

- The continued preference for traditional types of pottery on the part of the population through the Roman period despite of the apparently availability of wheel-thrown wares.

- The apparent distinction between the types of pottery used on sites of Roman character, such as forts, *vici*, and villas, and those from rural farming settlements, particularly notable in the differential use of calcite tempered wares.

These characteristics suggested that it was worth diverging from the established traditions of analysis which, while they have provided high quality datasets, have not yet provided insight into the sociology of production, circulation and consumption of pottery. For this reason it was decided to try to develop an alternative model for the understanding of the pottery, focusing on the specific characteristics of assemblages from East Yorkshire.

Conventions and abbreviations used in the text and the accompanying data tables are summarised in Table 15. Abbreviations used to denote specific vessel types are given in the sub-heading to each descriptive section in the type series below.

Methodology

The standard range of variables were recorded for each group of sherds, as defined by the fabric type, within each context: number of sherds, weight of sherds, estimated maximum number of vessels (ENV), estimated vessel equivalent (EVE) and rim diameter. Hitherto, relatively simple classifications for the definition of the vessel forms in pottery from settlements, as opposed to burials, have generally been used, with Rigby's attempt to provide a synthesis for sites to the north of Holderness being the most extensive to date. In this case it was decided to take a slightly different approach.

Abbreviation	Meaning
&	Denote joining sherds from different contexts
inc	Inclusion
w/	With
int	Internal
ext	External
U/Dec	Undecorated
U/ID	Unidentified
N/A	Not applicable
S-Ped base	Solid pedestal base
H-Ped base	Hollow pedestal base, aka ring-foot base
ASW	Average sherd weight
ENV	Estimated (maximum) number of vessels
EVE	Estimated vessel equivalent
PRIA	Pre-Roman Iron Age
LPRIA	Late Pre-Roman Iron Age
R-B	Romano-British
E R-B	Early Romano-British
SFN	Small find number
Fig	Figure
Diam	Diameter

TABLE 15: CONVENTIONS AND ABBREVIATIONS USED IN THE HAND-MADE POTTERY REPORT

A scheme based on that devised by Knight for the East Midlands (1998) was considered but such an approach would be unable to deal with the considerable minor variations at the level of individual vessels that would impede the creation of a usable type series. The implication of earlier work on comparable assemblages was that there were regularities in the shape of the vessels and that the individual vessel types reflected strong and persistent shared preconceptions of what a pot should be, what it should look like, and how it should be made. In practical terms, this is reflected in the relative ease of identifying parallels from across East Yorkshire for individual vessels from a given assemblage.

During the preliminary examination and recording, the rim sherds were extracted from their context groups, and rebagged separately. Final type descriptions were not determined until a series of basic vessel forms had been identified and described, on the basis of an overview of the entire assemblage. The aim was to identify broad classes of vessel while avoiding the small-scale variations in rim shape and detail that are inevitable when production at the household level is involved. In other words, to try to identify the potters' mental templates, as indicated by the remarkably stable regularities in vessel shape and size. The scheme presented here inevitably involves subjective choices and should be seen as provisional, to be refined and revised as new data becomes available in the future.

Pottery data tables have been compiled for all of the sites discussed in this report and summary tables extracted from these to highlight specific aspects of the assemblages. In the archive, the data is presented both as a single table listing all of the pottery from the site, sorted by context group, context, and fabric type, and as a series of smaller tables covering individual features or context groups and relating to specific sub-sections in each site narrative. These archive tables contain much information not repeated in the text and are intended to allow reinterpretation of the data in the light of future discoveries.

Fabric type series

The classification of the vessel fabrics was based upon the work of Didsbury (2004, 2006, 2009a, 2009b, unpublished, Didsbury and Vince 2011) and Rigby (2004) with the terminology modified from that of Didsbury. The basic distinction between calcite tempered and vesicular wares (H1/H4) and rock and quartz tempered wares was retained but with distinctions between the sub-types within the H2 group. While not identical to the scheme used for the Creyke Beck assemblage (Didsbury, unpublished), the scheme was intended to address some or all of the same issues of diversity within the broader groups. The fabric groups are defined in Table 16. It should be noted that these are fabric groups rather than fabric types; there is a significant degree of variation in density and size of the inclusions between vessels within groups.

The percentages of the different fabrics in each feature or context group were initially calculated according to the ENV figures. In cases where vessels are shattered into many small sherds, this over-represented certain fabrics, notably H4, and so the figures were recalculated using the weight of sherds, believed, in this instance, to be more representative.

Fabrics H1 and H4

The calcareous fabrics H1 and H4, including all subdivisions, were compared across all sites and phases to assess the nature and extent of any change in the representation of these wares. This is of interest in view of the suggestions (e.g. Swan 2002) that production of calcite tempered wares by potters working in the native tradition increased in the third or fourth century AD. The lack of any precision in the dating of the pre-Roman features, the unknown variables affecting the rate and patterns of the adoption and use of wheel-thrown wares and changes in patterns of settlement and land use, with consequent impacts on the patterns of deposition, all made the drawing of definite conclusions on this point difficult. Vessels with calcareous inclusions formed only a very small part of the totals across the sites.

Fabric group	Description
H1	Fabrics containing calcareous temper, including calcite, shell and chalk
H1 Calcite	Fabrics containing angular calcite grains, varying in size and angularity
H1 Shell	Fabrics containing shell inclusions
H1 Chalk	as CTW (Rigby 2004)
H2	The general category for fabrics which contain non-soluble stone temper, notably quartz and igneous rock fragments. Highly variable and sub-divided as follows:
H2 Fine	A distinctive fine sandy textured fabric normally containing abundant fine quartz grit (<0.2mm) and only occasionally a small proportion of larger quartz grit and generally no rock fragments
H2	A medium textured H2 fabric with varying proportions of quartz and rock fragments between 0.2mm and 0.5mm; background is fine quartz sand with sparse to common larger inclusions, sometimes approaching the H2 Rock group where rock temper is predominant
H2 Rock	Sherds containing common to abundant rock fragments between 0.2mm and 0.5mm usually in a fine matrix containing moderate to abundant quartz sand
H2 Coarse Rock	Sherds containing particularly prominent angular rock fragments between 0.5mm and 10mm
H2 Hyper-coarse	Very distinctive but rare fabrics containing large angular rock fragments 10mm and larger in size; quartz is normally present as sand-grade inclusions
H2 Flint	As H2 but with small quantities of flint, usually angular, sometimes slightly abraded; to be distinguished from early prehistoric quartz-tempered ware
H2 Vesicular	A very specific fabric group distinguished by its bright orange and light grey fabric with abundant fine quartz temper and large voids at the surface superficially resembling the vesicles in the H2/H4 wares described below. The voids are generally larger than those commonly found in the H4 group and are only present on the surfaces
H2 Red	An H2 fabric distinguished by the presence of soft, rounded red iron-rich inclusions, often with fine quartz and rock fragments
H2 Slag	H2 sherds which include black, glassy, vesicular grains believed to be iron slag
H2 Fuel Ash	H2 fabrics with the distinctive white vesicular inclusions, believed to be fuel ash slag
H2 Grog	H2 sherds with grog inclusions in addition to quartz sand
H2 Mica	Prominent biotite or muscovite inclusions (specified in the data tables), generally in a medium textured H2 or H2 Rock fabric
H3	Sherds containing both calcareous and non-calcareous inclusions, with variants as specified for H2, above
H4	Vesicular wares of type H1 which have been particularly badly affected by the action of acidic ground water resulting in the removal in solution of the calcareous inclusions.
H5 and H5 Fine	A very distinctive soft crumbly grey sandy fabric in coarser and finer variants superficially resembling Romano-British greyware; see discussion below.
HM type	Unidentifiable fragments of hand-made pottery, normally of H2 type
Fired clay	Small fragments of fired clay
Crucible	Crucible fragments distinguished by their distinctive form and heavily over-fired fabric

TABLE 16: FABRIC TYPES IDENTIFIED IN THE POTTERY ASSEMBLAGES

Structures 2 and 3 at Old Ellerby produced assemblages with a relatively high proportion of H1/H4 fabrics (13.1% and 15.6% respectively). Later features, including the first- to second-century ditches and gullies and the third- to fourth-century pits contained much lower proportions (up to 5.2% and 4.1% respectively). In other features percentages rarely rose above one per cent of the total.

The Burton Constable assemblage differs in several respects and there would seem to be some indication of a rise in the proportion of H1/H4 types over time. For the most part, the settlement features produced very low percentages of H1/H4, never reaching more that 2 per

cent in the features associated with the ring gullies. The large assemblage from Structure 5 is an exception to this, with over 18 per cent in this type. In the Roman features, the representation of H1/H4 is highly variable: Enclosures 2, 4, 6, the burial and particularly Enclosure 8 all produced high proportions while ditch **118934**, ditch **118927**, Enclosure 11 and the possible grain dryer, **9282**, contained more modest quantities. Ditch **118958** was unusual, with less than one per cent.

Brandywell showed a considerable degree of contrast between features, with Structure 1 containing a high proportion of H1/H4 (13.3%) while gully **25247** contained an unusually high proportion of H1 Shell (19.3%). Other features contained less that 5 per cent while the types were entirely absent from several. There does not seem to be any correlation with the presence of wheel-thrown pottery but none of the wheel-thrown wares are of a date later than the mid-second century AD.

H1/H4 types were present across the features at Nuttles but proportions were low, typically under 0.6 per cent, even in the second-century AD ditches. The general picture from Lelley resembles that from Nuttles with a regular but low representation across features up to late second-century date. The exception to this is pit **35465** where H4 wares contribute 75.2 per cent of the total. The situation at New York is not entirely dissimilar to that at Lelley. H4 wares were present in features across the site, generally below 10 per cent, irrespective of date. In ditch **117024**, the proportion was nearly 63 per cent.

Patrington shows a distribution similar in general terms to that at Lelley and New York, with a general occurrence of H1/H4, including H1 Shell, across the site and a small but distinct concentration (16.2%) in the second- to early third-century ditches. Scorborough Hill produced only a small quantity of H1/H4, all from pit **12081**. H1 Calcite and H4 sherds were present at Gilcross, H1 Calcite being particularly common in the earlier features. Out Newton Road produced very small quantities of H1 Calcite, H1 Chalk and H4 from pit **13020** and the later fills of ditch **13070**.

In his discussion of the supply of pottery to the site at Melton, Fenton-Thomas (2011) has suggested that following the Roman conquest, the local manufacture of pottery ceased and was replaced with a supply originating in north Lincolnshire. This included hand-made shell tempered ware (*ibid.* 393). The quantities of shell tempered ware (H1 Shell) were extremely low on all sites considered in this report but Fenton-Thomas's suggestion, based as it is on data from an extensively excavated site does raise a question that must be addressed.

H1 Shell wares were identified only at Burton Constable, Brandywell, Patrington and Dimlington Road, always occurring alongside quartz and rock tempered wares and sometimes alongside H1 Calcite wares. At Burton Constable, H1 Shell was notable by its absence from the ring gullies and the numerous features associated with the Iron Age settlement, with the exception of Structure 6. Small quantities were, however, present in several of the third- and fourth-century features. The picture was not as clear at Brandywell as the feature which contained the highest proportion of H1 Shell (gully **25247**; 19.3%) did not produce any wheel-thrown pottery. At Patrington, H1 Shell was present in the large second- to early third-century ditch. The earlier ditches in Dimlington Road contained a relatively high proportion of H1 Shell (7.8%) but did not include any wheel-thrown pottery.

Even allowing for issues of residuality, it is difficult to argue on this evidence that local production of pottery ceased after the Roman Conquest and was replaced by Lincolnshire wares, at least as far as sites in Holderness are concerned. It is possible that Melton, being located closer to a trans-Humber transport route was unusual in this respect or that the inhabitants of sites closer to the Humber generally preferred to obtain their pottery from Lincolnshire. This might be an indication that the population of Melton originated in Lincolnshire and retained a preference for familiar types of pottery in preference to the local rock tempered wares.

There are situations in which the proportions of H1/H4 sherds is higher than normal in certain features: this is the case for the northern arc of Old Ellerby Structure 3, Structure 5 at Burton Constable, Structure 1 at Brandywell, Structures 1 and 2 at New York and the structural features at Gilcross. If this occurrence was limited to the ring gullies then it might be of some significance to the question of structured deposition, but the situation is comparable in non-settlement features at Brandywell, Lelley, New York, Patrington, Bluegate Corner, Gilcross and Dimlington Road. It seems safe to conclude that these haphazard occurrences of small clusters are each the remains of only one or two large vessels and that their locations have no specific significance.

In all cases H1/H4 vessels form only a small part of the overall ceramic assemblage and it is clear that the preference among the inhabitants of the sites discussed here was for locally manufactured rock tempered wares over calcareously tempered wares, whether H1 Shell or H1 Calcite, throughout the periods of activity represented.

Fabric H3 and variants

Fabric H3 and its variants were rare types which included both calcareous and a variety of non-calcareous inclusions, usually rock and/or quartz. While present sporadically across the site at Burton Constable, its representation was highly variable, with concentrations associated with the later features, notably Enclosure 2 (11.4%), Enclosure 4 (5%), Enclosure 9 (28.3%) and Enclosure 11 (18.8%). With the exception of feature **118974**, the type was rare in features associated with the Iron Age settlement. The situation at Bluegate Corner was broadly similar with sherds associated with features of Roman date.

Smaller quantities, less than 3 per cent of the total assemblages, were present at Brandywell, Patrington and Scorborough Hill, largely from late first- to second-century contexts. Very small quantities were present at Old Ellerby, New York and Out Newton Road. Although sporadic in its occurrence, the type was represented in all phases at Old Ellerby. The sherds from New York and Out Newton Road were all from features of early Roman date. No H3 types of any sort were identified at the other excavation sites.

Fabric H5

The H5 Sandy Grey ware group was added to the basic scheme to cover a group of vessels with a very distinctive soft, crumbly mid-grey fabric which superficially resembled a soft Roman grey ware. The fabric was a rare one and was absent from Brandywell, Braemere Hill, Burstwick, Churchlands, Patrington, Weeton, Gilcross, Out Newton Road, Hull Road and Dimlington Road.

The fabric shows some variation in character between plots, perhaps suggesting that it was locally manufactured and that different potters were using different clay bodies, although intending to produce similar wares. As discussed below, the type was commonest on Lelley where the sherds are generally distinguished by very dense, even, fine quartz sand and sparse fine rock fragments, which give the cross-sections a distinctive appearance and the surface the texture of fine sandpaper. These sherds are extremely finely finished, with a wall thickness of around 4.8mm. Although on close examination it is clear that they were hand-made, the vessels may have been finished on a turntable. A much softer H5 fabric was also represented at Lelley and elsewhere, much more prone to abrasion and to shedding its surface as dust.

At Old Ellerby, Burton Constable, Nuttles, New York and Scorborough Hill, the type forms only a very small proportion of the assemblages. In contrast, it forms over 10 per cent of the feature assemblages from both Structure 1 and pit **35464** at Lelley and from ditch **120665** at Bluegate Corner. Although bearing a superficial resemblance, the type appears to pre-date the appearance of Romano-British grey ware on a number of the sites so the resemblance is, presumably, a chance one. Three samples of H5 were submitted for petrographic analysis (Ixer, this volume: samples P09, P10 and P11): all proved to be of probable local origin.

Fabric H2 and variants

The overwhelming majority of sherds from all sites and all phases were variants of the H2 group containing varying quantities and sizes of quartz sand and grit, rock fragments of various types, soft red inclusions, flint and other inclusions. This group includes Rigby's (2004, 25) Erratic Tempered ware (ETW) category.

H2 Grog

Grog tempered pottery was only identified from Old Ellerby and ditch **118954** at Burton Constable but the identification of grog inclusions in two of the petrographic samples suggests that it is present more commonly, but too small to be seen with the naked eye or hand lens. The small assemblage in pit **3043** at Old Ellerby contained a single grog-tempered sherd associated with wheel-thrown pottery dating to the late second to mid-fourth century AD. Ditch **118954** included four small fragments of probable grog tempered pottery.

H2 Coarse Rock and H2 Hyper-coarse

Two groups were identified as of particular interest by virtue of their distinctively coarse temper. Diverse tempering material is characteristic of the assemblages from eastern Yorkshire, normally assumed to result from the use of highly heterogeneous local clay sources. In the coarse and hyper-coarse categories, the inclusions are particularly visible at the surface and set the vessels apart, at least phenomenologically. The coarse inclusions may have been deliberately incorporated to increase stability during manufacture. However, while coarse temper seems generally to be associated with larger vessels, not all large vessels were coarsely tempered. A wedge-rimmed jar from Lelley (SF 272), for instance, and a flared-rimmed jar from Old Ellerby (Fig. 92.12) were both in fine fabrics, demonstrating that coarse fabrics were not required for larger vessels. In a small number of cases, the large inclusions are quartz, but rock fragments are far commoner. Individual rock fragments are generally angular and appear to have been freshly smashed stone rather than natural inclusions in the clay.

Hyper-coarse fabrics were identified from only Burton Constable and Burstwick. At Burton Constable the sherds were from unstratified contexts but those from Burstwick were associated with the ring gullies. Together with a group of slightly finer but still coarsely tempered sherds, they constitute over forty per cent of the feature assemblages. This concentration of coarse sherds might indicate that a number of similar vessels had been disposed of together, possibly after being used for some specific purpose.

The H2 Coarse Rock category was much more abundant than the hyper-coarse category. At Old Ellerby, the type, where present, varies between 6.5 per cent and 13 per cent of the feature assemblage, with no indication of any significant change over time. Two categories, H2 Coarse Rock and H2 Coarse Quartz, were identified in Burton Constable. The H2 Coarse Quartz type is rare and only present in contexts associated with Structure 5 and ditch **118958**. More generally, coarsely tempered wares are absent from the earliest deposits on the site. Structures 2 and 4 produced very high proportions: 40.3 per cent and 53 per cent respectively. By contrast, Structure 5 and ditch **118958**, both of which contained large pottery assemblages, included relatively modest proportions: 15.3 per cent and 13.3 per cent respectively. The same general pattern of high variability is also typical of the later features.

Elsewhere, there is a similar degree of variability. In Brandywell, Nuttles, Patrington and Out Newton Road the distribution suggests that the type was commoner in pre-Roman features than in those of Roman date. In Gilcross the type was absent from the earliest ditch and forms a small component within the settlement features. This apparent pattern is less visible at New York where high proportions are present in most of the feature assemblages. At Bluegate Corner, coarsely tempered wares were absent from all features and feature groups except for Structure 2, where the type forms 24 per cent of the total. The distribution from Burstwick is unusual and highly variable: in the ring gullies, the type forms 20.9 per cent of the total and in ditch **51026** it constitutes 60.8 per cent but elsewhere on the site the type was rare. Both types were rare at Lelley and confined to Structure 1. Very small quantities were present at Churchlands and Scorborough Hill but both types are absent at the other sites.

H2 Fine

The distribution of H2 Fine fabrics, often associated with the more distinctive vessel types, also varies widely between sites and between individual features. This variation does not seem to be related to chronology: at Burton Constable the proportions vary widely between features but the type is common in both the colluvial deposit **118979** and late Roman features such as Enclosures 3 and 4 and ditch **118957**. The other sites show a similar range of variation but in none is there any systematic variation over time.

H2 Slag and H2 Fuel ash

Two H2 variants, one with distinctive white vesicular inclusions resembling small fragments of white pumice stone and the other with hard, black, vitreous inclusions, stand out by virtue of their unusual and distinctive character and rare occurrence. The first of these could contain fuel ash slag (Doonan, pers. comm.). The second group are suspected of containing other types of slag, following the identification of iron slag in sherds from Dalton Parlours (Buckland *et al.* 1990). It should be noted that the petrographic reports (Ixer; Pitman and Doonan; this volume, page 170) indicate that what appeared as a black, vitreous slag-like material in samples P07 and P08 now seems to be an igneous rock inclusion while samples P09 and probably P10, not suspected of containing slag inclusions, probably do. Identification of slag temper is clearly not straightforward, implying that its true representation within the assemblages considered here is largely unknown.

The use of residues and waste from metal working as tempering agents in pottery manufacture (Buckland *et al.* 1990) may have had some specific cultural or economic link to pottery manufacture, as it has been suggested

that metal working and metal workers were accorded particular status in pre-Roman Iron Age society (Hingley 2006; Giles 2007). Perhaps more plausibly, the use of these residues might simply have been haphazard, as a convenient and abundant waste product from another productive activity taking place in the vicinity of pottery production. The apparent scarcity of vessels containing slag and slag-like temper, their sparse distribution and their lack of any clear association with specific significant contexts would lend weight to this view. There is no evidence that these were anything other than normal domestic vessels and while we know little of how the pottery was used, nothing in its character or distribution suggests that it was more than utilitarian in nature.

Of the two identifiable vessel types containing slag-like temper, one, from Brandywell, was a funnel-rim jar and the other, from Burton Constable, a vertical rim jar (see 'Type Series' below for vessel form descriptions). Four bases contained such inclusions: solid-pedestal types from Burton Constable, Brandywell and Scorborough Hill and flat from Burstwick. The limited chronological evidence would seem to suggest that slag-tempered wares were of late pre-Roman Iron Age or early Roman date and it may be significant that none of the sherds occurred in contexts containing wheel-thrown pottery of late second-century date or later.

Crucible fragments were recovered from seven of the excavation sites. Their presence indicates that non-ferrous metal working was undertaken on the plots from which they were recovered. The correlation with the plots which produced slag-tempered sherds is only partial, being limited to Burton Constable and Scorborough Hill: the implication is that the use of slag temper for pottery was not routine where metal working was taking place and may have been rather rare. While these observations do not rule out the possibility that there were links between different pyrotechnologies, either practical or symbolic, the association was probably not a regular one.

Pottery manufacture

Where it is possible to identify the precise method of manufacture of the hand-built pottery, slab-building, as opposed to coil building, appears to have been the preferred option. Clear examples of oblique slab-joins are common, particularly in the case of the larger vessels. This is not to imply that the pots were crude or poorly made. A number of variations in technique are possible and many of these are seen in the assemblages. The majority of the vessels are carefully finished with smoothed surfaces internally and externally and a high degree of regularity in the vessel forms. While it would perhaps be misleading to subdivide the assemblage into the traditional 'coarseware' and 'fineware' categories, there are distinctions between vessels which were reflected in their manufacture and may be related to their function. A relatively small number of the smaller vessels (notably VRGJ and VRSJ types) show a considerably greater degree of investment of time and labour in the finishing than do the larger vessels. These smaller types are thin-walled and elaborately shaped, often with burnished surfaces and ring foot or splayed bases. They show little or no sign of breakage along the slab joins and appear to have been thinned by careful working of the internal and external surfaces. While it would be going too far to describe these bases as 'turned' they had clearly been inverted and the bases modified while the vessels were close to leather-hard.

In the case of the flat and solid-pedestal bases, some at least seem to have been added as separate elements, as indicated by the characteristic fracture lines and the evidence of internal smoothing over the joins. In other cases, particularly with some of the globular vessels, the rims are elaborate and carefully finished: this elaboration not appearing to have any specific function. While the pottery was undoubtedly primarily utilitarian, its manufacture was not in any sense casual. The potters were more than competent at manufacturing vessels that were both adequate for their functions and conformed to shared perceptions as to the desirable characteristics of individual vessels. It is of interest to recall the observation on the broadly contemporary vessel from Mellor that, in spite of its rough appearance, the characteristics of the fabric suggest high preparation index (Ixer 2005, 39-40), implying that pottery production was more than a casual household task (see Feinman *et al.* 1981 for a suggested methodology to investigate this aspect of the pottery industry).

There seems to be a good case for arguing that the entire production process, from the procurement of the clay and temper to the firing was undertaken with due care and attention to detail even while the level of technical sophistication was relatively low. The selective use of coarse temper for some large vessels is entirely consistent with ethnographic evidence on the relationships between technology, function and cultural perceptions of the nature of pottery and its role in wider society, which can be complex and difficult to disentangle. This aspect of pottery manufacture might be more valuable in contributing to our understanding of craft production and its social correlates than further attempts to identify chronologically sensitive variations in vessel morphology.

Type series

The typology proposed here departs from existing schemes as these were found to lack the clarity in distinguishing the range of vessel types needed to order a body of material that poses numerous challenges to conventional analysis. A full review of existing schemes is beyond the scope of this report but would

appear to be a priority in any reconsideration of the later prehistoric and Roman archaeology of eastern Yorkshire, particularly given the apparent discrepancies between the information presented here and that of Rigby (2004). The scheme proposed here defines the range of vessel types identified in the assemblages from the various sites to allow comparison across time and space. As with any typological scheme, particularly where hand-made vessels are concerned, a simplification of reality has been necessary. The degree of fragmentation means that the majority of types are based primarily on the characteristics of the rims and in many cases the full vessel profiles remain unknown.

The scheme seeks to reconcile the contrasting evidence for variability within the defined groups with conformity to a set of conceptual templates which appear to have structured the production of recognisable vessel types across individual sites and seem to have been stable over a long period of time. Crucially, this conformity with a long-term tradition seems to have been robust enough to withstand both the arrival of wheel-thrown pottery in the Romano-British tradition and also the growth in use of calcareously tempered fabrics during the later Roman period (Swan 2002).

In spite of many years of detailed work and an increasing number of assemblages from developer-funded work, there remains no detailed chrono-typological scheme of the type that has been compiled for many other areas of the country (Rigby 2004; Didsbury unpublished 2011). This should not be seen primarily as a methodological problem but as an aspect of late prehistoric and Roman period society in the region. This report represents an opportunity to examine this aspect, with implications for the understanding of a range of social and economic issues.

The description of each individual class of vessels is followed by an examination of its distribution, both spatial and chronological. As the hand-made vessels themselves are only rarely chronologically diagnostic, most of the dating information has come from other sources: the Roman and Romano-British pottery data (Leary, this volume, page 174), the radiocarbon dating and a small number of individual hand-made vessel types that have parallels with material from other dated sites.

Because of the fragmentation of the vessels and the small numbers of complete profiles that were recovered, no attempt was made to distinguish large from small jars and priority was placed on the shape of the vessel irrespective of size. This decision was deemed to be justified because similar vessel forms seemed to be replicated in different sizes, and because attempts to classify vessels by size and presumed function, such as storage jar or cooking pot, have been criticised for the assumptions involved. A preliminary attempt to tackle the issue of vessel size was made using a comparison of the range of rim diameters within each class; overall, this was inconclusive but might be repeated more productively using a different methodology in the future.

Everted Rim Jar (ERJ)

The ERJ category is a very broad, with a large number of variations on the basic theme of pear-shaped, narrow-shouldered, round or globular bodied jars with rims varying in length and in the degree to which they rim is everted, from almost vertical to quite sharply. Some have pronounced necks (Fig. 96.105) but some do not (Fig. 97.109, 113 and 121). The type is distinguished from wedge-rimmed jars by the lack of thickening on the internal angle. Rather the rim and wall retain more or less the same thickness from the body, through the neck to the lip, the latter varying from square to round in cross-section. The ERJ class is also distinguished from vessels with small 'beaded' rims, which, while everted in the strict sense, barely extend beyond the thickness of the wall. A distinction has also been drawn between ERJ and flat-rimmed jars (FlRJ) with the latter having a rim that is so sharply everted that it is flat in relation to the base of the vessel.

Most of the everted rim jars are of small to medium size (Figs. 97.115, 121 and 123; 98.152) with a smaller number of larger 'storage jar' types (Figs. 94.59, 60 and 61; 95.104), the latter often with heavier clubbed rims. The class also includes some slightly unusual vessels (Fig. 96.101). Classifying the everted rims accurately and consistently was particularly difficult because of the degree of latitude possible in what is perhaps the most elementary of all jar forms. Variation includes the width of the rim and the degree of thickening of the rim above the neck: it may be possible at some stage to further sub-divide this class. Everted rim jars occur in all fabrics with finely finished vessels in finely vesicular fabrics (e.g. Fig. 98.146) to the commoner, more coarsely tempered wares.

Parallels

Everted rim jars are a ubiquitous form and as such are present in most assemblages of later prehistoric and Roman date. In many cases the class has been sub-divided, most notably by Rigby who has used body shape and specific details of the rims to define smaller classes. This was only rarely possible with the sites considered here, largely because of the fragmentation of the assemblages and the difficulty of relating rim form to overall vessel shape. Where larger profiles survived, they have been described in the data tables and specific examples have also been illustrated.

In general terms, parallels were noted for the type among Rigby's pear-shaped jar, chamfered jar, necked jar and necked storage jar forms and there may also be some overlap with her shapeless jar group (2004,

38-41, figs. 6 and 7). Other assemblages also reflect the degree of variety in the type including High Wold, Bridlington (Didsbury 2009a, figs 22.7; 23.30; 24.50), Atwick (Challis and Harding 1975, fig. 29.2 and 4), South Cave (Challis and Harding 1975, fig. 36.7), Driffield Aerodrome (Challis and Harding 1975, fig. 38.1), Faxfleet 'A' (Challis and Harding 1975, fig. 39.1 and 2), Sewerby Cottage, Bridlington (Didsbury 2009b, figs. 176.2, 3 and 14; and 177.37 and 38), Melton (Didsbury and Vince 2011, figs. 131.1 and 2; 132.6; 135.1, 6, 14, 15, 16 and 17), Wharram Percy (Didsbury 2004, figs. 102.23 and 43; 103.50; 104.92, 93 and 100) and the A1 Dishforth to Barton road-widening scheme (Cumberpatch unpublished 3, figs. 2, 6 and 10).

Dating and distribution

The difficulty of defining distinctions within the ERJ class renders it difficult to use as a chronological marker. A more detailed, statistical approach might yield information on changes to distribution over time but it is far from clear that this would be the case. However, there do appear to be some distinctions within the distribution of ERJs across the sites considered here. ERJ forms are extremely rare in the assemblages from New York, Burstwick, Churchlands, Patrington, Bluegate Corner, Weeton, Out Newton Road, Hull Road and Dimlington Road. This does not seem to be linked to chronological factors and may be because the form was functionally suited to some specific task or purpose or because of some less obvious cultural preference or requirement. Given the general absence of decoration it seems plausible to argue that vessel form may have played an important part in this.

At Old Ellerby, ERJ forms were present in structures and in boundary ditches, and the reason for their absence from some contexts is not immediately apparent. The type was more generally distributed at Burton Constable: although absent from some of the pit groups associated with the ring gullies, it was common in the structural features, most notably Structure 5. This rather patchy distribution was also noted on other sites.

Flat-Rim Jar (FlRJ)

Flat-rimmed jars (FlRJ) have a very distinctive, sharply everted rim on a rounded, usually shouldered body. The profile of the rims identified in this report tended to be slightly squarer than the example illustrated by Challis and Harding.

Parallels

Parallels for this form include Levisham Moor (Challis and Harding 1975, fig. 50.8) and Shiptonthorpe (Evans 2006, fig. 7.9, G08.4), the latter example being in a calcareous fabric.

Dating and distribution

Flat-rimmed jars were not a common form but appeared to have a broad distribution. At Old Ellerby they were present in both the earlier and later features, including those dated to the third or fourth centuries AD. A similar pattern can be seen at Burton Constable where examples occurred in Structure 5 as well as in ditch **118958**, although the actual numbers in any one feature were low. At Brandywell, FlRJs were present in Structure 1 and gully **25113**, and at Nuttles the type occurred in ditches containing wheel-thrown wares dating to the late first or second century. A similar date is suggested in the case of Scorborough Hill.

Square-Rim Jar (SqRJ)

Square-Rim Jars (SqRJ) are a distinctive but very rare form characterised by a heavy square or diamond-section rim on an open or pear-shaped jar body. Although distinctive, the form may share some characteristics with everted rim jars with heavy square rims (Fig. 93.20).

Parallels

The form is not one that is well-represented in the literature and the only clear parallel found was from Rudston Roman villa (Rigby 1980; fig. 27.8). This rare form requires further research.

Dating and distribution

Square rim jars should be considered to be part of the larger ERJ class. They were identified from only Old Ellerby, Burton Constable and Lelley and show a considerable degree of variation within what must be considered a loose group. The vessel from Old Ellerby (Fig. 93.32) is from Structure 2, the two examples from Burton Constable are both from ditch **118958**, while that from Lelley is from a context associated with Structure 3.

Vertical Rim Jar (VRJ)

The vertical rim jar category is an extremely broad one and encompasses diverse groups of vessel from large utilitarian vessels, the majority in the VRJ-CS, VRJ-CT sub-groups, to finely made and finished types, often with burnished surfaces, that might be said to constitute something approaching a 'fineware' category, as seen in the VRSJ and VRGJ sub-groups. The defining characteristic of the VRJ class as a whole is that the rim, while distinct from, and narrower than, the body, has little or no eversion even while the profile of the body may be similar to that of the ERJs, varying from globular and wide-shouldered to elongated, pear-shaped or narrow-shouldered with the rim standing almost vertically on the shoulder or neck. Lips may be rounded to a varying extent.

A significant distinction within the group is between the short stumpy vertical rims (VRJ-CS) and the longer, thinner vertical rims (VRJ-CT). The distinction between these vessels and some of the everted rim jars can be ambiguous (for example Fig. 96.106). Particularly with the smaller vessels and those with longer rims, there are possible overlaps between the two groups, but the VRJ-CS and -CT jars tend to be of a larger size and to have thicker walls and a generally coarser range of fabrics. The longer vertical rims tend to belong to smaller jars, often in hard, black sandy textured fabrics, with varying sizes and proportions of rock and quartz inclusions.

Vertical rimmed jars barely appear in Rigby's review of pottery from the region and one possible close parallel, the deep-collared shouldered jar (Rigby 2004, 39, fig. 6 and 192 fig. 77.4) in an unusual shell tempered fabric, is identified as unique. Given the virtual ubiquity of vertical rim forms on the sites considered here it maybe that there is some regional diversity in vessel forms although this does not seem to be borne out by Evans' distribution map (1995, fig. 5.7, type Li). Given the enormous expansion in the quantity of available data, largely the result of commercial work, since both the Pots in Pits project (1988 to 1992) and Evans' survey, there is probably a good case for revisiting the question of regionality in vessel form in eastern Yorkshire.

Dating and distribution

The vertical rim jar category with its numerous variants is among the commonest type identified and defined within the assemblage. The majority of examples of plain vertical rim jars are associated with ring gullies and pre-Roman or early Roman features with fewer from late Roman contexts. The Old Ellerby examples were commonest in the contexts associated with Structures 2 and 3 but were also present in the third- or fourth-century ditches and pits. Smaller numbers of VRJ rims were present in other features. VRJs were common throughout the Burton Constable site but commonest in the features comprising the earlier phases of activity. It part this may be due to the higher numbers of sherds generally associated with the settlement than those from the boundary and enclosure ditches and as such may be related more to patterns of disposal and discard than with changes in patterns of use.

At Brandywell, Nuttles, Lelley, Burstwick, Patrington, Weeton and Gilcross, VRJs were commonest in contexts related to structures but were also present in first- to second-century ditches. The absence of later Roman features from these sites means that comparison with Burton Constable was difficult. At Scorborough Hill, a large number of vessels were present in the assemblage from pit **12081**. VRJs were rare in other sites although, where present, were generally found in features of the pre-Roman or early Roman date.

Vertical Rim Jar – Coarse Short (VRJ-CS)

The short stumpy-rimmed VRJ-CS type is characterised by a rim of no more than 2cm in height and which may be almost as wide as it is tall. Vessels tend to be large and often have thick walls, and are made in coarse sandy fabrics, sometimes with rock or quartz inclusions of the coarser type although smaller examples in finer fabrics were also noted (e.g. Fig. 98.137, 140 and 153).

Parallels

Parallels for the VRJ-CS sub-type are numerous and include Eastburn (Challis and Harding 1975, fig. 31.7), Driffield Aerodrome (Challis and Harding 1975, fig. 38.2), possibly Saltshouse School (Challis and Harding 1975, fig. 41.3), Creyke Beck (Didsbury unpublished, figs. 19.10 and 15; 20.35; 26.139; 21.49; 22.65; 24.103, 105 and 106; 25.116 and 26.139), Melton (Didsbury and Vince 2011, fig. 137.4), Reighton By-pass (Cumberpatch unpublished 1, fig. 23.15, 56 and 58) and Hawling Road (Evans and Creighton 1999, fig. 7.16, G01-J24). Examples from High Wold, Bridlington (Didsbury 2009a) include those shown in figs. 23.28 and 29, and 24.39, the latter in an H4 fabric.

Dating and distribution

At Old Ellerby, VRJ-CS vessels were present in both early and late features with examples from Structures 2 and 3, ditch **3267** and from third- and fourth-century features. A broadly similar pattern was seen in Burton Constable where the type was found widely in contexts associated with the structures and settlement features belonging to the earlier phases of activity and more rarely in the late ditches, notably ditch **118958** with its unusually large and diverse pottery assemblage and possibly in ditch **118927**. At Brandywell, Nuttles, Lelley, New York, Scorborough Hill and Out Newton Road the type was present in pre-Roman contexts, especially ring gullies, and also present in first- to early second-century ditches but seemingly absent from later contexts, while at Burstwick and Patrington it was present only in pre-Roman features.

Vertical Rim Jar – Coarse Tall (VRJ-CT)

The tall vertical rim which defined the VRJ-CT sub-type was typically found on jars of a similar size to the VRJ-CS type but with a pronounced internal angle at the junction between the rim and body. This feature is particularly prominent on examples from Burton Constable but rather less so on examples from Nuttles. How far such differences are significant and how far they represent variations in practice between different potters is unclear. There was a considerable size range from the larger (Figs. 95.64 and 65; 98.132 and 99.169 and 170) to smaller examples (Figs. 92.22; 98.150; 99.172).

Parallels

Parallels for the type occurred at Garton Slack, Levisham Moor 'A' and Faxfleet 'A' (Challis and Harding 1975, figs. 33.2; 49.1; and 39.7, respectively). These examples had parallels in Burton Constable (Fig. 95.64 and 65) with a tall vertical rim on a large 'storage jar' sized body and a distinctive internal angle at the base of the rim. The type seems to have been a standard component of pottery assemblages across the region, although it may be rather less common than the VRJ-CS type, and other examples are known from Melton (Didsbury and Vince 2011, fig. 138.3), Creyke Beck (Didsbury unpublished, figs. 20.35; 21.49 (not as tall as some examples but with the distinctive definite internal angle); 27.156 and 161; and 28.182) and Dalton Parlours (Sumpter 1990, fig. 94.2). Possible examples from Rudston Roman Villa include those illustrated by Rigby (1980, fig. 46.205 and 206).

Dating and distribution

As with the VRJ-CS group, the VRJ-CT type appears preferentially in late Iron Age and early Roman contexts. In Old Ellerby the type was rare, occurring only in Structure 3 and the late first- to late second-century ditch **3267**. In contrast the type is relatively common in Burton Constable where it was associated with Structures 1, 2, 4 and 5 as well as ditches **118970** and **118954**. It also occurred sporadically in some of the pits in the area of the settlement but was rare in the later enclosure ditches with the exception of ditch **118958**. It was also represented at Nuttles, Lelley, New York, Burstwick, Patrington, Scorborough Hill and Out Newton Road, with an unstratified example from Gilcross.

Vertical Rim Jar - Fine Short Globular (VRJ-FSG)

The VRJ-FSG type is a large and internally diverse class of small to medium-sized vessels with a globular body and having a distinct vertical rim, sometimes slightly everted and markedly differentiated from the body. The word 'fine' in the type name is accurate as far as many of the vessels are concerned, but examples in gritty textured fabrics were also present.

Parallels

Vertical rim vessels were poorly represented in Rigby's classification and the only close parallel for the VRJ-FSG type was a collared globular jar (Rigby 2004, 40, 127, fig. 33.1) even though parallels for the type are recorded elsewhere. Examples include Pale End (Challis and Harding 1975, fig. 46.1), High Wold, Bridlington (Didsbury 2009a, figs. 22.10 and 24.45, Creyke Beck (Didsbury unpublished, figs. 19.11 and 22.63), Sewerby Cottage, Bridlington (Didsbury 2009b, fig. 176.5) and Melton (Didsbury and Vince 2011, fig. 135.12).

Dating and distribution

The VRJ-FSG type was a broad one and perhaps as a result it was found to be relatively common. It was widely distributed in Old Ellerby with examples from both the earlier structures and from the third- or fourth-century ditches and pits. In Burton Constable it was present sporadically in settlement features but absent from the later ditches, with the exception of ditch **118958**. It was also present at Bluegate Corner, in the later phase features. In other sites the type appears to have been absent from contexts of later than first- to early second-century date.

Vertical Rim Jar – Narrow Body (VRJ-NB)

The narrow-bodied vertical rimmed jars usually have only a narrow or vestigial shoulder and often a slightly dished internal profile to the vertical rim.

Parallels

Parallels for the form included examples from Emmotland (Challis and Harding 1975, fig. 31.6), Creyke Beck (Didsbury unpublished, fig. 27.155) and Melton (Didsbury and Vince 2011, fig. 131.3 and 9).

Dating and distribution

The VRJ-NB form was generally rare, with the exception of Out Newton Road where examples were present in both pre-Roman and early Roman contexts. A slightly earlier date range is suggested by the occurrence of examples from Burton Constable, Lelley, New York, Scorborough Hill and Gilcross.

Vertical Rim Open Jar (VROJ)

Vertical rim open jars formed an ambiguous category between shoulderless VRJ and Open Jar types. The distinguishing characteristic is a very narrow shoulder and body with a slightly narrower tall vertical rim, usually with a rounded lip. The form may be related to the VRJ-NB type.

Parallels

Few parallels were found for this form. They included Kilnsea (Challis and Harding 1975, fig. 21.6), Emmotland (*ibid.* fig. 31.6) and Melton (Didsbury and Vince 2011, fig. 134.1).

Dating and distribution

The VROJ form was identified only at Burton Constable and several examples were recovered from contexts associated with Structure 1 and features associated with the settlement. This might imply that the type is one that dates to the late pre-Roman period but it would be hazardous to draw conclusions from such a sporadic distribution.

Vertical Rim Shouldered Jar (VRSJ)

Vertical Rim Shouldered jars (VRSJ) form a very distinctive group characterised by their fine sandy H2 fabrics, and a tall vertical or slightly everted rim, often with a small clubbed or beaded rim on a wide, high-shouldered body that tapers from the shoulder to a narrower splayed or pedestal base. It is probable that some of the fine burnished splayed or pedestal-footed bases discussed below belong to VRSJ vessels (compare Figs. 97.111 and 95.79 with Figs. 93.19; 96.98 and 98.138).

The vessels were burnished externally giving a fine finish which complemented the thin walls and elaborate form. A tendency to break at the junction of the neck and shoulder makes definite attribution to the form difficult in the case of small rim fragments and body sherds: as a result the type may be under-represented. Sherds from Scorborough Hill, for example, noted as being from shouldered or carinated jars but unattributable to a definite form, may be of this type. The form also has some similarity with some of the VRJ-FSG vessels but the VRSJ fabrics were generally finer, the neck or rim taller and the external surfaces were burnished.

Parallels

The VRSJ form appears to have been rare in eastern Yorkshire (Didsbury unpublished, 29). The best parallels for the form are found among the late Iron Age shouldered jar forms of Lincolnshire and the east Midlands and in this respect the VRSJ group can be compared to the decorated sherds from Old Ellerby, Burton Constable and Nuttles. It should be emphasised that the fabrics were local ones and were not the shell tempered Lincolnshire types (see also Didsbury unpublished, 28-9). A further distinction may be their slightly simpler forms which lack the cordons and corrugations typical of the Lincolnshire vessels (*cf* Elsdon 1996, C13; Elsdon 1997, fig. 58.86 and 88; May 1996, figs. 19.34, 263; and 19.43, 429) and those from the East Midlands (including Leicester, Elsdon 1996, D17a); Gallows Nooking Common, Nottinghamshire, (Elsdon 1996, B7), and Weekley in Northamptonshire (Jackson and Dix 1986-7; fig. 40.171). This having been noted, corrugated vessels are not unknown in Yorkshire as the evidence from Weelsby Avenue, Grimsby (Elsdon 1996, C.6b) and Brantingham (Elsdon 1996, C.13) demonstrates.

Dating and distribution

The VRSJ group is of particular interest as a result of its distinctive form, careful manufacture and fine finish. Its distribution across the sites was unusual with particular concentrations at Scorborough Hill and Gilcross. Two examples, one of which was questionable, were identified from Old Ellerby. The single definite example was from a third- or fourth-century context. The single example from Burton Constable is from the large and diverse assemblage in ditch **118958**. Brandywell and Lelley both produced examples of the type from first- to second-century AD contexts while the example from Nuttles was probably somewhat earlier.

Pit **12081** at Scorborough Hill produced up to fourteen examples, as well as four other possibles. Body sherds from carinated jars were also identified. The assemblage from Gilcross included up to thirty-eight examples with one further possible example. These were all from contexts associated with wheel-thrown pottery, dating to around the period of the conquest. Given that these periods were well represented on other sites, where VRSJs were rare, it is possible that the concentrations at Scorborough Hill and Gilcross relate to some specific aspect of the sites. That the type is unusually finely finished with a very distinctive form may be significant in this respect.

Elsewhere, a plain shouldered jar from Old Sleaford (Elsdon 1997, fig. 77.365), alongside cordoned examples, dated to the site period 2 (*c.* AD10 to 65). The evidence from Dragonby would point to a slightly earlier date, but there is little doubt that these vessels are of later Iron Age: Late La Tène in Knight's (2002) terms, most probably spanning the period between the first century BC and the early to mid-first century AD.

Vertical Rim Globular Jar (VRGJ)

The VRSJ type seems to be part of a group which includes the smaller wedge-rim and beaded rim globular jars, particularly the latter, and a number of individual variants which do not fit easily into any rigid classificatory system. They are distinguished by the lack of any significant thickening of the rim.

Parallels

Parallels for this form were not abundant although Creyke Beck appears to have produced several (Didsbury unpublished, figs. 19.11; 24.103 and 111, and possibly 23.93) while another possible example came from Melton (Didsbury and Vince 2011, fig. 135.12). Examples were also identified from High Wold, Bridlington (Didsbury 2009a, figs. 22.10 and 23.26 and 29).

Dating and distribution

The VRGJ form was not widely represented and where identified, numbers were low. Four examples from Old Ellerby all came from Structure 2. Structure 4 at

Burton Constable produced two rims while a possible example of the type was identified in one of the contexts associated with Structure 5. Brandywell, Nuttles, Lelley and Scorborough Hill each produced single examples from late Iron Age or first- to second-century contexts.

Vertical Rim Jar type (VRJ type)

A number of jars with vertical rims did not fit into any of the categories defined above. Examples from Old Ellerby (Fig. 92.2) and Dimlington Road (Fig. 99.177) are illustrated.

Open Jar (OJ)

The Open Jar form was defined as a parallel sided jar having no constricted neck and more or less parallel sides. Some vessels had a shallow groove externally or had slightly everted walls towards the rim but no significant constriction that could be called a neck. The fact that the upper body and rim were vertical meant that they can be seen as similar to some types of VRJ, (particularly the VROJ group) and there were considerable problems in distinguishing small rim sherds; this accounts for some of the questionable attributions (?OJ, ?VRJ). The type was rare in H1/H4 fabrics but there was an example from pit **9665** at Burton Constable.

Parallels

Parallels for the open jar form were widespread in both space and time. Examples include Danes Graves and Garton Slack (Challis and Harding 1975, Figs. 31.2 and 33.11, respectively). While they seem to encompass Rigby's thick-walled, wide-mouthed shapeless jar category (2004, 38) the proposed early date range (900 to 600 BC) is not consistent with the evidence from the sites discussed here. Other examples include Creyke Beck (Didsbury unpublished, fig. 26.150), High Wold, Bridlington (Didsbury 2009a, fig. 22.2) and Melton (Didsbury and Vince 2011, fig. 136.1).

Dating and distribution

Open jars, while never a common form, occurred regularly. They were present in late first- to late second-century and third- or fourth-century features at Old Ellerby. At Burton Constable the form was present in both settlement features and in the Roman ditches and at Nuttles in the ring gullies and in the second-century ditch systems. The form appeared to be limited in its occurrence to the late Iron Age field system at New York while in Braemere Hill there was a single example from a pre-Roman context. A small number of OJ and OJ type vessels were present within pit **12081** at Scorborough Hill with further examples in the linear features. Examples from Gilcross were dated to the period around the time of the conquest while those from Out Newton Road were from both the Iron Age pit and the upper, early Roman fills of the enclosure ditch. Open Jars and a barrel jar were the only identifiable vessels from Hull Road. At Dimlington Road, Open Jars were present in the later prehistoric phases of the site.

Everted rim open jar (EROJ)

A distinctive variant on both the Open Jar and Everted Rim Jar forms, the Everted Rim Open Jar is characterised by a parallel-sided or slightly rounded body and a small, everted rim without any neck or upper body constriction. The rims may be a simple extension of the body without any thickening or can be slightly clubbed. The degree to which the rim is everted may vary: some examples are barely everted but are clubbed and others are not clubbed and are quite broadly everted.

Parallels

In general terms the EROJ type may be similar to Rigby's 'shapeless jar' category although this is such a broad group and the apparent lack of care in manufacture noted by Rigby (2004, 38) was not a general characteristic of the type as defined here. Parallels include Riggs Farm (Challis and Harding 1975, fig. 31.10), Sewerby Cottage (Didsbury 2009b, fig. 176.11), Melton (Didsbury and Vince 2011, fig. 135.10), Creyke Beck (Didsbury unpublished, figs. 20.29; 21.55; 23.83 and 25.128), High Wold, Bridlington (Didsbury 2009a, fig. 22.14) and the A1 Dishforth to Barton road-widening (Cumberpatch unpublished 3).

Dating and distribution

Although EROJ were never common forms they did occur regularly. The single example from Old Ellerby was from a context forming part of Structure 3. In Burton Constable they were commonest in contexts associated with the settlement, notably Structure 5. Examples were also recovered from ditch **118958** but were absent from the other Roman period features. Two EROJ rims were identified at Brandywell: one from Structure 1 and the other from a mid-first- to mid-second-century context. At Nuttles the type was limited in its occurrence to contexts associated with the settlement. Lelley produced one EROJ from Structure 3 and one EROJ type rim from pit **35464**.

Examples were present in the ring gullies and ditches at New York and two EROJ rims were recovered from ditch **4736** at Braemere Hill. At Burstwick, EROJ and EROJ-type sherds were present in pit **51048**, which pre-dated the appearance of wheel-thrown pottery. Sherds from Hull Road were also recovered from contexts lacking wheel-thrown pottery. By contrast, the EROJ sherds from Scorborough Hill were from early Roman features: pit **12081** and the enclosure ditch **12003**. EROJ

sherds from Out Newton Road came from both the pit and the later phase of the enclosure ditch.

Clubbed Rim Open Jar (CROJ)

CROJ was rare type characterised by a round, clubbed rim, on an open or barrel-shaped body, often slightly inturned. The rim was sometimes heavy in relation to the thin walls, as in examples from Brandywell, but sometimes thicker, as at Old Ellerby.

Parallels

Parallels for the CROJ type include South Cave (Challis and Harding 1975, fig. 36.5) but apart from this example the form seems to be a rare one.

Dating and distribution

Clubbed Rim Open Jars were rather less common that the EROJ vessels but occurred widely, if not abundantly. The single example from Old Ellerby is from Structure 2. At Burton Constable, single examples came from Structure 5 and from ditch **118958**. Two CROJ and one possible CROJ were identified in Brandywell from the first- to second-century AD ditches.

Wedge-rim Open Jar (WROJ)

This rare form is characterised by a generally open profile with a slightly constricted neck, and a 'rounded-wedge' internal profile and shallow neck externally. Although the form of the rim is similar to that of other wedge-rim types, the form of the vessel is more open.

Parallels

Challis and Harding have published a single example of a similar vessel from Faxfleet A (1975, Fig 39.3).

Dating and distribution

The WROJ form was so rare as to be either anomalous or a variation on other open jar types and so is considered here rather than with the other vertical rim jar types. There was one example from Brandywell (Fig. 96.89).

Wedge-Rim Globular Jar (WRGJ)

The Wedge-Rim Globular Jar class subsumes Rigby's bead-rim and wedge-rim globular jars as the distinction between the two is not clear (2004, fig. 7). As defined by her, the type is characterised by a short everted rim with the internal angle forming the 'wedge' which gives the type its name. Variations on the basic design include both the size of the vessels and the thickness of the vessel walls. At one extreme, Fig. 97.126 shows a large, thick-walled vessel with a very heavy rim while, in contrast, that shown in Fig. 95.69 is small and thin walled. More elaborate rims (for example Fig. 95.76) also occur occasionally. More commonly, medium-sized vessels with less extreme rim forms represented the type (Figs. 97.128 and 98.157). There is some overlap with everted rim jars and vertical rim jars with short rims and particularly with the wedge-rimmed jars described below.

Parallels

Published parallels for the type include Rigby's wedge-rim globular jar form (2004, figs. 7 and 26.3 and 5), which she dates to the period between 100 BC and 100 AD, and the bead-rim globular jar form with a similar date range. Challis and Harding have identified a similar vessel from South Cave (1975, fig. 36.2) while Didsbury has also published a somewhat similar vessel from Melton (Didsbury and Vince 2011, fig. 137.3) although this latter example is in a shell-tempered fabric (IASH) while the examples from the sites considered here were in H2 and calcite-tempered H1/H4 fabrics. A similar vessel is shown in Evans and Creighton 1999 (fig. 7.18, G32-J02).

Dating and distribution

Wedge-rim Globular jars were present in a number of early features in Old Ellerby including Structures 1, 2 and 3. Numbers were low but the form was notably absent from the large and diverse assemblage associated with third- and fourth-century activity. Numbers of sherds were also low at Burton Constable with a distribution chronologically more or less consistent with that at Old Ellerby. Another late occurrence of the type was in Bluegate Corner where a single sherd was recovered from the enclosure ditches, which also contained wheel-thrown pottery of mid-second- to late third-century date. The type was also present in later prehistoric and early Roman contexts at Lelley Structure 1, pit 12081 at Scorborough Hill, in several features at New York and in one of the ring gullies at Gilcross.

Wedge-rim Jar (WRJ)

The Wedge-rim Jar group has similar rim shapes to the wedge-rim globular jar group and the two could be subsumed into a single type. The principal difference between them is in the shape of the body rather than the rim. Although examples in H2 fabrics were not uncommon, the form was well represented by examples in H1/H4 fabrics.

Parallels

In general terms the type can be compared to the WRGJ vessels described above and also perhaps with two jars

of similar shape but different sizes from Wharram Percy (Didsbury 2004, figs. 105, 106 and 107), South Cave (Challis and Harding 1975, fig. 36.2) and Bridlington to Haisthorpe water pipeline (Cumberpatch unpublished 2, figs. 8 and 16).

Dating and distribution

The Wedge-rim Jar group, although very distinctive in shape, was relatively rare in its occurrence. Only two examples were identified in the assemblage from Old Ellerby, one each from Structures 1 and 2. The larger assemblage from Burton Constable produced examples of WRJ vessels in the vesicular H4 fabric (Fig. 94.53). The majority of examples came from late prehistoric and early Roman features, specifically Structures 1 and 5, including examples in the H4 fabric from gully 9420, with one H4 example, and undated pits. There was also an H4 rim in ditch 118958.

Structure 1 (Fig. 97.116) and pit 35465 at Lelley both produced examples, the latter in H4 fabric. A further example was present in a context associated with Structure 1 in Bluegate Corner while a second sherd from Structure 2 was in the commoner H2 fabric.

Funnel-Rim Jars (FRJ)

Funnel-rim jars form a distinctive group defined by their long, slightly everted rims, usually with flat or rounded lips but sometimes slightly bulged to give a beaded profile. The funnel-shaped profile of the rim is particularly marked when the rim is a long one; the shoulder/body can be rounded or narrow and probably rather pear-shaped. Typical examples are large, of storage jar size, but smaller examples were also identified. Fig. 93.24 shows a very tall example from ditch 3267 at Old Ellerby. The same context included several other examples of a similar form but the rims were not as tall and the lips were slightly flatter. The shorter examples may merge into the VRJ category and this element of overlap means that classification at the margins can be difficult, especially with small rim fragments.

Some of the H4 FRJs have a less pronounced funnel shape than the H2 examples and have been given the suffix (H4) to distinguish them. There are two distinct classes within the H4 group. One group has thin rims with no thickening while the other is closer to vessels in the H2 fabric with, generally, shorter thicker rims. There are examples of thin rims from the fill of ditch 3267 at Old Ellerby, the upper fill of pit 118095 at Burton Constable, as well as an unstratified find from at the south end of that site, and two examples from Bluegate Corner ditch 119970.

The thick group is more heterogeneous in character than the thin group. Pit 3279 at Old Ellerby, the charcoal-rich upper fill of pit 35465 at Lelley, and ditch 117024, to the west of New York provided typical examples, while an example from the lowest fill of intervention **9283** through ditch **118933** at Burton Constable has an unusual rim/lip with a flange. At the same site, the upper fill of the south-eastern terminal of Structure 5 produced an odd example, with a longer rim, and no clubbed lip.

Parallels

Parallels for the FRJ type are numerous and the form seems to have been both a popular and long-lived one, both factors which may account for the high degree of diversity in the rim shape and vessel size. Challis and Harding have published examples from Pale End (1975, fig. 46.1 and 4) and from Levisham Moor sites A and D (figs. 50.11 and 49.2). The form resembles three of Rigby's types; the flared-rim shouldered jar (2004, 39, fig. 6), the deep-flared shouldered jar (2004, 39, fig. 7) and possibly the necked jar (2004, 40, fig. 7). Didsbury has examples similar to the type as defined here from High Wold, Bridlington (2009a, fig. 23.23: with a distinctive internal flange on the lip) and Sewerby Cottage (2009b, fig. 177.30 (in H4) and 36 (in H2)).

It is of particular interest that the type is also present at the Romano-British site of Shiptonthorpe (Evans 2006, examples include: figs. 7.8: G01.1; 7.9: G01.2HM, G03.1; 7.10: G13.1, G27.4, G27.2B, G51.1A; and 7.11: G52.1.). The considerable range of variation in the Shiptonthorpe assemblage reflects the observed variation in the assemblages discussed here. Similar vessels are illustrated in the type series based upon the assemblage from Hawling Road, Market Weighton (Evans and Creighton 1999, see for example, figs. 7.17: G28-J01; 7.18: G60-J03). The references to Knapton type jars in both of these reports refers back to the vessels published by Corder and Kirk (1932, specifically fig. 30.1 to 9 inclusive). The relationship between the production of Knapton type and related wares (all in calcite tempered H1/H4 fabrics) and the production of the pottery used on pre-Roman Iron Age and Roman period 'native' sites (on the evidence from the sites considered here, principally quartz and rock tempered) requires further work.

Dating and distribution

Among the most distinctive of vessel types, with many parallels from other sites in the region, the Funnel-rim Jar form was identified in many of the sites considered here. The largest numbers came from Old Ellerby and Burton Constable. FRJ and FRJ-type vessels, including examples in the H4 fabric, were present consistently in contexts from Structures 1, 2 and 3 at Old Ellerby, through to the third to fourth-century features. The distribution in Burton Constable was similarly broad although they generally occurred as single examples from a feature, with the exceptions of Structure 5 and Ditch **118958** which contained 19 and 171 sherds respectively.

The distribution in Brandywell was also wide with twelve rim sherds in the first- and second-century ditches. A similar pattern can be seen in Nuttles where a general distribution across the major features, including the settlement, includes ten rim sherds from the late second-century ditches. All but one of the examples from Scorborough Hill were concentrated in pit **12081**, including a group of eighteen FRJ rims alongside other late forms including lugged jars and fine VRSJ vessels. At Lelley, nine examples were identified in contexts associated with Structure 1, with two, in H4 fabrics, from pit **35465**. There were two examples from Bluegate Corner, one in an unusual H3 fabric. Gilcross, New York, Braemere Hill and Burstwick also produced small numbers.

Globular jars and Barrel-shaped jars

The globular jar or barrel-shaped jar category is a broad one and encompasses a good deal of variability in size and in the details of rim shapes. The barrel jars, lacking any rim shape other than a plain termination, are the simplest form and merge into the open jar form at one extreme. The globular jars are rather more inturned than the barrel jars and have a variety of rim shapes which have been codified below although the degree of variability within each group should not be underestimated: the variations noted below can be seen as points on a continuum rather than strict distinctions.

Barrel Jar (BJ)

The term 'barrel jar' has been applied here in a slightly more restricted sense than that used by Didsbury (unpublished) and refers to a plain jar form with a rounded inturned rim forming the termination of a barrel-shaped body, as shown in Rigby's schematic illustration (2004, fig. 4). Other types of vessels may have barrel-shaped bodies but show a variety of different rim forms and so have been defined as separate types. This definition also sets barrel jars apart from globular jars which have a much more rounded body form, again with a variety of rim shapes.

Parallels

Parallels for the barrel jars are numerous and include Atwick and West Furze (Challis and Harding 1975, figs. 29:1 and 38.6, respectively), Dalton Parlours (Sumpter 1990, fig. 94.5), The Pit Site, Burton Agnes (Rigby 2004, fig. 16:1 and 3), Tuft Hill (Rigby 2004, figs. 35.2 and 50.11), Hanging Cliff (Rigby 2004, fig. 76.11), Melton (Didsbury and Vince 2011, figs. 135.2 and 5; 136.2 and 152.5), Creyke Beck (Didsbury unpublished, fig. 23.91) and High Wold, Bridlington (Didsbury 2009a, fig. 23.21). Further examples were identified in features excavated on the line of the Bridlington to Haisthorpe pipeline (Cumberpatch unpublished 2) and the A1 Dishforth to

Barton road widening scheme (Cumberpatch unpublished 3, figs. 5, 8). The broad range of sites with similar vessels appears to reflect the very long life span of this vessel type.

Dating and distribution

Barrel jars have a history stretching back to the Bronze Age and although Rigby dates their occurrence in East Yorkshire to the period 900 to 400 BC (2004, 31-34), their widespread occurrence on the sites considered here suggests that the type continued in use through the late pre-Roman Iron Age into the early Roman period and possibly later. Didsbury notes that 'the form is of little diagnostic value, being widespread in Iron Age regional assemblages, particularly from the third century BC' (unpublished, 25) while Challis and Harding (1975, 74) also see the type as having a much longer lifespan than that suggested by Rigby.

No barrel jars were positively identified at Old Ellerby although a small number of body sherds described as 'ovoid jars' may be from jars of this type. Barrel jars were widely present in Burton Constable, with four vessels each identified from Structures 4 and 5 and three from pit **9665**. Single examples were present in ditches **118970** and **118958**, and in pits **118975** and **118468**. Enclosures 4 and 6, both of which included late Roman material, each produced rim sherds, two in the case of Enclosure 4.

A date range up to early Roman would encompass the examples from New York, Braemere Hill, Patrington, Weeton, Gilcross, Scorborough Hill, Out Newton Road and Hull Road, while those from Churchlands and possibly Bluegate Corner were from contexts containing wheel-thrown pottery of up to late second- to third-century date.

Everted Rim Globular Jar (ERGJ)

Everted rim globular jars (ERGJ) were a rare but distinctive form, closely related to the ERJ group and with a passing similarity to some of the smaller VRGJ types. The form was characterised by a small everted rim on a wide-shouldered globular body.

Parallels

Parallels for the ERGJ group were not numerous but include examples from Reighton By-pass (Cumberpatch unpublished 1, fig. 23.61) and East Field, Burton Agnes (Rigby 2004, fig. 26.1).

Dating and distribution

Only Lelley and Patrington produced examples: both examples from Lelley came from contexts associated with the Structure 3 and the single example from Patrington (Fig. 98.143) was associated with the settlement. Rigby's dating of the example from East Field places the type in the period around 100 BC to AD 100.

Beaded Rim Globular jar (BRGJ)

Beaded Rim Globular jars are distinguished from the other classes of small globular jar by the presence of a small, distinct beaded rim.

Parallels

Parallels for the BRGJ type were not numerous but included the A1 Dishforth to Barton road widening (Cumberpatch unpublished 3, fig. 4), Wharram Percy (Didsbury 2004, figs. 103.60, 62 and 63 (with perhaps less rounded bodies) and 105.106 and 107), Great Ayton Moor (Challis and Harding 1975, fig. 46.12 and Creyke Beck (Didsbury unpublished, fig. 26.136).

Dating and distribution

The form was commonest at Burton Constable where it occurred in Structure 5, pits **118523** (Fig. 95.70) and **118712**, and ditch **118958**. At Dimlington Road, a single sherd came from the later ditches. Other sites produced smaller numbers of examples: Brandywell, Nuttles and pit **12081** at Scorborough Hill.

Hammer-Head Rim Globular jar (HHRGJ)

The Hammer-head Rim Globular Jar form is a variant on the globular jar type distinguished by the rim profile, which is elongated both internally and externally. The angle of the hammerhead can vary from flat to inclined, and examples of all types are included among the illustrated vessels.

Parallels

Published parallels for the type seem to be limited to Creyke Beck (Didsbury unpublished, fig. 26.138), Wharram Percy (Didsbury 2004, fig. 104.94), High Wold, Bridlington (Didsbury 2009a, fig. 24.47) and possibly Rudston Roman villa (Rigby 1980, fig. 37.134) although the latter example has a rather less elaborate rim than some of the examples considered here.

Dating and distribution

A highly distinctive but rare form, the Hammer-head Rim Globular Jar, was identified on only three sites, Old Ellerby, Burton Constable and New York. It was commonest in Burton Constable and the presence of seven examples compared with only one each from Old Ellerby and New York is interesting but not readily explicable. The sherd from New York (Fig. 97.127) was from one of the pits dated to the early Roman period by the presence of wheel-thrown pottery, while that from Old Ellerby (Fig. 93.37) was from Structure 2. In chronological terms this is consistent with all but one of the occurrences in Burton Constable. The exception, perhaps inevitably, is the late ditch **118958**, with its large residual component. The other occurrences are in Structures 1, 3, 4 (Fig. 95.73) and 5 (Fig. 95.66), and pits **118198** and **9140** (Fig. 95.67). The generally consistent impression is that the type was use in the late pre-Roman and early Roman periods.

Triangular Rim Jar (TriRJ)

This type shows a range of very distinctive rim shapes ranging from angular to rounded, but having a triangular profile in cross-section. Rim orientation may vary from almost vertical to everted.

Parallels

Published parallels for this form, or range of similar forms, were sparse. A vessel from Rudston Roman villa (Rigby 1980, fig. 37.132) appeared to be similar to the example from Burton Constable (Fig. 94.62) although possibly with a wider shoulder. No parallel for the more elaborate example from Old Ellerby was located.

Dating and distribution

The distinctive form occurred in chronologically diverse contexts although in relatively small numbers. At Old Ellerby, the type was present in contexts associated with Structure 2 (Fig. 93.33). Two examples were present in the large ditches related to third- or fourth-century activity. A similarly broad date range was seen in Burton Constable where the occurrence of the type in Structures 1, 5 and Structure 6, and in a series of pits associated with the settlement phase as well as in ditch **118958**. The assemblage from Brandywell consisted of just two rim sherds, one from Structure 1 and one from the second-century enclosure ditch.

Lugged jar (LJ)

Lugged jars were identified by the lugs or lug fragments, which, being solid and robust, survived well as identifiable fragments. Unfortunately none formed part of a reconstructable vessel and so the relationship of lugs and vessel types remains uncertain, although evidence from elsewhere suggests that everted rim and barrel-shaped forms were involved.

The majority of lugs had rounded profiles although there were exceptions, notably an example from Scorborough Hill which had a distinctive pointed shape (Fig. 99.159) paralleled at Ramsdale Park, Nottinghamshire (Elsdon 1996, B.6a:31), Rillington, Levisham Moor (Challis and Harding 1975, figs. 37.5 and 49.5 respectively) and less closely at Nafferton (Rigby 2004, fig. 63.7) with the latter vessel being closer to another example from Scorborough Hill (Fig. 99.160). Other lugs had the rounded shape similar to the example shown in Fig.

99.161, which seems to be the commonest variant. One lug from Dimlington Road (Fig. 99.178) was unusual in being oriented horizontally rather than vertically. No parallel has yet been traced for this vessel.

Parallels

Parallels for the vertical lugged jars were common and, in addition to the examples noted above, also included Great Kendal, Rillington, Thornton Dale (Challis and Harding 1975, figs. 27.7, 37.5 and 51.4 respectively), Rudston Roman villa (Rigby 1980, figs. 37.128; 50.267 and 268; and 53.310 and 311), Wharram Percy (Didsbury 2004, figs. 104.97 and 157.392), Hanging Cliff (Rigby 2004, fig. 83.4), Nafferton (Rigby 2004, fig. 63.7), Bridlington to Haisthorpe water pipeline (Cumberpatch unpublished 2, figs. 52 and 54) and Reighton By-pass (Cumberpatch unpublished 1, fig. 23.66).

Dating and distribution

Lugged jars are unusual in being one of the few vessel types to have a reasonably consistent date range attached to them. Rigby has suggested that the type dates to the period 400 BC onwards but, although she places it in two of her typological groupings (400 to 100 BC and 100 BC to AD 100), she notes elsewhere (2004, 40) that it 'continued to be popular until the end of the Roman period'. This late date is consistent with the evidence from the Bridlington to Haisthorpe water pipeline where lug fragments occurred consistently in association with wheel-thrown pottery of third- and fourth-century date (Cumberpatch unpublished 2). At Wharram Percy, a rounded lug handle was dated to the period between the late Iron Age and the second century AD (Didsbury 2004, 316).

Lugged jars were not a common form. Two features in Burton Constable produced fragments of lug-handled jars. These were Structure 5 and ditch **118921** (Fig. 94.45), a component of the late third- to early fourth-century AD Enclosure 11. Brandywell produced a single lug fragment from the first- to second-century AD ditch system. A similar, perhaps slightly narrower, date range also applies to pit **12081** in Scorborough Hill, which contained at least seven and possibly nine fragments. It is interesting to note the numbers of lugged jars, both hand-made and wheel-thrown, associated with the wells at the Rudston Roman villa (Rigby 1980) and at Dalton Parlours (Sumpter 1990, 235-245). Gully **120170** at Weeton, the Iron Age pit at Out Newton Road and ditch **120937** at Dimlington (Fig. 99.178) produced only single sherds.

Lid-seated jars (LSJ)

Lid-seated jars were not a common form in any of the assemblages and those rims that were identified as of this type formed a diverse group which included very fine examples with burnished surfaces to coarse rock tempered examples. As such they barely constituted a discrete group. Given the probability that the form seems to be an earlier rather than a later Iron Age one, as discussed below, their scarcity may be a reflection of the fact that most of the sites appeared to be of later Iron Age date. One possible ceramic lid was identified at Out Newton Road (Fig. 99.171). This took the form of part of an irregular disc, perhaps with part of a central lug or handle.

Parallels

Lid-seated rim jars appeared to be a regular if not a common form across eastern Yorkshire. Examples include those from Rudston Roman villa (Rigby 1980, fig. 27.1), Melton (Didsbury and Vince 2011, fig. 137.6 and 7), Creyke Beck (Didsbury unpublished, 27, figs. 20.34, 22.73, and 23.76 and 86) and Hanging Cliff (Rigby 2004, figs. 75.3 and 4; 76.8; and 78.2; see also Rigby 2004, 39 for further discussion).

Dating and distribution

Like the lugged jars, lid-seated rim jars are one of the few vessel forms for which specific and plausible date ranges have been proposed, in this case an earlier Iron Age date (Didsbury 2011, 196), although elsewhere there seems to be evidence that the form was somewhat longer-lived (Didsbury unpublished, 27).

The type was rare, examples being found on only two of the sites. In the case of Burton Constable, single examples were identified from the fill of ditch 118103 (Fig. 95.75), from Structure 5 and from a nearby pit, 9665 (Fig. 95.74). The sherd from pit 9665 has two large holes through the body below the rim: it is unclear whether these were made pre- or post-firing. The example from Scorborough Hill (Fig. 98.154) was from pit 12081.

Clubbed Rim Jar (CRJ)

Clubbed rim jar is a rather ambiguous and poorly defined type represented by small fragments of round clubbed rims on undefined bodies. Examples in the H4 fabric were characterised by a heavy rounded clubbed rim on the neck and wall with considerable variation between examples. One of the examples from Burton Constable had a rim decorated with angled finger impressions.

Parallels

The closest parallels for the form appeared to be from Lincolnshire with similar clubbed rim jars from Old Sleaford (Elsdon 1997, figs. 51.5, 10 and 14; and 58.79) and Dragonby (May 1996, figs. 19.26:120; and 19.28:170 and 171).

Dating and distribution

In addition to the decorated sherd from Burton Constable Structure 5 (Fig. 94.58), there was a second example at the site from ditch 118958 (Fig. 94.51). A sherd from Brandywell was an unstratified surface find. Examples from Nuttles and from Dimlington Road were both from contexts lacking wheel-thrown pottery, suggesting a late pre-Roman date, broadly consistent with the parallels from Lincolnshire.

Bowls and dishes

Bowls are a rare form in Iron Age assemblages from the area (Didsbury unpublished, 24): this makes the few definite examples which were positively identified of particular interest. The individual examples are shallow bowls or dishes but their profiles differed in a number of respects.

Parallels

It is notable that Rigby does not include any bowl forms in her general typology (2004), but in her account of the coarse wares from Rudston Roman villa, she includes a number of hand-made bowls in both Fabric 1 (= H2) and Fabric 2 (= H1/H4), notably Figs. 28.16; 30.29; 34.82; and 52.302 in addition to wheel-thrown examples. Two hand-made examples have been published by Didsbury (2009, fig. 177.21 and 22) but neither resembles the examples discussed here to any great extent. Chance finds from Flixton (Challis and Harding 1975, fig. 38.10) included a shallow bowl but again the resemblance to the examples discussed here was limited.

Dating and distribution

Three examples positively identified include an unstratified surface find from Nuttles (Fig. 96.94). At Bluegate Corner, a bowl (Fig. 98.144) was recovered from fill 119984 of ditch 120665, the earlier fills of which produced a wide range of hand-made pottery, mainly in fine H2 fabrics although fill 119984 also contained wheel-thrown pottery of late third- to fourth-century date. A bowl was present within the large assemblage from pit 12081 at Scorborough Hill (Fig. 98.156). Generally, it would seem that the bowls date to the Roman period and it might be argued did not form part of the traditional range of local wares, although these three examples were hand-made in standard local fabrics.

Bases

The classification of bases followed the typology set out by Knight (1998) with flat bases being distinguished from solid pedestal bases and both from ring-foot or hollow pedestal (H-Ped) bases. Some of the flat bases, particularly from Old Ellerby, showed clear evidence of manufacture, with the break lines indicating that the bases were made separately from the bodies and attached by smoothing the internal surfaces of the wall slabs to the base plates.

The flat and solid pedestal bases were both relatively simple forms but the ring foot and splayed pedestal bases imply rather more effort in the manufacture and finishing and probably belonged to 'fineware' VRSJ vessels (Figs. 92.17; 96.98 and 138). Few complete vessel profiles were recovered making it difficult to link ring foot bases with specific vessel types (but see Figs. 95.79 and 97.111) though the majority were in fine fabrics and with carefully finished smoothed or burnished surfaces. No functional or practical use for the ring foot could be adduced and it seems probable that these were the equivalent of tablewares.

The second distinctive type are flat bases perforated with a single hole, usually in the centre, or, more rarely, a double hole. They did not have the multiple small holes seen in Roman 'cheese presses' or early modern and recent stoneware colanders. The size and position of the hole gave them an unsettling resemblance to a modern flowerpot and it is perhaps not beyond the bounds of possibility that they were intended for the propagation of plants. A more plausible suggestion is that the perforated vessels were intended to be used as strainers, probably in combination with a wad of hay or straw placed inside the pot which would act as the filter while the hole allowed liquid to drain away (Gareth Perry, pers. comm.). In an Anglo-Saxon context it has been argued that such vessels were used in the brewing of beer (Perry, pers. comm.) but clearly they could have had a variety of domestic uses in addition to or as well as brewing.

Parallels

Parallels for the ring foot or hollow pedestal bases and splayed or pedestal bases appear to be rare in eastern Yorkshire. Rigby omits them entirely from her classification (2004, figs. 5 to 7) and they are also absent from Challis and Harding's catalogue. As with the decorated pottery discussed below, the best parallels seem to be from Lincolnshire and the east Midlands, although it should be emphasised that the vessel fabrics appear to be local ones. Parallels from Dragonby (May 1996) include figs. 19.27:141 and 157; 19.35:293; 19.39:351, 19.43:423, and 19.62:763 and 770-72. In the case of the latter examples it should be emphasised that, with one possible exception, none of the bases were decorated. Parallels for perforated bases include Bridlington to Haisthorpe water pipeline (Cumberpatch unpublished 2, fig. 45).

Dating and distribution

The type was rare with only four examples being positively identified, from Old Ellerby, New York (Fig.

97.118) and Scorborough Hill. Of these, the example from Old Ellerby was from the fill of late fourth-century pit **3040**. The example from Scorborough Hill was from pit **12081**.

Unusual and individual vessels and objects

From Old Ellerby, an ERJ type vessel with an unusual profile, a thin, sharply everted rim on a prominent angular shoulder (Fig. 93.31), may be a variant on the BRSJ type. No parallels are known for an unusual variant on a Vertical Rim Jar or Open Jar form with a heavy, clubbed rim on a vestigial neck and narrow body of uncertain form (Fig. 93.40). A small irregular thumb pot with a bevelled rim and finger impressions externally, from Burton Constable (Fig. 94.43) is paralleled by an example from Bridlington to Haisthorpe water pipeline (Cumberpatch unpublished 2, fig. 46). Burton Constable also produced a carefully finished 'teardrop' shaped solid lug or handle with shallow grooves across the top (Fig. 94.47) and a flat-topped clubbed rim on a rounded body (Fig. 95.83), possibly a variant on the VRJ-CS type.

An odd bowl or jar rim from Lelley had a pronounced internal angle and wide square-lipped everted rim (Fig. 97.117) though the body form is not clear. No parallels have been found for two pieces from Patrington: a short hollow tube handle (Fig. 98.136) and an unusual wide rim of uncertain form with three shallow grooves on the top (Fig. 98.142). An unidentified object broken into several non-joining parts from Gilcross (Fig. 99.64) is similar to an example at Old Ellerby.

Decorated vessels

Decoration is rare on pottery of later prehistoric date in eastern Yorkshire (Didsbury 2004, 148-9) and the assemblages from the sites considered here are no exception to this general rule. But decorated vessels were not unknown and included some finely finished examples bearing designs similar to those on pottery from Lincolnshire and the east Midlands. In addition, a number of sherds bore ambiguous marks which could have been deliberate or accidental: single incised or impressed lines; haphazard fingertip or fingernail marks; and signs of pinching, especially on rim sherds. Smoothed and burnished surfaces can also be considered as decoration and have been mentioned in the vessel form type series, as they seem to relate to specific vessel types. They were particularly notable in the case of the smaller and finer vessels such as the VRSJs and vessels with hollow pedestal or ring-foot bases which were typically burnished externally.

The meaning and significance of decoration on pottery has been widely debated but such discussions generally deal with situations where decoration is the norm rather than, as in the present case, where it is both rare but also clearly deliberate. It is hard to argue that decoration on the scale seen here could have had a significant role in such issues as the delineation of ethnic or social affiliation or that it could have played a significant apotropaic role in protecting the household or the contents of the pottery vessels. Indeed, the similarity of the decorative motifs with those found in Lincolnshire and the East Midlands would seem to argue explicitly against any role as defining the people of eastern Yorkshire as culturally distinct from other areas. In this respect, the use of pots defines East Yorkshire as significantly different to societies in the area immediately to the west, from modern South and West Yorkshire across the southern Pennines to the Cheshire Plain, where pottery use seems to have been extremely rare. Eastern Yorkshire has much more in common with Lincolnshire and the east Midlands in spite of the apparent role of the Humber as a boundary than it does with the geographically contiguous area to the west.

That the decorated pots were of local manufacture seems to be established by the fact that the fabrics were not in general, of exotic types. Few of the small number of vessels in the H1 Shell fabric were decorated and those in the H4 fabric which were decorated, predominantly with finger-impressed rims, appeared to have been calcite rather than shell tempered suggesting manufacture north of the Humber. An exception is the vessel that provided petrographic sample 02 (Fig. 94. 44) which included poorly preserved shelly material alongside burned out plant matter. A source in Lincolnshire is possible for this vessel. The same may be true of the everted rim jar in a fine H4 fabric from Bluegate Corner (Fig. 98.146) which also appeared to have been shell tempered.

Pending a wider study of the incidence of decorated vessels across eastern Yorkshire, no satisfactory explanation for the appearance of the small number of decorated vessels can be proposed. The apparent competently executed designs, notably those with the incised and impressed designs (IARC; Knight 1998), show no signs of experimentation or of being merely copies or imitations of regional imports, quite apart from the absence of evidence for any such imports. The existence of these shared designs appears to contradict other evidence for the insularity of later prehistoric society in the area.

Ring stamps

Two sherds bearing patterns of small repeated ring stamps were identified, at Nuttles (Fig. 96.97) and Burton Constable (Fig. 94.48). In neither case was it possible to determine the larger pattern although they appeared to be different, with the example from Burton Constable forming part of a larger pattern of intersecting lines of rings while the sherd from Old Ellerby featured parallel lines of ring stamps. Specific parallels are rare but include

examples from Weekley in Northamptonshire (Jackson and Dix 1986-7).

Rouletted decoration (single row)

Single rows of rouletted decoration were present on four sherds, one from Old Ellerby (Fig. 92.14) and three from Nuttles (Fig. 96.95, 99 and 101). Two of the examples from Nuttles were extremely similar both in the shape and style of the rouletting and in the fabric and it is possible that they were from the same vessel although they did not join. The other sherd from Nuttles was unusual, not only in combining fine vertical incised lines and fine vertical rouletting but also in its bright orange colour, which was generally rare. The sherd from Old Ellerby differed in that the decoration included only a single line of fine rouletting between and parallel to fine vertical incised lines.

Impressed linear and rouletted decoration

The most elaborate example of a decorated vessel, from Burton Constable (Fig. 94.44) bore composite decoration consisting of double square-ended rouletting (see Knight 2010, 263 for a description of the technique) with impressed lines, including linear infill. The sherd was too small for the full complexity of the design to be apparent but similar composite designs are known from a variety of sites across Lincolnshire and the north-east Midlands: notably Dragonby, Old Sleaford, Grimsby and Salmonby (Challis and Harding 1975; May 1996; Elsdon 1997). Of the vessels sampled for petrographic analysis, this vessel was the only one for which a non-local origin is likely (Ixer, this volume, sample P02).

Impressed linear decoration

The broad category of impressed linear decoration covers shallow grooves and lines with a rounded profile. While some of these lines clearly formed parts of larger designs, others were apparently haphazard and could well have been accidental: it was not always easy to make this distinction. Of the deliberate designs, the majority were from Burton Constable (Fig. 94.46, 50 and 52), with single examples from Old Ellerby and Brandywell, both of which were small and indistinct. Both curvilinear and rectilinear designs are represented. The haphazardly occurring impressed lines are a relatively common occurrence generally. Along with the much more extensive evidence of smoothing and burnishing, and perhaps even the use of coarse and hyper-coarse rock inclusions, this suggests that the surface appearance of pottery vessels was not without significance, even where it was not reflected in complex designs and motifs.

Impressed line and cordon

A group of sherds, from the terminal of Structure 1 at Lelley, probably from no more than one or two vessels, had complex decoration, including an impressed diamond grid pattern on the neck and a cordoned profile (Fig. 96.110 and 112). The sherds included the rim, neck, parts of the body and hollow pedestal or ring foot base. The underside of the base bore faint burnished lines which may have formed part of a design similar to those seen on the underside of bases from Dragonby (May 1996, fig. 19.17). Cordoned or corrugated profile vessels without decoration occur elsewhere including Creyke Beck (Didsbury unpublished, fig. 21.54). Petrographic analysis showed that its composition was distinctive, with significant quantities of fine grog, but that it was most probably of local manufacture (Ixer, this volume, sample P01).

Incised line and dot

Sherds with incised line and dot decoration were present at four sites. The most complex examples, from Brandywell (Fig. 96.84) and Nuttles (Fig. 96.96), closely resembled the IARC patterns defined by Knight (1998, 14) and are comparable to examples from Dragonby, although with the spaces between the incised lines infilled with dots. In contrast the examples from Old Ellerby (Fig. 92.13) have a 'running scroll' design similar to examples from Weekley in Northamptonshire but without the impressed dots. The sherd from Churchlands (Fig. 98.134) was unusual in apparently being the work of less accomplished craftsmanship. The incision was shallower and the lines were less assured in their execution. In this respect it seemed to resemble an example from Breedon-on-the-Hill (as illustrated by Challis and Harding 1975, fig. 13.10) but with short lines joining the main lines instead of the lines of dots seen on the Breedon example.

Combed, cordoned and cord-impressed decoration

No precise parallel has been traced. A single sherd, from Scorborough Hill, decorated with combing (Fig. 98.149). This small sherd had five fine combed lines externally. One vessel, from Out Newton Road, was decorated with a raised cordon; unusually among the decorated vessels, this was in a calcite tempered H4 fabric. It is probably of earlier date than the majority of the sherds considered in this report and it may even date to the Late Bronze Age. A vessel with cord-impressed decoration from Bluegate Corner (Fig. 98.146) was a finely finished everted rim jar in a very fine H4 fabric with a burnished surface. Although cord impressions seem to be commoner on earlier prehistoric pottery vessels, this example appeared to be of a later pre-Roman Iron Age type.

Pinched decoration

The most distinctive of the decorated vessels were those with pinched or 'pinch and twist' decoration. These vessels, generally in sandier textured fabrics than those of other decorated vessels, were commonest at Scorborough Hill (Fig. 98.151) although the most complete example was from Old Ellerby (Fig. 92.2). Another small sherd was present at Nuttles. The distinctive body finish was characterised by pinching, generally all over the surface. When a twist has been given to the pinching, the result is a very characteristic 'pinch and twist' pattern. Impressions of the potter's fingernails were clearly visible in several examples. Parallels for this technique are surprisingly sparse. Pinched decoration has been recorded from Scarborough Castle (Challis and Harding 1975, figs. 42 and 44) although only as decoration on raised cordons. A closer parallel may be Billingborough in Lincolnshire (Elsdon 1996, C2.2a:435, 346) which is dated to the late Bronze Age or early Iron Age. The examples discussed here were predominantly from contexts containing wheel-thrown pottery of Romano-British date and identifiable vessel forms were of later prehistoric type (VRJ, VRJ-FSG), although the dating of individual vessel forms remains difficult.

Herring bone impressed rims

Three angular VRJ-CS rims from Brandywell (Fig. 96. 84, 86 and 87) were decorated with very distinctive deeply impressed double herringbone patterns. No direct parallels could be traced although decorated rims are one of the few kinds of decorative motif to appear with any regularity in eastern Yorkshire. Although all from the same context, the sherds appeared to be from different vessels.

Finger impressed rims

Decoration of the types described above is generally rare, but finger impressed rims occur regularly, if not commonly, across eastern Yorkshire. Rims with finger impressions, in some case barely of sufficient depth and size to be deliberate, but in others certainly so, were present at Burton Constable (Fig. 94.52, 54 and 56) and Braemere Hill (Fig. 97.129). Two distinct sub-types were identified; angled finger impressions across all or part of a clubbed or thickened rim and round finger-tip impressions on the top of a clubbed or thickened rim. Variation in the techniques give slightly different results so there are few identical patterns but the general distinction seems to be replicated across the area and beyond (Rigby 2004, 27-8).

Examples of angled finger impressions from elsewhere in the region include Creyke Beck (Didsbury unpublished, figs. 20.24; 25.123; 28.179 and 187), Atwick and Garton Slack, (Challis and Harding 1975, figs. 29.3 and 53.3 respectively). Examples of round finger-tip impressions include Faxfleet A and Burradon I (Challis and Harding 1975, figs. 40.3 and 53.3 respectively) and Melton (Didsbury and Vince 2009, fig. 137.1). More generally examples have been discussed by Knight in the context of the assemblages from Market Deeping (2010b, 262) while Elsdon has drawn attention to the incidence of finger impressions of the rims of Scored ware vessels (1992, 84). Evans's distribution maps, which include vessels with finger-tip decorated rims (1995, figs. 5.3, 5.9) would now seem to be in need of updating to take account of the considerable amount of new work.

Tool impressed rims

A small number of vessel rims were decorated with tool marks. In examples from Burstwick and Patrington, these took the form of angled impressions on the top of the rim (Fig. 98.139). A shallow groove around the top of a rim from Scorborough Hill could be a further example. Such tool impressions are known from other sites, including Saltshouse School, Costa Beck (Challis and Harding 1975, figs. 41.4 and 51.11, respectively) and Wharram Percy (Didsbury 2004, 22).

Other decoration

An unusual raised circular design element on a sherd from gully 25247 at Brandywell is presumably decorative although it is unclear which part of the vessel was represented. The same could be said of deep stamped impressions on a sherd from New York (Fig. 97.119): no overall motif was identifiable. A sherd from Gilcross (Fig. 99.142) bore closely spaced stabbed decoration all over the external surface.

Scored ware

Scored ware (Elsdon 1992, Knight 2010, 262-3) was identified at Burton Constable and Burstwick, but the most notable example was from Churchlands. This had a scored surface combined with shallow parallel incised lines on the external surface (Fig. 98.135; *cf* Knight 2010, fig. 138.38 and 41). The sherd had been reused after breakage as a pot disc, one of many identified (see 'Pot discs' below) but the only one to be decorated.

Decoration and chronology

The limited numbers of examples precludes detailed analysis of the date range of decoration on later prehistoric pottery but several independent opinions seem to be in broad agreement: Didsbury's discussion of the incidence of decorated pottery at Wharram Percy (2004, 148-9) and the evidence from Hawling Road (Evans and Creighton 1999, figs. 7.16 and 7.17) point to a range spanning the end of the prehistoric period and the first century AD, broadly consistent with the conclusions of Challis and Harding (1975, 95) and Knight's Late La Tène phase (2002).

There are clear examples of residual assemblages from later features on a number of the sites considered in this report, presenting difficulties in elucidating the chronology of the decorated pottery from independent dating evidence. This is particularly so at Old Ellerby, where all but two of the decorated vessels were associated with wheel-thrown pottery, in four cases with types dated to the third century or later.

Relatively few of the decorated sherds from Burton Constable were associated with datable material other than sherds from Structure 5. Two sherds from Brandywell, neither of them bearing anything more than an impressed line, were associated with wheel-thrown pottery, of late first- to early second-century date. Other, more elaborate designs were undatable, at least by association. A similar date range is applicable to the comb-impressed sherd from Nuttles. The assemblage from pit 12081 in Scorborough Hill included a number of decorated sherds, the majority from contexts containing wheel-thrown pottery of mid- or late first- and early second-century date. No wheel thrown pottery was associated with the decorated sherds from New York, Braemere Hill, Burstwick, Churchlands, Patrington, Gilcross or Dimlington Road.

Overall, while the evidence is sparse, it seems that it may support a generally early date prior to, or within, the first and second centuries, consistent with the opinions expressed by other authors. The few cases at odds with this conclusion may indicate survival of decoration on hand-made pottery into the third or fourth century but are more likely to be examples of residuality.

Decoration: discussion

A high proportion of the decorated sherds could not be attributed to specific vessel types. This included some of the more complex rouletted and incised types of decoration. In one case (Fig. 97.110, possibly also 112) the vessel type, a cordoned beaker, seemed to be unique amongst the assemblages considered here. Impressed linear decoration was associated with VRJ-FSG forms (Fig. 94.52 and 50) and possibly with a VRSJ. One sherd bearing incised line and dot decoration (Fig. 96.85) was on an ERJ type vessel as was a rouletted pattern (Fig. 96.95) but other complex designs were associated only with body sherds.

Two of the three examples of the distinctive 'pinch and twist' decoration were associated with VRJs (Fig. 92.2) and one with a VRJ-FSG (Fig. 98.151). Other vessels appeared, from the curvature of the body sherds, to be medium-sized jars. Herring-bone impressed, finger- and tool-impressed rims were associated with medium and larger sized jars including VRJ-CS (Fig. 96.84, 86 and 87), FRJ, VRJ, ERJ, CRJ(H4) and EROJ forms. Finger-tip impressions were associated with FRJ rims but also occurred on ERJ, VRJ and EROJ forms.

The distribution of decorated pottery can be described generally as broad but sparse and the numbers of examples from individual site assemblages seem to be proportionate to the size of the assemblages: decorated vessels, while rare, were not concentrated on specific settlements. Patterning within individual plots was difficult to discern. Large assemblages, specifically those associated with Structure 5 in Burton Constable and pit **12081** at Scorborough Hill, included several examples of decorated sherds: this may be the result of chance although in other cases, notably ditch **118958**, the numbers seemed low in comparison with the size of the assemblage. Extensive excavation of Iron Age and Roman period settlements in their entirety will be needed to provide definitive answers.

Pot discs

Pot discs, also known as pottery roundels, gaming pieces or counters, are a common find on archaeological sites of all periods. Made from fragments of broken vessels, rather than being purpose-made, they vary in quality from roughly circular to ovoid to sub-rectangular objects with chipped edges to carefully finished discs with ground or polished edges. They are regularly found on medieval, post-medieval, early modern and recent sites in north-east England (Cumberpatch 2011) and are widespread on Iron Age sites across Europe, including Stradonice in Bohemia, Velem Szent Vid in Hungary and Aulnat in central France (Cumberpatch 1991, Collis pers. comm.). It came as little surprise to find them occurring equally regularly on the sites considered here. One example is made from a decorated sherd (Fig. 98.135) but the majority are from undistinguished body sherds. The quality of manufacture varied: one example from Burton Constable shows every sign of having been carefully finished while others were only roughly chipped to an approximate disc. They vary widely in size; the largest sub-rectangular examples are 120 by 94mm and 120 by 92mm, and the largest sub-circular example 95 by 90mm. The two smallest are 28.5 by 22.7mm and 26 by 25.5mm.

The most frequent explanation for these discs is that they were used for playing games or gambling although no definite examples of such a use have been documented, even in eighteenth- or nineteenth-century contexts. Explanations such as their use as missiles to scare birds from crops seem over complex, as pebbles or small stones would be equally appropriate and readily available on ploughed fields or in stream beds. The apparently haphazard variation in size would seem to rule out games such as chess in which the character of individual pieces is important, but may not preclude simpler games. Perhaps the oddest factor is that this tradition of using broken potsherds persisted from at least the first millennium BC until the late nineteenth century AD while the actual manufacture of clay discs

in their own right was not, to the best of the author's knowledge, ever substituted, in spite of the fact that it would have been a simple matter.

Repair holes

It is often assumed that the rather crude and utilitarian appearance of the hand-made pottery meant that it was of little value. The fact that a number of sherds bore deliberately bored holes, apparently intended to allow a broken vessel to be repaired, would seem to cast some doubt on this theory. There was no evidence for the use of metal rivets and it would seem that the pots were 'stitched' with some type of perishable material. Only seven examples were positively identified. It may be significant that two of the three rim sherds with repair holes were lid-seated jars, believed to be an early form. The only other form to be identified was an open jar. Five out of the seven vessels identified were in H2 Fine fabrics. Similar examples of perforated vessels include that illustrated by Didsbury (2010: fig. 130.1).

Vessel size

The fragmentation of the assemblages, the difficulty of reassembling individual vessels on more than an occasional basis and the difficulties of measuring the diameter of hand-made vessels with any accuracy precluded any detailed investigation of vessel size. It seemed clear, intuitively, that there were distinct vessel size classes within the assemblages and that certain stylistic traits, notably vertical and near-vertical rims, crossed these size classes while others, such as globular jars, were more limited in their occurrence. Data on vessel rim diameter and the percentage of the rim surviving were collected primarily to make such data available to future researchers and EVE calculations form part of the site archive. Rim diameters have been used here as a proxy for a more comprehensive measure of size such as vessel volume (*cf* Woodward and Blinkhorn 1997). There are few clear patterns in the data but some apparent trends can be identified.

Among the everted rim jars (ERJ) there seemed to be very little standardisation, with rim diameters varying between 9cm and 31cm although with a possible concentration between 15cm and 22cm. Funnel-rimmed jars (FRJ) also varied widely but seemed to cluster slightly between 14cm and 27cm. The very broad VRJ-FSG category was also diverse but showed a marked concentration between 9cm and 16cm. In contrast, VRJ-CS vessels were somewhat larger with a concentration between 13cm and 27cm with the full range lying between 12cm and 35cm. The finer VRSJ forms varied between 10cm and 19cm, although the majority lay between 10cm and 16cm. No real conclusions can be drawn with regard to the WRGJ vessels which ranged in size between 12cm and 28cm with no two examples

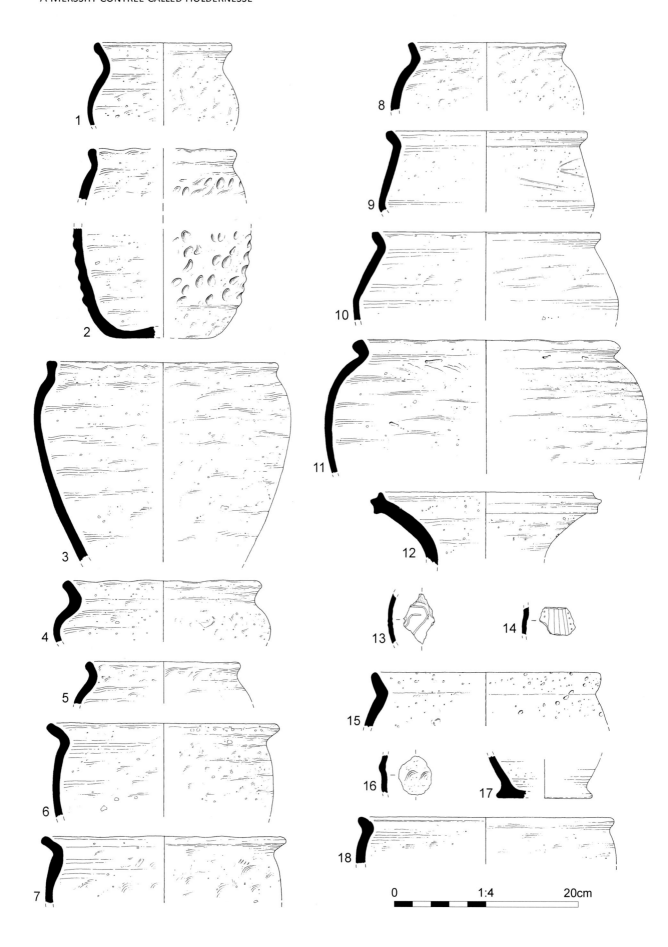

Fig. 92: Hand-made Iron Age tradition pottery, 1-18, Old Ellerby

Illustrated hand-made pottery 1

Old Ellerby

1. FRJ. DISTINCTIVE UNUSUAL H2 TYPE FABRIC, VESICULAR SURFACE, OCC. WHITE NON-CRYSTALLINE GRIT. FILL *3208*, CUT 3191, DITCH 3329

2. VRJ. FINE SANDY H2 BODY, OCCASIONAL ROCK FRAGS. PINCHED ALL OVER; IMPRESSED RIM; *CF* ELSDON 1996 C.2. BLACK DEPOSIT INT. FILL *3208*, FEATURE 3329

3. VRJ-CS. SANDY H2, SPARSE TO MOD. ROCK FRAGS UP TO 6MM, OCC.8MM PINCHED RIM, FLAT TOP. FILL *3134*, PIT 3133

4. ERJ. FINE H2 BODY, MOD. LARGE ANG. QUARTZITE ROCK FRAGS, OCC. V. LARGE GRIT, TO 1.5CM. EVERTED RIM ON SHOULDERED BODY. FILL *3081*, CUT 3061, STRUCTURE 2

5. ERJ. FINE SANDY H2 FABRIC, SPARSE ROUND QUARTZ TO 1MM. PINCHED RIM. FILL *3150*, CUT 3149, DITCH 3125

6. FRJ. SOFT SANDY H2 ROCK FABRIC, PITTED, ABRADED; MOD. WELL-SORTED ANG. ROCK FRAGS TO 4MM. SHARPLY EVERTED WIDE RIM. FILL *3064*, CUT 3063, STRUCTURE 3

7. FRJ. SANDY H2 FABRIC, SPARSE ROUNDED ROCK FRAGS TO 5MM, LIMITED ABRASION. WIDE FLARED RIM. FILL *3070*, PIT 3069

8. ERJ. HARD, FINE BLACK H2 FABRIC, ROCK FRAGS TO 4MM, MAINLY FINER. EVERTED, SLIGHTLY FUNNEL-SHAPED RIM, SLIGHT INT. ANGLE. FILL *3282*, PIT 3279

9. ERJ. FINE H2 BODY, SPARSE SUB-ANG. QUARTZ 1MM; EVERTED RIM, SLOPING SHOULDER, START OF SHOULDER ANGLE. FILL *3291*, STRUCTURE 2

10. ERJ. FINE SANDY H2 FINE FABRIC, SPARSE SUB-ANG. QUARTZ TO 2MM; SHORT, SLIGHTLY ANGULAR EVERTED RIM. SMOOTHED EXT. ?SAME AS ABOVE. FILL *3156*, TERMINUS, 3155, DITCH 3243

11. ERJ. H2 FABRIC. SHORT EVERTED ROUNDED RIM ON A GLOBULAR BODY; BLACK DEPOSIT ON SHOULDER ONLY. BURNISHED EXT; NOT ABRADED. FILLS *3180&3291&3306*, STRUCTURE 2

12. UNIQUE JAR. SLAB-BUILT FLARED RIM JAR OR ?BOWL FORM, SQUARE RIM WITH ELABORATE ANGLES. H2 FABRIC, QUARTZ TEMPER. FILL *3300*, STRUCTURE 2

13. HOLLOW WARE. FINE BLACK SANDY H2 FABRIC, SMOOTHED EXT. CURVILINEAR INCISED DESIGN ON EXT. FILL *3247*, CUT 3246, DITCH 3219

14. HOLLOW WARE. H2 FINE FABRIC. LINE AND DOT-IMPRESSED DECORATION FILL *3290* STRUCTURE 2

15. FRJ(H4). COARSE BLACK VESICULAR H4 FABRIC. FILLS *3282&3299*, PIT 3279

16. POT DISC. H2. FINE BLACK BODY. ABUNDANT QUARTZ GRIT TO 1MM; FILL *3281*, CUT 3279, STRUCTURE 2

17. JAR. H2 FINE FABRIC, QUARTZ TEMPER, SOFT RED INCS, GIVING VESICULAR INT. SURFACE. SMOOTHED EXT. DISTINCTIVE SPLAY-FOOTED BASE. FILLS *3229&3290*, STRUCTURE 2

18. WRGJ. FINE SANDY H2 FABRIC, ABUNDANT QUARTZ SAND, OCC. LARGER GRAINS. FILLS *3035&3324*, PIT 3034

having the same rim diameter. Open Jars (OJ) spanned a very wide range of sizes between 10cm and 39cm with no very clear concentration within this range. Much the same seemed to be true of the EROJ form although numbers were very low across the plots on which such types were represented with single examples ranging between 11cm and 29cm. This brief survey of a complex topic does little more than raise the possibility that there may be size classes within some of the vessel types defined in this report.

Old Ellerby

The Old Ellerby site assemblage of 3421 sherds weighing 60178g represents a maximum of 2995 vessels (ENV) with an overall average sherd weight of 20g. In common with the general situation on the sites considered in this report, H2 fabrics were predominant with a smaller proportion of vesicular (H4) wares, most probably originally tempered with angular calcite grit, present throughout the life of the site. The H4 wares may be over-represented in some features because of the presence of a small number of highly fragmented large vessels giving both high weight and ENV figures. The unusual and distinctive H5 fabric was associated with Structures 2 and 3, both of later Iron Age date, suggesting that the fabric was unlikely to be a copy of Roman grey ware, in spite of its appearance.

A wide range of vessel types was present in the ring gullies, with large jars particularly well represented in Structure 2. Vertical and everted rim vessels are common, and open jars and wedge-rimmed vessels were also present. Structure 2 is distinguished by the presence of an apparently unique vessel with an elaborate flared rim (Fig. 92.12) as well as a TRJ. The distinctive sandy grey H5 fabric is also represented, which, given their probable pre-Roman date, would tend to suggest that it was not created in an attempt to replicate the appearance of Roman-British grey wares, particularly as it is absent from later phases of activity on the site.

Structure 2

The substantial pottery assemblage from the Structure 2 ring gully includes a number of cross-context joins, all but one internal to the ring gully itself (Table 17). The assemblage is notable for the high proportion of vesicular H4 sherds which form 46 per cent of the total by ENV, but only 13.1 per cent by sherd weight. The discrepancy between these figures results from the large number of small sherds of this type from intervention **3179** close to the southern terminal of the ring gully. It is probable that these sherds were from a single large vessel, although their highly fragmented nature makes this hard to judge. Much smaller quantities of H4 pottery, more in line with the figures from other sites, were recorded from contexts **3062** and **3078**.

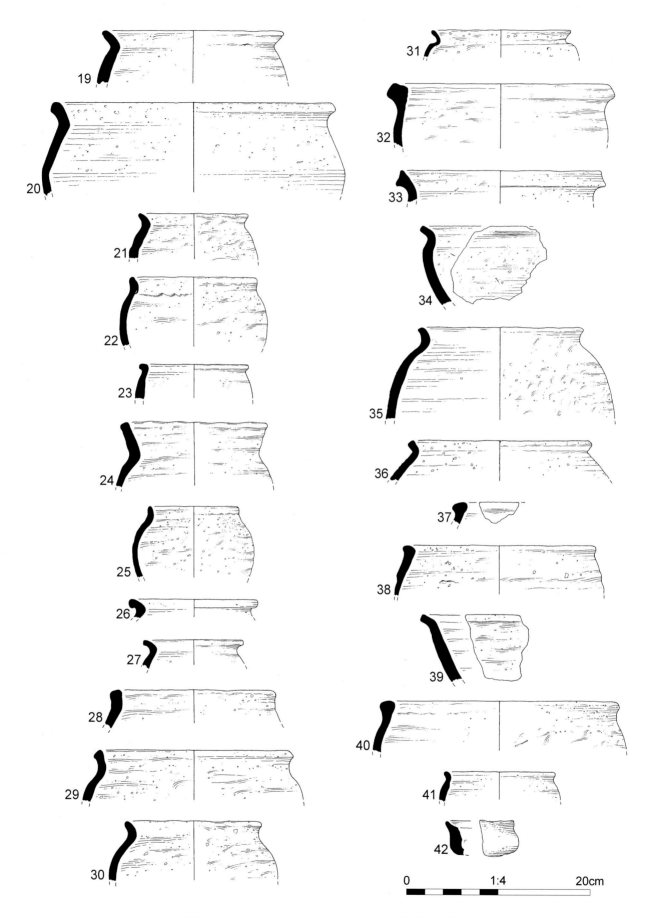

FIG. 93: HAND-MADE IRON AGE TRADITION POTTERY, 19-42, OLD ELLERBY

Illustrated hand-made pottery 2

Old Ellerby

19. FRJ. H2 FABRIC, REDUCED SANDY CORE, DULL ORANGE OXIDISED MARGINS, OCC. QUARTZ TO 2MM. RIM THINNER THAN THICK SHOULDER/BODY. FILLS, *3229&3290*, STRUCTURE 2

20. ERJ. AN EVEN, COARSE SANDY TEXTURED H2 BODY, MOD. SUB-ANG. ROCK FRAGS TO 2MM. SLIGHTLY ANGULAR RIM, *CF* FIG. 32A. FILL *3229*, CUT 3228, STRUCTURE 2

21. WRGJ. SANDY H2 BODY, OCC. LARGER GRAINS; BLACK CORE, BUFF TO GREY TO ORANGE SURFACES. SMOOTHED RIM, ROUGH BODY. FILL *3286*, STRUCTURE 3

22. VRJ-CT TYPE. BLACK H2 FABRIC, ROCK FRAGS TO 4MM. ROUND-LIPPED VERTICAL RIM ON NARROW SHOULDER/BODY. FILL *3286*, STRUCTURE 3

23. CROJ. FINE SANDY H2 FINE FABRIC, QUARTZ UP TO 0.5MM; FINELY SMOOTHED EXT. AND ROUND CLUBBED RIM. SLIGHTLY INTURNED BARREL-SHAPED BODY. FILL *3291*, STRUCTURE 2

24. FRJ. BLACK TO BUFF H2 BODY, GEN. FINE SANDY, SPARSE QUARTZ TO 4MM. TALL FUNNEL NECK/RIM, FLATTENED LIP. SMOOTHED EXT. FILL *3268*, DITCH 3267

25. VRGJ. HARD BLACK H2 QUARTZ FABRIC, ABUNDANT PROMINENT QUARTZ, MOD. MUSCOVITE TO 3MM; BLACK DEPOSIT EXT. SMOOTHED NECK. FILL *3290*, STRUCTURE 2

26. FLRJ. FINE BLACK SANDY H2 FABRIC, SHARPLY EVERTED, SLIGHTLY OVERHANGING RIM. FILL *3261*, CUT 3259, DITCH 3056

27. FLRJ. HARD FINE BLACK SANDY H2 FABRIC, OCC. LARGE ANG. ROCK FRAGS. SHARPLY EVERTED RIM. FILL *3229*, CUT 3228, STRUCTURE 2

28. VRJ-CS. FINE H2 ROCK FABRIC MOD. ANG. ROCK FRAGS. SHORT, THICK, VERTICAL RIM, FLAT TOP. CONTEXTS *3017&3207*, UNSTRATIFIED & FILL OF CUT 3187, STRUCTURE 2

29. ERJ TYPE. SANDY H2 FABRIC, ANG. ROCK FRAGS TO 3MM. SLIGHTLY EVERTED, ALMOST VERTICAL RIM, CLUBBED, DIAMOND PROFILE LIP. FILL *3027*, CUT 3049, STRUCTURE 2

30. ERJ TYPE. FINE H2 COARSE FABRIC, ABUNDANT PROMINENT LARGE ANG. ROCK FRAGS. SHORT SLIGHTLY EVERTED ROUNDED RIM, ROUND LIP ON NARROW-SHOULDERED BODY. FILL *3248*, CUT 3249, STRUCTURE 2

31. ERJ TYPE. FINE H2 QUARTZ FABRIC, ABUNDANT ANG. WHITE QUARTZ. V. THIN-WALLED, PRONOUNCED SHOULDER, SHARPLY EVERTED RIM. FILL *3282*, PIT 3279

32. SQRJ. FINE SANDY H2 ROCK FABRIC, SPARSE, WELL-SORTED ROCK, QUARTZ GRAINS TO 4MM, MAINLY FINER. UNSTRATIFIED FINDS *3017*

33. TRIRJ. BLACK H2 FABRIC, ABUNDANT QUARTZ SAND, OCC. ROCK FRAGS TO 5MM. DISTINCTIVE POINTED RIM WITH SHARP EXT. BULGE. FILL *3282*, PIT 3279

34. ERJ. H2 FABRIC, ABUNDANT QUARTZ GRIT TO 1MM, OCC. FLINT. SHOULDERED, PEAR-SHAPED, SHORT, SHARPLY EVERTED RIM. FILL *3282*, PIT 3279

35. ERJ. FINE, HARD SANDY H2 BODY, SPARSE ROCK FRAGS TO 6MM. SHORT, SHARPLY EVERTED RIM, SLIGHT TRACES OF PINCHING. FILL *3282*, PIT 3279

36. ERJ VARIANT. HARD BLACK H2 ROCK FABRIC, ANGULAR ROCK FRAGS TO 4MM IN FINE MATRIX. SHORT ANG. SLIGHTLY EVERTED RIM ON GLOBULAR BODY. FILL *3281*, PIT 3279

37. TRIRJ. FINE H2 FINE BODY, SPARSE ANG. ROCK FRAGS TO 3MM. FILL *3170*, CUT 3168, STRUCTURE 2

38. VRJ-CS TYPE. H2 RED SANDY TEXTURED PALE GREY BODY, BRIGHT ORANGE MARGINS, SOFT RED ROCK FRAGS. FILL *3299*, PIT 3279

39. EROJ. FINE H2 SANDY FABRIC, REDUCED CORE, BRIGHT ORANGE MARGINS. FILL *3093*, CUT 3092, STRUCTURE 3

40. VRJ VARIANT. SANDY H2 ROCK FABRIC, ROCK FRAGS TO 6MM. FLAT-TOPPED, CLUBBED VERTICAL RIM, CONSTRICTED NECK, NARROW BODY. FILL *3016*, PIT 3014

41. VRJ-FSG. FINE BLACK SANDY H2 FABRIC, BLACK DEPOSIT EXT, SMALL, SLIGHTLY EVERTED ROUND-CAPPED RIM. FILL *3180*, CUT 3179, STRUCTURE 2

42. UNIDENTIFIED OBJECT. SANDY H2 FABRIC, OCC. ANG. ROCK FRAGS. FILL *3186*, FEATURE 3329

Cut	Contexts	ENV	Wt/g	ASW/g
3155	3156	58	1654	28.5
	3291	30	1334	44.5
3179	3180	630	6909	11.0
	3180&3306&3291	1	1309	1309.0
	3306	8	196	24.5
3249	3248	4	206	51.5
	3311	10	351	35.1
3168	3171, 3170	3	3769	1256.3
3255	3256	56	1180	21.1
	3300	8	1318	164.8
3266	3262	1	14	14.0
3187	3207	26	283	10.9
U/S&3187	3017&3207	1	104	104.0
3061	3062, 3081, 3082	44	455	10.3
3074	3078	51	1105	21.7
3049	3027	31	318	10.3
3228	3228, 3229, 3273, 3290	309	7631	24.7
3020	3020	16	196	12.3

TABLE 17: DISTRIBUTION OF HAND-MADE POTTERY IN STRUCTURE 2, OLD ELLERBY INCLUDING CROSS-CONTEXT AND CROSS-FEATURE JOINS

The surviving parts of the northerly section of the ring gully closest to the presumed location of the terminal, contexts **3229**, **3273** and **3290**, produced slightly over one quarter of the total pottery by ENV and 28.5 per cent by weight. This includes a fine splay-footed base (Fig. 92.17), possibly part of a VRSJ or similar vessel. Quantities of pottery are lower from interventions elsewhere around the circuit of the ring gully. Fill **3180** may be unusual in view of the presence of the high number of H4 sherds, although these possibly represent only one or a few vessels.

Vessels from the fills of the ring gully include FRJs, (Figs. 92.11; 93.20), the rim and shoulder of an ERJ (Fig. 93.20), and two similar vessels (Fig. 92.4 and 9), and a VRJ-FSG (Fig. 93.41). A number of rarer vessel types were also represented including a CROJ (Fig. 93.23), a VRGJ (Fig. 93.25), an HHRGJ, an FlRJ (Fig. 93.27), the rim of a VRJ-CS (Fig. 93.28) and three ERJ type vessels (Figs. 92.10; 93.29 and 30). There is also one decorated sherd (Fig. 92.14).

Structure 3 (Gullies 3124 and 3125)

The southern gully, **3125**, produced an assemblage of 238 sherds weighing 3175g, representing a maximum of 233 vessels (ENV) with an average sherd weight of 13.6g. As with Structure 2, sherds in vesicular fabrics with fine angular voids are present and concentrated in a single context (**3150**) probably indicating the presence of a substantial part of a single vessel. The fifty-eight sherds represented 24.8 per cent of the total from the group by ENV but only 10.9 per cent by weight. Identifiable vessel types include an EROJ (Fig. 93.39) and an ERJ (Fig.92.5).

Cut	Contexts	ENV	Wt/g	ASW/g
	3288	63	1326	21.0
3086	3087	13	189	14.5
	3287	7	8	1.1
3149	3150	131	1321	10.1
3092	3093	19	331	17.4
3053	3053	13	103	7.9
3053	3054	48	1313	27.4
	3286	158	2903	18.4
3063	3064	11	291	26.5
	3285	7	232	33.1
3101	3102	42	1029	24.5
	3284	5	51	10.2
3103	3104	78	812	10.4
3101	3102&3104	1	118	118.0

TABLE 18: DISTRIBUTION OF HAND-MADE POTTERY IN STRUCTURE 3, OLD ELLERBY, INCLUDING CROSS-CONTEXT AND CROSS-FEATURE JOINS

Gully **3124** to the north, produced 433 sherds weighing 6852g, representing a maximum of 363 vessels (ENV) with an average sherd weight of 18.8g (Table 18). H4 fabrics constituted 14.8 per cent of the total by weight and 28 per cent by ENV. The pattern of distribution is not clear: while the eastern terminal produced 10.4 per cent of the pottery, by weight, this was outweighed by the material from intervention **3286** which lay nearer to the centre of the feature. Vessel types include a WRGJ and a VRJ-CT type (Fig. 93.21 and 22) and an FRJ (Fig. 92.6).

Ditches 3075 and 3267

The small size of the assemblages from ditches **3075** and **3267** would be consistent with them having been, at least in part, boundary ditches that might be expected to contain less pottery than contexts more closely associated with domestic activities such as the ring gullies. The assemblage from ditch **3075** is dominated by H2 fabrics with only two sherds of H4. A single rim sherd from an FRJ, somewhat shorter than the usual, is the only diagnostic sherd but the type does not appear to be chronologically significant.

Ditch **3267** included a high proportion of rim sherds in both H2 and H4 fabrics alongside vertical rimmed jars and individual examples of open jars, everted rim jars and an FRJ (Fig. 93.24). The hand-made wares are associated with wheel-thrown pottery of late first- to late second-century date. Although consisting predominantly of vessels in rather undistinguished H2 fabrics, context **3317** also produced a group of fine vesicular (H4) hand-made wares, including the rim of an FRJ, resembling those from Structure 3 described above.

Gully 3219

Gully **3219** produced a group of twenty-nine sherds weighing 264g and representing a maximum of twenty-eight vessels, with an average sherd weight of 10.5g. The group is distinguished by the presence of two decorated sherds bearing incised curvilinear designs (Fig. 92.13) but other diagnostic sherds are limited to the rims of two FRJs. Other than using parallels for the incised decoration, there is little contribution that the hand-made pottery can make to the dating but the evidence of the decorated sherds would tend to suggest a later Iron Age date. All is in undistinguished H2 fabrics with the exception of a piece of the vesicular H4 type from context **3247**.

Gully 3329

A small assemblage recovered from gully **3329** has a relatively high incidence of joining sherds, in large part due to the presence of a highly distinctive and unusual vessel from context **3208**. This is a vertical rimmed jar, which was decorated with pinching all over the external surface (Fig. 92.2). This vessel is not unique, with other examples present at Nuttles and Scorborough Hill, but it is unusual and has few parallels from the wider region.

Vessel forms include wedge-rimmed and VR jars, with a single example of a TRJ. This is a broadly similar pattern to that seen in ditch **3267**, although the small size of the groups should be taken into account in such comparisons. In contrast to Structure 2, all of the pottery from the feature was of H2 type, H4 being notable by its absence. The rim and body of an FRJ has an unusual fabric (Fig. 92.1) but one that still falls within the H2 range.

Third- to fourth-century ditches

Many of the features dated to the third and fourth centuries AD were cut into the top of ring gully **3020** and as a result may have contained residual material. This may explain both the amount of material and the diverse range of vessel types present in the later features.

Curvilinear ditch **3056** produced sixty-five sherds, weighing 606g, and representing the same number of vessels. An ASW of 9.3g is comparable to that of the earlier ditches but lower than that of the contemporary features discussed below. Dated by the wheel-thrown pottery to the period between the later third and early fourth centuries AD the fills of the ditch produced a relatively small assemblage of hand-made wares, all of them in H2 fabrics. Vessel types include Open Jars, VRJ forms including a VRSJ of probable first-century BC to mid-first-century AD type, an FRJ and a flat-rimmed jar (Fig 93.26).

The assemblage from ditch **3243** consists of 154 sherds weighing 3011g and representing a maximum of 143 vessels. Average sherd weight is 21g (ENV). The assemblage is composed predominantly of body sherds in the normal diverse range of H2 fabrics with a number of identifiable rims including ERJ in H2 and H3 fabrics (Fig. 92.10) and an ERGJ, FRJ and a TriRJ. Small groups of vesicular H4 sherds are present. Much of the assemblage is likely to be residual and the range of vessel types broadly reflects that seen in earlier phases of the site. Recut **3175**, in the southern terminus of the ditch, produced nine sherds including the rim of a VRJ-CS and a base.

Irregular linear features 3314 and 3139

Only four body sherds, with an ASW of 17.2g, were recovered from feature **3314**, associated with wheel-thrown pottery dating to the second to mid-fourth centuries. The larger and more diverse hand-made pottery assemblage from feature **3139** consists of fifty-seven sherds weighing 3151g representing a maximum of twenty-six vessels (ENV). The high ASW of 121.1g is the result of the presence of two large jar bases: twenty-three joining sherds weighing 1502g, and eight joining sherds weighing 1281g. Removing these two vessels gives an ASW of 10.2g, more consistent with figures from other features. Identifiable vessel forms include an FRJ, a VRJ-FSG and the two large jar bases.

The pottery from two fills, **3298** and **3296**, includes sherds in a very distinctive bright orange vesicular fabric, which may all have belonged to the same vessel, an ERJ, although no cross-context joins were identified; similar sherds were also noted in the fill of pit **3309**, cutting feature **3139** and in fill **3256** of ring gully **3020**, through which feature **3139** was cut. Pit **3133**, also cut into the fill of feature **3139**, produced an assemblage of twenty-three sherds weighing 687g representing a maximum of twenty vessels. The average sherd weight, 34.3g, is raised by the presence of two joining sherds, together weighing 423g, forming the rim and body of a VRJ-CS jar with a pinched rim (Fig. 92.3), the only identifiable vessel in the assemblage.

The assemblage from pit **3236**, which contained a human cremation and returned a radiocarbon date of AD cal 210 to 390, was limited to two small hand-made body sherds.

Third- to fourth-century pits

The majority of the twenty-four sherds, weighing 179g, from pit **3043** are unidentifiable body sherds but include two rim sherds from an unidentified type of jar. Pit **3040** produced forty-one sherds weighing 755g representing maximum of thirty-seven vessels giving an average sherd weight of 18.4g. The group includes body sherds with a distinctive ovoid shape, a perforated 'flowerpot-type' base and rim sherds from an FIRJ, a VRJ and a VRJ-FSG. All the fabrics are of H2 types, the majority of them finer types.

Pit **3279** contained 121 sherds weighing 2564g from a maximum of 108 vessels. The average sherd weight is 21.2g. H2 fabrics predominate, though there is a small group of H4 sherds, including an ERJ variant rim sherd (Fig. 93.36), and the rim and body of an FRJ(H4) (Fig. 92.15). Identifiable vessel forms include a TriRJ (Fig. 93.33) and VRJ-CS types (Fig. 93.38) but the majority are ERJ (see, for example, Figs. 92.8; 93.32, 34 and 35) with one ERGJ.

The diverse assemblage of pottery from pit **3034** consists of fifty-two sherds weighing 857g and representing a maximum of forty-three vessels. Cross-context joining sherds link fill **3035** and the unstratified context **3324** through the rim of a WRGJ (Fig. 92.18). Other forms include FIRJ, VRJ-CS, ovoid jar and possible OJ and ERJ types. All of the fabrics are H2 types.

131

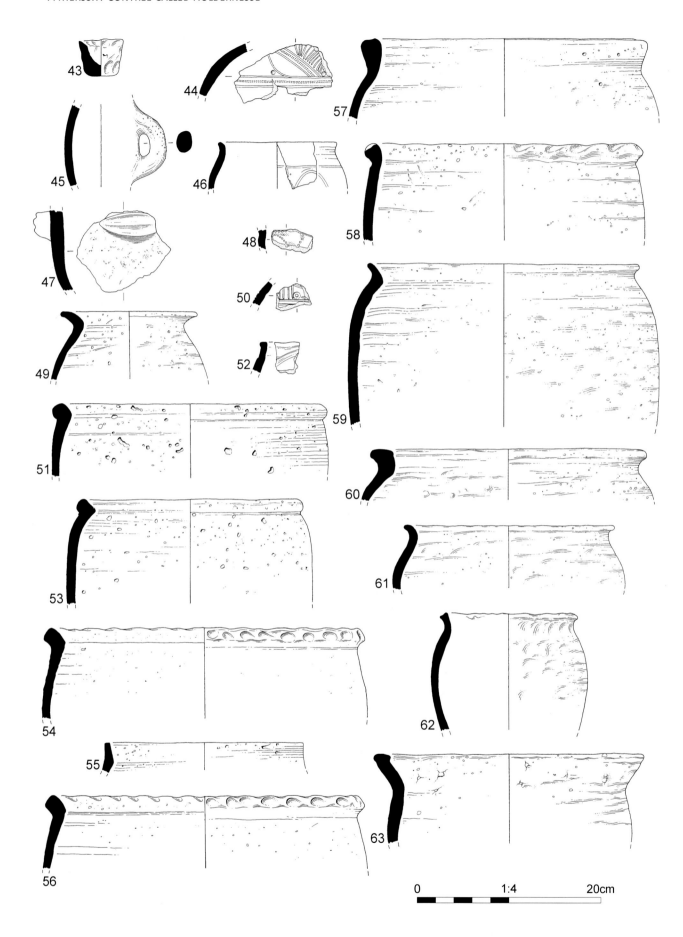

Fig. 94: Hand-made Iron Age tradition pottery, 43-63, Burton Constable

Illustrated hand-made pottery 3

Burton Constable

43. Thumb pot. H2 Fine fabric, black. Bevelled rim, uneven base; small finger prints. SF 1219. Fill *118128*, pit 118198

44. Hollow ware. Double square-ended rouletted lines and impressed curvilinear lines, linear infill. H2 Fine fabric. Fill *118504*, feature 118503, overlying SE terminal Structure 5

45. Lugged jar. H2 Quartz fabric, abundant, well-sorted ang. to sub-ang. quartz to 4mm. Smoothed ext. Fill *9527*, ditch 118921, Enclosure 9

46. VRJ-FSG type. Horizontal impressed line on narrow shoulder and arc on body, burnished surface. H2 Fine fabric. Fill *118911*, cut 118617, Structure 5

47. Handled jar. H2 Rock fabric; sandy, common well-sorted large ang. rock frags to 8mm, occ. larger. Horizontal oval lug handle, not pierced, shallow grooves on handle. Fill *118450*, curvilinear feature 118949

48. Hollow ware. H2 Fine fabric. Intersecting lines of impressed ring stamps. Upper fill *9841*, cut 9842, Structure 5

49. ERJ(H4). Black, vesicular H4 fabric, rounded quartz. Very pronounced everted rim on a round-bodied jar. Fill *9548*, cut 9847, Enclosure 2

50. Hollow ware. Horizontal impressed line, multiple vertical lines and ring stamp on body. H2 Fine fabric. Fill *118505*, cut 118057, Structure 5

51. CRJ(H4). Heavy round clubbed rim; probably finished on turntable. H4 fabric coarsely vesicular, decayed calcite grains. Fill *118596*, cut 118595, Structure 5

52. VRJ-FSG type. Shallow impressed double curving line on neck and body. H2 Fine fabric. Fill *118130*, cut 118112, ditch 118958

53. WRJ(H4). Short wedge-shaped rim, slightly dished top. H4 fabric, vesicular, frags of decayed calcite internally; black deposit ext. Fill *118596*, cut 118595, Structure 5

54. EROJ type. Angular rim, thin cordon on top and angled impressions on external angle. H2 Quartz fabric. Fill *118505*, cut 118057, Structure 5

55. VRJ(H4) type. Vertical, flat-topped rim. Vesicular throughout. Possibly LBA/EIA open jar form; *cf.* Reighton Fig. 23; 8, 9, 10. Alluvial layer *118912*, overlying southern end of site

56. EROJ type. Angled finger impressions on top and external angle of rim. H2 Rock fabric. Fill *118520*, cut 118057, Structure 5

57. VRJ(H4) variant. Short, rounded inverted wedge-shaped slightly off-vertical rim, wide flat top. Vesicular throughout; *cf* CXT *118842* and *9487*. Fill *118596*, cut 118959, Structure 5

58. CRJ(H4). H4 Calcite fabric, angled finger impressions on round clubbed rim; smoothed surface. Fill *118505*, cut 118057, Structure 5

59. ERJ. Short slightly everted rim on narrow bodied jar. H2 Rock fabric, sandy textured body, moderate well-sorted angular rock frags to 6mm, occ. larger. Smoothed exterior. Fill *118670* of pit 118669

60. ERJ type. H2 Rock fabric, abundant sub-ang. rock frags to 6mm, rarely larger. Large jar, short, thick vertical rim, pronounced ext. lip angle and int. angle at base of neck. Fill *9469*, gully 118984

61. ERJ. H2 Fine, occ. larger grains. Small irreg. everted rim on short neck, shouldered body. Fill *118505*, cut 118057, Structure 5

62. TriRJ type. Small triangular rim, pinched pointed cap on curving neck. H2 Fine sandy fabric, rare sub-rounded quartz to 5mm. Slight striations ext. Fills *118521&118159&118035*, intercutting pits 118523, 118160 and 118036

63. FRJ. H2 Coarse Rock fabric, common coarse ang. rock frags to 8mm, occ. Tall, thick, funnel shaped rim, neck with slight int. flange. Fill *118277*, cut 118278, Structure 5

Pit **3014** contained an assemblage of seventy-seven sherds weighing 1132g with an average sherd weight of 14.7g. Wheel-thrown pottery of Romano-British type was also present. Vessel types were limited to VRJ and VRJ-FSG types (Fig. 93.41) with a single possible ERJ. One sherd had a semi-vitrified, vesicular deposit on one side, suggesting that it had been associated with some form of high-temperature industrial activity (see Pitman and Doonan, this volume, page 171).

Other features

Postholes **3116**, **3120** and **3307**, cut into the top of ring gully **3020**, contained collectively, seventeen body sherds weighing 151g, in a variety of fine H2 fabrics. Pit **3112** produced a possible VRSJ and an ERJ variant associated with two base sherds of Roman date, while pit **3126** produced nine sherds weighing 32g. From opposite ends of the excavation area, pit **3069** and feature **3140** both contained rim sherds of FRJ type (Fig. 92.7). Pit **3088** produced three body sherds and a rim, weighing 23g in total and elongated pit **3130** produced a small assemblage in H2 fabrics. Pit **3166** had a single 12g body sherd.

Unstratified contexts

A considerable quantity of hand-made pottery was recovered from unstratified contexts, including

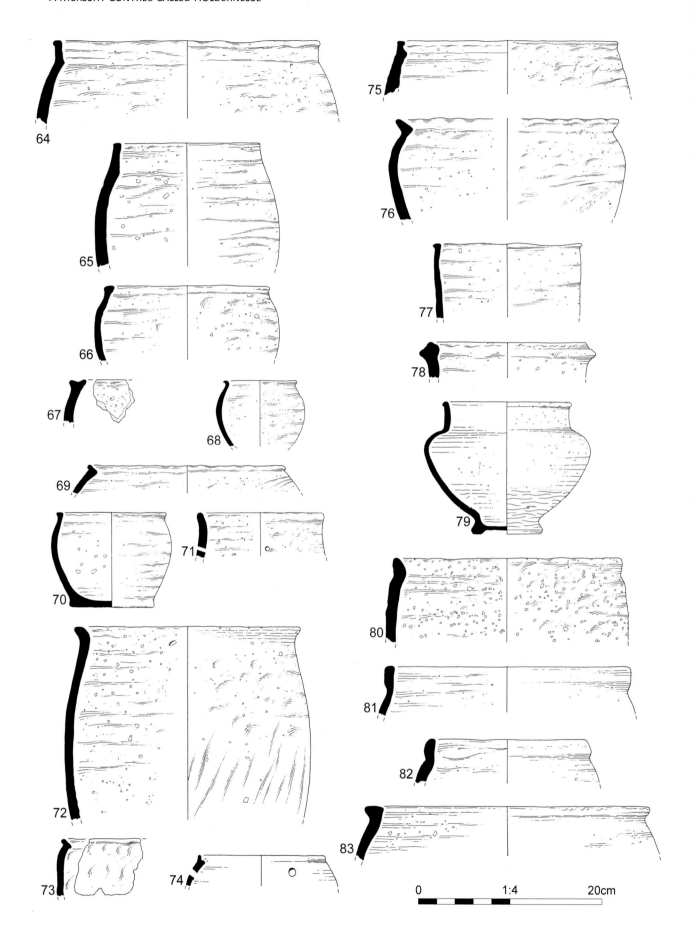

FIG. 95: HAND-MADE IRON AGE TRADITION POTTERY 64-83, BURTON CONSTABLE

Illustrated hand-made pottery 4

Burton Constable

64. VRJ-CT. DENSE BLACK H2 ROCK FABRIC, ANG. ROCK FRAGS UP TO 5MM VERTICAL NECK, FLAT-TOPPED BEADED RIM ON BARELY ROUNDED LARGE JAR BODY, PROMINENT INTERNAL ANGLE. FILL *118014*, CUT 9967, STRUCTURE 5

65. VRJ-CT. FINE BLACK H2 ROCK, ANG. ROCK FRAGS TO 6MM, OCC. LARGER VERTICAL FLAT TOPPED RIM ON NARROW-SHOULDERED BODY. FILL *118827*, CUT 9972, STRUCTURE 5

66. HHRGJ. FINE BLACK H2 ROCK FABRIC, MOD. POORLY SORTED ANG. ROCK FRAGS TO 4MM. SHORT SQUARE-SECTIONED HAMMERHEAD RIM. SMOOTHED INT. FILL *118597*, CUT 118595, STRUCTURE 5

67. HHRGJ. H2 COARSE ROCK FABRIC, COMMON COARSE ANG. ROCK FRAGS TO 4MM. FLAT TOPPED HAMMERHEAD RIM, WIDE, SHALLOW GROOVE ON TOP. FILL *9141*, PIT 9140

68. WRGJ. H2 FINE, SANDY TEXTURED BLACK FABRIC, RARE QUARTZ TO 6MM, MAINLY FINER. DISTINCTIVE ROUND JAR WITH V. SMALL BEADED RIM. LAYER *9912*, OVERLYING CUT 9911, STRUCTURE 5

69. WRGJ. H2 FINE, SMALL WEDGE-RIM ON A GLOBULAR BODY; FINE SANDY BLACK H2 W/ OCCASIONAL ROUNDED ROCK FRAGS UP TO 4MM. SURFACE FINDS *9001*

70. BRGJ. H2 ROCK SANDY FABRIC, ABUNDANT FINE QUARTZ, MOD. ANG. ROCK FRAGS TO 5MM. SMALL, FLAT-TOPPED BEADED RIM. FILL *118521*, PIT 118523

71. OJ. H2 ROCK FABRIC, COARSE ANG. ROCK FRAGS TO 6MM. SLIGHTLY EVERTED ROUND-LIPPED VERTICAL RIM ON OPEN BODY; REPAIR HOLE. SMOOTHED SURFACES. FILL *118483*, DITCH 118970

72. EROJ. H2 ROCK&QUARTZ FINE SANDY FABRIC, MOD./ ABUNDANT ANG. QUARTZ, ROCK FRAGS TO 6MM. LARGE OPEN JAR, SMALL EVERTED RIM. FILL *9789*, CUT 9788, STRUCTURE 1

73. HHRGJ. H2 ROCK FABRIC, BLACK, SPARSE ANG. ROCK FRAGS TO 6MM. BEADED HAMMERHEAD RIM, NO NECK. FILL *118115*, CUT 118114, STRUCTURE 5

74. LSJ. H2 FINE, SANDY TEXTURED, VERY FINE FABRIC, FINE SUB-ANG. QUARTZ SAND. DISTINCTIVE BIFID RIM (*CF.* 118352). TWO LARGE HOLES BORED THROUGH UPPER BODY. BURNISHED EXT. SURFACE FINDS *9001* & FILL *9008*, CUT 9009, STRUCTURE 3

75. LSJ. H2 COARSE ROCK, ABUNDANT ANG. ROCK TEMPER TO 6MM. V. DISTINCTIVE LID-SEATED RIM. FILL *9992*, PIT 118103

76. WRGJ. PROMINENT INT. ANGLE, POINTED LIP, IRREGULAR RIM, FINGERMARKS. HARD BLACK H2 ROCK FABRIC, ANGULAR ROCK FRAGS TO 5MM. FILL *118677*, DITCH 118676

77. OJ TYPE. IRREGULAR BEADED RIM ON AN APPARENTLY CYLINDRICAL VESSEL; H2 ROCK FABRIC, FINE SANDY, POORLY SORTED ROCK FRAGS TO 6MM, MAINLY FINER. FILLS *9439*&*118522*, DITCH 118958, PIT 118523

78. SQRJ VARIANT. FINE SANDY H2 ROCK BODY, MOD. WELL-SORTED ANG. ROCK FRAGS TO 6MM (*CF* CXT *9001*). THICK, SQUAT SQUARE PROFILED RIM. FILL *118341*, DITCH 118958

79. VRSJ. H2 FINE, REDUCED SANDY BODY, OCC. LARGER GRAINS. VERTICAL NECK, HIGH-SHOULDERED BODY, PEDESTAL BASE. BURNISHED EXT. FILL *118341*, DITCH 118958

80. OJ. H2 COARSE FABRIC; ABUNDANT ANG. ROCK FRAGS TO 6MM, OCC. LARGER, PROTRUDING THROUGH BRIGHT ORANGE SURFACE. DISTINCTIVE LARGE OPEN JAR. FILL *118046*, CUT 118047, STRUCTURE 2

81. VROJ. H2 ROCK FABRIC, SANDY, ANG. ROCK FRAGS TO 6MM, OCC. TO 11MM. VERTICAL RIM, DEEP COLLAR ON NARROW OPEN BODY SMOOTHED EXT. ALLUVIAL LAYER *118912*, OVERLYING SOUTHERN END OF SITE

82. VROJ. SHORT VERTICAL RIM ON NARROW BODY, CONSTRICTED NECK. SANDY H2 QUARTZ FABRIC, SPARSE QUARTZ GRAINS TO 3MM. FILL *9861*, DITCH 118978

83. FRGJ. WIDE, SQUAT, FLAT-TOPPED EVERTED RIM; H2 ROCK & QUARTZ. FABRIC, SANDY, MOD. WELL-SORTED ROCK FRAGS TO 6MM, MAINLY FINER QUARTZ. FILLS *118505*&*118895*, CUTS 118057, 118351, STRUCTURE 5

surface subsoil spreads and remnant furrows **3091**, **3221**, **3032** and **3017**, surface find contexts **3196** and **3324**, and fill **3235** from an intervention to find the relationships between features **3034**, **3219** and **3040**. A wide range of rim sherds from context **3017** included one of the rarer forms, a SqRJ (Fig. 93.32). Otherwise, identifiable vessel forms were only found in context **3091** and were limited to the apparently ubiquitous ERJ and VRJ types with one unidentified jar distinguished by apparently deliberate impressed lines externally. A body sherd from the same context was decorated with a more complex design of incised lines forming a curvilinear pattern.

Burton Constable

The Burton Constable site produced the largest and most complex assemblage of pottery from the pipeline: a total of 9946 sherds weighing 148,354g and representing up to 9101 vessels.

Colluvial layers and associated features

Colluvial layer **118979** produced an assemblage of 204 sherds weighing 239g representing a maximum of 187 vessels and with an average sherd weight of 11.9g. A wide range of fabrics include the vesicular H4 type which is represented by a VRJ rim, in context **9487**, as well as by body sherds. Other vessel types, all in H2 fabrics, include VRJ, VRJ-NB and an ERJ. Abrasion is common throughout the assemblage, as might be expected with a colluvial deposit.

Pit **9476** contained forty-four sherds of pottery weighing 1729g representing a maximum of thirty-five vessels. The ASW is unusually high at 49.4g, largely through the presence of five joining sherds forming the rim of an ERJ. In spite of the small size of the assemblage, the number of identifiable vessels is high, with rims from large VRJ-FSG, VRJ, VRJ-CS vessels all present. Measuring accurately the diameters proved difficult because they are extremely uneven but body sherds with a large radius of curvature show that they are from vessels at the larger end of the size range. H2 Rock fabrics are predominant with just one small flake in an H4 fabric and a small piece in an H2 Fine fabric with a burnished external surface. Pit **118843**, cut by the ring gully of Structure 5, produced just seven small abraded sherds in a fine sandy H2 fabric.

Structure 1

Penannular gully **118974** produced an assemblage of 206 sherds weighing 4138g and represented a maximum of 143 vessels with an ASW of 28.9g (Table 19). A single sherd of wheel-thrown pottery from context **9599** was probably intrusive.

Contexts **9493** and **9789** stand out by virtue of their high ASW figures and the fact that they contained the highest proportion of pottery, by weight, from the feature although both of these can be seen as the result of the presence of substantial parts of two large EROJ vessels, one in each context (Fig. 95.72). None of the identifiable vessel parts (types EROJ, VRJ-CS, VRJ-CT, and ERJ) were chronologically diagnostic.

The quantities of pottery in deposits possibly associated with the ring gully are summarised in Table 20. The contrast between the lower ASW figures for the fill of ditch **118978** (11.5g) and colluvial layer **118980** (14.0g) and those of gullies **118984** (25.7g) and **118977** (20.6g)

may be the result of deliberate decisions or variability resulting from different processes relating to deposit formation.

The range of fabrics was wide with a small quantity of H3 and H4 sherds as well as a variety of H2 types. A sherd of H5 from this group is worthy of note as an example of the fine sandy grey fabric bearing a visual resemblance to the Romano-British grey ware, which it appears to pre-date.

The range of vessel forms was particularly wide with VRJ forms particularly well represented and diverse in the degree of variation within the broad type. Forms which do not form a major part of the repertoire were also well represented including EROJ, HHRGJ, TriRJ, VROJ (Fig. 95.82) and WRJ(H4). Forms FRJ and ERJ (Fig. 94.60) were also present. Context 9861 also contained a fragment of a crucible rim, probably used for making leaded tin bronze (Pitman and Doonan, this volume, sample 20).

Structure 2

The pottery assemblage from ring gully 118944 consists of fifty-one sherds weighing 748g and representing a maximum of forty-six vessels (Table 21).

One context, **118046**, stands out as containing a small number of significantly larger sherds of pottery but given the limited extent of the surviving ring gully and the consequent uncertainty over the location of the entrance it is difficult to determine if this is significant or simply

Feature	ENV	Wt/g	ASW/g
118978	68	779	11.4
118980	363	5081	13.9
118984	117	3003	25.6
118977	54	1114	20.6

TABLE 20: SUMMARY OF HAND-MADE POTTERY FROM FEATURES ASSOCIATED WITH STRUCTURE 1, BURTON CONSTABLE

Context	Cut	ENV	Wt/g	ASW/g
9920	9921	3	3	1
9850	9851	3	7	2.3
118044	118047	3	43	14.3
118045	118047	17	268	15.7
118046	118047	6	262	43.6
118129	118113	3	38	12.6
118629	118628	7	18	2.5
118826	finds ret	4	109	27.2

TABLE 21: DISTRIBUTION OF HAND-MADE POTTERY FROM STRUCTURE 2, BURTON CONSTABLE

Context	Cut	ENV	Wt/g	ASW/g
9493	9492	10	1054	105.4
9511	9510	10	43	4.3
9599	9598	7	93	13.2
9767	9766	40	795	19.8
9789	9788	34	1514	44.5
9863	9862	41	638	15.5

TABLE 19: DISTRIBUTION OF HAND-MADE POTTERY IN STRUCTURE 1, BURTON CONSTABLE

the result of chance factors. The range of vessel types is rather narrow with single examples of BJ, ERJ and VRJ-CT types with two OJ rims (Fig. 95.80) and the remainder unidentified hollow wares. H2 is the only fabric group represented although within this group the range is wide and includes coarsely tempered types.

Features associated with structure 2

Ditch **118954** produced a group of 201 sherds weighing 5491g representing a maximum of 184 vessels, with an average sherd weight of 29.8g. The majority of the fabrics are variants of the H2 type but the assemblage also includes small quantities of both H1 Calcite and H4 types. The range of vessel types is considerably wider than that from the ring gully and includes OJ and ERJ forms, although the majority are variants on the VRJ type.

Ditch **9957** produced seven body sherds, two of which are flint tempered. Flint is occasionally present in sherds of H2 type (H2 Flint), but in these two sherds the inclusions are both larger and commoner than is normally the case, and it may be that they are fragments of earlier prehistoric types residual in a later feature. The fills of features **118342** and **118344** also produced small groups of body sherds, all of them in H2 type fabrics. No identifiable vessels are present from either of these contexts.

Structure 3

The two parts of the ring gully, **9010** and **9007**, produced a total of 118 sherds of hand-made pottery weighing 882g and representing a maximum of 111 vessels (Table 22).

Although the absolute quantity of pottery from the feature is relatively small, there is some indication of patterning in the distribution. The south-east terminal produced just two large sherds while the intervention to the south-west of the terminal contained a larger

Context	Cut	ENV	Wt/g	ASW/g
9978	9977	2	52	26
9011	9012	21	92	4.3
9008	9009	8	89	11.1
9011&9008		1	25	25
9021	9022	1	16	16
9023	9024	2	10	5
9006	9007	15	230	15.3
118011	9010	61	368	6

TABLE 22: DISTRIBUTION OF HAND-MADE POTTERY FROM STRUCTURE 3, BURTON CONSTABLE

number of small sherds. The sherds from the western side are larger than any from elsewhere, apart from the south-eastern terminal. The intervention closest to the truncated north-eastern terminal produced the greatest quantity by weight.

The range of identifiable vessel types is diverse, with single examples of FRJ, EROJ, HHRGJ and an LSJ, the last possibly indicating an earlier Iron Age date for the feature. This vessel appears to have been repaired with two prominent drilled holes (Fig. 95.74). The presence of the unusual EROJ and HHRGJ types may link the structure with Structure 1, although neither form has any clear chronological significance. Fabrics are H2 Fine and H2 Rock with a single small sherd in the vesicular H4 fabric.

Features associated with Structure 3

Ditch **118970**, to the north of Structure 3 produced eighty-two sherds weighing 1122g, representing a maximum of seventy-six vessels (ASW: 14.7g). The group is dominated by H2 Rock fabrics with smaller quantities of other H2 types. Vessels include single examples of BJ, possible ERJ, VRJ and VRJ-CT as well as an Open Jar with a repair hole (Fig. 95.71). Feature **9071**, which may have been the terminus of ditch **118970**, produced eleven body sherds weighing 159g (context **9070**). All of the fabrics are H2 types and there are no identifiable vessels in the group. Fill **118823** of posthole **118753** produced two sherds of pottery in H2 Rock fabrics weighing 10g. One sherd is the base of a jar but no specific vessel forms are identifiable.

Structure 4

Ring gully **118056** produced a total of 771 sherds of hand-made pottery weighing 16116g representing a maximum of 670 vessels (Table 23).

The considerable variation in number of sherds and ASW around the circuit of the ring presumably reflects patterns of differential disposal. Contexts in, and adjacent to, the terminals produced the largest quantity of pottery with contexts at the western side producing smaller numbers.

There is a high proportion of H2 Coarse Rock fabric, with a small quantity of H4 and a variety of other H2 types. The range of vessel types is similar in broad terms to those from other structures and related features. Vertical rimmed vessels predominate but OJ and BJ forms are also present together with FRJ and more elaborate forms such as HHRGJ which has parallels in the assemblages from Structures 1 and 3. A vessel from fill **9937**, with a joining sherd from fill **9938**, is distinguished by its unusual orange to grey sandy fabric. A similar vessel, with a slightly longer neck, in a similar

Context	Cut	ENV	Wt/g	ASW/g
9970	9972	1	16	16
9979	9972	11	50	4.5
118827	9972	46	1417	30.8
9937	9868	85	1928	22.6
9938	9868	81	4337	53.5
9937&9938	9868	1	393	393
9869	9868	26	765	29.4
Sub-total		*251*	*8906*	*35.4*
118819	9888	12	130	10.8
118820	9888	16	465	29
9926	9888	34	740	21.7
9889	9888	51	557	10.9
Sub-total		*113*	*1892*	*16.7*
9965	9967	6	128	21.3
9966	9967	18	103	5.7
118014	9967	9	555	61.6
118015	9967	3	108	36
Sub-total		*36*	*894*	*24.8*
118277	118278	34	761	22.3
118221	118223	12	38	3.1
Sub-total		*46*	*799*	*17.3*
118115	118114	7	158	22.5
118220	118114	19	171	9
Sub-total		*26*	*329*	*12.6*
118809	118041	73	516	7.0
118810	118041	10	265	26.5
118042	118041	7	119	17
118043	118041	3	79	26.3
Sub-total		*93*	*979*	*10.5*
118829	118052	3	78	26
118053	118052	47	470	10
118423	118424	19	1375	72.3
118824	118424	17	127	7.4
118825	118424	19	267	14
Sub-total		*105*	*2317*	*22.0*

TABLE 23: DISTRIBUTION OF HAND-MADE POTTERY FROM STRUCTURE 4, BURTON CONSTABLE

The distribution of the pottery around the circuit of the ring does not appear to show any marked distinctions between zones. The range of fabrics is wide with small quantities of H1 (Calcite and Calcite and Flint), H3 and H4 types and a quantity of the soft grey fabric, H5. The H4 sherds appear to have been entirely calcite-tempered, judging by the size and shape of the voids and the small amount of surviving calcite. The large and diverse H2 group includes the normal wide range of inclusions and a small quantity of fuel ash tempered sherds. A significant group consists of sherds with distinctively coarse angular rock temper, similar to that noted above in the case of Structure 4. A small number of crucible fragments are also present (see Pitman and Doonan, below).

The range of vessel forms is wide and includes numerous unusual and rare vessels among the ubiquitous VRJ, ERJ and FRJ types. Many are represented by small, irregular rim fragments for which neither the diameter nor the percentage figure can be determined. The more unusual vessels include an HHRGJ similar to the examples from Structures 3 and 4, a TriRJ (*cf* Structure 1) and a wide range of wedge-rimmed jars, including examples in the H4 fabric. Two fragments of lugged jars, from fills **118251** and **118386**, both in H4 fabrics, could be dated to around 400BC to AD100. A lid-seated jar rim from fill **118352** is of a type which has been linked with sites dating to the earlier part of the pre-Roman Iron Age.

Pit 118975

Pit **118975**, running south from the south-western edge of the ring gully towards the centre of the arc of the Structure 1 gully, produced seventy-eight sherds representing a maximum of 73 vessels and weighing 699g, giving an ASW of 9.5g. The assemblage includes a wide range of fabrics, including H1, H3 and H4, a possible crucible fragment and a single sherd of Scored ware type. The date range of Scored ware, from the mid-third century BC to early or mid-first century AD, is broadly consistent with dating evidence from the Structure 5 contexts.

'Structure 6'

The group of poorly defined features within and overlying the Structure 5 ring gully, including ditches **118986**, **118676**, **118512**, **118514**, **118621**, **118510**, **118695**, **118751**, **118744**, **118746** and **118748**, may have been the truncated remains of a later structure. Collectively, they produced a total of 355 sherds weighing 3880g and representing a maximum of 333 vessels. The average sherd weight is 11.6g. The range of vessel types, while narrower than that seen in the case of Structure 5, is still relatively wide, and includes HHRGJ, EROJ and WRGJ (Fig. 95.76) although with ERJ and

fabric, is present in the assemblage from ditch **118958**. None of the identifiable vessel types from the feature as a whole can be considered chronologically diagnostic.

Structure 5

Structure 5 produced a large assemblage of hand-made pottery with only three sherds of wheel-thrown Romano-British wares (Table 24). The ring gully was recut on at least two occasions and was also cut by later pits, so a degree of residuality and intrusion will have affected the composition of the pottery assemblage.

Contexts	Cut	ENV	Wt/g	ASW/g
118596	118595	486	8211	16.9
118634	118595	3	26	8.7
118597	118595	62	888	14.3
Sub-total		*551*	*9125*	*16.6*
118896	118057	22	86	3.9
118907	118057	73	122	1.7
118908	118057	30	229	7.6
118505	118057	936	16173	17.3
118505&118058&118596	118057	1	868	868
118505&118895	118057	1	245	245
118542	118057	3	4	1.3
118058	118057	69	713	10.3
118520	118057	5	170	34.0
Sub-total		*1140*	*18610*	*16.3*
118352	118351	142	1590	11.2
118895	118351	25	184	7.4
Sub-total		*167*	*1774*	*10.6*
118253	118252	21	83	4.0
118384	118383	3	52	17.3
118251	118250	24	183	7.6
118387	118383	2	52	26.0
Sub-total		*29*	*287*	*9.9*
118902		19	144	7.6
118883	118553	5	29	5.8
118885	118553	2	27	13.5
Sub-total		*7*	*56*	*8.0*
118386	118385	13	103	7.9
118904		43	833	19.4
118901		4	57	14.3
118554	118553	8	137	17.1
118556	118555	20	221	11.1
118558	118557	22	441	20.0
118899	118644	9	248	27.6
118910	118609	12	107	8.9
118909	118651	12	152	12.7

Contexts	Cut	ENV	Wt/g	ASW/g
118971	118620	12	260	157
118659	118658	14	1152	82.3
118842	118841	1	29	29.0
9904	9842	5	44	8.8
9841	9842	77	1083	14.1
9912&9841		1	134	134.0
9910	9842	13	254	19.5
Sub-total		*96*	*1515*	*15.8*
118854	118855	16	276	*17.3*
118856		9	68	7.6
118802	118801	14	384	27.4
118893	118364	4	46	11.5
118892	118364	6	111	18.5
118366	118364	5	106	21.2
118369	118367	3	64	21.3
118371	118370	4	27	6.8
118373	118372	3	43	14.3
Sub-total		*25*	*397*	*15.9*
118850		6	192	32.0
118191	118190	17	214	12.6
118193	118192	4	20	5.0
118195	118194	14	173	12.4
Sub-total		*35*	*407*	*11.6*
118249	118207	15	245	16.3
118246	118205	13	232	17.8
118247	118205	7	189	27.0
118248	118205	11	106	9.6
118245	118206	7	39	5.6
Sub-total		*53*	*811*	*15.3*
118243	118203	44	708	16.1
118894	118203	5	91	18.2
Sub-total		*49*	*799*	*16.3*
118731	118730	19	114	6.0
118182	118183	4	4	1.0
118714	118712	12	174	14.5
118178	118179	12	30	2.5
118400	118398	16	212	13.3

TABLE 24: DISTRIBUTION OF HAND-MADE POTTERY FROM STRUCTURE 5, BURTON CONSTABLE

VRJ types predominant. Fabrics include H1 Calcite and H1 Shell with H4 types and the H2 group includes sherds apparently tempered with slag or similar residue, perhaps reflecting the presence of fuel ash slag in Structure 5.

In the same part of the site, the seven sherds from ditch **118949** include an unusual oval or 'tear-drop' shaped lug handle (Fig. 94.47) for which no parallels have been found. Ditch **118760** contained a group of twelve sherds, the majority in coarse rock tempered fabrics, including the rim of a barrel jar.

Other deposits associated with the Iron Age settlement

In addition to the ring gullies, many of the ditches, gullies, pits and postholes in the southern part of the excavation area produced assemblages consisting predominantly of body sherds in H2 fabrics with varying numbers of different types of rims which indicate general similarity with the material derived from the ring ditches. Full details are in the project archive.

The assemblage from pit **118198** includes six identifiable vessels: an HHRGJ similar to those from the ring ditches, a BROJ, a VRJ-CS, an ERJ, a VRJ and, the most unusual item, a small thumb pot (Fig. 94.43) which was unique as far as the sites considered in this report are concerned. It is paralleled by a similar vessel, although decorated with fingernail impressions, from Bridlington to Haisthorpe water pipeline (Cumberpatch 2009b, fig. 46). Both vessels came from pits and neither appears to be a crucible although their actual purpose is unclear. Subsoil layer **9912** overlying Structures 4 and 5 also produced a range of vessel types (ERJ, VRJ, BRGJ (Fig. 95.70) although the fabrics are, with the exception of a small quantity of possible H3, all of H2 type, including H2 Fuel Ash.

Other notable contexts include fill **118096** of pit **118095**, which produced four fragments of ceramic furnace lining (see Pitman and Doonan, below, page 171). Pit **118707** is distinguished by the large number of thick-walled sherds, many of which are abraded. No chronologically diagnostic sherds were identified although both HHRGJ and TriRJ type vessels are present. The range of fabrics is normal with H2 types predominant and small quantities of H3 and H4 types also present. Gully **9420** includes a quantity of sherds, including a range of vessel rims, in unusual soft sandy fabrics (H2 Soft Sand and H2 Soft Sand and Rock) apparently unique to this feature. A lid-seated jar rim was recovered from the fill of a small depression formed above ditch **118954** (Fig. 95.75).

Roman enclosure system

The assemblages from the enclosure ditches are generally smaller than those associated with the earlier structures (Table 25). This could be because the use of hand-made pottery had declined by the later Roman period but it could equally relate to the context of deposition with features in the immediate vicinity of domestic structures more likely to see the accumulation of domestic and craft-related waste.

Inhumation 9794

The inhumation pit produced sixteen sherds weighing 49g, representing a maximum of eleven vessels. The ASW is 4.4g and all of the sherds are abraded fragments, many little more than flakes, with only one identifiable vessel: an ERJ in the vesicular H4 fabric. There is nothing in the character of the assemblage to suggest that the pottery was deliberately included in the grave.

The possible grain dryer

Contexts associated with the possible grain dryer (**9279**, **9233** and **9250**) produced seventeen sherds and fragments of hand-made pottery some of which might have been fired clay rather than vessel fragments. No identifiable vessels are present and all the sherds are in H2 Fine and H2 type fabrics.

Ditches 118957, 118927 and 118958

The two intersecting ditches towards the southern end of the excavation area, ditches **118927** and **118957** had similar assemblages (Table 26). In both cases, the range of fabrics is dominated by H2 types with small quantities of H1 Shell and H4 types in ditch **118927** and three sherds of H4 in ditch **118957**. Identifiable vessel forms are few but include OJ types and a VRJ-CS from ditch **118927** and two ERJs from ditch **118957**.

By contrast, the large assemblage from ditch **118958** includes a wide variety of vessel and fabric types. Fabrics include H1 Calcite, H1 Shell, H3 and H4 alongside a range of H2 types, with H2 Coarse rock and H2 Fine both

Enclosure	ENV	Wt/g	ASW/g	Comments
1	3	39	13.0	One vesicular H3 type, other two H2 types, one of which part of the base of a jar
2 and 3	70	1091	15.5	Sixty per cent (by ENV) of the sherds were recovered from ditch 118934 and this group also included a fragment of furnace lining
4 and 5	100	436	4.3	two barrel jars and an FRJ in an H4 fabric
6, 7 and 8	36	776	21.56	Includes three large sherds, one the rim of a barrel jar H1. Calcite and H4 were the commonest types; also a sherd in a shell-tempered fabric. All in calcite fabric from one or more thin-walled vessels
9 and assoc. features	73	646	8.8	Identifiable vessels limited to a lugged jar (9527) and two probable VRJs (9625 and 9530). Unclear whether lugged jars enjoyed a longer lifespan than 400BC – 100AD proposed by Rigby or if these sherds residual. Significant proportions of H1 Calcite, H3 types and H4 fabrics.
10 and 11	13	228	17.5	Only one shapeless fragment in a coarse rock tempered H2 fabric from enclosure 10. Enclosure 11 includes 3 flat bases. Majority of sherds in H2 Fine fabrics but H3 and H4 types also present

TABLE 25: SUMMARY OF HAND-MADE POTTERY FROM THE ROMAN ENCLOSURE DITCHES, BURTON CONSTABLE

Ditch	ENV	Wt/g	ASW/g
118927	87	743	8.5
118957	59	507	8.5
118958	923	16516	17.8
118934	16	135	8.4

TABLE 26: SUMMARY OF HAND-MADE POTTERY FROM THE LATER DITCHES, BURTON CONSTABLE

represented. Fourteen joining sherds (SF 1232) form part of an FRJ and there is another, substantially complete, FRJ in H2 Quartz. Vessel forms include a number of distinctive minor types with parallels among the assemblages from the ring ditches (BRGJ, CRJ, CROJ, HHRGJ, SqRJ, TriRJ) alongside the commoner ERJ, VRJ, BJ and OJ types. The assemblage also includes a VRSJ of probable first-century BC to first-century AD date. The distinctiveness of this assemblage probably resulted from it cutting through Structures 2 and 4 and other deposits relating to the Iron Age settlement.

The overall character of the small assemblage from ditch **118934** has more in common with those from ditches **118927** and **118957** than with ditch **118958**. The range of fabrics is limited and the only identifiable vessels are a possible VRJ and an FRJ.

Unstratified material

Although of limited use in contributing to the overall understanding of the site, three vessels from unstratified contexts have been selected for illustration as good examples of their type: an early VRJ (Fig. 94.55) in a vesicular H4 fabric with parallels from Reighton By-pass site (Cumberpatch unpublished 1, fig. 23:8, 9 and 10); an H2 Rock fabric (Fig. 95.81) and a WRGJ (Fig. 95.68).

Brandywell

The assemblage from Brandywell consisted of 1972 sherds of pottery weighing 27,346g and representing a maximum of 1855 vessels (ENV) with an overall average sherd weight of 14.7g. The range of fabrics is typical of the sites considered here, with a preponderance of H2 types and relatively small quantities of H1 and H4 types, but there are a number of distinctive features. H1 Shell wares are present in unusual quantities, notably from gullies **25249** and particularly **25247** while small quantities of other H1 fabrics are noted elsewhere. H3 wares are also present, notably from the first- to second-century field boundaries. Among the H2 fabrics, H2 Fine is particularly common, and nondescript H2 wares, lacking the larger inclusions seen in the other varieties, are also common, suggesting that the use of coarse

temper was less on this site than on the other sites along the pipeline route.

Vertical rim jar types are common throughout the site, as are FRJ forms, with other vessel types present in small quantities. The close similarity in the date range as indicated by the wheel-thrown wares as well as general similarities between the hand-made assemblages suggest that the activities represented were not widely separated in time. The absence of wheel-thrown wares from ditch **25209** suggests closeness in date to the ring gullies, also devoid of wheel-thrown pottery.

Structure 1

The four ring gully sections considered to be elements of Structure 1 produced a total assemblage consisting of 369 sherds weighing 4637g and representing a maximum of 354 vessels (ENV) with an average sherd weight of 13.1g (Table 27). The postholes within the area enclosed by the ring gullies add a further eighteen sherds. This includes two large sherds, used as post-packing in posthole **25199**.

The range of fabrics is wide with a small quantity of H1 and a larger quantity of H4 sherds (0.13% and 13.3% respectively) alongside the normal range of H2 types. The latter include a freshly broken pot disc. The unusual concentration of H4 fabrics may be due to the presence of a single vessel, although the shattered nature of the sherds precludes the identification of any internal joins. Vessel forms include ERJ, EROJ, FlRJ, FRJ, TriRJ and various VRJ types.

Structure 2

Group	ENV	Wt/g	ASW/g
25238	231	2503	10.8
25239	64	1162	18.1
25243	9	107	11.8
25119	50	865	17.3
Posthole 25199	10	463	46.3
Posthole 25193	2	5	2.5
Posthole 25214	3	17	5.7
Posthole 25220	1	15	15.0

TABLE 27: DISTRIBUTION OF POTTERY FROM STRUCTURE 1, BRANDYWELL, AND ASSOCIATED FEATURES

Gully	Sherds	Wt/g	ENV	ASW/g
25129	11	112	11	10.1
25137	84	2710	74	36.6

TABLE 28: DISTRIBUTION OF POTTERY FROM STRUCTURE 2, BRANDYWELL

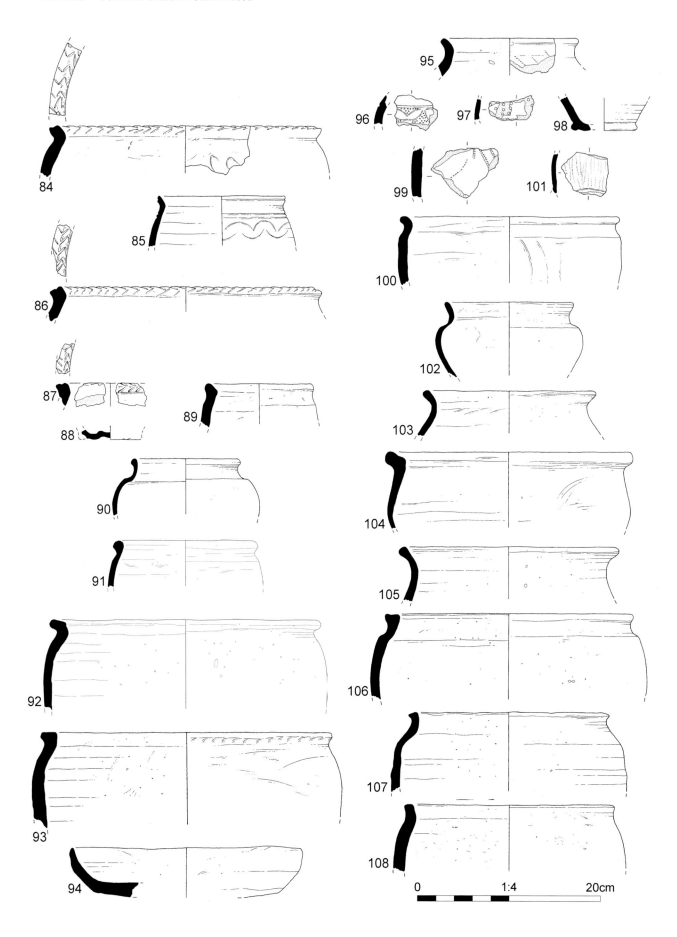

FIG. 96: HAND-MADE IRON AGE TRADITION POTTERY 84-108: BRANDYWELL AND NUTTLES

Illustrated hand-made pottery 5

Brandywell

84. VRJ-CS. H2 FINE FABRIC, RARE QUARTZ AND ROCK TO 5MM. IMPRESSED CHEVRON/HERRINGBONE PATTERN ON RIM. FILL *25115*, GULLY 25113

85. ERJ TYPE. *CF.* MAY 1996. FIG 19.54, 647, 649, 19.58 BUT IN SANDY BROWN H2 FINE FABRIC; SMALL SHARPLY ANGLED RIM. CURVILINEAR IARC AND DOT DECORATION EXT. FILL *25138*, GULLY 25137

86. VRJ-CS. H2 FINE FABRIC, RARE QUARTZ AND ROCK TO 5MM. CHEVRON/HERRINGBONE PATTERN ON RIM FILL *25115*, GULLY 25113

87. VRJ-CS? H2 FINE FABRIC. DEEPLY IMPRESSED CHEVRON DESIGN ON RIM; RIM FORM UNCERTAIN. FILL, *25115*, GULLY 25113

88. HOLLOW WARE. H2 FINE FABRIC, BLACK QUARTZ TEMPER. RAISED CIRCULAR DECORATION. FILL *25124*, PIT 25167

89. WROJ. H2 FINE BROWN SANDY FABRIC; SHORT WEDGE-RIM JAR, SLIGHT NECK ON OPEN BODY. SMOOTHED EXT. FILL *25186*, GULLY 25216

90. VRSJ. H2 FINE BROWN SANDY QUARTZ, V. FINE FABRIC. DISTINCTIVE FORM, EXCEPTIONALLY THIN-WALLED. RIM BURNISHED EXT AND INT. FILL *25009*, DITCH 25168

91. CROJ. ROUNDED CLUBBED RIM ON THIN NECK; FINE SANDY H2; OCC. ANGULAR QUARTZ. FILL *25100*, CUT 25097 OF DITCH 25116

92. FLRJ. FLAT SHARPLY EVERTED RIM ON ROUND JAR BODY. H2 RED FABRIC. LIGHT BUFF SURFACE, GREY CORE; ROUND RED INCS AND ROCK FRAGS. FILL *25202* OF POSTHOLE 25201

93. VRJ-CS. H2 ROCK, ANGULAR ROCK FRAGS TO 4MM SHORT, SQUARE-SECTION VERTICAL RIM ON A LARGE ROUNDED BODY. FILL *25202* OF POSTHOLE 25201

Nuttles

94. IRB. FINE, HARD SANDY H2 FABRIC. SHALLOW INTURNED RIM BOWL; ?ROMAN FORM. SMOOTHED INT AND EXT. SUBSOIL *3105*

95. ERJ. FINE SANDY H2 FABRIC, OCCASIONAL QUARTZ GRIT TO 1MM, SINGLE FLINT 6MM. CURVED EVERTED RIM, ROUND LIP. ANGLED COMB IMPRESSED LINES ON NECK. SUBSOIL *31001*

96. HOLLOW WARE. FINE SANDY H2 FABRIC, SPARSE WHITE QUARTZ GRIT TO 1.5MM. IARC, DOT INFILL AND DEEP INCISED LINE. SUBSOIL *31001*

97. HOLLOW WARE. FINE SANDY H2 FABRIC. PARALLEL LINES OF RING STAMPS. SUBSOIL 31001

98. JAR. FOOTED BASE. SHALLOW GROOVE FOOTRING. BLACK H2 FINE FABRIC. BURNISHED EXT. FURROW *31003*

99. JAR. ??SAME VESSEL AS 97; FINE H2 FABRIC. COMB IMPRESSED LINES EXT. FILL *31023*, CUT 31022, STRUCTURE 1

100. ERJ TYPE. ROUNDED RIM WITH PRONOUNCED NECK. HARD, H2 FINE FABRIC, V. FINE. SMOOTHED RIM AND NECK. VERT. STRIATED BODY. FILL *31052*, DITCH 31518

101. HOLLOW WARE. VERTICAL LINES OF SINGLE FINE, DEEP IMPRESSIONS. VERY FINE SANDY H2 TYPE FABRIC, MOD. FINE ROUNDED QUARTZ GRIT, SOFT RED INCS. FILL *31096*, DITCH 31523

102. VRSJ. QUARTZ TEMPERED BLACK SANDY H2 FINE FABRIC. EVERTED RIM ON SHOULDERED GLOBULAR BODY. BURNISHED EXT. FILL *31082*, RING GULLY 31519

103. ERJ TYPE. TALL THIN EVERTED RIM, IRREGULAR LIP ON CURVED NECK. BROWN TO ORANGE SANDY H2 FINE FABRIC, OCC. LARGER GRIT. FILL *31127*, DITCH 31145

104. ERJ. THICK EVERTED RIM WITH CONCAVE INT. PROFILE ON A THIN BODY; FINE H2 FABRIC. SMOOTHED EXT. FILL *31048*, GULLY 31516

105. ERJ. EVERTED RIM WITH LONG NECK AND CLUBBED LIP; H2 FINE SANDY BODY; UNUSUAL FORM. SMOOTHED INT. AND EXT. FILL *31506* OF CUT 31505, PIT 31523

106. VRJ-CS VARIANT. SHORT, FLAT-TOPPED CLUBBED RIM. H2 FABRIC, MOD. ANGULAR QUARTZ TO 4MM, RARELY LARGER. SMOOTHED RIM AND NECK. FILLS *31083&31112*, STRUCTURE 1

107. VRJ-CS. H2 MICA FABRIC. ABUNDANT ANGULAR WHITE QUARTZ TO 4MM, BIOTITE; BLACK DEPOSIT INTERNALLY. SMOOTHED NECK, PINCHED RIM. FILL *31063*, CUT 31062, STRUCTURE 1

108. VRJ-CS. SHORT FLAT-TOPPED VERTICAL RIM. SOME SOOTING EXT. H2 FINE FABRIC, OCC. ROCK AND QUARTZ TO 6MM. SMOOTHED NECK. FILL *31083*, CUT, 31085, STRUCTURE 1

The pottery assemblage from contexts constituting Structure 2 consists of ninety-five sherds weighing 2822g representing maximum of eighty-five vessels. The average sherd weight is 33.2g (Table 28). The assemblage from gully **25137** is notably larger in size and consists of larger sherds (as indicated by the ASW) than the assemblage from gully **25129**.

Gully **25137** included identifiable rim sherds (ERJ, BJ, ?FRJ) as well as the bases and body sherds from at least two large jars in distinctive H2 Coarse fabrics, and a sherd with IARC

curvilinear and dot decoration, of a probable late Iron Age date (Fig. 96.85). In this respect the assemblage is a distinctive and unusual one. Pit **25117**, cut by gully **25129**, produced as small assemblage predominantly of H2 Fine type. Two rim sherds, probably from the same vessel, a TriRJ, are the only sherds in a slightly coarser rock tempered fabric.

Gully 25113

The curvilinear gully cutting the Structure 2 ring gully produced an assemblage of 275 sherds weighing 4191g and representing a maximum of 269 vessels, giving an ASW of 15.5g. The assemblage is distinguished by the fact that it includes a high proportion of rim sherds (mainly VRJ-CS with ERJ, FRJ and BRGJ types). Smoothed and burnished body sherds are also common and fine H2 fabrics predominate. Two contexts include rim sherds with impressed chevron decoration (Fig. 96.84, 86 and 87). The VRJ-CS rims are typically short, slightly everted and with round or slightly clubbed lips. The bodies appear to be of a narrow or pear-shaped form rather than the wider globular form.

Structure 3

Gully **25228** produced three sherds, including a fragment of a base, in H2 Rock fabrics. Feature **25234**, possibly a continuation of the same gully, also produced three sherds.

Mid-first to early second-century ditches

The range of fabrics from ditches **25116**, **25208** and **25209** was wide with H1, H3 and H4 types all represented in small quantities alongside the H2 wares, of which H2 Fine is the commonest sub-type (Table 29). The range of vessel forms is somewhat wider than that from the earlier structures. VRJ types, including the fine VRSJ and VRGJ types, are the commonest forms with smaller numbers of CROJ, EROJ, ERJ, FRJ, Globular and lugged jars. As in Structure 1, smoothed and burnished sherds are common but more elaborate types of decoration are absent.

Second century enclosure ditch

Ditch **25168** produced an assemblage of 107 sherds weighing 1410g and representing a maximum of 87 vessels, giving an ASW of 16.2g. One small sherd of H3 Chalk fabric is present among an assemblage consisting predominantly of H2 Fine fabrics. The numbers of identifiable vessel types is low although the range was wide, given the small size of the assemblage. The group includes one VRSJ with parallels in the earlier ditches and a TriRJ, a rare type also present in Structure 1.

Gully **25064**, which appeared to drain into the north-eastern arm of the ditch, produced three small sherds in H2 Fine fabrics, while pit **25250**, which may also have drained into the ditch through gully **25030**, included the base of a small jar

Ditch	Sherds	ENV	Wt/g	ASW/g
25116	549	540	7242	13.4
25208	44	43	378	8.8
25209	78	74	1035	14.0
Total	**671**	**657**	**8655**	**13.2**

TABLE 29: DISTRIBUTION OF POTTERY IN FIRST- TO SECOND-CENTURY DITCHES, BRANDYWELL

in an H2 Quartz fabric, along with body sherds, the majority in H2 Fine fabrics.

The rectangular structure

The group of postholes adjacent to ditch **25208** produced thirteen sherds weighing 58g representing a maximum of twelve vessels, giving a relatively low ASW of 4.8g. H2 Fine sherds are the commonest type represented. A VRJ-FSG is the only identifiable vessel type. The sherds are generally abraded, consistent with a slow accumulation of weathered material as the posts decayed and the postholes filled up. Two small gullies in the same part of the site, **25038** and **25093**, produced body sherds in similar H2 Fine fabrics.

Second century burials

The fill of burial **25184** contained an assemblage of eighteen sherds weighing 260g with an ASW of 14.4g. Two rims are identifiable, an ERJ and a VRJ-CS. The three sherds, weighing 58g, from child burial **25059** are body sherds in differing H2 fabrics, showing a moderate to high degree of abrasion, similar to that seen in the non-funerary contexts.

Pits

Pit **25167** produced sixty-eight sherds weighing 719g and representing maximum of 67 vessels. The ASW is 10.7g. Sherds in H3 and H1/H4 fabrics are present in the group but the majority of sherds are of the H2 Fine type. Rims include Tri-RJ, ERJ and VRJ-FSG types. Specific sherds of note include a pot disc and an unusual base with a raised element in the centre (Fig. 96.88).

Two other small pits cut though the earlier ring gullies: pit **25173** which produced a small group of body sherds, all in fine fabrics containing occasional flint grains, and pit **25230**, which contained the rim of a VRJ-FSG and the base of a jar, the latter in the H4 fabric along with body sherds in a variety of H2 fabrics and, in one case, H3.

Gullies

Forty sherds, weighing 527g, from gully **25247**, which cut through Structure 2 and pit **25167**, represent a maximum of thirty-nine vessels. The assemblage consists primarily of H2 fabrics but also includes a group of shell tempered sherds (H1), forming 19.3 per cent of the total, a slightly unusual occurrence in an area dominated by H2 and H1 calcite tempered wares. Identifiable vessel types include two ERJ rims and an FRJ rim.

The 135 sherds, weighing 1736g and representing up to 99 vessels, from the fills of gully **25249** include a wide variety of vessel types: Barrel jars, VRJ types, FRJ, WROJ (Fig. 96.89) and unidentified jars. Two bases in coarse rock tempered fabrics appear to be from jars of a large size although exactly how large is unclear. Fine

H2 fabrics are common among the rims although less so among the body sherds. A single small sherd of shell tempered pottery (H1 Shell) is unusual but is paralleled in gully **25247** and pit **25167**.

Gully **25177**, parallel to gully **25249**, produced small groups of body sherds, all in fine fabrics. The majority of the twenty-one sherds, weighing 195g, from feature **25210** are of the H2 Fine type although the group also includes rock tempered sherds and the rim of an FRJ in an unusual fabric with possible slag inclusions. The group also includes two VRJ-FSG rims.

Nuttles

The importance of the Nuttles site assemblage lies especially in the presence of wheel-thrown wares of second-century AD date alongside substantial hand-made assemblages: 1229 sherds weighing 24,679g and represented a maximum of 829 vessels (ENV) with an average sherd weight of 29.7g. Taken alone, a comparison of the range of vessel types and fabrics present in the Iron Age contexts with those from the second-century ditches does not seem to indicate any significant change in the types of vessel being made and used. The major categories, the ERJ, OJ and VRJ groups, remain significant throughout and the differences in less common types (BRGJ, CRJ, CROJ, EROJ, TriRJ) are based on single occurrences which hardly seems a reliable basis upon which to propose significant chronological differentiation.

The second-century ditches yielded more in the way of H5 fabrics and variants than the earlier features, but again the quantities are too low for this to be asserted as a distinction. Other unusual types, including the H2 Fuel Ash and H2 Flint types, remain broadly constant.

Late Iron Age settlement

Dating evidence from this phase of activity was sparse and there was little that was self-evidently chronologically distinctive in the hand-made pottery assemblage. No Romano-British pottery was associated with any of these contexts.

Gully **31522**, the southern section of the Structure 1 ring gully, produced 188 sherds weighing 5919 representing a maximum of 122 vessels with an overall ASW of 48.5g. Fragments of three vessels, a VRJ-CS (Fig. 96.106), a VRJ-CT and a large jar, linking contexts **31083** and **31112**, largely account for the high average sherd weight. Other contexts in the same part of the ring gully produced a wide range of vessel types including open jars (OJ and EROJ) vertical rimmed jars (VRGJ, VRJ-CS (Fig. 96.108), VRJ type), globular or round-bodied vessels (BRGJ, ERGJ) and everted rim forms (ERJ).

Bases and base/body combinations attest to the presence of several large jars from context **31083**. Four sherds from context **31041** are tempered with white, vesicular fragments believed to be fuel ash (Pitman and Doonan, this volume, page 171). The pottery was associated with burnt deposits of charcoal, heat-affected clay, and charred plant remains.

The larger northern section of the ring gully, **31514**, produced 187 sherds weighing 3586g and representing a maximum of twenty-nine vessels with an average sherd weight of 123.6g. As with the southern section, the distribution of sherds varies considerably between different contexts (Table 30). Most notably the assemblages include substantial parts of two large vessels, one FRJ and one VRJ-CS (Fig. 96.107). The group also includes a sherd bearing comb-impressed lines (Fig. 96.99). Bases are flat or with short, solid pedestals.

Gully **31519** also contained an assemblage of relatively large sherds, with twenty-two sherds weighing 725g representing a maximum of eighteen vessels with an ASW of 40.2g. The range of vessels is broadly similar to those from the groups discussed above in that it includes a VRJ-CS jar rim, eleven body sherds from a large jar and the rim and body of a fine VRSJ with a burnished surface (Fig. 96.102). During initial cleaning of the site, the base and lower body from a large jar (SF 321), weighing 1805g in total, were recovered from the surface of this feature, along with a small group of H4 sherds.

Context	Cut	ENV	Wt/g	ASW/g
Structure 1				
31024	31022	4	31	7.7
31023	31022	1	42	42
31063	31062	14	1900	135.7
31053	31062	3	1441	480.3
31061	31056	2	55	27.5
31057	31056	5	117	23.4
31112	31114	20	185	9.25
31083&31112		3	3076	1025.3
31083	31085	5	51	10.2
31084	31085	65	2077	31.9
31041	31042	17	413	24.2
31021	31020	12	117	9.75
Total		**151**	**9505**	**1867.3**
Structure 2				
31082	31081	6	273	45.5
31043	31044	12	488	40.6
Total		**18**	**761**	**42.3**

TABLE 30: DISTRIBUTION OF POTTERY FROM STRUCTURES 1 AND 2, NUTTLES

Ditch **31518** contained thirteen sherds, representing the same number of vessels, and weighing 459g, giving an ASW of 35.3g. The assemblage includes two rims, one from a funnel-rimmed jar, the other an everted rim jar with a smoothed neck and scored shallow vertical striations (Fig. 96.100). The striations are reminiscent of Scored ware but are less marked, and the form is not typical of Scored ware (Elsdon 1992), suggesting that the resemblance may be fortuitous. Shallow vertical scoring is not an unusual feature in the assemblages from the pipeline as a whole.

A group of pits within the area defined by the Structure 1 ring gully produced only a small pottery assemblage. Four abraded body sherds in a fine H2 fabric from pit **31059**, the base of a jar in a rock-tempered H2 from pit **31124**, two small sherds in a fine sandy H2 fabric with smoothed external surfaces from pit **31129**; and a single small body sherd from pit **31148**.

Late Iron Age or early Roman features

Ditch **31520** produced an assemblage of twenty-three sherds weighing 173g representing a maximum of twenty-two vessels, giving an ASW of 7.8g. The sherds are generally small and often abraded. A VRJ-CS from context **31135** is the only identifiable vessel, and there is one other unidentifiable rim sherd. Fine textured H2 fabrics predominate (77.4%) with a single small sherd of vesicular H4. The group includes a small fragment of a solid pedestal base.

Gully **31521** produced a small group of twelve rims and body sherds together with a footring base, the only sherd of distinctive character in the group, the rim sherds being small, in poor condition and only identifiable as of possible ERJ and FRJ type. The assemblage weighs 141g in total, representing a maximum of eleven vessels and is exclusively of H2 type fabrics.

Ditch **31516** produced ninety-two sherds, weighing 1460g, representing a maximum of eighty-eight vessels. The sherds are in a variety of H2 fabrics, including examples with fuel ash and flint temper, with a single sherd of H1/H4 type. The average sherd weight is 16.5g. The range of identifiable vessel forms is wide with FRJ, OJ, ERJ (Fig. 96.104), VRJ-FSG and VRJ-CS types all present.

Second century features

Contexts dated by the presence of Romano-British wheel-thrown pottery alongside the hand-made wares produced a collective assemblage of 351 sherds weighing 7103g representing a maximum of 317 vessels. The average sherd weight of 20g is high for linear features but significantly lower than the average weights recorded from the earlier settlement contexts.

The identifiable vessels from ditch **31145** are dominated by funnel-rimmed jars, with only one rim from another type of vessel, a flat-rimmed jar. Fine H2 fabrics predominate although small numbers of other types are also present, including a sherd with the vesicular fuel ash slag temper noted from Structure 1 and sherds with flint temper. There are also some sherds in the unusual H5 fabric. Context **31127** was originally assigned as the fill of a supposed feature cut by ditch **31145**, but subsequently reinterpreted as part of the same ditch. This interpretation is supported by several instances where sherds are so similar, in the appearance of the fabric, to sherds from the fills of ditch **31145** that it is probably that they came from the same pot or from pots of very similar type. Similarly, FRJ sherds from the two contexts are likely to be from the same vessel as they have very similar profiles. Of particular note is a sherd with pinched decoration. The combined fills of **31145** and context **31127** together produced 121 sherds, weighing 3846g from a maximum of 102 vessels, giving an unusually large ASW of 37.7g.

The western and central intervention through ditch **31515** produced only four body sherds, weighing 56g, all in H2 fabrics. However, the eastern terminus of this ditch, **31508**, yielded an additional 47 sherds, representing up to 42 vessels and weighing 642g.

Feature **31523** contained a modestly sized pottery assemblage of sixty-three sherds weighing 942g and representing a maximum of sixty vessels. The ASW is 15.7g. The range of identifiable vessels is wide and includes FRJ, VRJ-CS, VRJ type and ERJ (Fig. 96.105). The range of H2 fabrics, which includes fuel ash tempered types, is also wide. No direct parallels have been found for an unusual comb-impressed sherd in an H2 type fabric with a bright orange exterior surface (Fig. 96.101).

An assemblage of 116 sherds weighing 1617g and representing a maximum of 109 vessels was recovered from the large ditch at the southern end of the excavation area. The average sherd weight, 14.8g, is typical of those from the other second-century features. A wide range of fabrics includes a variety of H2 types and small numbers of H4 and H5 sherds. Three funnel-rim jars along with a single ERJ type are represented, along with the shoulder and neck of an unidentified jar. The group also includes a small crucible fragment.

Other contexts

Residual finds from medieval or later furrows **31003** and **31071** include VRJ-FSG and ERJ rims, and a footring base. Fabrics are of the H2 and H5 type. Unstratified finds from the subsoil surface include some of the less common types of vessel (TriRJ and CROJ) alongside ERJ, FRJ and OJ forms. Of particular interest are three decorated sherds: a sherd which bore incised IARC designs with a deep incised line and dotted infill (Fig. 96.96) in a very fine sandy fabric similar, at least superficially, to a sandy H2 type; a sherd which bears parallel lines of ring stamps (Fig. 96.97); and the rim of an ERJ with comb impressions on the neck (Fig. 96.95). The profile of an inturned rim bowl (Fig. 96.94) suggests that it may be a copy of a wheel-thrown Romano-British form, an unusual occurrence given the general persistence of traditional forms throughout the Roman period.

Lelley

The total assemblage of handmade pottery from the site comprises 2770 sherds, weighing 43,066g, and representing a maximum of 2491 vessels. The overall average sherd weight is 17.2g.

Structure 1

Structure 1 produced over 70 per cent of the total site assemblage: 1943 sherds weighing 37,879g representing a maximum of 1772 vessels, giving an average sherd weight of 21.3g (Table 31). The range of vessel types is wide, particularly among the vertical rimmed vessels. Cross-context joins are particularly common, including two cases with an unstratified context (35592) and in one case with a subsoil context (3501). In two cases, cross-context joins link groups of sherds recorded as small finds, a VRJ (SF 272) and a VRJ-FSG (SF 275). In another case (SF 268), not all of the sherds join but the similarity between the fabrics suggests that they are from the same vessel, a jar of ERJ type but with a small, scarcely everted rim.

The distribution of pottery within the feature was uneven with contexts the south-eastern terminus 35288 and the adjacent intervention 35294, producing 56 and 18 per cent of the total assemblage by ENV, respectively. Other aspects of these contexts, particularly fill 35287, are unusual and distinctive. The greater part of the assemblage from this fill is characterised by general homogeneity represented by a brown to grey sandy textured H2 body with varying proportions of quartz and rock grit, sometimes with angular and rounded (pebble-like) grit in the same sherds. The overwhelming impression is of a broadly similar range of H2 fabrics which cuts across distinctions in the vessel forms, represented by rims and bases.

This fill also includes a group of sherds in the distinctive sandy grey H5 fabric. This fabric contained sparse, well sorted rock grains up to 3mm and occasional quartz grains of a similar size. The overall appearance of the fabric is superficially similar to Romano-British grey ware and the sherds are well-finished with only limited signs of being hand-made. It is unclear how many

Cut	Contexts	ENV	Wt/g	ASW/g
35288	35287, 35296	1064	25842	24.3
35294	35295	331	5273	15.9
35367	35368	97	1201	12.3
35192	35193	60	1273	21.2
35209	35208	14	465	33.2
35218	35219	55	148	2.6
35238	35239, 35236	169	1973	11.7
35231	35232	7	234	33.4
35252	35253	2	84	42
35273	35274	2	33	16.5
Joins				
35288/35294	35287&35295	32	661	20.6
35192/35209	35193&35208	16	450	28.1
35294&35238	35296&35239	1	128	128
35288&35367	35287&35368	1	104	104

TABLE 31: DISTRIBUTION OF HAND-MADE POTTERY FROM STRUCTURE 1, LELLEY

vessels are represented but it may be no more than two or three in total. Abrasion on these sherds is pronounced and joining sherds were rare. Similar sherds were identified in context 35368, 35296 (SF 275), 35295 (SF 273, and tall, funnel-shaped rims) and 35239.

Twelve sherds, some joining, are in a third distinctive fabric: soft, fine brown with a slightly soapy finish and fine vesicles in cross-section, neither obviously shell tempered nor quartz tempered. These sherds have a distinctive finish with burnished cross-hatching on the neck and linear striations on the body interrupted by narrow vertical panels or stripes (Fig. 97.110 and 112). A ring-foot or hollow pedestal base from the same context is probably from the same vessel. Parallels include Dragonby (May 1996, fig. 19.37:303; ceramic stages 10-11, pre-Flavian to late first century AD) which may indicate an origin in Lincolnshire.

Intervention 35238 produced the next largest group of sherds, with links with other parts of the ring gully through cross-context joins. The group includes two joining sherds from the base of a jar distinguished by abundant angular rock and flint fragments which appear to have been freshly crushed for inclusion in the clay body. Otherwise, this context is dominated by sandy textured H2 wares containing sparse to moderate quantities of rounded inclusions. The other interventions produced much smaller groups of sherds, appearing to represent clear evidence for non-random or structured deposition. The distinct groups identified during the excavation (SFs 272, 273 and 275) lend credence to the suggestion that these deposits were in some way unusual or distinctive.

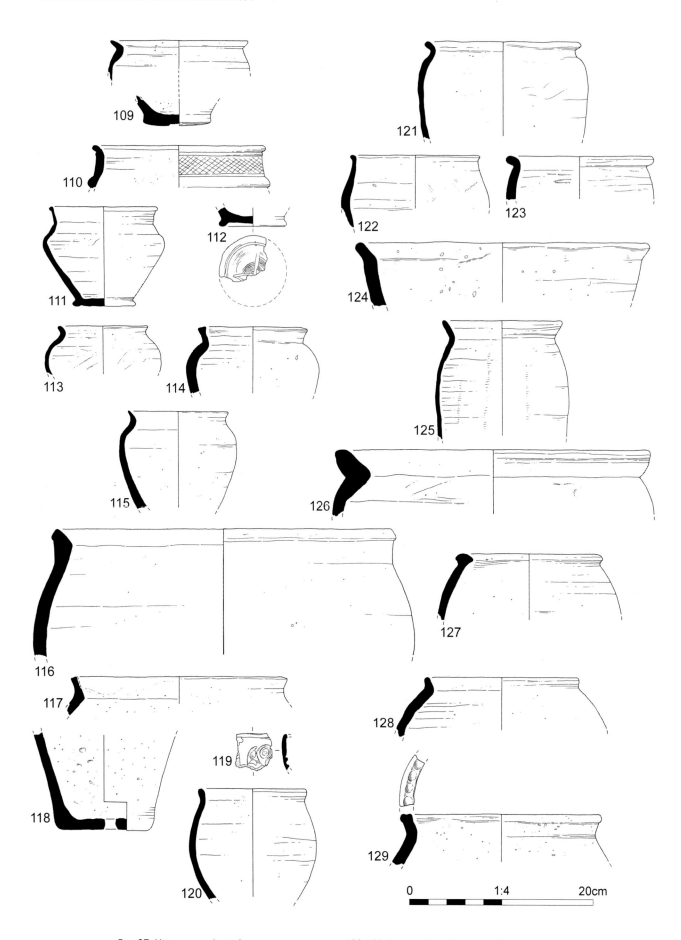

FIG. 97: HAND-MADE IRON AGE TRADITION POTTERY 109-129: LELLEY, NEW YORK AND BRAEMERE HILL

Illustrated hand-made pottery 6

Lelley

109. ERJ. H2 FINE BLACK FABRIC; UNUSUAL LAMINATED FRACTURE. SMOOTHED EXT. FILL *35287*, CUT 35288, STRUCTURE 1

110. CORDONED BEAKER. UNUSUAL SOFT BROWN SOAPY H2 FINE FABRIC. FILL *35287*, CUT 35288, STRUCTURE 1

111. VRSJ TYPE. HIGH-SHOULDERED JAR, H2 FINE BLACK SANDY BODY, RARE QUARTZ GRIT TO 2MM, OCC. LARGER; THIN BLACK DEPOSIT ON THE BURNISHED SURFACE. FILLS *35462&35463*, PITS 35464 AND 35465

112. CORDONED BEAKER. UNUSUAL SOFT BROWN SOAPY H2 FINE FABRIC. FILL *35287*, CUT 35288, STRUCTURE 1

113. ERGJ. H2 FINE BLACK SANDY BODY; GLOBULAR BODY, SMALL EVERTED RIM. SMOOTHED EXT. FILL *35374*, CUT 35375, STRUCTURE 3

114. VRJ-FSG. SANDY GREY H5 FABRIC, SPARSE BUT REGULAR ROUNDED QUARTZ AND OCC. ROCK GRIT TO 4MM; ALMOST VERTICAL WEDGE-SHAPED RIM ON SHOULDERED BODY. FILL *35462*, PIT 35464

115. ERJ. HIGH SHOULDERED JAR WITH SHORT EVERTED RIM IN A BLACK SANDY H2 FINE FABRIC; TRACES OF BLACK DEPOSIT EXT. SMOOTHED EXT FILL *35537*, PIT 35534

116. WRJ. LARGE JAR. H2 FINE SANDY FABRIC, DISTINCTIVE RIM. SMOOTHED INT. AND EXT. FILL *35287*, CUT 35288, STRUCTURE 1

117. ERJ VARIANT. BRIGHT ORANGE H2 QUARTZ FABRIC, ABUNDANT FINE QUARTZ SAND, MOD. WELL SORTED SUB-ANGULAR QUARTZ TO 3MM. LAYER *35502*, UNDERLYING POSSIBLE OVEN

New York

118. 'FLOWERPOT'. H2 FABRIC, ABUNDANT ANGULAR ROCK FRAGS TO 8MM; HOLE IN CENTRE OF BASE. FILL *119250*, CUT 119249, STRUCTURE 1

119. V. UNUSUAL STAMPED DECORATION. H2 FINE SANDY FABRIC. FILL *119138*, DITCH 120024

120. VRJ TYPE. ROUND-LIPPED, SLIGHTLY EVERTED VERTICAL RIM ON A ROUND BODY. BROWN SANDY H2 FINE FABRIC. FINELY SMOOTHED EXT. FILL *117025*, DITCH 117024

121. ERJ. FINE BROWN SANDY H2 FABRIC. SMOOTHED EXT. FILL *117025*, DITCH 117024

122. VRJ-NB TYPE. SMALL VERTICAL BEADED RIM, VESTIGIAL NECK ON NARROW-SHOULDERED BODY. BROWN SANDY H2 COARSE FABRIC, OCC. QUARTZ TO 3MM. BURNISHED EXT. FILL *119814*, DITCH 120030

123. ERJ. DISTINCTIVE ROUNDED EVERTED RIM JAR. BROWN SANDY H2 FINE FABRIC, FINE SMOOTHED FINISH INT. AND EXT. FILL *117023*, PIT 117022

124. EROJ. H2 COARSE FABRIC, PROMINENT SUB-ANGULAR WHITE QUARTZ TO 6MM; SLIGHTLY EVERTED PINCHED RIM ON AN OPEN BODY. FILL *119803*, CUT 119840, STRUCTURE 4

125. FRJ TYPE. COARSE SANDY H2 ROCK FABRIC, ABUNDANT ANGULAR ROCK FRAGS, DISTINCTIVE BARREL-SHAPED BODY, PROMINENT FUNNEL NECK/RIM. FILL *3626*, DITCH 3619

126. WRGJ. V. THICK, SHARPLY EVERTED RIM. SANDY, H2 FINE FABRIC, OCC. ANGULAR QUARTZ TO 2MM. FILL *119139*, DITCH 120025

127. HHRGJ. H2 FINE FABRIC, ABUNDANT FINE QUARTZ SAND, SPARSE LARGER GRAINS. FILL *119139*, DITCH 120025

128. WRGJ. SHORT VERTICAL RIM ON GLOBULAR BODY. H2 ROCK FABRIC, MOD. ANGULAR ROCK FRAGS TO 4MM. FILL *119138*, DITCH 120024

Braemere Hill

129. FRJ TYPE. H2 ROCK FABRIC. SPACED ROUND FINGERTIP IMPRESSIONS ON FLAT LIP OF RIM. UPPER FILL *4726*, DITCH 4736

Vessel types are diverse. A high frequency of VRJ forms in context **35287** conceals a considerable degree of variability in the size of the vessels and the exact shape of the rims which range from thick-walled, medium sized vessels to the much smaller, finer vessels. Other vessels include ERJ types (Fig. 97.109), open jars, funnel-necked jars, wedge-rimmed jars (Fig. 97.116) and globular jars. Large jars, as indicated by body sherds with a broad curvature, are also well represented.

The presence of the late hand-made form, VRSJ, provides the only indication of the date range of the feature: the VRSJ form seems to date to between the first century BC and the early or mid-first century AD. To suggest that the absence of wheel-thrown wares indicates a date in the earlier part of this range may be to over-interpret the data.

Structure 2

The pottery assemblage from Structure 2 consists of just eighty-seven sherds weighing 272g representing a maximum of eighty-five vessels with an average sherd weight of 3.2g, a striking contrast to the assemblage from Structure 1. With the exception of a small number of sherds in the H1 Fine and H4 fabrics all of the sherds are in H2 fabrics and show the usual range of variation in the size and character of the inclusions. The distinctive fabric H5 is absent. The distribution of the pottery shows no particular bias towards a particular area although the truncation of the southern section of the gully may have obscured possible variation.

Structure 3

The partial ring gully of Structure 3 produced an assemblage of 242 sherds of pottery weighing 1510g and representing a maximum of 226 vessels (ENV) with an average sherd weight of 6.6g. The fabrics are of various H2 types with a single small sherd of H4. The distinctive H5 fabrics seen in Structure 1 are notable by their absence. Vessel rims are well represented, with various ERJ and VRJ forms present, including an ERGJ (Fig. 97.113), as well as a WRGJ and an unusual square-rimmed jar, although the range is smaller than that from Structure 1.

Pit 35465

Pit **35465** produced 219 sherds weighing 1100g. These represent a maximum of 212 vessels, giving an average sherd weight of 5.1g, but were probably the remains of a much smaller number of smashed vessels. The assemblage is notable for the strikingly high proportion of fabric type H4, which constitutes 75.4 per cent of the total (ENV). Vessel types in H4 fabrics include VRJ, ERJ, FRJ and WRJ.

Pit 35464

The pottery assemblage from pit **35464**, just to the north of pit **35465**, consists of seventy-five sherds weighing 563g and representing a maximum of forty vessels. The average sherd weight is 14g, closer to that of Structure 1 than to Structure 2 or pit **35465**. The range of fabrics includes H2 and H2 Fine (87.5% of the total) with smaller quantities of the H4 and H5 types. The assemblage includes two rim sherds (EROJ and VRJ-FSG) and the complete profile of a fine VRSJ with a burnished surface (Fig. 97.112).

Residual pottery from later contexts

A high proportion of the hand-made pottery from the site was residual in medieval features. A number of distinctive vessels are present: they include a VRF-FSG (Fig. 97.114), an ERJ (Fig. 97.115) and an ERJ variant (Fig. 97.117).

New York

The total site assemblage consists of 770 sherds weighing 11424g and representing a maximum of 647 vessels with

Structure	Ring gully	ENV	Wt/g	ASW/g
1	119840	20	61	3.1
2	120027	7	120	17.1
3	120028	7	32	4.6
4	119840	20	377	18.9
4	119842	2	25	12.5
Total		**56**	**615**	

TABLE 32: SUMMARY OF HAND-MADE POTTERY ASSEMBLAGES FROM STRUCTURES, NEW YORK

an average sherd weight of 17.6g. Of particular note, ninety-one crucible fragments provide evidence for non-ferrous metal working. Non-ferrous metal working seems to have been locally organised on a relatively small scale: as such it would share a basic structure in common with pottery production and presumably with other kinds of craft production and manufacture.

Iron Age settlement

The pottery assemblages from the four ring gullies are of poor quality in that they consist of only small groups of heavily abraded sherds. Most are in H2 fabrics, with a few examples of the vesicular H4 fabric (Table 32). The assemblages from Structures 1, 2 and 3 consist only of body sherds, but ring gully **119840** included a rim sherd, from an EROJ (Fig. 97.124).

It is not clear whether the limited size and poor condition of the sherds is the result of the apparently severe truncation suffered by these structures or because they had a function, perhaps industrial, that did not primarily involve the use of pottery. This paucity of material contrasts with the often substantial pottery assemblages from ring gullies elsewhere on the pipeline.

Late Iron Age ditch systems

In contrast to the ring gullies, the later boundary ditches produced larger groups, although scarcely more informative. Two features stand out: ditches **120026** and **120030**.

Sixty-one sherds of pottery weighing 1187g and representing a maximum of twenty-four vessels recovered from ditch **120026** have an average sherd weight of 49.4g. The disparity between the number of sherds and the ENV figure and the high ASW figure is attributable to the presence of five sherds forming the flat base and lower body of a jar (SF 1383) and twenty-nine sherds forming the profile of a VRJ-FSG vessel (SF 1384) with a flat base. Both vessels resemble each other in the character of their fabrics and are distinctive within the group by virtue of the inclusion of prominent angular rock fragments, probably freshly smashed, in a very distinctive fine matte black body. Other vessels include an everted rim jar, an open jar and an everted rim open jar.

The assemblage from ditch **120030** consists of seventy-four sherds of pottery weighing 1796g and representing a maximum of sixty-eight vessels with an average sherd weight of 26.4g. Vessel types include open jars with both plain and everted rims, a barrel jar and two VRJ types (Fig. 97.122; VRJ-NB type). With the exception of a single very small abraded sherd of H4 type, all the fabrics are of H2 types with coarsely rock tempered sherds particularly common in the upper fill of intervention **119815**. Ditch

120029 produced only eight abraded body sherds, the low average sherd weight of 5.5g, perhaps indicating a higher level of residuality. Ditch **119155** produced two joining sherds in a rock-tempered H2 fabric, while ditch **119153**, probably a continuation of the same feature, produced a single small sherd in a fine H2 fabric.

Reorganised field system: ditches 120024 and 120020

The fills of the intersecting ditches **120020** and **120024** together produced 117 sherds weighing 1499g and representing a maximum of 108 vessels with an average sherd weight of 13.8g. This combined figure conceals a marked disparity in average sherd weights: 15.8g for ditch **120024** and 6.7g for ditch **120020**. The ranges of fabrics from the two assemblages are similar, both including small quantities of H4 sherds alongside a variety of H2 types; the terminus of ditch 120024 also includes a small sherd in the sandy grey H5 fabric.

All of the diagnostic sherds came from the central intervention through ditch **120024** and include the rim of a VRJ-CS with shallow finger impressions on the rim, two EROJ rims and a WRGJ (Fig. 97.128). No parallel has been traced for an unusual decorated sherd: flat with deep stamped circular and curvilinear decoration externally (Fig. 97.119). The fabric is extremely fine and sandy in texture and the shape of the sherd is not attributable to any specific vessel type. Part of a broken pot disc was also present in this context.

Ninety crucible fragments from intervention **119137** in ditch **120024** include rims and spouts and some possible mould fragments. The soft, crumbly sherds had suffered considerably from abrasion. The sherds were pale grey in colour and had a very light, light cindery texture (see Pitman and Doonan, this volume, page 171). Their presence in a boundary ditch is of interest in that metal working seems to have normally been carried out at some distance from dwellings and other structures, perhaps for safety reasons (Giles 2007:399, see also Hingley 2006). A possible crucible fragment was also recovered from intervention **119224** ditch **120020**, which otherwise contained only abraded body sherds and flakes in H2 fabrics, in most cases fine grained types. The crucible fragments from the site weigh 213g in total and up to eighty-five vessels, though probably far fewer, are represented.

Early Roman enclosure ditches 120022 and 120034

The larger of the two enclosure ditches, **120022**, contained only a single small sherd from the rim of a globular jar in a fine sandy H2 fabric. Ditch **120034**, partially overlying Structure 1, contained an assemblage of eighteen sherds weighing 137g representing a maximum of seventeen vessels with an average sherd weight of 8g, in addition to wheel-thrown wares. Body sherds predominate and

diagnostic sherds are limited to rim sherds from a VRJ and jar of unidentified type. Abrasion was once again a feature of this assemblage. A small group of body sherds in various H2 fabrics from ditch **3618**, recorded during evaluation trenching (Savage 2011) include the rim and body of an FRJ type vessel (Fig. 97.125). Pit **119249** contained a perforated 'flowerpot' style base of a jar (Fig. 97.118) probably used in conjunction with a pad of hay or straw as a strainer.

Pits 120035, 120025 and 119829

The average sherd weights for pits **120035**, **120025** and **119829** are 10.4g, 21g and 48g respectively, suggesting rather different formation processes were operating in each case. Pit **120035** contained a single VRJ-CS type jar rim on a globular body along with small and abraded body sherds. The relatively wide range of vessel types represented among the thirty-six sherds, weighing 652g and representing a maximum of thirty-one vessels, from pit **120025** includes a barrel jar, a WRGJ (Fig. 97.126), a bowl or open jar in a vesicular H4 fabric and a very distinctive globular jar with an unusual hammerhead rim (Fig. 97.127). The assemblage from pit **119829** includes a VRJ-CS with a pinched rim and a group of sherds in a coarse grey H2 fabric, containing abundant angular rock fragments.

Other contexts

The fill of a shallow feature, **117022**, overlying the central area of the excavation area, produced a group of thirty-six sherds weighing 418g representing a maximum of twenty-six vessels, giving an average sherd weight of 16g. The majority of the sherds were in fine H2 fabrics and a number had smoothed or burnished surfaces; two vessel types were identified, a WRGJ and an ERJ (Fig. 97.123).

Ditch **117024**, recorded during monitoring of topsoil removal 180m to the west of the excavation area, produced 176 sherds weighing 2371g representing a maximum of 158 vessels. The average sherd weight is 15g. Unusually, the group includes a significant proportion of vesicular H4 fabrics, with two ERJ(H4) rims. Vessels in the generally commoner H2 fabrics include an ERJ (Fig. 97.121) and a VRJ (Fig. 97.120) together with a perforated base similar to the example from pit **119249**, above.

Braemere Hill

The overall site assemblage of 249 sherds, weighing 3835g, represents a maximum of 225 vessels. Average sherd weight is 17g. The linear feature contained a more diverse assemblage of vessel types than did the ring gully; this could indicate a difference in date or relate to some other factor: the range of activities carried out in their immediate vicinities, or the nature of the formation processes that led to the creation of the deposits.

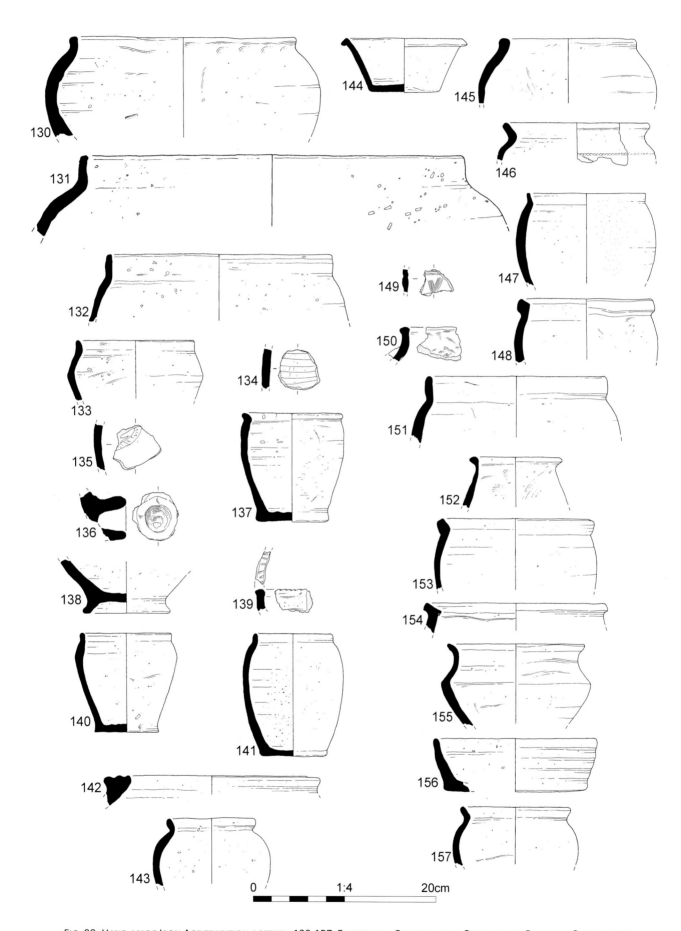

FIG. 98: HAND-MADE IRON AGE TRADITION POTTERY, 130-157, BURSTWICK, CHURCHLANDS, PATRINGTON, BLUEGATE CORNER AND SCORBOROUGH HILL

Illustrated hand-made pottery 7

Burstwick

130. VRJ-CS. V. SHORT, FLAT-TOPPED RIM, SLIGHTLY EVERTED. H2 COARSE ROCK FABRIC, ABUNDANT ANGULAR ROCK FRAGS TO 6MM IN SANDY BLACK BODY. FILL *51098*, RING GULLY 51148

131. FRJ. H2 HYPER-COARSE FINE BLACK FABRIC, V. LARGE (8-10MM), ABUNDANT ANGULAR ROCK FRAGS. SLIGHTLY DISHED, FUNNEL PROFILE RIM. FILL *51098*, RING GULLY 51148

132. VRJ-CT. THIN, IRREGULAR VERTICAL RIM ON A NARROW BODY. H2 COARSE ROCK FABRIC, SANDY, ABUNDANT ANGULAR ROCK FRAGS TO 7MM. FILL *51101*, RING GULLY 51145

133. VRJ-FSG. PROFILE CARINATED RATHER THAN GLOBULAR. SANDY H2 FINE BODY, OCC. ROCK TO 2MM., FILL *51060*, PIT 51048

CHURCHLANDS

134. HOLLOW WARE. FINE BLACK SANDY H2 ROCK FABRIC, FINE ANGULAR ROCK, QUARTZ FRAGS TO 3MM. INCISED CURVILINEAR DESIGN. FILL *119533*, PIT 119534

135. SCORED WARE. POT DISC 43x50MM; ABUNDANT ANGULAR QUARTZ GRIT 1MM TO 3MM. FILL *119498*, PIT 119499

Patrington

136. ?LID. H2 FABRIC, ABUNDANT FINE TO MEDIUM ANGULAR QUARTZ GRIT; SHORT TUBE HANDLE (NOT SPOUT). FILL *88013*, DITCH 88171

137. VRJ-CS. H2 COARSE, HARD BLACK SANDY BODY; LARGE ANGULAR ROCK FRAGS TO 8MM. FILL *88063*, DITCH 88171

138. JAR. H2 FINE FABRIC, SANDY TEXTURE, ROCK AND QUARTZ GRIT TO 1MM. V. DISTINCTIVE BASE. BURNISHED EXT SURFACE. FILL *88112*, DITCH 88171

139. VRJ TYPE. HARD BLACK H2 ROCK BODY, SPARSE ROCK FRAGS TO 3MM. (*CF*; RIGBY 2004 FLARED NOTCHED BOWL:FIG 8). ANGLED IMPRESSIONS ON TOP OF RIM *88117*, DITCH 88171

140. VRJ-CS TYPE. SMALL JAR 107MM HIGH; PINCHED ROUNDED RIM, FLAT BASE. H2 ROCK FABRIC, COARSE ROCK, QUARTZ GRIT TO 8MM. UNSTRAT. *88167*

141. VRJ-NB. V. DISTINCTIVE DENSELY TEMPERED H2 QUARTZ FABRIC, ANGULAR QUARTZ TO 1.5MM. SMALL VERTICAL RIM, ROUND LIP. UNSTRAT. 88167

142. ?JAR. HARD, DARK GREY H2 ROCK&QUARTZ BODY, ABUNDANT ANGULAR QUARTZ, ROCK TO 2MM. V. UNUSUAL RIM WITH PROMINENT GROOVES. FILL *88063*, DITCH 88171

143. ERGJ. FINE H2 BLACK FABRIC, COMMON SUB-ROUNDED QUARTZ TO 2MM, DULL ORANGE MARGINS. SMOOTHED RIM, SHOULDER. FILL *88043*, CUT 88016, STRUCTURE 1

Bluegate Corner

144. UNUSUAL SHALLOW BOWL OR DISH FORM. BLACK H2 FINE FABRIC. ABUNDANT ROUNDED QUARTZ. SMOOTHED INT. AND EXT. FILL *119984*, DITCH 120665

145. VRJ-CS. V. SHORT FLAT-TOPPED VERTICAL RIM, FLAT TOP. BLACK SANDY H2 FINE FABRIC. BURNISHED RIM AND UPPER BODY. FILL *117081*, CUT 119890 STRUCTURE 1

146. ERJ(H4). SOFT BLACK FINELY VESICULAR SHERDS IN H4 TYPE FABRIC. IMPRESSED CORD DECORATION ON SHOULDER. FILLS *117075&119935*, CUTS 119883, 119934, STRUCTURE 1

147. VRJ-FSG. FINE GREY REDUCED SANDY H5 FABRIC. FINELY MADE BARREL-BODIED JAR, SHORT VERTICAL RIM. FILLS *119968&11997*, DITCH 120665

Scorborough Hill

148. OJ VARIANT. VERTICAL POINTED RIM, INTERNAL BEVEL, PRONOUNCED NECK BUT OPEN FORM. SANDY H2 QUARTZ FABRIC, SPARSE ROUNDED QUARTZ TO 4MM. BURNISHED BELOW RIM. FILL *12086*, DITCH 12003

149. HOLLOW WARE. V. FINE BLACK SANDY H2 FINE WARE; UNUSUAL FINE-COMBED DECORATION EXT. FILL *10410*, PIT 12081

150. H2 FINE. VRJ-CT. UNUSUAL NARROW-BODIED JAR WITH TALL NECK AND RIM, AND NARROW CONSTRICTED NECK. H2 FINE FABRIC. FILL *10421*, PIT 12081

151. VRJ-FSG. SHORT VERTICAL RIM, CLUBBED FLAT-TOPPED LIP; PINCHED BODY (*CF*. *10413* AND *10421* AND PLOT 31). H2 FINE FABRIC. FILL *10410*, PIT 12081

152. ERJ TYPE. ROUNDED CLUBBED RIM ON A THIN NECK AND SLOPING SHOULDER. H2 ROCK FABRIC, BLACK THROUGHOUT, COARSE ANGULAR ROCK FRAGS TO 4MM. FILL *10432*, PIT 12081

153. VRJ-CS. SHORT THICK VERTICAL RIM ON A ROUNDED BODY. FINE SANDY OXIDISED H2 RED BODY, SOFT ROUND RED GRIT TO 5MM. SHALLOW GROOVE ON TOP OF RIM. FILLS *10421&10437&10438*, PIT 12081

154. LSJ TYPE. SANDY H2 FINE. FABRIC, OCC. LARGER QUARTZ GRAINS. LID-SEATED RIM, PROMINENT INT. FLANGE. FILL *10437*, PIT 12081

155. VRSJ. H2 FINE FABRIC, SANDY, OCC. QUARTZ TO 2MM. SMOOTHED NECK AND INT. SURFACE. FILLS *10438&10451*, PIT 12081

156. BOWL. SOFT, ABRADED, H2 TYPE SANDY FABRIC, SPARSE ANGULAR ROCK FRAGS. APPEARS TO BE SHALLOW WIDE BOWL, PLAIN RIM, FLAT BASE. FILL *10413*, PIT 12081

157. WRGJ. BROWN SANDY H2 FINE FABRIC, SPARSE QUARTZ TO 1MM; SMALL EVERTED RIM, PROFILE VARIES AROUND CIRCUMFERENCE. SMOOTHED NECK. FILLS *10447&10451*, PIT 12081

Ditch 4736

Ditch **4736** produced an assemblage of eighty-six sherds of pottery weighing 1670g representing a maximum of seventy-six vessels, giving an average sherd weight of 21.9g. All the sherds are of H2 type although within this there is considerable variety in the tempering material. The range of vessel types is also wide with vertical and everted rim jars, open jars, barrel jars and a funnel rimmed jar. Three vessels have finger-tip impressed rims, a rare example of decoration on locally manufactured vessels. The barrel jar rims are in a hard and dense black fabric with a laminated fracture and distinctive smooth, pimply surfaces internally and externally. The fill of feature **4737** produced a further nine hand-made sherds, weighing 35g. All are body sherds or small flakes recovered from the environmental samples and all are in fabrics of H2 type.

Structure 1

The three segments of the ring gully produced an assemblage of 141 sherds weighing 2048g, representing a maximum of 134 vessels with an average sherd weight of 15.2g. In spite of the relatively large average size, the sherds show considerable evidence of abrasion. A limited number of identifiable sherds are present, the range of vessel types more limited than in the assemblage from ditch **4736**, being largely restricted to VRJ types, including VRJ-FSG, and VRJ-VCS. Fabrics are predominantly of the H2 type with only six sherds of H4. The north-western segment of the ring gully contained over 70 per cent of the total assemblage including a substantial part of the rim and upper body of a large jar with a short, thick vertical rim (VRJ-CS). Other rims are also of the vertical type apart from a small fragment of a clubbed rim. Posthole **19090** produced three abraded body sherds in H2 fabrics. Unstratified finds from the subsoil above Structure 1 include ten flaked and abraded sherds, eight of which join to form the pinched rim of a small vertical rim jar.

Burstwick

The site produced 1006 sherds of pottery, weighing 20,210g and representing a maximum of 883 vessels (ENV), giving an overall average sherd weight of 22.8g. Vessel forms are dominated by VRJ types with OJ types forming a significant component only in pit **51048**. Large vessels seem to be common in the ring gully fills, shown by the curvature of body sherds as well as the presence of VRJ-CS and VRJ-CT vessels and six FRJ vessels. Coarse and hyper-coarse fabric variants occur widely but are absent from the first enclosure ditch; they are particularly common from the ring gullies. Apart from the sherds of second-century Romano-British pottery from ditch **51025**, dating evidence is limited to the two sherds of Scored ware type from the first enclosure ditch.

If the date range of these sherds is similar to that of true Scored ware, then they suggest a date between the mid-third century BC and the mid-first century AD, but this should not be considered definite dating evidence.

Structure 1

The assemblage from intervention **51100** is distinguished by the presence of a significant number of sherds containing coarse and hyper-coarse rock fragments. These are set in a fine sandy matrix and the rock fragments are very visible at the surfaces internally and externally giving the vessels a particularly distinctive appearance and texture. Even when the inclusions are not hyper-abundant they were highly distinctive simply because of their size and angularity. The vessels appear to be quite large with thick walls although no complete vessel profiles can be identified. With one exception, an open jar, the rims are all of the vertical type, although they display considerable variation of body shape and length of the rims. It is clear that the size of the vessels also show considerable variation. Intervention **51111** also produced rock tempered H2 wares, including a vertical rimmed jar and an unidentified jar rim, but the very coarse fabrics are absent.

In the recut ring gully, rock tempered fabrics again predominate with a significant proportion of hyper-coarse fabrics, including an FRJ rim (Fig. 98.131). VRJ rims are again common, and include a VRJ-CS rim (Fig. 98.130), but open jars with flat-topped rims, distinguished from the VRJ and ERJ forms by the lack of any constriction forming a neck or any significant angling of the rim, are also present. The diameter of some of the body sherds indicate that some of the vessels were of large size.

Eight sherds, spread between both the gully and its recut, appear to form three sections of the same rim and upper body of a VRJ with a thick globular body. Although this vessel was a large, thick-walled one, it was one of the few in which the large angular rock fragments are sparse rather than very abundant. It has a sandy fabric. The form

Gully	Cut	ENV	Wt/g	ASW/g
51145	51097	2	41	20.5
51145	51100	77	2452	31.8
51145	51111	91	1142	12.5
51145	Sub-total	*170*	*3635*	*21.38235*
51148	51124	184	6588	35.8
51148	51109	4	763	190.7
51148	Sub-total	*188*	*7351*	*39.1*
Total		**358**	**10986**	**30.7**

Table 33: Distribution of hand-made pottery from Structure 1, Burstwick

is also rather more globular than the other large vessels. More generally, it may be noted that interventions **51097** and **51100** contained an apparent concentration of larger vessels (including a VRJ-CT: Fig. 98.132). Other contexts produced rims of small jars, mainly VRJ types.

Ring gully 51106

The fill of cut **51106** contained only four sherds and two pieces of fired clay, weighing 43g in total. All of the sherds are of H2 type and none are diagnostic. The disparity in the pottery assemblages from Structure 1 and gully **51106** suggest significant differences in the formation processes responsible for these two assemblages and might indicate different functions for the structures.

First enclosure ditch

Twenty-two sherds, weighing 440g and with an average sherd weight of 22g, were recovered from ditch **51149**. Although only body sherds are present, the group is diverse in the range of H2 fabrics represented, and includes two non-joining sherds identified as Scored ware (Elsdon 1992). These sherds are distinguished by the presence of coarse striations externally which had clearly been deliberately applied. The fabric is not significantly different from other H2 Rock and Quartz types, suggesting local manufacture rather than the import of Scored ware vessels from the East Midlands. The date range for Scored ware extends from the mid-third century BC to the mid-first century AD.

Pit 51048

Cut **51048**, the first phase of a large sub-circular feature overlain by the corner of the first phase of the enclosure ditch, produced an assemblage of 202 sherds of pottery weighing 3880g and representing a maximum of 185 vessels (ENV) from three contexts. These groups include a small number of coarse rock-tempered sherds, but the majority are in a much finer fabric than those from the ring gullies. While still of H2 type they contain only small sub-angular rock and quartz inclusions and only one large body sherd can be described as coarse. Flint is also a notable inclusion and, while never being the commonest type, it appears regularly alongside rock fragments and quartz. Rims fall into two distinct types: open jars, the majority with small everted rims, and vertical rim jars of various types, including a VRJ-FSG (Fig. 98.133). Two sherds are burnished externally.

Pit recut 51108

Two contexts in the recut of pit **51048** contained pottery, an assemblage which consists of seventy-two sherds weighing 1827g, representing a maximum of seventy-one vessels. The average sherd weight is slightly higher than was the case in the first phase of activity (25.7g) but

the range of fabrics and vessel types is broadly similar, although with the inclusion of a small rim of ERJ type.

Second enclosure ditch

Ditch **51026** produced a total of 148 sherds weighing 1633g representing a maximum of 102 vessels giving an average sherd weight of 16g. With the exception of two vertical rimmed jars the sherds are undiagnostic bases, body sherds and small abraded flakes and chips. Finer rock tempered fabrics predominate although one flat base is tempered with coarse angular rock fragments. One sherd is of a vesicular H4 type fabric, an unusual occurrence on this site.

Features enclosed by ditch 51026

The only other sherd from the site in vesicular H4 fabric was retrieved from posthole **51099**, one of six similar postholes in the area enclosed by ditch **51026**. A rim of a VRJ-FSG vessel from posthole **5127** is the only sherd of diagnostic form from this area. Nineteen body and base sherds from pit **51057** include a group of in a coarsely rock tempered fabric, similar to that from the ring gullies. The remainder of the sherds are finer but only one small fragment could truly be described as fine. The majority are featureless body sherds but they include an unidentified jar rim.

Ditch 51025

Ditch **51025**, at the eastern end of the site, produced thirty-nine sherds of pottery weighing 311g representing a maximum of thirty-seven vessels. They include sherds from a wheel-thrown bowl and a sherd of undated Roman grey ware, along with two small body sherds of H2 Fine fabric from a hand-made vessel. With the exception of a small fragment from an everted rim or open jar and two base sherds, none of the sherds are diagnostic and all are in variants of the H2 fabric, including fine examples.

Other contexts

The fill of pit **51055** contained eight body sherds weighing 144g, representing a maximum of seven vessels. None of the sherds is identifiable to a specific vessel type and all are in various kinds of H2 fabric. Feature **51052**, possibly a recut of this pit, produced a single sherd in rock-tempered H2 fabric.

A small group of body sherds and shattered flakes from pit **51104** are all in H2 fabrics, three falling into the coarse category, similar to examples seen elsewhere on the site. A small posthole nearby, **51129**, produced single sherd in rock-tempered H2 fabric.

Churchlands

The site assemblage of 224 sherds of pottery weighing 3435g represents a maximum of 214 vessels (ENV). The average sherd weight of 16g conceals wide variation between features. Generally speaking, rock tempered H2 fabrics are common but the inclusions are relatively fine. Although some of the sherds are clearly from large vessels, the coarse abundant rock fragments seen in some of the other sites, such as Burstwick, are absent. The assemblage as a whole is characterised by a high level of abrasion and relatively few joining sherds, which may indicate that the filling of the features occurred over a period of time and involved material that had spent some considerable time on the surface of the ground. The range of fabrics is limited to H2 types with no calcareous tempered wares from any of the features. Identifiable vessel forms are few in number but cover a range of typical wares including barrel jars, everted rim jars, open jars and various vertical rimmed jars.

Structure 1

An assemblage of sixteen sherds weighing 47g includes only one rim sherd: a very small piece of a vertical rimmed jar. The small size of this assemblage and the very low average sherd weight of 3g may indicate that this structure had a function other than domestic occupation.

Boundary ditch and fence lines

Ditch 119353 produced a small group of ten sherds and a lump of fired clay, weighing 89g in total, with an average sherd weight of 8g. Two rim sherds are included in the group, one from a barrel jar, the other unidentifiable. A heavily abraded sherd from posthole 119367 is in a fine H2 fabric. Three slightly coarser sherds recovered from the fill of posthole 119549 are in H2 Quartz and H2 Rock tempered fabrics.

Irregular ditches

Ditch 120115 contained three sherds, weighing 35g. Two are in standard rock tempered fabrics while the third is somewhat finer and burnished externally. The larger assemblage of thirty-one sherds, weighing 293g with an average sherd weight of 9.4g, from ditch 120117 includes two small rim fragments, belonging to a barrel-shaped jar and a VRJ-FSG jar. A small group of sherds are in fine H2 fabrics but the remainder are in coarser rock tempered fabrics of undistinguished type. One sherd is burnished externally. The assemblage from ditch 120120 consists of thirteen sherds weighing 216g. Eleven sherds are small and heavily abraded; of the other two, the larger is a body sherd from a large jar, indicated by its curvature, while the smaller sherd has sparse flint temper among the commoner rock fragments. The large sherd inflates the average sherd weight to 16.6g but when this is removed, the average falls to 6g, more consistent with other context groups across the site.

Pit 119406

The largest of the pits, 119406, contained, in addition to sherds of Bronze Age date and a single Roman-British sherd (discussed elsewhere), ten sherds weighing 387g with an unusually high average sherd weight of 38.7g. With the exception of a small rim sherd from an everted rim jar, all are featureless body sherds although the curvature of the largest, in a coarse rock tempered fabric, suggests that it came from a large jar. The majority of the sherds are of H2 rock or coarse rock type although three are much finer.

Other pits

Pits 119383, 119493, 119499, 119518, 119520, 119532, 119534 and 120107 all produced small quantities of pottery, of which most of the sherds are undiagnostic and many are abraded. Pit 119499 includes a pot disc made from a sherd of Scored ware, of mid-third-century BC to early or mid-first-century AD date (Fig. 98.135). The shallow impressed lines on the external surface of a sherd from pit 119534 may have been accidental, but the same pit also in includes a sherd with a deliberate incised design (Fig. 98.134). A vessel from pit 119518 has a burnished surface and the same context produced the base and lower walls of a large jar in a coarse quartz and rock tempered fabric.

Double-ditched enclosures

The outer ditch of the double-ditched enclosure, 119547, contained only four body sherds of pottery weighing 41g. Their average sherd weight is 10.2g. Three are in a standard H2 Rock tempered fabric but the fourth is in an unusual, very soft brown sandy fabric of an unfamiliar type. The inner ditch, 120123, produced five body sherds weighing 41g in total, including a possible broken pot disc, all in typical H2 sandy or rock tempered fabrics.

Post-medieval extraction pits

An assemblage of hand-made pottery consisting of twenty sherds weighing 240g, residual in pit 120124, includes the rim of an everted rim jar and a small footed base along with part of a large jar.

Patrington

The total site assemblage of 797 sherds, weighing 13,279g, represents a maximum of 643 vessels. The overall average sherd weight is 20.6g. The range of vessels from the enclosure and settlement features is dominated by vertical rim types although these vary considerably in size and detail. Large vessels of undetermined type are indicated by the presence of body sherds of large diameter. The number of distinct fabrics is lower in contexts associated with the three structures than in the earlier enclosure ditch although it is unclear if this represents anything more than chance. Quartz and rock tempered fabrics were predominant throughout all phases of the site with calcareous tempers in the minority; these include, unusually, shell-tempered sherds.

Ditch 88171

The diverse assemblage from ditch **88171** consists of 271 sherds weighing 5274g and representing a maximum of 247 vessels (ENV), giving an average sherd weight of 21.3g. It includes sherds from large jars, some with wide vertical striations externally, and from finer vessels represented by burnished hollow pedestal bases (e.g. Fig. 98.138), probably wares of higher quality or which were intended for some particular purpose. The smaller vessel forms are dominated by vertical rimmed jars although it seems unlikely that these rims belonged to the pedestal-based jars as the exterior surfaces were not burnished. A number of unusual items include a tube handle (Fig. 98.136), a vertical rimmed jar with definite decoration in the form of angled impressions on the rim (Fig. 98.139), a small vertical rimmed jar (VRJ-CS type) with possible fingernail decoration (Fig. 98.137) and an unidentified jar rim with prominent grooves (Fig. 98.142).

A further 110 sherds, from a maximum of 50 vessels and weighing 3056g, included in the analysis as context **88167**, probably also derived from the fills of ditch **88171**. Parts of some large, coarsely rock tempered vessels and also two, or possibly three, small vertical rimmed jars (Fig. 98.140 and 141) are present. Other sherds include a finger impressed base, the rim of an everted rim jar and fragments of large jars, as indicated by the curvature and thickness of body sherds.

Structure 1

The assemblage from the earliest group of ring gullies consists of 175 sherds of pottery weighing 1686g and representing a maximum of 122 vessels (ENV), giving an average sherd weight of 13.8g. A small piece of Roman pottery dated to the mid-first or second century was also recovered. With the exception of a sherd in the soft orange/grey sandy H3 fabric, all the sherds from this group are of H2 type. Vessel forms are unexceptional, particularly when compared with the unusual items from the earlier enclosure ditch, and include vertical rimmed jars, an everted rim globular jar and a barrel jar. There is nothing to set the assemblage from the terminal apart from the remainder of the assemblage.

Structure 2

The assemblage from the Structure 2 ring gully, which cut through Structure 1, consists of sixty-seven sherds weighing 1316g and representing a maximum of sixty-three vessels. Apart from a higher average sherd weight

of 20.8g and fewer sherds in the H2 Fine fabric group, it is broadly similar to the assemblage from the earlier ring gully. Rim sherds are limited to vertical rimmed vessels and a barrel jar although the curvature of some of the body sherds indicates that they had belonged to a jar with a large circumference. Fabrics show some degree of variation within this broad H2 group.

Structure 3

Although small in size, with forty-four sherds weighing 442g representing a maximum of forty-two vessels and with a low average sherd weight of 10.5g, the pottery assemblage from Structure 3 includes three rim sherds: two vertical rimmed vessels and an open jar. The range of fabrics is wider than those from Structures 1 and 2 in that it includes seven sherds in vesicular H4 fabrics. H2 Fine fabrics are present but coarser rock and quartz tempered types are commoner.

Curvilinear gully 88018

The possible truncated remains of a fourth ring gully, **88018**, produced only one fragment of pottery, a small body sherd, weighing 4g, in a fine H2 fabric.

Roman enclosure ditches

Contexts firmly dated to the Roman period produced forty-four sherds of hand-made pottery, weighing 603g and representing a maximum of forty vessels, with an ASW of 15g. Sherds are often abraded while others are mere flakes. The large ditch running across the site, **88174**, accounts for twenty-one of these sherds, weighing 362g, with an ASW of 18.1g. Fine H2 fabrics predominate, some of them with burnished surfaces, but the group also includes two sherds in H1 shell tempered fabrics and five sherds in a vesicular H4 fabric. A round-bodied jar from a small ditch cut into the fills of ditch **88174**, weighing 168g, is the only specific vessel type identified. The remaining twenty sherds, weighing 73g, derive from the small rectilinear features at the south-eastern end of the excavation area.

Twenty-one small sherds recovered from ditch **119562**, almost certainly the same feature as ditch **8803**, produced an unusual group in a soft, soapy-textured black H3 type fabric with fine vesicles: Fine H3 fabrics are a feature of this ditch. This group includes a very small section of beaded rim and a sherd with an odd lobate form. Vessel forms, tentatively identified from small rim sherds, appear to be of the distinctive fine vertical rim shouldered jar type in both H2 Fine and H3 Vesicular fabrics.

Bluegate Corner

The site assemblage from Bluegate Corner consists of 494 sherds of pottery weighing 6315g and representing a maximum of 436 vessels (ENV). The overall average sherd weight is 14.4g. A number of unusual vessels are discussed in greater detail above, in the type series. Wheel-thrown wares were absent from the ring gullies and associated pits but present in the enclosure ditches, suggesting that the earliest boundaries remained in use into the late Roman period, and possibly later than the small group of gullies in the north of the site. In these gullies, second- to third-century pottery was associated with a vertical rimmed jar in an H4 fabric and a barrel jar. The larger enclosures ditches produced a much wider range of vessel types including OJ, ERJ, FRJ, VRJ-FSG, VRSJ and WRGJ. In the latter case the wide date range indicated by the wheel-thrown wares makes it difficult to link any hand-made form with a particular period while the narrow range of vessels from the ring ditches, which differ little from the types in the enclosure ditches, seems to both confirm the long-lived character of hand-made forms and the difficulty of identifying any significant change in vessel types through the pre-Roman Iron Age and into the Roman period. Similarly, there seems to have been little change in fabric types throughout the life of the activity at the site.

Structure 1 and associated pits

The small assemblage from the Structure 1 ring gully includes the thick base of a single large jar (SF 1531) in intervention **119904** accounting for the unusually high average sherd weight (Table 34): without this vessel, the average sherd weight reduces to a more typical 16.7g. Although not large in size, the group is notable for the diversity of fabrics, which include a variety of H2 types along with a battered and flaked wedge-rimmed jar in vesicular H4 fabric. This vessel may have originated outside the region, possibly in north Lincolnshire although no precise parallels for it have been identified. Other distinctive sherds include the rim of a VRJ-CS jar with a burnished rim and upper body (Fig. 98.145) and a second similar vessel.

Pit **119883**, cut by intervention **119890**, produced part of the rim of a finely vesicular H4 everted rim jar with impressed cord decoration on the shoulder (Fig. 98.146). A joining sherd is present in the assemblage from intervention **119934** through the ring gully. Pit **119936**,

within the ring gully, contained a single small flake of pottery, but the assemblage from pit **119896** is larger: twenty-six sherds weighing 261g. All are of H2 type with the majority being of the common fine black sandy type. Only one rim was present, a small fragment of a vertical rimmed jar.

Structure 2

Ring gully **119967** produced an assemblage of 158 sherds weighing 706g, representing a maximum of 145 vessels (Table 35). Vessel fabrics are limited to H2 types with notably coarse sherds from context **119999**. A VRJ-FSG from context **119942** and a wedge-rimmed jar from context **119944** are the only identifiable vessel types.

The distribution of pottery in Structure 2 is very biased with 61 per cent by weight of the locatable sherds deriving from the south-eastern terminal and the two adjacent sections, while the rest of the southern arc contributes a further 22 per cent of the total.

Ditches 120664, 119962, 120665 and 120666

Forty-four sherds, weighing 416g and representing a maximum of forty vessels, giving an average sherd weight of 10.4g, were recovered from the fills of ditch **120664**. The majority are plain body sherds in H2 or H2 Fine fabrics, with coarser types notable by their absence. Diagnostic sherds are limited to a possible ERJ, an open jar, a vertical rim jar and a possible funnel-rimmed jar. The group also includes part of a solid pedestal base and a small fragment of heavily burnt clay with a slag-like deposit on one side. The upper fill of ditch **119962** produced two small body sherds in H2 fabrics, one of which is considerably abraded.

The assemblage from ditch **120665** consists of 214 sherds weighing 2393g and representing a maximum of

Cut	Context	ENV	Wt/g	ASW/g
119890	117081	2	134	67
119904	119905, 119915	8	2102	262.75
119906	11907	6	27	4.5
119934	119935	4	42	10.5
	119903	1	1	1
Total		**21**	**2306**	**109.8**

TABLE 34: DISTRIBUTION OF HAND-MADE POTTERY FROM STRUCTURE 1, BLUEGATE CORNER

Context	ENV	Wt/g	ASW/g
119942	6	120	20.0
119943	56	169	3.0
119994	20	18	0.9
119944	19	72	3.8
119995	1	31	31.0
119996	6	86	14.3
119949	1	10	10.0
119999	16	84	5.3
119965	1	16	16.0
119966	1	4	4.0
119967	18	94	5.2
Total	**145**	**706**	**4.9**

TABLE 35: DISTRIBUTION OF HAND-MADE POTTERY FROM STRUCTURE 2, BLUEGATE CORNER

183 vessels with an average sherd weight of 13g. Fabrics are unusually diverse, with H2, mainly fine sandy textured bodies but including flint and soft red inclusion tempered variants, H3, H4 and H5, albeit in relatively small quantities. The range of vessel types, as represented by the varying rim forms, is also wide and includes fine VRSJ and WRGJ alongside the commoner VRJ and ERJ. A very unusual hand-made dish with an everted rim (Fig. 98.144) may have been based on a Romano-British type. Three vessels are represented by cross-context groups: a globular jar, lacking a rim, in a fine H2 fabric; the rim of a VRJ type vessel in an unusual fine vesicular H3 fabric; and a vessel, represented by the rim and body and a number of non-joining sherds, in a fine sandy grey reduced fabric with abundant fine rounded quartz sand defined as type H5 which, superficially at least, resembles a Romano-British form (Fig. 98.147). Ditch **120666** produced five body sherds weighing 19g, all in fine sandy H2 fabrics.

Roman ditches and pits

The pottery from gully **119866** consists of just three sherds, all in H2 fabrics, including the round, inturned rim of a barrel jar. Gully **119892**, also at the northern end of the site, produced eight sherds, all in vesicular H4 fabrics and including a single VRJ rim. This small concentration of H4 sherds is unusual in that the fabric is generally rare and infrequently found alone. The small size of the group might suggest that this is a chance occurrence rather than an indication of any more general change in the representation of H1/H4 fabrics in the Roman period.

Weeton

The site assemblage from Weeton consists of 188 sherds of pottery weighing 1953g and representing a maximum of 161 vessels. The overall average sherd weight is 12.1g. The paucity of identifiable vessel types and the small quantity of wheel-thrown pottery precludes an extensive discussion of the significance of the assemblage but in general terms it shows a similar range of vessel types and fabrics to those of the other sites considered here.

Ditches 120164 and 120223

The twenty sherds from ditch **120164** weigh 149g, with an average sherd weight is 7.4g. Only three rim sherds are present, two VRJs and one VRSJ(H4), the latter providing a broad date range from the first century BC to the early to middle first century AD. All but this rim are in various H2 fabrics, the majority being H2 Fine.

The assemblage from ditch **120223** consists of fifty-five sherds weighing 605g representing a maximum of forty-nine vessels with an average sherd weight of 12.3g. The group is predominantly of fine H2 fabrics and H1/H4

was notable by its absence. Diagnostic sherds are rare, with only three barely identifiable rims and two flat bases. Abrasion is common and some groups of sherds consist of little more than flakes and abraded fragments.

Curvilinear gully 120170

Gully **120170** produced an assemblage of eighty-seven sherds weighing 1037g representing a maximum of seventy-one vessels, and with an average sherd weight of 14.6g. The majority of sherds are in fine sandy H2 fabrics and include a VRJ rim, a ring foot (hollow pedestal) base and a rounded lug handle, the latter suggesting a date range between 400 BC and AD 100. The most unusual item in the assemblage is a group of thirteen joining sherds which appear to have a smoothed edge, as if the broken edge of a vessel had been ground down after breakage. There are no parallels for this object from the other assemblages in this report although the secondary use of broken pot sherds as pot discs is common.

Roman gullies

A group of six small, heavily abraded fragments were recovered from intervention **120153** through gully **120226**, while the northern intervention, **120202**, contained two small sherds in a fine H2 fabric. Five joining sherds from gully **120225** are from a jar in an H2 fabric, and a similar number of sherds, weighing 41g, from feature **120195** are all body sherds in H2 fabrics. Of four body sherds, weighing 32g, from gully **120224**, there are two that join: these are in an unusual light buff vesicular fabric, while the remaining sherds, one of which may be a broken pot disc, are in quartz and rock tempered H2 fabrics.

Scorborough Hill

Of the total hand-made pottery assemblage from Scorborough Hill, comprising 2238 sherds weighing 34,847g and representing a maximum of 2051 vessels (ENV), over 90 per cent by weight and 88 per cent by sherd count were recovered from the fills of a single feature, the large pit **12081**. The significance of this material is considerably heightened by the large and unusual assemblage of early Roman wheel-thrown wares recovered from the same contexts. Average sherd weight for the whole site is 16.9g.

Ditches 12096, 12103 and 12113

The three assemblages, from ditches **12096**, **12103** and **12113** differ slightly in character with average sherd weights of 24g, 14.5g and 4.5g respectively, perhaps indicating rather different deposit formation histories. None of the assemblages total more than eighteen sherds, with ditch **12113** only producing two small abraded sherds. The largest assemblage, from ditch **12103**, contains the widest range of identifiable vessel types with rims from VRJ, OJ and FRJ vessels, in all cases too small or irregular to permit EVE data to be collected. The generally rather abraded character of the assemblage is consistent with accumulation in the ditch during silting. Ditch **12096** includes just one identifiable sherd, a large fragment of a VRJ-CS, the size of which skews the average sherd weight to 24g. Without this sherd the ASW is only 9.7g, more consistent with values from the other ditches.

Pit 12081

The various fills of pit **12081** produced 1981 hand-made sherds, weighing 31,607g and representing a maximum of 1813 vessels, alongside a large and notable assemblage of wheel-thrown wares, dated to the mid-first to early second centuries AD. The average sherd weight of the hand-made component is 17.4g.

The range of vessel types represented in the assemblage is wide when compared with other features on the site and there is considerable variation within the ERJ, VRJ and OJ classes. The assemblage also includes examples of forms for which possible date ranges can be suggested, including two LSJ rims likely to be of earlier Iron Age date. In one case, the LSJ was accompanied by a fragment of a lugged jar with a date range of 400 BC to AD 100 AD or later, in the same context.

Other datable types include a group of distinctively fine VRSJ vessels, which could include carinated jar bodies from fills **10427** and **10444**, and a splayed base from fill **10447**. A date range spanning the first century BC to the early to mid- first century AD seems appropriate for these vessels although a slightly later date, more consistent with the wheel-thrown wares is also possible. A similar date range may be appropriate for the single VRGJ vessel from fill **10438**. A bowl from fill **10413** (Fig. 98.156) may also be a late type, perhaps a copy of a Roman form.

Several lugged jars were identified. As discussed elsewhere, Rigby (2004) has suggested a date range between around 100 BC and AD 100 but the evidence from the sites discussed in this report may indicate the continuing production of such vessels into the later Roman period. The concentration in pit **12081** recalls the association between wells and lugged jars seen at Rudston Roman Villa and at Dalton Parlours (Rigby 1980, Sumpter 1990).

Large jars and FRJ forms are common as well as the smaller, finer vessels. Other types, undated, include OJ, EROJ and BRGJ, WRGJ types. The assemblage also includes a single example of the perforated 'flowerpot' type base.

Decorated vessels are rare but include burnished and smoothed surfaces on the smaller vessels, notably the VRSJ and related vessel types. Other decorated sherds include fine combed lines (Fig. 98.149), impressed and incised lines, although these could include accidental markings. The assemblage also includes several examples of the distinctive 'pinch and twist' design (Fig. 98.151), also seen in the assemblages from Old Ellerby and Nuttles. A VRJ-VCS vessel is decorated with a shallow impressed groove around the rim. There are a number of pot discs, including the two largest identified from any of the sites considered in this report.

The suggestion that the wheel-thrown assemblage is an unusual deposit (Leary, this volume, page 178) is certainly consistent with the character of the hand-made pottery assemblage, unusual in both its size and the diversity of the range of vessel types represented. It should be emphasised, though, that while the group includes a wide range of vessel types, these were not, generally speaking, unique and all have parallels elsewhere, as set out in the type series, even the unusual pinched-surface vessels. Taken together with the dated wheel-thrown pottery, the group would appear to provide a useful cross-section of the types of pottery in use during the early Roman period.

Some caution should perhaps be exercised in adopting this interpretation, however, not only because of the apparently wide date range seemingly indicated by the co-occurrence of the LSJ, VRSJ and Lugged Jar types but also because individual assemblages with similarly large and diverse compositions have been identified elsewhere. At Burton Constable, both Structure 5 and ditch **118958** produced broadly comparable assemblages and in the case of the ditch it is likely that residual material from earlier features was at least partially responsible for the range of material involved. This is not to imply that the same was necessarily true in the present case, as different types of formation process may have superficially similar outcomes, but it should perhaps be taken into consideration.

If this is not the case and the assemblage was created through the destruction of a domestic assemblage, it would seem to suggest that hand-made pottery was being used alongside the wheel-thrown wares. It would also suggest that the lid-seated jars remained in use until the first or second century AD, thus eliminating them as an indicator of an early date, as has been argued elsewhere (Rigby 2004, Didsbury and Vince 2011).

Ditch 12003

The pottery assemblage from ditch **12003** consists of ninety-five sherds weighing 1052g and representing a maximum of eighty-nine vessels with an ASW of 11.8g. Although primarily of body sherds, it also included a small but diverse group of rims representing range of vessel types: EROJ, OJ (Fig. 98.148), ERJ and FRJ. Fine fabrics were common and the group included a number of abraded sherds and fragments of fired clay. The largest group of sherds, from fill **12011**, was not associated with any wheel-thrown pottery but, although consisting primarily of finer textured H2 fabrics, in some cases with burnished surfaces, it did not appear to display any characteristics, other than its size, to set it apart from other assemblages within the feature.

Other contexts

Ditch **12018** produced just two sherds, one a small flake, the other a larger sherd from a jar with a burnished external surface. Both are in H2 Fine fabrics. A small group of hand-made pottery from ditch **10412** includes a crucible fragment (context **10416**; see Pitman and Doonan, this volume, page 171) and two rims: a possible open jar and a VRG-FSG. Feature **12016**, a shallow area of root disturbance between the recorded sections of ditches **12018** and **12023**, also contained a VRJ-FSG rim.

Gilcross

The site assemblage from Gilcross, 708 sherds weighing 8500g, represents a maximum of 654 vessels (ENV). The overall average sherd weight (ASW) of 12.9g conceals considerable variation at the level of individual contexts and context groups which indicate rather different processes of deposit formation operating within the ditches and the ring gullies. The ring gullies produced a wide range of vessel types with vertical rimmed vessels predominating and a particular concentration of the fine vertical rimmed shouldered jars. The presence of the crucible fragments and unusual objects should also be noted.

While the ring gullies and pits produced a wider range of fabrics than did the ditches, it is difficult to be certain of the significance, if any, of this, given the discrepancy in the sizes of the assemblages from the different groups of features. Coarse rock tempered sherds are noticeably more common in the ring ditches and pits and it may not be unreasonable to link this with the different range of activities to be expected in the settlement; if significant this pattern should also be expected on other sites, although there is scant evidence of this. A small number of sherds of Romano-British type from two contexts associated with the settlement suggest a very late Iron Age date or a date around the time of the conquest.

Iron Age ditches

Ditch **121102** contained a small group of fragmentary abraded sherds and fragments of fired clay in quartz-rich H2 fabrics. The average sherd weight is 5.2g. Two rim sherds appear to come from open vessels, possibly bowls,

Context	ENV	Wt/g	ASW/g
121068	33	305	9.2
121091	13	67	5.2
121023	1	2	2
120969	2	19	9.5
121093	7	101	14.4
120961	1	71	71
121045	6	11	1.8
121094	13	111	8.5
121086	15	157	10.5
121095	2	63	31.5
120981	7	211	30.1
121028	1	46	46
Total	**101**	**1164**	**11.5**

TABLE 36: DISTRIBUTION OF HAND-MADE POTTERY FROM STRUCTURE 1, GILCROSS

but both are small and in poor condition. Ditch **121006** produced ten sherds with an average sherd weight of 3.9g, the majority of them in a calcite tempered H1 fabric. While contexts in which H1/H4 fabrics predominate are rare, the small size of this assemblage means that few definite conclusions can be drawn from it. Ditch **121049** produced a similar small group. All are body sherds in sandy H2 fabrics, the majority very small and abraded, giving an average sherd weight of 2.2g.

Structure 1

The assemblage from Structure 1 was diverse in character and included a wide range of H2 fabrics (Table 36). Diagnostic sherds include examples of everted rim open jars, vertical rimmed jars and a globular or barrel-shaped jar (Fig. 99.166). Decoration is limited to smoothed external surfaces, one example of which is burnished.

Context	ENV	Wt/g	ASW/g
121071	4	113	28.2
121026	17	142	8.4
121083	11	234	21.3
121082	23	165	7.2
120952	14	105	7.5
121081	20	574	28.7
120966	7	52	7.4
121080	38	1054	27.7
121079	28	670	23.9
Total	**162**	**3109**	**19.2**

TABLE 37: DISTRIBUTION OF HAND-MADE POTTERY FROM STRUCTURE 2, GILCROSS

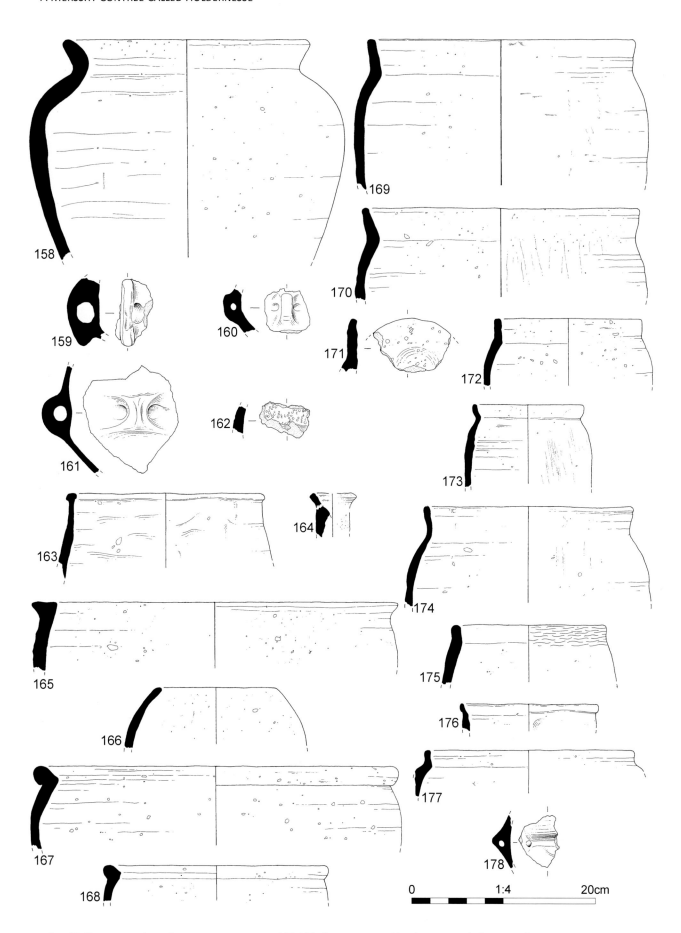

Fig. 99: Hand-made Iron Age tradition pottery, 158-178: Scorborough Hill (continued), Gilcross, Out Newton Road and Dimlington Road

Illustrated hand-made pottery 8

Scorborough Hill

158. FRJ. SHARPLY EVERTED FUNNEL-PROFILE RIM, NO NECK. H2 RED FABRIC, ABUNDANT SOFT RED INCS TO 5MM, QUARTZ SAND TO 1MM, RARELY TO 8MM. SMOOTHED EXT FILL *10432*, PIT 12081

159. LUGGED JAR. H2 FINE QUARTZ TEMPERED BODY. FILL *12051*, PIT 12081

160. LUGGED JAR. H2 RED FABRIC, OCC. SOFT ROUNDED RED GRIT, ROUNDED QUARTZ TO 1MM. FILL *10438*, PIT 12081

161. LUGGED JAR. H2 FINE FABRIC, SANDY, ROUNDED QUARTZ TO 2MM. FILL *10421*, PIT 12081

Gilcross

162. HOLLOW WARE. FINE BLACK SANDY H2 FABRIC, MOD. WELL SORTED ROCK FRAGS TO 2MM; STABBED ALL OVER EXTERNALLY. FILL *121036*, CUT 121029, STRUCTURE 3

163. OJ. FINE HARD BLACK SANDY H2 FABRIC, OCC. ROCK FRAGS TO 5MM; SMALL IRREGULAR CLUBBED RIM ON AN OPEN BODY. FILL *121036*, CUT 121029, STRUCTURE 3

164. RIM OF AN UNIDENTIFIED CYLINDRICAL OBJECT; H2 FINE SANDY FABRIC. FILL *121041*, PIT 121040

165. OJ TYPE. UNUSUAL FLAT TOPPED RIM, WIDE EXTERNAL FLANGE. H2 COARSE ROCK FABRIC, ABUNDANT ANGULAR ROCK FRAGS TO 8MM PROMINENT AT SURFACE. FILL *121080*, STRUCTURE 2

166. BARREL JAR TYPE. H2 QUARTZ. COARSE SANDY FABRIC, ABUNDANT ANGULAR QUARTZ GRIT AND OCC. ANGULAR ROCK FRAGS. FILL *120979*, CUT 120981, STRUCTURE 1

167. WRJ(H4). THICK ROUND EVERTED RIM, PROMINENT INTERNAL ANGLE; POSSIBLY WHEEL-TURNED. H4 FABRIC, COARSE, BUT SPARSE VESICLES. FILL *121097*, PIT 121078

168. WRJ(H4). CLUBBED RIM, EXTERNAL BULGE. CHIPPED AND DAMAGED. COARSELY VESICULAR H4 FABRIC. FILL *121097*, PIT 121078

Out Newton Road

169. VRJ-CT. LARGE JAR, TALL EVERTED RIM. H2 COARSE ROCK FABRIC, ABUNDANT ANGULAR ROCK FRAGS TO 8MM; PROMINENT SLAB-JOINS. SMOOTHED EXT. FILL *13021*, PIT 13020

170. VRJ-CT. TALL ALMOST VERTICAL RIM, ROUND LIP; H2 COARSE ROCK FABRIC, ANGULAR ROCK FRAGS TO 8MM. SMOOTHED EXT. FILL *13021*, PIT 13020

171. DISC OR LID. POSSIBLE LUG OR KNOB STUMP IN CENTRE; H2 COARSE ROCK FABRIC, ANGULAR ROCK FRAGS TO 6MM. FILL *13021*, PIT 13020

172. VRJ-CT. ROUND-LIPPED VERTICAL RIM ON NARROW SHOULDERED BODY, PRONOUNCED INT. ANGLE; SHORTER THAN SOME CT TYPES. H2 ROCK FABRIC, ABUNDANT WELL-SORTED ANGULAR ROCK TO 4MM. FILL *13021*, PIT 13020

173. VRJ-NB. THIN VERTICAL RIM, SLIGHTLY DISHED; DEPOSIT ON NECK EXT. H2 ROCK FABRIC, ANGULAR ROCK FRAGS TO 2MM. SMOOTHED EXT. FILL *13021*, PIT 13020

174. VRJ-NB. TALL VERTICAL RIM ON NARROW-SHOULDERED BODY; H2 ROCK FABRIC, ROCK FRAGS TO 6MM, GENERALLY FINER. SMOOTHED EXT. FILL *13021*, PIT 13020

175. OJ TYPE. SIMPLE ROUNDED VERTICAL RIM WITH SLIGHT NECK/SHOULDER; H2 ROCK FABRIC, ANGULAR ROCK FRAGS TO 3MM IN BLACK BODY. SMOOTHED NECK AND RIM. UPPER FILL *13039*, CUT 13040, DITCH 13070

176. OJ TYPE. VERTICAL RIM, SLIGHTLY DISHED INT, EXTERNAL COLLAR, COULD BE VRJ BUT NO TRACE OF SHOULDER. H2 ROCK FABRIC, ANGULAR ROCK FRAGS TO 2MM. SMOOTHED INT. AND EXT. FILL *13021*, PIT 13020

Dimlington Road

177. VRJ TYPE. SMALL VERTICAL RIM, PRONOUNCED EXTERNAL SHOULDER. FINE H2 QUARTZ FABRIC, SPARSE SUB-ANGULAR QUARTZ TO 5MM. FILL *120939*, DITCH 120937

178. LUGGED JAR. H2 FINE SOFT BRIGHT ORANGE SANDY FABRIC; ABRADED EDGES. FILL *120909*, DITCH 120937

Structure 2

Sherds in H2 rock tempered fabrics predominate in the assemblage from the Structure 2 contexts, in contrast to the more diverse assemblages from other contexts (Table 37). Diagnostic vessels include an open jar and small fragments of the rims of vertical and everted rimmed jars: somewhat irregularly finished, to the extent that their diameters can not be reliably measured. Less typical is an OJ rim (Fig. 99.165). The association of one of the VRJs with possible wheel-thrown pottery of later prehistoric or mid-first-century date in the fill of cut **121079** is of interest here and is similar to the date range proposed for upper fill of cut **120981** in Structure 1 (Leary, this volume, page 178).

Structure 3

Structure 3 produced a diverse range of vessel forms, with examples of an open jar (Fig. 99.163) and a finely finished vertical rimmed jar. Bases are of both the flat and solid pedestal type. Two sherds are of unusual character: a body sherd decorated with closely spaced stabbing (Fig. 99.162) and a sherd of unknown function perforated before firing.

Pits

Feature **121078**, possibly a continuation of the Structure 3 ring gully, produced thirty-seven sherds weighing 959g and representing up to thirty-four vessels. Average sherd

Context	ENV	Wt/g	ASW/g
121029	4	122	30.5
121076	15	171	11.4
121075	4	117	29.3
121046	8	41	5.1
121074	2	40	20
121056	3	63	21
121073	18	166	9.2
121060	12	154	12.8
121072	3	131	43.7
121103	69	1005	14.6

TABLE 38: DISTRIBUTION OF HAND-MADE POTTERY FROM STRUCTURE 3, GILCROSS

weight is 28.2g. The range of fabrics is greater than that from the ring gullies, in that it includes sherds in H4 fabric as well as H2 types. The range of forms is also diverse and includes an everted rim jar, a clubbed rim jar and a wedge-rimmed jar.

The small assemblages from pits **121011**, **121012** and **121058** were predominantly body sherds in a range of H2 fabrics. The only rim sherd, from an open jar, is from the upper fill of pit **121011**. This pit stands out, with a high average sherd weight of 25g and a relatively low incidence of abrasion. In contrast, pit **121012** contains a large number of small, often abraded sherds with an average weight of 6.8g. Like pit **121011**, pit **121058** contains only a small number of sherds although the average weight is lower at 10.2g and closer to that of pit **121012**.

The burial and crucible group

The pottery assemblage from pit **121040** is notable in that it includes fragments of crucibles (Pitman and Doonan, this volume, page 171), parts of an object of unidentified character (Fig. 99.164) and an odd rounded sherd resembling a sagging base. The group also stands out among the material from the site as a whole in that it includes a higher than normal proportion of fine H2 fabrics, although the vessels were, as usual, fragmentary with an average sherd weight of 9.2g. A tall, funnel-shaped jar rim from fill **121043** is one of a number of vessels in a fine, sandy grey H2 fabric. The same context also produced a turned ring foot base in a fine H2 fabric. It is probable that other fine sherds are from vessels similar to a VRSJ from the pit fill. The distinctive character of the assemblage suggests that it was related to the use of the pit as a grave, although it should be noted that the assemblage does not include any complete vessels and the pottery was not placed in any particular arrangement with reference to the skeleton.

Feature 121105

Diagnostic sherds from linear feature **121105** are limited to everted rim jar types, including one in an H1 Calcite tempered fabric and a small fragment of a rim sherd from a vertical rimmed jar.

Out Newton Road

The site assemblage of 1047 sherds of pottery weighing 12,503g represents a maximum of 1018 vessels, with an overall average sherd weight of 12.2g. The pottery forms a homogeneous group both in the limited range of vessel forms and the range of fabric types, with a high proportion of coarse rock tempered fabrics. In particular, the rim sherds are distinctly homogeneous, with hard, dark grey, rather coarse fabrics and with a distinctive group of vertical rims on narrow jars, the rims slightly dished internally. The similarity of the assemblages from the enclosure ditch and from the large pit suggests that they are similar, both chronologically and in their origins. Despite the evidence of the wheel-thrown pottery, there is little in the hand-made pottery assemblage to indicate any significant difference between the two phases of filling of the ditch, reflecting the apparent lack of typological development within the hand-made pottery assemblages.

Iron Age enclosure 13070; early phase

In total, ninety-six sherds weighing 1750g were recovered from the earlier fills of the large enclosure ditch, **13070**. This combined assemblage represents a maximum of ninety vessels, including large jars in coarse rock tempered fabrics and vertical rimmed jars.

Pit 13020

The 754 sherds, weighing 8917g, from pit **13020** represent a maximum of 736 vessels but include some substantial groups of small, shattered sherds, so this is almost certainly a significant overestimate of the real total. The assemblage includes two small crucible fragments (Pitman and Doonan, this volume, page 171), both from the upper fill of the pit. Additionally, fragments of fired clay from the main fill of the pit have surface vitrification, suggesting that they too had been involved in a high-temperature process, although none could be positively identified as crucible fragments.

In other respects the assemblages from these two fills resemble each other closely, with a distinct split between H2 Fine fabrics and coarser H2 Rock and Coarse Rock fabrics tempered with large angular rock fragments. In some cases the curvature of the sherds indicates that the coarse fabric sherds were from large diameter jars; although there are few joining sherds, it seems likely that a relatively small number of large jars are represented.

The assemblage also includes a small quantity of H1 Chalk tempered sherds and two vesicular H4 sherds.

Identifiable vessel types are dominated by rims from a variety of small vertical rimmed jars (Fig. 99.169, 170 and 172) with two much larger tall vertical rims in coarse rock tempered fabrics: (Fig. 99.173 and 174). The group also includes part of a flat ceramic disc, possibly part of a lid (Fig. 99.171). The vertical rims are highly fragmented precluding the measurement of the diameter or calculation of the EVE figure, although enough survives for the identification of the vessel type to be reasonably certain. Other vessel types include the rim of an Open Jar (Fig. 99.176) and part of the lug from a lugged jar, the latter suggesting a date range between around 400 BC and 100 AD or later. The absence of wheel-thrown pottery suggests that a date within the later part of this range is less probable.

Early Roman infilling of ditch 13070

The combined assemblage from the later fills of enclosure ditch **13070** consists of 196 sherds weighing 1820g and representing a maximum of 191 vessels. Diagnostic sherds indicate that a similar range of vessel types is represented as in the earlier phase, although with a less diverse range of vertical rim jars (Fig. 99.175) and slightly greater variability in the open and barrel shaped jars. Fill **13041** produced two unusually thick bases, probably from large vessels, both heavily abraded. This context also produced the only dated wheel-thrown pottery from the site, suggesting a date in the second century AD or later.

As elsewhere on the site, the fabrics are predominantly quartz and rock tempered although H1 Calcite and H1 Chalk fabrics are also represented by a very small number of sherds. Fill **13017** produced a single sherd in an unusual H3 calcite and rock tempered fabric.

Hull Road

The Hull Road site assemblage, 185 sherds weighing 1656g and representing a maximum of 182 vessels, is homogeneous, all of the fabrics being of the H2 type with rock temper predominating. Of four vessel rims, three are from open jars and the fourth from a barrel jar, although fragments of shouldered jars suggest that either everted or vertical rimmed vessels are also present.

Ditch 120760

Ditch **120760** produced ninety-five sherds weighing 857g and representing a maximum of ninety vessels. Average sherd weight is 9.5g. The group includes two Open Jar rims and the shoulders of two jars of unidentified type.

Structure 1

The assemblage from Structure 1 consists of seventy body sherds and fragments along with a single small rim sherd from an Open Jar, from the southern arc of the ring gully. Average sherd weights from the two elements of the ring gully differ considerably: 12.5g and 5.5g respectively for the northern and southern arcs.

Enclosure ditch 120763

Just four body sherds were recovered from the first phase of the substantial enclosure ditch, **120763**. The later recut, **120762**, added a small group of body sherds and flakes in H2 fabrics with a single rim sherd from a barrel-shaped jar.

Dimlington Road

The site assemblage from Dimlington Road consists of 244 sherds weighing 2473g and representing a maximum of 221 vessels. The overall average sherd weight is 11.1g. The quantities of pottery from the features are low, making comparison within the site, or between this site and others, difficult and potentially misleading. The assemblages from the three structures are particularly small: this may be due as much to their truncated nature as to any other factors.

Iron Age settlement features

Structure 1, in the western excavation area, produced just two small body sherds, weighing 5g, in typical H2 type quartz tempered fabrics. Pit **120944** produced two undiagnostic body sherds, both in quartz-tempered fabrics one of which is in an unusual bright orange fabric.

Only one context from Structure 2 produced pottery: fill **120457** of gully **120543**. The assemblage of fourteen sherds weighs 32g. Most of the sherds are little more than flakes and scraps, not attributable to any specific vessel type. All are in H2 fabrics, the majority fine in texture. One body sherd in a typical H2 Rock fabric, weighing 7g, was recovered from posthole **120485**.

Ring gully **120565** contained a body sherd, broken into three pieces, and a flake. The flake is in a fine H2 fabric; the body sherd is somewhat coarser. Ring gully **120630** produced just one sherd, the rim of a VRJ CS/CT type vessel in a slightly unusual dense, oxidised body, smoothed externally. Pit **120586** contained a single small abraded sherd in a fine H2 fabric.

Ditches 120945, 120937, 120615 and 120616

In the western excavation area, the 17 sherds, weighing 155g, from ditch **120945** include the rim of a CRJ(H1) in a shell tempered fabric. The fills of the stratigraphically later ditch **120937** produced an assemblage of thirty-five sherds weighing 255g and representing a maximum of thirty-four vessels. The average sherd weight is 7.5g. One VRJ (Fig. 99.177) and one lugged jar (Fig. 99.178) were identified, the lugged jar being unusual in having a lateral rather than a vertical pierced lug. The vessel is in an unusual bright orange fabric (*cf* Knight 1998).

Ditch **120615** produced 11 sherds weighing 111g, including two open jar (OJ) rims in H2 Fine fabrics. Ditch **2250**, probably a continuation of ditch **120616**, produced eighteen sherds weighing 268g, representing a maximum of fourteen vessels, giving an average sherd weight of 19.1g. In spite of the small size of the group, three different vessel types are represented: OJ, BRGJ and an ERJ type. Fabric types vary with H2 and H3 types both present.

Pits

Two of the stone-filled pits, **120506** and **120572**, produced small quantities of pottery, all body sherds and all in H2 fabrics. Of the other pits, several produced small quantities of hand-made pottery but the only identifiable vessels are three open jars from pits **2253** and **120592** and an unidentified jar from pit **120587**. Smoothed surfaces are common on the sherds from pit **2253**.

The seventy-six sherds, weighing 664g and representing up to sixty-seven vessels, from pit **120592**, form an unusual assemblage with forty-five sherds in H4 fabrics rather than H2. These include sherds from a cordoned jar, similar in general respects to the Bronze Age bucket jars illustrated by Rigby (2004; 31, fig. 4). It is possible that all of the vesicular H4 sherds are from the same vessel although as so often with this fabric, identifying joining sherds is difficult because of the shattered nature of the sherds. The rim is unfortunately absent which renders a positive identification of the form impossible.

Hand-made pottery: discussion

The foregoing description of the pottery assemblages presents a body of data that both builds on previous work in the area and also opens up some possible new approaches to the material. This section attempts to offer a preliminary interpretation of the data which will contribute to the development of broader research themes in eastern Yorkshire. Previous research has emphasised the specific themes of landscape archaeology and the archaeology of death and burial (e.g. Bevan 1999a, Giles 2000, Fenton Thomas 2011) but while there have been extensive descriptive accounts of the artefactual record, there has been relatively little synthetic or interpretative analysis. In part this has been the result of the fissioning of archaeological research in Britain into two traditions: academic scholarship and, more recently, development funded investigations. With the concentration of the

latter on interpretation of individual sites, investment in the production of broader regional or sub-regional narratives has failed to keep pace with the accumulation of data. This dichotomy caricatures the real situation: academic researchers are aware of the importance of artefact production and exchange just as commercial archaeologists appreciate the wider context of their assemblages. But broadly, and for practical reasons, the dichotomy persists in the published and grey literatures and has had an impact on the nature of the archaeological narratives about the later prehistoric period in eastern Yorkshire.

A second fissure lies deep in the history of archaeology and concerns the effects of the Roman Conquest on archaeological research, which have resulted in the emergence of 'prehistoric' and 'Roman' archaeologies as sub-disciplines, separated both conceptually and institutionally. This distinction has been exacerbated by the generally malign effect of a handful of Classical sources on perceptions of late prehistoric societies (Collis 2003, 13-26). Attempts in the 1980s and early 1990s to write accounts of 'different Iron Ages' and to bring traditions of research within 'prehistoric' and 'Roman' archaeologies together had some impact at the academic level and have subsequently influenced fieldwork, notably in a growing interest in structured deposition, but generally the distinction between the two sub-disciplines remains strong. Pottery specialisation tends to split along traditional lines: on the one hand, studies of 'hand-made' pottery in the native tradition and on the other, 'wheel-thrown' Roman and Romano-British pottery. The considerable personal investment made by individuals in gaining proficiency in one or other of these areas of specialisation and the practical difficulty of moving between the two tends to reinforce the dichotomy, even when the data indicates a high degree of continuity within a complex and changing socio-historical context. This distinction has been reinforced by the routinisation of commercial archaeology, which has also impeded attempts to break away from traditional structures of practice. The following discussion is intended as a preliminary attempt to delineate some areas where further research would be both possible and fruitful and to propose some avenues of investigation which have not hitherto been explored.

In her survey of prehistoric pottery manufacture and exchange Morris (1994, 1996) has presented a model of pottery production based principally upon archaeological data from southern England and on the ethnographic data presented by Arnold (1985). Although references are made to northern England, the summary tables and maps (1996, Tables 4 and 5, fig. 3; 1996, Tables 5.2, 5.3, fig. 5.2) show a clear bias towards those areas which have seen the most extensive and detailed excavations. While this is entirely understandable given the disparities in research (Robbins 1999), the effect has been to create a homogenised 'northern Britain' where regional differences are either not apparent due to an absence of data or are elided under a general scheme of 'local production and distribution'. Eastern Yorkshire, where pottery manufacture and use was a strong and well-established tradition, is treated alongside modern South and West Yorkshire, the southern Pennines and the Cheshire plain, where pottery use in the later prehistoric period was so limited that many societies can be described as aceramic, notwithstanding a small number of isolated occurrences on sites such as Mellor (Nevell and Redhead 2005) and Sykehouse (Roberts 2003). Furthermore, the definition of 'local' production used by Morris, where raw materials were acquired from less than ten kilometres from the location where the pottery was utilised may not be as universally applicable as the ethnographic data implies given the suggestion that in north-east Yorkshire at least 'there was ... significant movement of pottery and/or raw materials within the region, sometimes between closely neighbouring sites, but sometimes over distances of more than 20 kilometres. ... Limited evidence has been found also for the import of pottery from farther afield' (Leslie *et al.* 2004, 23).

Being limited in scope to the pre-Roman period, Morris' model does not address the evidence for the continuity of local production into the Roman period in eastern Yorkshire alongside the use of wheel-thrown wares in the Romano-British tradition and the later development of the large-scale manufacture of calcite-gritted wares at sites such as Holme-on-Spalding-Moor, Norton and Malton (Evans 1988, Swan 2002).

How then might we move discussion of the pottery industry and wider later prehistoric and Roman-period society on? A broad regional approach, extending that of Rigby (2004) to the whole of eastern Yorkshire would represent a significant research project; such an approach would have to engage constructively not only with the evidence for local production of hand-made pottery but also with the relationship between hand-made and wheel-thrown pottery, the very different social and economic contexts of their production and the wider implications of their co-occurrence and evidence for consumption and use. It is perhaps more feasible in the present context to focus on some of the details of the production and use of hand-made pottery as a preliminary to a broader investigation in a research context.

David Peacock's proposal for seven modes of pottery production within the Roman world (1982, 6-11; see also van der Leeuw 1976 and Cumberpatch 1991 for further discussion) includes two which might be deemed relevant to the manufacture of hand-made pottery in the later prehistoric and Roman periods. Household production is defined as the simplest level of manufacture within which each household produces pottery for its own use, using the simplest technology and involving

vessel types which are 'strictly functional and will be made according to time-honoured cultural recipes' (1982, 8). The limited scale of production will preclude investment in technology 'and neither wheel or kiln will be used; moreover it is unlikely that a turntable will be available' (1982, 8). This model is perhaps the one which fits best with Morris's picture of later prehistoric pottery manufacture mentioned above.

At a more complex level is the household industry in which production is in the hands of a few individuals within a community who will undertake it on a seasonal basis using simple technology, which may include a turntable and perhaps a basic kiln. Pottery may be marketed outside the immediate household and this may be detectable when petrographic or other methods of analysis are employed. Peacock acknowledges that the distinctions between his modes of production may become blurred when translated into the real world and that they should be considered as points on a continuum rather than as fixed stages in a quasi-evolutionary scheme, although this would have the effect of distancing them from the Marxian formulation upon which they are based, and will necessitate more detailed discussion of their status and significance if they are to be considered as more than simply descriptive. The situation in eastern Yorkshire can be seen as somewhat more complex than household production but it does not entirely conform to the criteria of a household industry. In particular there is, as yet, no firm evidence of any form of kiln from the area (although see Didsbury and Vince 2011, 196 for a tentative suggestion of the use of kilns) and production remained based on slab and coil building throughout the Roman period, even though the potters could hardly have been unaware of the principle of the wheel.

At the most basic level, the preparation of the clay would seem to indicate some degree of concern for aspects of the pottery which reflects Woodward's assertion that 'in all periods from the Neolithic to Iron Age it has been possible to suggest that pottery fabric may have been of extreme symbolic importance' (2002, 111).

Ixer has pointed out (this volume, page 170) that, for the samples analysed as part of this project, the temper could have occurred naturally in the clay and may not have involved the deliberate addition of inclusions. It is not clear to what extent the clay was cleaned before being used. Conversely, the use of apparently deliberately prepared coarse and hyper-coarse rock fragments for some, but not all, of the larger vessels might imply a concern for the character of the clay or the finished vessels. This may have been related to their function but might also relate to less tangible aspects of their place in society.

The variability in temper recalls Woodward's observations on the regularities observable in fabrics from the Neolithic to the Iron Age in southern England cited above. It is not clear, for example, whether particular kinds of rocks were being selected for inclusion as coarse angular temper or why only a very small proportion even of the larger vessels contained hyper-coarse inclusions. While conventional petrographic techniques may be of limited value in provenance studies in eastern Yorkshire with its extensive glacial clay deposits, there may be a significant role for studies of grain size and angularity in producing a more sophisticated fabric classification to that employed in this report. Such a classification might allow a closer and more objective correlation between fabric type and vessel form and thus open up interpretative possibilities that are not available using currently accepted definitions.

The issue of variation in temper is clearest when we consider the significance of the principal distinction in assemblages of hand-made pottery, that between those vessels with calcareous temper (H1/H4), those with quartz and rock temper (H2, H5) and the minor role of hybrid tempers (H3). This is of particular interest given the distinction between rock tempered and calcite tempered wares in the later Roman period. Differentiation between various types of calcite-gritted ware (Evans 1988) may also be of significance.

Calcareous temper presents greater technical challenges, particularly for firing, than does rock temper, but for the pots supplied to Romanised small towns, rural sites and villas in eastern Yorkshire it seems to have been used almost exclusively. In contrast, the production of quartz and rock tempered vessels appears to have continued on 'native' settlements into the third and probably the fourth centuries. Inevitably a lack of chronological resolution poses problems in delineating precisely the extent of this dichotomy and the suggestion that there was a reorganisation of the landscape in the late second or third century further complicates the matter. There is a good case for further investigation of the relationship between hand-made rock tempered fabrics, calcite tempered wares and wheel-thrown wares and the populations who used them.

More broadly, the widely varying proportions of different fabric types on different types of sites across the region is a particular problem and there seems to be no simple way of identifying the site-specific causal factors which resulted in the composition of the assemblages without a major research project which will cut across professional and institutional boundaries that currently hamper our understanding of the situation as a whole.

Beyond the issue of the fabrics, the question of technology is also one of considerable importance. While the majority of vessels seem to have been made using slab and coil techniques the smaller, thin-walled vessels (VRSJ, WRSJ and similar) and those with ring-

foot and splayed bases required the use of simple but specialised tools and techniques, perhaps including some form of turntable (and see Didsbury and Vince 2011, 196 for a suggestion that some vessel rims from Melton may have been wheel-formed). Even if the vessels were rotated on a simple mat or wooden base rather than a turntable, the investment in time implies something more than a concern for basic functionality. Even though relatively small numbers of vessels are involved, there may be a case for developing a classification of hand-made vessels that acknowledges differentiation on the basis of labour input as well as vessel morphology (cf Feinman et al. 1981).

It has been comparatively easy to locate parallels from the area for most of the vessel forms defined in the type series and many of these are cited in the vessel type descriptions. The same is more generally true and it has frequently been observed that one of the chief characteristics of hand-made pottery in eastern Yorkshire is the lack of variation in form from the Middle Iron Age into the second century AD and probably later. This degree of standardisation and its longevity, which is an impediment to the creation of conventional chrono-typologies, is in its own way an important aspect of the pottery industry and one with significant implications for our understanding of the society that produced and used the pottery.

Such continuity, particularly in the face of a major economic, political and presumably social change as that represented by the arrival of the Romans with a range of easily available alternative types of pottery vessels, would seem to imply a society that was both stable and highly conservative in its attachment to long-established traditions of technological practice. How far this also implies conservatism in wider fields of social practice remains to be determined and will require the synthesis of information derived from several distinct strands of archaeological investigation.

The production of any artefact follows cultural rules and prescriptions which determine the choice of technology, the investment of time and effort in manufacture, and such culturally specific norms and values as are believed to be embodied in the artefact. These rules and prescriptions describe the *habitus*, as defined by Bourdieu (1992, 52-65), of the production of the artefact. The existence of structure within pottery assemblages, revealed in the classifications used by archaeologists, in anthropological terms the *etic* classifications, implies the existence of practical cultural rules regarding the manufacture of individual vessels, irrespective of how these may relate to the *emic* classifications employed by the makers and users of the pottery. These rules will reflect the duality that exists between social structure and individual agency (Giddens 1984, 25) and embody beliefs about the relationship of human beings to the wider world, ranging from the mundane to broader areas of concern such as cosmology.

While all other social and cultural variables may be different, the essential case, that material culture embodies aspects of the world views of its makers and users, is as valid for later prehistoric pottery as it is for medieval and post medieval pottery (Cumberpatch 1997, 2003). The historically specific question at issue is not the existence of habitual structures within later prehistoric society in eastern Yorkshire but the nature of those structures which gave them the strength to endure from the early or middle Iron Age, into the third century and beyond. The identification of such structures and the habitual cultural rules that constituted them is beyond the scope of this report and requires not only a regional approach to pottery production but also the integration of data from other crafts such as iron-working and non-ferrous metallurgy (cf Giles 2007). The strength of these habitual structures and the communities of practice that facilitated their transmission and survival in the face of the pressures to adopt Romanised ways of life, which proved potent in other geographical areas, set eastern Yorkshire aside from other parts of England but as yet have hardly been addressed, at least in the literature familiar to the author.

Turning to the issue of the possible movement of pottery or of raw materials between settlements or over longer distances, the nature of the clay deposits and their origin as glacial drift over much of Holderness appears to preclude any realistic possibility of linking individual vessels with precise source areas, at least using established techniques. The results of the petrography undertaken as part of the Pots in Pits project (Rigby 2004) have been mentioned above, and the detailed analysis of the assemblage from Melton showed that at least eleven distinct vessel fabrics were represented (Didsbury and Vince 2011, 195). There are a number of factors which can contribute to a particular compositional profile for an individual assemblage and, while sites in Holderness may be less ideally located than Melton to receive local or regional imports, the pottery assemblages do suggest some degree of inter-regional interaction.

The very small quantity of shell tempered ware (H1 Shell) identified in the assemblages suggests a limited degree of cross-Humber movement, as Lincolnshire appears to be the most obvious source for these vessels (cf Didsbury and Vince 2011, 196). How far the chalk (H1 Chalk) and calcite (H1 Calcite) gritted vessels, the latter including most of the vessels in the H4 fabric, can be assumed to have originated on the Wolds is unclear. Chalk and calcite are present in local glacial drift deposits and chalk nodules can be collected in abundance from the clay cliffs of Holderness but whether such clays could have been cleaned of all their non-calcareous rock fragments seems unlikely. Taking account of the relatively small

numbers of such vessels, it seems more likely that they reached Holderness from sites to the west and north, either as entities in their own right or as containers of some type of commodity.

The case of the decorated vessels may be somewhat different. The limited programme of petrographic analysis carried out by Rob Ixer indicated that at least some of the decorated vessels were of local origin and the fabrics of the remainder were certainly not of East Midlands type (Knight, pers. comm.). This having been noted, designs were executed with a degree of competence equal to that seen on similar vessels from Lincolnshire and the East Midlands, which might suggest that the vessels were made, or at least decorated, by individuals familiar with the techniques and who must also have possessed the necessary tools, including roulette wheels. One possibility therefore is that it was not the pots that were moving but the potters.

There is scant evidence for habitually itinerant potters, and Peacock has suggested, on the basis of ethnographic parallels, that potters working within household industries tend to be women: the possibility of patrilocal exogamy, the inter-regional exchange of marriage partners, is one that cannot be ruled out. Female potters, or women whose socio-economic roles included the manufacture of pots, might well have brought their tools and techniques with them and employed them in their new homes, despite a prevailing lack of interest or even hostility to innovation in pottery manufacture.

Future studies of bone chemistry might be useful in evaluating this, admittedly speculative, suggestion and in this connection it is of interest to note that the individual buried in the Ferry Fryston 'chariot' burial may have come from eastern Yorkshire (Brown et al. 2007, 154). The evidence for a high degree of conservatism in the manufacture and use of pottery in eastern Yorkshire might also be seen as consistent with the very limited presence of pottery on sites in the region to the west. If there was some form of contact between the communities in East Yorkshire and areas to the south and west which involved the exchange of marriage partners, it is perhaps not beyond the bounds of possibility that the small quantities of pottery on sites to the west represent the traces of individuals who left eastern Yorkshire but who took with them the knowledge of potting and a desire to use pots. The fact that pottery was not adopted on any significant scale in this large zone suggests that social norms and values were as strong in this area as they were in eastern Yorkshire, even if they were diametrically opposed. This may be substantiated by the evidence for resistance to the adoption of Roman pottery in the area, which broadly parallels the situation in eastern Yorkshire.

A final issue to be noted is the nature of pottery production in use in the later fourth and early fifth centuries AD and the question of the character of early post-Roman pottery. Here again, inter-disciplinary studies involving co-operation between individual specialists will needed to identify and characterise assemblages dating to the period that saw the end of production and use of Roman styles of pottery. Once again, close attention needs to be paid to well-dated assemblages of this period and their characteristics, as well as the definition of what constitutes post-Roman pottery.

In conclusion it may be said that the volumes of pottery, both hand-made and wheel thrown dating to the later prehistoric and Roman periods, that have been unearthed as a result of recent infrastructure work in eastern Yorkshire represent a remarkable opportunity to add considerable detail to the picture of later prehistoric and Roman period societies which has hitherto been largely dominated by studies of land division and funerary rites and rituals. The quantity and quality of the data emerging from developer-funded work surely demands some degree of investment in the production of interpretative accounts of the archaeology of the region to do justice to the significant commercial investment.

Petrographical analysis of the Iron Age pottery

Rob Ixer

Eleven sherds were examined using a x20 hand lens and their colour compared with the Geological Society of America Rock-Color Chart. Standard thin sections were prepared in the usual manner and examined: macroscopically with a x20 hand lens, noting their colour, and microscopically in transmitted light. Detailed petrographical descriptions, paying particular attention to all possible anthropogenic components within the non-plastics, are included in the site archive, and the findings summarised below.

Sample	Site	Context	Feature
P01	Lelley	35287	35288
P02	Burton Constable	118504	118503
P03	Burton Constable	118341	118283
P04	Lelley	35463	35464
P05	Burton Constable	118522	118523
P06	Nuttles	31041	31042
P07	Brandywell	25211	25210
P08	Burton Constable	118172	118095
P09	Burton Constable	9494	layer
P10	Lelley	35368	35367
P11	Lelley	35295	35294

TABLE 39: SAMPLES SELECTED FOR PETROGRAPHIC ANALYSIS

Manufacture

The majority, and perhaps all, of the pots are tempered. Samples P01 and P02 are both grogged; in P01 the amount suggests intentional grogging to a clean clay. P02 also has significant grog within a very packed or possibly tempered clay; in addition to quartz sand the clay has cut straw, or similar material, and non-local fossil material.

Sample P03 is plant tempered: either cut grass or cereal stems have been added to a naturally fine sandy clay, or cut straw and fine sand added to a clean, or deliberately cleaned clay. The size range of the natural non-plastics suggests the former. The fabric is like many Iron Age plant tempered pots found in the English Midlands.

Samples P05 and P06 are tempered with fly ash. Most of the fly ash clasts are larger than the natural, sub-rounded to rounded, non-plastic components. The size range of the natural non-plastics suggests that fly ash has been added to a natural, fine sandy clay rather than fly ash and fine sand added to a clean, or cleaned, clay. Similar natural raw materials have been used in both pots.

Samples P07 and P08 carry dolerite temper; although the igneous clasts are larger than most of the non-plastics they are not present in large amounts. In both samples quartz-rich sand grains are more abundant, suggesting the clay is naturally silty, or that fine-grained sand was added in addition to olivine dolerite to a clean clay. Sample P08 has a more varied set of igneous rock clasts within a very uniform temper and may be tempered with glacial sand.

Samples P04, P09, P10 and P11 have a quartz-rich sand as the main non-plastic component and may be untempered naturally sandy clays or tempered with fine-grained sand.

Provenance

The clay component is of little help in provenancing the pots. Samples P01, P03, P04, P05, P06, and P07 have a clay that carries very fine-grained quartz and white mica (187µm in diameter) as would be expected from most glacial sediments but in samples P02 and P08 to P11 small, white mica laths are absent or very minor, an unusual occurrence.

Larger, natural clasts, that may be sand temper, include monocrystalline quartz, plagioclase, potassium feldspars, including microcline and perthite, together with accessory minerals dominated by zircon and tourmaline but also include possible garnet. Rock clasts are more variable both in amount and in their lithologies, although in most pots (other than P07 and P08) quartz-rich sediments are more common than igneous and far more common than metamorphic rocks. This rock and mineral assemblage is quite consistent with an origin in the glacial deposits, including till, outwash sands and gravels and diamicton (poorly sorted clay to cobble size material), that are present throughout Holderness. The deeply buried chalk bedrock has contributed nothing.

The igneous rocks are dominated by dolerite and by lesser amounts of microporphyry; there is little or no coarse-grained granite. The composition of the rocks suggests that they initially came from north of Holderness, perhaps Northumberland and the Cheviot Hills (Ixer and Vince 2009), and were entrained within glacial deposits that were restricted to the north-east coastal region of England.

The pots can be grouped by the nature of their temper. Sherds P07 and P08 are both tempered with dolerite though not the same: P07 has an analcime-bearing altered ophitic dolerite and P08 an altered non-ophitic dolerite. The limited material does not suggest that either is from the quartz dolerite Whin Sill of northern England although this is the most obvious and likely source. It is of note that the dolerite tempered pots from Mellor in Derbyshire were not from Whin Sill erratics but probably from locally sourced igneous outcrops. In the absence of locally suitable igneous outcrops in East Yorkshire and in light of the association of the dolerite with other igneous rocks in the paste, it is probable that the dolerites are erratic material: if so, the rocks have been selected from the till.

Samples P05 and P06 are tempered with anthropogenic material: a glassy fly ash. This shows a surprisingly wide size range, and no metal slag was recognised. Trace amounts of metal slag, with olivine, but no fly ash, present in P09 and possibly in P10, are not temper but adventitious.

Sample P03 is tempered with straw or other plant material, and samples P04, P09, P10 and P11 are quartz sand tempered. They are similar to many Iron Age pots in middle England and no specific origin for their raw materials is possible although, as all the non-organic components are probably glacial in origin, they could be local.

Samples P01 and 02 carry significant amounts of grog or auto-grog but have quite different pastes to each other. In both pots the composition of the grog is very similar to the main clay and intentional grogging rather than dirty work practice cannot be shown for certain; however, it is more likely in P01. Pot P02 has,

in addition, a minor shell component in both main paste and in the grog, which may suggest that it was manufactured away from Holderness. It is the only pot that suggests an exotic origin and even here the evidence is very slight.

Conclusions

The petrography of the pots strongly suggests that, other than P02, all the pots could have been locally or very locally produced and were manufactured by adding locally sourced temper to glacial clays or by firing suitably silty clays.

Analysis of crucibles and metal-working residues

Derek Pitman and Roger Doonan

Ceramics recovered from Old Ellerby, Burton Constable, Nuttles, New York, Bluegate Corner, Scorborough Hill, Gilcross and Out Newton Road were characterised to identify material and technological origin (Table 40). Metallurgical surface residues were identified using a Thermo-Niton pXRF surface analyser. Elevated levels of metal species indicate contact with molten metal and, in some cases, suggest the compositions of the alloys. Internal and external surfaces of samples were analysed for copper, arsenic, lead and zinc; a subsample of suspected crucible fragments, comprising samples 17, 18, 19, 20 and 23, were also analysed for the presence of tin. Suspected slag tempered ceramics were sectioned and mounted in resin, ground and polished to 1μm for examination using a Nikon Optiphot 2 Trinocular Microscope.

XRF analysis

Results are presented semi-quantitatively in Table 41. Most of the samples examined exhibited elevated levels of metal species on their internal surfaces in comparison to their exterior surfaces. The possible slag tempered wares showed significantly less metallic enrichment on their internal surfaces when compared to the suspected crucible sherds.

All of the copper readings on the external surfaces of the sherds were below 200ppm. This is in contrast to the internal surface where copper concentrations ranged from

Type	Mass/g	No.	Description
Possible slag tempered ware	271.3	10	No sign of excessive vitrification; macroscopic examination shows slag or other vitreous material used as temper
Possible crucible sherds	60.7	6	Signs of vitrification and some morphological characteristics of a crucible such as shape or metallic residue
Possible furnace lining	31.3	4	Clay with glassy, highly vitrified surface; other surface less vitrified.
Non-diagnostic high temperature ceramic	263.6	96	Evidence of excessive heating but no morphological characteristics of function.

TABLE 40: SUMMARY OF THE MATERIALS ANALYSED FOR EVIDENCE OF METAL WORKING

Sample	Site	Context	Feature	Ident	Mass/g	Interior	Exterior
11	New York	119138	119137	Poss. mould frags	212.4		
12	Nuttles	31116	31103	Crucible	6.0	Pale grey	Pale grey
13	Out Newt. Rd	13019	13021	Furnace lining	3.7	Dark grey glassy	Pale brown
14	Scorbro' Hill	10416	10412	Crucible	4.2	Pale grey; white glassy concretion	Pale grey
15	Gilcross	121041	121040	Crucible	6.6	Pale grey	Pale grey
16	Gilcross	121043	121040	High temp. ceramic	4.2	Pale grey	Pale grey
17	Gilcross	121043	121040	Crucible	4.0	Dark grey/red	Pale grey
18	Burton Const.	118912	unstrat	Crucible	24.8	Pale grey	Pale grey
19	Burton Const.	9603	9601	High temp. ceramic	14.3	Pale grey	Pale grey
20	Burton Const.	9861	9860	High temp. ceramic	4.6	Pale grey	Pale grey
21	Burton Const.	9378	9377	Furnace lining	3.2	Glassy dark grey	Pale brown
22	Burton Const.	118094	118080	Furnace lining	19.1	Bloated, pale grey	Pale brown
23	Burton Const.	118505	118057	High temp. ceramic	22.1	Pale grey	Pale grey
25	Out Newt. Rd	13021	13020	Crucible	15.1	Pale grey, bloated	Glassy, grey; some dark red corrosion.
26	Old Ellerby	3016	3014	High temp. ceramic	6.0	Pale grey	Glassy brown
28	Bluegate C'nr	119979	119977	Furnace lining	5.3	Glassy dark grey	Red/brown

TABLE 41: DETAILS OF SAMPLES ANALYSED FOR EVIDENCE OF METAL WORKING

EX	External surface
IN	Internal surface
-	Not present
•	<100 ppm
••	101-1000 ppm
•••	1001-10,000 ppm
••••	>10,001 ppm

TABLE 42: KEY TO THE SEMI QUANTITATIVE XRF RESULTS

undetectable to over 1%. Arsenic was mostly undetected on the external surfaces of the sherds. On the internal surfaces however, the concentration ranged from undetectable to 500ppm. Lead was only present in trace amounts (less than 35ppm) on the external surfaces but was significantly enriched (to over 0.1%) on the internal surfaces. Zinc was generally present at below 100ppm on the external surfaces but levels of 5000ppm were detected on internal surfaces. Tin similarly showed a significant increase on the inner surface, with external concentrations less than 200ppm and the internal concentrations as high as 0.1%.

When present in significant amounts, all of the elements show a strong positive correlation, particularly copper, tin and lead.

Sample	12		13		14		15		16		17		18		19		20	
Surface	EX	IN	EX	IN	EX	IN	EX	IN	EX	IN	EX	IN	EX	IN	EX	IN	EX	IN
Cu	•	••••	•	•	•	••	•	•••	•	•••	••	•••	•	••	•	•	•	••••
As	-	•	-	-	-	•	-	••	-	•	-	•	-	•	-	-	•	••
Pb	•	••	•	•	•	-	•	•••	•	••	•	••	•	••	•	••	•	••••
Zn	••	•••	••	••	•	•	•	••	••	••	••	•••	•	••	••	••	•	••
Sn											••	••	-	••	-	••	-	••••

Sample	21		22		23		25		25		26		27		28	
Surface	EX	IN	EX	IN	EX	IN	EX	IN	EX	IN	EX	IN	na	na	EX	IN
Cu	•	••	•	•	•	••••	•••	•••	••	•••	•	-	-	-	•	••
As	•	•	-	-	-	••	-	•	•	-	-	•	•	•	-	-
Pb	•	•	-	•	•	••	-	•	-	-	•	•	•	•	•	•
Zn	••	••	••	••	••	••	-	•	•	•	•	•	•	•	•	•
Sn					••	••••										

TABLE 43A AND B: RESULTS OF XRF ANALYSIS OF HIGH TEMPERATURE CERAMICS/CRUCIBLES

Sample	11.1		11.2		11.5		11.6	
Surface	EX	IN	EX	IN	EX	IN	EX	IN
Cu	●	●●●	●	●●	●	●●●	●	●●
As	●	●	-	-	-	●	-	●
Pb	●●	●●	●	●	●	●●	●	●●
Zn	●	●	●	●	●	●	●●	●●●

TABLE 44: RESULTS OF XRF ANALYSIS OF POSSIBLE MOULD FRAGMENTS

Site	Sherds	Weight/g
Old Ellerby	441	5319
Burton Constable	956	13305
Brandywell	132	1949
Sproatley	50	662.3
Nuttles	125	1791
Lelley	4	25.6
New York	22	456.9
Burstwick	12	211.2
Churchlands	3	97.8
Winestead	20	158.8
Patrington	65	1757
Bluegate Corner	513	5760
Weeton	4	13
Scorborough Hill	392	5371
Gilcross	4	95.6
Out Newton Rd	3	34.5
Dimlington	6	8.9

TABLE 45: QUANTITY OF WHEEL-THROWN ROMANO-BRITISH POTTERY FROM EXCAVATION AREAS

Reflected light microscopy

Reflected light microscopy was carried out on samples 3, 4 and 5, the micrographs confirming the presence of vitrified inclusions and suggesting that slag had been incorporated in the ceramic as an intentional temper. These inclusions show little evidence of crystallinity. Colours range from light grey to black. Occasional free silica inclusions are present, and the rounded pore structure resembles that of an over-vitrified ceramic or a silica-rich slag. There are rare instances where iron oxides and possible iron silicates are visible, similar to the structures expected on iron slags. There are no diagnostic phases which would allow the slags to be assigned to a specific process but the absence of metallic inclusions suggests they are unlikely to derive from copper or other non-ferrous metallurgy.

Discussion

Crucibles

Most samples exhibit elevated levels of metal species on their internal surface. These elevated levels, especially copper, lead, tin and arsenic, in conjunction with evidence of vitrification, suggest that many samples can be correctly identified as crucible fragments. Samples 13, 14, 19, 21, 22, 26, 27, 28 do not have enhanced levels of metal species, but are similar in both fabric and morphology to the other sherds and may represent unused vessels.

The most enriched samples, 20 and 23, showed exceedingly high values; particularly copper lead and tin. It is likely that such high values are due to residual metal on the surface, rather than just the result of contact with a molten metal. The co-presence of copper, tin and lead suggests that this was a leaded tin Bronze alloy, typical for the Iron Age (Dungworth 1997).

The morphology of the crucibles is also notable; particularly sample 18, which retains a full internal wall from rim to base. The crucible depth of around 40mm is smaller than the typical value of around 70mm. The curvature of the base seems to suggest a triangular plan: a common characteristic of late prehistoric, especially Iron Age, crucibles (Lucas and Paynter 2010, Gregory 1992).

Furnace lining

Three fragments of possible furnace lining, samples 13, 21 and 22, were characterised by a single, significantly vitrified surface. Analysis of the vitrified and un-vitrified surfaces showed little increase in metallurgical enrichment on either surface.

Slag tempered ware

The analysis of the inclusions in the slag tempered ware was inconclusive as to the specific metallurgical process, although it is certain that these inclusions derive from a high temperature process. If metallurgical then it would most likely be some aspect of iron metallurgy as the analysis shows only minor increases in non-ferrous elements.

Conclusions

This assemblage, though fragmentary, presents an interesting case study into late prehistoric craft production. The material can be broadly split into two categories; ceramics resulting from high temperature industrial processes, and ceramics tempered with debris that likely originated in a high temperature activity. It is likely that the glassy material which was used to temper the latter group was drawn from metallurgical activities carried out nearby, indicating a relationship between different kinds of craft practice.

The identification of metallurgical debris in association with Iron Age features is not uncommon being a typical feature for a range of settlement sites, from farmsteads to hillforts. The alloys melted within the crucibles are consistent with Iron Age metallurgical practice.

Romano-British pottery

R. S. Leary, with Felicity Wild (samian) and Kay Hartley (mortaria)

The quantities of pottery sherds recovered from the excavated areas are shown in Table 45. The pottery was examined in context groups and catalogued according to the Guidelines of the Study Group for Romano-British Pottery (Darling 2004). Fabrics were recorded and described using standard terminology (as Peacock 1977) with reference to the National Fabric Collection where appropriate (Tomber and Dore 1998). Forms, decoration, conditions and cross joins were described and pottery was quantified by sherd count, weight and rim percentage value.

Wares and forms

The pottery fabric was examined by eye or, where necessary, under an x30 binocular microscope, and sorted into ware groups on the basis of colour, hardness, feel, fracture, inclusions and manufacturing technique. It was possible to identify examples of early grey wares from industries based in north Lincolnshire such as at Dragonby and Roxby (Swan 1996 and Rigby and Stead 1976). Fabrics such as the late hard and fine Holme-on-Spalding-Moor group and the Crambeck grey wares were readily identified, but several of the other grey ware fabrics merged into each other and many could not be attributed to a kiln source, in the absence of a diagnostic form. This problem has been encountered frequently by other specialists working on Yorkshire Romano-British pottery (Evans 1985, 260-5, Monaghan 1997, 900-1).

The earliest wheel-thrown pottery was made in a grey-brown quartz-tempered ware, which included a fine and a medium tempered fabric, BSA1 and BSB1, used to make bowls and wide-mouthed jars. These were of pre-Flavian and Flavian type with grooves and cordons on the upper body and bead or everted rims. Some may be late Iron Age in date. In addition to these were a number of beakers, including a girth beaker and simple everted rim beakers, and plain-rim platters. The coarser fabric was also used to make jars with upright flat-topped rims of a type found in late Iron Age, as at Scratta Wood (Challis and Harding 1975, fig. 17.13-14), and early to mid-Roman groups (Gregory 1996, 517 where it was called proto-Dales ware). These vessels are similar to types found in north Lincolnshire, in form but perhaps not fabric, since the Lincolnshire late Iron Age vessels are more commonly shell-tempered. A wide-necked flagon in a white ware associated with these wares at Scorborough Hill is likely to come from an imported flagon of Hofheim type dating to the mid-first century.

Grey ware fabrics GRB4 and 6, related to these transitional wares, were probably obtained from the kilns at Dragonby and Roxby. These included 'foreign' types known from the Flavian kiln 4 at Dragonby, such as a tripod bowl and an early flagon in a coarse off-white ware, and the early second-century kiln waste group F2567 at Dragonby, such as the flanged dish (Swan 1996, fig. 20.34: 1458). Tripod bowls were common in France (Swan 2009; Tuffreau-Libre 1992, 76; Cool 2006, 41-2) and found predominantly on military or urban sites in Britain in the first century: Colchester (Symonds and Wade 1999, 470), Verulamium (Frere 1972, 282: 231; 284: 234), London (Davies et al. 1994, 75, fig. 65. 379; 130, fig. 111.708), Caerleon (Zienkiewicz 1986, 60, fig. 1.18). They are present in Yorkshire at York itself and at Castleford (Rush et al. 2000, 109: 135-6) in fabric 81, a coarse grey ware with quartz, sedimentary rock and occasional grog inclusions, and Malton (Wenham and Heywood 1997, 86: 237) in calcite-gritted ware (Corder 1930b, fig. 1.19).

Recent work by Tyers (1996, 142) has demonstrated that early tripod bowls at Colchester (Cam 45b) are imports. The vessels are very rare on rural settlements but their presence in kiln 4 at Dragonby, dated by Swan to the early to mid-Flavian period (1996, 575-577: 1418), along with other 'exotic' elements, such as flagons, rusticated jars, samian bowls copies and a cheesepress, as well as the use of oxidising firing conditions and the form of the kiln, led Swan to conclude that the potter involved, although perhaps local, was working primarily for the military establishments to the north at Brough-on-Humber and beyond. Swan posited that later kilns at Dragonby worked for similar military markets on the basis of the presence of military types such as samian copies, a collared bowl of Continental type and tazze. The form of the Dragonby vessel compares most closely to our tripod bowl. The tripod bowls from the military and urban sites of Colchester, Caerleon, and Verulamium have straight walls and flat bases whereas the Dragonby example has curved walls and slightly rounded base as at Scorborough Hill. Those from Castleford and London also have this profile but the Malton examples had straighter walls and plain rims. At Dragonby, Swan argues that the presence of tripod bowls implies the presence of soldiers, or potters paid by the army, from northern or western Gallia Belgica who prepared food in a different way to the native Britons.

Types made in the north Lincolnshire kilns in the late first and second centuries were present and encompass the main second-century wheel-thrown types. Dish types comprise one with an inturned rim and one with a wide, flat, grooved rim, both internally decorated with zones of burnishing. Both types were made at Roxby (Rigby and Stead 1976 types H and no. 78) and Dragonby (Swan 1996, fig. 20.34: 1458, 1474 and 1477, dated by Swan to the early second century). They were common at Dragonby, particularly with the triangular zones of burnished decoration from the early second to the mid-

Fabric code	Description
BBT1	Dark grey/black, hard with hackly fracture. Moderate, medium, subangular quartz with rare medium, rounded grey inclusions. Probably a black burnished ware copy
BSA1	Dark brown with buff margins and darker core. Hard, smooth with finely irregular fracture. Abundant, fine quartz and sparse medium subangular quartz.
BSB1	Dark brown sometimes with buff/lighter brown margins. Hard and sandy where not smoothed. Hackly fracture moderate, rounded and subrounded medium quartz, rare rounded sandstone, subangular ?flint and rounded calcareous inclusions ?chalk
CTB1	Brown fabric, hard with rough feel. Medium ill-sorted medium shell or platey vesicles
CTB2	As CTB1 with moderate, medium subangular quartz
CTA2	Dales ware. Tomber and Dore 1998 DAL SH
CTA4	Grey, hard with irregular fracture. Moderate medium, round and platey white inclusions, shell and oolitic limestone? And moderate medium subrounded quartz and dark grey inclusions, perhaps igneous
DR20	Dressel 20 amphora. Tomber and Dore 1998 BAT AM
EYCT	East Yorkshire calcite-gritted wares. Examples with quartz coded EYCT gritty
FLA1	White. Hard and smooth with smooth fracture. Sparse fine quartz and rare medium rounded brown inclusions
FLA2	White or pinkish cream. Oft, powdery with fine fracture. Sparse, medium, subrounded quartz and rounded brown inclusions
FLA3	Cream with grey core Hard, slightly sandy feel. As GRB12 but cream surfaces
FLA4	White, fairly hard with powdery feel and finely irregular fracture. Moderate, fine angular quartz and rare, medium and coarse, rounded red/brown inclusions.
FLB	As OAB with traces of white slip
GRA1	Grey with buff margins and darker grey core. Soft, smooth with fairly smooth fracture. Rare medium subangular quartz
GRA2	Hard medium grey with smooth feel and finely irregular fracture. Abundant fine subangular and subrounded quartz, rare, burnt organics
GRB1	Medium to light grey. Hard, slightly sandy with irregular fracture. Moderate fine to medium. Subangular quartz
GRB2	Medium grey ware with moderate medium quartz and sparse fine to medium white inclusions GRB2B with brown margins
GRB3	Holme-on-Spalding-Moor fine grey ware. Tomber and Dore 1998 HSM RE
GRB4	Dragonby coarse. Grey with buff margins and grey core. Sometime grey/brown with brown margins Sandy, gritty feel and hackly fracture. Abundant, medium, subangular and subrounded quartz, sparse fine to medium white calcareous inclusions and rounded red/brown inclusions.
GRB5	Dark faced grey ware abundant medium subangular quartz
GRB6	Dark grey with buff/brown margins and dark grey core.? Transitional ware. Hard, slightly sandy feel and irregular fracture' studded' with sparse to moderate medium subangular quartz and sparse fine white inclusions. Perhaps related to bsb1.
GRB7	As GRB4 but medium grey with buff margins and grey core.
GRB8	Or 9th-11th C very gritty early transitional ware. Grey with brown margins. Hard and gritty feeling. Hackly fracture. Abundant, well-sorted. Medium to coarse rounded and subangular quartz
GRB9	Medium to dark grey with buff margins and dark grey core. Fairly smooth, hard with slightly irregular fracture. Moderate fine-medium, subangular and subrounded quartz and rare, fine rounded brown inclusions.
GRB10	Dark grey with buff margins and orange/brown core. Gritty, hard with irregular fracture. Moderate, medium, subangular and subrounded quartz with sparse, ill sorted fine to coarse, rounded red/brown inclusions
GRB11	Dark grey slightly sandy, hard with irregular fracture. Moderate, ill-sorted, fine quartz and sparse, medium, subangular quartz and brown oxides
GRB12	Grey with buff margins and dark to medium grey core. Soft fairly smooth with fairly smooth fracture. Sparse medium and fine quartz and fine white inclusions, calcareous.
GRB13	Grey with buff margins. Sandy, hard with hackly fracture. Moderate, coarse subangular and rounded quartz and long thin vesicles
GRB14	Brownish grey with grey core. Soft with sandy feel and finely irregular fracture. Moderate to sparse, fairly fine-medium, subangular and subrounded quartz and sparse rounded grey./brown inclusions.
GRB15	Grey copies of BB1 and 2. Medium grey, hard with hackly fracture. Sometimes with brown margins. Abundant , well sorted medium subangular quartz, rare vesicles . Similar to GRB4 in texture. BB copies

Fabric code	Description
GRB16	Dark grey, hard and gritty with hackly fracture Abundant, well-sorted medium angular quartz
GRB17	Dark grey with light grey core. Soft, powdery with irregular fracture. Abundant, fine to medium quartz and sparse coarse rounded white inclusions and grey/black inclusions.
CRA RE	Crambeck grey ware. Tomber and Dore 1998 CRA RE. CRA RE BUFF= same fabric with buff core
GRC1	Light grey, very hard with bumpy feel. Sparse subangular coarse and medium/fine quartz and rounded brown and grey inclusions
GRC2	Buff, hard with gritty feel and irregular fracture. Sparse, coarse rounded quartz and brown ferric inclusions, possibly some igneous inclusions. Micaceous
GRC3	Grey sometimes with brown margins. Hard, sandy with finely irregular fracture. Moderate fine to medium, subangular quartz and sparse, coarse subangular quartz, ?igneous inclusions, sandstone and medium, subrounded vesicles/white calcareous inclusions
GRC4	Dark grey /brown with darker core. Gritty feel and hackly fracture. Abundant, medium, subrounded quartz and igneous inclusions with sparse subrounded soft grey inclusions and rare angular vesicles.
GRC5	Grey, sometime brown margins, sandy feel with moderate fine to medium, subangular quartz and sparse, very coarse subangular quartz, subrounded ?igneous inclusions, and medium, subrounded vesicles/white calcareous inclusions. Some of the vesicles are somewhat flat and thin as shell. A similar fabric is used for the hm dales type ware
GTA8/GTA8G	Brown or grey ware with medium grog/clay pellets, sparse to moderate medium quartz and sparse medium shell inclusions
GTA10	Grey ware with moderate, subangular, medium quartz and sparse coarse, angular grey grog or argillaceous inclusions.
GTA14	Fine brown ware with grog/clay pellets and sparse fine calcareous inclusions
MCRA PA	Crambeck parchment ware mortarium
MCRA WH	Crambeck white ware mortarium
MEBOR	Ebor type mortarium
MMALTON	Ebor/Malton area mortarium
MOWS	White slipped oxidised mortarium
MW	White mortarium
NV	Nene Valley colour coated ware
OAA	Orange with grey core. Soft. Smooth and finely with irregular fracture. Moderate, medium, subangular quartz and sparse soft, red/brown inclusions.
OAB	Oxidised ware. Moderate medium, subangular and subrounded quartz. Predominantly very abraded undiagnostic sherds
RS	Orange with darker orange/red slip. Hard and smooth with finely irregular fracture. Moderate, fine, angular and subangular quartz.
RS IMP PR6	Pompeian red ware fabric 6
TS	Samian ware

TABLE 46: ROMANO-BRITISH POTTERY: FABRIC DESCRIPTIONS

third century (Gregory 1996, 519-20: 843 and 932). Darling (1984, 85-6: 43-4) gave the dish form a date range starting in the late first century and continuing as late as the early third.

Some jar forms present were also common at the north Lincolnshire kilns (Roxby A-D) typically with everted or rebated rims and grooved wavy line decoration on the shoulder or rustication. A carinated bowl form, (Roxby type E) with distinctive shelved carination form was common. Wide-mouthed jars with sharply everted rims compared to Roxby F, although it was not always possibly to differentiate these from later, third-century wide-mouthed jars with everted rims, particularly in the

case of rim fragments. Some lugged jars may also belong to this period but it is not easy to differentiate these from later lugged jars. Some narrow-necked jars with zones of rouletting or burnished linear decoration probably date to this period. Ring and dot beakers in both oxidised and grey wares date to the earlier part of this period and may be traded from further south.

A distinctive fabric with grog inclusions or clay pellets (GTA wares) was used to make jars with an everted rim or a bead rim, overhanging internally, and also the rebated-rim jar form made at Roxby in grey ware. These compare in fabric and form to vessels made at Dragonby kiln 3 (Rigby and Stead 1976, fig. 64.4) and belong to a group

Ware	Sherds	Sherd wt	Rim %
Old Ellerby			
BSB1	1	11.3	7
CRA RE	2	69.1	12
CT	1	4	
CTA2	123	1213.5	213
EYCT	30	438.6	71
GRA2	9	191.6	34
GRB	13	45.9	
GRB1	48	354.5	
GRB10	6	101.4	7
GRB13	7	68.3	
GRB14	63	1045.4	47
GRB15	24	354.6	87
GRB16	1	42.4	
GRB17	1	88.8	5
GRB2	3	109.2	21
GRB3	32	699.6	116
GRB4	49	768.7	56
GRB5	3	14.3	
GRB7	24	166.1	19
GRC	1	11.6	
GTA10	2	29	
GTA8	19	405.4	65
GTA8G	8	102.2	
MMALTON	2	87	10
MW	1	12.3	
NV	5	27.5	12
OAB	8	32.4	5
TS	15	115.6	1
H	3417	60705	1255
Total	**3918**	**67315.3**	**2043**
Burton Constable			
BSB1	1	42.2	
CRA RE	10	293.2	16
CT	8	15.2	
CTA2	191	1169.5	59
CTA4	12	227.9	69
CTB1	3	57.8	12
CTB2	1	17.8	
EYCT	136	2065.1	197
GRB	30	191.4	8
GRB1	108	1234.3	132
GRB10	24	346.2	15
GRB11	1	2	
GRB13	23	313.2	9
GRB14	92	932.5	46
GRB15	16	136	5
GRB2	34	873.6	99
GRB3	147	3445.1	315
GRB4	26	262.3	13

Ware	Sherds	Sherd wt	Rim %
GRB5	18	228.5	5
GRB6	10	197.6	24
GRBY	1	6.9	
GRC3	27	765.8	77
GRC4	4	29.1	11
MCRA PA	4	85.3	15
MCRA WH	8	309	30
MOWS	6	49.3	5
NV	4	22	10
OAB	13	103	11
Ox	1	2.6	
TS	4	25.1	9
H	9946	148354	
Total	**10909**	**161803.5**	**1192**
Brandywell			
BSA1	9	76.3	
BSB1	11	110.1	30
CTB1	10	354.3	85
DR20	10	594.2	
FLB	1	1.4	
GRA1	1	5.5	
GRB	6	22.8	
GRB2	13	207.1	15
GRB4	13	342.8	36
GRB6	26	326.9	77
GTA8	1	13.7	
GTA8G	3	70.4	25
GTA8G/10	23	431.4	8
OAA	8	36.6	27
OAB	8	62.3	
H	1971	27350	535
Total	**2114**	**30005.8**	**838**
Sproatley			
BSB1	4	16	6
GRB	2	16.7	
GRB1	4	13.8	
GRB3	1	49.2	5
GRB4	5	15.9	
GT	1	6.8	
GTA10	7	186.9	50
MEBOR	1	315.1	15
OAB	1	13.7	
TS	24	28.2	
H	169	1349	
Total	**219**	**2011.3**	**76**
Nuttles			
BBT1	1	6.8	
BSB1	1	21.4	
FLA	1	7.6	
GRA	2	6.8	

Ware	Sherds	Sherd wt	Rim %
GRB1	48	568.1	58
GRB2	3	24.1	9
GRB4	31	449.8	67
GRB6	20	425.7	57
GRB7	9	134.88	27
GTA8G	4	68.7	
MOR	1	53.8	
OAB	4	23.8	
H	1228	24673	541
Total	**1353**	**26464.48**	**759**
Lelley			
CRA RE	1	6	
GRB4	1	3.2	
GRB6	2	3.4	
NV	1	2	
OAB	2	1.5	
TS	2	17.6	5
H	2765	42921	1113
Total	**2774**	**42954.7**	**1118**
New York			
GRA	1	68	
GRA1	2	12.8	
GRB1	6	12.9	
GRB2	1	30.6	
GRB8	3	122.8	
GTA8G	1	159.9	
OAB	5	12.6	
TS	3	37.3	
H	770	11424	227
Total	**792**	**11880.9**	**227**
Burstwick			
CT	1	10.2	
GRB	1	1.7	
GRB1	1	21.4	
GRB7	9	177.9	28
H	1004	20190	181
Total	**1016**	**20401.2**	**209**
Churchlands			
GRB1	3	97.8	8
H	224	3435	10
Total	**227**	**3532.8**	**18**
Winestead			
BBT1	1	3.6	
CRA RE	2	34.4	
EYCT	1	7.8	5
GRB1	5	37.3	
GRB2	1	5.7	5
GRB3	3	57.3	
NV	1	7.1	
OAB	2	4.6	
Ox	4	1	
H	15	432	

Ware	Sherds	Sherd wt	Rim %
Total	**35**	**590.8**	**10**
Patrington			
CTA2	36	600.3	29
GRA1	2	70.8	18
GRB	1	2.6	
GRB1	15	673.5	39
GRB5	5	236.3	11
MMALTON	1	79	11
TS	5	94.4	29
H	797	13279	299
Total	**862**	**15035.9**	**436**
Bluegate Corner			
CT	15	56	
CTA2	109	447.4	48
EYCT	1	20.7	5
FLA1	12	119.8	
GRA1	5	26.8	16
GRB	34	99.4	
GRB1	43	337.9	42
GRB10	63	911	49
GRB11	4	87.5	51
GRB12	32	179.9	37
GRB3	39	1016.5	150
GRB4	17	217.2	47
GRB5	5	28.5	3
GRB6	5	24.1	
GRB7	6	37.5	
GRB9	50	1105.8	81
GRC	1	7.2	
GRC1	13	93	
GRC2	14	316.8	
GTA10	1	12.2	
GTA8G	3	77.3	
MLNV WH	39	521.7	43
OAB	2	15.9	
H	491	6284	151
Total	**1004**	**12044.1**	**723**
Weeton			
GRB	2	2.4	
GRB3	1	8.1	11
GRB4	1	2.5	
H	188	1953	25
Total	**192**	**1966**	**36**
Scorborough Hill			
BSB1	61	751.1	204
CTB1	2	38.3	8
FLA1	5	68.2	
FLA3	5	56.6	65
FLA4	1	50.7	
GRA1	6	115	3
GRA2	2	108.5	16
GRB	5	5.5	

Ware	Sherds	Sherd wt	Rim %
GRB1	17	169.4	
GRB10	4	40.9	
GRB13	18	394.2	21
GRB4	124	2402.8	310
GRB6	37	277.5	106
GRB7	81	672.5	110
GRC3	3	55.9	5
GRC5	3	36.8	5
GTA10	1	19.7	
GTA8G	1	25.2	6
OAA	1	3.7	
OAB	8	65.2	11
RS	1	0.9	1
RS IMP PR6	4	29.7	7
TS	8	70.9	
H	2194	34578	786
Total	**2592**	**40037.2**	**1664**
Gilcross			
BSA1	4	95.6	5
H	703	8444	192
Total	**707**	**8539.6**	**197**
Out Newton Rd			
GRB1	3	34.5	
Total	**3**	**34.5**	
Dimlington Rd			
GRB	6	8.9	
Total	**6**	**8.9**	
Grand total	**28745**	**444934.9**	**9558**

TABLE 47: POTTERY WARES BY SITE

of jars in this general form made around Humberside and with a greater variety of everted and rebated rims in the Trent Valley (Todd 1968).

One very small rim sherd with an internal step in what seems to be a red-slipped fabric may belong to a type of platter made at Lincoln in the late first century (as Darling 1981, fig. 23.2: 2). In addition to the imported white ware flagon, a bodysherd from a North Gaulish mortarium of late first- to early second-century date was also present and a Pompeian red ware flat rim bowl or dish fabric 6 was identified. This fabric may have been imported from west Flanders (Tomber and Dore 1998, 45).

Some grey ware copies of black burnished bowls with bead rims and dishes with plain or grooved rims and everted-rim jars with burnished linear decoration belong to the later second to mid-third century. To these may be added Dales and Dales-type jars and plain-rim dishes which date to the third to mid-fourth century increasing numerically from around the mid-third century. Shouldered, wide-mouthed jars and lugged jars belong to this period but can be difficult to distinguish from later examples and the biconical bowls with everted rims are typical of third-century groups. These types can be paralleled in the Norton kilns near Malton but are more likely to have been made at contemporary local kilns (Hayes and Whitley 1950, types 6, 4 and 10 respectively). Traded fine wares in the third century included a very small amount of Nene Valley colour coated ware, beakers and a Castor box, and flanged and collared rims of the late second to third century perhaps from Malton, or elsewhere in Yorkshire.

	bowl	bowl/dish	dish	platter	cup	small jar	beaker	flagon	jar	narrow-necked jar	wide-mouthed jar	storage jar	tripod	mortarium	box	lid	Indet	Total rim %	Handmade vessels	all
Old Ellerby	98	1	109	35			12		368	30	118			10			7	788	1255	**2043**
Burton Const	278	32	193				22		250	192	115	27		50	10	12	11	1192	-	**-**
Brandywell	80		1				37		135		50							303	535	**838**
Sproatley	6											50		15		5		76	0	**76**
Nuttles	72	10	3				35		92								6	218	541	**759**
Lelley		5																5	1113	**1118**
Burstwick			28															28	181	**209**
Churchlands		8																8	10	**18**
Winestead																5	5	10	0	**10**
Patrington	18		7	23					29		49			11				137	299	**436**
Bluegate C	249		15						130	86	38			43		11		572	151	**723**
Weeton	11																	11	25	**36**
Scorb'ro Hill	284		62	45		31	19	65	225		46	6	72			1	22	878	786	**1664**
Gilcross											5							5	192	**197**
All project	**1096**	**56**	**418**	**80**	**23**	**31**	**125**	**65**	**1237**	**308**	**425**	**83**	**72**	**129**	**10**	**34**	**51**	**4**		**4**

TABLE 48: VESSEL FORMS BY SITE

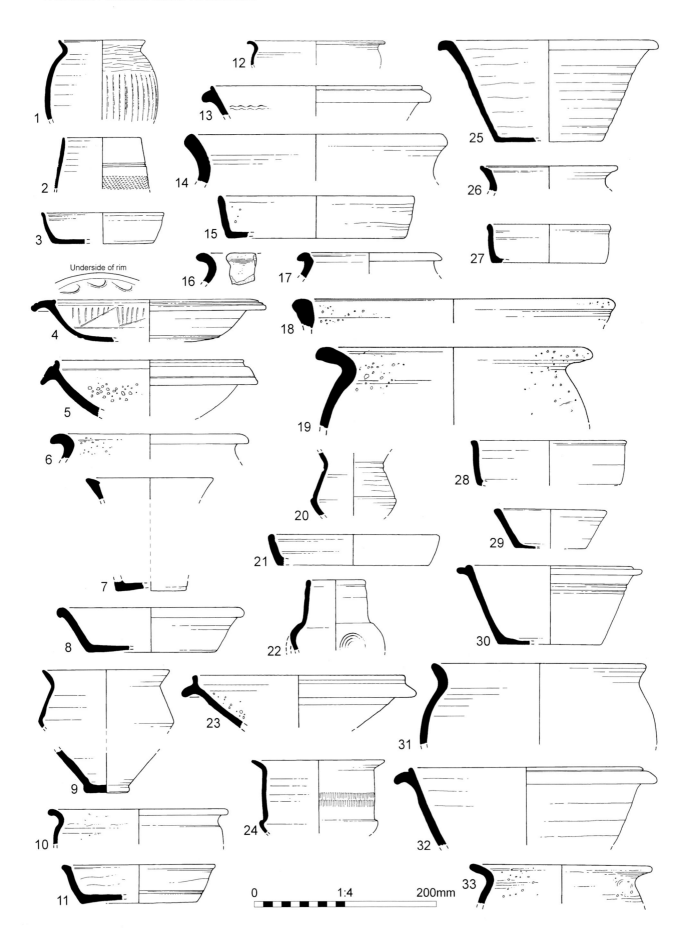

Underside of rim

FIG. 100: ROMANO-BRITISH POTTERY: 1 TO 37

Illustrated Roman pottery 1

Old Ellerby

1. GRB15 EVERTED-RIM JAR; VERTICAL BURNISHED LINES. SLIGHT GROOVE INSIDE THE RIM. FILLS *3282* AND *3299*, PIT 3729 AND UNSTRATIFIED

2. NV1 PLAIN-RIM BEAKER; ROULETTED BODY. FILL *3282*, PIT 3729

3. GRB4 PLATTER OR DISH; GROOVED RIM. FILL *3317*, DITCH 3267

4. GRA2 DISH; FLAT FLANGED RIM; DOUBLE GROOVE AT DISTAL END. BURNISHED WAVY LINE UNDER FLANGE AND TRIANGULAR ZONES OF BURNISHED VERTICAL LINES INSIDE BODY. FILL *3268*, DITCH 3267

5. MORTARIUM, SOFTISH, POWDERY FABRIC, BUFF-BROWN ON INSIDE SURFACE, VERY ORANGE-BROWN ELSEWHERE; NO TRACES OF SLIP; MODERATE, ILL-SORTED AND RANDOM INCLUSIONS: QUARTZ WITH SOME RED-BROWN AND BLACK MATERIAL. TRITURATION GRIT: VARYING KINDS OF QUARTZ, HACKLY FRACTURE AND RARE QUARTZ SANDSTONE, RED-BROWN AND BLACK MATERIAL. FILL *3224*, CUT 3223, DITCH 3219

6. EYCT HUNTCLIFF-TYPE JAR RIM. LOWER FILL *3041*, PIT 3040

7. CTA2 DALES WARE JAR. LOWER FILL *3041*, PIT 3040

8. GRB HOS BEAD RIM DISH. UPPER FILL *3042* PIT 3040

9. GRB14 CARINATED BOWL/JAR; WALL SLOPING IN TOWARDS RIM. UPPER FILL *3042*, PIT 3040

10. GRB14 EVERTED-RIM WIDE-MOUTHED JAR. UPPER FILL *3042*, PIT 3040

11. GRB2 LIPPED DISH. UPPER FILL *3042*, PIT 3040

12. GRB10 EVERTED-RIM WIDE-MOUTHED JAR. FILL *3204*, CUT 3203, DITCH 3056

13. CRA RE DEVELOPED FLANGED BOWL; INTERNAL WAVY LINE BURNISH. FILL 3222, PIT 3043

14. GRB17 WIDE-MOUTHED JAR; EVERTED RIM. FILL *3227*, CUT 3226, DITCH 3243

15. EYCT PLAIN RIM DISH. FURROW *3091*

16. EYCT PROTO-HUNTCLIFF JAR RIM. FURROW *3091*

17. EYCT HUNTCLIFF-TYPE JAR RIM. FURROW *3091*

Burton Constable

18. CTB1 OXIDISED SHELL-TEMPERED RIM FROM LARGE JAR/ STORAGE JAR. FAIRLY UPRIGHT RIM, RATHER TRIANGULAR. FORM COULD BE LATE IRON AGE OR EARLY ROMAN IN DATE (MAY 1996 FIG. 19.8 GROUP 20 AND FIG. 20.1 H1 JARS). UPPER FILL *118387*, CUT 118383, STRUCTURE 5

19. EYCT LARGE JAR; ALMOST HORIZONTAL EVERTED RIM. FILL *9378*, CUT 9377, DITCH 118934

20. GRB1 SMALL CARINATED BOWL; INSLOPING UPPER WALL AND EVERTED RIM. FILL *9378*, CUT 9377, DITCH 118934

21. GRB15 SHALLOW PLAIN-RIM DISH. BURNT. FILL *9378*, DITCH 118934

22. GRB14 LONG NECKED GLOBULAR BEAKER. ONE NON-ADJOINING BODYSHERD SUGGESTED THIS MAY HAVE BEEN INDENTED BEAKER. FILL *9378*, CUT 9377, DITCH 118934

23. CRA WH MORTARIUM. CAMBECK TYPE 6 (CORDER AND BIRLEY 1937, FIG. 3) BUT COARSENESS OF OATMEAL CREAM FABRIC AND THE BRIGHT SALMON-PINK CORE SUGGESTS FROM LOCAL WORKSHOP WORKING IN CRAMBECK TRADITION. FREQ. TINY, MODERATELY WELL SORTED QUARTZ INCLUSIONS, AND SMALL AMOUNT OF RED-BROWN MATERIAL. IRON SLAG TRITURATION GRIT. FOURTH CENTURY. SOME WEAR. FILL *9378*, CUT 9377, DITCH 118934

24. GRB3 CARINATED BOWL; UPRIGHT WALL AND EVERTED RIM AS AT THROLAM KILNS (CORDER 1930A FIG. 16 NO 103-5). LATE THIRD TO FOURTH CENTURY. FILL *9830*, CUT 9829, DITCH 118922

25. GRB2B LIPPED RIM BOWL. NEARLY ALL PRESENT. SF 1215, FILL *9830*, CUT 9829, DITCH 118922

26. GRC4 DALES-TYPE JAR; GROOVE ON UPPER FACE. FILL *9657*, CUT 9437, DITCH 118922

27. CTA4 LIPPED DISH. FILL *9658*, PIT 9728

28. CTA4 LIPPED DISH, TALLER THAN ABOVE. FILL *9658*, PIT 9728

29. GRB3 PLAIN-RIM DISH. FILL *9658*, PIT 9728

30. GRB3 DEVELOPED FLANGED BOWL. FILL *9658*, PIT 9728

31. GRB13 WIDE-MOUTHED JAR. FILL *9658*, PIT 9728

32. GRB3 DEVELOPED FLANGED BOWL. FILL *9148*, CUT 9127, DITCH 9621

33. EYCT PROTO-HUNTCLIFF JAR RIM. WORN WHERE LID WOULD REST, SUGGESTING MID-FOURTH CENTURY DATE. UPPER FILL *9387*, CUT 9385, DITCH 118929

The hard grey fabric of the late Holme-on-Spalding-Moor wares was present and is dated from the late third to fourth century. However it is suspected that some of the sherds in fabric GRB1 were Holme-on-Spalding-Moor products also, with slightly coarser inclusions and with softer fabrics, which may be a result of burial conditions. Forms included developed bead and flange bowls, carinated bowls with straight walls, lugged jars and everted-rim wide mouthed jars (Halkon and Millett 1999, types B09-11, B04, J01 and B01 respectively). The bead and flange bowls, wide-mouthed jars and lugged jars were also present in a slightly coarser grey ware which is likely also to be a Holme-on-Spalding-Moor fabric. The small amount of Crambeck grey wares have a similar date range and include developed bead and flange bowls, a beaker, lugged jars and a spouted jug form. Only one flanged bowl has the internal burnished wavy line characteristic of the late fourth century.

A small amount of oxidised, medium-quartz-tempered ware was identified but the source of this is not known.

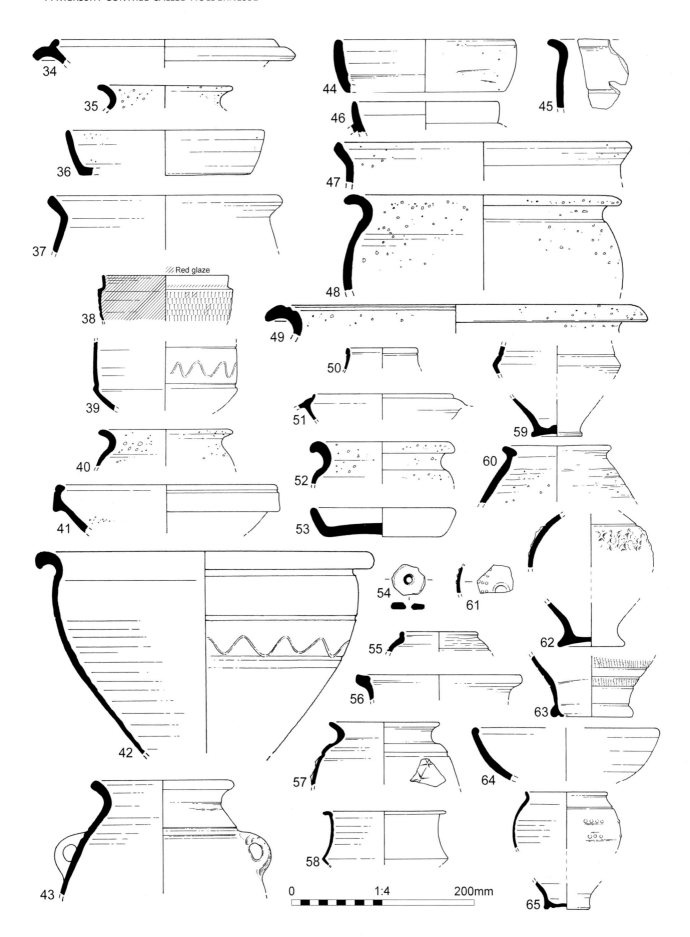

Red glaze

Fig. 101: Roman pottery, 34--54 Burton Constable, 55-65 Brandywell

Illustrated Roman pottery 2

Burton Constable

34. CRA WH MORTARIUM. FABRIC ALMOST BROWNISH-CREAM, TEXTURE MADE VERY SANDY BY THE PRESENCE OF MINUTE MOSTLY QUARTZ PARTICLES, PERHAPS A CONSTITUENT OF CLAY USED, BUT FINER TEXTURE. HEAVILY BURNT ON FLANGE AND BEAD. RIM-PROFILE A VARIANT OF CRAMBECK TYPE 6 WITH HIGH, INWARD SLOPING BEAD. FOURTH CENTURY. UPPER FILL *9387*, CUT 9385, DITCH 118929

35. EYCT PROTO-HUNTCLIFF WARE JAR RIM. UPPER FILL *9637*, CUT 9638, DITCH 9825

36. CTA4 PLAIN-RIM DISH. UPPER FILL *9637*, CUT 9638, DITCH 9825

37. GRC3 JAR; TALL EVERTED RIM; ROUNDED BLUNT END. UPPER FILL *9272*, CUT 9768, DITCH 9825

38. NV1 CASTOR BOX RIM AND BODY. SHARPLY EXECUTED SHOULDER SUGGESTS THIRD CENTURY DATE. UPPER FILL *9272*, CUT 9768, DITCH 9825

39. GRB3 BODY OF CARINATED BOWL; UPRIGHT BODY AND WAVY LINE BURNISH. FILL *9882*, CUT 9883, DITCH 118934

40. EYCT PROTO-HUNTCLIFF JAR RIM. FILL *9882*, DITCH 118934

41. CRA PA CREAM FABRIC FIRED PALE BROWNISH ON INSIDE SURFACE; FABRIC TENDING TO LAMINATE AT POINT OF CHANGE. FREQ. TINY OR SMALL INCLUSIONS, MOSTLY QUARTZ, SOME RED-BROWN AND BLACK MATERIAL. TRITURATION GRIT ENTIRELY BLACK SLAG. VARIANT OF CRAMBECK TYPE: *CF* YORK MINSTER (HARTLEY 1995, FIG.126, NOS. 44-49) BUT NOT A CRAMBECK FABRIC: LOCAL WORKSHOP USING INFERIOR CLAY. RIM-WALL PLAIN, NOT PAINTED AS IS OFTEN THE CASE WITH THIS FORM. FINE 'PARCHMENT WARE' TYPE LINKED TO PERIOD AFTER AD 370 (CORDER AND BIRLEY 1937, FIG.3 AND 398-413; BIDWELL 2005). UPPER FILL *9887*, CUT 9885, DITCH 118917

42. MUCH OF A GRB3 WIDE-MOUTHED JAR; WAVY LINE BURNISH OUTSIDE BODY. LOWEST FILL *9081*, CUT 9082, DITCH 118917

43. GRB3 NARROW-MOUTHED EVERTED RIM JAR; GROOVE ON SHOULDER. LOWEST FILL *9081*, CUT 9082, DITCH 118917

44. GRB3 PLAIN-RIM DISH. LOWEST FILL *9081*, CUT 9082, DITCH 118917

45. GRB14 EVERTED RIM WIDE-MOUTHED JAR. LOWEST FILL *9081*, CUT 9082, DITCH 118917

46. MOWS WALL-SIDED FLANGED BOWL, RATHER THAN MORTARIUM. LOWEST FILL *9081*, CUT 9082, DITCH 118917

47. GRC3 JAR; TALL EVERTED, BLUNT-ENDED RIM. FILL *9773*, DITCH 118928

48. EYCT PROTO-HUNTCLIFF JAR. FILL *9106*, CUT 9107, DITCH 118920

49. EYCT RIM FROM HUNTCLIFF-TYPE JAR; DOUBLE LID SEATING. UPPER FILL *9447*, CUT 9445, DITCH 118931

50. GRB1 BEAD RIM OF LONG NECKED BEAKER. UPPER FILL *9447*, CUT 9445, DITCH 118931

51. GRB6 INCOMPLETE RIM AND BODYSHERD FROM COLLARED BOWL. LATE FIRST TO EARLY SECOND CENTURY (SWAN 1996 FIG. 20.34 NOS 1459-60). FILL *9508*, CUT 9509, DITCH 118960

52. EYCT PROTO-HUNTCLIFF SHOULDERED AND NECKED JAR. UPPER AND MIDDLE FILLS *9624* AND *9625*, CUT 9622, FEATURE 9717

53. GRC3 SEVERAL ABRADED SHERDS FROM BASE BODY AND RIM OF PLAIN RIM DISH. A LONG-LIVED TYPE BUT THE GRC WARES SEEM TO INCREASE NUMERICALLY IN THE LATER PHASES AND BOTH BIDWELL AND CROOM (2010, 31) AND BELL AND EVANS (2002, 407) SUGGEST LATE THIRD TO FOURTH CENTURY RANGE FOR GRITTY GREY WARE GROUP. MIDDLE FILL *9624*, CUT 9622, FEATURE 9717

54. GRB1 BODYSHERD MADE INTO SPINDLE WHORL. MIDDLE FILL *9624*, CUT 9622, FEATURE 9717

Brandywell

55. BSB1 SMALL JAR OR BEAKER; ROUNDED SLIGHTLY EVERTED RIM AND SHOULDER GROOVE BELOW BURNISHED ZONE. FABRIC SIMILAR TO LATE IRON AGE AND EARLY ROMAN FORMS WARES FOUND IN TRENT VALLEY. FILL *25231*, PIT 25230

56. BSB1 UPRIGHT, FLAT-TOPPED RIM OF JAR. NUMBERED 25169: PROBABLE MISREADING FOR FILL *25109*, CUT 25108, PIT 25250

57. GRB6 RIM AND BODYSHERDS FROM GIRTH BEAKER. A NON-ADJOINING BODYSHERD WITH RUSTICATION PROBABLY COMES FROM THIS VESSEL. UPPER FILL *2505*, CUT 2504, DITCH 25116

58. GRB6 CARINATED BOWL; EVERTED RIM AND SHELVED CARINATION. LOWER FILL *2506*, CUT 2504, DITCH 25116

59. GRB2 SPLAYED BASE AND LOWER BODY OF RUSTICATED JAR. LOWER FILL *25112*, CUT 25106, DITCH 25116

60. GRB6 SHOULDER OF CARINATED BOWL; SHELVED CARINATION AND BASE IN SAME FABRIC. LOWER FILL *25112*, CUT 25106, DITCH 25116

61. CTB1 NECKLESS JAR; TRIANGULAR SHAPED RIM FORMED BY FOLDING CLAY IN TO FORM FLAT TOPPED RIM; INTERNAL REBATE. LOWER FILL *25112*, CUT 25106, DITCH 25116

62. GRA1 BODYSHERD FROM RING AND DOT JAR. LOWER FILL *25112*, CUT 25106, DITCH 25116

63. BSA1 FOOTRING BASE AND LOWER BODY OF BEAKER; ZONES OF ROULETTING. MIDDLE AND LOWER FILLS *25062* AND *25060*, CUT 25043, DITCH 25168

64. GRB4 DISH; INTURNED ROUNDED RIM. MIDDLE FILL *25060*, CUT 25043, DITCH 25168

65. OAA1 SMALL EVERTED RIM BEAKER; SHOULDER GROOVE AND BARBOTINE DOT PANEL; NON-ADJOINING FOOTRING BASE. MIDDLE FILLS *25060* AND *25045*, CUT 25043, DITCH 25168

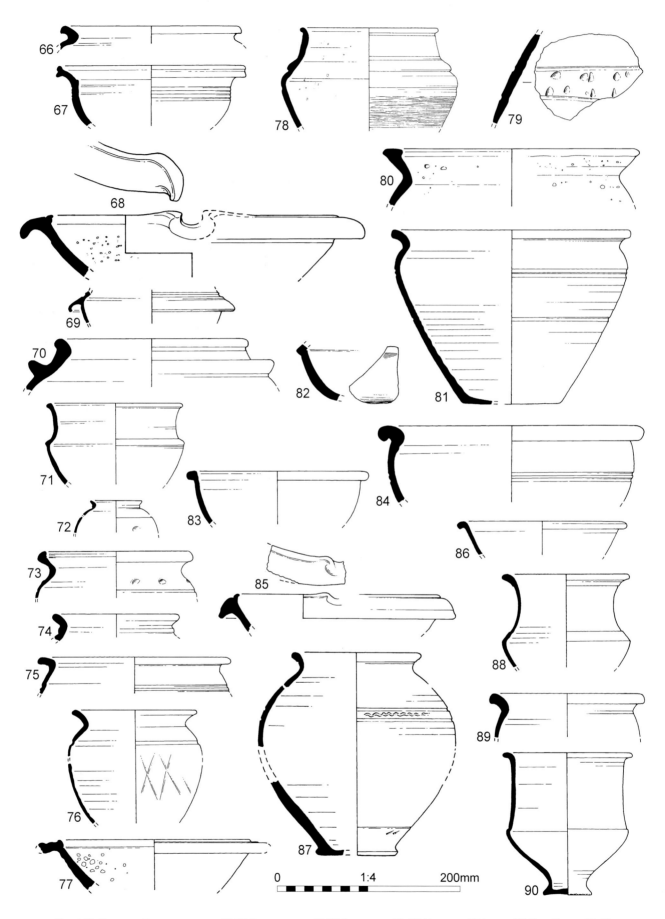

FIG. 102: ROMANO-BRITISH POTTERY, 66-67 BRANDYWELL, 68-70 SPROATLEY, 71-77 NUTTLES, 78 LELLEY, 79 NEW YORK, 80-85 PATRINGTON, 86-90 BLUEGATE CORNER.

Illustrated Roman pottery 3

Brandywell

66. GTA8G 'NATIVE' JAR; EVERTED RIM. PRIMARY FILL *25011*, CUT 25008, DITCH 25168

67. GRB4 BIFID FLANGED BOWL AS ROXBY TYPE S (RIGBY AND STEAD 1976). LOWER FILL *25027*, PIT 25025

Sproatley

68. MORTARIUM. HARD, DEEP ORANGE-BROWN FABRIC; MAY HAVE HAD THIN SELF-COLOURED SLIP. FREQ. TINY TO SMALL INCLUSIONS: QUARTZ AND BLACK PARTICLES. TRITURATION GRIT ENTIRELY QUARTZ-LIKE. FROM UNLOCATED NORTHERN ENGLAND WORKSHOP. RIM-PROFILE SUGGESTS DATE BEFORE AD 140: COULD BE CONSIDERABLY EARLIER. SPOUT BROKEN BUT VISIBLE R-FACING SIDE SUGGESTS COULD BE AS EARLY AS AD 80/85. OPTIMUM LATE FIRST TO EARLY SECOND CENTURY. UPPER FILL *26097*, CUT 26096, PIT 26428

69. GRB1 FLANGED HEMI-SPHERICAL BOWL. HADRIANIC-ANTONINE. RIGBY AND STEAD 1976, FIG. 68 NO. 70 AND DARLING 1984 FIG. 15 NOS 45-6. MIDDLE FILLS *26062* AND *26063*, PIT 26059

70. GTA10 EVERTED RIM NARROW MOUTHED JAR; SHOULDER FLANGE. UNSTRATIFIED *26021*

Nuttles

71. GRB4 CARINATED BOWL; SHELVED CARINATION. UPPER FILL *31096*, CUT 31095, DITCH 31523

72. GRB1 SMALL BEAKER; SHORT EVERTED RIM, TRACES OF APPLIED DECORATION: PROBABLY BARBOTINE DOTS. UPPER FILL *31096*, CUT 31095, DITCH 31523

73. GRB7 REBATED, EVERTED RIM JAR. RIGBY AND STEAD 1976, ROXBY TYPE A. FILL *31126*, CUT 31145, DITCH 31515

74. GRB4 EVERTED RIM; ROUNDED EXPANDED TIP (RIGBY AND STEAD 1976 ROXBY TYPE B). UPPER FILL *31119*, DITCH 31103

75. GRB1 EVERTED-RIM JAR; DOUBLE SHOULDER GROOVE. FILL *31127*, DITCH 31145

76. GRB4 EVERTED-RIM JAR; DOUBLE SHOULDER GROOVE AND ACUTE LATTICE BURNISH. *c.*AD 120 TO 200. FILL *31127*, DITCH 31145

77. INCOMPLETE HORIZONTAL REEDED RIM AND BODY OF MORTARIUM. OATMEAL CREAM FABRIC, TINGES OF ORANGE-BROWN BELOW SURFACE; ORANGE-BROWN, OCC. BLACK, STREAKS IN BODY OF FABRIC; SLIGHTLY ROUGH TO THE TOUCH; NO SLIP SURVIVES. FREQ. ILL-SORTED INCLUSIONS: TINY TO MEDIUM-SIZED QUARTZ, RED-BROWN AND BLACK. TRITURATION GRIT OF RED-BROWN AND BROWN SANDSTONES, ANGULAR BLACK QUARTZ, AND PROBABLY OTHER ROCKS. FILL *31127*, DITCH 31145

Lelley

78. GTA14 NON-ADJOINING SHERDS FROM CARINATED BOWL. VESSEL HAS BEAD RIM, UPPER BODY DECORATED; LATTICE BURNISH ABOVE A CARINATION; AT LEAST TWO CORDONS.

THE LOWER BODY HAS MULTIPLE STRIATIONS PRESUMABLY FROM THROWING AND THE BASE HAS A FOOTRING. FILL *35287*, CUT 35288, STRUCTURE 1

New York

79. GTA8G SHERD FROM A LARGE STORAGE JAR; ZONE OF DOUBLE STABBED DECORATION. MIDDLE FILL *119245*, CUT 119243, DITCH 120022

Patrington

80. CTA2 DALES WARE LID-SEATED JAR. FILL *88162*, CUT 88026, DITCH 88174

81. GRB1 SHOULDERED WIDE-MOUTHED JAR; EVERTED RIM. DOUBLE GROOVES AROUND SHOULDER, SINGLE GROOVE AROUND LOWER BODY. COMPARES BETTER TO SECOND AND EARLIER THIRD CENTURY TYPES (RIGBY AND STEAD 1976, ROXBY TYPE F) THAN TO MID-THIRD- TO FOURTH-CENTURY WIDE-MOUTHED JARS. FILL *88081*, CUT 88026, DITCH 88174

82. GRB1 INCOMPLETE RIM AND BODY FROM DISH; INTURNED RIM, WORN INSIDE BODY. A COMMON FORM IN NORTH LINCOLNSHIRE AT DRAGONBY AND ROXBY (GREGORY 1996, 519-20 CITING INSTANCES FROM FLAVIAN PERIOD TO MID-THIRD CENTURY; RIGBY AND STEAD 1976 FIG. 67 NOS 41-2, WHO CITE OCCURRENCES IN FLAVIAN TO ANTONINE CONTEXTS AT BROUGH). FILL *88135*, CUT 88133, DITCH 88174

83. GRA1 OPEN VESSEL; ROUNDED, SLIGHTLY RECTANGULAR-SHAPED RIM. A DISH COPYING VARIOUS BB1 AND BB2 FLAT AND BEAD RIM DISHES OF SECOND AND THIRD CENTURIES (MONAGHAN 1997 DP5). FILL *88105*, CUT 88107, DITCH 88173

84. GRB5 DARK GREY WARE WEAKLY SHOULDERED WIDE-MOUTHED JAR; CHUNKY EVERTED RIM, UNDERCUT, AS IN THIRD CENTURY TYPES MADE AT NORTON (HAYES AND WHITLEY 1950 TYPE 6). FILL *88121*, CUT 88123, DITCH 88174

85. MORTARIUM. ORANGE-BROWN FABRIC WITH SLIGHT VARIATION IN CORE, TENDENCY TO LAMINATE; TRACES OF CREAM SLIP. INCLUSIONS OF RANDOM, ILL-SORTED, QUARTZ WITH SOME RED-BROWN AND BLACK MATERIAL. A FEW TRITURATION GRITS SURVIVE; INCLUDING QUARTZ AND RED-BROWN ?SANDSTONE. BLACKENED ON END OF FLANGE AND PART OF BEAD: MAY BE DUE TO REDUCING CONDITIONS AS KILN WAS CLOSED TO SLOW DOWN COOLING AFTER FIRING (*CF* BROUGHAM-HACKTHORPE: REPORT IN PREP). FILL *8837*, PIT 8838

Bluegate Corner

86. GRB5 BEAD-RIM DISH COPYING BB2 TYPES OF MID-SECOND TO MID-THIRD CENTURY. MONAGHAN 1997 TYPE DP5. FILL *119960*, CUT 119964, DITCH 120664

87. GRB10 MANY SHERDS FROM NARROW-MOUTHED JAR; EVERTED RIM AND ZONE OF BURNISHED WAVY LINE ON THE UPPER BODY. FABRIC NOT TYPICAL OF LATER KILNS AT HOLME-ON-SPALDING MOOR AND THE FORM IS A LONG-LIVED TYPE. A SECOND TO THIRD CENTURY RANGE MIGHT BE

SUGGESTED. FILLS *119968* AND *119978*, CUT 119970, DITCH 120665

88. GRB4 CARINATED BOWL; SHELVED CARINATION AN EVERTED RIM. TYPICAL OF NORTH LINCOLNSHIRE KILNS AS AT ROXBY IN SECOND AND EARLY THIRD CENTURIES (RIGBY AND STEAD 1976 TYPE E). FILL *119968*, CUT 119970, DITCH 120665

89. GRB4 EVERTED-RIM JAR. SIMILAR TO ROXBY JARS TYPES B-D (RIGBY AND STEAD 1976). FILL *119968*, CUT 119970, DITCH 120665

90. GRB3 EVERTED-RIM, CARINATED BOWL; UPRIGHT UPPER BODY. (HALKON AND MILLETT 1999, TYPE B04). SWAN CONSIDERED THE VERTICAL WALL TYPE A LATER DEVELOPMENT DATING TO THE LATE THIRD TO EARLY FOURTH CENTURY AND LATER (2002 FIG. 15 NO. 204). FILL *119983*, CUT 119938, DITCH 120665

Illustrated Roman pottery 4

Bluegate Corner

91. GRB11 DALES TYPE JAR. SIMILAR IN FORM, BUT NOT FABRIC, TO SHIPTONTHORPE JAR DATED TO LATER THIRD TO MID-FOURTH CENTURY (EVANS 2006, 154 G08.1 AND 2). FILL *119983*, CUT 119938, DITCH 120665

92. GRB4 EVERTED-RIM JAR, SIMILAR TO NO. 35. FILL *119983*, CUT 119938, DITCH 120665

93. GRB9 DEVELOPED FLANGED BOWL. HALKON AND MILLETT 1999, TYPE B08. LATE THIRD TO FOURTH CENTURY. FILL *119983*, CUT 119938, DITCH 120665

94. MLNV REEDED RIM MORTARIUM. GREY FABRIC FIRED TO CREAM AT SURFACES, ALL OF WHICH SUFFERING FROM EXFOLIATION, FABRIC HAS TENDENCY TO LAMINATE. FABRIC IRREGULARLY VESICULAR, FREQUENT TINY TO SMALL QUARTZ GRAINS, SOME ILL-SORTED RED-BROWN AND RARE BLACK MATERIAL. MUCH OF TRITURATION GRIT FALLEN OUT, BUT PROBABLY ALL BLACK SLAG. SURFACES HAVE SUFFERED SOME ABRASION BECAUSE OF IMPERFECT QUALITY OF FABRIC. INTERIOR SURFACE SHOWS EVIDENCE OF CONSIDERABLE WEAR. FILL *119983*, CUT 119938, DITCH 120665

95. GRB3 SHERDS GIVING COMPLETE PROFILE OF BOWL; TRIANGULAR RIM (HALKON AND MILLETT 1999, TYPE B06), SECOND TO FOURTH CENTURY; IN FINER FABRIC, MORE LIKELY TO DATE TO LATE THIRD TO FOURTH. FILL *119984*, CUT 119947, DITCH 120665

96. GRB9 SHERDS GIVING COMPLETE PROFILE OF DEVELOPED FLANGED BOWL. HALKON AND MILLETT 1999, TYPE B08. LATE THIRD TO FOURTH CENTURY. FILL *119984*. CUT 119947, DITCH 120665

Scorborough Hill

97. GRB4 TRIPOD BOWL. FILL *10421*, PIT 12081

98. GRC3 FLAT-TOPPED UPRIGHT RIM OF JAR. FILL *10421*, PIT 12081

99. BSB1 EVERTED-RIM JAR, PERHAPS HANDMADE. FILL *10427*, PIT 12081

100. FLA1 NECK OF WIDE-MOUTHED HOFHEIM TYPE FLAGON; MULTI-RIBBED HANDLE STUB. FILL *10427*, PIT 12081

101. GRB4 FRAGMENT OF GIRTH BEAKER; STABBED DECORATION. FILL *10427*, PIT 12081

102. GRB4 EVERTED RIM FROM BOWL OR JAR; DOUBLE GROOVE FORMING CORDON ON SHOULDER. FILL *10442*, PIT 12081

103. FLA3 EVERTED RIM FLAGON; CORDONED NECK; RIBBED HANDLE FILLS *10447* AND *10410*, PIT 12081

104. BSB1 BOWL; CONCAVE NECK AND RIM GROOVED EXTERNALLY AND INTERNALLY, POSSIBLY HAND MADE. FILL *10438*, PIT 12081

105. BSB1 SCORCHED JAR; EVERTED RIM AND GROOVED SHOULDER, SCORCHED. FILL *10438*, PIT 12081

106. BSB1 BURNT PLAIN-RIM PLATTER OR DISH. FILL *10438*, PIT 12081

107. GRC5 UPRIGHT RIM; FLAT TOP. FILL *10438*, PIT 12081

108. MOST OF A GRB4 DISH; INTURNED RIM. FILL *10438*, PIT 12081

109. BSB1 BEAD-RIM SHERD FROM BOWL, PROBABLY CORDONED. FILL *10447*, PIT 12081

110. GRA2 DISH; FLAT FLANGED RIM, DISTAL GROOVE AND GROOVED INTERNALLY JUST BELOW RIM AND AT ANGLE OF WALL AND BASE; FAINT TRACES OF BURNISHED WAVY LINE INSIDE BODY AND UNDER RIM. FILL *10409*, PIT 12081

111. BSB1 EVERTED RIM SMALL JAR OR BEAKER; SLIGHT INTERNAL OVERHANG TO RIM. FILL *10444*, PIT 12081

112. GRA1 SHERD; BARBOTINE DOT DECORATION. FILL *10408*, PIT 12081

113. GRB4 BEAD RIM BOWL. FILL *10440*, PIT 12081

114. RS IMP RED-SLIPPED OPEN VESSEL; FLAT RIM. AS MONAGHAN 1993 NO. 2901. FILLS *10440* AND 10428, PIT 12081

115. GRB4 EVERTED-RIM JAR. FILL *10405*, DITCH 12018

116. GRB4 GIRTH BEAKER SHERD; STABBED AND COMBED DECORATION. FILL *12005*, DITCH 12003

117. GRA1 ROULETTED BODYSHERD FROM BEAKER. FILL *12007*, DITCH 12003

118. GRB13 REBATED RIM JAR; GROOVED WAVY LINE ON SHOULDER. FILL *12007*, DITCH 12003

119. GRB7 EVERTED RIM JAR; ACUTE LATTICE BURNISH. FILL *12086*, DITCH 12003

120. GTA10 LUG FROM LARGE JAR. FILL *12024*, DITCH 12003

121. GTA8G EVERTED RIM FROM STORAGE JAR. SUBSOIL *12001*

122. RED-SLIPPED RIM; INTERNAL GROOVE, PERHAPS FROM PLATTER AS DARLING 1981 FIG. 23.2 NO. 2 MID- TO LATE FIRST CENTURY. SUBSOIL *12001*

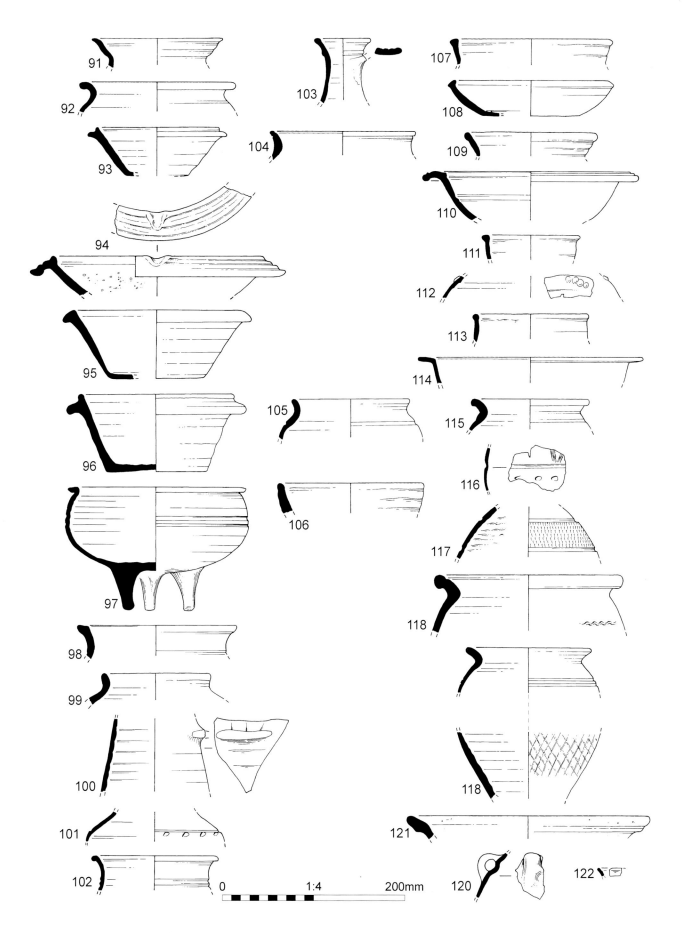

FIG. 103: ROMANO-BRITISH POTTERY, 91-96 BLUEGATE CORNER, 97-122 SCORBOROUGH HILL

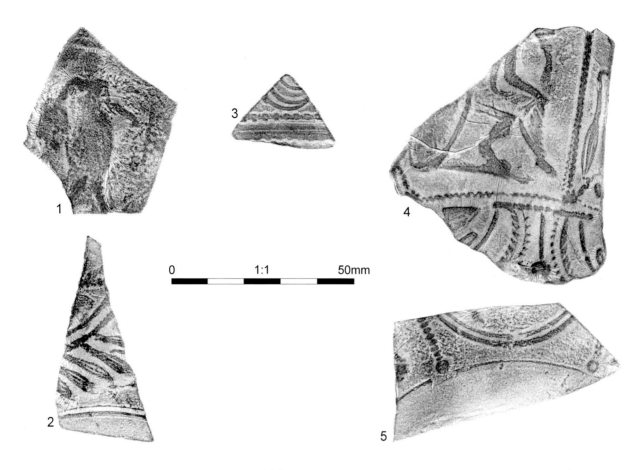

Fig. 104: The samian pottery: 1 to 5

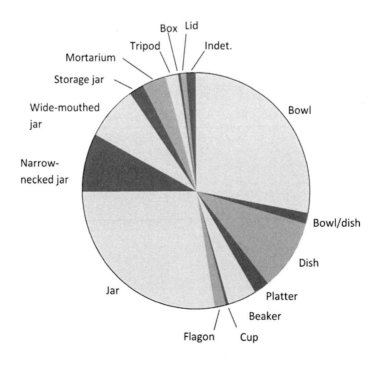

Quantification of Romano-British pottery by vessel types by rim percentage values

Illustrated samian sherds (Felicity Wild)

1. FORM 37, CENTRAL GAULISH. ABRADED SHERD SHOWING PANEL CONTAINING VENUS (O.293A). OF THOSE POTTERS KNOWN TO HAVE USED THE TYPE, PERHAPS DIVIXTUS IS THE MOST LIKELY, OR HIS SLIGHTLY LATER ASSOCIATE ADVOCISUS. NO DETAILS TO INDICATE THE POTTER MORE PRECISELY, BUT LIKELY TO DATE TO c.AD 150-180. UPPER FILL *3296*, CUT 3295 OF DITCH 3139, OLD ELLERBY

2. FORM 37, CENTRAL GAULISH, SHOWING PART OF A BOAT MADE UP OF A DOUBLE FESTOON WITH OARS (ROGERS 1974, U171). AN IDENTICAL BOAT APPEARS ON A BOWL IN THE STYLE OF SERVUS III (STANFIELD AND SIMPSON 1958, PL. 138, 2) c.AD 160-190. UNSTRATIFIED FINDS *35592*, LELLEY

3. FORM 29, SOUTH GAULISH. SMALL FRAGMENT OF UPPER ZONE WITH SCROLL DECORATION. THERE IS NOTHING TO INDICATE THE POTTER, BUT THE BOWL IS LIKELY TO BE, AT LATEST, c.AD 70-85. FILL *10410*, OF PIT 12081, SCORBOROUGH HILL

4. FORM 37, SOUTH GAULISH, SHOWING PANEL DECORATION WITH SEATED MARS (O.139) AND SALTIRE OVER A ZONE OF FESTOONS CONTAINING STIRRUP LEAVES. THE DECORATION IS TYPICAL OF THE LATE FLAVIAN-TRAJANIC PERIOD, c.AD 85-110. UPPER FILL *10431*, OF DITCH 10430, SCORBOROUGH HILL

5. FORM 37, CENTRAL GAULISH, SHOWING LOWER PART OF PANEL DECORATION. THE BEAD ROWS ENDING IN SMALL CIRCLES ARE TYPICAL OF ANTONINE POTTERS SUCH AS, FOR EXAMPLE, CINNAMUS, THOUGH NO OTHER DISTINCTIVE FEATURES SURVIVE FROM WHICH TO MAKE AN ATTRIBUTION. c.AD 150-180. FILL *12039*, OF DITCH 12040, SCORBOROUGH HILL

Apart from a fragment with ring and dot decoration, no diagnostic forms were found.

Proto-Huntcliff S-bend or hooked rim jars lacking the internal lid seating of true Huntcliff type jars or with necks and everted rims were present and date from the late third to mid-fourth century (Bell and Evans 2002, types 6.2-5 and J9.1). Rather fewer true Huntcliff type jars or late double lid-seated jars and late Crambeck forms datable to the late fourth century were identified.

Only two of the mortaria, from Old Ellerby and Patrington, are attributable to a known workshop. Distribution suggests that it is located in the Malton area; it was probably active in the late second to early third century. The mortarium from Sproatley is from an unlocated workshop in northern England which was active in the late first- to early second-century period. All the remaining mortaria, at least seven judging from rim fragments, are probably the products of perhaps a single unlocated 'local' workshop, to which Burton Constable, Nuttles and Bluegate Corner all had access. It was producing mortaria in the Crambeck and Lower

Nene valley traditions and presumably had potters who had come from those workshops. All of the products of this workshop could fit a date in the fourth century and quite possibly not earlier than the mid-fourth century.

Seven of the excavation areas produced samian, though only Old Ellerby and Scorborough Hill produced groups larger than four sherds. In total, the samian ware amounted to 40 sherds from a maximum of 30 vessels.

Old Ellerby

From contexts relating to the Iron Age settlement features, the only wheel-thrown sherds recovered were single body sherds, in GRB4 and GRB7 fabrics, from fills **3027** and **3256** of cuts **3049** and **3255** respectively.

First- to second-century ditches

A sherd from primary fill **3052** of ditch **3075** may have been a piece of samian with none of the surface slip surviving. If so, it is likely to be Central Gaulish, dating to around AD 150 to 180.

The fills of ditch **3267** give date ranges spanning the mid-/late first to early second century to the late second to third century. Several sherds in the GTA range were identified. This is similar to a type known from north Lincolnshire and the Trent Valley in the mid-/late first to second century. As well as these, sherds in the GRB4 and GRB7 fabric groups point to a late first- to second-century date range. These include a platter copying Gallo-Belgic platters or perhaps samian form 18 of first-century date (Fig. 100.3). This vessel is similar to one made at the Flavian kiln 4 at Dragonby (Swan 1996, fig. 20.32: 1420). A BSB1 sherd from a cordoned bead rim bowl of late La Tène type is of similar date range. The same ditch also produced an abraded and burnt body mortarium sherd in a fine-textured cream fabric with small mostly transparent quartz trituration grit, and a flat-flanged grey ware dish with grooves and zones of burnished lines under the flanged rim and inside the body (Fig. 100.4).

In ditch **3219**, a fine grey ware flanged dish (GRA2) of the same type as that found in Scorborough Hill (Fig. 103.110, below) dates to late first to early second century (Swan 1996 fig. 20.34: 1458 from early second-century kiln waste; present in Roxby Antonine kiln group no. 78 though Swan thinks a survival; at Malton, Corder1930b, fig. 17: 4 in an early group late first to early second century). A GRB2 wide-mouthed jar with short everted rim compares to vessels from the Hadrianic-Antonine kiln 5 at Dragonby and second-century vessels at Roxby (Swan 1996, fig. 20.33: 1437 and 1444; Rigby and Stead 1976, type R, fig. 68.74). A decorated samian sherd of form 37 (Fig. 104.1) is likely to be Central Gaulish and to date to the period around AD 150 to 180. A mortarium sherd (SF 1103, Fig. 100.5) can be attributed to a workshop probably situated somewhere south of Malton. The type was being made in the first half of the third-century, though some production in the late second-century cannot be ruled out. A probable joining sherd was also recovered from pit **3274** (see below). Overall, this assemblage seems to be contemporary with the later material from ditch **3267**.

Later ditches

The larger assemblage from the later phases was dominated by ware groups such as Dales ware and fabric groups GRB3 and GRB14, in types made at the Holme-on-Spalding-Moor industry. Also present were Huntcliff and proto-Huntcliff type jars, Crambeck grey ware and Nene Valley colour-coated wares. The presence of Huntcliff type jars and a Corder type 1b developed flanged bowl demonstrates activity continued at least as late as around AD 360/370 when manufacture of these types commenced (Bidwell and Croom 2010, table 4.1: 2 and 12).

The fills of ditch **3056** included a Crambeck grey ware beaker base, a GRB3 wide-mouthed jar and a sherd from a Nene Valley beaker. A date range in the later third to fourth century is implied by the Crambeck ware, and the presence of a Huntcliff type jar rim demonstrates infilling continued as late as around AD 360. Ditch **3243** produced sherds from a GRB17 wide-mouthed jar of third- to fourth-century date (Fig. 100.14), a sherd from a third-century Nene Valley colour-coated indented beaker, and two samian sherds: one of form 31 and the other a dish of uncertain form. Both are likely to be Central Gaulish and to date from the second half of the second century AD. Collectively, these suggest that the feature belonged to a date range overlapping with that of ditch **3056**, in the third century.

Pits and small linear features

Pit **3274**, cut into the top of ditch **3219**, produced a fragment from a collared mortarium in an oxidised ware comparable to mortaria from the York area or Malton, belonging to the late second to third century (Bidwell and Croom 1997, fig. 26.147). This group has vessels dating as early as the late first century to as late as the late second century. As most of the types are second century, it is likely that the infilling took place at this time with the earlier platter and cordoned bowl being deposited perhaps while the ditch was still in use, in the mid- to late first century.

Three of the four sherds from fills **3192** and **3186** of feature **3329** were in GRB4 fabric and date to the later first or second century. The other sherd was from a GRB1 jar with burnished lines, perhaps as a black burnished type jar, and a second-century date is likely.

The assemblage from pit **3279** jar included several relatively unabraded sherds from the base, body and rim of a GRB15 everted rim jar with internal groove (Fig. 100.1), of mid-second- to mid-third-century type copying BB2 jar forms (Monaghan 1997, type 3J3: AD 150/60-220/40). Accompanying this vessel was a moderately large sherd from the rim and upper body of a rouletted beaker of Nene Valley colour-coated ware (Fig. 100.2), also dating to the late second to mid-third century (Perrin 1999, 121). The condition of both of these sherds suggests that the infilling of the pit dates to around this time. A sherd of a samian dish, likely to be East Gaulish and to date to the late second, or possibly third century, was also recovered.

A late Crambeck grey ware flanged bowl with internal wavy line burnish (Fig. 100.13) gives a date after around AD 370 for fill **3222** of pit **3043** and sherds from a Huntcliff type jar (Fig. 100.6) from the primary fill **3041** of pit **3040** provide a date after around AD 360. Other vessels from this pit include: twenty-one sherds from a Dales ware jar (Fig. 100.7); most of a bead rim dish, in a fine ware, comparable to Holme-on-Spalding-Moor grey ware (Fig. 100.8); a GRB2 sherd from a lipped rim dish in a coarser fabric with calcareous inclusions; eight GRB14 sherds from a biconical bowl with everted rim and insloping walls (Fig. 100.9), a type common in the third century; and GRB14 sherds from a wide-mouthed jar (Fig. 100.10). A sherd of a Central Gaulish samian vessel, of uncertain form but likely to date to the second half of the second century, was also recovered.

Pit **3034** included several sherds from a Dales ware and two sherds from a Huntcliff type jar with grooved shoulder from primary fill **3035** giving a *terminus post quem* in the mid-fourth century (Bidwell and Croom 2010, table 4.1: 3). A GRB1 basal sherd from fill **3113** of pit **3112** cannot be closely dated within the Roman period although it is not diagnostic of early type.

Linear feature **3139** included sherds from a biconical bowl with insloping walls like that from pit **3040** and many small abraded sherds from a Dales ware jar came from the fill of **3314** with sherds from a lugged jar. These again point to a date in the later third or early fourth century. An abraded sherd from a Form 37 Central Gaulish samian vessel (Fig. 104.1) showing a panel containing Venus (O.293A), is likely to date to around AD 150 to 180.

Two samian sherds were also recovered from spread layer **3091** overlying the northern side of Structure 2: a bowl likely to be East Gaulish and late second or possibly third century, and a Form 31 Central Gaulish vessel likely to date to the second half of the second century.

Old Ellerby: general

Creighton demonstrates from the evidence from Holme-on-Spalding-Moor that many of the forms were present from the earliest to the latest phases and there was little change in the fabrics (1999, 164, tables 5.16 and 17). He also notes that the change in forms relate to specialisation within the kilns. Swan has suggested an overall date range of third to early fourth century for the Holme-on-Spalding-Moor industry with trade dating to after AD 220-30 (2002, 63-5). She dated some types to the late third to early fourth century such as the 'bobbin shaped' mouth jar, the carinated bowl with vertical walls and the developed flanged bowl (Swan 2002, fig. 15.196, 204 and 208), but manufacture of many types runs right through the production period. Swan gives the biconical bowl with insloping walls an earlier date range than that with straight walls (2002, fig. 15.205). Evans suggested this type was not introduced until the late third to fourth century based on the sequence at Brough-on-Humber and other sites, and the earlier examples of the form attributed to Holme-on-Spalding-Moor at Rudston were from the Norton kilns (1985, 246 and 303-304). At Shiptonthorpe, Evans gave examples of the carinated bowl with insloping walls a late third- to fourth-century date (2006, R07.29). Additionally, he extends the date range of the industry into the later fourth century.

The Dales ware vessels would point to a third- to mid-fourth-century date range. Some controversy exists over the start date for Dales ware: Swan (1992) suggests an early third-century date for Dales type ware and Creighton follows this dating for Dales type forms at Holme-on-Spalding-Moor. At Lincoln, Darling noted Dales ware did not appear in any quantity until after the mid-third century and similarly at Brough-on-Humber Evans recorded that, although Dales ware was present in early to mid-third-century groups, it was not common until the late third century (1985, 273-5). Evans also gives Holme-on-Spalding-Moor Dales type ware a late third- to early fourth-century date range (1985, 278-9) and observed at Shiptonthorpe that a similar local type continued in use into the second half of the fourth century (2006, 132).

Thus there is some difficulty in deciding how early these groups may date. However, relative frequency of Dales ware would support a date in the later third century while the absence of late Holme-on-Spalding-Moor vessel types might favour a third- rather than a fourth-century emphasis. This would agree with the lack of very hard fired fabrics, characteristic of the later production at Holme-on-Spalding-Moor. The small amounts of Crambeck grey ware and Huntcliff type ware would also point to a diminution in activity by the fourth century although the proximity of the industry at Holme-on-Spalding-Moor meant that Crambeck and Huntcliff type wares might be expected to be less common even in the

mid- to late fourth century and so the absence of these chronological markers may be less significant. Overall the pottery would favour a date range from the later third extending into the fourth century, to as late as the mid-fourth century.

Burton Constable

The assemblage of wheel-thrown pottery from this site comprised 956 sherds, weighing 13.3kg. The diagnostic sherds from the assemblage indicate a late date range in the later third to early fourth century with some sherds dating to the mid- to late fourth century and a small amount of material dating from the late Iron Age to mid- to late first century AD.

Settlement features

One small, GRB1 rim sherd, an everted rim, was found in fill **9599** of the Structure 1 ring gully. The fabric is not an early ware of the first or earlier second century but, beyond that, this small sherd cannot be closely dated within the Roman period.

Five early Roman sherds of the mid/late first to early second century were recovered from the various fills of Structure 5. A rim and upper body sherd in an early shell-tempered ware, CTB1, came from upper fill **118505** of intervention **118057**. The fabric fits with a north Lincolnshire source and the form is a cordoned bowl derived from late Iron Age vessels in that area. This vessel could be late Iron Age in date. From the contiguous context **118596**, a GRB4 sherd with channels, probably a cheesepress, is of slightly later date in the Flavian-Trajanic period. This form was made in kiln 4 at Dragonby, given an early to mid-Flavian date by Swan (Swan 1996, fig. 20.32: 1417). Two sherds from a shell-tempered storage jar from the upper fill, **118387**, of ditch **118617** also dated to the first century. A BSB basal jar sherd from fill **118400** of cut **118398**, close to the northern terminal, was of similar date range. A tiny scrap of fine oxidised ware was found in the upper fill, **118531**, of the eastern terminus of 'Structure 6' feature **118986**.

Enclosure 1

Fill **9050** of ditch **9955** produced a single sherd from GRC3 coarse grey ware wide-mouthed jar. This compares to a type of third- and fourth-century date.

Enclosures 2 and 3

Terminal **9724** of ditch **118922**, and its precursor, ditch **9835**, both had sherds of East Yorkshire calcite-gritted ware in proto-Huntcliff and Huntcliff types giving date ranges of early to mid-fourth century, and later than around AD 360, respectively. Crambeck grey ware sherds were also present in ditch **9835**. Ditch **118934** contained sherds from several vessels of late third- to mid-fourth-century date. These included a carinated bowl with insloping walls and everted rim, developed flanged bowls of the same date range and everted rims from narrow and wide-mouthed jars in medium and fine grey wares GRB1 and GRB3. The forms would be consistent with a source at the Holme-on-Spalding-Moor kilns. In addition to these, burnt sherds from a GRB15 shallow, plain rim dish and a GRB14 long necked beaker were in a coarser fabric but give a similar date range. A Crambeck white ware type 6 mortarium dates to the fourth century and a proto-Huntcliff jar with everted, almost flat rim is of early to mid-fourth-century date. The absence of Crambeck ware and Huntcliff type jars suggests a date range in the late third to early fourth century before these became more common.

Pit **9728**, cutting the eastern end of ditch **118922**, also contained significant amounts of Romano-British pottery and vessels included a fragmented Dales ware jar, two lipped dishes in a calcareous ware CTA4, a grey ware plain-rim dish and a developed flanged bowl and a coarser grey ware wide-mouthed jar. These types point to a date in the late third or early fourth century with two small sherds of Crambeck grey ware and no Huntcliff type ware being present.

Ditch **118922** contained much of a Dales ware jar, a GRC3 Dales ware type rim, most of a lipped GRB2B bowl, a substantial proportion of a carinated bowl with upright wall as those made at the later Throlam kiln in the Holme-on-Spalding-Moor industry and rim sherds from a shell-tempered double lid seated jar of late fourth-century type and from a proto-Huntcliff jar of early to mid-fourth-century date. The vessels for which a substantial proportion were present point to a late third- to early fourth-century date while the lack of Crambeck ware and classic Huntcliff type jars suggest little activity after the mid-fourth century.

Fill **9148** of ditch **9621** was dated to the late third to fourth century by a developed flanged bowl sherd in a fine grey ware similar to the Holme-on-Spalding-Moor fine grey wares.

Enclosures 4 and 5

None of the sherds from ditch **118922** were closely datable although the fine fabric and hard firing of a basal sherd from ditch **118933** compared well to the later Holme-on-Spalding-Moor grey wares. Sherds recovered from ditch **118929** include a Crambeck grey ware developed flanged bowl, a proto-Huntcliff jar rim of early to mid-fourth-century type, the rim of a GRB3 narrow mouthed jar, probably lugged, a type 6 Crambeck white ware mortarium of the fourth century, a small scrap from a Dales ware jar, a sherd from a double lid-seated jar of mid- to late fourth-century date and sherds

from a carinated bowl with insloping walls. These types indicate a date not significantly later than Enclosures 2 and 3.

Pottery from features internal to Enclosure 4 included sherds from developed flanged bowls, present in ditches **118933** and **118960**, and sherds from a necked proto-Huntcliff jar of early to mid-fourth-century type from fills **9624** and **9625** of feature **9717**, along with a GRC3 shallow plain-rim dish. A GRB1 bodysherd reused as a spindle whorl was also present in this feature. A sherd from a Crambeck grey ware developed flanged bowl, dating to the late third to fourth century was present in oven **9519**. Small and abraded sherds from ditch **118941** included highly fragmented scraps from an EYCT plain-rim dish of late third- to fourth-century date and a basal sherd from a fourth-century Crambeck white ware mortarium along with undiagnostic grey ware scraps. A fairly large rim sherd from a Huntcliff type jar with double lid seating came from ditch **118931** with an abraded rim sherd from a GRB1 long necked beaker with bead rim of late third- to mid-fourth-century type.

What appeared to be a sherd from a bowl of much earlier type came from fill **9508** of ditch **118960**. The rim was incomplete and was in a fabric comparable to GRB4, a ware similar to products of the Dragonby kiln. The form compares well to a collared bowl from there, dating to the late first to early second century (Swan 1996, fig. 20.34 nos. 1459-60). Swan points out that the bowl was of a type common on the Rhineland and Pannonia suggesting tentatively that its manufacture may indicate the presence of military craftsmen or veterans from this area.

Enclosures 6, 7 and 8

The date range again lay in the late third to fourth century although a Crambeck type 7 mortarium with a date after around AD 370 was present. However no Crambeck grey ware or classic Huntcliff type jars were present suggesting the Crambeck mortarium was a late addition and these features fall within the same ceramic period as the earlier enclosures. Significant proportions of a GRB3 narrow-mouthed jar and a GRB3 wide-mouthed jar of late third- to fourth-century type were found in fill **9081** of ditch **118917**.

Enclosure 9

A Proto-Huntcliff jar rim from primary fill **9526** of ditch **118921** gives a *terminus post quem* in the early to mid-fourth century. The sherds from this ditch were small and abraded and may have been largely redeposited. No fresh deposits of large unabraded sherds were present. The pottery from ditch **118964** was similar but included sherds from a Crambeck grey ware lugged jar and a classic Huntcliff type jar in fill primary fill **9932** giving a date after around AD 360 for infilling.

Burial 9794

Grave **9794** contained small and abraded sherds, including EYCT and Crambeck white ware, giving a late third- to fourth-century date range.

Later ditches

Most of the pottery sherds from the later ditches were small, abraded and largely undiagnostic bodysherds. Sherds from a Dales ware jar and a proto-Huntcliff jar from ditch **118924** gives a date in the first half of the fourth century for final infilling. Apart from the Huntcliff type vessel, most of these sherds were not significantly later in date to the pottery from the preceding phases.

General: Burton Constable

The proportion of Dales ware jars, East Yorkshire proto-Huntcliff and Huntcliff type jars, Crambeck wares and late Holme-on-Spalding-Moor grey wares was high while the early mid/late first- to early second-century wares and second-century Roxby types were noticeably rare. One collared bowl dating to the late first to early second century was present (context **9508**) and fragment from an oxidised shell-tempered storage jar from **118387** is of similar date range. A small number of second-century types were also present, bowls and dishes with flat rims copying second-century BB vessels and a scrap of samian.

A number of vessels may date to the third century. The carinated grey ware bowls are typical of this period and the Dales and Dales type wares including jars and simple plain-rim dishes were common in the third to mid-fourth century. The wide-mouthed jars include types datable from the third to fourth century as well as examples in the hard grey ware typical of the late Holme-on-Spalding-Moor kilns. Late third to fourth-century developed bead and flange bowls in grey ware, including the late hard Holme-on-Spalding-Moor ware, were common and a long necked indented beaker was also of late third- to mid-fourth-century date. Grey ware lugged jars with vertical linear burnish were present and carinated bowls with straight walls in the late Holme-on-Spalding-Moor fabric were identified. The majority of the East Yorkshire calcite-gritted ware jars had proto-Huntcliff forms with outcurving or hooked rims, which lacked the internal lid seating, or necked form with everted rims. One EYCT plain rim dish was present. Both lugged jars and developed bead and flange bowls in Crambeck ware were identified. Two wall-sided oxidised mortarium dated to the fourth century and several Crambeck white ware type 6 mortaria dated to the late third to fourth century. Fragments of a Castor box were of third-century type.

A small number of Huntcliff type ware jars and double lid-seated jars of the mid-to late fourth century were

present as were four sherds of Crambeck parchment ware mortaria (type 7) and these indicate some activity after around AD370. Overall, the range and quantities of the types suggest small amounts of activity in the late first to second century with a peak in the later third to mid-fourth century and reduced activity in the second half of the fourth century.

Brandywell

The assemblage from this plot included sherds in fabrics most common in the mid/late first to early second century. Forms included sherds from a Dressel 20 amphora originally holding olive oil from southern Spain, rusticated jars, Roxby type A jars, the jars with everted rims, overhanging internally typical of mid/late first- to early second-century production in north Lincolnshire and the Trent Valley (Rigby and Stead 1976, fig. 64.4); the carinated and shallow bowl forms made at Roxby and found from the Flavian period to the second century as well as the shallow dish form with upturned rim (Rigby and Stead 1976 types E, S and H). One grey ware rim sherd was of Dales ware type dating to the third to mid-fourth century. The majority of the forms and fabric present suggest a late first- to early/mid-second-century date range.

Features in the area of the ring gullies

BSB1 sherds from a small jar or beaker from the primary fill of pit **25230** are of late Iron Age or very early Roman date. The vessel appears to be wheel-thrown and a Conquest period or early Roman date in the first century is suggested. The form would fall into Elsdon's group 11 at Dragonby dating from the conquest to Flavian period (1996, 415). A sherd in the same fabric, also with external burnishing was present in fill **25186** of gully **25249**. These sherds compare to a ware group known around the Trent Valley and north Lincolnshire in relatively small quantities used to make platters, cordoned and carinated bowls, butt beakers and small beakers such as this one. The rim was formed by folding in the clay in the same way as the jar from ditch **25116** fill **25112**. These jars resemble the later Dales ware type jars and can easily be confused with them. At Scratta Wood an example was found in a pre-Roman Iron Age assemblage.

Earlier Roman ditches

Sherds from the earlier phase of ditches included the well-known carinated bowl form made in the north Lincolnshire kilns, with distinctive shelved carination from the late first to early third century. In this fabric, late first to early second century would be appropriate. In addition, sherds from two rusticated jars, one a waisted jar type with nodular rustication in fabric GRB6 and the other in a GRB2 ware with more subdued spidery rustication. The waisted rusticated jar is of mid-first-century date and the GRB2 jar may be late first to early second century. The GRA1 ring and dot beaker sherd gives a Flavian-Trajanic date range and the distinctive CTB1 jar was a common type in north Lincolnshire and down the Trent Valley in the mid-first to mid-second century (Rigby and Stead 1976, fig. 74.11-12 and fig. 76.37-8; Darling 1984, 88 and fig. 15.60-63). This example has an early appearance.

A sherd from the upper fill of ditch **25116** was in a grog-tempered grey ware and came from a jar with a grooved wavy line, perhaps as Roxby type A in the second century (Rigby and Stead 1976). Sherds from an early Dressel 20 oil amphora also came from this ditch. Ditch **25208** contained four small abraded wheel-thrown sherds: two are undiagnostic grey ware, one is a bodysherd in GRB1 and the fourth a white-slipped oxidised sherd. These are not closely datable. Apart from the 'native' jar type, these are military pottery types with no pre-Roman ancestry in this region. The rusticated jars are closely associated with the movement of the military as are ring and dot beakers. The north Lincolnshire carinated bowl form points to the origin of this group although whether the movement was of pots or potters is difficult to establish.

The large enclosure ditch

The wheel-thrown pottery from ditch group **25168** is similar in date to that from the earlier ditches. The BSA rouletted beaker with its zones of rouletting and dark grey/brown fabric has an early character and may be pre- or early Flavian while the barbotine beaker and inturned rim dish are of Flavian-Trajanic type, the dish type continuing through the second century. A GTA8G everted-rim jar is typical of 'native' jars from the Trent Valley and Humber Estuary area in the late first to early second century. Pit **25250** contained vessels made in the rather gritty grey ware GRB4. These included a small rusticated sherd, an everted rim jar similar to Roxby B in form and a flanged bowl Roxby type S of Hadrianic-Antonine date (Darling 1984, 86 and 47; Rigby and Stead 1976). Fill **25109** of this pit contained base and bodysherds with an everted rim sherd from a jar in a grog-tempered ware which is commonly used in the Trent Valley for 'native' type jars from the later first to mid-second century. The gritty wares and later forms suggest a date in the first half of the second century for this group. A rim sherd belonging to the native jar series with upright, flat topped rim in a gritty quartz and shell-gritted ware, probably also derived from this context although it was misnumbered as **25169**.

General

This plot is unusual in having sherds of Dressel 20 amphora, imported from southern Spain for its olive oil. These large vessels were frequently reused, often modified by the removal of handles or rims to facilitate ease of access. The presence of such a vessel here perhaps is more likely to be the result of this sort of recycling rather than the purchase and consumption of olive oil. The other wheel-thrown vessels are types made by the military and are predominantly bowls and beakers. The non-local jars are of a type found commonly in north Lincolnshire and the Trent Valley and perhaps indicate the source of all the wheel-thrown vessels. These jars are not noticeably superior to the local handmade types and may have been traded for their contents.

Sproatley

Very little stratified Romano-British pottery came from this site. Sherds from a grey ware flanged, hemispherical bowl came from the upper fill of elongated pit **26428**, and from a fill of pit **26059**. This form can be compared to examples from Roxby (Rigby and Stead 1976, fig. 68.70) and Lincoln (Darling 1984, fig. 15.45-6) dated to the Hadrianic-Antonine period with one Flavian-Trajanic example from Winterton (Rigby and Stead 1976, fig. 76.52). Pit **26428** also contained a grooved-rim dish from the mid-second to mid-third century, and an oxidised flanged mortarium (Fig. 102.68).

This mortarium was in a hard, deep orange-brown fabric and may have had a thin self-coloured slip. The frequent, tiny to small-sized inclusions consist of quartz and black particles, and the trituration grit is entirely of quartz-like rock. The mortarium is not from any major or even minor known source, but an unlocated workshop in northern England. It is well-made and the rim-profile should belong to a date before AD140 at the latest: it could be considerably earlier. The spout is broken, but the beginning of the right-facing side is visible and it could be as early as AD 80 or 85. The optimum date is late first to early second century. Seven sherds and scraps from a badly fragmented samian dish, probably of form 18/31R or 31R, were present in the lowest fill of cut **26401** of ditch **26454**. This vessel was Central Gaulish and of Antonine date.

A GTA sherd from the surface of the flint spread **26020** is of uncertain date. Other unstratified sherds from the site include BSB sherds from an early vessel with combed chevron decoration and cordons, probably a girth beaker type, a bead rim from an early GRB4 carinated bowl and a developed flanged bowl in a fine grey ware is probably from the Holme-on-Spalding-Moor kilns dating to the late third to fourth century. There were also grey grog-tempered GTA10 sherds from a large jar with everted rim with a very unusual flange on the shoulder. Wares of this type are common in the Trent Valley in the late first to mid-second century and the rim form would fit in with the types made. The shoulder flange, however, is quite unparalleled.

The stratified sherds give dates in the second century perhaps into the third century. The unstratified sherds widen this date range to include mid-first- to early second-century activity with one late third- to fourth-century piece.

Nuttles

The small number of wheel thrown sherds identified dated mostly to the second century. Types present included early grog-tempered ware, sherds from carinated bowl of late first- to second-century type, Roxby type jars with everted and rebated rims, a small grey ware beaker with barbotine dots, a flat-rim bowl or dish copying second-century BB1 types, and BB1 type jars with acute lattice burnish. One vessel was of somewhat later date: a mortarium, from fill **31127** of ditch **31145**, with a reeded rim projecting horizontally is a type produced in the Lower Nene Valley potteries in the fourth-century (Johnson 1983, fig. 44, nos. 233-235), possibly mid-fourth century or second half of the fourth century. The fabric and suite of trituration grit, however, clearly indicate production in a small local workshop. The trituration grit used consistently throughout the third and fourth centuries in the Lower Nene valley is black slag and this must be the first example recorded with multi-coloured trituration grit.

The second-century sherds came from ditches **31145**, **31515**, **31523** and **31103**. The absence of later material, bar one sherd, suggests activity ceased by the end of the second century if not earlier. Forms included jars, one beaker, bowls or dishes of black burnished type, and one white ware bodysherd perhaps from a flagon. The assemblage was dominated by Lincolnshire types as is typical of this period with no distance-traded wares represented. Overall, the nature of the assemblage gives the impression that the excavated area lay at some remove from the focus of domestic settlement in this phase.

Lelley

A GRB8 sherd from posthole **35188**, in the base of ditch **35190**, was likely to be of early Roman date, perhaps in the mid-first to second century as was a concave body sherd in a similar fabric from secondary fill **35244** of ditch **35245** and a bodysherd in this ware from fill **35468**. The cordoned bowl is the most diagnostic piece from the features as regards date. This vessel falls into Elsdon's group 4 (1996) and this general form spans the Conquest at Dragonby with wheel-thrown vessels appearing in late pre-Roman Iron Age groups. Elsdon noted that the earlier forms had cordons and burnished vertical lines. It is very difficult to date this firmly in a pre- or post-Conquest date range. Generally Lincolnshire types do not appear in this region until the Roman period. However Lincolnshire-type vessels are now being recognised in this area (Didsbury unpublished) and elsewhere in

Yorkshire in certain pre-Conquest contexts (Evans 2005, 142). A bowl from excavation at Aram, of similar type to that from context **35287**, was given a date in the early first century BC (R. Mackey pers. comm.).

A colour-coated beaker sherd from the fill of posthole **35401** is probably from the Nene Valley industries and is likely to be of the late second or third century at the earliest. Unstratified material included a sherd from a Crambeck grey ware spouted jug of late third- to fourth-century date as well as two samian sherds, both Central Gaulish: one is Form 31 and of Antonine date; the other (Fig. 104.2) of Form 37 (Rogers 1974, U171). A boat identical to that shown on the illustrated piece appears on a bowl in the style of Servus III and dated to around AD 160 to 190 (Stanfield and Simpson 1958, Pl. 138.2).

New York

A sherd of a footstand from a samian bowl or dish, probably East Gaulish, was recovered from the middle fill of cut **119234** through ditch **120022**. No close parallels to the form are forthcoming. The sherd, which shows two rivet holes, can be dated to the late second or third century. Two sherds from fill **119245** of the same ditch: an oxidised quartz-tempered sherd and a GTA8G sherd from storage jar with two row of stabbed decoration on the body (Gregory 1996, fig. 20.8: 877) suggest a mid/late first-to early second-century date. Undiagnostic grey ware sherds of Roman date were present in fill **119258** of the smaller ditch, **120034**, and in the fill of pit **119829**. The pottery from ditch **3619**, possibly a continuation of ditch **120022**, included a grey ware concave sherd from a carinated bowl of the late first to second century and a grey handmade jar with tall everted rim which could also belong to this date range.

Burstwick

Eight abraded sherds from a flat-rim dish, dating to the second century, and an undiagnostic grey ware sherd came from cut **51007** of ditch **51025**.

Churchlands

Two grey ware sherds were recovered from stratified contexts: a basal sherd from a bowl or dish from the fill of pit **119532** dating to the second century or later, and a rim sherd from a bead-rim bowl, from the upper fill of pit **119406**, which belonged to the mid-second to mid-third century.

Winestead

A small group of small abraded sherds was recovered from this excavation. Diagnostic sherds gave a date range in the late third to fourth century and comprised a Crambeck grey ware lugged jar from ditch **73112**, a late Nene Valley colour-coated dish or bowl base from ditch **73097** and, from unstratified contexts, a Holme-on-Spalding-Moor lugged jar and an East Yorkshire calcite-gritted lid. Very abraded scraps of abraded grey ware from fills of ditches **73020** and **73201** were diagnostically early Roman. Other grey ware sherds were not closely datable within the Roman period although sherds from ditch **73091** and **73203** compared well to the fine fabric from Holme-on-Spalding-Moor kilns of the later third to fourth century.

These few sherds indicate activity in the later Roman period, with no sherds which need be dated earlier than the third to fourth century. The early Roman wares of Lincolnshire type, of first- and second-century date, were not present and the condition, size and number of Roman wheel thrown sherds suggests a site at some distance from domestic settlement.

Patrington

Sherds from a Dales ware jar were recovered from the fills **88080**, **88081** and **88162**; these fills were from a section, **88026**, targeting the early phase ditch **88171** but which inadvertently sampled ditch **88174**, which, at the time, was thought to be a shallow surface feature. Pottery of this type was made from the beginning of the third century, but was not appearing in this area until around the mid-third century. The same intervention also produced a base sherd of a Form 31 Central Gaulish samian vessel and sherds from a GRB1 wide-mouthed jar similar in form to jars made at Roxby in the second to early third century while one of pair of joining sherds of another samian vessel was recovered from the same intervention; its counterpart was unequivocally from ditch **88174**. This vessel, of Form 33, was of Antonine date. The walls of the Form 31 vessel had been trimmed off, presumably after breakage, and the outer surface had unfortunately flaked off where the stamp would have been. The assemblage from ditch **88174** also included a large sherd giving the complete profile of a very similar vessel and a GRB1 dish with inturned rim, dating from the late first to second century and continuing as late as the mid-third century at Dragonby. Sherds from Dales ware jars also suggest a third-century date for this ditch. Fill **88121** produced several sherds from a wide-mouthed jar in a dark faced grey ware GRB5 compared better to wide-mouthed jars from the third-century kilns at Norton (Hayes and Whitley 1950, type 6).

Sherds from a GRA1 dish with rounded rim from the rectilinear enclosure ditch **88173** belong to a range of flat and bead-rim dishes copying BB1 and BB2 dishes and bowls of the second and third century. This example compares to types at York dating to the mid-second to mid-third century (Monaghan 1997, DP5). A small group of sherds from enclosure ditch **88096** included a sherd of a Form 18/31 Central Gaulish samian vessel of Hadrianic

or Antonine date. The fill of pit **8838** contained a sherd from the shoulder of a GRB1 carinated bowl of a type most common in north Lincolnshire in the late first to early third century, a GRB1 everted rim from a wide-mouthed jar, probably of second-century date along with a sherd of mortarium (Fig. 102.87).

This mortarium sherd is in an orange-brown fabric of a kind associated with small, somewhat convex rim-profiles, divided into three parts. They post-date the practice of stamping. Their distribution is centred on north-east Yorkshire: York (Monaghan 1997, fig. 374.3404); Malton (Wenham and Heywood 1997, fig. 27.156 and fig. 26.147; also several unpublished old finds); Langton (Corder and Kirk 1932, fig. 12.7; fig. 24.6, 7 and 18); Rudston (Stead 1980, fig. 42.154 and fig. 43.177 with four others mentioned). Production within this area is certain, perhaps somewhere south of Malton. The evidence from Rudston and Langton point to a production date perhaps in the first half of the third-century though a beginning in the late second-century is not impossible.

An overall date range from the mid-second to mid-/late third century is suggested by the forms and fabrics present in this group. Sherds from the carinated bowls, inturned rim dishes and wide-mouthed jars with everted rims of types similar to those made at Roxby were present and these, together with the samian form suggest activity in the Antonine period, the mid- to late second century. Another grey ware wide-mouthed jar compared better to types made at Norton in the third century and a bead-rim bowl probably also belongs to the late second to mid-third century. The Dales ware jar sherds are probably the latest vessel dating to the second half of the third century or early fourth century. The absence of fourth-century types suggest activity ceased or moved within the late third century.

This small assemblage includes several north Lincolnshire forms and, although they may have been made in East Yorkshire, these demonstrate the close relationship between the south and north sides of the Humber estuary. The Dales ware indicates trade with north Lincolnshire in the third century but the grey wares are likely to be from Yorkshire.

Bluegate Corner

The assemblage comprised a group of second- to third-century vessel types, such as everted rim wide-mouthed jars, dishes with inturned rims, bead-rim bowls copying BB2 types, lugged jars and carinated bowls of Roxby type and three rusticated jar sherds, along with a group of late third- to fourth-century types such as Holme-on-Spalding-Moor type carinated bowls with straight walls, developed bead and flange bowls, a Dales ware jar, a grey Dales type jar and a lower Nene Valley reeded rim mortarium. From the topsoil stripping, an East Yorkshire calcite-gritted ware rim from a jar with hooked rim but no lid seating dates to the fourth century, probably in the mid-fourth century and is the latest Roman sherd.

The earlier group was present in the shallow gullies **119866** and **119892**, the southern ditches, **119962** and **120664**, and the various fills of the northern ditch **120665** while a dump of the later vessels was present in the upper fills **119983** and **119984** of ditch **120665** at the junction with ditch **120666**. These later groups included fairly large sherds giving whole profiles. A cream ware flagon, of which twelve sherds from the base and neck are present, is Roman and most probably of mid-first- to second-century date but the burnt condition makes identification difficult. Since other sherds from this context dated to the second or early third century this date range is likely.

Apart from the abraded rusticated sherds, the fabrics and form point to a second- to third-century date range perhaps extending into the early fourth century. The absence of Crambeck ware, East Yorkshire calcite-gritted ware and Huntcliff type ware suggests activity had ceased in the area before the arrival of these wares. The second- and earlier third-century forms and fabrics compare well to north Lincolnshire types while the later third- to early fourth-century vessels can be found in the Holme-on-Spalding-Moor range.

Distance trading is only represented by the Lower Nene Valley mortarium, though the fabric indicates a local workshop. The profile is entirely typical of reeded mortaria with finger-depression spout produced in the Lower Nene Valley within the period AD250-400+ (generally similar to Perrin and Hartley 1996, fig.114, M32). This is a type which is very difficult to date with confidence, but if the potters working in the Crambeck and Lower Nene valley traditions were working in the same workshop (the fabrics of Fig. 101.41 and this piece appear to be identical and to be fired in the same way) then this piece is likely to be fourth-century. There is no obvious reason to assume that the workshop was active over more than a century and it could be considerably less.

Weeton

Gully **120226** produced a small scrap of grey ware only broadly datable to the Roman period, and an everted rim from its upper fill, which compares to late Holme-on-Spalding-Moor products (Tomber and Dore 1998 HSM RE) of late third- to fourth-century type. The rim is probably from a biconical bowl (Halkon and Millett 1999, typeB03a, Gillam 1970: 178 dated AD 290-350). Single undiagnostic scraps of grey ware from gullies **120224** and **120225** were not closely datable.

Scorborough Hill

A large group of pottery from this site included early imports and unusual vessel types. Types ranged in date from the late Iron Age/Conquest period to the early second century. The assemblage included: a range of bead and everted rim, necked bowls with high shoulders or carinated shoulders, burnished externally; at least one platter; a girth beaker; a white ware flagon of first-century type, probably imported or from Lincoln; an early flagon, probably from the Flavian kiln at Dragonby (Swan 1996 fig. 20.32: 1424-5); and rusticated ware and a near complete tripod bowl closely comparable to vessels made at the Flavian kiln at Dragonby (Swan 1996, 575-577: 1418).

Later contexts included vessel types datable to the early second century including Roxby type jars (Rigby and Stead 1976, fig. 65) and bowls, including a flat rim bowl with burnished internal decoration, present at Dragonby (May 1996, fig. 20.34: 1458) from early second-century kiln waste and in the Antonine kiln group at Roxby (Rigby and Stead 1976, fig. 68.78), although Swan thought this was a survival at that date. This bowl form was also present at Malton (Corder 1930b, fig. 17.4) in a late first- to early second-century group and in a late Antonine context at Brough (Wacher1969, Fig 60.158). A dish form, which often has similar decorative treatment, was present at Roxby (Rigby and Stead 1976, fig. 67.41-2, who cite occurrences in Flavian to Antonine contexts at Brough) and at Dragonby (Gregory 1996, 519-20 citing instances from the Flavian period to the mid-third-century). Carinated bowls with the typical stepped carination of north Lincolnshire products of the late first to second century were present (Rigby and Stead 1976, fig. 66.29; Gregory 1996, 520; Darling 1984, fig. 16.94 with Flavian to Severan examples cited). The presence of a Pompeian Red ware flat-rim bowl fabric 6 is unexpected. A small scrap of red-slipped ware from the subsoil was from a rim with groove or step inside the body similar perhaps to a form made in red-slipped ware at Lincoln (Darling 1981, fig. 23.2: 2).

The site produced eight sherds of samian. This assemblage proved unique among all the sites on this pipeline and the contiguous Ganstead to Asselby pipeline, in that the samian was almost entirely South Gaulish and of first-century date.

Early ditches

The upper fill **10431** of ditch **10430**, produced a Form 37, South Gaulish samian sherd (Fig. 104.4) with decoration typical of the period around AD 85 to 110. A sherd of Pompeian red ware, which joined with a sherd from the upper fill of pit **12081**, was also recovered from this ditch.

Pit 12081

The two lowest pit fills, taken together, contained the transitional fabric BSB1 used to make necked bowls and carinated bowls of mid- to late first-century date with some possibly belonging to the late pre-Roman Iron Age. Fabric GRB4 was common in this fill used to make carinated bowls with shelved carination, plain rim platter, tripod bowl and girth beaker type all point to a Flavian-Trajanic date range, late first to early second century, and compare to types made in the Dragonby kiln 4. Most of the GRB4 tripod bowl was present in this fill, with many adjoining sherds as if deposited more or less complete. GRB6 may be a finer version of GRB4 and two sherds of this were present in this fill, from a bead-rim bowl of late first- to early second-century date. A large sherd from the neck of a fine white ware wide-necked flagon of Hofheim type supports such a date (Hawkes and Hull 1947, types 161-5). This vessel is not local but may be from Lincoln (Darling 1984, fabric 1) and date to the first century. A plain Form 27 samian vessel of Flavian or Trajanic date was also recovered from the lower fill.

The coarse wares point to a date in the late, or mid- to late, first century. Tripod bowls at Dragonby were dated by Swan to this period (2009, 45) and her detailed consideration of this type suggested that this form went out of use after the Flavian period (2009, 55). Also present was a jar with a tall, upright, rather flat rim in a gritty grey ware GRC3. This type was present in kiln 5 at Dragonby dated to the Hadrianic-Antonine period by Swan. She considered this form intrusive because she associated it with Dales ware and Dales-type ware forms, which she dated from the second decade of the third century (1996, 577). Gregory, however, recorded these in his horizon III dated early second to early third century and suggested they derived from late Iron Age and earlier Roman types (1996, 517). Other evidence for deriving this form from late Iron Age and early Roman forms can be found. At Scratta Wood in north Nottinghamshire a jar form with this form of rim was found (Challis and Harding 1975, fig. 17.13-4). It is found in the Trent Valley and is not dissimilar to the rim form of a cordoned neck jar of late pre-Roman Iron Age to early Roman date (Leary 2006 and 2009). A prototype occurred at Chesterfield, Derbyshire in 'Trent Valley ware' in a mid- to late first-century context and also at Rampton in the Trent Valley (Ponsford 1992, fig. 19.18). Rigby had also traced the form at Winterton and Old Winteringham in earlier groups of Antonine date (1976, 189-90, fig. 79.6-8 and fig. 81.45-9).

Similar material was found in the next fill in the sequence, including examples of sherds from the same vessels. In addition a cream ware flagon with a flaring rim and cordoned neck was present in a fabric similar to GRB4 but oxidised. This form compared to flagons made at the mid- to late Flavian kiln at Dragonby (Swan 1996 fig.

20.32: 1424-5). Also present in this fill were sherds from GRB4 rusticated jars and everted-rim jars and vessels in a medium grey ware, GRB7 which compares to samples from Roxby. This last fabric was used to make a plain-rim platter or dish and a dish with inturned rim as Roxby type with a date range from the late first to early third century (see above discussion, Rigby and Stead 1976, fig. 67.41-2). The fabric and form of this vessel suggests a later date range for this fill. Two pieces of samian pottery were present in this fill: a small fragment of a South Gaulish Form 29 bowl (Fig. 104.3) likely to date to around AD 70 to 85, and a piece of the footstand of a Type 18R or 18/31R vessel of Flavian or Trajanic date.

During excavation, a deposit thought to be possibly the remains of a cremation was identified within this fill. Significant numbers of sherds from burnt fine white ware flagon were present as well as a burnt shallow platter/dish. Flagons commonly accompany the dead either as pyre goods or grave goods.

The later fills contained less pottery, but of a similar type to that from the underlying fills, although with the addition of a flanged dish in fabric GRA2 in a form related to the dish with inturned rim found at Dragonby and Roxby which Swan dated to the early second century. A South Gaulish Type 18 or 18/31 samian vessel of Flavian or Trajanic date was also recovered. The assemblage from these fills contained very little of the first-century types and was dominated by grey wares GRB1, GRB7 and GRB10, suggesting a later date when the first- to early second-century wares BSB, GRB4 and 6, had gone out of use. The upper ditch fill also had sherds from a Pompeian red ware vessel. The ware compared closely to samples of Pompeian red ware T3 from York which Monaghan correlated to Peacock's fabric 6 (1997, 884-5) and dates to the second century. An adjoining sherd from this vessel was recorded from the upper fill of ditch **10430**.

Pit **12081**, therefore, began to fill up in the Flavian period with later material being added in the early second century. Some of the material from the early fill could belong to the late pre-Roman Iron Age in the early to mid- first century AD but sherds of Flavian date came from the same fills. The presence of near complete vessels such as the tripod bowl and the inturned rim dish in pit **12081** raises the possibility that there may have been an element of deliberate placement as part of ritual activity. However, there was nothing in the arrangement or positioning of the vessels within the ditch to support this interpretation.

Later features

Three GRB4 basal sherds from a jar were present in ditch **12096**. GRB4 fabric was used to make north Lincolnshire types dating from the late first to early second century. A samian sherd from ditch **12040**, thought to be a southern continuation of the same ditch. This was from a Form 37 Central Gaulish vessel (Fig. 104.5). It dates from around AD 150 to 180.

A second large pottery assemblage from the site was recovered from ditch **12003**. This had a slightly later date range than that from pit **12081**. The lower fills produced sherds from a GRB4 carinated bowl with shelved carination of late first- to second/early third-century date and further sherds from a vessel of the same type along with many sherds from an everted-rim jar with acute lattice burnished coping BB1 jars of the second century. However, a GRB4 sherd from a vessel with stabbed decoration and combed chevrons comes from a girth beaker type vessel of the mid- to late first century and is very similar in form and fabric to a sherd from an early fill of pit **12081**. The upper fill contained a jar of Antonine type with a rebated rim as Roxby type A and a GRB4 sherd with a zone of rouletting, perhaps of the late first or early second century. These vessels compare to the group from the later fills of pit **12081** in fabric and date range, belonging to the second century.

Ditch **12018** contained several sherds from a GRB4 jar with everted rim probably of second-century type (Rigby and Stead 1976, type B).

Scorborough Hill, general

Overall, the assemblage from this plot has remarkable characteristics in terms of the wares, the vessel types, and their early date. It contrasts strongly with the assemblages expected from rural settlements of this date and has a strong military character. The tripod bowl has been extensively discussed by Swan (2009) who demonstrated their Gallic ancestry, association with the military and their early date in Britain, no later than the Flavian period. Swan argued that they represent people movement from Gaul, either soldiers or their dependants, who maintained cooking practices brought from their homeland using these tripod vessels. Such vessels would have facilitated rapid heating and cooking of foodstuffs, contrasting with the slow cooking of food in jars, 'casserole-style' common in Britain. Such slow cooking was particularly suited to northern provinces, where fires would be kept going all day for warmth (Swan 2009, 18 and 51-2). The presence of such a vessel here is of great interest. It has clearly been used since at least one tripod leg and adjoining base is scorched. The tripod bowl compared favourably in form and fabric to those made at Dragonby. Although tripod bowls were present at York, these were either Gallic imports or from north Lincolnshire (Monaghan 1997, 880 and Swan 2009, 39).

Fragments from a Pompeian red ware dish in Peacock's fabric 6, thought to come from Belgium, suggest another exotic culinary element to the group. Such dishes are thought to have been used for the making of bread and used principally by the military population (Cool 2006, 76). Pompeian red ware fabric 6 (Monaghan 1997, 884) was also present at York. The presence of a suite of north Lincolnshire type tableware, such as carinated bowls, platters, a flagon and jars, as well as non-local types such as the Hofheim type flagon and the Pompeian red ware vessel, all point to the site being the home of a family with military connections, perhaps a veteran of Gallic origin, possibly from Brough-on-Humber with trading links with York.

Gilcross

A rim sherd from the upper fill of cut **121079** through ring gully **121101** was in a quartz-tempered dark grey ware with brown margins similar to early Roman wares in north Lincolnshire. The rim was slightly everted and appeared hand-made rather than wheel thrown and may belong to the late Iron Age or conquest period. Three further sherds in a similar fabric came from the upper fill of cut **120981** through ring gully **121089**. These came from a broken pedestal base and would fit a similar date range.

Out Newton Road

A grey ware bodysherd from fill **13030** of cut **13018** through enclosure ditch **13070** came from a wide-mouthed jar. The fabric and form suggest a date from the mid-second to mid-third century before the products of the late Holme-on-Spalding-Moor kilns were common. An undiagnostic grey ware sherd from **13041** fill of cut **13040** is likely to date in or after the second century.

Function and site status

The high proportions of hand-made wares on the sites indicate a rural status and contrast with assemblages from small towns such as Shiptonthorpe. Jars predominate on all sites and tablewares are rare. However the assemblage from Scorborough Hill is very unusual in having more table ware vessels such as flagons, beakers, bowls and dishes and exotic vessel types indicating a foreign method of cooking and early imports as well as first-century wheel thrown or turned vessels of north Lincolnshire type but perhaps not fabric. The presence of these types at this site indicate an unusual character and, although hand-made 'native' type vessels were still dominant, the exotic character of some of the vessels, types considered exotic even at Dragonby, suggest the presence of a person of Gallic origin. A similar explanation might be put forward for the presence of a collared bowl of Pannonian type at Burton Constable although, in this case, the vessel does not imply foreign cooking habits and may simply be a chance acquisition of a bowl made by a potter of foreign origin working in the region (Swan 1996, 579) and the rest of the assemblage from this plot does not include any other exotic elements and is of generally later date.

Samian was present on some sites but in all cases the relative proportion of the total assemblage was less than 1 per cent, although the assemblages from Sproatley, New York and Patrington have somewhat higher proportions of samian than those from the other sites. No amphora sherds were present. Similarly there was only a handful of traded fine ware and even mortaria, a type usually present at a constant level on all settlement types (Evans 1993, 103), were scarce.

Trade and exchange

All the assemblages were dominated by the locally produced hand-made jars of native type. The group from Scorborough Hill is the only assemblage with Lincolnshire types and exotic elements present in the mid- to late first century. The connection with Lincolnshire is visible in the second-century groups along the pipeline and can be paralleled at Shiptonthorpe although Evans noted that quantities of second-century Lincolnshire type grey wares on rural sites in the region were markedly lower than at Shiptonthorpe and pointed to this as evidence of a lack of economic cohesion between the small town and surrounding rural sites. Certainly the sites along the pipeline show a similar picture with assemblages dominated by hand-made native wares contrasting with 10 to 20 per cent at Shiptonthorpe (Evans 2006, 140). However it would appear that the small amount of second-century wheel-thrown pottery that was acquired came from the same Lincolnshire sources as served Shiptonthorpe.

In the later second and third century the Lincolnshire link continued, with Dales ware jars being obtained, but most grey ware was probably of local origin at this time and continued to be until the arrival of Crambeck wares and Huntcliff type wares in the fourth century. These wares seem to be obtained only in small quantities, as a result of competition from the local Holme-on-Spalding-Moor industries.

Throughout the Roman period, imported and traded wares were very rare on settlements along the pipeline. The assemblage from Scorborough Hill is exceptional both in the presence of Lincolnshire types in the mid- to late first century and a small amount of imported pottery from Gaul and perhaps West Flanders.

Taphonomy

Extensive study of the distribution of sherds within features was not carried out but it is clear that although most of the assemblages comprise domestic rubbish, deposited in earth-dug features, deliberate deposition of complete or near complete pots was being practised. This is likely to relate to ritual activities of different types including cremation rites, at Scorborough Hill, and closure deposits or boundary deposits (Merrifield 1987, 37-50) at, perhaps, Old Ellerby, Burton Constable and Bluegate Corner: these would have marked rites which accompanied changes in the layout of the boundaries.

Post-Roman pottery

Jane Young, with Peter Didsbury

Introduction

A total of 2249 post-Roman pottery sherds were submitted for examination. The pottery was recovered from sixty-five different fields along the pipeline route, but Lelley was the only excavation site to produce a substantial group, comprising 1714 sherds.

Methodology

The material was recorded at archive level in accordance with the Medieval Pottery Research Group's Guidelines (Slowikowski *et al.* 2001). Quantification was by number of sherds, weight and vessel count within each context. Full data is included in the site archive. Every effort was made to identify cross-context joins. Relevant characteristics needed to assess the assemblage, such as condition, usage and decoration, were also noted. Fabric identification of the medieval and earlier pottery was confirmed by x20 binocular microscope examination. The pottery has, where possible, been subdivided into previously published East Yorkshire or National types (Watkins 1987; 1991; 1993; Didsbury and Watkins 1992). Otherwise the expanded coding system (CNAME) initially developed for the Lincoln Ceramic Type Series (Young et. al 2005) and further developed for sites in North and North-east Lincolnshire (Boyle and Young 2008) and Yorkshire (Vince and Young 2007) was used. In agreement with Peter Didsbury, two new East Yorkshire ware types (EYEMCS and EYQC) were allocated. The ceramic data was entered on an Access database using these fabric codenames. Individual sherds were dated in the archive with the exception of the assemblage from Lelley where a probable ceramic deposition date for each context was noted.

Condition

The pottery is in a variable condition although most sherds are at least slightly abraded with sherd size mainly falling into the small to medium size range (1g to 30g). In total, fewer than nine hundred vessels are represented by more than one sherd and twelve vessels have cross-contextual joins. A number of vessels have external soot residues showing that they have been used over an open fire, several of which appear to have broken during use as the soot is found to continue over the broken edges. Some vessels also have internal soot or carbonised deposits suggesting that the contents of the vessel have burnt. At least one jug base has evidence for charcoal heating rather than use with an open flame. Other indications of usage include wear marks, post-firing holes, and white internal 'kettle fur' deposits caused by the heating of water or containment of urine.

Code	Full name	Date range	Sherds	Vessels
BBAS	Black Basalt	1768 to 1900	1	1
BERTH	Brown glazed earthenware	1550 to 1800	13	12
BEVO1	Beverley orange Fabric 1	1100 to 1230	473	349
BEVO1T	Beverley Orange-type Fabric 1	1100 to 1230	321	202
BEVO2	Beverley Orange Fabric 2	1230 to 1350	168	154
BEVO2T	Beverley Orange-type Fabric 2	1230 to 1350	1	1
BL	Black-glazed	1550 to 1750	23	23
BS	Brown stoneware	1680 to 1850	1	1
CHPO	Chinese Export Porcelain	1640 to 1850	2	2
CIST	Cistercian-type	1480 to 1650	4	4
CREA	Creamware	1770 to 1830	12	11
DONC	Doncaster Hallgate-type	1170 to 1250	1	1
ECHAF	Early to mid-Anglo-Saxon organic-tempered	450 to 800	8	1
EMHM	Early Medieval Handmade	1100 to 1250	8	8
EMLOC	Local Early Medieval fabrics	1150 to 1230	2	2
EMX	Non-local Early Medieval fabrics	1150 to 1230	4	3
ENGS	Unspecified English Stoneware	1750 to 1900	58	53
ENPO	English Porcelain	1744 to 1900	4	4
EYEMCS	East Yorks Early Medieval Coarse Sandy	1100 to 1250	22	16
EYQC	East Yorks Quartz and Chalk tempered	1170 to 1250	550	465
FREC	Frechen stoneware	1530 to 1680	4	3
GRE	Glazed Red Earthenware	1500 to 1650	4	4
GSS	Greensand and shell	1050 to 1250	5	4
HEMGG	Humber Early Medieval Glazed Gritty	1130 to 1230	4	2
HUM	Humberware	1250 to 1550	81	66
HUMB	Humber Basin fabrics	1250 to 1500	9	9
INDUS	Industrial ceramic building material	Roman to 1900	1	1
LERTH	Late earthenwares	1750 to 1900	9	9
LFS	Lincs Fine-shelled	970 to 1200	2	2
LHUM	Late Humber-type	1550 to 1750	13	12
LKT	Lincoln kiln-type shelly	850 to 1000	8	4
LMLOC	Late Medieval local fabrics	1350 to 1550	1	1
LONS	London Stoneware	1670 to 1800	1	1
LSH	Lincoln shelly	850 to 1000	4	3
LSX	Non-local late Saxon fabrics	870 to 1080	0	0
MEDLOC	Medieval local fabrics	1150 to 1450	38	4
MEDX	Non Local Medieval Fabrics	1150 to 1450	6	5
MISC	Unidentified types	400 to 1900	17	15
NCBW	19th-century Buff	1800 to 1900	5	5
NFREM	North French	1150 to 1250	2	1
NGR	Northern Gritty	1180 to 1450	1	1
NLFMSW	North Lincs Fine to Medium Sandy	1150 to 1450	2	2
NLG	North Lincs Gritty	1050 to 1200	16	12
NLQC	North Lincs Quartz and Chalk-tempered	1050 to 1220	40	35
NOTS	Nottingham stoneware	1690 to 1900	8	8
PARIAN	Parian	1840 to 1900	1	1
PEARL	Pearlware	1770 to 1900	9	6
REDCH	Reduced Chalky	1070 to 1230	46	27
RYDALE	Rydale	1550 to 1750	1	1
SCAR	Scarborough	1150 to 1350	1	1
SLIP	Unidentified slipware	1650 to 1750	17	16
SNX	Non-local Saxo-Norman Fabrics	870 to 1150	52	2
ST	Stamford	970 to 1200	2	2

Code	Full name	Date range	Sherds	Vessels
STAXT	Staxton-type	1150 to 1500	6	6
STMO	Staffordshire/Bristol mottled-glazed	1690 to 1800	6	5
STSL	Staffordshire/Bristol slipware	1680 to 1800	1	1
TORK	Torksey	850 to 1100	12	5
TORKT	Torksey-type	850 to 1100	27	18
TOYBT	Toynton Bourne-type	1300 to 1500	1	1
TPW	Transfer printed	1770 to 1900	42	38
UNGS	Unglazed Greensand-tempered fabrics	950 to 1250	9	8
WEST	Westerwald stoneware	1600 to 1800	1	1
WHITE	Modern whiteware	1850 to 1900	36	32
YG	Yorkshire gritty	1050 to 1250	14	10
YORK	York glazed/York White	1150 to 1300	4	2
YORKD	York D	870 to 1030	1	1
YW	Anglo-Scandinavian York	850 to 1000	3	2
		Totals	**2249**	**1708**

TABLE 49: POST-ROMAN POTTERY TYPES; GENERAL DATE RANGE AND QUANTITIES

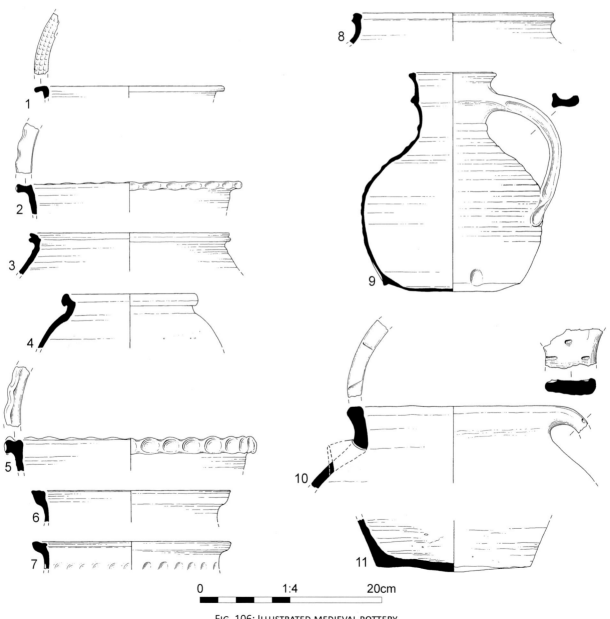

0   1:4   20cm

FIG. 106: ILLUSTRATED MEDIEVAL POTTERY

Range and variety of materials

A range of sixty-five different, identifiable post-Roman pottery ware types and fifteen miscellaneous vessels were identified (Table 49) ranging in date from the early Anglo-Saxon to early modern periods and including local, regional and imported vessels. Vessel forms are mainly limited to various types of jugs, jars and bowls, but more unusual vessels include examples of bottle, chamber pot, dish, pipkin, cup, drinking jug, saucer and plate.

Early Anglo-Saxon: fifth to eighth centuries

Eight sherds from a single jar in an organic-tempered fabric (ECHAF) were recovered from layer **35270** at Lelley. The fabric contains abundant carbonised vegetable matter, including chaff with sparse mixed quartz. A single incised line suggests that the vessel was decorated, but this need not imply an Early Saxon date as similar incised decoration is also found on middle Saxon pottery in North Lincolnshire (Young and Vince 2009). Pottery tempered almost entirely with carbonised vegetable matter, not a common tradition in either Yorkshire or Lincolnshire, seems to span the period between the fifth and eighth centuries.

Illustrated post-Roman pottery

1. YORK D WARE; SMALL BOWL WITH SQUARE ROLLER-STAMPING ON RIM TOP. TOPSOIL DEPOSIT *35000*, LELLEY

2. EAST YORKSHIRE QUARTZ AND CHALK-TEMPERED; BOWL OR 'PEAT POT' WITH PRESSED RIM EDGE. TOPSOIL DEPOSIT *35000*, LELLEY

3. BEVERLEY 1-TYPE; JAR WITH DEEPLY GROOVED RIM. SUBSOIL DEPOSIT *35001*, LELLEY

4. TORKSEY-TYPE; JAR WITH EVERTED RIM. FILL *35350* OF DITCH 35328, LELLEY

5. TORKSEY-TYPE; LARGE JAR WITH PRESSED RIM. FILL *35072* OF DITCH 35073, LELLEY

6. BEVERLEY 1-TYPE; JAR WITH WEDGE-SHAPED RIM. INNER RIM EDGE IS WORN. FILL *35591* OF CUT FEATURE 35590, LELLEY

7. BEVERLEY 1-TYPE; JAR WITH PRESSED SHOULDER. UNSTRATIFIED FIND *35592*, LELLEY

8. BEVERLEY 1-TYPE; JAR. FILL 35554 OF POSTHOLE 35555, LELLEY

9. BEVERLEY 1-TYPE; JUG WITH SOOT ON UNDERSIDE OF BASE. FILL *35533* OF PIT 35614, LELLEY

10. UNIDENTIFIED NON-LOCAL SAXO-NORMAN; PITCHER WITH INCISED LINES ON RIM. FILLS *117055* AND *117056* OF DITCH 117054, RECORDED DURING MONITORING OF TOPSOIL STRIPPING

11. LOCAL MEDIEVAL; JUG WITH TOOL MARKS ON BASE INTERIOR. FILL *9072* OF FEATURE 9074, BURTON CONSTABLE

Anglo-Scandinavian (mid-/late ninth to mid-eleventh century)

In total fifty-five sherds of certain Anglo-Scandinavian date were recovered from along the route of the pipeline. These sherds represent thirty-three vessels and were mainly recovered from Lelley. Nine of these vessels can be dated with certainty to the period between the mid-/late ninth and the late tenth centuries. The Torksey-type vessels cannot, however, be closely dated although they are likely to be of pre-conquest date.

Eight sherds from four undecorated jars are in mid-/late ninth- to late tenth-century Lincoln Kiln-type Shelly ware (LKT). Another three vessels are in a similar shell-tempered ware (LSH), also produced in Lincoln and similarly dated. Lincoln appears to have been the main producer of well made wheel-thrown shell-tempered Anglo-Scandinavian pottery and vessels appear as far afield as Birka in Sweden (Selling 1955). Most of the pottery however was traded across the East Midlands and into parts of East, South and West Yorkshire as well as being found in mid-ninth- to tenth-century deposits at York (Mainman 1990, 415-421).

Five vessels in Torksey-type fabrics (TORK) are in similar fabrics to those recovered from the thirteen known kiln sites at Torksey itself (Young *et al.* 2005 and Young and Perry forthcoming). Four of these vessels are jars of undiagnostic type and could date anywhere between the late ninth and mid-eleventh centuries. The fifth vessel is a bowl with a flanged rim. This sherd and one of the jar sherds incorporate a small amount of carbonised vegetable matter within the fabric. This phenomenon had not been noted among any of the material recovered from Torksey itself until recent trial-trenching by Sheffield University, when sherds with a small amount of carbonised vegetable matter were recovered from Test Pit 1 near to the site of Kiln 3 (Young and Perry 2011).

A further eighteen vessels are in variant fabrics which may or may not have been produced in Torksey (TORKT). Nine of these vessels are in a fabric that contains moderate to common, mainly well-rounded iron-rich grains, but may also include fragments of iron slag. Two of the sherds also include sparse to moderate carbonised vegetable matter. This fabric variation has previously not been noted by the author, either among the kiln waste from Torksey or from excavated groups. These vessels include a large jar with a pressed rim edge (Fig. 106.5) indicating a late tenth-century, or later date. Another jar rim in this fabric is typical of the period between the late tenth and early/mid-eleventh centuries. None of the other vessels are chronologically distinct. Two vessels contain moderate to common carbonised vegetable matter and are similar to vessels recovered from 23 Clifford Street, York (Young 2011).

A single small flanged bowl with square roller-stamping on the rim edge (Fig. 106.1) is of York D ware type (YORKD). The bowl, from layer **35000** at Lelley, is of mid-/late ninth- to tenth-century date (Holdsworth 1987 and Mainman 1990) and is likely to be from an unknown production centre in East or West Yorkshire. Three wheel-thrown sherds from two jars, also from Lelley, have been tentatively identified as York ware vessels (YW) of probable mid-/late ninth- to tenth-century date (*ibid.*). Two of these sherds are from a jar with a wire-cut base. At Lurk Lane Beverley, York ware and York D ware were found in roughly equal amounts (Watkins 1991, 73-74) but York ware is more common at Coppergate in York (Mainman 1990), although this may be a chronological difference.

Saxo-Norman: late ninth to late twelfth centuries

Eighty-four sherds of Saxo-Norman date were identified. All six of the pottery ware-types present (GSS, LFS, SNX, ST, UNGS and YG) have long life spans, making close dating difficult. Two small sherds of Lincolnshire Fine-shelled ware (LFS), both from Lelley, are of general late tenth- to twelfth-century date. The eight vessels in Unglazed Greensand (UNGS) fabrics are likely to have been produced in the vicinity of the Lincolnshire Wolds. The type was in production from the tenth to mid-thirteenth centuries and no chronologically diagnostic sherds were recovered. Only two Stamford ware (ST) sherds were found, one of which is the rim of an unglazed jar of late tenth- to eleventh-century date. The other sherd, from either a glazed pitcher or a jar, in Fabric B is of post-conquest late eleventh- to twelfth-century date.

Two sherds from a single small jar in a Greensand and shell-tempered fabric (GSS) were found at Lelley. Similar vessels are found concentrated on sites along the east coast from East Anglia to Northumbria and are thought to have been made in the Yarmouth area between the eleventh to twelfth centuries (Alan Vince pers. comm.). A total of ten Yorkshire Gritty ware vessels (YG) were recovered from along the route of the pipeline. At least three different fabrics are represented, including one example of a newly defined micaceous fabric (Fabric 1) thought to be of late eleventh- to mid-twelfth-century date (Young and Didsbury forthcoming). The other vessels are not chronologically significant but should belong to the period between the late eleventh and mid-thirteenth centuries.

A single small jar sherd in a fine light oxidised fabric is unlikely to have been produced locally. The thin-walled vessel, from Lelley, appears to be a Stamford ware variant and may have come from a production site in Yorkshire such as the one recently discovered at Pontefract (Roberts and Cumberpatch 2009). Fifty-one sherds from a single vessel, possibly a pitcher, from ditch

117053 (Fig. 106.10) were in a fairly fresh condition with large mainly freshly broken sherds, not all of which were recovered. The vessel is in a mottled part reduced, part oxidised coarse gritty fabric of unknown type. It is possible that this vessel is related to a reduced gritty fabric (HMYG) found at Wetherby, Ripon and York (Mainman 1997 and Young and Didsbury forthcoming), but without chemical analysis it would be impossible to be certain, and it is well away from the known distribution of the type. It would be unusual for a pitcher of this form to post-date the mid-twelfth century in the East Midlands or the early twelfth century in Yorkshire.

Early Medieval: late eleventh to early/mid-thirteenth centuries

The largest quantity of post-Roman pottery, 1493 sherds in total, is of early medieval type. These vessels in fourteen different post-conquest to mid-thirteenth-century ware-types are discussed briefly below. Six of these ware types post-date the early/mid-twelfth century and have probably ceased production by the mid-thirteenth century. Production of the rest of these types was conservative and vessel form-type, manufacture and decoration changed little over the 100 to 150 years of their production.

Beverley-type 1 vessels are the most common ware type of early medieval date along the pipeline. For the purposes of this report these have been divided into vessels that have a fabric, form and manufacture similar to products that are known to have been made in Beverley (BEVO1 with 473 sherds) and those either with variant inclusions, form types or being possibly part hand-made (BEVO1T with 321 sherds). This classification however does not imply that all of the BEVO1 vessels were produced in Beverley, or that none of the BEVO1T was made there.

The majority of the BEVO1 sherds recovered are from plain undecorated jugs, although at least fifty-seven jars and five possible bowls were also found. Early jugs with thick walls and sparse 'splashed' glazes may date to the first half of the twelfth century (P. Didsbury pers. comm. 2011). Most of the vessels however, are well executed and have thin and even walls, suggesting that they belong to the second half of the twelfth century or to the earlier part of the thirteenth (Watkins, 1991, 80 and Didsbury and Watkins 1992). Examples of 'splashed' and suspension glazes abound at Lelley but the sherds from elsewhere are mainly too abraded for the glaze to survive. Six of the BEVO1 jugs have combed decoration and one small jug with a 'splashed-type' glaze has applied decoration. The cross-hatched combed decoration on a jug from pit **35066** is similar to that found on a jug from Lurk Lane, Beverley (Watkins 1991, fig. 67, 134) from a pre-1188 fire horizon deposit. An unusual occurrence is that of an early pipkin handle in pit **35066**. This straight handle has a curved end and a raised central rib. The underside

Site fabric	Vessels
4	9
5	5
7	10
8	13
9	41
10	9
Total	**87**

TABLE 50: VESSEL COUNTS FOR SAMPLED SITE FABRICS FOR BEVERLEY 1-TYPE WARE

has numerous small slashes, presumably to aid even firing. Such vessels are often attributed to the thirteenth century or later, but there is increasing evidence that this form originates in the later part of the twelfth century in both Yorkshire and Lincolnshire (Watkins 1991 and Young 2012).

The two hundred and two vessels classified as BEVO1T include a number of coarseware vessels that appear to have been part hand-made. Most of these vessels are in site-specific fabrics 8 and 9, the fabric of which is not dissimilar to the range classified as Fabric A at Beverley (Didsbury and Watkins 1992, 108-111), but the manufacture and rim forms cannot be paralleled in material so far recovered from Beverley itself (P. Didsbury, pers. comm. 2011). The same fabrics appear to have been used for both fully wheel-thrown and partially thrown vessels, although they rarely seem to have been used for fineware forms. More than twenty different fabric variations fell within this group, although several fabrics were only represented by a single vessel. Most of these fabrics contain a small amount of chalk, but it is never a major inclusion. The minor fabric representations may just reflect an odd batch within the main Beverley production, or they could signal production centres outside of Beverley itself.

Six main groups of fabrics emerged during the study (Site Fabrics 4-5 and 7-10). None of these fabrics differ significantly from the range classified as BEVO1 'Fabric A' in Beverley. A sample of eighty-seven vessels from Lelley rigorously subdivided into these six fabrics at x20 microscopic level (Table 50) suggested that Fabric 9 was the most common type forming 47 per cent of the sample. Fabric 9 contained common sub-round to round quartz grains of 0.1 to 0.3mm together with larger rounded quartz of 0.8 to 1.0mm and moderate to common iron-rich grains. Fabric 8, although superficially similar, contained abundant finer quartz grains of a slightly larger size range (0.2 to 0.4mm) and sparse calcareous grains. Fabrics 4 and 5 had almost identical quartz and iron-rich inclusions but Fabric 5 lacked the moderate to common calcareous grains present in Fabric 4. Fabric 7, although containing a similar quartz grain size to that of Fabric

8, tended to have more grains at the 0.4mm edge of the range. Fabric 10 appeared slightly different to the other fabrics in this group having a fine background quartz content below 0.1mm and containing common rounded quartz of 0.1 to 0.5mm, together with moderate iron-rich grains and moderate calcareous grains.

Fabrics 4 to 5 and 7 to 9 could have come from the same production site with the textural differences relating to the preparation of different clay batches, but Fabric 10 is likely to have utilised a different clay source entirely. These fabrics do occur at Hedon within Hayfield's Coarse-Sand-tempered and Finely Sand-tempered traditions, but need not necessarily have been manufactured there as proposed by Hayfield (Hayfield and Slater 1984, 68-69). The nomenclature used in the Hedon report is somewhat misleading as the terms 'Coarse Sand-tempered' and 'Finely Sand-tempered' (*ibid.* 25-29) do not necessarily refer to the quartz size within the fabrics, but appear just to represent a 'coarseware' and a 'fineware' tradition. The fabric descriptions also do not contain reference to the common chalk inclusions often present. The presence of incidental glaze on a few coarseware vessels found in Hedon suggests that they are being fired together with glazed finewares. This phenomenon is also found at Nottingham (Nailor and Young 2001) where coarsely-sanded oxidised jars appear to have been fired with the white-fabric glazed jugs, as attested by stacking scars on the bases of the jars, and at Lincoln where wasters in a shell-tempered fabric have been found in a kiln producing mainly glazed quartz-tempered jugs (Young 2012).

Only eight of the BEVO1T vessels can positively be identified as jugs. One of these, a jug rim found in cut **35165**, of ditch **35608** has a thick smooth suspension-type glaze. The fabric of this vessel is extremely coarse and falls outside the range of those usually found in Beverley. However the shape of the upright rim is fairly typical of jugs found in deposits dating to the last quarter of the twelfth century there. The other jugs have either a splashed or a heavily pocked suspension glaze. Pit **35614** produced sixty-eight sherds from a single BEVO1T jug forming a near-profile (Fig. 106.9). The heavily pocked suspension glaze and rim type suggest that this jug is also of mid-/late to late twelfth-century date. The jug is competently manufactured being very thin-walled and carefully finished but is not typical of Beverley production (Peter Didsbury, pers. comm.). A similar jug was found in ditch **35439**.

A single potential jug sherd, found in ditch **35180**, is in one of the defined site fabrics (Fabric 9). The 129 jars identified include both completely wheel-thrown examples and those that have been partially hand-formed. The rim profiles of most of these jars can be paralleled among the material recovered from Hedon (Hayfield and Slater 1984, figs. 9-30). A jar with pressed shoulder decoration in Site Fabric 8 (Fig. 106.7) is similar to several vessels found at Hedon (*ibid.* fig.12.61 and fig.14.110-111). The wedge-shaped rim with an internal lip found on this jar, is a common shape among the BEVO1T material recovered, as is a similar thicker wedge-shape rim without the internal lip (Fig. 106.6). Wear marks found on the inner rim edge of some of these jars suggest the use of either a lid, or continual stirring. Many of these jars have an abrupt colour change from an oxidised exterior to a reduced internal surface indicating that they have been fired upside down on a flat surface.

Six of the BEVO1T jars had deep external rim grooves rims (Fig. 106.3) and a further vessel has a less pronounced groove (Fig. 106.8). This type of rim is not found on known Beverley products although at Annie Reed Road (Didsbury and Holbury 2009, fig. 14.49 and 57) some rims do have a slight rim groove. These rim shapes however are known at Hedon (Hayfield and Slater 1984, fig. 17.179-180 and fig. 18.205, 221 and 222) and are also found in other northern coarseware industries such as those at Coulston (McCarthy and Brooks 1988, fig. 118.575 and 583) as well in the Yorkshire and Northern Gritty ware traditions (Vince and Young 2007, figs. 158.11 and 159.28 and 35).

Five hundred and fifty-sherds in fabrics containing quartz and chalk inclusions have been grouped together to form a new ware type: East Yorkshire Quartz and chalk-tempered (EYQC). Examination under a x20 binocular microscope suggests that a wide range of individual fabric types are represented, but that the majority of vessels fall into Site Fabrics 1, 2 and 11. The chalk inclusions vary in frequency between sparse and moderate, but are rarely as common as those found the Reduced Chalky ware or North Lincolnshire Quartz and Chalk traditions. The quartz varies between common and abundant in frequency but is almost always round to sub-round in shape and within the 0.2 to 0.8mm size range. Other inclusions are mainly iron-rich grains and the occasional fragment of flint. Most of the vessels are completely hand-made, although on a number of jars the rims appear to have been wheel thrown or turn-tabled. Similar fabrics occur at Hedon where they are grouped together as Coarse Sand-tempered fabrics (Hayfield and Slater 1984, 27). Hayfield suggests that these fabrics are products of kilns in Hedon itself, but without a kiln group being located and further scientific analysis, this cannot be proved. It is likely that a number of production sites in East Yorkshire, are making this type of pottery, probably including Hedon.

Almost all the identifiable vessel forms are jars, although at least one bowl or peat-pot with a thumb-pressed rim is also present (Fig. 106.2). Rim shapes are more varied than those found on the BEVO1T vessels and include wedge-shaped, grooved-rim, everted, triangular, square and collared examples. This may reflect a greater number of production sites, or a longer production period with rims changing shape over time. Many of the vessels have external soot residues suggesting their primary use as cooking vessels. Further study is needed to determine the exact chronological sequences of this type, although the date range for most fabrics is likely to fall within the twelfth to mid-thirteenth centuries.

The second new ware type to be created for this report comprises a small group of coarse quartz-tempered vessels now termed East Yorkshire Early Medieval Coarse Sandy ware (EYEMCS). Sherds tempered with coarse sand were found in twelfth-century deposits at the Lurk Lane and 33-35 Eastgate excavations in Beverley, but were thought to be intrusive examples of medieval Coarse Sandy ware (Watkins 1991, 88 and Didsbury and Watkins 1992, 117). These vessels are tempered with common to abundant coarse sub-round to subangular quartz of up to 1mm unlike the gritty wares (YG and NGR) which are tempered with angular Millstone grit. All identifiable vessel forms amongst the sixteen recovered vessels are jars. Two of the three jar rims have deeply grooved rims and the third is triangular-shaped.

The remaining Early Medieval vessels can be divided into unglazed coarsewares (EMHM, EMX, NLG, NLQC and REDCH) and glazed tableware or serving wares (DONC, EMLOC, EMX, HEMGG, NFREM and YORK). The coarseware vessels are mainly jars although one bowl was identified. These vessels mostly have external soot residues confirming their use as cooking vessels. These hand-made types belong to a widespread tradition that probably originates in the later eleventh or early twelfth centuries and extends from East Anglia to East Yorkshire. All of the early medieval coarsewares recovered from along the pipeline are likely to have been produced within Yorkshire or northern Lincolnshire.

Thirty-five vessels, mainly jars but also including a single bowl, are in North Lincolnshire Quartz and Chalk-tempered ware (NLQC). At St Peter's Church Barton in North Lincolnshire this is the major coarseware type until it is superseded by medieval quartz or shell-tempered fabrics in the thirteenth century (Boyle *et al.* 2011). The type is generally found on sites in North and North-east Lincolnshire in deposits of late eleventh- to mid-thirteenth-century date and may have been made in the area. Five of the rims are of the grooved-rim type, which is fairly commonly found on vessels in Lincolnshire.

The second largest group, of twenty-seven vessels, is also tempered with medium to coarse quartz and chalk (REDCH) but is more commonly found in East Yorkshire. This Reduced Chalky ware (Watkins 1991, 79-80) is a loose grouping of primarily reduced quartz-tempered fabrics, all of which contain common chalk grains. It forms the main coarseware present at Lurk Lane, Beverley, from the mid- to late twelfth century (Watkins 1991, 64-66) and may be a fairly local product.

Only two jars rims are present in the group one of which is of the heavily grooved-rim type whilst the other is triangular-shaped.

Eight sherds in fine quartz-tempered fabrics are of Early Medieval Hand-made type (EMHM). The fabrics of all but one of the vessels do not contain chalk, but the main difference in this type is the method of manufacture. These vessels are thin-walled and comparable to those found in East Anglia (Jennings 1981, fig. 14) and Lincolnshire (Young *et al.* 2005, 121-122). They appear to have been widely traded, either as vessels in their own right or as containers, and find their way inland to sites such as Doncaster (Buckland *et al.* 1988) and Nottingham (Nailor and Young 2001). Sixteen sherds from twelve vessels are in North Lincolnshire Gritty ware (NLG). This type usually dates to between the late eleventh and early/mid-thirteenth centuries in Lincolnshire and contains coarse non-angular quartz grains of up to 15mm in size. One abraded sherd has traces of glaze and may come from a jug. A single fine quartz-tempered jar sherd from Lelley is from an unknown non-local production site (EMX).

Two jugs are not in the Beverley ware tradition but have fabrics that suggest a local origin (EMLOC). Both vessels were recovered from Lelley and are represented by small undiagnostic sherds. A single unglazed sherd is probably from a Doncaster Hallgate Fabric B jug or jar (DONC). This type is usually found in groups of late twelfth- to early/ mid-thirteenth-century date but could be of slightly earlier or later date (Buckland *et al.* 1979). Two light-bodied jugs with bright copper-green glazes are of York Glazed ware type (Brooks 1987). One jug, possibly an early knight jug, is represented by two small body sherds and an applied limb. Such jugs may have their origins in the late twelfth century as is attested by a York-type jug with applied decoration from Beverley (Watkins 1991, fig 53.9), although the jug from Lelley is likely to be of thirteenth-century date. The other jug is decorated with applied scale decoration. Four other glazed jugs are from unknown regional centres. The two Humber-type Early Medieval Glazed Gritty ware jugs (HEMGG) from Lelley are of a type that is occasionally found in late twelfth- to early thirteenth-century deposits in North Lincolnshire but no production site has been identified for the type (Boyle and Young 2008). Both jugs are wheel-thrown and have a thick splashed-type glaze. Two other glazed vessels are from unknown regional centres (EMX). The only medieval continental import to be recovered is a North French jug (NFREM) with applied vertical strip decoration, from the subsoil surface at Lelley. Similar jugs have been found in deposits of mid-/late to late twelfth-century date in Lincoln, where they were grouped as Fabric A (Young *et al.* 2005, 131).

Medieval: thirteenth to fifteenth centuries

Three hundred and thirteen sherds in ten ware-types of thirteenth- to fifteenth-century type are discussed briefly below. The pottery can be divided into coarsewares, mainly intended for use in the kitchen or dairy, or industrially, and finewares used for serving, lighting, at table or more specific use, although sometimes the same industry produced both types. For the earlier part of the thirteenth century this distinction is quite marked with coarse quartz-tempered wares forming the main coarsewares and finer sand-tempered, mainly glazed, wares forming the finewares. The medieval-type coarseware industries mostly had their origins in the later part of the twelfth century and the low numbers present, only eight vessels, may be explained by a chronological overlap with the early medieval type coarsewares. This distinction is largely lost by the late thirteenth century by which time the two major local pottery industries at Beverley (BEVO2) and Cowick (HUM) produced large numbers of jars and bowls alongside their jugs.

The most common medieval ware type to occur along the pipeline is Beverley 2 ware (BEVO2) with one hundred and sixty-eight sherds representing a maximum of 154 vessels. A single variant sherd had common calcareous inclusions (BEVO2T). Almost all of the sherds recovered were from Lelley and are identifiable as jugs or occasionally jars, ranging in size from small to large. Two sherds from a single potential bowl were recovered from an unstratified context at Scorborough Hill. Only three of the jugs are decorated, two with applied decoration and one with combed wavy lines. The majority of the sherds are in Fabric B (Didsbury and Watkins 1992) which spans the life of the ware type from the thirteenth until at least the early/mid-fourteenth centuries. None of the eleven vessels in Fabric C, which is more common in the late thirteenth to early fourteenth centuries, came from Lelley suggesting that this site had been largely abandoned by the late thirteenth century.

From the late thirteenth century onwards the Beverley-type vessels were supplanted by Humberware (HUM) produced at several centres in East Yorkshire (Watkins 1987, 98 and Watkins 1993, 76-90), in York at Blue Bridge Lane (Vince and Steane 2005) and probably also in North Lincolnshire. This ware type remained in production until about the middle of the sixteenth century and small undiagnostic sherds are often hard to closely date. Of the sixty-six Humberware vessels recovered from along the pipeline, most are small to medium-sized jugs, although one drinking jug and one very large jug were also found. Nine other vessels, four of which come from the evaluation site at Hollym Road, are also likely to be products of kilns operating in the Humber Basin (HUMB). These vessels are all likely to be jugs of thirteenth- to mid-sixteenth-century date and include a possible drinking jug.

A small but wide-ranging group of other medieval finewares was found along the pipeline, mostly in unstratified topsoil or subsoil contexts. Only one of these vessels is from an identifiable production site elsewhere in Yorkshire (SCAR), although three other vessels are possibly fairly local products (MEDLOC). The single Scarborough (SCAR) ware sherd is from a jug with a copper-coloured glaze and is likely to date to the thirteenth or fourteenth centuries. The three fineware vessels likely to have been made at as yet unknown centres in East Yorkshire (MEDLOC) include thirty-five sherds from a single large jug in a fine bright oxidised sandy fabric (Fig. 106.11). The vessel is in an extremely fragmentary and brittle condition and could represent waste material. The base appears freshly broken and is unusual in having multiple pressing marks from the end of a stick on the internal surface. This was probably to push-out the base after an unsuccessful removal from the wheel (J. Hudson, pers. comm. 2011). Two jugs are in North Lincolnshire Fine to Medium Sandy ware (NLFMSW) which was probably produced in the area around modern Scunthorpe in the thirteenth and fourteenth centuries (Young 2009). Five unidentified non-local jugs are regional imports (MEDX) from unknown kiln sites, probably in Yorkshire and Lincolnshire.

Only eight medieval-type coarseware vessels were recovered from the pipeline, with six examples of Staxton-type ware (STAXT) from the Lelley excavation site. Included in the group is a finger-pressed rim from a jar or bowl that is likely to date to between thirteenth and mid-fourteenth centuries. Staxton-type ware appears to have been the most common type of coarseware in use in Beverley between the early/mid-thirteenth and early fourteenth centuries (Watkins 1991, 87 and Didsbury and Watkins 1992, 111) but was not important in Hull (Watkins 1987, 109-110). A very abraded sherd of Northern Gritty ware (NGR), found during evaluation trenching to the north of Southside Road, Halsham, is probably from a jar of twelfth- or thirteenth-century date. These gritty fabrics are found on a number of sites in West and North Yorkshire with known production sites including Baildon, Brunthwaite, Follifoot and Upper Heaton (Vince and Young 2007, 274). The earliest vessels are found in late eleventh- to twelfth-century contexts there and the type continues in use until the late fifteenth or sixteenth centuries. This industry produced both unglazed coarsewares and glazed jugs and bowls. A single very abraded jar sherd in a local medium sandy fabric (MEDLOC) may be equivalent to the finer end of medieval Coarse Sandy ware in use in Hull in the later thirteenth and fourteenth centuries (Watkins 1993, 76).

Late medieval to early post-medieval: mid-fifteenth to sixteenth centuries

Only nineteen sherds can be considered to be of possible late medieval to early post-medieval date. Most of the sherds are of a Late Humberware-type (LHUM) and could date anywhere between the mid-sixteenth and eighteenth centuries (Humber 5 at Hull; Watkins 1987, 106-107). Five of the twelve Late Humberware vessels are identifiable as large bowls and one sherd with an internal and external glaze may be from a jug. A single sherd recovered from the Hollym Road evaluation has internal purple/black glaze spots and is probably from a locally manufactured jug or jar of fourteenth- to sixteenth-century date (LMLOC). The sherd is too coarsely sanded to be considered a typical Humberware type. Three of the four Cistercian ware sherds recovered from the pipeline are from small cups of general late fifteenth- to sixteenth-century date. The fourth sherd, from ring gully **121101** at Gilcross, is from a tall cup and is of sixteenth-century type. The only other vessel of this period is represented by a single jar sherd in a rarely found ware type (TOYBT). Archaeological investigations near Ingoldmells in Lincolnshire produced seven vessels in this new Toynton-type ware of late medieval to early post-medieval date. Visually these vessels look like a slightly sandy post-medieval Bourne ware (BOU); however when examined at x20 magnification it is obvious that the fabric is similar to the Toynton wares and does not resemble any known Bourne product. Similar vessels were recovered some years ago from Bicker in Lincolnshire but were not characterised at the time. These vessels are likely to date to between the fifteenth and sixteenth centuries.

Post-medieval: sixteenth to eighteenth century

Seventy-one of the sherds examined are of sixteenth- to eighteenth-century date; these include coarsewares, slipwares and stonewares. Forty-one sherds in four ware types are post-medieval coarsewares of late sixteenth- to eighteenth-century date (BERTH, BL, GRE and RYDALE). Vessel forms are mainly large bowls and jars probably intended for use in the kitchen. Other vessels include drinking vessels and a chamber pot. Most of these coarseware vessels are likely to be of fairly local provenance although some of the sherds may come from a Lincolnshire source (possibly Boston, Grimsby or Bolingbroke) and the Ryedale bowl originated in the Howardian Hills (Brooks 1987, 162-3).

Sixteen slipware vessels, probably mostly made in Yorkshire (SLIP), include decorated press-moulded dishes and thrown bowls. Some of these vessels probably date into the nineteenth century. A single press-moulded dish in a light orange fabric may be a Staffordshire product (STSL), although recently similar vessels have been found at a production site near Leeds. Five vessels including two bowls, a small jar and a mug or cup, are in eighteenth-century Staffordshire Mottled ware (STMO). Despite the name these vessels were made in other centres including London, Bristol and Yorkshire.

A single example of a eighteenth- or nineteenth-century London Stoneware bottle (LONS) and three imported German Frechen stoneware vessels (FREC), are all plain drinking jugs of late sixteenth- to seventeenth-century date, were also recovered. The sherd of Westerwald Stoneware (WEST) from the subsoil surface in the same field as the Burstwick excavation area is from an eighteenth-century chamber pot and is decorated with a blue infill.

Early modern: mid-eighteenth to twentieth century

Sherds of late eighteenth- to twentieth-century date include earthenwares, stonewares and industrial finewares. Nine unglazed orange earthenware vessels (LERTH) are all likely to have been intended for use as flowerpots or larger garden pots. Eight Nottingham Stoneware (NOTS) vessels include jars and bowls of eighteenth to mid-nineteenth date. A single Brown Stone ware sherd (BS) is possibly from an eighteenth-century jug or jar. A modelled fox head in Parian (PARIAN) may have formed the knob of a lid. A sherd of Black Basalt (BBAS) may have come from a small jar. Fifty-three other stoneware vessels (ENGS), including bottles, flagons and jam or lard jars, are of later, nineteenth- to twentieth-century date. Industrial late eighteenth- to twentieth-century fineware vessels are mainly plates, dishes and cups and include Creamware (CREA), Pearlware (PEARL), transfer-printed (TPW), porcelain (ENPO), Buff ware (NCBW) and white wares (WHITE). Two fragments of eighteenth-century Chinese Export Porcelain (CHPO) were recovered: one from a plate and the other from a small drinking bowl with underglaze blue and over-glaze red painted decoration.

Discussion

A single early Anglo-Saxon vessel recovered from Lelley is the only ceramic evidence for fifth- to eighth-century occupation. No pottery of middle Saxon type was found on any site, but the excavation site at Lelley provided evidence for Anglo-Scandinavian occupation, material which includes vessels produced in both Lincolnshire and Yorkshire with Torksey and Torksey-type vessels being the most common type found. The presence of three York ware vessels indicates pre-mid-/late tenth-century occupation (Mainman 1990, 411); otherwise few of the Anglo-Scandinavian vessels can directly be attributed to the early part of this period. A large Torksey-type jar with pressed rim decoration suggests a late tenth-century or later date for activity indicating more than one period of occupation. A small group of sherds recovered during evaluation may also indicate occupation in the vicinity of Daisy Hill farm, Burstwick.

With the exception of the vessel from ditch **117053** to the south of Southside Road, Halsham and a couple of stray finds, pottery of Saxo-Norman type was limited to Lelley. By the twelfth to early/mid-thirteenth centuries, however, pottery was being discarded in the vicinity of nine locations along the pipeline route in addition to Lelley. The ceramic profile of this period suggests a similar general pattern to that found at Hedon (Hayfield and Slater 1984), with most of the pottery probably being manufactured within East Yorkshire, but lacking the greater number of regional imports found at that site. Jars are overwhelmingly the main twelfth-century vessel type, but jugs seem to become an important factor in the assemblage from the late twelfth century.

Pottery from the high medieval period was recovered from forty-four of the fields along the pipeline route, with the Lelley site, despite having declined from its earlier predominance, still contributing forty-six per cent of the sherds. Most of the material from this period is Beverley 2 jugs with very few coarseware fabrics occurring. Again few regional imports and no continental imports of this period were recovered. Little pottery attributable to the fourteenth to sixteenth centuries was recovered, possibly reflecting a change in agricultural practices or the depopulation of villages after the mid-fourteenth century. A slight increase occurs in the number of vessels of late seventeenth to nineteenth century again suggesting a change in land usage.

Worked stone

Ruth Shaffrey

Old Ellerby

A single large complete perforated whetstone (SF 1102, Fig. 107.1) measuring 258mm in length, found in spread layer **3091** overlying Structure 2, may relate to metal working associated with the activity in the Iron Age or Roman period. It is made from a fine-grained grey sandstone with infrequent muscovite mica, probably from the Coal Measures. The presence of mica would seem to preclude its identification as Kentish Rag from which two similar sized whetstones at Fiskerton were made (Parker Pearson 2003, 122). A study of whetstone lithologies from five large Romano-British assemblages showed that Coal Measures sandstone types were second in number to those of Kentish Rag (Moore 1978). This pattern was replicated in a later study of London whetstones, which showed that the most popular lithology was from the nearest suitable source of whetstone material, Kentish Rag (Rhodes 1986, 240).

Coal Measures sandstones of types suitable for sharpening outcrop in many places in Yorkshire (Moore 1978, 68 referencing Farey 1811). A scan of the

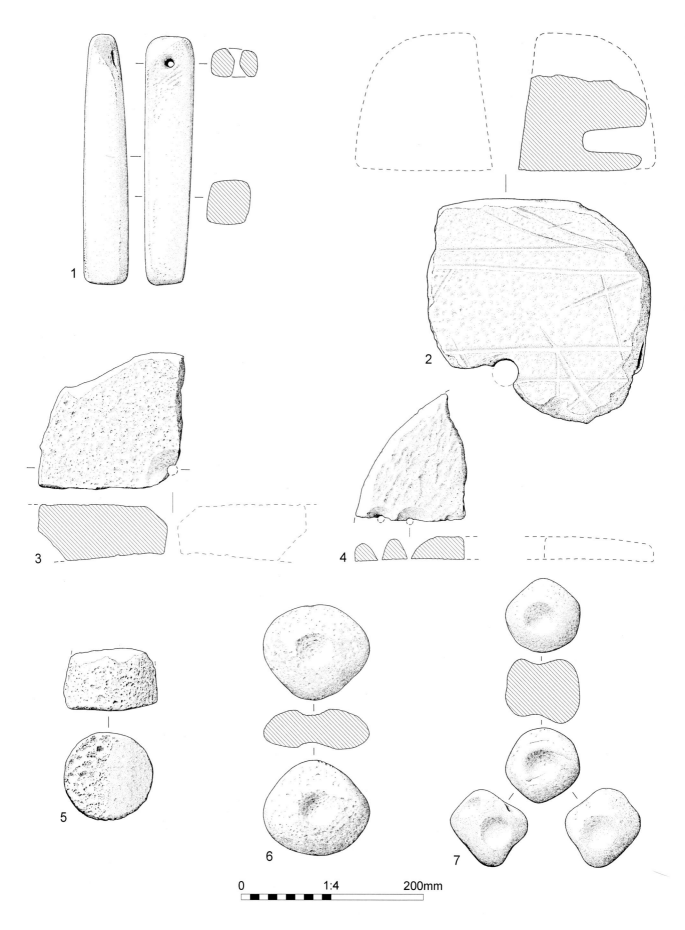

Fig. 107: Worked stone objects

Illustrated stone artefacts

1. COMPLETE LARGE WHETSTONE, FINE-GRAINED, MICACEOUS GREY SANDSTONE, PROBABLY FROM COAL MEASURES. FINE PECK MARKS OVER LARGE PARTS. ALL FACES USED, WITH AREAS WORN SMOOTH. ARRISES SHARP WHERE USED ACROSS FACES. 7MM DIAM. CIRCULAR PERFORATION; 258MM BY 27-46MM BY 50-40MM (ONE END SQUARE, OTHER RECTANGULAR). WT 1252G. SF 1102, LAYER *3091* ABOVE DITCH 3243, OLD ELLERBY

2. UPPER BEEHIVE ROTARY QUERN FRAG. GREY GREEN, FINE GRAINED IGNEOUS ROCK, PROBABLY ERRATIC. HANDLE SOCKET 67MM DEEP, 28MM DIAM. FEED PIPE 21MM DIAM. PECKED ALL OVER. GRINDING SURFACE FLAT. 280-340MM DIAM. 130MM THICK. WT 9600G. SUBSOIL *118912* ACROSS SOUTH END, BURTON CONSTABLE

3. UPPER ROTARY QUERN, SHAP GRANITE. FLAT SURFACES, GRINDING SURFACE WORN VERY SMOOTH. EDGES MISSING. HOPPER ONLY 50MM DIAM. FEED PIPE 16MM DIAM. >300MM DIAM. 64 MM THICK. SF 288. WT 2400G. FILL *25138* OF RING GULLY 25137, BRANDYWELL

4. UPPER ROTARY QUERN, PROB. LOCAL JURASSIC SANDSTONE, FINE OR MEDIUM GRAINED MOD. SORTED TEXTURE. NO OBVIOUS INCLUSIONS, BUT BURNING SLIGHTLY OBSCURES. THIN DISC TYPE, ROUGHLY PARALLEL FACES, PECKED ALL OVER, SIDES SLOPE IN SLIGHTLY. GRINDING SURFACE SLIGHTLY CURVED, CONCAVE, NOTICEABLY WORN TOWARDS CIRCUMFERENCE. HEAVILY BLACKENED. UPPER SURFACE HAS TWO HOLES APPARENTLY THROUGH TO GRINDING SURFACE, THOUGH MIGHT BE RESULT OF EXTENSIVE WEAR. 370MM DIAM. BY 24MM MAX. THICKNESS. WT 443G. SF 265, FILL *35183* OF PIT 35184, LELLEY

5. MINIATURE COLUMN SECTION. MILLSTONE GRIT. MEDIUM-COARSE GRAINED POORLY SORTED FELDSPATHIC CREAM SANDSTONE. PECKED CIRCUMFERENCE. ONE END WORN. 100 MM DIAM. BY >63MM. WT 889G. SUBSOIL *3508*, LELLEY

6. PROCESSOR SF 1382. FINE-GRAINED GREY GREEN SANDSTONE PEBBLE WITH HOLLOW, ROUGH INSIDE, IN EACH FACE. EDGES OF PEBBLE ALSO HAVE SOME PERCUSSION WEAR. 112 BY 98 BY 42MM. WT 658G. FILL *119150*, CUT 119151 OF DITCH 120026, NEW YORK

7. ROUGHLY CUBOID CREAM QUARTZITE COBBLE PROCESSOR. DEEP DEPRESSIONS ON TWO OPPOSING FACES; MUCH SHALLOWER ON TWO ADJACENT FACES. MOST AREAS RETAIN FINE PECKING MARKS. ALL DIMENSIONS 72-74MM. WT 656G. SF 1601, FILL *120156*, CUT 120157 OF DITCH 120170, WEETON

published literature shows that whetstones are mainly identified as 'local sandstone'; the use of general descriptive terms probably due to the difficulty in identifying lithology in hand specimens. It is difficult to see the mineralogy in whetstones with their fine-grained texture and their typically worn surfaces. 'Local sandstone' could encompass Kentish Rag, or local micaceous sandstone, including that from the

Coal Measures (Clarke 1998, 258; Clarke 1990, 126; Wenham and Heywood 1997, 39; Gwilt 2006, 244-245). A single Coal Measure sandstone whetstone was identified at Thurnscoe (Wright 2004, 58).

Although the whetstone may be of typical material, it is unusual in both its size and the fact that it is perforated. It is 100mm longer than the Thurnscoe example and significantly longer than most other whetstones in the region. Perforations are also more typical of smaller examples of whetstones. None of the 16 items found at nearby Dragonby are as large or are perforated (Wright 1996, 378). A review of other sites in the region revealed none that were pierced and the largest comparable example was one of 172mm from Castleford (Clarke 1998, 258; Clarke 1990, 126; Wenham and Heywood 1997, 39; Gwilt 2006, 244-245).

Elsewhere in the country, however, large whetstones do exist: two, measuring 320 and 340mm length, were found at Fiskerton in Lincolnshire (Parker Pearson 2003, 122) and a group of more than a hundred whetstones measuring close to a Roman foot (296mm) were found together at Wroxeter (Atkinson 1942, 129). Although similar in length, the whetstones from both of these sites are far slimmer than the current example. They are comparable to an example of similar size and shape found in London, where analysis indicated that these longer thinner whetstones may be typically later Roman. The same analysis also indicated that early Roman whetstones tend to be less formalised in dimensions and usually thicker (Rhodes 1986). It is possible the Fiskerton, Wroxeter and London examples belong to a later tradition of whetstone production but future work may show that there is a spatial difference in whetstone form.

It is evident that this is an unusual example of a large, heavy, neatly finished and perforated whetstone, most likely to have belonged to a toolkit of a craftsman of some experience and skill. Perforations are usually assumed to be an indication that the whetstone was suspended from a tool belt but the size and weight (1252g) of this whetstone would probably have precluded it being comfortably carried. It is more likely that it was hung from a nail or peg in a workshop. The overall size of the whetstone and the wear found on it is consistent with its use for sharpening large blades such as scythes or swords (Parker Pearson 2003, 122).

Burton Constable

Two rotary querns, one hone and a stone used for rubbing were recovered. The rubber (SF 1228), from pit **9617**, is a large cobble with one flat pecked and worn face. The hone (SF 1201), from ditch **118934** at its intersection with ditch **118933**, also makes use of a cobble, although it is only a piece broken from a larger stone. It has not been humanly modified other than having one noticeably worn face with some scratches.

Of two rotary querns recovered, one is a fragment of thick beehive quern (Fig. 107.2). From an unstratified context, it is of Iron Age form, although these continued in use into the Roman period. The small surviving section of complete profile indicates the presence of a small hopper and enough of the circumference survives to show that the quern is not of the rare three handled type and had either one or two handles originally. The handle socket and feed pipe are both very neatly and uniformly circular so that they were probably made with a metal tubular bit (Heslop 1988, 63). Both the handle hole and the feed pipe are smooth inside but their different diameters indicate that they were formed with different drill bits. The perfectly cylindrical shape of the handle socket suggests it was fitted with a wooden handle (Heslop 2008, 51), as an iron handle would have caused the socket to wear differentially.

The second quern fragment (SF 1216), from the terminal of the Structure 4 ring gully, may also have been of beehive form, although it is much thinner and insufficient survives to be sure of much other than that the grinding surface was flat. This quern also has a small basin on the non-grinding face, which is not a hopper. The centre of the quern is missing and it is not possible to tell if the basin was a feature of manufacture or added later during reuse; basins are a common feature on beehive rotary querns in the region (Heslop 2008, 26).

Both quern fragments are made of igneous rock that probably originated as glacial erratics. Shap granite occurs as erratic boulders in the Vale of York and possibly further east (Wilson 1948, 72) and need not have been transported any great distance. Boulders of a selection of rocks originating in the Pennines and Scandinavia are also found along the Yorkshire coast (Wilson 1948, 72). Despite the likely local origin for the stone used for these querns, their presence is noteworthy as rotary querns made from erratic boulders are not common. None were recovered from the Rudstone Dale and Thorpe Hall sites on the Ganstead to Asselby pipeline, some 30km westwards (Shaffrey 2011), although at Dragonby a number of querns were probably made from boulders from the glacial drift, including one of granite (Wright 1996, 367). A single example in Shap granite was also recorded at Cawthorne near Barnsley (Hayes, Hemingway and Spratt 1980, 308). Elsewhere in the northern counties, an erratic of gneiss was used at Catterick for a lower stone (Wright 2002, 267). Several querns of glacial erratics were found in Romano-British phases of activity at High Wold, Bridlington although two were most likely to be from saddle querns and none could be confirmed as definitely from rotary querns (Heslop and Gaunt 2009).

Along with the two querns found at Brandywell and the example at Patrington (below), these hint that erratic exploitation might be greater in the Holderness peninsula

than elsewhere in Yorkshire. Three of these four rotary querns are of beehive form and one of flat disc form, suggesting that the practice of exploiting erratics occurred over a period of time, probably sporadically given the numbers in question. Exploitation may have occurred when access to more usual supplies of querns was not possible, perhaps indicating a low status to the site. Elsewhere, it has been suggested that rotary querns made from non-typical stones may have been considered exotic, which may in turn have afforded them a luxury status (Heslop 2008, 16), but that is not supported by the evidence here.

Brandywell

Two rotary querns were recovered, both from the fill of ring gully **25137**. One of these is the lower stone of a beehive rotary quern with a 27mm diameter spindle socket, 49mm deep. The quern is made from a grey green micaceous igneous rock; part of the original face of the boulder survives on the base, demonstrating that it is from an erratic. The upper rotary quern (SF 288; Fig. 107.3) is also from an erratic, in this case Shap Granite (see Burton Constable, above). The entire circumference of this quern is damaged, possibly deliberately, but it is of Roman disc form with a small hopper and narrow feed pipe of 16mm. It is not known whether it had a handle socket.

Lelley

Four items of worked stone were recovered: three rotary quern fragments and one piece of miniature column. The three querns include one fragment of disc style lava quern of an estimated 600mm diameter and thus probably from a millstone (SF 264). This was recovered from a fill of ditch **35195**, one of the recuts of ditch **35608**, where it is cut by ditch **35609**. Two further quern fragments were recovered. One (SF 279), incorporated into the kerb, **35437**, of the oven, is made of a medium-grained sandstone containing frequent polished grains, probably Spilsby Sandstone. The other (SF 265; Fig. 107.4) is made from a non-diagnostic fine to medium grained sandstone, possibly from the Jurassic. Both are fragments from flat disc style rotary querns, and could be either Roman or medieval in origin. The use of one in the structure of an oven and the burning of the other prior to deposition in pit **35184**, indicate that they had been fragmentary for some time prior to their final deposition.

A fourth item provides a tantalising hint of something different. It is a fragment of coarse grained poorly sorted feldspathic sandstone, probably Millstone Grit that has been shaped into a small column (Fig. 107.5). It was recovered from an unstratified subsoil context and is probably Roman in origin; it would have been used decoratively and indicates the presence of a villa or other reasonably high status building somewhere in the vicinity.

New York

A pebble with a hollow formed in each opposing face (SF 1382, Fig. 107.6) and with some percussion wear on the edges caused by use for pounding, was recovered from ditch **120026**. The function is unclear: a possibility is that it was a crude form of nut cracker, with the nut placed under the hollow to secure it in place before being bashed to crack it open.

Patrington

A single rotary quern was recovered from pit **8840**. Most of the original surfaces do not survive so it is not possible to reconstruct its form, although a basin on one face may be part of the original hopper. It is made from a glacial erratic. The use of glacial erratics is discussed in more detail in the report for Burton Constable (above).

Weeton

A single item of worked stone was found in the fill of ditch **120170**. It is a quartzite river cobble crudely formed into a cuboid with pecking and shaped so that it has deep depressions on two opposing faces with shallower basins on two adjacent ones (Fig. 107.7). The hollows may be purely decorative and the overall shape of the stone is similar to items identified as missiles or ballista balls at Carlisle (Shaffrey 2009, fig. 546) although this identification drew heavily on the military associations of that site, which are not present here. Assuming a decorative function for the hollows, stones such as this could also have functioned as weights. Alternatively, the hollows may have been used, perhaps for the cracking of nuts, a theory posited for the similar stone (SF 1382) from New York (above). At present it remains enigmatic.

Fired clay

Lisa M. Wastling

Nine of the excavation sites produced significant fired clay assemblages. As is usual with such differentially preserved material, the majority of fragments were non-diagnostic. The range of diagnostic material consists of structural fired clay or daub, objects associated with the manufacture of textiles, non-ferrous metal working mould fragments, and briquetage: the fired clay associated with salt manufacture. The bulk of material dated to the Iron Age or Early Roman period; however, a single object of Bronze Age date was also recovered and some of the structural fired clay derives from deposits of late Saxon to medieval date.

Methodology

The fired clay was examined by eye, with routine use of a hand lens at x10 magnification and occasional use of binocular microscope at x20 magnification. The hand lens used has a millimetre scale at its base.

The fabric-types were grouped on the basis of temper and the natural constituents of the clay. Those designated Q were mainly quartz-based, and of silty or sandy character. V denotes vegetable temper such as grass or chaff. QV contains both Q and V characteristics. Fabrics containing calcareous inclusions, consisting of rounded chalk fragments, are coded as QC when the level of chalk fragments is moderate or above, though not when chalk fragments are sparse. U was used for pieces too small to categorise. A separate list of fabric-types was derived for each site assemblage. Those for the larger groups are tabulated below; those for the smaller assemblages are stored with the project archive. A copy of the assemblage data for each site in an access database also forms part of the project archive.

Where wattle impressions were present, these were measured using templates with 5mm increments; thus the 10mm template group includes wattle impressions of 10 to 14mm diameters, the 15mm template 15 to 19mm and so on.

Old Ellerby

A small number of fired clay mould fragments from Old Ellerby are of intrinsic interest; the remainder are non-diagnostic fragments. Initially, the mould fragments were assigned to a number for unstratified finds as they were collected as a group from a newly-machined surface. However, a tiny sliver of fired clay weighing just 0.12g recovered from context **3016** has a fresh break, which refits one of the unstratified sherds. Therefore it is highly likely that this group of fired clay fragments originated in the upper fill of pit **3014**, cut into the Structure 2 ring gully. Six sherds were recovered including the sliver, with a total weight of 38.9g. Two or possibly three moulds are present.

The fabric of the moulds is a very sandy fine matrix with extremely well-sorted angular to sub-angular quartz sand grains. There are occasional larger grains and sparse red or brown rounded ferrous-rich pellets, under 1mm diameter. One piece (Fig. 108.3) has been harder fired, and therefore is less abraded than the others. The quartz-rich fabric would give the moulds refractory qualities to reduce the likelihood of distortion during the casting process. There are no surviving areas of flat mating surfaces or luting clay to indicate that they are of two-piece moulds and an insufficient proportion survives to suggest the use of one-piece moulds. There is also an insufficient amount of the matrices surviving to determine the types of objects being cast.

The largest fragment (Fig. 108.1) has the complete profile of the sprue cup with an elongated runner, which

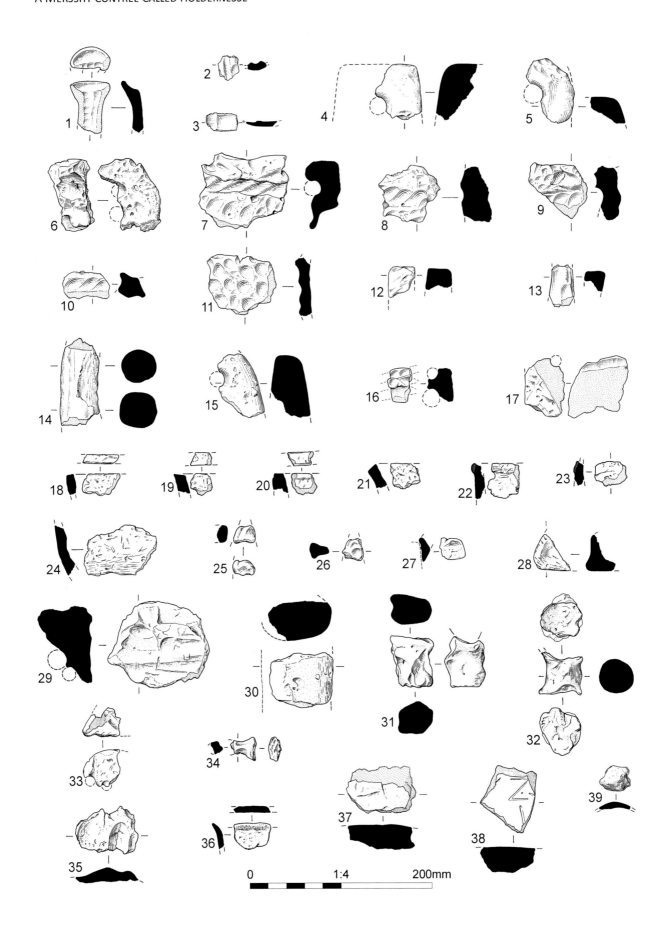

FIG. 108: FIRED CLAY: METAL-WORKING MOULD, DAUB AND BRIQUETAGE

Illustrated fired clay artefacts

Old Ellerby

1. MOULD. SPRUE-CUP AND NECK OF NON-FERROUS METALWORKING MOULD. TWO JOINING SHERDS AND ONE NON-JOINING. ABRADED. ELONGATED RUNNER: ?SPLIT INTO TWO LINEAR RUNNERS TO FILL MOULD. OXIDISED EXT. SURFACE, REMAINDER REDUCED TO DARK GREY. H: 53MM; MAX DIAM: C50MM; MIN DIAM: *c*.30MM. UNSTRATIFIED FINDS *3324*, ABOVE RING GULLY 3020

2. MOULD. FRAG. OF NON-FERROUS METALWORKING MOULD, ?PART OF 1 (ABOVE). ABRADED. PART OF OBJECT MATRIX WITH CURVING OR SINUOUS PROFILE. OXIDISED EXT. SURFACE, REMAINDER REDUCED TO DARK GREY. L: 23MM; W: 21MM; TH: 8MM. UNSTRATIFIED FINDS *3324*, FROM REGION OF RING GULLY 3020

3. MOULD. TWO JOINING FRAGS. OF NON-FERROUS METALWORKING MOULD. HARDER FIRED THAN THOSE ABOVE AND OF DIFFERENT MOULD. OXIDISED EXT. SURFACE, REMAINDER REDUCED TO V. DARK GREY. OBJECT MATRIX BEARS GENTLE CURVE AND HAS BLACK PITTED SLAGGY RESIDUE ADHERING TO PARTS OF SURFACE. L: 35MM; W: 19MM; TH: 6MM. LARGER PIECE FROM UNSTRATIFIED CONTEXT *3324*; FINE SLIVER FROM FILL *3016* OF PIT 3014

Burton Constable

4. PYRAMIDAL LOOMWEIGHT. OXIDISED THROUGHOUT. ROUNDED CORNER OF TOP OF WEIGHT, BROKEN AT PERFORATION. PERF. DIAM: *c*.15MM. FABRIC Q1. H: 56MM; W: 48MM; TH: 36MM; WT: 90G. CONTEXT *9698*, COLLUVIAL LAYER *118979*

5. PYRAMIDAL LOOMWEIGHT. OXIDISED THROUGHOUT. ROUNDED CORNER OF TOP OF WEIGHT, BROKEN AT PERFORATION. PERF. DIAM: 20MM; L: 70MM; W: 46MM; TH: 32MM; WT: 71G. CONTEXT *118518*, SUBSOIL OVERLYING COLLUVIAL LAYER *118979*

6. DAUB FRAG. BEARS TWO PARALLEL ROD IMPRESSIONS: 10MM AND 15MM IN DIAM. ORIGINAL SURFACES OF STRUCTURE NOT PRESENT ON PIECE. L: 84MM; W: 45MM; TH: 45MM. UPPER FILL *118191* OF DITCH 118190, STRUCTURE 5 RING GULLY

7. DAUB; TWO JOINING FRAGS BEARING TWO PARALLEL ROPE IMPRESSIONS: UPPERMOST SO WELL-PRESERVED THAT BOTH STRANDS AND FIBRES OF THE ROPE CAN BE CLEARLY SEEN. WET CLAY HAS DISTORTED DOWNWARDS OVER UPPERMOST ROPE, WHICH GIVES EVIDENCE OF ORIENTATION. ROPE DIAM: *c*.18MM. L: 92MM; H: 75MM; TH: 45MM. FILL *118809* OF DITCH 118041, STRUCTURE 4 RING GULLY

8. DAUB FRAG. BEARS SINGLE ROPE IMPRESSION. ROPE DIAM. *c*.18MM; L: 60MM; W: 57MM; TH: 35MM. FILL *118809* OF DITCH 118041, STRUCTURE 4 RING GULLY

9. DAUB FRAG. BEARS SINGLE ROPE IMPRESSION. ROPE DIAM. *c*.18MM. L: 57MM; W: 57MM; TH: 30MM. FILL *118809* OF DITCH 118041, STRUCTURE 4 RING GULLY

10. DAUB FRAG. BEARS SINGLE ROPE IMPRESSION. ROPE DIAM. *c*.18MM; L: 53MM; W: 35MM; TH: 35MM. FILL *118809* OF DITCH 118041, STRUCTURE 4 RING GULLY

11. DAUB. THREE JOINING FRAGS WHICH BEAR FLAT OUTER SURFACE WITH ROWS OF NEAT EVENLY-SPACED FINGER-TIP IMPRESSIONS, ?DECORATION. L: 72MM; W: 62MM; TH: 18MM. FILL *118809* OF DITCH 118041, STRUCTURE 4 RING GULLY

Brandywell

12. BAR OR SLAB FRAG. PART OXIDISED, PART REDUCED. SUBJECT TO BURNING POST-BREAKAGE. TH: 27MM; W: >23MM; L: >30MM. FILL *25109* OF PIT 25108

13. BAR OR SLAB FRAG. OXIDISED THROUGHOUT. SUBJECT TO BURNING POST-BREAKAGE. TH: 25MM; W: >25MM; L: >42MM. FILL *25138* OF RING GULLY 25137

14. ROD FRAG. OVAL IN SECTION, SLIGHTLY TAPERED. OXIDISED SURFACE, CORE REDUCED TO BLACK. MAX. DIAM: 38-41MM; L: >92MM. FILL *25161* OF GULLY 25160, RING GULLY 25243

15. PYRAMIDAL LOOMWEIGHT OR THATCH-WEIGHT. EXT. SURFACE OXIDISED, CORE REDUCED. TOP OF LARGE WEIGHT, BROKEN AT PERFORATION. PERF. DIAM: 20MM; H: 64MM; W: >45MM; TH.>55MM; WT: 167G. FILL *25112* OF CUT 25106, DITCH 25116

Lelley

16. DAUB. SMALL FRAG. BEARING THREE ROD IMPRESSIONS: 10MM AND 20MM DIAM., OTHER NOT MEASURABLE. L: 26MM; H: 35MM; TH: 27MM. LAYER *35505*, UNDERLYING MED. OVEN

17. DAUB FRAG. BEARING PART OF FLAT OUTER SURFACE FINGER-SMOOTHED AND WITH SINGLE ROD IMPRESSION ON REVERSE, OF 10MM DIAM. L: 60MM; H: 55MM; TH: 50MM. LAYER *35505*, UNDERLYING MED. OVEN

Braemere Hill

BRIQUETAGE CONTAINERS

18. CONTAINER RIM SHERD. FLAT-TOPPED CUT RIM. VESSEL EXT. SMOOTH, INT. ABRADED, ROUGH. FABRIC V1. L: 41MM; H: 23MM; TH: 10.5MM. FILL *4726* OF RECUT 4720, DITCH 4736

19. CONTAINER RIM SHERD. FLAT-TOPPED CUT RIM. BOTH LATERAL SURFACES SMOOTH. FABRIC V1. L: 23.5MM; H: 21MM; TH: 12MM. FILL *4726* OF RECUT 4720, DITCH 4736

20. CONTAINER RIM SHERD. FLAT-TOPPED CUT RIM. THICK-WALLED. VESSEL EXT. SMOOTH, INT. SLIGHTLY ROUGHER. HORIZONTALLY-SCORED LINE 5MM BELOW RIM. FABRIC V1. L: 28MM; H: 22MM; TH: 15MM. FILL *4709* OF CUT 4706, DITCH 4736

21. CONTAINER RIM SHERD. EXTERNALLY-BEVELLED RIM. VESSEL EX. SMOOTH, INT. ABRADED, ROUGH. FABRIC V1. L: 32MM; H: 26.5MM; TH: 11.5MM. FILL *4726* OF RECUT 4720, DITCH 4736

22. Container body sherd. Strip of luting on ext. prob. repair. Vessel ext. smooth, int. abraded, rough. Fabric V1. L: 33mm; H: 37mm; Th: 11mm. Fill *4726* of recut 4720, ditch 4736

23. Container body sherd. Strip of luting on ext. prob. repair, as above. Vessel ext. smooth, int. abraded, rough. Fabric V1. L: 33mm; H: 24mm; Th: 11mm. Fill *4726* of recut 4720, ditch 4736

24. Container body sherd. Large, longitudinally straight in form, showing curvature in vessel height. Vessel ext. smooth, int. abraded, rough. Fabric V1. L: 75mm; H: 53mm; Th: 13mm. Fill *4726* of recut 4720, ditch 4736

Supports and stabilisers

25. ?Spacer-clip. Hand-squeezed frag. bearing flat surface; shows evidence of being squashed and pressed onto another object with flattish surface. Fabric Q1. L: 22mm; W: 18mm; Th: >15mm. Fill *4707* of recut 4720, ditch 4736

26. Poss. spacer-clip. Hand-squeezed frag, similar nature to above, bears two small flat areas. Fabric Q1. L: 22mm; W:22mm; Th: 19.55mm. Fill *4707* of recut 4720, ditch 4736

27. ?Spacer-clip. Hand-formed wedge-shaped frag. One flat side pushed against an object, other near flat with depression in centre ?where pressed. Fabric Q1. L: 26mm; W: 25mm; Th: 13mm. Fill *4726* of recut 4720, ditch 4736

28. ?Pedestal or other support, such as bar. Corner. Obj. has been placed onto slightly rough surface before firing. Under base is reduced to grey, other surfaces oxidised, orange. Small patch of light buff 'salt coloration'. Fabric QV1. H: 43mm; W: 41mm; Th: 38mm. Fill *4726* of recut 4720, ditch 4736

Chuchlands

29. Daub frag. Outer surface finger-smoothed, bearing elongated oval thumb or finger impression. L: 106mm; H: 87mm; Th: 55mm. Upper fill *119516* of pit 119518

30. Cylindrical ?loomweight. Burnt post-breakage. Part of body of large weight; none of perforation survives. Diam: *c.*90mm; H: 64mm; Th: 54mm; Wt: 167g. Fill *119498* of pit 119499

Weeton

31. Pedestal. Complete hand-squeezed pedestal with lumpy undulating surface, evidence of being squashed between palm and fingers. Surface bears patches of whitish 'salt-scale'. Base flat, top concave, to seat base of evaporation container. Fabric QV1. H: 50mm; max. diam: 43mm. Fill *120209* of ditch 120223

Scorborough Hill

Supports and Stabilisers

32. Pedestal. Complete squat pedestal with circular section. Both ends concave. One end has regular concavity with lip, other more uneven. Fabric QV1. H: 40mm; max. diam: 47mm. Fill *12005* of cut 12006, ditch 12003

33. ?Pedestal base frag. Basal angle. Object placed onto slightly rough surface before firing. Is linear indentation under base, ?from twig. Part oxidised, part reduced. Fabric QV1. H: 30mm; W: 37mm; Th: 34mm. Fill *10410* of cut 10407, ditch 12081

34. ?Spacer-clip. Hand-squeezed piece roughly T-shaped in form. Regular curve on one side; more uneven one on other. Fabric Q2. L: 28mm; W: 25mm; Th: 13mm. Fill *10444* of cut 10441, ditch 12081

Structural Briquetage

35. Two joining frags. Undulating outer surface. Salt coloration throughout fabric. Patchy buff to whitish. L: 67mm; H: 50mm; Th: 11mm. Lower fill *10431* of ditch 10430

Gilcross

Briquetage Containers

36. Container body sherd. Straight vessel edge showing curvature in height of sherd. Vessel int. smooth, ext. abraded. L: 41mm; H: 27mm; Th: >8mm. Upper fill *121015* of pit 121012

Structural Briquetage

37. ?Floor frag. Slab-like, flat, slightly worn near surfaces. Patchy whitish 'salt' skin. Mostly oxidised orange, though outer 5mm ranges from buff to light and mid-greys. L: 71mm; W: 47mm; Th: >29mm. Upper fill *121043* of pit 121040

38. ?Floor frag. Slab-like flat, slightly worn near surfaces. Lower surface rougher. Remnants of whitish 'salt' skin. Mostly oxidised orange, though small section of upper surface reduced to mid-grey. L: 62mm; W: 55mm; Th: 25mm. Upper fill *121043* of pit 121040

Metalworking mould fragment

39. ?Non-ferrous metal-working mould frag. Convex. Oxidised ext., patch of pinkish coloration indicating intense heat. Remainder reduced to dark grey. L: 33mm; W: 25mm; Th: 7mm. Upper fill *121043* of pit 121040

possibly narrows to split into two in order to channel the molten metal into the object matrix; alternatively, the narrow section forms part of the object matrix itself. The elongated form of the sprue cup, suggests that it was formed in the same operation as the body of the mould rather than being attached separately. The other pieces include part of an object matrix with a curving or sinuous profile (Fig. 108.2) and a smooth, slightly curved surface, showing no detail (Fig. 108.3). This may be part of an object such as a vessel.

The survival of this small group is unusual. Moulds are very friable objects post-casting and often end up in extremely small fragments. As moulds are broken open at their site of usage they generally do not travel far from the metal-working site. It is likely that they were incorporated in the fill a short time after use. There was a small amount of slag recovered from the site, some ferrous-based and the remainder non-diagnostic. It has been suggested that fired clay moulds are very suitable for use as grog during pottery manufacture (Spratling 1979, 141), which is one reason that they could possibly be removed from the production site, though there is no evidence for pottery production within the finds assemblages.

Energy dispersive X-ray fluorescence provided supporting evidence for one of the fragments (Fig. 108.1) having been part of a non-ferrous metal-working mould (Jones, this volume, page 223). Although the other evidence for metal-working on the site was largely limited to non-diagnostic slags, it seems most likely these two fragments result from metal working at or very near the site itself. Although superficially similar and from the same context, the other pieces investigated (Fig. 108.2 and 3) had no evidence of contact with molten metal but one of them (Fig. 108.3) had a carbonised surface deposit, for which the infrared spectrum suggests a starch-based source. This piece may therefore have had a different function, perhaps involving food preparation.

Burton Constable

A total of 573 fragments of fired clay weighing 4939g were recovered from Burton Constable, from 112 contexts, the overwhelming majority not diagnostic. Six fabric-types were identified in this assemblage, the majority being of fabric Q1.

Fragments of two pyramidal loomweights were recovered from the spread layer at the southern end of the site, contexts **9698**, and **118518** (Fig. 108.4 and 5). Both are well-fired, hard and of fabric Q1. Hard-fired and sandy fabrics, containing stones within the matrix, are common for pyramidal loomweights in the East Riding.

The 426 pieces of fabric-type Q1 constitute 92 per cent by weight and 74 per cent by quantity of the total from the site. Apart from the loomweights, most is likely to represent structural fired clay or daub, which has been fortuitously preserved by burning, either as a result of its function or due to demolition or accidental destruction by fire. Fifty pieces have a part of a smoothed flat surface and two pieces bear an arris. Six fragments have wattle impressions, though in only two cases is there sufficient surviving to measure the round-wood diameters. These parallel impressions of 10 and 15mm on a single piece (Fig. 108.6) are both likely to represent rods, the woven horizontal elements in a wattle panel. One piece from the upper fill of ditch **118938**, in fabric QV1, has a layer of coarse chaff. This is similar in form to the layers of chaff often found in the interior core of the walls of kilns and other structures exposed to high temperature processes. This fragment is however, fully oxidised, which suggests a different type of function.

Of particular interest are a group of forty-four Q1 pieces from the upper fill, **118809**, of the Structure 4 ring gully. It is highly likely that almost all derive from a single structure. What makes them extremely unusual, if not

Code	N	Wt/g	Description	Use
Q1	426	4657	Sandy; occ. small stones up to 3mm and sparse stones up to 6mm, occ. rounded voids and very sparse calcareous (?chalk) inclusions	Loomweights; structural/daub.
Q2	1	4	Silty, inclusion-free; very smooth in texture; hard fired.	All pieces undiagnostic
Q3	1	5	Fine silty; sparse organic grass/chaff inclusions, mod. rounded ?chalk voids and occ. very fine ?hair.	All pieces undiagnostic
V1	13	58	Sandy; abundant fine grass/chaff temper, low density; sparse stones and calcareous ?chalk inclusions less than 2mm.	Structural?
QV1	11	63	Sandy; mod. coarse grass/chaff temper: 2-3mm diam and more than 35mm long, forming mesh-like layers within the clay matrix, occ. small stones up to 3mm and sparse stones to 6mm, occ. rounded voids.	All pieces undiagnostic
QV2	30	104	Sandy; mod. fine grass/chaff temper: 2-3mm, sparse fine ?hair, occ. rounded ?chalk voids; low density.	All pieces undiagnostic
U	91	48	Uncatagorised	
Total	**573**	**4939**		

TABLE 51: FIRED CLAY FABRICS, BURTON CONSTABLE

unique, is that the impressions of the organic framework onto which the clay was daubed indicate that it was manufactured partly of rope, of around 18mm diameter. The twist of the rope strands can be clearly seen in the impressions: one impression is so clear that the individual fibres of the strands are visible (Fig. 108.7 to 10). This use of rope is strange as the manpower needed to produce the rope would make it a more highly prized item than more easily obtained roundwood. It may be that the form of the structure could not be produced using either a wholly wattle roundwood or basketry frame, and that the rope was therefore more suitable. The form of this structure is however, elusive. That pieces of this fired clay structure join and have a relatively large fragment size suggests that they are also within primary deposition, whereas much of the other fired clay is highly fragmented.

Eight pieces possess a flattish surface bearing rows of neat finger-tip indentations, which may have been a decorative, rather than a functional aspect (Fig. 108.11). These may have been part of the structure with the rope impressions, though there are no joins to provide conclusive evidence for this. By contrast, another piece from fill **118809**, bearing a wattle impression of 10mm diameter, is somewhat denser than that with the rope impressions and it is more likely to have derived from a different structure.

Brandywell

Sixteen fragments from Brandywell, ten of which were featureless pieces, collectively weighed 595g. The assemblage was ascribed to five different fabrics. One fragment from primary fill **25136** of ditch **25247** is vitrified with only a small portion retaining the characteristics of fired clay. Another small piece is of a fabric and type often found in kilns: hard, reduced clay bearing long grass or chaff temper in mesh-like layers within the matrix. This type of clay may also occur as part of structures used for other industrial high temperature processes: furnaces, smithing hearths and ovens.

Identifiable objects include two bar or slab fragments, an oval sectioned rod and a pyramidal loomweight. The two bar fragments Fig. 108.12, 13) and the rod are in a very

sandy fabric (Fig. 108.14) containing occasional larger sand grains around 1mm in diameter. Rectangular and square sectioned bars and slabs are relatively common fired clay objects from sites in the late Iron Age. They are commonly interpreted as fire bars, oven slabs or kiln material, and are part of the suite of objects often referred to as 'Belgic bricks'. Fired clay rods are also not uncommon. All three objects are likely to have performed some kind of role involving supporting other objects during processes where heat is involved. These types of objects also appear within briquetage assemblages, although there is no evidence to suggest that they were used as part of the process of saltmaking at this site.

The weight (Fig. 108.15) is of pyramidal form, the most common loomweight type in East Yorkshire from sites of late Iron Age and Roman date. It is, however, a particularly large example and may have been utilised instead as a thatch-weight. It has a coarse sandy fabric bearing frequent grit-sized grains and larger stones up to 4mm in length.

Lelley

A total of 149 fragments of fired clay weighing 935g were recovered from Lelley. Three fabrics were present, the majority of the assemblage assigned to fabrics QC1 or QV1.

Most of the pieces of fired clay are likely to have been structural daub. Of the rest, some probably derived from fired clay objects, although none show any diagnostic features. Fourteen per cent of the fragments bear one flat surface.

The fired clay from fill **35505** contained four fragments of daub with wattle rod impressions. These are likely to derive from a demolished wattle and daub structure, and have been preserved by burning, either accidentally or as part of a demolition process. One piece bears three roundwood rod impressions, the measurable diameters of which are 10mm and 20mm (Fig. 108.16). Another has two impressions, one of 15mm, and the other not measurable, and two have a single impression, of 10mm diameter in one case (Fig. 108.17) while the other is

Code	N	Wt/g	Description	Use
Q1	19	85	Sandy, grainy texture; abundant sand, occ, small stones to 3mm, mod. larger quartz sand grains	?Daub
QC1	81	598	Sandy matrix; mod. calcareous inclusions of rounded chalk fragments to 5mm, chalk likely to have been a natural constituent of clay rather than added temper, v.sparse grass/chaff temper	Daub
QV1	47	248	Sandy; mod. small grass/chaff temper, sparse stones to 12mm diam. may contain v. sparse small chalk fragments to 2mm diam.	?Daub
U	2	4	Pieces too small to be assigned to the other groups	
Total	**149**	**935**		

TABLE 52: FIRED CLAY FABRICS, LELLEY

again not measurable. The fragment with the single wattle diameter of 10mm also bears part of the flat external surface indicating that the thickness of the clay adhering to one side of the wattle panel was 40mm.

None of the impressions present are sails, the uprights around which the rods are woven. The rod diameters are within the range seen at sites where large numbers of wattle impressions have been found, such as Flixborough, where the maximum rod diameter was 20mm (Wastling 2009, 158).

Braemere Hill

The fired clay from Braemere Hill, 226 fragments in total, weighing 746g, was all recovered from the north-western excavation area. The majority of fragments were of briquetage: types consist of containers, stabilisers and a possible support, with container sherds manufactured using an organic-tempered fabric being the most common. Five fabrics were identified, most of the collection being assigned to fabrics V1 or Q1.

Some of the pieces exhibit 'salt coloration', typically certain pinks, lavender, buff and very light greys indicating the presence of salt (Morris 2001, 41 after Matson 1971 and Rye 1981). Pinkish hues can, however, be occasionally observed on other clay artefacts associated with high temperature processes, such as metal working. Contact with brine can also cause a salt 'skin' or 'scale' to form: a thin white- to buff-coloured surface layer, which can appear slip-like.

Briquetage containers (Fig. 108.18-24)

Of the organic-tempered V1 fabric, 114 fragments were deemed to be container sherds. There are none in other fabrics. Although the assemblage of sherds is relatively small, there are enough features present (or absent) to tentatively suggest that the containers may have been half-

cylindrical or semi-conical gutter-shaped forms, possibly bearing flat ends. Of the five rim sherds present, four are flat-topped cut rims, one of which (Fig. 108.20) bears incised scoring below the rim in order to guide the cut marks, whereas the fifth (Fig. 108.21) is externally bevelled.

Most of the larger body sherds show curvature, though in none of the pieces is there enough present to be able to estimate the potential width of the vessel. Twenty-nine sherds exhibit the full thickness of the vessel wall, ranging from 6mm to 15.5mm, though most are over 9mm. None of the sherds bear a basal angle. Two sherds possess a strip of luting across the exterior surface of the vessel (Fig. 108.22, 23) suggesting that they have been used more than once and repaired during the period of usage. The container rims were cut when the clay was in a leather-hard state after which the vessels were pre-fired prior to use at the saltern.

These containers were used during salt-manufacture to heat and concentrate brine, eventually leading to the formation of salt crystals. One interesting feature of the container sherds is that in cases where both the interior and exterior of the vessel wall are present the interior surface is abraded, with flakes of the interior walls missing in most cases. This suggests damage from scraping out of the salt at the end of the manufacturing process. This type of abrasion is a common feature of many of the container sherds examined during the Fenland Management Project in Lincolnshire (Lane and Morris 2001, *passim*) and probably indicates that the salt was not distributed or stored in the manufacturing vessels, allowing them to be re-used.

Briquetage stabilisers

Three squeezed lump-like pieces were present and a single flatter 'clip'. All four were made from fabric Q1. The lump-like squeezed pieces (Fig. 108.25-26) are all

Code	N	Wt/g	Description	Use
Q1	20	44	Sandy, grainy texture; abundant sand, lack of other temper; relatively soft-fired; mid-orange, oxidised throughout	Supports: squeezed pieces, clips (stabilisers)
Q2	7	40	Silty; inclusion-free; v. smooth texture; hard fired; colour from orange to dark grey-brown	All pieces undiagnostic
QV1	3	44	Sandy; mod. well-sorted grass/chaff temper, sparse stones to 12mm; colour from orange to mid grey-brown, occasionally buff, with variations occurring on single pieces.	Briquetage, possibly supports: pedestals or bars
V1	117	573	Fine silty; sparse sand grains, abundant well-sorted grass/chaff temper impressions; temper voids generally less than 10mm. Mostly mid-orange, some pieces with reduced cores; some with occ. patches of pinkish 'salt' coloration or buff to white 'skin' on the surface.	Briquetage containers
U	79	45	Pieces too small to be assigned to the other groups.	
Total	226	746		

TABLE 53: FIRED CLAY FABRICS, BRAEMERE HILL

incomplete though their form and size suggests that they may belong to 'clips': pieces placed between the container rim or upper body as lumps of wet clay, and which were subsequently hardened by the heat of the saltern hearth or oven. The flatter clip would have served the same purpose, but takes a different form (Fig. 108.27) and would have been placed across the top of the rim of the vessels. The choice of clip form used during the process may have been determined by the spacing of the containers. The corner of a single object tentatively identified as a support (Fig. 108.28), was also retrieved.

Discussion

The fired clay assemblage from Braemere Hill consists mainly of briquetage container fragments in a grass or chaff tempered fabric. Most was recovered from fills **4707** and **4709** of ditch, **4736**. A recut produced two further fragments of briquetage container, and sixty container fragments were recovered from fill **4725**, an area of more recent disturbance to the north-eastern part of the ditch. There is no reason to believe that these fragments did not originate within ditch **4736**.

Although the form of container could not conclusively be ascertained, the nature of the rims and the fabric type used bear similarities to the semi-conical gutter-shaped containers of the late Iron Age and early Roman period recovered from sites south of the Humber, in Lincolnshire and Norfolk, for example.

There is a noticeable paucity of briquetage supports within the assemblage and a complete lack of structural briquetage. The portable containers may have been carried some distance from the saltern in order to scrape out the salt and were subsequently broken and discarded. The fact that two sherds bear repairs suggests that they were usually re-used. Although none of the excavated features are likely to have formed part of a saltern complex, the fact that the containers were re-used and the heightened level of charcoal and ash recorded within the ditch fills may suggest that the salt is likely to have been manufactured in the near vicinity.

Incised scoring, as exhibited by some of the examples here (for instance Fig. 108.20), is known from containers of middle Iron Age date in Lincolnshire, mainly in limestone-tempered fabrics, but this type of treatment does not occur on late Iron Age vessels in Lincolnshire (Morris 2001, 325-6). That scoring occurs on vessels here within the late Iron Age may indicate that forms of briquetage within the East Riding of Yorkshire are likely to have as many differences as similarities when compared with other salt manufacturing areas, and to constitute a distinct regional suite of objects and vessels.

Churchlands

Of the eleven fragments, weighing 641g in total, from Churchlands, five bear no diagnostic features. Two fragments are of interest. A large piece of daub, from the upper fill of pit **119518**, bears two parallel roundwood impressions (Fig. 108.29). The upper impression is 2cm in diameter, the lower is not measurable. These impressions show the positions of two horizontal rods, set at slightly different angles within the weave of a wattle panel. The flat outer surface of the daub has been finger-smoothed and also bears an elongated impression of a finger or thumb. On the reverse of the piece the clay has been extruded between the two rods and has sunk down slightly over the top if the lower wattle, enabling the orientation of the piece to be ascertained. The fabric of this piece has a sandy matrix with added fine grass/chaff temper.

The second piece of interest, from the fill of pit **119499**, is part of a cylindrical fired clay object, of around 90mm diameter (Fig. 108.30). This is within the usual diameter range of cylindrical loomweights of Bronze Age date; with the presence of residual Bronze Age pottery in the same pit, this piece lends weight to the possibility of domestic settlement in the vicinity of the site in this period. The object is in a fabric with a sandy matrix containing small stones up to 3mm in length and occasional iron-rich inclusions.

Weeton

The assemblage from Weeton comprises twelve fragments, together weighing 247g, in two different fabrics. Ten of the fragments are undiagnostic. Though small, the assemblage provides further evidence for saltmaking: a complete hand-squeezed pedestal, a flat-surfaced piece of structural briquetage or working-floor fragment, and an undiagnostic piece bearing a patch of pinkish-lavender salt coloration.

The pedestal (Fig. 108.31) is broadly comparable to well-known examples from Iron Age and Roman saltern sites in Lincolnshire: Helpringham Fen (Chowne and Healey 1999 fig. 8.22), Holbeach St Johns (Bell 1999, fig. 42.31-35) and Cowbit (Morris 2001, fig. 21.44-50). However, this example from Weeton and the one from Scorborough Hill (below) are, if not the first, then among the first of this type to be positively identified from East Yorkshire. The upper end of the pedestal is concave in order to seat a container during the evaporation process. The shape of the concavity suggests the basal form of this vessel is likely to have been elongated or cylindrical. The fabric of the pedestal is sandy, bearing sparse fine grass or chaff temper.

The fragment with the flat surface is of compacted hard clay, the surface appearing worn and abraded, and may derive from the clay floor of a saltern oven. Such pieces are relatively common from *in situ* saltern ovens.

Code	N	Wt/g	Description	Use
Q1	12	172	Matrix with abundant sand, occ. grit-sized grains, occ. Stones: 1 to 3mm	?Structural briquetage.
Q2	9	76	Well-sorted, sandy, with lack of other inclusions	Stabilisers.
Q3	1	26		
QV1	44	352	Sandy; abundant fine grass/chaff temper, occ. chalk and other stone to 2mm	Briquetage supports
QV2	5	44	Sandy; abundant fine grass/chaff temper, abundant red ?iron rich grains to 2mm	Not known.
U	11	10	Pieces too small to be assigned to the other groups	
Total	**82**	**680**		

TABLE 54: FIRED CLAY FABRICS: SCORBOROUGH HILL

Scorborough Hill

Eighty-two fragments, weighing 680g in total, were recovered. Most are featureless fragments but five pieces pertain to the manufacture of salt. These briquetage fragments are a stabiliser, two supports and two pieces of possible structural material. The majority of fragments and objects were assigned to Fabrics QV1 or Q1 (Table 54).

The relatively small Scorborough Hill assemblage augments the evidence for salt manufacture along the length of the pipeline. Though none of the excavated features could be identified as part of a saltern complex, saltmaking activity is likely to have been undertaken nearby.

Briquetage pedestals

A complete pedestal takes the form of a near-cylindrical hand squeezed rod, with concave slightly expanded ends (Fig. 108.32). A similar pedestal was recovered at Helpringham Fen in Lincolnshire, where it was referred to as a 'seat' (Chowne and Healey 1999, 17). A second possible support consists of the flared basal angle of a pedestal (Fig. 108.33). The angle at which the base narrows precludes an interpretation of this piece as part of a pyramidal loomweight.

Briquetage stabilisers

A small irregular, roughly T-shaped finger-squeezed spacer-clip (Fig. 108.34) from fill **10444** of pit **12081** is likely to have been placed between briquetage containers in order to stabilise them during the heating process. The smooth regular concavity may have been used to seat the base of an evaporation container.

Structural briquetage

Two joining fragments of possible structural briquetage (Fig. 108.35), also from fill **10444**, bear an uneven outer surface and show salt coloration. These fragments may have been part of a briquetage hearth or oven structure.

Gilcross

In total, thirty-nine fragments of fired clay weighing 731g were recovered from Gilcross. Twelve of these are featureless fragments, twenty-six are briquetage sherds, and a single piece may be a fragment of a metal-working mould. The saltmaking evidence consists of container sherds and possible structural material, adding further evidence of salt manufacture to the corpus of briquetage from the Easington to Ganstead pipeline. In addition, a modicum of evidence for non-ferrous metal working complements the findings of crucible fragments at the site.

Briquetage containers

The twenty-six container sherds were all body sherds and were all in the same fabric: a fine sandy matrix, with abundant grass/chaff temper. The temper was very well sorted and generally under 5mm in length. Occasional pieces showed tiny areas of whitish salt coloration on the surface, particularly remaining in the temper voids. The largest sherd shows enough of the length to indicate that it was not part of a circular-rimmed vessel but appears to derive from a vessel with relatively straight sides (Fig. 108.36). This would tentatively fit with the half-cylindrical or semi-conical gutter-shaped forms suggested at Braemere Hill (above). The wall thickness of these sherds ranged from 5 to 8mm, relatively thin for briquetage containers, though such slight walls are not unknown. The narrowest from Braemere Hill was 6mm and others of comparable dimension are known from Lincolnshire and Norfolk: of the Middle Iron Age container sherds from Langtoft, Lincolnshire, for example, 88.2 per cent were under 7mm thickness (Morris 2001, 368).

Structural Briquetage

The structural briquetage consisted simply of thick slab-like pieces, of variable thickness, bearing a flat, smoothed surface and a rough underside (Fig. 108.37, 38). Eight such pieces were recovered. Four of these had a whitish salt skin on the surface and one also had areas of pinkish-lavender salt coloration. The fabric has a silty matrix with occasional larger sand-sized grains up to 1mm in length and sparse organic inclusions, possibly of grass or chaff.

These pieces are dense and of a similar character to clay domestic hearth bases. They are likely to derive from a saltern oven or hearth floor and have been fired *in situ* during the heating process. In some pieces, only the upper portions seem to have been preserved by firing: these were presumably sufficiently thick to have prevented the base reaching firing temperature, or were simply subjected to lesser heat. One piece (Fig. 108.38) possesses a full thickness of 25mm and has been placed upon a slightly rough, flat surface, possibly the ground, while the clay was plastic. The presence of the 'salt' skin on half of these fragments points to their probable use in saltmaking process, although there is also evidence for non-ferrous metal working from the feature from which they were recovered. The structural briquetage was present in all three fills of pit **121040**, which contained a human burial. The briquetage is likely to be residual material, either from disturbed deposits which have been truncated, or from the contemporary ground-surface at the time the burial occurred.

A probable metal-working mould fragment

A small fragment of possible non-ferrous metal working mould (Fig. 108.39) was also recovered from pit **121040**. This is a small rounded fragment of near identical fabric to that of the mould fragments from Old Ellerby (above): a very sandy fine matrix with extremely well-sorted angular to sub-angular quartz sand grains. There are occasional larger grains and sparse red or brown rounded ferrous-rich pellets, under 1mm diameter. None of the object matrix survived. The pit also produced crucible fragments with high levels of copper on their internal surfaces (Pitman and Doonan, this volume, page 171). A small quantity of slag was not diagnostic of any specific high-temperature process (Mackenzie 2010).

Conclusion

The combined fired clay assemblage from the project is relatively small, but it incorporates evidence for a range of functions: textile-working, non-ferrous metal working, structural fired clay and most importantly, the manufacture of salt. The date range of this material extends from the Bronze Age to the medieval period, though the majority is of Iron Age or early Roman date. With regard to the fabric types represented, there are no inclusions present in any of the fired clay examined that would lead one to surmise that any other than local clays and locally available tempers were used.

Non-ferrous metal-working moulds were recovered from two sites near the opposite ends of the pipeline: Old Ellerby and Gilcross. Unfortunately the form of objects manufactured could not be ascertained. However, the fact that the mould clays on these two sites were near identical is of note.

Briquetage is concentrated in two separate areas along the route. There is a good assemblage from Braemere Hill and a cluster of sites producing small amounts of briquetage towards the Easington end of the pipeline: Weeton, Scorborough Hill and Gilcross.

None of the features at these sites can be conclusively identified as being part of a saltern complex, though the salt is likely to have been manufactured in the near vicinity of each excavation, as briquetage, with the exception of some types of container, is generally considered to not travel far from its place of primary usage. This fired clay assemblage is of some importance in the history of the identification of this functional group in the East Riding of Yorkshire. Until comparatively recently there has appeared to be a relative paucity of saltmaking evidence from the region, considering that the area borders the Humber Estuary and contains the low-lying former wetlands of Holderness. A number of 'salt' place names occur within this area.

Evidence from the East Riding was noticeably absent at the seminal conference on saltmaking held at the University of Essex in 1974 (de Brisay and Evans 1975, *passim*). Reference to the 'salt' place-names and the suggestion that this material should be expected to be found was mooted in 1990 (Didsbury 1990, 95,338) and the previous year a small amount of briquetage had been published from Faxfleet, on the western side of the Wolds (Sitch 1989, 13). This suggested that the salinity was sufficient for salt-production so far west and therefore favourable conditions would also occur further east along the estuary.

In 1995, briquetage was recovered during a watching brief in Preston Road, Hull at the eastern edge of the city, though it was not initially identified as such. When this material was seen, around a year later, it was recognised as the debris from saltmaking activity (Peter Didsbury, pers. comm.). Further briquetage was recovered in small amounts within, as yet unpublished, assemblages, from 2000 onwards, excavated in the vicinity of North Cave, following which the author re-examined some old material from the same area excavated from the mid-1980s to mid-1990s. Saltmaking evidence was indeed present, though misidentified as kiln material and detritus from metal working. Unfortunately, much of this evidence had not come to light prior to the distribution map of salt-producing areas of the later Iron Age presented in the ground-breaking volume covering a millennium of saltmaking in the Fenland, edited by Lane and Morris (2001, Fig. 123). Therefore, the map shows a gap between Lincolnshire and Teesside, giving the impression that the East Riding was not a salt-producing area.

Further briquetage recovered from Easington in the mid-2000s, thought to be only the second instance of briquetage being found within the East Riding (Morris 2011), should now perhaps be considered rather the second group to reach publication. This material in conjunction with that from this project forms a concentration around the Easington area, ranging in date from the late Bronze Age to the early Roman period.

In retrieving evidence for Iron Age or Roman saltmaking from four sites along this narrow strip of land between Easington and Ganstead, the investigations along the pipeline route have given some idea of the density of distribution of saltmaking within the region, and indicated that it may, in fact, have been commonplace. While sites in the East Riding may be harder to detect, because of the sedimentology of much of the area and the potential for alluvial deposits to obscure the evidence, the manufacture of salt may have been of comparable importance and scale to that from the Fenland areas of Eastern England.

This fired clay assemblage provides sufficient evidence for a start-point to the classification of saltmaking evidence in the area and raises the possibility of future standardised typologies. It is hoped that this assemblage, along with others currently in the analysis stage from recently excavated pipelines within East Yorkshire, may augment the evidence listed above and start to redress the imbalance of evidence so that the East Riding of Yorkshire is rightly recognised as an area of salt production.

Analysis of metal-working mould fragments

Jennifer Jones

Four pieces of ceramic (fragments 1a, 1b, 2 and 3) from Old Ellerby, identified as possible metal-working mould fragments (Wastling, above), were examined under x16 magnification for traces of surface residue. No metal-working residue was observed, but a bubbly, black deposit, covering half of the inside surface of fragment 3 was noted.

Energy dispersive X-ray fluorescence (EDXRF) surface analysis of the internal and external surfaces of each of the four fragments was carried out, using an Oxford Instruments ED2000 instrument. Significant peaks in each spectrum were examined. The analyses are qualitative: results should not be compared with quantitative or semi-quantitative analyses.

In addition, a small sample of the black, bubbly material from fragment 3 was detached for examination by scanning electron microscopy (SEM), and by energy dispersive X-ray (EDS) and infrared spectroscopy.

Results

All four samples were found to contain iron alongside a background of earth element traces, as would be expected for ceramic objects. The spectra of all four are visually very similar, but fragments 1a and 1b, the joining sprue cup and neck, show low levels of copper, zinc and lead on the inside surface (Fig. 109), suggesting the mould may have been used to produce a leaded brass object.

A sample of the black deposit on the inside of fragment 3 was mounted for examination and analysis using a Hitachi TM3000 SEM facility. The images show a vesicular, glassy material and EDS analysis found high levels of carbon and oxygen along with calcium and other earth elements, suggesting that the material could be organic. The infrared spectrum of the deposit, measured using a Perkin Elmer UATR Two instrument, was compared against a range of reference spectra. As is often the case with archaeological material, an exact match could not be found, but the sample spectrum shows similarities in the position of the major spectrum peaks to that of a library spectrum for starch. This would be consistent with identification of the black deposit as a carbonised foodstuff.

Conclusion

The four sherds are similar in appearance and produced similar background EDXRF spectra, suggesting they were made from similar fabric, but only fragments 1a and 1b show evidence to support use as a metal-working mould. Fragment 3 has a starch-based carbonised surface deposit, suggesting it is from a pot used for cooking, and is therefore not likely to be part of the same vessel as fragments 1a and 1b.

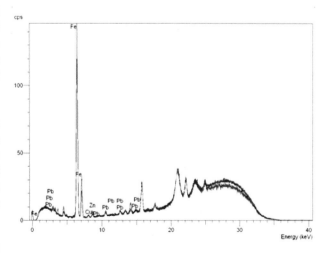

FIG. 109: EDXRF SUPERIMPOSED SPECTRA FROM INSIDE SURFACES OF FRAGMENTS 1A (BLUE) AND 1B (RED), SHOWING DETECTED TRACES OF COPPER, ZINC AND LEAD

Section 4: People, Economy and environment

Human remains

Katie Keefe and Malin Holst

Introduction

Six inhumation burials along with disarticulated remains of a possible seventh were excavated, at five different sites along the pipeline route (Table 55).

Three cremation burials were also located (Table 56), two in simple pits and one, 13013, within the backfill of the enclosure ditch at Out Newton Road. None were urned or accompanied by any grave goods.

Three assemblages of disarticulated human bone from Brandywell were also examined. Fills **25060** and **25062** of ditch **25168** contained a total ten fragments of human bone. The context which contained perinatal skeleton **25067** also produced bone of a slightly older infant or young juvenile. A large fragment of human tibia, broken into four pieces, was recovered from fill **10438** of pit **12081** at Scorborough Hill.

Preservation

The state of preservation of the skeletons was assessed and their completeness expressed as a percentage (Table 55). The quantity of cremated bone recovered from the three cremation burials ranged from 1.9g to 390.5g. It is likely that only a portion of bone was selected from the pyre for burial, but truncation of the burials would also have caused some loss of bone.

The bone from burial **117008** was very well burnt, causing the complete loss of the organic portion and producing a white colour throughout. By contrast, the bone fragments from burial **3237** varied in colour, ranging from white and brown to black. Notably, the identifiable fragments of pelvis and femur tended to be black or brown. Burial **13013** was reasonably well burnt, with occasional blue/grey or black coloration of the internal surfaces of some bones. Dark coloration implies that there was either not enough time, oxygen, fuel or a sufficiently high temperature to complete the cremation process fully. Of particular note is the black coloration on internal surfaces, resulting from the bone being burnt in

Skeleton	Cut	Site	Orientation (head first)	Preservation	% complete
9796	9794	Burton Constable	W-E, supine	Mod.	75%
25183	25184	Brandywell	N-S, on right side	Good	90%
25218	25059	Brandywell	N-S, on right side	Good	75%
25067	25066	Brandywell	Disarticulated	Mod.	20%
26354	26353	Sproatley	Probably N-S	Very poor	1%
35042	35044	Lelley	Possibly W-E	Mod.	15%
121051	121040	Gilcross	SW-NE, Supine	Mod.	25%

TABLE 55: SUMMARY OF ARCHAEOLOGICAL INFORMATION OF INHUMED SKELETONS

Burial	Cut	Bone colour	Preservation	Wt/g
3237	3236	Mostly white externally with black or grey internal surfaces, bones of pelvis black; some long bone fragments brown	Moderate	390.5
117008	117007	White, occasionally blue grey on internal surfaces	Moderate	130.2
13013	13014	White, occasionally blue grey on internal surfaces	Moderate	1.9

TABLE 56: SUMMARY OF CREMATED BONE ASSEMBLAGES

Context	10mm		5mm		2mm		< 2mm		Total wt/g
	Wt/g	%	Wt/g	%	Wt/g	%	Wt/g	%	
3237	76.6	19.6	168.1	43.0	123.7	31.7	22.1	5.7	390.5
117008	13.5	10.4	63.5	48.8	51	39.2	2.2	1.7	130.2
13013	0	0	1.9	100	0	0	0	0	1.9

TABLE 57: CREMATED BONE FRAGMENT SIZE

an oxygen-starved environment (Herrmann 1970). This suggests that bones remained intact during cremation, inhibiting oxygen access to these internal surfaces, fragmenting after burning had taken place. The degree of fragmentation suggests that the bone was disturbed while still hot, although fragmentation could also have been caused by post-depositional disturbance. In the case of burial **3237**, the pyre may have undergone a degree of localised collapse, causing the bones of the pelvis and upper legs to become buried and starved of oxygen.

A high proportion of the bone in each of the three cremation burials (Table 58) could be identified, the majority being either from long bone shafts or from the skull: these included recognisable cranial bones, parts of the mandible and tooth roots, as well as generic vault fragments. Since the cranial vault is very distinctive and easily recognisable, even when severely fragmented, it often forms a large proportion of identified bone fragments in cremated remains (McKinley 1994), but bones representing all parts of the body were found, including the small bones of the fingers, parts of vertebrae, ribs and identifiable bones from the arms and legs. Unspecified long bone fragments, however, formed a significant proportion of the remains.

Assessment of age

Three of the inhumed individuals appeared to be adults. Due to heavy fragmentation and poor survival of certain skeletal elements only a limited number of techniques used to assess age could be employed. Ageing estimates for skeleton **9796** relied solely upon dental attrition and suggested an age between 36 and 45 years. Skeleton **25183** was difficult to age: multiple techniques providing varied ranges, some parts of the skeleton suggesting a younger age, but on balance it is likely to have been a mature adult, aged 46 years or older. Of the two non-adults from Brandywell, the dental development and developmental changes in the axial skeleton of skeleton **25218** suggested a juvenile aged between three and four years, while skeleton **25067** was a perinate. The ageing of this individual relied on the presence of a maxillary deciduous root crown and measurements of long bones which were incomplete, and therefore provided only a minimum age. The disarticulated bone from the same context belonged to an infant or young juvenile, while that recovered from ditch fills **25060** and **25062** were from an adult.

The extremely small quantity and fragment size of the bone recovered from skeleton **26354** from Sproatley meant that it was not possible to estimate its age. Based on long bone measurements, skeleton **35042** from Lelley was aged at least 36 weeks *in utero* and was either a late term foetus or a perinate. Dental attrition and degenerative changes in the hips suggested that skeleton **121051** from Gilcross was aged between 26 and 35 years. The disarticulated bone from Scorborough Hill belonged to an adult.

Because none of the criteria normally used for age determination were represented in any of the cremation burials, age determination was based on less reliable criteria. The bone robusticity and dental development of all burials suggested that each of the three individuals was at least sixteen years old, but may have been considerably older.

Sex determination

It was possible to estimate the sex in all three of the inhumed adults: skeleton **9796** was male, as was the mature adult skeleton **25183**. Skeleton **121051** was a probable female but there was a paucity of sexually dimorphic skeletal elements. None of the cremation burials, or the disarticulated bone assemblages contained any sexually dimorphic skeletal elements.

Non-metric traits

The extreme fragmentation of all of the inhumed skeletons precluded any metrical analysis. Only a very few non-metric traits were observed. Skeleton **9796** exhibited extra bones in the sutures at the back of the skull: an ossicle at lambda; bilateral ossicles at lambdoid. Bennett (1965) has suggested that the formation of ossicles in these sutures may be related to stresses placed on the growing cranium during foetal life and early infancy. There were also small holes at the top of the skull and behind the ear and a small nodule of bone at the base of the skull: bilateral parietal foramen, bilateral mastoid foramen extrasutural, sutural mastoid foramen and a precondylar tubercle. Post-cranial traits included bilateral hypotrochanteric fossa: pronounced muscle development is likely to have been the cause of these depressions at the top of the femur shaft.

Cremation	Skull		Axial		Upper limb		Lower limb		Unid. limb		Total identified		Total unid.	
	Wt/g	%	Wt/g	%	Wt/g	%	Wt/g	%	Wt/g	%	Wt/g	%	Wt/g	%
3237	13.6	3.5	13.5	3.5	3.8	0.7	36.7	9.4	122.2	31.3	189.8	48.6	200.7	51.4
117008	12.1	9.3	5.5	4.2	0	0	0	0	49.4	37.9	67.0	51.5	63.2	48.5
13013	0	0	0	0	0	0	1.9	100	0	0	1.9	100	0	0

TABLE 58: IDENTIFIABLE ELEMENTS IN THE CREMATION BURIALS

Skeleton **25183** also exhibited bilateral parietal foramen, along with small extra hole at the base of the skull and nodules of bone on the internal surface of the mandible: a double anterior condylar canal and a bilateral mandibular torus. Post-cranial traits included variations in the humerus, femur and patella: a septal aperture, bilateral Allen's fossa; hypotrochanteric fossa; third trochanter, a vastus notch, and vastus fossa. There were also variations in the articular surfaces of the lower leg and ankle: bilateral tibial squatting facet, bilateral medial talar facet and bilateral peroneal tubercles.

Pathology

Bilateral periosteal reactions were evident on the tibia and fibula shafts of skeleton **9796**. The bone appeared to be well remodelled and had become reincorporated into the bone cortex, suggesting that the inflammation was no longer active at the time of death. Skeleton **25183** also exhibited bilateral new bone formation along the shafts of his tibiae. On the left tibia, a thick plaque-like deposit was discernable among the striated lamellar bone on the central third of the medial surface of the shaft (Fig 110). The deposit of bone was slightly thicker than the surrounding striated bone, with a smooth surface and an irregular outline. The lesion was sub-circular in shape and a second lesion similar in appearance but smaller in size was located on the distal third of the medial surface of the same bone. It is possible that the thickened deposits of bone were the results of ulcerations of the soft tissue.

The disarticulated tibia shaft from pit **12081** at Scorborough Hill showed evidence of lamellar periosteal reaction on the medial and lateral surfaces of the shaft. Skeleton **9796** had mild new bone formation in the right maxillary antrum indicative of chronic sinusitis.

Actinomycosis

Skeleton **25218** exhibited multiple porotic lesions believed to correspond to the bacterial infection caused by actinomycosis (Fig. 111). This is a rare bacterial infection, affecting humans and cattle. It is most common in individuals between the ages of 15 and 35 years (Aufderheide and Rodríguez-Martín 1998, 194). Infection is usually the result of an injury to the tissues in regions of the body where the bacterium is normally found: the mouth and throat, gastrointestinal tract and the female genital tract (Ortner 2003, 319). The ventral (anterior) surface of the surviving sacral bodies of skeleton **25218** exhibited smooth edged, lytic lesions, with an absence of reactive periosteal bone formation, and exposure of the underlying trabecular bone. These lesions have the general appearance of enlarged vascular foramina. The distribution of lesions in this case is characteristic of gastrointestinal actinomycosis (Ortner and Putschar 1981, 218).

Tuberculosis

Two forms of tuberculosis can be identified in the skeletal record, *Mycobacterium tuberculosis* and *Mycobacterium bovis* (Ortner 2003). Because of the differing modes of infection it may be possible to differentiate between the two strains within skeletal material; the former manifesting in the thoracic spine and ribs, from infection originating in the lungs, and the latter concentrating on the lumbar vertebrae and pelvis, with the infection originating in the stomach and intestines, although these lesions are not mutually exclusive (Knüsel pers. comm. 2007). Gastrointestinal tuberculosis is caused by *Mycobacterium bovis* and is contracted through the intake of meat or milk from infected cattle, thus

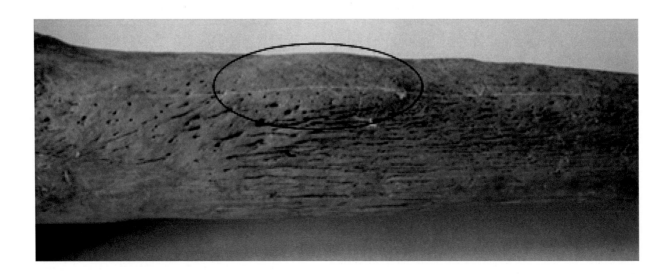

FIG. 110: STRIATED LAMELLAR BONE AND DENSE PLAQUE DEPOSIT (CIRCLED) ON THE LEFT TIBIA OF SKELETON 25183

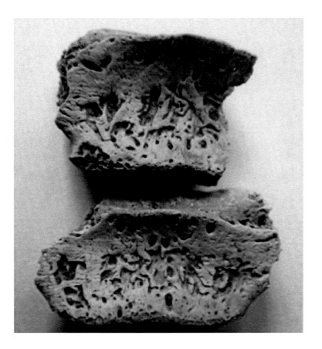

FIG. 111: VASCULAR LESIONS AND DISORGANISED BONE ON THE SACRUM OF SKELETON 25218

FIG. 112: LYTIC DESTRUCTION OF ANTERIOR BODY OF THIRD LUMBAR VERTEBRA OF SKELETON 25183

transmitting the infection to the human gut (Roberts and Cox 2003, 119), though less commonly the disease can be transmitted through droplet infection (Roberts and Manchester 2005, 187). The initial stage is largely asymptomatic (Aufderheide and Rodríguez-Martín 1998, 119), but can be fatal. The secondary stage of the infection can be caused by re-infection with the bacilli, or through bacilli being released from a dormant primary lesion (*ibid.* 120).

Lytic lesions in fifth to eleventh thoracic vertebrae and first to third and fifth lumbar vertebrae (Fig. 112) were evident in the spine of skeleton **25183**, mostly involving the destruction of the superior and inferior surfaces of the anterior vertebral bodies. The margins of the lesions were irregular, and often multi-focal, consisting of smaller lesions which had coalesced. Little to no blastic activity (bone formation) was recorded. The wedge-shaped appearance of the eighth and ninth thoracic vertebrae may have been caused by crush fractures; it is possible that the multiple destructive lytic lesions compromised the structural integrity of the vertebral bodies and caused the bodies to collapse under the weight of the torso.

Skeletal involvement only occurs in a small percentage of individuals with tuberculosis, and archaeological examples are relatively uncommon, making the lesions observed in skeleton **25183** of significant scientific importance. Roberts and Cox (2003, 120) suggest that the crude prevalence rate tuberculosis lesions in Roman Britain was just 0.5% and that most individuals with tuberculosis were from relatively urban settlements. A TB strain did appear to be present in the extracted DNA

from Skeleton **25183**, but the DNA was of a very poor quality and further analysis was thought unlikely to provide a definitive confirmation of the *Mycobacterium tuberculosis* complex (Abi Bouwman and Charlotte Roberts, pers. comm, October 2010).

Possible brucellosis

Possible evidence for infection was observed in the left pelvis of skeleton **9796**. A large lytic lesion, measuring 36.1mm (superiorly/inferiorly) by 11.6mm (anteriorly/posteriorly) and up to 7.0mm deep, with an irregularly undulating base and sides (Fig. 113) appeared to have eroded the superior margin of the acetabulum of the left hip. Surrounding the lesion was an area of disorganised new bone, suggesting that the lesion was both proliferative and destructive. The right hip was severely damaged *post mortem* and it was not possible to ascertain whether the lesions were bilateral; however, a fragment of anterior inferior iliac spine exhibited similar disorganised new bone formation and may suggest that both hips were involved. Brucellosis is usually transmitted through the ingestion of infected milk, milk products or meat. Although it rarely affects the skeleton, a Roman skeleton from York had a similar lesion (Holst 2010).

Miscellaneous Infection

All four individuals with observable eye orbits, the adult skeletons **9796**, **25183** and **121051** and the juvenile skeleton **25218** showed lesions of *cribra orbitalia*. Skeletons **9796** (Fig. 114) and **121051** both exhibited mild vascular impressions in the orbit roofs, while the two

FIG. 113: POSSIBLE BRUCELLOSIS LESION ON THE LEFT HIP OF
SKELETON 9796

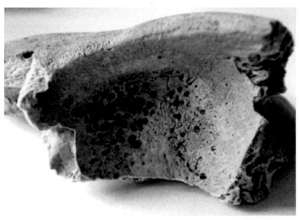

FIG. 114: *CRIBRA ORBITALIA* LESIONS IN ORBIT, SK 9796

individuals from Brandywell expressed small pinpoint and larger coalesced porotic lesions. Roberts and Cox (2003, 141) suggest that a crude prevalence rate of *cribra orbitalia* of 19 per cent has been observed in the Iron Age and 9.64 per cent in the Roman period in Britain.

Skeleton **25183** showed evidence for degenerative joint disease (DJD) in the left hip, with mild osteophyte formation and porosity of the joint surfaces of the acetabulum and femoral head. Roberts and Cox (2003) suggest a crude prevalence rate of 0.3 per cent for hips affected by DJD in Roman Britain, with males three times more likely to be affected than females. DJD was also observed in the left elbow on the superior articular surface of the ulna of skeleton **9796**. The young middle adult female from Gilcross also exhibited bilateral, mild porotic lesions on the tempero-mandibular joint of her lower jaw. Two fragments of bone from the disarticulated bone assemblage from context **25062** also showed evidence for DJD: a first sacral vertebra and a lumbar vertebral body fragment had marginal osteophyte formation.

Skeleton **25183** has a probable *Calcaneus secundarius* lesion: a roughened and irregular crescent shape on the anterior talar facet of the right calcaneus. *Calcaneus secundarius* is an accessory bone, formed by a secondary centre of ossification connected to the rest of the calcaneus in life by cartilage (Mann and Murphy 1990, 130). Although the small accessory bone is rarely recovered archaeologically, the notch left on the calcaneus is distinct, with a roughened porotic appearance (*ibid.*). According to Mann and Murphy (1990), such lesions are not uncommon, occurring in between 1.4 and 6.0 per cent of all populations. The same individual also probably had *hallux valgus* in both first metatarsals, where the big toe deviates away from the midline resulting in the formation of bunions, which can become inflamed. This condition can produce lytic lesions very similar in appearance and location to those caused by gout (Mays 2005). In this case, *hallux valgus* is likely to be congenital (*ibid.*).

Other pathological lesions noted included mild inflammatory lesions on the shins of the male adults

from Burton Constable and Brandywell, and in the disarticulated adult tibia from Scorborough Hill. Skeleton **9696** had suffered from chronic sinusitis. Mild degenerative disease was observed in at least one joint of the adults from Burton Constable, Brandywell and Gilcross, as well as the disarticulated remains from Brandywell.

Trauma

The disarticulated adult fibula from context **25060** showed evidence for a well-healed fracture of the shaft of the bone. It is likely that this was caused by direct trauma to the bone, producing a transverse fracture (Dandy and Edwards 1998, 260). Usually, no immobilisation is required for isolated fibula fractures (*ibid.*).

Dental health

Teeth and jaws were examined macroscopically for evidence of pathological changes. Skeletons **9796**, **25183**, **25218** and **121051**, all had partial or complete dentitions available for examination. Prevalence rates for individuals have been calculated as a percentage of tooth positions affected, where appropriate (e.g. AMTL, abscesses), and as a percentage of teeth affected (e.g. caries, calculus). In total 73 permanent teeth were present and seven deciduous (milk) teeth in skeleton **25218**. A total of 84 adult tooth positions and seven non-adult tooth positions were present. Two permanent teeth (2.4%) had been lost *post mortem*.

Two individuals had suffered from *ante mortem* tooth loss (AMTL): a total of nine teeth (10.7%). Possible causes include dental caries, abscesses, alveolar resorption and perhaps manual extraction. The greater degree of AMTL observed in skeleton **9796** may be related to his advanced age. Skeleton **25218** had two small carious lesions on the occlusal surface of the deciduous first molars (28.6% of its observable teeth). Skeleton **121051** exhibited a large carious lesion on the lingual surface of the root of her left third molar (3.6% of her observable teeth). Overall, 2.5 per cent of teeth were affected by caries.

All of the individuals with observable dentitions exhibited some degree of calculus on their teeth. Skeleton **9796** from Burton Constable exhibited only slight deposits in the interstitial spaces between six of his sixteen observable teeth. The mature adult male from Brandywell, **25183**, exhibited flecks to slight deposits in the interstitial spaces between all of his thirty-one observable teeth and the juvenile from the same site, **25218**, exhibited only slight deposits on the buccal surface of a single maxillary molar (1/7 teeth available for observation). Skeleton **121051** from Gilcross had moderate to heavy deposits on all of her observable teeth, affecting the buccal and lingual surfaces and the spaces between her teeth. Overall, 80% of all teeth recovered exhibited calculus deposits. Only one individual, **25183**, exhibited evidence of enamel hypoplasia: faint hypoplastic lines on many of the teeth in his anterior dentition (10/31, 32.3% of his observable teeth, 12.5% of all teeth).

Dental health appeared to be generally good in those teeth available for examination from both Burton Constable and Brandywell. However, Skeleton **121051** exhibited surprisingly poor dental health, with advanced deposits of calculus observed, evidence of *ante mortem* tooth loss and caries, despite being relatively young. It is possible that her poor state of dental health may have been the result of a particularly rich diet, or alternatively low levels of oral hygiene. Skeleton **25218** from Brandywell exhibited two lesions on two of its deciduous teeth. Deposits of mineralised plaque were noted on the majority of teeth, suggesting perhaps that overall dental hygiene was poor.

Animal bone

Jennifer Wood

Introduction

A total of 14,940 (101,472g) fragments of animal bone were recovered by hand with a further 2194 (528g) fragments from sieved environmental samples. Most of the excavation sites produced only limited quantities, and only the assemblages from Burton Constable, Brandywell, Lelley, Scorborough Hill and Out Newton Road were judged to warrant further analysis. Bone from unphased, modern, post-medieval and topsoil contexts have been excluded from this analysis.

Methodology

The recovered bone from the whole pipeline route has been fully recorded into a database, included in the project archive. Bone was identified with access to a reference collection and published guides. Remains were counted and weighed, and where possible identified to species, element, side and zone (Serjeantson 1996). Fusion data, butchery marks (Binford 1981), gnawing, burning and pathological changes were noted when present. Ribs and vertebrae were only recorded to species when they were substantially complete and could accurately be identified. Undiagnostic bones were recorded as micro (rodent size), small (rabbit size), medium (sheep size) or large (cattle size). Where possible, the separation of sheep and goat bones was carried out using the criteria of Boessneck (1969) and Prummel and Frisch (1986) comparison with reference material, but is otherwise recorded as sheep/goat.

The condition of the bone was graded using Lyman's (1996) criteria. However, there was little discernable pattern of variation, either between sites or between phases, the hand-collected assemblages generally averaging 3, while the condition of the sieve-collected material tended to be poorer, averaging 4. Quantification of species was carried out using the total fragment count of bone and teeth, calculated for each taxon. Where fresh breaks were noted, fragments were refitted and counted as one. Tooth eruption and wear stages were measured using a combination of Halstead (1985), Grant (1982) and Levine (1982), and fusion data was analysed according to Silver (1969). Measurements of adult, that is fully fused, bones were taken according to the methods of von den Driesch (1976).

Burton Constable

A total of 4343 (30,476g) fragments were recovered by hand and a further 487 (81g) from sieved environmental samples. For the purposes of analysis, features have been grouped into four broad stratigraphic phases:

A: Contexts pre-dating the ring gullies.

B: Iron Age ring gullies.

C: Late Roman enclosures.

D: Realignment of Roman ditches.

Pathology

Four fragments display evidence of pathological change. Two cattle first phalanges, from cuts **118609** and **118462** of the Structure 5 ring gully, have osteophytic lipping on the margins of the proximal articulation. A fragment of equid tibia recovered from ditch **118927** has heavily marked muscle attachments on the posterior shaft and a fragment of cattle innominate recovered from ditch **118958** displays evidence of polishing on the acetabular surface. These changes can be attributed to wear and tear and stress responses in reaction to pressure on the joints and ligaments; such as would occur in animals utilised for traction.

Butchery

Fifty fragments show evidence of butchery. The majority of the butchery marks are knife cuts and chop marks consistent with disarticulation and jointing of the carcase. The various fills of the large curvilinear gully of Structure 6, feature **118986**, produced over one third of the butchered remains from the site, including a sheep horncore chopped through the base and the tip, presumably to retrieve the horn for working.

Worked bone

Worked fragments of bone include two cattle metatarsals, one from pit **118198**, with a possible drilled hole through the proximal articulation and the other, from cut **118364** of the Structure 5 ring gully that definitely has had a hole drilled in the same place. A hole through another long bone articulation fragment from cut **118367** of Structure 5 may have also been deliberately drilled. A red deer antler from cut **118529** of the Structure 6 gully has been sawn through both ends and hollowed through the centre. An equid metapodial posterior shaft (SF 1210) from ditch **118954** has been sawn through the proximal and distal ends, has holes drilled though the shaft at each end and has a slightly polished finish. Ditch **118977** produced a fragment of worked bone (SF 1207, Fig. 90.2) which tapers at both ends to form a double ended point, though both ends are broken off.

Burning

Of the total of 122 fragments of hand collected burnt bone and 118 sieve-collected fragments, twenty three per cent were recovered from the western most cut, **9842**, through the Structure 5 ring gully. The burnt bone probably represents hearth sweeping and incidental burning events.

Gnawing

Fifty fragments of gnawed bone represent approximately one per cent of the overall assemblage. This low proportion suggests that the bone was, in general, rapidly buried, reducing the access of scavengers.

Species representation

The identified taxa from the assemblage are summarised in Tables 59 and 60.

Sheep/goat

Sheep/goat remains are the most abundantly represented species group within the assemblage (Table 60), with sheep being positively identified, but with no evidence specifically for goat. Tooth wear for the Iron Age settlement phase shows a distinct peak at 3 to 5 years of age, with a slightly smaller peak at 20 to 34 months. Only two mandibles were recovered from contexts relating to the late Roman enclosures, both indicating slaughter at an age associated with meat production. Epiphyseal

Taxon	Phase A	B	C	D	Total
Equid (Horse Family)	2	20	7	8	37
Cattle	8	180 *(1)*	79	73	340 *(1)*
Sheep/goat	4	329	25	106	464
Sheep		9	3	2	14
Pig	2	92	10	12	116
Dog	2	2	3		7
Red Deer *(Cervus elaphus)*		1			1
Goose *(Anser sp.)*				1	1
Domestic Fowl *(Gallus sp.)*			1		1
Rodent	*(6)*	*(1)*			*(7)*
Passeriform (song bird family)		19			19
Large mammal	30	467 *(6)*	184	123	804 *(6)*
Medium mammal	18 *(1)*	585 *(8)*	45 *(3)*	151	799 *(12)*
Small mammal		2			2
Micro mammal	*(16)*	*(6)*	*(2)*		*(24)*
Unidentified	42 *(90)*	1079 *(307)*	400 *(40)*	217	1738 *(437)*
Total	**108 *(113)***	**2785 *(329)***	**757 *(45)***	**693**	**4343 *(487)***

TABLE 59: IDENTIFIED TAXA, HAND- (AND SIEVE-) COLLECTED ANIMAL BONE, BY PHASE, BURTON CONSTABLE

Taxon	A	B	C	D
Horse family	1	1	1	1
Cattle		1	5	5	4
Sheep/goat	2	12	3	6
Pig		1	3	1	2

TABLE 60: MINIMUM NUMBER OF INDIVIDUALS (MNI), BY PHASE, BURTON CONSTABLE

fusion ageing generally reproduces the patterns shown by the tooth wear scores, with a majority of individuals being slaughtered when skeletally mature, of an age where several fleeces would have been produced.

High fragmentation meant that opportunities to calculate withers height measurements were limited, but those that were possible were within a range of 0.51m to 0.63m, with no noticeable variation between phases. This lack of variation suggests that there was no significant stock improvement or variation in breeds during the occupation of the site. Both meat-bearing bones and those normally discarded are well represented within each phase, suggesting that both food waste and butchery discard are present. Again, there is little variation in this pattern over time

Cattle

Cattle are the next most abundant species. The tooth wear scores for cattle show a certain amount of variation between phases. The Iron Age settlement contexts have a double peak, at 18 to 30 months and at old adult age, while there is a greater emphasis on older animals from the late Roman enclosures. This may indicate an enhanced importance for milk production and traction, as against meat production, in the later phases.

Opportunities for both epiphyseal fusion and withers height calculations for cattle are generally more limited than for sheep/goat, as the bones are usually subject to greater amounts of processing during butchery, but the epiphyseal fusion data for cattle indicate a similar pattern to the tooth wear scores, although with more of an emphasis on adult remains. Only three withers height estimations were possible, all from Iron Age settlement contexts, with one individual at 1.0m and two at 1.12m.

Pig

Though consistently present, pigs did not contribute to the site economy to the same extent as cattle and sheep/goat. Tooth wear age scores, only available for the Iron Age settlement contexts, show one immature, three sub-adult and three adult individuals, with no very old animals. The epiphyseal fusion data provides a slightly different pattern, suggesting that none of the scoreable animals within the assemblage were above the age of

2½ years. Taken together, the two methods indicate that most of the pigs were slaughtered as soon as sufficiently fattened, with some animals being kept into adulthood for breeding. Skeletal element analysis again indicates that meat-bearing bones and butchery discard are both present suggesting that the carcase was processed and utilised on site. A predominance of meat-bearing bones from the Iron Age settlement contexts may, however, indicate that consumption rather than processing predominated during this phase of use.

Equid (horse family)

As with pigs, equid remains were regularly present within the animal bone assemblages for most phases of activity on site, though not in large numbers. Ageing data is limited to three teeth, all from Iron Age contexts, which provide scores of 3 to 6½ years, 7 to 9½ years and 11 to 15 years of age. Butchery evidence was noted on two radius fragments, from pit **118523**, and from cut **118803** of the Structure 5 ring gully. It is not uncommon for horse carcases to be processed for meat and bone after the animal is found to be no longer useful.

Other species

As well as the small number of dog bones recovered, the presence of carnivore gnawing on bones of other species suggests dogs were present throughout. Single fragments of goose and domestic fowl were recovered from ditches **118958** and **118917** respectively. A mostly complete skeleton of a small song bird from ring gully **118041** is thought unlikely to have been caught for food and probably represents a natural death.

A single fragment of worked red deer *(Cervus elaphus)* antler was recovered from ditch **118529**. As deer antler is shed seasonally and is regularly utilised for working, this may have been imported to the site rather than indicating the local presence of red deer.

Rodent and rodent-sized remains were recovered from a number of environmental samples. Rodents are often commensal animals attracted to refuse from settlement, but their presence probably has no other cultural significance.

Discussion

Analysis of the animal bone suggests that both breeding and utilising animals was occurring at Burton Constable. The underlying economy in all phases was based upon sheep/goat and cattle, the contribution of cattle to the site diet probably more important because of the higher meat yield per carcase. Husbandry practices were based on a mixed economy, balancing the production of meat while maximising secondary products such as wool, milk and traction. Numerically, cattle remains slightly predominate in the late Roman enclosure contexts. This may be seen as a move from traditional Iron Age farming practices: it is thought that a higher demand for grain in the Roman period increased the need for cattle to provide traction and manure (Grant 1989:138). The change in the pattern of age distribution of cattle, if not merely random, would support this theory.

Pigs made a smaller contribution to the diet and may have been kept in smaller numbers, foraging in the remaining woodland while prime grazing was utilised for cattle and sheep. The diet economy also suggests occasional consumption of goose and domestic fowl. Generally, there is no evidence to suggest high-status consumption.

Brandywell

A total of 1216 (8184g) fragments of bone were recovered by hand and further 295 (34g) from sieved environmental samples. The archaeological activity on site has been attributed to three phases:

1: Iron Age ring gullies

2: Late first- to second-century radiating field system ditches.

3: Second-century boundary and enclosure ditches

Fourteen fragments (36g) of burnt bone from the hand collected assemblage, and a further twenty-five fragments (2g) from the sieved remains, were fairly evenly distributed between features and phases.

Pathology

Evidence of macro-porosity and slight proliferation of osteophytic growth around the margin of the proximal articulation on a fragment of equid metatarsal, from ditch **25043**, may have been caused by infection or trauma to the joint.

Butchery

Seven fragments, all recovered from Phase 1 contexts, show evidence of butchery. With the exception of two fragments of cattle horncore with chop marks consistent with horn removal, this takes the form of cut marks from disarticulation of the carcase.

Gnawing

Gnawing was noted on seven fragments spanning all three phases. This low occurrence, approximately 0.5 per cent of the overall assemblage, suggests that most of the bone was rapidly buried, reducing access for scavengers.

Species representation

The identified taxa from the assemblage are summarised in Tables 61 and 62.

Sheep/goat

The MNI calculations show an emphasis on utilisation of sheep/goat in the assemblages from each phase, in comparison with cattle and pig. Tooth wear and epiphyseal fusion data are both limited, but taken together are consistent with slaughter of young animals for meat and retention of older individuals for wool production. Two innominates and a humerus from animals aged of less than 10 months, two bones from an infant lamb and a tibia from an animal aged less than 1-2 years, all from Phase 2, indicate that lambing was taking place.

Cattle

Cattle are the second most abundant species identified within the assemblage. As with sheep/goat, tooth wear score data for cattle is fairly limited and the epiphyseal fusion data provides little further information. The majority of the remains are from skeletally mature animals, over four years old. Bones from younger animals include a tibia from Phase 1 from an animal aged less than 2 years, and from Phase 2: a second phalanx and humerus from animals aged below 13 to 18 months and a metatarsal from an animal aged below 2 to 3 years. In addition, pit **25083** contained a partially complete cattle skeleton from an animal aged less than 7 months. The presence of these post-cranial remains from younger animals suggests a

Taxon	Phase 1	2	3	Total
Horse family	3	13	1	17
Cattle	42 (1)	39	29	110 (1)
Sheep/goat	73	41	12	126
Sheep	2	4		6
Pig	22 (2)	6	4	32 (2)
Dog	1			1
Bird		1		1
Large mammal	39 (2)	74	40	153 (2)
Medium mammal	69 (3)	47	27 (7)	143 (10)
Unidentified	279 (15)	129	148 (265)	556 (280)
Total	**530 (23)**	**354**	**261 (272)**	**1145 (295)**

TABLE 61: IDENTIFIED TAXA, HAND- (AND SIEVE-) COLLECTED ANIMAL BONE, BY PHASE, BRANDYWELL

Phase	1	2	3
Horse family	1	2	0
Cattle	2	2	2
Sheep/goat	7	5	4
Pig	2	2	2

TABLE 62: MINIMUM NUMBER OF INDIVIDUALS (MNI), BRANDYWELL

dairy based economy, with a predominance of adult animals retained for milk production and breeding, and a cull of excess male calves.

Pig

The MNI calculations suggest that pigs may have been present in similar numbers to cattle, although the possible sources of bias and small assemblage sizes preclude a firm conclusion. Where possible to assess epiphyseal fusing, most appear to be from young animals aged below 1 to 2 years, although a femur from an animal aged over 3½ years is present in the Phase 2 assemblage. Two mandibles of sub-adult animals from Phases 1 and 3 provide the only tooth-wear ageing data.

Other species

Fourteen fragments of equid remains were recovered. A single tooth from 2 ditch **25207** was from an animal aged 7-9½ years of age. Only a single fragment of dog bone was recovered, from curvilinear gully **25113**, but carnivore gnawing is evident in all phases and it is likely that dogs were consistently present.

Discussion

The assemblage, although too small to provide significant data on age at death profiles, provides hints as to animal utilisation and husbandry practices. The underlying economy supplying the site was predominantly based on sheep/goat, with cattle and pig also contributing to the site diet. Animal husbandry practices were based upon a mixed economy, balancing the production of meat while maximising secondary products: wool, milk and traction. Skeletal elements associated with both butchery and domestic food waste are present. Horn core removal cut marks, noted from Phase 1, provide evidence of small-scale craft working.

Lelley

A total of 1250 (9058g) fragments of bone were recovered by hand, with a further sixty-one (34g) from sieved environmental samples.

The archaeological activity on site is attributed to the following phases:

1. Late Iron Age settlement
2. Eleventh-century enclosure system
3. Twelfth- to early thirteenth-century enclosures
4. Mid-thirteenth-century field boundaries
5. Early fourteenth-century field systems and pits

Identified taxa from the assemblage are summarised in Tables 63 and 64.

Butchery

Sixteen fragments of bone show evidence of butchery, consistent in each case with disarticulation and jointing of the carcase. The medieval phases of activity show an increase in chop marks, suggesting that the use of cleavers had become routine.

Burning

Thirty-seven burnt fragments were recovered by hand collection and a further seven from the sieved samples. Sixty percent of the remains are from ring gullies **35288**, **35367** and **35367**. These fragments probably represent hearth sweeping or incidental burning.

Gnawing

Gnawing was noted on twenty-four fragments of animal bone, from all phases. This low proportion of the overall assemblage suggests that the bulk of the bone was rapidly buried.

Sheep/goat

The MNI calculations suggest that, in most phases, sheep/goat and cattle were represented in fairly equal numbers. Ageing data is limited, with only six mandibles spread across the five phases. Where recording of epiphyseal fusion is possible, most were skeletally mature, greater than 3 to 5 years old. Exceptions include a tibia from animal aged below 1 year in Phase 2, and an axis from an animal aged under 4 years age in Phase 5.

Cattle

MNI calculations indicate cattle numbers roughly equal to sheep/goat. Tooth wear data is fairly limited: an old adult mandible was recovered from Phase 2, a mandible from an animal aged 30 to 36 months from Phase 4 and two mandibles from animals aged 30 to 36 months from Phase 5. Where possible to score the epiphyseal fusion, most were from skeletally mature animals, more than 4 years old. Bones from younger animals included a metatarsal from Phase 1 and a metacarpal from Phase 2 both from animals under two years of age; and a femur from an animal aged below 3 years, recovered from Phase 5. These animals were slaughtered around prime meat age, of 30 to 36 months, but otherwise there is a predominance of adult animals, retained for milk production, traction and breeding.

Pig

Pigs were present on site in small numbers in each phase. Ageing data was limited to a mandible of a sub-adult animal from Phase 1 and a fused tibia of an animal aged over 2 years from Phase 4.

Taxon	Phase 1	2	3	4	5	Total
Horse family	1	2	1	4	10	18
Cattle	14	17	13	28	22	94
Sheep/goat	11 *(2)*	13	16	28	45	113 *(2)*
Sheep				1	3	4
Pig	5	1	1	5	5	17
Dog *(Canis* sp.*)*				2	1	3
Cat *(Felis* sp.*)*				5	2	7
Goose *(Anser* sp.*)*			1	1	1	3
Domestic fowl *(Gallus* sp.*)*				1		1
Crow *(Corvus* sp.*)*				1		1
Bird				9	1	10
Hare *(Lepus lepus)*			1			1
Rabbit *(Oryctolagus cuniculus)*					1	1
Brown rat *(Rattus norvegicus)*			3			3
Large mammal	31 *(3)*	31	35	79	44	220 *(3)*
Medium mammal	14 *(7)*	26	21	29	22	112 *(7)*
Small mammal		1		1		2
Micro mammal			3			3
Unidentified	120 *(57)*	47	99	291	80	637 *(57)*
Total	**196 *(69)***	**138**	**194**	**485**	**237**	**1250 *(69)***

TABLE 63: IDENTIFIED TAXA, HAND- (AND SIEVE-) COLLECTED ANIMAL BONE, BY PHASE, LELLEY

Phase	1	2	3	4	5
Horse family	1	1	1	1	1
Cattle	1	2	2	2	2
Sheep/goat	2	2	2	2	2
Pig	1	1	1	1	1

TABLE 64: MINIMUM NUMBER OF INDIVIDUALS (MNI), LELLEY

Taxon	Feature group A	B	C	D	Total
Equid	6	17		1	24
Cattle	20	35	6	3	64
Sheep/goat	24	60	36	2	122
Sheep			2		2
Pig	3	6			9
Dog		1			1
Large mammal	29	73	13	6	121
Medium mammal	47	113	22	1	183
Unidentified	17	84	37		138
Total	**146**	**389**	**116**	**13**	**664**

TABLE 65: IDENTIFIED TAXA, HAND-COLLECTED ASSEMBLAGE, BY FEATURE GROUP, SCORBOROUGH HILL

Equid

Eighteen fragments of equid were recovered, with small numbers in all phases. Two teeth, from Phase 4 and from Phase 5, both derive from animals aged 4-6½ years. The majority of the post-cranial remains are from skeletally mature individuals, over 3½ years old, but an unfused humerus from an animal aged under 3 years was recovered from Phase 2. As equids were commonly utilised for traction and riding, most were generally retained until old age and slaughtered and processed when no longer useful. The younger animals may be natural deaths.

Other animals

Three fragments of dog bone, from Phases 4 and 5, were recovered, but there is evidence of carnivore gnawing in all phases of activity. Seven fragments of cat bone were recovered from ditch **35444** and pit **35066**. The remains from ditch **35444** probably come from a single individual, likely to have been around 9 to 10 months old at the time of death (Habermehl, 1975:177).

Isolated fragments of goose were recovered from Phase 3, 4 and 5, and domestic fowl from Phase 4. A fragment of crow *(Corvus* sp.*)* from Phase 4 is likely to have been a wild bird, present as a scavenger, although crows are edible. Wild species included hare *(Lepus lepus)* and brown rat *(Rattus norvegicus)* from Phase 3, and rabbit *(Oryctolagus cuniculus)*, from Phase 5. Hare and rabbit would have been hunted species occasionally supplementing the diet of the site. The identification of the rat species was based largely on its size; it is unlikely to have been misidentified unless it was an unusually large black rat. Unlike black rat, the brown rat is a burrowing species and its occurrence here within a medieval context is almost certainly intrusive, as it is generally not thought to have first arrived in Britain until much later.

Discussion

In general, skeletal elements are a mixture of remains commonly associated with both butchery and domestic food waste and most likely represent general domestic activity. The Iron Age contexts show a slight emphasis on sheep/goat, whereas the medieval phases suggest a more mixed economy with cattle and sheep/goat being present in fairly equal numbers. However, cattle would have contributed more to the diet as a result of their much larger carcase size. Pig, goose, domestic fowl and occasionally hare and rabbit would have also contributed to the medieval diet. Animal husbandry practices would have balanced the production of meat with the maximisation of secondary products such as wool, milk and traction.

Scorborough Hill

A total of 664 refitted fragments of bone, weighing 6639g, were recovered from four feature groups:

A: Ditches pre-dating pit **12081**

B: Pit **12081**

C: Ditch **12003**

D: Ditches post-dating pit **12081**

The assemblages from each group are summarised in Table 65. The total included 136 fragments (196g) of burnt bone, of which pit **12081** accounted for 96 fragments, 72 per cent of the total. Most appear to be sheep/goat and medium mammal-sized. The burnt bones were recovered from a variety of contexts and therefore do not represent a single event; a series of cooking events are more likely or the disposal by burning of the remains from feasting or frequent hearth clearings.

Butchery

Nine fragments of bone, from pit **12081**, together with a single piece from ditch **10430**, have knife cuts consistent with disarticulation and jointing of the carcase. In addition, a cattle mandible from ditch **12003** displays a chop mark.

Gnawing

Thirteen fragments of bone have signs of carnivore gnawing, nine of them from pit **12081**.

Sheep/goat

Sheep/goat remains are the most abundant species group within the assemblage, roughly twice as numerous as cattle. Two metapodials from ditch **12003** can be identified as from sheep. A single sheep/goat metatarsal from ditch **12003** provides a withers height estimation of 0.60m. Tooth wear data is limited to two mandibles from animals aged 20 to 34 months from pit **12081**. Epiphyseal fusion, where possible to observe, indicates skeletally mature animals, over 3½ years old, with the exception of a tibia from an animal under one year of age, and two metapodials and a tibia from animals aged under 2 years. This limited ageing evidence is consistent with a mixture of both meat and wool production.

Cattle

Tooth wear data for cattle is limited to an old adult mandible from ditch **12081** and a mandible from a senile animal from ditch **12003**. Epiphyseal fusion data indicates that the majority of remains are from skeletally mature animals, over 4 years old. Exceptions include a metatarsal from an animal aged under 2 years and a femur from an animal less than 3 years of age, both from pit **12081**. Measurements of a single metacarpal recovered from recovered from pit **12081** provided a withers height estimation of 1.10m.

Other species

Pig remains are very limited within the assemblage but were present in pit **12081**, and in ditch **10430** truncated by pit **12081**. Twenty-four fragments of equid, mostly loose teeth, were recovered, seventeen of which are from pit **12081**. Six upper molars provide ageing data: one from an animal 8½ to 11½ years old, three from an animal aged 7 to 9½ years, and one each from animals 2½ to 5 years and 3 to 6½ years old. Post cranial remains, where possible to assess, are from animals at least 3½ years old.

Discussion

Skeletal elements show a general bias towards those associated with butchery discard. The series of deposits from pit **12081** containing burnt sheep/goat and medium mammal remains, possibly representing successive hearth clearing events or small feasting events, are worthy of note. Ageing data from the assemblage suggest that some sheep/goats were slaughtered at prime meat age whereas others were retained breeding and the production of wool. Cattle ageing data is more limited but is consistent with mixed husbandry practices, producing meat and milk. Pigs would have been utilised to supplement the diet, while equids and dogs, the latter represented by a single tooth from pit **12081**, would have been present as working animals.

Out Newton Road

A total of 1639 (10,153g) fragments of bone were recovered. Contexts have been divided into two phases:

1: The early fills of the late Iron Age enclosure ditch and the infilling of pit **13020**.

2: The later infilling of enclosure ditch in the early Roman period.

The identified taxa are summarised by phase in Tables 66 and 67.

Butchery

Nine fragments of bone, from both phases, display evidence of butchery: mostly cut marks associated with disarticulation and jointing of the carcase. A single equid phalanx recovered from ditch section **13046** has cut marks circling the midshaft, typical of skinning.

Worked bone

Two fragments of worked bone were recovered from the early Roman phase in section **13040**: a single deer antler fragment, sawn through the base and the outer surface trimmed; and a sheep/goat metatarsal (SF 282) with a hole drilled through the proximal articulation and the broken midshaft trimmed and polished to form a point.

Burning

Of the 188 fragments of burnt bone recovered, 180 are from pit **13020**. The majority of are from sheep/goat or medium mammal sized animals. Context **13021** within pit **13020** contained a large number of fragments which may have been from the same individual, possibly

the remains of a single cooking or feasting event. The remainder of the burnt bone probably represents hearth sweeping and incidental burning.

Gnawing

Gnawing was noted on eight fragments, spanning both phases. Only around 0.5 per cent of the bones are gnawed, suggesting that the majority of the assemblage was rapidly buried, reducing the access of scavengers.

Sheep/goat

Fragment counts and MNI calculations show that sheep/goat remains are the most abundant species group within the assemblage. Two goat horncores are present but there is no positive evidence of sheep. A single radius recovered from Phase 1 pit **13020** provides a withers height estimation of 0.56m.

Ageing data is very limited. A single mandible from a Phase 2 context in ditch **13070** is from an animal aged 20 to 34 months. Where it is possible to observe epiphyseal fusion, the majority of the remains are over 3½ years old. Exceptions, all from Phase 1, were an innominate and a radius from animals less than 10 months of age; a metapodial from an animal under one year of age; an unfused calcaneus from an animal aged less than 2½ years; and two femurs from an animal aged less than 3 years.

The skeletal element representation for sheep/goat is limited but most elements are represented for both phases of activity, suggesting a mixture of butchery and food waste is present, possibly with a slight emphasis on food waste elements in Phase 1.

Cattle

MNI calculations suggest that the numbers of cattle in Phase 1 were roughly equal to equids and pigs, whereas in Phase 2 cattle were present in greater numbers, though slightly fewer than sheep/goat.

Tooth wear score data for cattle is limited to two mandibles from adult animals from Phase 1, and a mandible from an animal aged 8 to 18 months from Phase 2. A single unfused femur from an animal under 3 years of age was recovered from Phase 2. Though numbers are limited, most skeletal

| | **Phase** | | |
Taxon	1	2	Total
Horse family	12	7	19
Cattle	47	51	98
Sheep/goat	70	31	101
goat	2		2
Pig	52	13	65
Dog	6	1	7
Cat		1	1
Deer		1	1
Large mammal	182	151	333
Medium mammal	196	67	263
Unidentified	501	248	749
Total	**1068**	**571**	**1639**

TABLE 66: IDENTIFIED TAXA, ANIMAL BONE ASSEMBLAGE, BY PHASE, OUT NEWTON ROAD

	Phase	1	2
Horse Family		2	1
Cattle		2	2
Sheep/goat		8	3
Pig		2	1

TABLE 67: MINIMUM NUMBER OF INDIVIDUALS (MNI), OUT NEWTON ROAD

elements are represented, consistent with a mixture of butchery and food waste being present in both phases.

Pig

Pig remains are present in small numbers in each phase. A single mandible from an adult animal was recovered from a Phase 1 context in ditch **13070**. Post-cranial remains, where possible to assess, are unfused apart from a radius and second phalanx, indicating animals over one year of age, and two metapodials from animals aged over two years, all from Phase 1 contexts. The skeletal element representation, though limited, suggests a predominance of butchery refuse.

Equid

Two equid teeth provide ageing data: in Phase 1 from animal aged 7-9½ years and in Phase 2 from an animal aged 9-11½ years. Butchery marks on a phalanx recovered from Phase 1 ditch **13046** indicates the animal may have been skinned.

Other species

Of the seven fragments of dog bone recovered, six from Phase 1 pit **13020**, are most likely from the same individual. Phase 2 contexts in ditch **13040** produced a cat mandible and a fragment of worked deer antler. As antler is seasonally shed and a useful commodity for working, this piece could have reached the site through trade over some distance so its presence does not necessarily imply that deer were present and hunted in the immediate vicinity.

Discussion

In Phase 1, the late Iron Age enclosure showed a strong emphasis on sheep/goat, with cattle, equid and pig in smaller number. In Phase 2, though sheep/goat still predominates, cattle become slightly more prominent, with equid and pig still present in small numbers. The ageing data suggests that animal husbandry was based on a mixed economy: sheep/goat being utilised for meat and wool and cattle for meat and milk, with pigs providing variety to the diet.

Overall discussion and conclusions

The five sites selected for further analysis all featured late Iron Age or early Roman period relating to settlement on or near the site. Additionally, Burton Constable had activity in the late Roman period while Lelley was a site of medieval settlement.

There appears to be little variation in the general patterns in all five late Iron Age to early Roman assemblages, all being fairly typical of rural producer sites. There is no specific

evidence to suggest that extensive trade was undertaken at any of the sites, although very local trade is highly probable. In all cases, husbandry of sheep, or goat, was an important element of the economy, with both meat and wool being produced. Cattle remains appear to show an age structure with a fairly high proportion of older individuals, beyond the age that animals would have been commonly slaughtered for meat. This suggests that production of milk and use for traction were important. Although cattle were generally not represented in as high quantities as sheep/goat, beef would have still been well represented within the diet, as a cattle carcase has a considerably a higher meat yield than that of a sheep. Diet would have been frequently supplemented with meat from pigs, and more rarely with birds such as goose or domestic fowl. Working animals would have included horses, dogs and cats. Wild species were notably rare in the assemblage, an exception being deer antler fragments, often showing evidence of working.

The animal bone from Scorborough Hill does not show any particular deviation from the patterns of husbandry and utilisation of the other contemporary sites along the pipeline route. Though the pottery assemblage might suggest the presence of non-local residents, the inhabitants of the site were undertaking similar activities to the indigenous population, with no obvious indications of extensive trading of animal produce or of a more exotic way of life.

Few contemporary sites have been investigated within southern Holderness, but comparison with larger and broadly contemporary assemblages from slightly further afield show that patterns described above appear to be fairly typical. Despite their different landscape settings in the western Wolds, both Shiptonthorpe (Mainland, 2006) and Hayton (Jaques, 2004) had a mixed economy of meat and wool production predominantly based upon sheep/goat, with cattle supplementing the site economy with meat, milk and traction.

The assemblages from the medieval deposits at Lelley show only limited deviation from the patterns of the earlier assemblages, suggesting that the settlement had a similar small producer economy, although with cattle slightly more prominent. Animal utilisation would have been little different from that of the late Iron Age, but beef would have made a more important contribution to the diet. Pigs did not play any more of a role, but additional species, such as domestic fowl, goose, hare and rabbit provided a more varied diet.

The general lack of variation of animal husbandry and utilisation, either geographically through the terrain traversed by the pipeline, or over the timescale of the excavation sites, suggests that the rural agricultural practices were barely influenced by economic, social or cultural change. The site economies are likely to have been optimised for the requirements of making a living from the local lowland landscape.

Plant macrofossils and other organic remains

Don O'Meara

Introduction and methods

An initial archaeobotanical assessment of soil samples recovered from the excavations was undertaken by Patricia Shaw and Don O'Meara of North Pennines Archaeology. Ten litre subsamples from each of 809 bulk soil samples were processed and assessed. This concluded that the aerobic, well-drained nature of the majority of the samples allowed for the penetration of modern roots and provided poor conditions for the preservation of plant remains and that there was very little charred plant material in any of the samples. Charred grain in particular was limited in most samples and positive identification could not be made due to a lack of chaff or the grain being too fragmentary or otherwise damaged.

Nevertheless, fifty-seven of the samples were thought to be of sufficient value to justify full archaeobotanical analysis. The remaining portion of each sample, generally a further 30 litres, was processed and their archaeobotanical and other archaeologically significant components were identified and quantified. The whole earth samples were manually floated and sieved using a Sīraf-style flotation tank (Williams 1973). The residue was collected using a 1mm plastic mesh and was air-dried and sorted by eye for any material that might aid understanding of the deposit. This included charred plant remains, bones, pottery, burnt clay and charcoal. Charcoal fragments were retained for later identification or for use in radiocarbon dating. Recovered artefacts have been included in the analyses carried out by the relevant specialist for each material type.

Residues were also scanned with a hand magnet to retrieve magnetic material, in particular flake and spheroidal hammerscale, fuel-ash slag and vitrified material, which might be indicative of high processes. Processing procedures and nomenclature follows the conventions set out by the Archaeological Datasheets of the Historical Metallurgical Society (1995) and English Heritage guidelines (Bayley *et al.* 2001).

An experienced environmental archaeologist examined all of the dried residues as it was appreciated from the assessment that the heavy clay soils might not allow a completely efficient separation of the charred organic remains from the inorganic residue. The washover, or flot, was collected in a 0.4mm mesh, dried slowly and scanned at x40 magnification for charred and uncharred botanical remains. Identification was undertaken by comparison with modern reference material held in the Environmental Laboratory at North Pennines Archaeology and by reference to relevant literature (Cappers *et al.* 2006; Berggren 1981; Jacomet 2006). Plant taxonomic nomenclature follows Stace (2010).

Relative abundance was recorded on a scale from 1 (lowest) to 3 (highest). For cereals, the individual items were counted. The other plant remains have been recorded on a scale from A to E, where A=1, B=2 to 10, C=11 to 30, D=30 to 100, and E= greater than 100. Where seeds could not be identified, the numbers of unidentified species was recorded rather than their relative abundance. For clarity, 'seed' is used for the seed or fruit structures (propagule or disseminule) unless otherwise stated. For cereals, 'grain' refers to the charred caryopsis. Chaff fragments were recorded as: rachis, palea, lemma, glume, awn, or culm or culm node. Sedge (*Carex* sp.) nutlets were classed as either lenticular or trigonus: further identification was not undertaken as these plants did not occur with particularly high frequency: the genus provides a general indication of wet environments, but it was not thought that detailed examination would provide any further useful knowledge of their contexts.

Inferences made regarding local environmental conditions or anthropogenic activity are viewed with the understanding that post-depositional processes differentially preserve different plant remains (Green 1982, 40-41). Thus charred remains preserve better than desiccated material and within the suite of desiccated material a similar differential preservation occurs; robust remains such as elder, goosefoot and nettle seeds can be interpreted as evidence of poor preservation when they dominate an assemblage (Kenward *et al.* 1986). Indeed it has been suggested that the presence of elder seeds (*Sambucus* sp.) could be used as a benchmark to assess overall preservation (Murphy and Wiltshire 1994, 2), though it may be argued from the results presented here that goosefoots (Chenopodiaceae species) may make a better bench mark when dealing with rural sites. To understand what is present it must be appreciated that much has also been lost.

The recorded data and full report on the samples analysed will form part of the project archive: site-by-site accounts included here concentrate on samples that provided the more significant findings.

Old Ellerby

Iron Age ring gully **3020** produced fragments of unidentified charred cereal grain from cut **3266**. From the Roman phases, the fill of pit **3279**, cut into the top of ring gully **3020**, was the richest sample analysed from this site, yielding, in addition to fragments of four unidentified charred cereal grains, low numbers of seeds of a *Fragaria* species (possibly wild strawberry; *Fragaria vesca*), sedges, goosefoots (Chenopodiaceae) and docks (including sorrel *Rumex acetosella*). This assemblage suggests a ruderal community of plants, as would be expected in an open environment in an area of herbaceous wayside.

Burton Constable

The fill of pit **118198** at the south-western edge of the excavation area produced three charred grains, two of

238

which may be cultivated cereals, while the third is probably a wild grass as it is very small, less than 4mm by 1.5mm. Low numbers of fragmentary Chenopodiaceae seeds were also recovered.

Desiccated seeds, mainly blinks (*Montia fontana*) with low numbers of dock (*Rumex* sp.) and a single seed of spiny sow thistle (*Sonchus asper*) were recovered from the ring gully of Structure 3. Two indeterminate cereal grains and four fragments of chaff, only partially charred, were present in the same sample.

From Structure 4, two fragments of charred material from cut **9888** may be grass rhizomes (*Poa* sp.), but could not be firmly identified. The primary fill in cut **9972** produced a single fragment of spelt wheat (*Triticum spelta*) glume base along with single seeds of trigonus sedge and dock (*Rumex* sp.) but the presence of desiccated pine needles may indicate modern contamination of this sample. Desiccated seeds of spiny sow thistle, goosefoot (Chenopodiaceae), stinging-nettle (*Urtica dioica*) and field penny cress (*Thlaspi arvense*), a common plant of waste and arable land, were recovered from the two lower fills of cut **118052** along with a single charred indeterminate cereal grain.

Samples from the Structure 5 ring gully were notable for their paucity of organic remains but the secondary fill of cut **9842** produced seeds of goosefoot, and a single desiccated seed of spiny sow thistle as well as two charred grains of wheat (poss. *T. aestivum*). Charred straw, including internode fragments, were also revered. The presence of desiccated plant remains, such as the sow thistle seed, may indicate modern contamination, but the charred cereal is more likely to be contemporary with the backfilling of the feature.

Eleven charred grains recovered from the large pit, **118523**, just to the east of Structure 5, are pitted and partially fragmented making identification difficult. Six wheat (*Triticum* sp.) grains are recognisable, as well as one grass seed (*Bromus* sp.). Numerous charred plant fragments were recovered, including straw fragments, possibly from grass rhizomes; the significance of this material is discussed below. A small number of seeds of *Danthonia decumbens*, a grass of acid grassland environment as well as goosefoots (Chenopodiaceae) and dock seeds (*Rumex*) were also recovered.

From the Roman features in the northern part of the site, charred grains within the charcoal-rich fill of the early phase ditch **9955** included five oat, one spelt wheat (*T. spelta* type) glume base, six barley (*Hordeum vulgare*) and around forty grains that were too heavily charred to identify.

The two uppermost fills of ditch **118927** both produced high quantities of elder seeds (*Sambucus nigra*) and seeds of a duckweed (*Lemna* sp.) while the lower of these also had seeds of a water crowfoot (*Ranunculus* sp.) and

fragmented seeds that may be of wild strawberry. A single charred barley grain was also recovered. The occurrence of so many duckweed seeds and the presence of water crowfoot suggest that this linear feature held standing water. The fill of ditch **118958** produced a single heavily charred cereal grain and charred poppy (Papaveraceae) seed although there was also a desiccated grain from a grass species which may indicate modern contamination. Poppy is a common weed of cereal crops and it is possible the seed and the cereal grain were grown in the same crop, though the link is tenuous given the low quantities of each.

The sample from the fill of oven **9519** produced moderate amounts of desiccated campion seeds (*Silene* sp.) as well as two heavily charred cereal grains. The condition of the grain from this sample is consistent with Boardman and Jones' (1990, 4) preservation number 6, being vesicular, heavily pitted and clinkered, implying exposure to a high temperature process. The campion species could not be identified beyond genus level and therefore provides limited environmental information as the genus as a whole can occupy broad ecological ranges. Two samples from the fill the L-shaped feature **9282** produced single charred grains of barley (*Hordeum vulgare*) and oat (*Avena fatua* type) as well as over fifty unidentifiable grains and four poorly preserved glume bases and fifteen other chaff fragments. This sample also produced low numbers of seeds from a cinquefoil (*Potentilla* sp.). Pit **9235**, cut into the northern end of the L-shaped ditch, yielded charred oat and nine charred spelt-type grains, along with twenty *T. spelta*-type glumes and three charred vetch seeds (*Vicia* sp.).

Overall, the samples from Burton Constable did not produce the large flot samples that would allow a detailed assessment of the wild or domestic plants utilised by the Iron Age or Roman population. Remains of cereals are present in over 60 per cent of the samples, providing evidence of a general spread of cereals through a range of contexts. However, charred grains occurred at an average frequency of only 0.2 grains per litre: when the two richest samples from features **9282** and **118595**, which produced forty-eight and eleven grains respectively, are discounted, the frequency drops to 0.05 charred grains per litre. There is clearly a distinction between these two relatively rich samples and the others. Feature **9282** appears to have acted as a basin of deposition for an unprocessed or part processed cereal crop, inferred from the fifteen fragments of rachis. There is an indication of a mixed crop with roughly equal frequencies of naked wheat and hulled barley.

The assemblage of wild plant remains does not present a particularly strong indication of specific ecological niches. The domination of assemblages by robust remains, such seeds of goosefoots and stinging nettle, probably reflect the poor preservation conditions for organic remains. However, in a general sense, the picture of an open landscape of slightly acidic grassland can be seen. Unusually for an often ubiquitous species, elder (*Sambucus nigra*) was limited to two samples, both from ditch **118927**. Their occurrence here is likely to have been the result of local factors: a cache of the berries from a small mammal, an elder bush growing very close by, or conditions such as the presence of standing water or rapid silting that favoured the preservation of these seeds. The relatively high frequency of blinks (*Montia fontana*) in the Structure 3 ring gully has parallels in a number of the occupation sites along the pipeline route: the possibility that it is related to the use of turf is discussed below (page 243).

Brandywell

Few botanical remains were retrieved from Iron Age contexts. The fill of ring gully **25246** produced a single seeds from goosefoot (Chenopodiaceae) and bedstraw (*Galium*) species, and the fill of gully **25137**, yielded one charred wheat grain (*Triticum* sp.) along with desiccated seeds of speedwell (*Veronica hederifolia*), goosefoot (Chenopodiaceae), blinks (*Montia fontana*) and dock (*Rumex* sp.).

From the possible post-built building, **25248**, post-hole **25066** produced low numbers of seeds of elder (*Sambucus nigra*) and goosefoot (Chenopodiaceae) and the fill of feature **25093** yielded a single charred oat grain; it is not clear whether this is a wild or cultivated form as its state of preservation was poor. Low numbers of desiccated seeds of ivy-leaved speedwell (*Veronica hederifolia*) and goosefoot were also recovered. Pit **25083**, which may also have been associated with building **25248**, produced three charred barley grains as well as charred grass seeds, at least one of which was tentatively identified as a *Bromus* species. Other charred remains included a trigonus sedge and low numbers of goosefoot.

The cereal remains recovered are broadly consistent with the remains from samples elsewhere, particularly Burton Constable (above). Limited numbers of hulled barley and naked wheat were recovered along with many grains that could not be identified to genus. The non-cereal plant remains were at low frequencies, hindering any detailed interpretation of the immediate environment.

Sproatley

Additional analysis of samples at this site was aimed chiefly at recovery of dating evidence, but the samples processed from possible Bronze Age barrows confirmed that there were minimal archaeo-botanical remains.

An exception to the general lack of charred organic remains at this site was provided by pit **26428**. Three analysed samples from the fill collectively yielded around 400 charred grains. Of these, at least sixty-five were oat grains, though not sufficiently preserved to distinguish between wild and domestic forms. Other grains were all heavily charred but some barley type grains were tentatively identified, as well as bread wheat (*Triticum aestivum*, including club wheat forms: subsp. *compactum*) and spelt wheat (*T. spelta*) forms. Over 200 spelt-type glume bases were also present in one of the samples, the concentration suggesting a local deposit of discarded chaff from winnowing. Three charred vetch-type peas were also recovered. The smaller pit, **26059**, cutting pit **26428** produced approximately one hundred further charred grains, including five oat and four barley grains. The majority of the remainder were of general naked wheat morphology.

Nuttles

The fill of ring gully **31514** produced four charred cereal grains of which three were wheat (*Triticum* sp.) and the other not identifiable. Desiccated seeds of stinging nettle (*Urtica dioica*), small nettle (*Urtica urens*), a Brassicaceae species, (either *Thalaspi* sp. or *Lepidium* sp.), blinks (*Montia fontana*) and dead nettle (*Lamium* sp.) were recovered in moderate amounts. Charred material recovered from this sample consisted of only a single sedge nutlet and a dock seed (*Rumex* sp.). There is a strong indication here of plant remains that may be linked to the collection of turfs, as discussed below, page 243).

Lelley

The terminus of the ring gully of Structure 1 produced seeds of blinks (*Montia fontana*), a trigonus sedge and dock (*Rumex* sp.), approximately half of which are charred. A single charred grain is suggested as oat, the level of charring creating difficulty in identifying whether this is a wild or cultivated form. The sample from the terminus of the ring gully of Structure 3 had a rather different composition, with six wheat (*Triticum* sp.) grains, a single charred barley grain, a fragment of an oat grain and four indeterminate fragments of cereal. Low numbers of charred trigonus sedge and low numbers of what were interpreted as charred grass grains were also recovered. The wild plant remains suggest an open ruderal landscape.

Some of the later phases produced much larger assemblages of cereals. Eight separate samples from the fills of rectangular feature **35611** collectively produced around 160 charred grains, the bulk of which were recovered from the residue rather than the flot. The grain morphology suggests that club wheat (*T. aestivum* subsp. *compactum*) may constitute much of the grain assemblage, while a limited number of grains show spelt wheat (*T. spelta*) characteristics. Seven grains were identified as barley (*Hordeum vulgare*) or bearing relatively clear barley morphology, and two as oat (*Avena* sp.). It should be borne in mind that identifications are based on the general morphological characteristics and that most of the grains were heavily charred. Three charred hazelnut shell fragments, three vetch-type members of the pea family were also recovered.

Two contexts associated with the possible oven produced comparatively rich charred grain assemblages. Fifteen heavily charred grains, including one possible fragment of oat and two of a naked bread wheat species, were recovered from the oven floor, layer **35371**, while pit **35529**, underlying the floor, produced over 200 charred grains, of which oats, wheat, and barley could be identified. Seed of goosefoot (Chenopodiacae), bulrush (*Scirpus* sp.) and willow herb (*Epilobium* sp.) were also recovered.

Around 90 per cent of the 450 charred grains recovered from pit **35059** were identifiable as wheat varieties, generally club-wheats: naked hexaploid types (*T. aestivum* subsp. *compactum*). Less than 20 examples each of charred oat and vetch (*Vicia* sp., all less than 5mm) were also present. Though chaff was not recovered to provide postitive confirmation, it is suggested that the oats were cultivated varieties, with some of the charred grains up to 8mm long. Two-row hulled types seemed to be present among the very limited quantities of barley. In general the grains from this sample represent some of the best recovered material from the project and indeterminate grains were in the minority for this sample. The very narrow range of material recovered, along with the absence of chaff, suggests that this is not general domestic waste but material from a cleaned grain source, perhaps accidently charred while being dried before milling.

Linear feature **35080** cutting pit **35059** had a similarly grain-rich lower fill: over 400 grains. Of these around one hundred seemed to be bread wheat types (*Triticum aestivum*), in particular, the rounded grains of club wheat (*T. aestivum* subsp. *compactum*). Five spelt-type grains (*T. spelta*) were identifiable by their parallel sides and drop shaped or round embryo, though no chaff was recovered. The heavily charred nature of the approximately 50 oat grains (*Avena* sp.) precludes firm differentiation of cultivated oats (*A. sativa*) from wild species, but their average size is typical of cultivated varieties. Barley was recovered with roughly the same frequency as oat grains, though this may provide a conservative estimate of numbers, as oat grains can remain distinctive after heavy charring whereas heavily charred barley grains may be confused with wheat forms. A similar bias may over-emphasise the importance of club wheat, which will maintain its very rounded appearance when charred while other wheats, such as spelt, lose their distinctive appearance. Approximately twenty-five charred peas were recovered: generally less than 5mm in diameter suggesting that they are vetch varieties, although two examples over 8mm in size may be cultivated varieties.

Of the wild plants, charred dock seeds occurred very frequently. Lesser amounts of charred corn marigold (*Glebionis segetum*) and thistle (*Cirsium* sp.) were also recovered. It is notable that the samples from this feature contained much more frequent weed seeds than the sample from pit **35059**.

Around eighty-five grains were recovered from the fills of ditch **35594**, all heavily charred. Eighteen could be provisionally identified as oat, and possible hulled barley (*Hordeum vulgare*) and naked wheat grains were also noted, but the condition of the assemblage makes a secure identification difficult for the rest.

The analysed samples from pit **35066** produced nine heavily charred grains of which two were oat-type and two bread wheat type, at least one of which was club wheat (subsp. *compactum*). Two heavily charred grains from pit **35111** were tentatively identified as club wheat and barley (*H. vulgare*). Three fragments of charred pea (*Pisum* sp.) from the same sample were interpreted as a cultivated form, as they were greater than 8mm in diameter.

New York

The ring gully of Structure 4 produced low numbers of blinks (*Montia fontana*) and a goosefoot species (Chenopodiaceae), in both cases the seeds being desiccated rather than charred. A single fragment of a charred barley grain was identified from another intervention through the same ring gully, as well as desiccated seeds of Chenopodiaceae and chickweed (*Stellaria media*) and charred seeds from a trigonus sedge, blinks, dock (*Rumex* sp.) and a meadow grass (*Poa* sp.). A possible umbellifer (Apiaceae) seed was also noted. The assemblages from the two samples show evidence for open grassland. The possible use of turf is also suggested.

Braemere Hill

Samples from the ring gully of Structure 1 produced low numbers of charred sedge, goosefoot species (Chenopodiaceae) and charred meadow grass (*Poa* sp.) seeds. Two charred wheat grains were recovered, of a naked type (possibly *T. aestivum*) along with six unidentified grains. Desiccated seeds of a *Polygonum* species, blinks (*Montia fontana*) and dock (*Rumex* sp.) were also recovered. Possible charred straw or rhizome fragments were present in very low quantities. The wild plant species suggest an open ruderal environment.

Burstwick

The charred seeds and plant remains from the fill of pit **51108** included moderate amounts of lenticular sedges with lower quantities of dock (*Rumex* sp.).

Desiccated remains were represented by goosefoots (Chenopodiaceae), chickweed (*Stellaria* sp.) and blinks (*Montia fontana*). Small amounts of charred straw fragments were also recovered along with charred meadow grass-type grains (probably *Poa* sp.). There was little to support the supposition that the pit was used as a well or watering hole: the species represented could have lived near a waterlogged area, but there is no evidence of aquatic species that would specifically indicate that the feature contained standing water.

Winestead

The sample from the fill of intervention **73141** of ditch **73097** contained approximately sixty charred grains. Four could be identified as barley and ten as wheat, of an oval or rounded *T. aestivum*. The majority of the remaining grains could also be classed as *T. aestivum*. A small number of grains, less than ten, were of an oat type, but were too heavily carbonised for a clear identification. Along with a small awn fragment recovered, this suggests that oats formed at least a portion of the assemblage.

The presence of charred seeds of cornflower (*Centaurea cyanus*) and black bindweed (*Polygonum convolvulus*), both common weeds of open grassland or cereal crop, is likely to be the result of an incomplete cleaning of the processed grain. The absence of chaff could be seen as evidence that the grain here was already winnowed (but see below for an alternative interpretation). It is likely that some charred weed seeds would survive the cleaning process into the finished product. Low numbers of desiccated seeds of elder (*Sambucus nigra*) and goosefoot (Chenopodiaceae) were also recovered, their presence with grains and seeds from an arable cereal field perhaps indicating that remains of plants from different environmental niches have been incorporated into this deposit.

The residue and flot from the sample from the fill of cut **73106** of ditch **73097** produced approximately ninety charred grains in total. Ten were wheat grains and twelve were barley, the remainder being too heavily charred to identify to genus. It was not possible to tell whether the barley was of a hulled variety. The wheat was of an oval-round form suggesting a naked variety of either *T. aestivum* or *T. compactum*. A charred fragment of oat awn was also recovered. Charred seeds of dock (*Rumex* sp.), grass (*Poa* sp.), and goosefoot (Chenopodiaceae) were also recovered. A single uncharred buttercup (*Ranunculus* sp.) seed was probably a modern contaminant.

Similar quantities of charred grain were recovered from ditch **73137**, including nine grains of wheat (*Triticum* sp.), fourteen of barley (*Hordeum* sp.) and three grains of oat. It was unclear whether the oat was a wild or cultivated form. The barley appeared to be of a hulled variety, as it showed dorsal scars on the grain. The wheat was identified as a naked hexaploid form, possibly *Triticum aestivum*, though the absence of chaff and the heavily charred nature of the material preclude completely confident identification. Charred seeds of a *Brassica* species, common knotgrass (*Polygonum aviculare*), a small pea species (*Pisum* sp.), valerian (*Valerianella* sp.), meadow grass (*Poa* sp.) and lenticular sedge were also recovered, as well as a single uncharred dock (*Rumex* sp.). This range suggests that this fill was well sealed, in comparison to other deposits from the site.

Taken together, these three samples contain the bulk of the charred cereal remains recovered from this pipeline as a whole. The ditches that they derived from were initially dated to the Iron Age, but the presence of naked hexaploid bread wheat and the weed seeds recovered broadly suggests material from the later, medieval, period.

Patrington

The fill of the south-eastern terminal of Structure 3 produced low amounts of desiccated seeds of stinging nettle (*Uritca dioica*), field penny-cress (*Thlaspi arvense*), nipplewort (*Lapsana communis*), knotgrass (*Polygonum* sp.) and chickweed (*Stellaria media*). These remains are of plants that would be expected in waysides or waste places. Two heavily charred cereal grains recovered from the Structure 1 could not be identified to genus. Charred fragments that may be from grass rhizomes (*Poa* sp.) were also recovered, as well as charred seed pods of wild radish (*Raphanus raphanistrum*), a plant that grows in a broad range of environments from cultivated areas to rough or waste ground.

The fill of the north-western terminal of ditch **88171** produced a single charred indeterminate grain as well as low numbers of a lenticular sedge, seeds of blinks (*Montia fontana*), chickweed (*Stellaria* sp.) and stinging nettle. Fragments of charred straw, presumably from local burning activity, were also recovered, as well as possible charred rhizome fragments. The fill of the Structure 2 ring gully produced seeds of blinks and chickweed, along with desiccated seed from an umbellifer (Apiaceae) species.

There was little direct evidence for cultivated plant remains from this site, with only three indeterminate grains. The general picture that emerges is of an open but quite wet environment.

Bluegate Corner

The Structure 1 ring gully produced, in total, twelve charred cereal grains: four of wheat and eight which could not be identified to genus. Three pieces of charred rachis segment were also recovered, one identifiable as *T. aestivum* type. Small numbers of charred lenticular and trigonus sedges and a single charred *Brassica* seed, as well as desiccated seeds of speedwell (*Veronica hederifolia*), blinks (*Montia fontana*), buttercup (*Ranunculus* sp.), chickweed (*Stellaria media*), stinging nettle (*Urtica dioica*) and a goosefoot species (Chenopodiaceae) were also present. This assemblage may show evidence of the use of turfs in the construction of Structure 1, particularly from the association of the *Ranunculus*, sedges and blinks. The fill of the Structure 2 ring gully produced a single desiccated fumitory (*Fumaria* sp.) seed and a poorly preserved seed of a goosefoot.

Skeffling

The fills of pits **120307**, **120301** and **120312** all produced similar assemblages of desiccated seeds. All three samples had numbers of a trigonus sedge, while pit **120307** produced a single seeds of goosefoot (Chenopodiaceae*)* and chickweed (*Stellaria* sp.) and pit **120312** had a goosefoot seed and an unidentified seed, probably an umbellifer (Apiacea) species such as burnet saxifrage (*Pimpinella major*). Evidence from the three samples suggests the pits were in an area of open wet ground.

Dimlington Road

Six charred grains were present in the sample from the upper fill of ring gully **120456** of which two can be identified as wheat (*Triticum* sp.) the others being eroded and unidentifiable. A single fragment of chaff was also unidentifiable. Desiccated remains of a fumitory (*Fumaria* sp.) were recovered, as well as a trigonus sedge nutlet and a single seed of chickweed (*Stellaria media*).

The south-eastern terminal of the Structure 3 ring gully had a comparatively high number of charred grains, approximately eighty recovered in total, though almost all were heavily charred fragments and not readily identifiable. A minority were barley, though it was not possible to say whether these might be naked or hulled types. The rest of the identifiable remains consisted of approximately twenty grains of charred wheat, which appear to be naked varieties (*T. aestivum* group) and included rounded or oval remains as well as some drop-shaped examples. The absence of chaff does not allow further differentiation of these grains at this stage. Low numbers of desiccated seeds of nipplewort (*Lapsana communis*) were recovered from this sample. A high proportion of the charred grains were recovered from the residue fraction, emphasising the need for careful examination of the residues of processed samples as well as the flots, particularly when samples are taken from heavy clay deposits.

Fragments of charred plant stems, including charred nodes and internode fragments, were notable in the sample from ring gully **120921** of Structure 1. This material seems to represent charred straw from a meadow grass (*Poa* sp.). Charred lenticular and trigonus sedges were recovered, as well desiccated seeds of goosefoot (Chenopodiaceae)

and blinks (*Montia fontana*). This sample may preserve evidence of turf. The material may have become charred if it had been used in the construction of a building subsequently destroyed by fire, or if it had been exposed to a domestic fire. The charred seeds of sedges, charred herbaceous material and seeds of blinks may also have resulted from the burning of turfs as a low grade fuel.

Low numbers of desiccated seeds of a fumitory, chickweed and goosefoot were recovered from pit **120596** at the eastern end of the excavation area.

Conclusions

The cereal remains recovered from these samples do not represent either the volume or the levels of preservation that would challenge our knowledge of agriculture and cereal production during the Iron Age to Roman period. The low levels of chaff present difficulties as, in many cases, the identification of wheat or barley beyond their genus level can only be made when chaff has been recovered. At least on some of the sites, the scarcity of chaff may be linked to the heavily charred nature of many of the grains. Experimental charring methods (Boardman and Jones 1990) have shown that chaff is the first component of the cereal ear to be rendered to ash and does not survive high temperatures as well as grains. It is suggested that when cereal grains show evidence of being exposed to temperatures which render them vesicular, heavily pitted and clinkered, the chaff will, by this stage of heating, have already been turned to ash, and therefore will not survive to be recovered by the archaeo-botanical methods utilised here.

A detailed palaeoecological study of this project is hindered by the consistently low numbers of plant remains, both wild and domestic species. However, one significant pattern may be emerging: tentative evidence, from the sites with ring gullies, for the exploitation of turfs. In particular, the relatively common occurrence of blinks (*Montia fontana*) has been noted in other studies that have tried to identify the use of turfs. The presence of sedge (*Carex sp.*) and heath grass (*Danthonia*) remains in addition to charred rhizomes or charred herbaceous plant material, occurring alongside blinks, can be taken as further supporting evidence for the use of turfs.

In their regional review of archaeobotanical material from the East Riding area, Hall and Huntley (2007) highlighted the possible use of turfs for building or burning several times and there are number of sites in the unpublished literature from this region where turf construction may be noted in the archaeo-botanical record. Similar evidence may be noted in many of the Easington to Ganstead samples. The evidence for turf use, however, is no means completely clear, and confident identification can only be made when it is supported by reference to the archaeological excavation findings.

Pollen

Tudur Burke Davies

Pollen analysis was carried out on three samples, 460, 463 and 465 in descending order, taken from the lower part of a vertical sequence of eleven samples from intervention **25043** of ditch **25168** at Brandywell. The three bulk soil samples were sub-sampled under laboratory conditions and subsequently processed by standard techniques (Moore and Webb 1978; Moore *et al.* 1991), with the addition of Lycopodium spore tablets to enable the calculation of relative pollen concentrations. Pollen counts of to 500 grains per sample were undertaken using a light microscope at x400 magnification, and at x1000 magnification with oil immersion for critical identifications. Identifications were carried using the reference collection at the University of Sheffield Archaeology Department and keys provided by Moore and Webb (1978), Moore *et al.* (1991) and Faegri and Iversen (1989). Pollen nomenclature follows the classifications of Bennet (1994). Discussions of the characteristics of vegetation types are based on the work of Clapham *et al.* (1987) and Grime *et al.* (2007).

Results (Fig. 114)

Herbaceous pollen dominates the majority of the pollen assemblage in all three samples, with smaller proportions of tree and shrub pollen; heaths although present are very scarce. There is little variation in pollen percentages between the three samples, the largest divergence being a larger quantity of *Cichorium intybus*-type pollen in sample 460 and a larger number of willow (*Salix*) pollen in sample 463. Smaller differences between samples include peaks in alder (*Alnus glutinosa*) and undifferentiated sedge (Cyperaceae) pollen in sample 460, higher cereal-type pollen values in sample 463, and lower numbers of ribwort (*Plantago lanceolata*) numbers in sample 460. The greatest difference observed in relative pollen concentration is the increased pollen concentration in sample 465, which has more than double the value of the other two samples. Otherwise, the variations seen between the percentage pollen diagrams for sample 460 and 463 are similar to those seen in the relative concentration diagrams.

Discussion

Pollen preservation and catchment

Pollen grains of different species show varying susceptibility to decay, which can in turn provide a biased representation of the original pollen assemblage. For example, alder (*Alnus glutinosa*) and ling (*Calluna vulgaris*) pollen can be over represented in relation to oak (*Quercus* sp.) as they have a lower susceptibility to oxidation or corrosion (Havinga 1964, 1967). Other indicators of poor preservation include the proportion of damaged pollen grains or by a low concentration of pollen grains (Moore and Webb 1978). The high levels of *Cichorium intybus*-type pollen in all three samples could be an indicator of differential pollen preservation, as this type is highly resilient to oxidation (Havinga 1967). However, in this instance, given that species, such as oak, that are far more susceptible to decay occur in relatively high numbers, the results indicate that the pollen assemblage within the samples examined are not significantly biased by differential preservation.

The higher concentration of pollen in sample 465 might indicate better preservation compared with samples 460 and 463, but the proportion of damaged pollen grains in all three samples is fairly similar. Therefore, this difference in concentration is more likely to represent a difference in the accumulation rates of the fills of the ditch. There is a risk of contamination from modern sources of pollen as the sub-samples for analysis were not retrieved directly from sealed deposits but from bulk samples. However, pine (*Pinus sylvestris*) pollen is scarce in all three samples, whereas samples from Willow Garth and the Bog at Roos, the nearest comparanda sites, show a characteristic increase in the numbers of pine in the most modern deposits.

Samples taken in bulk do not represent specific 'episodes' in time (Dimbleby 1985). If a deposit is naturally accumulating, bulk samples from that deposit will either represent pollen from a mixture of ages within a profile, or possibly a random point in time during that period of accumulation. Although the pollen samples from Brandywell were not acquired from a clear stratigraphic sequence, they were taken from progressively deeper points within the same ditch profile, and represent sequentially earlier periods of pollen deposition, though it is impossible to determine the time lapsed between those three periods.

The size of pollen catchment increases with the size of the sampling basin (e.g. Jacobsen and Bradshaw 1981; Sugita 1991). For a small basin such as the ditch sampled in the current study, the majority of the contemporary pollen represented in the samples will derive from very local vegetation communities. There will also be a smaller contribution from the general pollen rain. Pollen could derive from a number of secondary sources (Dimbleby 1985: 88), such as erosion from nearby palaeosols or enclosure banks. Biological and anthropogenic activities associated with the site may also result in concentrations of specific species. It is often observed that reworked pollen derived from palaeosols appears darker in colour than pollen from contemporary sources (Dimbleby 1985): such a phenomenon was not apparent in the pollen assemblages from Brandywell.

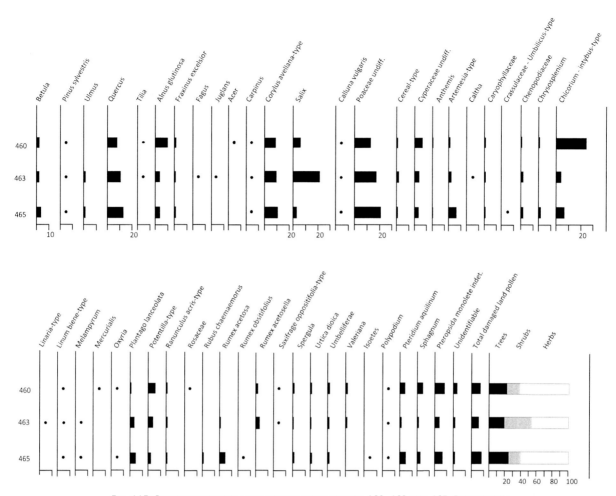

FIG. 115: PERCENTAGE TOTAL LAND POLLEN FROM SAMPLE 460, 463 AND 465, BRANDYWELL

The only two taxa that occur in large enough frequencies to suggest an artificial concentration are willow (*Salix* sp.) in sample 463 and *C. intybus*-type, in sample 460. The high occurrence of *C. intybus*-type pollen, which includes pollen of common arable and wayside weeds such as dandelion, may be related to the use of animal fodder, but could equally be related to an increase in local abundance, possibly within the ditch itself. The increase in willow appears to coincide with a decrease in herb communities, suggesting it is related to changes in the local environment.

It would therefore appear that the majority of the pollen within the samples is contemporary with the accumulation of the deposits from which they were taken and, owing to the nature of the sampling basin, is likely to be derived from the area or the settlement site immediately surrounding the ditch.

Environmental characteristics

The dominance of herb pollen within all three samples would suggest that the landscape immediately surrounding the settlement was largely open during the time the ditch fills were accumulating. All three samples contained indicators

of both arable (Cereal-type, *Anthemis*, Caryophylaceae, Chenopodiaceae, *Linaria* and *Melampyrum*) and pastoral (*Linum bienne*-type, *Plantago lanceolata* and *Rumex acetosella*) agriculture. These were also the prevalent conditions during the Roman period at the Bog at Roos (Beckett 1975, 1981) and also at Willow Garth (Bush and Ellis 1987; Bush 1993). All three sites have similar levels of woodland and shrub pollen combined with indicators of arable and pastoral agriculture. The largest difference between the vegetation communities at each of these three sites, however, is the high frequency of heath pollen at Roos which is all but absent at the other two sites. This may therefore indicate that the heathland so prevalent at the Bog at Roos was a local phenomenon, rather than a characteristic of the region as a whole.

The presence of walnut (*Juglans regia*) in sample 463 is intriguing. This is not a native tree and its presence may be an indicator of ornamental planting or woodland management. However, the impact of this activity on herbaceous communities is unlikely to have been significant given the scarcity of this pollen type.

As some species included in the *C. intybus*-type favour wetland habitats, its increase in sample 460 may be related

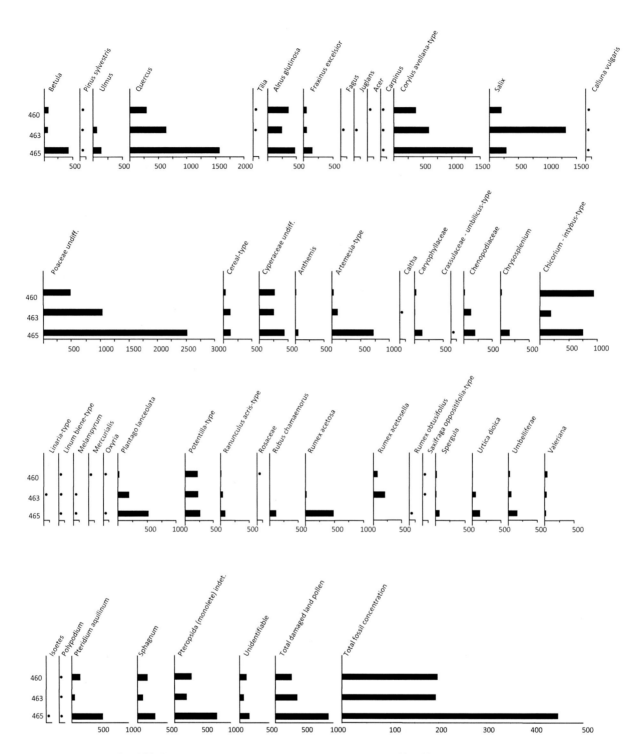

FIG. 116: RELATIVE CONCENTRATION OF POLLEN FROM SAMPLE 460, 463 AND 465, BRANDYWELL

to the increase in indicators of wetland communities in this sample (e.g. *Alnus glutionsa*, Cyperaceae, *Valeriana* and *Sphagnum*). Interestingly, the peak in wetland taxa coincides with a decrease in indicators of arable agriculture, possibly indicating a reduced production during this period because of an apparent climatic downturn. There is evidence of episodic increase in rainfall at both Willow Garth and the Bog at Roos early in the first millennium A.D. (*cf* Bush and Ellis 1987; Bush 1993; Beckett 1975, 1981), but establishing contemporaneity with sample 460 is very difficult in the absence of secure dating.

Molluscs

Matt Law

Complete mollusc shells and distinctive fragments were identified using a reference collection, although in some cases key diagnostic features had been lost through damage to the shells or were obscured by concreted deposits in the shell openings. For each gastropod taxon within a sample, the most commonly represented non-repetitive element, usually the shell apex, umbilicus, or body whorl with mouth, was counted to determine the minimum number of individuals (MNI) present. This avoids underestimation when only shell apices are counted (Giovas 2009). In the case of *Bithynia tentaculata*, counts of both operculae and shells were recorded. Principal sources for the biology of the recorded species were Kerney and Cameron (1979), and Davies (2008). Nomenclature of non-marine species follows Anderson (2008).

Only four of the excavation sites had land snail assemblage of sufficient size to have any interpretative value. The small numbers of marine molluscs, from various sites, were mostly the common food species: oyster, mussel, cockle, whelk and dog whelk, although the more unusual *Boreotrophon truncatus*, found subtidally on stony or gravelly shores in the North Sea (Hayward *et al.* 1995, 532), was recorded from ditch **35594** at Lelley.

Burton Constable

Fill **118304** of ditch **118958** shows signs of slow deposition, with reasonable molluscan diversity. A number of freshwater and wet ground taxa are present, suggesting that the ditch went through periods of flooding. The lowest fill, **9300**, of ditch **118927** also shows signs of flooding, with high numbers of *Anisus leucostoma*, which is tolerant of seasonal drying out.

Brandywell

The assemblage from the lowest fill of intervention **25043** of ditch **25168** indicates a well developed freshwater habitat. *Hippeutus complanatus* in particular requires a well vegetated environment (Davies 2008, 168). The presence in moderately high numbers of *Trochulus striolatus* suggests long vegetation on the margins of the ditch, although short, possibly closely grazed, grassland in the local environment is implied by the presence of *Vallonia costata*, *Vallonia* cf *excentrica* and *Pupilla muscorum*.

Lelley

Three samples from ditch **35609** all show signs of the presence of standing water: *Planorbis planorbis*, *Bithynia tentaculata* and *Radix balthica* in particular being early colonisers of freshwater habitats. One shell of *Anisus leucostoma* was deformed, either genetically or as the result of an infection.

Out Newton Road

The sample from the upper fill of enclosure ditch **13070** appears to show evidence for seasonal flooding although no true freshwater taxa are present. There are strong indications of short, closely-grazed grassland, with reasonably high numbers of *Vallonia* cf *excentrica*, *Pupilla muscorum* and *Vertigo pygmaea*. The relatively high number of shells in this sample may reflect a long period of deposition. Other samples from Out Newton Road add support the picture of short grassland and seasonal flooding.

Conclusions

Although preservation of mollusc shells is poor owing to acidic soils, the results show that shell-rich contexts do exist, especially within deeper features. These have the potential to reveal details of land and drainage management regimes, especially where vertical columns of samples through different fills are available. This has implications for future work in southern Holderness, especially in the design of sampling strategies to take into account the possibility that preservation may exceed expectations.

Section 5: Discussion

The early Mesolithic period

It is only at the very end of the Palaeolithic period, following the retreat of the ice sheets, that the inhabitants of East Yorkshire begin to emerge into the archaeological record. Earlier finds are limited to reworked flints and stone tools recovered from glacial gravels, such as a handaxe and flake from a quarry to the south-east of Burstwick and a flint axe and other tools from south-west and south of Burstwick (Brigham, Buglass and Steedman 2008, 74). At Brigham, in the Hull valley near Driffield, over 4400 pieces of worked flint were recovered during gravel quarrying in 1962-3 (Manby 1966, 211-228; Wymer and Bonsall 1977, 432; Loughlin and Miller 1979). The nature of this assemblage shows signs of the shift in hunting methods, with the development of small, specialised implements that mark the transition between the late Palaeolithic and the early part of the Mesolithic periods (Van de Noort and Davies 1993, 49).

The study of Mesolithic activity in the wider Yorkshire region, and indeed through much of northern Britain and beyond, is dominated by the site at Star Carr, in the Vale of Pickering, first investigated by Grahame Clark in the late 1940s and early 1950s (Clark 1954, 1972). The rich artefactual remains from the site include worked antler, bone points, shale beads and a large assemblage of flint tools, along with well-preserved environmental remains. The site is the subject of ongoing investigations and research, but it is likely to have been part of a much larger settlement, preserved where the land has remained as wetland. The settlement could have been occupied year-round, over an extended period of time, and served as a focal point for groups of hunter-gatherers seasonally migrating over a wide area.

Within Holderness, Clark excavated a site of similar date to Star Carr at Brandesburton (Clark and Godwin 1956). This site produced bone harpoons or notched points, which have also been recorded from deposits in the former Skipsea Withow and Hornsea meres and from the foreshore at Hornsea and at Gransmoor (Sitch and Jacobi 1999). In the Hull valley near Eske, north of Beverley, Stone Carr, which occupies a localised area of sand and gravel, produced a scatter of around 750 flints characteristic of the later Mesolithic period (Chapman *et al.* 2000, 160-168, Metcalfe *et al.* 2003). At this time, there seems to have been a move to a more sedentary, less nomadic existence, perhaps based around meres and valley bottoms.

In southern Holderness, Mesolithic finds have been largely limited to scatters of diagnostic flints. Systematic fieldwalking as part of the Humber Wetlands Project identified eighty assemblages, of varying sizes (Van de Noort 2004, 36). Elsewhere, a wooden stake recovered in 1994 from Round Hill, one of the sites originally excavated by Thomas Boynton (see page 5), was radiocarbon dated to 8350 to 7949 cal BC (Head 1995, 220-221). The stake resembled those excavated by Boynton and appeared to have been driven into the same peat levels (Fletcher and Van de Noort 2007).

Sproatley in its setting

The flint-working remains from the Sproatley site constitute by far the largest assemblage of early Mesolithic flint from the southern part of Holderness, complementing the findings from sites further north, such as Brigham and Stone Carr. The larger of the two concentrations of flints at Sproatley had been disturbed by small-scale pit digging in the Bronze Age but over much of its area there seems to have been minimal disturbance, with flint-working waste lying where it had initially fallen.

The gentle topography of the surrounding landscape is misleading when considering the setting of the Sproatley and Brandywell sites during the Mesolithic period. Borehole cores from the Keyingham and Roos valley systems suggested that in the early Mesolithic period the valley bottoms were more than 9m lower than today (Dinnin and Lillie 1995). Similar results were obtained in the Hull valley at Stone Carr (Lillie and Gearey 2000, 64-69). The natural forerunners of the Sproatley and Wyton Drains would have occupied deeper incised channels in a pronounced, actively eroding valley system. The Sproatley site would therefore have occupied a far more prominent position than it does today: an open aspect with wide visibility southwards towards the Humber and westward to the Hull valley.

The underlying drift geology would have been an important factor in the location of this site. Till deposits dominate southern Holderness, with alluvium in the valley bottoms, but the Sproatley site lies on the edge of a small discrete deposit of glaciofluvial sands and gravels. During the excavations, the difference in the surface geology of the Sproatley and Brandywell sites was apparent, the superficial sands and gravels of Sproatley contrasting with the till deposits of Brandywell. In part, the flint-working utilised this local gravel as a raw material.

The general picture of the changing environment of the region provided by pollen studies (e.g. Van de Noort and Davies 1993, 14) suggests that pine and willow would have replaced the birch scrub that developed on the open tundra of post-glacial landscape by the time that the Sproatley site was being used. Hazel and elm would

248

also have been increasing. Fairly dense woodland is likely to have covered the Holderness claylands, while the free-draining sand and gravels at Sproatley may have had a more open landscape, more attractive to Mesolithic communities. A similar argument has been advanced for the siting of Stone Carr (Lillie *et al.* 2003) in a similar open landscape.

In the absence of any clear stratigraphic differentiation within the flint deposits, it is not easy to arrive at a reliable estimate the lifetime of the activity at Sproatley. While the site may have been active for no more than a season, a more extended existence, spanning a number of seasons, is perhaps more probable.

Elsewhere along the pipeline route, unstratified Mesolithic flints were collected from eight of the excavation sites as well as eight other plots of land. For the most part, these were stray finds, but it is possible that the group of flints from the small site at Skeffling may have been contained within a remnant piece of contemporary subsoil, preserved within a slight hollow, and similar, though on a much smaller scale, to the *in situ* deposit at Sproatley. These small assemblages of stray flints indicate brief periods of activity or short periods of occupation, as would be expected in a landscape supporting small semi-nomadic groups of hunters. A more intensely used site, such as Sproatley, would have formed a base, to which small groups of hunters or trappers would periodically return, allowing them to replenish supplies of flint from the gravels, but also no doubt providing a forum for social interaction between groups.

The later Mesolithic and early Neolithic

Diagnostic flint from the later Mesolithic period was limited to a single piece, from Sproatley. It is hard to believe that this contrast between the earlier and later Mesolithic periods is simply a result of the pipeline route sampling an unrepresentative transect through the landscape; it seems more reasonable to conclude that there was a genuine contraction in activity in this part of Holderness.

Changes to the landscape, especially in response to the rising sea level, may be invoked as a possible cause. With slower run-off from the land, the channels of watercourses would have silted up. The increase in wetland is shown in the pollen record as alder becoming widespread, while oak came to dominate the claylands, with lime on the freer draining gravels (Metcalfe *et al.* 2000, 112). There is a striking contrast with the rivers of the Humberhead Levels, where half of the Mesolithic scatters recorded by the Humber Wetlands Survey had flints diagnostic of the later Mesolithic or early Neolithic (Van de Noort 2004, 37).

These changes may have led to the abandonment of the Sproatley site for more favourable locations higher up the valley systems, The rising sea level would have also profoundly affected the wider setting of South Holderness: with the flooding of the Doggerland plain, the region no longer lay on the borders of a wide lowland area and became a maritime province with two very different coastlines, to the east and south. This changing landscape would have altered the way in which the area was utilised, the loss of a large area of land, over a relatively short period, progressively restricting the ambit of itinerant hunters.

As with the later Mesolithic, the early Neolithic seems to be poorly represented within Holderness. Only two of the flints from the pipeline were diagnostic of the early Neolithic period: a laurel leaf point from Sproatley and a leaf-shaped arrowhead found on the stripped subsoil surface at Fosse Hill, Skeffling. Recent studies of the period of transition from Mesolithic to Neolithic have emphasised the complexity of the changes (e.g. Robb and Miracle 2007), and the defining characteristics of the transition, a new suite of flint tools, the adoption of a settled agricultural lifestyle, the use of pottery and the construction of landscape monuments, were adopted at different times, and with considerable geographical variation. The impression from the pipeline results, that there was a broad similarity between the late Mesolithic and early Neolithic periods, would be consistent with this view.

The later Neolithic and early Bronze Age

Cut features dating from the Neolithic period are scarce in southern Holderness, and are mostly limited to pits, with examples from the excavations at Leven and Creyke Beck. A notable exception, however, is the site at Easington Warren, where a hengiform monument with nearby evidence of occupation, including possible hearths and a post-built structure, were sealed beneath a Bronze Age barrow (Evans and Steedman 2001, 69-73). Finds included flint tools, pottery, part of a large polished adze and a fired-clay loomweight. Pollen analysis produced no evidence for crops being grown (Van de Noort 2004, 51) although fragments of a saddle quern indicated the processing of grain. In the wider region, at Sewerby Cottage Farm in Bridlington excavations produced evidence for Neolithic settlement, in the form of five possible buildings, thought to indicate episodic occupation spanning at least 500 years (Fenton-Thomas 2009).

Otherwise, evidence of Neolithic Holderness rests largely on unstratified and often poorly located finds. These include considerable numbers of polished stone tools collected by nineteenth-century farm workers for sale to collectors and museums (Manby 1988, 35) as well as unstratified finds recovered during excavations or from fieldwalking surveys. Their distribution reveals something of the patterns of activity in the period, with a possible weighting towards areas close to contemporary rivers or meres (Dinnin and Van de Noort 1999, 74; Manby *et al.* 2003, 259). The common occurrence of Mesolithic, Neolithic and Bronze Age finds, as, for instance, at Brandesburton (Head 1995 193-194) and Easington (Evans and Steedman 2001, 73), suggests continuity of use over very considerable periods of time. Pollen sequences suggest localised declines of tree species at sites such as Withow Gap near Skipsea, Brandesburton, and Gills Mere, to the north of Roos (Lillie *et al.* 2003), but widespread forest clearance does not appear to have occurred until later. Following the Europe-wide decline in elm, dominant tree cover in Holderness was provided by oak, hazel and lime, with pine in sandy or dry areas (Taylor 1995).

Barrows at Sproatley

The two possible round barrows investigated at Sproatley join close to one hundred listed in the Humber sites and monuments record in South Holderness, with particular concentrations in the Aldbrough and Withernwick areas and, nearer to the pipeline, around Burstwick. In the absence of excavation it is not possible to be certain of the nature of these SMR sites, overwhelmingly identified from cropmarks showing in aerial photographs, but their number suggests that ploughed out barrows are a frequent feature of the landscape.

Only two examples to the east of the Hull valley have been previously excavated in recent times, both at Easington Warren (SKEALS n.d, Evans and Steedman 2001, 69-73). These barrows seem to have been part of a group which includes at least four more possible barrows showing as cropmarks at Kilnsea, and almost certainly others lost to coastal erosion: sherds of cinerary urn and a complete vessel of the same type, dated to the late Bronze Age or early Iron Age, were found on the beach at Kilnsea Warren in 1957. The alluvial coverage of Bronze Age land surfaces along the Humber could conceal further examples of barrows in the area. Cremated bone from two excavated pits at the Langeled Gas Terminal at Easington, which returned Bronze Age radiocarbon dates (Richardson 2011, 7-8), also provides evidence of funerary activity in the area.

The Easington barrows were smaller than the annular features at Sproatley, although the diameters quoted were for the extents of the monuments rather than enclosing ditches; indeed, the more southerly of the Easington barrows did not appear to have been surrounded by a ditch, consisting only of a mound 16m across (Evans and Steedman 2001). The 'small' barrow at Easington had an enclosing ditch defining an area approximately 9m in diameter but also had an external bank taking the full width of the monument to 17m. This contrast in

the morphologies of the two Easington Warren barrows suggests that they may have been different classes of monument to one another, and to the examples at Sproatley; they also serve as a reminder that the presence of a large mound is not common to all classes of round barrow, and the absence of surviving mounds at Sproatley is not necessarily wholly attributable to plough damage.

The fifty-one small fragments of plain Beaker pottery recovered from the Sproatley site were found some distance from the possible barrows, from two locations: at least 50m from the excavated barrow ditches, and from deposits 20m from the line of the putative third barrow, inferred from the geophysical survey. Nevertheless, they demonstrate that there was early Bronze Age activity close by. Beaker pottery is rarely found in Holderness, but is commonly associated with round barrows. The similarity of the Sproatley sherds to those recovered at the southern barrow at Easington Warren (Manby, this volume, page 100) lends support to the supposition that this was a funerary site. The small features cut into northern flint scatter returned radiocarbon dates that fall firmly within the Beaker period, and later Neolithic and Bronze Age flint was a significant minor component of the assemblages from both Sproatley and Brandywell, immediately adjacent.

Other Bronze Age activity

Because they often form clear cropmarks, Bronze Age barrows are over-represented in the archaeological record when compared to other remains of the period. The results of large development projects that sample large areas of the landscape can help to redress this bias. Excavations at Catwick Quarry (summarised by McCoy 2008) revealed features indicating possible early Bronze Age occupation. Occupation may also be represented by pits excavated on the Leven to Brandesburton bypass (Steedman 1993, 5), middle Bronze Age food vessels and a cup recovered during gravel extraction at Barff Hill north-east of Beverley in the 1930s, and hearths identified at Easington Warren (Evans and Steedman 2001, 69). An isolated pit, probably the remains of a cremation burial, was found on the north-western outskirts of Preston village on the Salt End to Aldbrough cable route (Manby, in Savage 2014). Sherds of Beaker pottery were also recovered from a site at Swine on the Ganstead to Asselby pipeline (Daniel *et al.* forthcoming).

The sites at Churchlands, Skeffling and Dimlington Road all produced indications of Bronze Age activity, as did pit **119574**, to the west of the Gilcross site. Three sherds of later Beaker pottery from this pit, the only dating evidence, suggest that the feature was dug in the Bronze Age. The same could be true of the small pits at Skeffling, of which two returned dates of 1760 to 1610 cal BC and 1750 to 1490 cal BC. A plausible though speculative suggestion, prompted by the presence of fire-cracked stones, is that the fills of the pits incorporated material from the remnants of a possible Bronze Age burnt mound, through which the pits were cut.

As well as producing one of the larger assemblages of worked flint along the pipeline route, with Mesolithic and Neolithic or early Bronze Age pieces, including a bifacially worked awl and the broken tip of what may originally have been a fine leaf-shaped knife, the Churchlands site produced sixteen pieces of Biconical Urn probably dating to 1700 to 1500 BC. A possible cylindrical loomweight recovered from the site, may also date from the Bronze Age. The Biconical Urn sherds are of some significance to the southern Holderness region as such pottery is scarce in East Yorkshire and, indeed, in the East Midlands, and is found mainly in funerary contexts, although at Caythorpe and Rudston, urn fragments occurred in pits associated with settlement (Manby, this volume, page 102).

Bronze Age activity at the Dimlington Road site is demonstrated by a radiocarbon date of 1490 to 1310 cal BC and sherds of possible Bucket Urn, from adjacent features. It is worthy of note that the sample for the radiocarbon date was from a charred cereal grain: a small but significant piece of evidence for cereal use in the area. Holderness must have witnessed huge changes in the subsistence strategies of its population in the time periods discussed here, from hunting to herding, through pastoral nomadism to settled agriculture, but evidence for these changes, and especially their timing, is fleeting. This tiny grain is perhaps an indication that the Bronze Age community was sufficiently stable to support investment in arable production. Here, as at Churchlands, the pottery may have been associated with a cremation burial, within what seems to have been a larger and long established funerary landscape, which also suggests a social investment in a settled place.

Distribution of Neolithic and Bronze Age activity

In all, struck flint was recovered from fifty-nine of the ninety fields on the pipeline route, of which forty-one had pieces that could be confidently dated to the later Neolithic or Bronze Age periods. These assemblages tended to be small, with only the Burton Constable, Brandywell and Sproatley excavation sites producing more than fifty flints. The Burton Constable assemblage includes an apparently abandoned, unfinished arrowhead, a discarded attempt, perhaps, to produce a leaf or barbed and tanged form. Although all of the Burton Constable assemblage was residual in later contexts, eight flints recovered from ditch **118957** are in fresh condition suggesting that they had not moved far from their original place of deposition. This would point to the focus of activity being centred close to the southern end of the site, the area subsequently settled in the Iron Age.

The distribution along the pipeline route gives an indication of the pattern of activity across the landscape and could potentially identify areas that were more intensively utilised. The raised densities of flints at the sites discussed above can be taken as an indication that they were being selectively utilised in the Neolithic or Bronze Age periods, although a considerable bias will have been introduced by the intensity of scrutiny that the excavation areas received, when compared with land elsewhere on the pipeline, where the flint assemblages consist of finds from fieldwalking, monitoring of construction and, in some cases, evaluation trenching. The extensive sampling procedure at the Sproatley site will have further skewed the distribution data.

This lack of a project-wide systematic sample collection, together with the small proportion of chronologically diagnostic forms within the flint assemblage, precludes a strictly quantitative analysis. Excluding the Mesolithic spreads at Sproatley, however, the majority of the diagnostic flints are of broad Neolithic or Bronze Age date and it is reasonable to assume that the same is approximately true of the total number of struck pieces: this number can be taken as a rough proxy for the Neolithic or Bronze Age material.

In order to investigate whether the flint distribution showed any influence of topographic setting, a comparison was made between the numbers of flints and heights OD for each field along the pipeline route. The major concentrations, at Burton Constable, Brandywell and Sproatley, lay above or very close to the 10m contour, but overall 77 per cent of the flints were from fields in parts of the route above 10m OD, 15 per cent in fields between 5m and 10m, and 8 per cent from fields below five metres. Along the pipeline route as a whole, sixty-four per cent of the land lies above the 10m contour, 24 per cent between 10m and 5m, and 12 per cent below 5m (calculations based on OS Panorama data). Taking into account the uncertainties of the data, the discrepancies between these two sets of figures are unlikely to be significant, and it seems reasonable to conclude that exploitation of the lower wetland zones may have been just as important as exploitation of the higher drier areas. But if the larger assemblages represent the locations of settlements or temporary camps, these seem to have been positioned well above the wetland zone. The small amount of Bronze Age pottery recovered also derived from sites at or above the 10m contour.

Although the distribution of flint away from the main concentrations was fairly even, there were two stretches of the pipeline route of over 1.5km in length which each produced only a single piece of flint: the areas between Arables Lane and Weldon's Plantation, Winestead, and to the North of Ploughlands Farm, Welwick. It may be significant that both of these areas rise to over 20m OD; it seems to be that the effect of the topography on the distribution of activity is most marked in the highest and perhaps most exposed parts of the landscape.

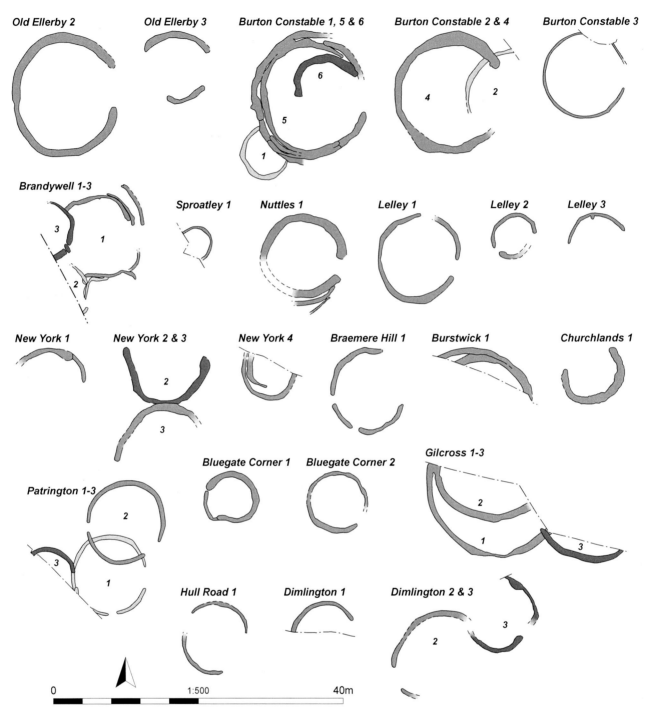

FIG. 117: IRON AGE RING GULLIES

Death and burial in the Iron Age, and beyond

Although square barrow cemeteries are typical of the East Yorkshire Iron Age on and around the Wolds, individual square barrows or small groups occur over a much wider distribution, from the 'warrior burials' at Brisley Farm in Kent (Stevenson 2012) to Boyscack Mills in Angus (Murray and Ralston 1997). The evidence for their distribution in south Holderness comes mostly from cropmark features. These include three possible examples Elm Tree Farm, Halsham (SMR MHU 19291), a single example 300m

north east of the Braemere Hill excavation site (MHU 2854) and possibly two more 750m to the south-west of Braemere Hill at Stockdale Farm, Burstwick (MHU 19316). Further afield, there are others to the east of Roos (MHU 18873) and at Mill Hill, East Garton (MHU 18844), at Leven (Brigham, Buglass, and Steedman 2008) and in the north of Holderness at Barmston (MHU332) and Fraisthorpe (MHU10044). To the east of the Hull valley, two possible examples have recently been investigated at Whitehill Farm Gas Storage Facility (NAA n.d.). But if the interpretation of the feature at Sproatley is correct, it is a rare, if not unique, example of an excavated square barrow in the southern part of Holderness.

One side had been lost to a later Iron Age ditch and another apparently recut but the form and dimensions of the feature fit within the normal range of those in the well-characterised square barrow cemeteries of the Wolds. Dating evidence from the feature is limited to a large fragment of pottery and a radiocarbon date from a small sample of charcoal from the fill of the ditch. The radiocarbon determination indicates a much earlier date than the range of dates typical of square barrows, while the pottery vessel, though not closely datable, does not differ from hand-made pottery recovered elsewhere, and assumed to be of broadly Iron Age date. The pottery is unlikely to have been intrusive, unless it was within the fill of an unrecognised feature cut into the top of the ditch, whereas there is a strong possibility that the fragment of charcoal used for dating could have been residual. The pottery is therefore considered to be the more reliable indicator of the date of the feature.

There was no sign of a primary burial within the area enclosed by the barrow ditch; this is not uncommon in square barrow burials, the grave being usually shallower than the ditch and therefore more susceptible to loss by truncation (Stead 1991, 9). However, a later grave had been cut across the top of the infilled ditch. Secondary burials occur fairly frequently in square barrows, though more usually aligned parallel, rather than across, the ditch. Dent (1995) notes that Bronze Age round barrows and the square barrows of the Iron Age do not, as a rule, share similar distributions, the Iron Age barrow builders seemingly ignoring the positions of the Bronze Age monuments. The Sproatley site may be unusual in this respect, with barrows of both periods occurring, if both interpretations are correct, within 200m of one another.

None of the other skeletal remains recovered are unequivocally of Iron Age provenance, although the Gilcross burial was probably of late Iron Age or early Roman date. The simple inhumation from Burton Constable and the adult, child and neonate remains from Brandywell were all from Roman contexts, as were the cremated remains from Old Ellerby and Out Newton Road. The Lelley neonate and the isolated cremated remains from the area north of the Burton Constable site were both undated.

Iron Age settlement

The most striking result from the investigations is the number of sites with Iron Age ring gullies. Counting the widely separated features at Dimlington Road as separate locations, there were sixteen such sites along the 32km-long pipeline. At least twenty-eight complete or partial ring gullies were excavated, along with perhaps another seven possible examples. If this density of remains is repeated throughout Holderness, it implies the presence of four thousand or more similar sites, a figure that could be a considerable underestimate, as many sites must have been lost since the Iron Age as a result of ploughing and erosion.

The term 'ring gully' has been used to describe these features, so as not to pre-empt consideration of their possible functions, discussed in more detail in the next section, but Iron Age ring gullies are generally interpreted as evidence of roundhouse-type structures, and therefore the remains of settlement sites. How many of these sites were occupied at any one time depends, of course, on their longevity but their number seems to indicate that the Iron Age landscape supported a relatively large population.

This richness of Iron Age settlement sites in Holderness has, until recently, not been reflected in the archaeological literature, but recent developer-funded investigations have begun to redress this balance. At the Aldbrough gas storage facility, a square enclosure surrounded the remains of at least five roundhouses (Bradley and Steedman 2014). The largest, around 10m in diameter, was defined by a ring gully, with two opposing entrances, surrounded by a larger concentric ring ditch. Two further ring gullies showed evidence that they had each been replaced on at least one occasion. One of these gullies also had two opposing entranceways. Two clusters of overlapping ring gullies, seven in total, were excavated 1.5km to the south-west, on the route of the electricity cable to the gas storage facility from Salt End power station (Savage 2014). The largest had an internal diameter of 14m.

Excavations at the Langeled gas terminal in Easington (Richardson 2011) revealed the disturbed remains of two ring gullies, positioned between north-to-south aligned ditches, interpreted as parts of a system of enclosed fields. The Easington to Paull pipeline route added a further seven ring gullies from five sites nearby (Rowland and Wegiel 2012).

Near to Ganstead village, excavations on the route of the Teesside to Salt End Ethylene Pipeline revealed a ring gully, 7.9m in diameter, cut through a cobbled surface (Evans and Atkinson 2009, 258-289). A series of regularly spaced oval pits were interpreted as the remains of a second roundhouse, while other postholes may have formed an earlier rectilinear fenced enclosure. Nearby domestic activity can also probably be inferred from Iron Age features excavated on the route of the A165 Leven to Brandesburton bypass and in advance of quarrying of sand and gravel at Catwick and Sandsfield Quarries (Evans and Atkinson 2009, 252).

There has been a similar accumulation of known Iron Age settlement sites in the Hull valley and the eastern fringes of the Wolds. At Creyke Beck (summarised in

Evans and Steedman 2001), the earliest of the seven probable roundhouses survived only as a dense group of postholes but the later examples were represented by ring gullies, ranging from 8m to 14m in diameter. A considerable assemblage of pottery indicated occupation into the early first century AD. A site at Saltshouse Road, on the north-eastern outskirts of Hull, excavated in 1962, also seems to have been occupied into the first century AD but to have gone out of use before distinctively Roman pottery became available. During construction of the Ganstead to Asselby pipeline, the remains of at least eight possible roundhouses, in the form of surviving ring gullies and posthole groups, were recorded at a site straddling Shepherd Lane, south of Beverley (Daniel *et al.* forthcoming). Geophysical surveys on the route of the Beverley southern relief road showed this site to be a small part of a much more extensive area of settlement extending northwards towards the outskirts of the town, and excavations by AOC Archaeology have revealed four ring gullies, as well as post-built structures (Kirsten Holland, pers. comm.). A ring gully 7m in diameter was also excavated during an evaluation at Hull High School in Anlaby (Fraser 2004).

The ring gullies: what did they surround?

None of the excavated ring gullies showed a coherent pattern of internal features that would provide unequivocal evidence that they surrounded a roundhouse-type structure, and the supposition that they did rests largely on the analogy with the better characterised examples from elsewhere in the country, together with the artefactual evidence. These comparanda include the well preserved and well characterised post-built roundhouses of the chalk downlands of southern England, as well as the more typical examples from much of the rest of lowland Britain, especially the claylands, where all that commonly survives is a penannular gully with occasional internal pits and postholes. In these cases, there will always be a case for questioning whether the interpretation as the remains of roundhouses is valid.

With regard to their form, the excavated Easington to Ganstead ring gullies were generally penannular or, where they were partly outside of the working width or truncated by later features, were consistent with having been penannular. Possible exceptions included structures 2 and 3 at New York, Structure 2 at Dimlington Road, and Structure 1 at Churchlands, which were incomplete irregular arcs. Where the breaks in the penannular circuit were visible, they were, in most cases, on the east or south-east side; this is by far the commonest orientation (Pope 2003, 176). There are good utilitarian reasons why a roundhouse should have an east or south-east facing entrance, both in the provision of shelter from prevailing westerly winds and, perhaps more importantly, making best use of the light and heat of the sun in the early part of the day (*ibid.*). The positions of the entranceways of some of the smaller ring gullies,

notably Churchlands and possibly Lelley Structure 2, were anomalous, and these gullies may have had a distinctly different function. Ancillary structures might, for instance, have had an entrance oriented towards their parent building. The possibility that ring gullies provided drainage around something other than a building, such as a hayrick or a working area, should also be borne in mind.

Typical roundhouse gullies cited in the literature range from 8m to 15m in diameter but with examples occurring beyond both ends of this range. The measured or estimated diameters of the Easington to Ganstead ring gullies range from 5m to 19.5m with a mean of 10.5m. Four stand out as having diameters of over 17m: the three at Gilcross and the recut gully at Burstwick. In all four of these cases, the ring lay only partially within the limits of excavation and the quoted diameter is based on extrapolation of the visible arc: it is quite possible they have been overestimated, especially if they deviated markedly from perfect circularity. Of the ring gullies that were wholly within their respective excavation areas, Old Ellerby Structure 2 and Burton Constable Structure 5 were the largest: both around 14m in diameter.

The environmental evidence from the Easington to Ganstead examples is unfortunately very limited, although there is a tentative suggestion that may indicate the use of turf, possibly as a component of the structure or for fuel. The artefactual evidence is far more compelling, with assemblages that are typical of the detritus from normal domestic activity within small rural settlements, in some cases in considerable quantities: Old Ellerby Structure 2 and Lelley Structure 1 both produced around 30kg of pottery. It is noteworthy that even some of the very shallow and heavily truncated ring gullies, such as the Hull Road example, produced comparatively large pottery assemblages. A lower level of domestic activity may be indicated by those examples where finds were scarce, such as Churchlands, Structure 1 at Bluegate Corner and Structures 2 and 3 at Lelley. These ring gullies were generally towards the smaller end of the size range and, as with the position of entrances, their atypicality may indicate an ancillary function.

There was a marked bias in the occurrence of pottery towards the ring gully terminals, with both the quantity of pottery and the size of sherds being generally greater. This bias in the distribution of finds towards the entranceways may have a purely functional explanation, as the likely area where activity is concentrated, but the material correlates of ideologically inspired practices within the social and economic realm have attracted much interest and debate in recent years (for instance Hill 1995, Chadwick 2009) and an entranceway is likely to have a deep cultural and symbolic significance. It is notable that a high proportion of the pottery finds appeared to have been originally deposited as complete, or substantially complete, vessels. This raises the possibility that they were deliberately deposited as 'structured' or 'placed' deposits.

Generally, then, the Easington to Ganstead ring gullies fit the common pattern of Iron Age roundhouse gullies, and they can be confidently interpreted belonging to this class of structure. This suggests that cultural practices in the East Yorkshire were similar to those in other lowland areas of later prehistoric Britain, despite other evidence of a degree of distinctiveness in the region.

Ring gullies: the form of the possible structures

The various possible interpretations of roundhouse ring gullies can be divided into two broad groups: they either held part of the structure, or they had a water-management function. A third alternative, that they served simply to demarcate their internal space, is not necessarily exclusive of the other two. Terminology varies, but Harding (2009, 71) uses 'ring groove' to designate a structural gully: 'a continuous circular trench into which upright posts, stakes or planks could be bedded'. This wide definition encompasses the possibility of the ring groove holding either load-bearing posts, the supporting framework of a curtain wall, or horizontal 'sill-beams or wall-plates, into which upright posts, stakes or planks could have been jointed'. Of the examples given by Harding, the positions of most seem to correspond to the second of these alternatives, the groove probably having held the uprights of a wattle wall woven *in situ*.

As a drainage feature, the traditional view of a ring gully is that it collected water dripping from the eaves of the building, possibly even being formed or maintained by the erosional action of water running from the roof. Perhaps more importantly, the gully would also act to deflect surface storm waters away from the base of the wall, and, if of sufficient depth, would serve to drain the space that it enclosed, by lowering the water-table. This would have been enhanced if it incorporated a run-off channel or if it was actively emptied.

The question that therefore needs to be posed for the Easington to Ganstead ring gullies is whether these features were ring grooves or drainage gullies. Various criteria can be applied in order to discriminate between these two possibilities (see, for instance, Pope 2003, 73). Being backfilled as part of the construction process, a ring groove, unlike a drainage gully, would not be open to receive finds during the period of use of the structure it surrounded. It would be expected to have a deliberately deposited fill consisting of the excavated topsoil and subsoil, with finds that were either residual or possibly votive. By contrast, a drainage gully is likely to have silt layers within its fill, possibly showing episodes of cleaning and recutting to keep it open and maintain its function, and to have finds derived from activities within and around the structure.

The optimum form of a ring groove would be vertical-sided and of approximately the same width as the timbers

that it was designed to hold, whereas a drainage gully, even if dug with vertical sides, would erode over time, in most soils, to approach a V- or shallow U-sided profile. Additionally, to support the wall, or other structural element, a ring groove would closely reflect the form of the complete structure and there is every indication that Iron Age builders were aware of the structural advantages of a perfectly circular form. By contrast, a drainage gully could deviate from circularity, especially on sloping ground, without seriously compromising its function.

Most of the Easington to Ganstead examples would fit the criteria for drainage gullies rather than ring grooves. Burton Constable Structure 5, with its finds-rich fills and multiple recuts, provides the clearest example. Structure 3 at the same site is probably the only one which could reasonably be interpreted as a ring groove. Although its close juxtaposition with Structure 5 over-emphasises its relative slightness and regularity, it was the most closely circular of any of the penannular gullies. Surviving to a depth of only 0.03 to 0.14m, it showed a steep-sided profile in the deepest of its excavated sections. Conversely, the quantity of pottery recovered, fifty-one sherds, weighing over 500g in total, suggests that the gully had been open to receive finds for some time. An interpretation as the base of a drainage gully, which would originally have been considerably deeper but has been truncated by ploughing, is perhaps more tenable, even in this case.

In Structure 5 at Burton Constable, the stratigraphy was consistent with the numerous shallow pits, postholes or stake-holes within the internal space of the ring gully being broadly contemporary with the ring gully. However, these features lacked any coherent pattern and they are more likely to have held either small internal fixtures or temporary supports used during construction of the building rather than permanent, integral, load-bearing elements. At the same site, Structures 3 and 4 also had internal postholes, but it was not clear whether these were contemporary with the ring gullies, and in both cases their disposition appeared to be rather random, lacking any obvious relationship to the geometry of the structure. The same is true of the internal postholes of the structure at Nuttles and the group of small discrete features within Structure 2 at Patrington.

The general lack of evidence for posts with a clear structural function prompts the question as to whether the structures were supported in some other way. A lack of postholes does not necessarily imply an absence of posts, as a post does not necessarily need to be deeply set in the ground if it is part of a structure that provides internal bracing, perhaps using a ring of lintels joining the tops of the posts. Posts could also have rested on a circle of sill beams or post pads placed on the ground surface (Harding 2009, 73-75). The posts in such arrangement would have needed support during construction, but a large circular post-built house could have nevertheless stood without leaving any evidence of postholes (Harding 2009, 56), or at least none that would survive later ploughing. Such a design of roundhouse might have been especially favoured in wetland areas, such as Holderness, where earthfast posts would have been particularly susceptible to rotting in damp ground.

A suspicion remains, however, that the past concentration of research excavation on better preserved sites, especially in the south of England, may have coloured views of how the roundhouses were constructed. Experimental reconstructions, pioneered at Butser Farm in West Sussex (Reynolds 1979) but subsequently carried out on many other sites throughout the country, have provided a wealth of information, especially useful for elucidating the constraints on the form and dimensions of roundhouses but have had a strongly normative effect on how these structures have been interpreted and visualised. The generality of Iron Age roundhouses may be quite different, especially if skills, tools and human resources needed for construction were not locally available. Smaller roundhouses, in particular, might have been altogether humbler structures, perhaps with a roof supported by thick turf walls rather than rings of posts.

The excavation sites produced some direct evidence of construction materials. Daub with roundwood impressions was found at Burton Constable, Lelley and Churchlands; fired clay recovered from Bluegate Corner, Old Ellerby and Brandywell was probably also daub. These examples clearly suggest that at least some of the structures used daub in their construction. This would normally have been supported on woven withies, a plentiful resource in the undrained wetlands of Holderness. More intriguing, however, is the rope-impressed daub in Burton Constable Structure 4. The rope seemed to have been laid in parallel lengths, with no sign of it having been knotted, as would be expected if it was tying timbers together. It is possible that rope could have been tied around the circumference of the walls to resist the radial forces from the weight of the roof but it is perhaps more likely that it had been pressed into service for repairs.

The use of turf as a construction material is hinted at by the composition of some of the arachaeo-botanical assemblages from ring gullies at Burton Constable, Nuttles, New York, Bluegate Corner and Dimlington Road. As a heavy material, its use in walls rather than roofing is perhaps more likely. Turfs stacked and faced with wattle and daub panels, could have formed a sturdy and weatherproof wall. As to the roof, a spread of material over Roundhouse 27 on the A63 Junction at Melton was interpreted as the remains of thatch (Fenton-Thomas 2011, 81-82); the Easington to Ganstead structures could have been similarly roofed.

The diameter of the roof can be estimated by assuming that a ring gully would be positioned so as to intercept rainwater running from the eaves of the structure, so the diameter of the ring gully would approximately equate to the extent of the roof. Without knowing the width of the eaves, and the thickness of the wall, any estimate of the internal area of the structure involves a considerable degree of conjecture, but an external diameter of at least 1.5m smaller than the diameter of the ring gully is a reasonable assumption.

The break in the ring gully at Nuttles had formed a focus for other features but there was no clear evidence at any of the sites for external porches to the structures. Postholes within, or just inside, the entrance gaps at Structure 4 at Burton Constable, and Structures 1 at Braemere Hill and Hull Road, possibly indicate the presence of some form of door. The Braemere Hill ring gully and Structures 1 and 2 at Patrington may have had two entrances, although in the case of Patrington the second breaks in the rings could have resulted from later truncation. This was probably the case with other double breaks, such as that of Structure 2 at Lelley. Double entranced ring gullies are, however, known from other nearby sites, notably the double-ringed gully at Aldbrough gas storage facility (Bradley and Steedman 2014) where the symmetry of the arrangement leaves little room for doubt that this was a deliberate element of the design.

The lack of any evidence for hearths is worthy of note. Later plough damage could be invoked, but no surviving hearth was recorded in Roundhouse 27 at Melton, where internal surfaces had been preserved beneath the remains of its collapsed roof (Fenton-Thomas 2011, 371). Heating provided by a hearth raised off the ground may be a possibility, the supports perhaps accounting for some of the internal features at Burton Constable Structure 5 and elsewhere. This is more likely to have been a practical possibility if the fuel was charcoal, rather than raw timber.

The ring gullies in context

The sites with Iron Age remains typically had one or more ring gullies along with pits and linear features. With a few exceptions, such as Patrington, the ring gullies are in the earliest stratigraphic phases, pre-dating all of the linear features. The greatest complexity was at Burton Constable, but even here there is no indication from the stratigraphy that any more than two roundhouses were in contemporary use, and it is possible that the remains represent a single roundhouse successively rebuilt in slightly different locations. The same is also true of the other sites with multiple ring gullies.

The common pattern of rebuilding within a slightly displaced footprint must have had some significance, as cutting a new drainage gully would almost certainly take more effort than emptying out an existing one, even one that had largely silted up. Recutting in exactly the same place is, of course, archaeologically difficult to detect, and that may have been the normal practice. However, if sufficient time had elapsed for the original ring gully to completely infill, it may have no longer been visible, though the siting of its replacement in roughly the same area would imply that the location was either physically or culturally constrained. Other possibilities are that the original structure may have been sullied in some way, requiring part of the footprint to be excluded, or the re-siting may have been a deliberate symbolic break with the past.

Although the working width of the pipeline allowed only a restricted view of the archaeological deposits, there was little to suggest that any of the sites were any more than small dispersed farmsteads. This is consistent with the evidence from other recent excavations on Iron Age sites within southern Holderness (Richardson 2011; Bradley and Steedman, 2014; Savage 2014; Rowland and Wegiel 2012).

Historically, the study of the British Iron Age has been hugely influenced by work on large defended settlements, far removed from the reality of life for the farmers of south Holderness. This influence is seen in the emphasis on the distinctions between enclosed or unenclosed settlements. Of the Easington to Ganstead sites, Out Newton Road, would certainly qualify as an enclosed settlement. The ditch, up to 1.7m deep and 6m across, if accompanied by a bank and possibly a hedge or fence, would have formed an imposing barrier conveying an unequivocal message about access to the space within. As far as can be inferred from the dating evidence, this site falls within the same chronological range as the other ring gully sites, so it is unlikely that its distinctive morphology is a simple correlate of its date. This implies that the site was functionally different to the other ring gully sites, perhaps serving as a centre of temporal or spiritual authority.

None of the other excavation sites showed anything comparable to the Out Newton Road enclosure, although the Burstwick ring gully may have been located within a ditched enclosure, of which two sides were visible. Extrapolating a north-western corner, where the ditch had been truncated, and two corners to the south of the limit of excavation would produce a rectilinear enclosure around the ring gully, for which parallels can be seen in cropmark sites in the Wolds (Stoertz 1997, 49-51). However, the finds from the enclosure ditch indicate that it infilled later than the ring gully and it may have originated after the ring gully infilled. If so, it fits what seems to be a common pattern at a number of the excavation sites, of rectilinear landscape features developing during the lifetime of settlement in the area but post-dating, where stratigraphic relationships are available, the ring gullies.

On a larger scale, the pipeline route did not cross anything which looked like a major boundary; there was nothing comparable to the linear monuments seen on the Wolds, commonly interpreted as territorial boundaries (but see Giles 2012, 53-62). Beyond their immediate extended family group, the inhabitants of all of these settlements are likely to have seen themselves as belonging to a single wider community.

Settlements in the landscape

The ring gully sites were, broadly speaking, spread along the entire length of the pipeline, but their distribution was not even. Dividing the pipeline route into three roughly similar lengths, the westernmost third, from Old Ellerby to the site at Braemere Hill, a distance of 10.5km, contained eight such sites, the 13.6km-long central section from there to Patrington contained two locations, while the south-eastern section, to the end of the pipeline at Easington, contained six ring gully locations in a length of 8.1km. These figures correspond to ring gully sites averaging less than 1.5km apart in the north-western and south-eastern sections, and over 6.5km apart in the middle section.

Considering the possible reasons for this distribution favouring of the two ends of the route, it is unlikely that differential preservation would have introduced a significant bias. The pipeline route ran almost exclusively through rural areas dominated by arable land (Middleton 1995, 20-22) and there is little doubt that all of the sites had been affected to some degree by ploughing, the effects of which were visible either as medieval or post-medieval furrows, or as more recent plough scores. However, there was no indication that the land in the central portion of the pipeline route had been more heavily or more frequently ploughed than either of the ends. As it is dominated by the Keyingham and Burstwick valley systems the opposite is more likely to have been the case, as the damper valley bottoms are likely to have been used in the past for permanent pasture or hay meadows.

In the wider Holderness region there is a correlation between locations of known settlements and the occurrence of gravel outcrops, towards the western side of the Holderness plain. To some extent, this may be a reflection of the distribution of recent development work, many of these sites having been discovered during quarrying of the deposits. A similar bias could be invoked to account for sites in the coastal zone, found as a result of the development of the natural gas industry.

Masking of sites by alluvium, laid down during or after the Iron Age, is another possibility. Superficial alluvial deposits are known to cover around 2.4km of the total length of the pipeline route (Holgate and Ralph 2006, quoting BGS maps and borehole records) and the presence of alluvium was broadly corroborated by observations during monitoring of the excavation of the pipe-trench. No evidence of deeply buried archaeological remains was noted during this monitoring, though it should be remembered that a pipe-trench provides a very imperfect window onto the sub-surface archaeology.

If differential preservation and alluvial masking are discounted, and the distribution of sites did not simply arise as a random sample, the observed pattern of settlement must reflect the original choices of location by the Iron Age inhabitants. Poor drainage and susceptibility to flooding are possible factors affecting this choice, the middle part of the pipeline route being dominated by the Keyingham and Burstwick valleys. But despite their vulnerability to flooding, the valley sediments would have produced fertile soils and, away from the meres, marshes and carrs, would have formed valuable meadowlands. Access to water, especially for grazing stock, would also have been important. Taking into account these factors, the distribution of the excavated settlement sites can perhaps be best explained as a balance between proximity to the resources of the lower-lying valley bottoms and the higher, drier land.

The observation that none of the excavated ring gully sites lay below the 9m contour, with the exception of Braemere Hill, at 5.5m OD, prompted the conjecture that land below this height was too wet for permanent settlement in the Iron Age. A number of sites in southern Holderness, such as Aldbrough (Bradley and Steedman 2014, Savage 2014), Langeled Receiving Facilities (Richardson 2011) and Withernwick (Steedman pers. comm.) are consistent with this view, counter-examples are provided by settlement sites south of Ottringham (SMR MHU7486), between Ganstead and Bilton (HFA 2001), and at Creyke Beck (Evans and Steedman 2001, 67-69). More recently, the sites on the Easington to Paull pipeline (Rowland and Wegiel 2012) are also much lower lying. The effect of local topography on Iron Age settlement location is clearly more complex.

The hydrological changes in the Iron Age and Roman landscape of the region are poorly understood (Dinnin and Lillie 1995) but it is likely that the sea level rise of the earlier post-glacial period continued into the early Iron Age. Increasingly, though, the isostatic rebound of the continental crust, as it slowly recovered from the effects of the weight of ice it had borne, became

Lab. Ref.		Str.	Contxt	RC date	δ13C	Calibrated date	Sample type
SUERC-	GU-				‰		
Old Ellerby							
38657	26354	2	3248	2075 ± 30	-21.6	180 (91.3%) 36 BC; 31 (1.9%) 19 BC; 13 (2.2%) 1 BC	Cattle molar
Burton Constable							
36190	24867	4	9979	2245 ± 30	-24.9	400 (29.2%) 340 BC; 320 (66.2%) 200 BC	Charcoal
38658	26355	2	118058	2000 ± 30	-21.8	86 (0.8%) 80 BC; 54 BC (94.6%) 71 AD	Cattle vertebra
38659	26356	1	9493	2000 ± 30	-22.2	86 (0.8%) 80 BC; 54 BC (94.6%) 71 AD	Cattle phalanx
Brandywell							
38660	26357	1	25200	2070 ± 30	-23.9	174 (02.3%) 19 BC; 13 BC (3.1%) 1 AD	Charred seed
Nuttles							
38666	26360	1	31024	2125 ± 30	-27.0	348 (7.1%) 318 BC; 207 (88.3%) 52 BC	Charred wheat
New York							
38667	26361	4	119836	2105 ± 30	-25.8	201 (95.4%) 46 BC	Charred cereal
Braemere Hill							
38668	26362	1	119066	2195 ± 30	-25.0*	367 (95.4%) 181 BC	Charred wheat
Patrington							
36194	24871	1	88051	2210 ± 30	-24.0	380 (95.4%) 190 BC	Charred grain
Bluegate Corner							
38669	26363	1	119907	2110 ± 30	-25.0	336 (0.6%) 331 BC; 204 (94.8%) 47 BC	Charred wheat
Hull Rd							
36201	24876	1	120708	2280 ± 30	-24.7	410 (55.8%) 350 BC; 300 (39.6%) 200 BC	Charcoal
Dimlington Rd							
36202	24877	1	120907	1980 ± 30	-26.2	50 BC (95.4%) 80 AD	Charred grain
36203	24878	2	120457	1485 ± 30	-25.0	AD 530 (95.4%) 650	Charcoal
36204	24879	3	120471	3125 ± 30	-22.7	1490 (1.7%) 1470 BC; 1460 (93.7%) 1310 BC	Charred grain

*assumed

TABLE 68: SUMMARY OF RADIOCARBON DATES FROM RING GULLIES

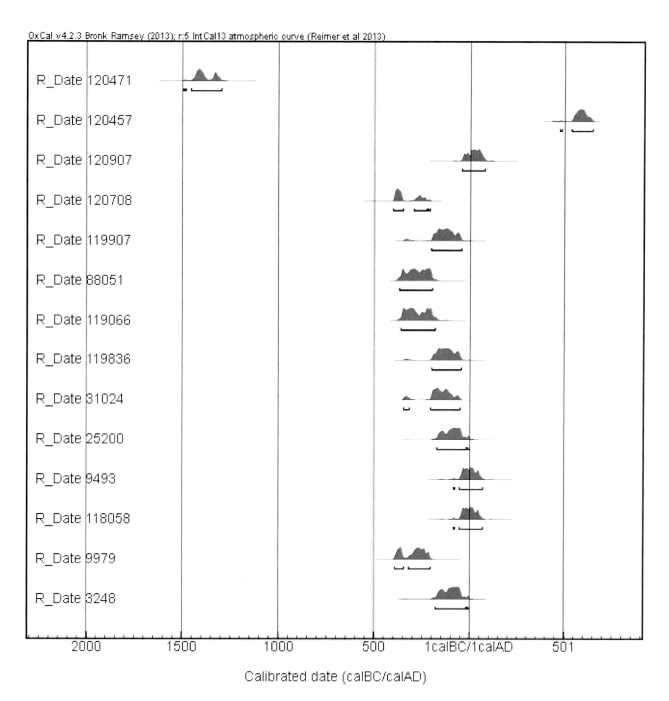

FIG. 118: PLOT OF CALIBRATED RADIOCARBON DATES FROM RING GULLIES

a significant determinant of the relative levels of land and sea. By 1000 BC, land below a height of 1.5m OD, would have been wetland (Van de Noort 2004, 25-27) but in the later Iron Age, the lower parts Holderness probably became drier: fertile alluvial land, separated by freshwater rivers and creeks. This would have allowed occupation closer to the present-day Humber shoreline, but it is likely that the accumulation of sediment in the valley systems further inland still impeded drainage, so that these remained susceptible to seasonal flooding. The boundary of the wetland zone would therefore have been a function of the distance from the Humber shoreline, as well as the contemporary sea level.

Social constraints would also have affected the distribution of settlements. Because of the lack of temporal definition, it is not certain which sites were contemporary, but even so, the density of settlements in the north-western and south-eastern sections of the route suggests that each would have been either directly in view of its nearest neighbour or at least in view of the smoke from the fires of nearby settlements. Though this was a landscape of dispersed farmsteads, these were not necessarily isolated. The meres and marshlands, waste and uncleared forest would have imposed a degree of separation, but the general lack of ditched boundaries perhaps suggests that this was a society which shared sufficient common interests between communities that it did not require formalised land divisions. Life in a remote and unforgiving landscape would not have been easy, and co-operation with neighbours would have been vital.

The chronology of the Iron Age settlements

The Bronze Age funerary sites and findspots imply that the area was quite widely settled at the beginning of the first millennium BC, but these settlements have left little evidence in the archaeological record. Any structures, of which there must surely have been some, seem not have significantly penetrated the ground to a depth below the subsequent plough zone. This raises difficulties in gauging the extent to which there was a significant increase in the number of settlements in the later part of the Iron Age, but the number of sites suggests that there was, if not a population explosion, at the very least an absolute increase, probably combined with a greater degree of permanence of settlement.

A number of reasons could be proposed for this increased colonisation of the landscape. Falling sea levels or possibly climatic amelioration in the earlier part of the Iron Age could have produced more exploitable land while changes in agricultural practice and technological advances, not least the availability of iron tools, would have increased the rate at which woodland could be cleared to create grazing areas for livestock, and allowed the heavy soils to be tilled. More stable agricultural regimes and, perhaps, more stable social organisation would have also facilitated moves to an increasingly sedentary lifestyle.

Establishing a clear chronological framework for the Iron Age settlements along the pipeline route is not straightforward. Radiocarbon dating is not kind to the Iron Age: the calibration curve flattens out between 800 and 400 BC and again between 400 and 180 BC so that determinations within these ranges have wide margins of error and dates are liable to variation as a result of minor refinements of the calibration curve, giving a false impression of accuracy. These problems were compounded on the Easington to Ganstead sites by the sparsity of suitable samples. Soil conditions were such that little organic material survived. Some contexts that would have been very useful to date yielded no suitable material, and in other cases the only available material was poorly preserved charcoal fragments that could not be closely identified.

Otherwise, dating is reliant on artefactual analysis or site morphology. The division of the European Iron Age based on the stylistic development of metal artefacts at the cemetery of Hallstatt in Austria and the lakeside settlement at La Tène in Switzerland is useful for high status funerary sites, but diagnostic metalwork is otherwise seldom found. The pottery assemblages from sites in the south of England, especially the Thames Valley and Wessex areas, can be divided into characteristic early, middle and late Iron Age dates, but elsewhere in Britain, this neat classification is generally not possible. Some characteristic earlier forms can be tentatively identified in East Yorkshire ceramic assemblages, but the local hand-made wares show little variation in form or fabric throughout the period and, on rural sites, hand-made, bonfire-fired vessels, are largely unchanged in both form and fabric throughout much of the Iron Age, and remained the predominant pottery type into the second century AD or beyond.

Although some decorated sherds offer the possibility of enhanced precision, the bulk of the pottery from the pipeline therefore offers little help in dating and phasing of sites. Wheel-thrown Roman pottery appeared in Holderness in the later first century AD and thereafter dating becomes easier, although characteristic regional wares are limited, refinement in dating relying on the presence of imported fine wares. Where a pottery assemblage from a feature solely comprises Iron Age tradition wares, narrowing the possible date range for the feature is problematic. Unless stratigraphic or morphological evidence suggests otherwise, a date before the later part of the first century can be fairly safely assumed for a feature that contains a large and varied assemblage of such pottery, but for smaller assemblages, a lack of wheel-thrown wares may be a purely random occurrence, at least until the third century, when such wares became common. Proposed dates for some features may therefore reflect the small size of the diagnostic assemblages and be more apparent than real.

The earliest of the settlement features may be Burton Constable Structure 4, which produced eight pottery sherds for which an early to middle Iron Age date might be appropriate, within a large assemblage of undiagnostic Iron Age tradition pottery. The date suggested by these eight sherds is not inconsistent with a radiocarbon date of 400 to 200 cal BC (SUERC-36190: Fig. 118) from a sample of charcoal from the ring gully. At the same site, the nearby Structure 5 ring gully produced three sherds of similar pottery, but the assemblage also contained four sherds dated as middle to later Iron Age, and a cattle vertebra from the fill of intervention **118057** gave a calibrated radiocarbon date of 86 BC to AD 71 (SUERC-38658). The same calibrated date range was obtained from a cattle phalanx recovered from Structure 1 (SUERC-38659). Both the charcoal and earlier pottery in the Structure 4 ring gully may have been residual although the balance of evidence perhaps suggests that a middle Iron Age date for Structure 4 and a late Iron Age date for Structure 5 are appropriate.

Two sherds of pottery similar to that from Burton Constable Structure 4 were recovered from the Burstwick ring gully. In the absence of diagnostically later pottery, an earlier Iron Age date for the establishment for the feature cannot be discounted. A sherd of middle to late Iron Age pottery and a radiocarbon date of 348 to 52 cal BC (SUERC-38666) from a charred wheat grain could indicate a middle Iron Age date for the ring gully at Nuttles.

At Braemere Hill, the radiocarbon date of 367 to 181 cal BC (SUERC-38668) from a charred wheat grain is at odds with the remains of vertical rimmed jar, possibly dating to AD 70 to 120 from the same ring gully. There is a possibility that the pot was deposited in an unrecognised feature cut into the top of the ring gully, but it seems more likely that the charred grain was residual. The presence of the grain, however, might imply that arable crops were being grown and processed in the vicinity at the earlier date.

A middle Iron Age date is implied by the radiocarbon date, 380 to 190 cal BC (SUERC-36194) from Patrington Structure 1. The date is not contradicted by any of the pottery from the ring gully. Possible middle Iron Age settlement is also indicated by the radiocarbon date of 410 to 200 cal BC (SUERC-36201) from charcoal in the ring gully at Hull Road, while the date range of 336 to 47 cal BC, (SUERC-38669) from a charred wheat grain in the ring gully of Bluegate Corner Structure 1 is broad enough to encompass a middle Iron Age date for the feature.

One of the larger assemblages of possible early or middle Iron Age pottery is the thirty-one sherds recovered from the Scorborough Hill site, all of which was residual in features securely dated to the early Roman period. The presence of these sherds would indicate a relatively high degree of activity at or near the site during the earlier part of the Iron Age. There is also tentative evidence for middle Iron Age activity, in the form of residual pottery, from Brandywell and Lelley. The eastern end of the Easington to Paull pipeline (Rowland and Wegiel 2012) provided an additional settlement site dating to the first half of the Iron Age.

The available dating evidence for all of the remaining gullies suggests that later Iron Age dates are appropriate. The calibrated radiocarbon dates all fall within the range 200 cal BC to 80 cal AD, and there was an almost total absence of any Roman pottery or native wares influenced by Roman forms, or any other type of find which could be confidently dated to the Roman period.

When did the roundhouses fall out of use?

The absence of wheel-thrown pottery is not in itself necessarily an indicator that these features had fallen out of use prior to the Roman period, as the uptake of Roman material culture on rural settlements in the East Yorkshire area is known to have been slow in the early years of the occupation. It has been argued that much of the pottery from the period was manufactured by military potters, or those under direct control of the military, primarily for a military market (Swan 2002, 35-39). Its absence at settlements in southern Holderness, where evidence of military presence is sparse, should therefore come as no surprise. There is also likely to have been resistance to Roman culture among the indigenous population, as well as cultural factors that meant that the traditional hand-made pottery types were more appropriate to the uses for which they were required.

What is striking, however, is the contrast between the ring gullies and the other features, such as pits and linear ditches, at many of the settlement sites. Pottery dated from the Roman period, including probable first to early second-century wares, were recovered from these other classes of feature at seven of the ring gully sites, and second- to early third-century types at a further four sites. With the exception of Scorborough Hill, these wares were only present in very small quantities but they are, nevertheless, a persistent element of the pottery assemblages. At Burton Constable there was almost certainly a hiatus between the Iron Age activity and the subsequent Roman phases of use, but at the other sites it is quite possible that use of the site, though not of the roundhouses, continued with little or no interruption from the late Iron Age through to the second century AD. Ditches, possibly representing parts of field systems or enclosures, were established at six of these sites, including Old Ellerby, Brandywell, Nuttles, New York, Burstwick and Patrington.

Three related inferences can be made. Firstly, Roman or Romanised wares appear to have been available to the local population from a relatively early post-conquest date. Secondly, there was continuing activity at many of the settlement sites. And thirdly, that the ring gullies had almost certainly gone out of use and had largely infilled by this time, and were no longer open to receive finds.

Evidence from other excavations within Holderness and the Hull valley is generally consistent with these findings, but for the most part these were single sites and the overall pattern was not so starkly illuminated. Examples include Creyke Beck (Evans and Steedman 2001, 67-69), where seven excavated ring gullies were all considered to date from the first and second centuries BC, and at Sandsfield Quarry near Brandesburton (Evans and Atkinson 2009, 252). No Roman or Romanised pottery was identified among the assemblages from the ring gullies on the Salt End to Aldbrough cable route in Garton parish, despite late first- and second-century Roman pottery being recovered from enclosure ditches on the same site (Savage 2014). Shepherd Lane, on the Ganstead to Asselby pipeline, also fits this pattern: the roundhouses seemingly out of use by the Roman period, while the field boundaries continued to function, with some modifications, and did come to contain Roman pottery.

The settlements at the Langeled Receiving Facilities near Easington (Richardson 2011) and the Gas Storage Facility at Aldbrough (Bradley and Steedman 2014) were interpreted as extending into the Roman period, but the only Roman finds recovered from any of the ring gullies at either of these sites seem to have been a single grey ware sherd from Building 3 at Aldbrough and a small fragment of Roman tile from Easington. This was despite the presence of Roman pottery in other features at both sites.

If the possibility that these few finds could have been intrusive is accepted, then all of the excavation results are consistent with roundhouses having fallen out of use in southern Holderness before the territory came under Roman control, and possibly even before the end of the first century BC. Many of the sites, however, continued to be used, although in the absence of clear evidence of structural remains, the nature of this use is uncertain. There is certainly an increase in land division, possibly reflecting changes in agricultural practice.

It should be reiterated that this argument is speculative, reliant as it is on negative evidence: the lack of diagnostic Roman pottery and of radiocarbon dates from the post-conquest period from any of the ring gullies. Also, it assumes that the ring gully sites were relatively long-lived. If they were short-lived, then each would provide a snapshot of, perhaps, their ten or twenty year lifespan within the several hundred years of the period of the currency of the form. It would then be statistically unremarkable if the final years of this period were not represented.

Longevity of roundhouses has been the subject of much debate. Spans of occupation of several hundred years have been suggested for sites in the south of England where greater resolution in the dating of Iron Age pottery assemblages can be achieved, while arguments for their being much shorter-lived structures hinge on the scarcity of evidence for replacement of posts and on experimental results on the lifetimes of post-built structures (Harding 2009, 278-9). In the case of the Easington to Ganstead sites, the quality of preservation does not allow such inferences but there was clear evidence for maintenance of the ring gullies at several of the sites, and for replacement of buildings in overlapping locations, implying some duration of occupation. Sites may well have endured for as long as the household unit, probably an extended family grouping, survived. It is evident that many of these sites attracted later activity, discussed further in the next section, suggesting that they had become established as definite 'places' in the Iron Age, rather than mere sites of temporary occupation.

A difficulty that needs to be acknowledged relates to the taphonomy of the finds: it has been tacitly assumed that the ring gullies infilled only when the roundhouses went out of use, the finds assemblages being thus deposited largely towards the end of the life of the ring gully. This is a reasonable assumption if the gullies were functional throughout the lifetime of the roundhouse; to continue to act as drains, for instance, they would need to be regularly cleaned out. However, if they were of use only during the construction of the roundhouse, as ring grooves to hold the base of a wattle wall or to act as a stob against which posts could be raised, the finds assemblages from their fills would accumulate very soon after they were first dug. There is also a possibility that deposition within the gullies involved a degree of selection: complete or substantially complete vessels may have been placed in the ring gullies for other than purely utilitarian reasons. If there were cultural reasons for the choice of local, hand-made wares for these purposes, it could again produce misleadingly early dating evidence.

As these counter arguments illustrate, the suggestion that roundhouses, occurring individually or in small groups, had ceased to be the general form of settlement in southern Holderness by the time of the Roman conquest is not much more than conjecture, but in the absence of further excavation data it is a plausible reason for the lack of distinctively post-conquest finds from the ring gullies.

Holderness and the Wolds

The suggested dating for the currency of the ring gullies certainly overlaps and may broadly coincide with that of the square barrow cemeteries of the Wolds region. With the notable exception of Garton-Wetwang, there are few recorded settlement sites associated with the barrow cemeteries; this is mirrored in the relative scarcity of recorded square barrow sites in Holderness. One possibility might be that the population was largely living in the lowlands but burying their dead on the higher ground of the Wolds. However, the Garton-Wetwang excavation provided a very clear example of settlement directly associated with a square barrow cemetery, and the apparent lack of other excavated examples may reflect the different archaeological histories of the Wolds and Holderness region. The early antiquarian work in the East Riding was very much concentrated on the artefact-rich funerary sites, possibly at the expense of settlement evidence, and the Wolds valleys have seen relatively few developer-funded investigations.

The material culture of the two areas was similar, however. Pottery assemblages from Holderness, for instance, are directly comparable to those from the Wolds. There was clearly communication between the two areas, probably more so in the north of the region where the wetlands and flood plain of the River Hull would have not have been an obstacle to overland movement. Of the possible interpretation of the long-distance linear monuments on the Wolds, one of the more plausible is that they relate to the movement of stock to upland grazing (Fenton-Thomas 2003), highlighting the possibility that the inhabitants of Holderness may have practised some degree of transhumance: moving from summer grazing in the damp pastures of Holderness to wintering grounds in the higher and drier, but less fertile, valleys of the Wolds. The sites at the north-western end of the pipeline, especially Old Ellerby and Burton Constable, would have been the least remote, at least by overland transport, from the Wolds and from the wider world, and it is perhaps unsurprising that these were artefactually the richest of the Iron Age ring gully sites.

Why were the roundhouses abandoned?

At the Iron Age settlement sites where activity continued into the second or early third centuries AD, notably Old Ellerby, Brandywell, Nuttles, and Bluegate Corner, the hand-made assemblages from the later linear features are very similar to those from earlier phases, apart from the occurrence of a small proportion of diagnostic Roman wheel-thrown pottery and a slightly wider range of fabric types. The implication is that the activities that produced the hand-made assemblages of the ring gullies continued largely unchanged: there was still occupation at, or very near, these sites. In these cases at least, it would be hard to argue that the disappearance of the ring gullies was simply a consequence of the abandonment of the settlements. A change of architecture, rendering settlement structures less archaeologically visible, seems more likely.

Apart from a few postholes which may, or may not, by contemporary with the ring gullies, the ring gullies themselves were all that remains, or at least all that was recognisable, of the Iron Age structures. A change of practice which obviated the need for a gully around a structure would therefore render the structure archaeologically invisible. Roundhouses may well have continued to be the normal form of domestic structure, but without their surrounding gullies or with shallow gullies that did not penetrate below the depth of the present day plough soil. But the disappearance of the ring gullies seems to correspond to increasing subdivision and drainage of the sites. At some stage, it is likely that rectangular buildings became the norm, reflecting this rectilinearisation of the landscape.

Pursuing this argument, the disappearance of the roundhouse would have been linked to changes in the apportionment of land. This could have had a myriad of causes: increased population pressure, greater economic productivity, trade and movement, or diffusion of cultural practices. The general trend, seen especially in the Wolds, seems to have been towards settlement

sites with contiguous ditched enclosures developed and maintained over an extended period of time and often concentrated along routeways (Giles 2000, 179). The Easington to Ganstead sites demonstrate the same trend.

The Roman period

At the ring gully sites, the evidence for continuing activity rests largely on the artefact assemblages from linear features and pits: pits and postholes at Brandywell and Burstwick may be the remains of post-built buildings, but otherwise there is nothing that could be interpreted as a domestic structure from the Roman period. On a smaller project, this would have been dismissed as nothing more than sampling error, the excavation area having, by chance, intersected Iron Age structures but failed to impinge on any of Roman date, with the recovered artefacts being taken as an indication that there was settlement nearby, beyond the limits of excavation. However, the relatively large sample offered by the Easington to Ganstead pipeline makes such an interpretation increasingly unlikely. If archaeologically visible Roman period structures occurred with anything close to the same frequency as the Iron Age ring gullies then it is very unlikely that they would not have been found.

With the exception of Burton Constable and Scorborough Hill, wheel-thrown Roman pottery was scarce at all the excavation sites, and was generally accompanied by much larger quantities of hand-made wares. The hand-made pottery in Roman contexts had a smaller average sherd weight than that in exclusively hand-made assemblages, probably indicating the inclusion of a proportion of residual sherds, but the character of these assemblages, especially the slightly greater range of fabric types, suggests that they were broadly contemporary with the wheel-thrown wares, and that residuality was not a major factor in the composition of the assemblages. As argued above, it seems likely that there was continuing occupation at these sites, persisting into the second or early third century, but using an archaeologically less visible form of structure.

This continuity of activity seems to imply that Roman rule, established when the army crossed the Humber around AD 71 or 72 (Cunliffe 2005, 215), initially had little effect on the overall distribution of rural settlements. Life carried on much as before, possibly with new proprietors who initially saw little need for change to a functioning system of land apportionment and use. This is not to imply that the late Iron Age society was static; there may well have been an ongoing process of aggregation of settlement, with the dispersed ring gully sites of the Iron Age gradually condensing into fewer but larger settlements.

There is little evidence of military presence in south Holderness, with the nearest well-attested establishments, north of the Humber, at Brough, York and Malton. Possible military stations at Swine, surrounded by a gated double rampart 'large enough to accommodate two to three thousand men' (Allen 1851, 270-71), and at Easington (Sheppard 1922, 208-209), are open to other interpretations.

In this context, the site at Scorborough Hill is of considerable significance, as showing a distinct Roman presence at an early date. The pottery assemblage from the site has a strong military character and a suggestion of a connection with northern Gaul. The site is difficult to interpret as the excavation area gave only a limited view, dominated by a single, large and rather strangely shaped elongated pit. It was at the northern limit of an extensive area of geophysical features, extending towards the Humber along the side of a creek, where Weeton Beck now discharges into the estuary. This creek would have provided access to trade routes to the North Sea, and upriver to Brough and York. Pre-construction work for the Easington to Paull gas pipeline located a possible tile kiln in this area, containing the remains of at least twenty-six *tegula* or *imbrex* tiles along with fragments of kiln furniture (Allen 2008, 9). Whether destined for trade or roofing a nearby building, the tiles confirm that there was a greater Roman influence or presence in this area than is generally the case in rural Holderness.

The Scorborough Hill site did not continue in use beyond the second century, and at only three of the excavation sites were there significant remains dating to the later third and fourth centuries. There needs to be a note of caution, as the dating of Roman pottery in the East Riding relies heavily on a limited number of diagnostic types, and a lack of later third- and fourth-century wares, especially from sites in the eastern part of the pipeline route, could reflect their distance from production centres rather than a lack of activity at this time. Nevertheless, it is striking that later Roman pottery is restricted in its occurrence to a very few sites, most notably Burton Constable and Old Ellerby at the western end of the pipeline route, with a relatively short later phase of activity at Patrington, probably following a period of abandonment after the Iron Age ring gullies went out of use.

The Roman phases at Burton Constable stand out from the generality. The apparently clear break after the Iron Age is striking and implies something more than an evolution in settlement form, as invoked elsewhere to explain the continuation of sites from the Iron Age roundhouses to the small enclosures of the earlier Roman period. The Iron Age settlement, at least that part lying within the excavation area, seems to have been abandoned, perhaps for 250 to 300 years, before the group of contiguous ditched enclosures were instigated, in the later third century. No features from the Roman phases could be definitely identified as structural remains, but the nature of the artefact assemblage, as well as features such as oven **9519** and the possible grain dryer, would strongly suggest domestic occupation.

The siting of this re-established settlement, in close proximity to the earlier remains, may have been accidental, influenced by the same factors that affected the choice of situation in the earlier period. But while it is unlikely that much trace of the original settlement remained visible after such a long period of disuse, the pattern of land clearance and land division may have been such that the site still formed the focus of an area of agricultural land, especially as the nearby site at Old Ellerby continued to be used, possibly intermittently, throughout the Roman period. The timing of the establishment of the Roman settlement at Burton Constable following the final demise of activity on most of the other excavation sites suggests a fairly extensive re-ordering of the landscape during the third century, with, perhaps, the consolidation of land holdings.

This picture from the Easington to Ganstead sites is largely consistent with other excavated sites in south Holderness. At Aldbrough (Bradley and Steedman 2014), the domestic buildings, enclosure and field system of the earlier phase of the site were replaced with a substantial series of ditches, creating larger enclosures which continued in use into the third century, although with a notable absence of domestic building remains. Two phases of Roman occupation were recorded on the Leven to Brandesburton bypass (Evans and Steedman 1997, 125). Ditches and slots of second-century date and a larger and more complex area of ditched enclosures a short distance to the south continued in use into the fourth century. Further south at Ganstead, the Iron Age site excavated on the Teesside to Salt End Ethylene pipeline continued into the early Roman period (Evans and Atkinson 2009, 263-265), when field boundary ditches were reinstated and a metalled track established. The main period of settlement at the Langeled terminal site at Easington (Richardson 2011) probably dated from the later Iron Age although two of the ring gullies may have still been open in the early Roman period; activity continued until at least the second century AD. The Iron Age ring gully site excavated on the Salt End to Aldbrough cable route (Savage 2014) similarly had a later phase of first- to second-century ditches.

The economy of the Iron Age and Roman sites

The agricultural economy

The excavation sites produced only limited evidence of agriculture, the soil conditions being generally not conducive to the preservation of organic material and environmental remains. Bone, shell and charred plant material were all depleted to a greater or lesser extent, but provisional inferences can perhaps be drawn. The animal bone from Iron Age contexts indicates that sheep, cattle and pigs were all being exploited. Minimum numbers of individuals calculated for the five sites with the largest assemblages seem to indicate that sheep were generally the most numerous animals, although cattle, because of their larger size, probably contributed more to the diet of the population. Small numbers of horse bones were also present.

In so far as it is possible to judge, this pattern is consistent across the sites. It suggests a mixed pastoral economy, probably using both the lower-lying wetland margins and the drier, higher ground. The low numbers of pigs might indicate that only a relatively small proportion of the land was still wooded. It provides an interesting contrast with the remains from the square barrow cemetery sites, where the carcases of young pigs were commonly included with the grave goods, along with joints of lamb or mutton. Stable isotope analysis on the human remains from the Wetwang and Garton cemeteries indicated that young pigs formed a significant contribution to the adult diet (Jay and Richards 2006). Apart from a solitary vertebra from the large pit at Out Newton Road, no fish bones were recovered; it is a common finding that there was little exploitation of marine or freshwater fish in the Iron Age (Dobney and Ervynck 2007; Willis 2007).

There is a hint, far from statistical significance, that there may have been a move towards greater use of cattle during the Roman phases at Burton Constable. A similar widespread pattern has been noted elsewhere in the country (Albarella 2007) and a link to a higher demand for grain, has been suggested, increasing the need for cattle to provide traction and manure (Grant 1989, 138). The cattle from these phases are generally of an older age-group, consistent with the theory that traction and milk production were of higher importance than meat production. A greater emphasis on arable cultivation may be linked to the increase in land division that is seen in the Roman phases. Investment in cultivation of crops requires security of land tenure; the development of systems of ditched enclosures would more clearly demarcate areas of exclusive use, as well as providing drainage for arable plots. Communal harvesting and storage of grain perhaps led to more centralised storage and possibly more aggregated settlement.

Though datable evidence from it was sparse, the extensive ditch system at Sproatley seems to have dated wholly from the Iron Age, however. This ditch system is unusual, its convergent form suggesting that it may have been designed to funnel livestock grazing on the marshes up towards a central collecting point.

The extensive programme of bulk soil sampling provided some direct evidence for crop use, with charred grain and chaff occurring in many samples but only in very small quantities and often not sufficiently preserved to identify to species. Spelt and bread wheats, barley and oats were positively identified in Iron Age contexts, though it was not clear whether the oats were cultivated or wild. The same species were also present in the Roman contexts, in slightly higher quantities, but nowhere near sufficient to provide any indication of their relative economic importance.

A few features did provide fairly sizable quantities of charred grain, including feature **9282** at Burton Constable and pit **26428** at Sproatley, both from later Roman phases. Querns of typical Iron Age or early Roman form, from Burton Constable, Brandywell and Patrington, show that these sites at least were producing their own meal. The lack of charred grain from the earlier features may, to some extent, reflect a genuine lack of grain cultivation and processing but it is much more likely that the comparative richness of these Roman pits was a consequence of a function related to the processing of grain.

The pollen sequence from the wet organic fills of the substantial ditch at Brandywell provided a direct view of the environment of the site and indicated open landscape used for both pastoral and arable agriculture. The changes in composition of the pollen assemblages through the sequence also suggested that this site may have undergone a period of temporary abandonment, allowing regeneration of scrubland vegetation, before being reoccupied and cleared once again. If this was the case, it might hint at a general pattern of regular short-term occupation of settlement sites interspersed with periods of fallowing.

Industry and trade

The earliest examples of iron artefacts in Britain, generally from anaerobic waterlogged contexts and considered to have been votive deposits, are all imports from Europe, but indigenous iron smelting was quickly established, producing, by the late Iron Age, La Tène-style artefacts of comparable quality to European examples (Stead 1984). The Foulness Valley, in the Vale of York to the west of the Wolds, formed an early centre of iron production (Halkon and Millett 1999, Halkon 2004) and around fifty sites with significant quantities of smelting slag have been identified within an 8km radius of Holme-on-Spalding-Moor (Halkon and Millett 1999). The five tonnes of slag from Moore's Farm makes it one of the largest Iron Age slag heaps discovered in the country (Halkon 2008). Evidence of iron working to the east of the Wolds, however, is very sparse, with the hearth bottoms, tap-slag and tuyère fragments from the Langeled site (Richardson 2011) providing a notable exception. The presence of crucibles at this site also suggests working of non-ferrous metals. Concentrations of slag from iron working, along with a crucible and mould fragment were also found at Shepherd Lane (Daniel et al., forthcoming).

The small quantities of ferrous slags recovered from Iron Age contexts at Old Ellerby and Patrington, and from Roman contexts at Burton Constable, most likely relate to iron smithing, rather than smelting. Fragments of a mould, which was probably used for casting lead bronze, were recovered from Old Ellerby and probably derived from a Roman pit cut into the top of the Structure 2 ring gully. Other possible moulds were recovered from Gilcross and New York from early Roman and probable later Iron Age contexts respectively. Ceramic fragments from crucibles were identified at Burton Constable, Nuttles, Scorborough Hill and Gilcross; the high concentrations of metal residues on the internal surfaces of two samples from Burton Constable indicate that they had probably been in contact with molten tin lead bronze.

Solidified drips of copper alloy from Burton Constable and New York were probably waste from metal casting. Copper alloy waste fragments were also found in Iron Age and early Roman contexts at Burton Constable, Nuttles and Gilcross. Fragments of furnace lining from Burton Constable and Out Newton Road indicate that high-temperature processes were being carried out. In addition, Iron Age contexts at Bluegate Corner and Weeton had industrial residues, impossible to assign to a particular production source (Mackenzie 2010).

Metal working was clearly widespread, with some level of practical knowledge forming part of the set of skills of most households. However, while there would have been a degree of functional self-sufficiency in everyday metal working, there would have been few nearby sources of raw materials and metal would probably have been obtained through trade, as bars or scrap, to provide the material for forging or casting. The products of this industry were less in evidence, metal finds being especially rare in secure Iron Age contexts, although this could be explained by poor preservation in aggressive soil conditions. The occurrence of fresh flint debitage in an Iron Age context at the Burstwick excavation area highlights the possibility that flint tools may have continued to be used alongside iron implements.

Textile production is likely to have been a largely or wholly domestic activity. At Burton Constable, there is evidence in the form of loomweights from an Iron Age context and, probably residual, in a later ditch. A fired clay object from a Roman context at Brandywell could have been another loomweight, although a structural function as a thatch weight is an alternative possibility. A double-ended bone point recovered from Iron Age ditch **118977** at Burton Constable is a possible textile or leather processing tool. Other examples of worked bone were scarce: isolated cattle or sheep metapodials with drilled holes from Burton Constable and Out Newton Road, a sawn horse bone from Burton Constable and fragments of sawn antler from Out Newton Road. Horncores showing cut marks are evidence for horn-working at Burton Constable and Brandywell.

That there had been little or no previously recorded evidence of salt production in south Holderness was surprising, considering the copious evidence of production sites south of the Humber on the Lincolnshire coastline. The briquetage recovered, most notably from the Iron Age ditch at Braemere Hill but also from Iron Age contexts at Gilcross and Roman contexts at Brandywell and Scorborough Hill, suggests that saltern sites along the northern shore of the Humber await discovery. The contrast with Lincolnshire may reflect the lack of recent development work along the Holderness foreshore or more probably the masking of sites by subsequent alluvial aggradation. The locally produced salt would presumably have been traded inland, along the estuary and possibly further afield.

Lab. Ref. SUERC-	GU-	Feature	Context	^{14}C date	δ13C ‰	Calibrated date	Sample
Old Ellerby							
36186	24866	Cremation	3237	1755 ± 30	-23.2	AD 170 (1%) 190; AD 210 (94.4%) 390	Charcoal
Burton Constable							
36191	24868	Grain dryer	9250	1840 ± 30	-22.7	AD 80 (95.4%) 250	Charcoal
Winestead							
36193	24870	Enc.ditch	73196	1265 ± 30	-21.4	AD 660 (93.1%) 830; AD 840 (2.3%) 860	Charred grain
Skeffling							
36196	24874	Pit	120311	3390 ± 30	-26.2	1760 (95.4%) 1610 BC	Charcoal
36200	24875	Pit	120306	3335 ± 55	-27.9	1750 (95.4%) 1490 BC	Charcoal
Dimlington Road							
38670	26365	Stone-filled pit	120539	1570 ± 30	-21.9	AD 420 (95.4%) 557	cow-size long bone

TABLE 69: SUMMARY OF RADIOCARBON DATES, MISCELLANEOUS FEATURES

The querns from Burton Constable, Brandywell and Patrington were in igneous rocks, including Shap granites, but these rocks are most likely to have been glacial erratics, which occur on the Wolds and possible further east into Holderness. The rope-impressed daub from Burton Constable serves as a reminder of the many artefacts made from organic materials that would have been used at these sites and that have subsequently perished. Rope would have had a host of uses around a farmstead: tethering beasts or hauling timber, hanging meat or tying together hurdles.

The most common evidence of human activity from Iron Age and Roman contexts was, of course, the large assemblage of local, hand-made pottery. Although none of the excavation sites showed any traces of pottery manufacture, it is likely that it was made locally, perhaps with each settlement routinely producing its own pottery by simple bonfire firing, as needed, using the local clays. There is also likely to have been trade between settlements, either of pots themselves or as containers for other commodities.

Roman contexts, with their greater range of artefacts, provided more traded goods: the objects in jet or shale could have been made from occasional material collected from local beaches but are much more likely to have been traded along the coast from the Whitby area, either as raw material or as finished artefacts. The glass beads of the necklace worn by the young child buried at Brandywell are also likely to have been acquired by trade rather than of local manufacture, while the glass bangles from Scorborough Hill seem to have been a product of a location somewhere between the Humber and southern Scotland, judging from the distribution of finds of this class of artefact.

In addition, imported pottery, though never occurring in large quantities, is a very tangible demonstration of trade with other parts of the empire. The first-century South Gaulish samian sherds from Scorborough Hill are particularly significant. Rather later Central and Eastern Gaulish wares were present at Old Ellerby, Burton Constable, Sproatley, Lelley, New York and Patrington.

Anglo-Saxon and Anglo-Scandinavian

In south Holderness, as elsewhere, the fourth-century sites seem to have rapidly fallen into disuse in the fifth century. The only clear evidence of Anglo-Saxon activity came from Lelley, where there was little or no Roman activity after the demise of the Iron Age settlement, Winestead, where the system of poorly dated enclosure ditches are thought to date to the period, and Dimlington Road, which unexpectedly produced radiocarbon dates from the period.

At Lelley, eight sherds from a single jar with a temper of carbonised vegetable matter, typical of the period spanning the fifth to eighth centuries, indicate there was at least some activity here between the abandonment of the roundhouses, and apparent reoccupation of the site in

the Anglo-Scandinavian period. Thereafter, settlement at the site may well have been continuous until the thirteenth or possibly the early fourteenth century. The presence of pottery vessels from kilns in Lincoln, Torksey and York demonstrated that the site had ready access to traded goods from beyond the local region during the Anglo-Scandinavian period.

From Winestead, the pottery is limited to sherds of undiagnostic hand-made pottery, including the substantial remains of a single large crudely made vessel, and abraded sherds of four vessels dated to the late third- or fourth-century: Crambeck and Holme-on-Spalding-Moor lugged jars, a Nene Valley colour-coated dish or bowl base, and an East Yorkshire calcite-gritted lid. The possibility that the site could be of a later date was raised by Don O'Meara, based on the oval to round form of the charred wheat grains, which gave them 'a very medieval feel' (pers. comm.). One of the charred grains subsequently returned a radiocarbon date of 660 to 830 cal AD.

The distinctive system of round-cornered enclosure ditches was unlike any of the other sites on the pipeline route. The general scarcity of finds might suggest that it had a purely agricultural function, but because of the low archaeological visibility of Anglo-Saxon rural settlement sites, the possibility of occupation should not be discounted. The overall alignment of the enclosures was parallel to the historic parish boundary between Winestead and South Frodingham. This boundary, less than 50m south-west of the excavation area, formed the northern limit of Winestead New Park, shown on a map of 1636 (Neave 1991, 19). Winestead village is known to have pre-Norman origins: the name occurs in a charter of 1033 (Ekwall 1960) as well as in the Domesday entries for Patrington and Kilnsea.

Excavated Anglo-Saxon sites in Holderness are sparse and consist mostly of burials, including small cemeteries at Swine, Burton Pidsea, Hornsea, Ganstead and Aldbrough (Loveluck 1999, 228; 2003, fig. 40). The seventh-century gold and garnet Holderness Cross from Burton Pidsea (MacGregor 2000) and a pottery vessel from Great Hatfield are also likely to have come from burial contexts. Nearer to the pipeline route, a single pit containing middle Saxon pottery, along with animal bone, was identified in the course of an evaluation adjacent to the Easington gas terminal, undertaken in 1998. This site, in the eroding cliff edge, was thought to be the final remains of what was once a settlement (Atkinson 1999, 24).

Little material evidence is known from the area, in comparison with the preceding periods, partly because the typically low-fired pottery of the period does not survive well, and is easily confused with Iron Age and hand-made Roman wares. Cropmarks of settlements and field systems are similarly not easy to distinguish from Iron Age and Roman remains, although most prove to date to the earlier periods when investigated. An exception is provided by a site to the north-east of Skeffling village, excavated on the Easington to Paull pipeline (site SPE3, Rowland and Wegiel 2012, 51-59), that may have been part of a similar, though probably earlier, system of enclosures to that at Winestead.

The two features at Dimlington Road that unexpectedly returned radiocarbon dates from the Anglo-Saxon period included a shallow curvilinear gully, considered to be an element of Structure 2. This had been disturbed by a later furrow, and there is a strong possibility that the charcoal sample used for dating could have been intrusive. The same could be true of the bone sample from one of the very distinctive rectangular stone-filled pits, as these flat-based pits were shallow and it is easy to imagine a bone fragment in the ploughsoil becoming lodged in the interstices between the stones. However, the bone was of reasonably fresh appearance making it less likely, though still feasible, that it was residual and, in the absence of a clear date and functional interpretation for the stone-filled pits, the possibility that this sample provides a true date for the feature is perfectly plausible. An undated feature at Burstwick may have had the same function, suggesting that these stone-filled pits could be of wide occurrence in the area. Should similar features be revealed in any subsequent works nearby, the possibility that they are of Anglo-Saxon date should be further explored.

Medieval

Occupation appears to have continued at the Lelley site through the Norman Conquest, probably without interruption. The site had been previously identified from aerial photographs and associated with the manor of Lund Garth. The early history of this manor is poorly documented but it would have taken its name from the Lund or Lound family, who held land in the area around Preston village in the thirteenth century (Allison 1984, 193).

The earliest documentary reference to Lund Garth seems to be in 1589, when the manor was sold by the Sheffield family to Nicholas Girlington. In the eighteenth century, it was held by the Helme, Sissison and Burril families (*ibid.*). The dating evidence implies that settlement in the vicinity of the excavation area had been abandoned in the thirteenth century, long before these documentary references, perhaps in favour of the site now occupied by Lund Garth Farm. The bulk of the post-Roman pottery from the site is of early medieval type, from industries flourishing from the late eleventh to the early or mid-thirteenth centuries. While the quantity of finds implies that there was domestic occupation on the site, possible structural remains were limited to a rectangular feature in the south-west corner of the site, associated with a nearby oven, and remains of a crushed chalk floor surface. The occupation seemed to fit within an extensive group of periodically renewed contiguous rectangular ditched enclosures. This group of enclosures can be very clearly seen on the geophysical survey results, continuing to the east for at least 100m and suggesting that the settlement consisted of three or more adjacent house plots.

Elsewhere on the pipeline route, medieval finds consisted mostly of pottery sherds on the surface or in the ploughsoil, no doubt largely deposited as a result of manuring. A notable exception was the group of sherds of Saxo-Norman pottery recovered from the fills of a small ditch, **117053**, investigated during monitoring of the topsoil stripping, 150m to the south of Southside Road, Halsham (NGR: 528625 426785). This ditch ran 12m to the west of a parallel field boundary shown on Halsham Tithe Map of 1847, and recorded during construction as a substantial ditch, **119055**.

Section 6: Conclusions

Taken overall, the Easington to Ganstead investigations have clarified the picture of the development of the south Holderness landscape, from the Mesolithic to the present day. It has particularly brought into sharp focus the flourishing Iron Age communities dispersed throughout the claylands of Holderness. As the largest study carried out in the region to date, it has expanded the baseline of data on which future work in Holderness can build. The rural settlement patterns suggested by this study, and the way in which they evolved through the late Iron Age and beyond, will undoubtedly need to be refined as more data is gathered, but provide a model against which other findings can be compared.

Inevitably, a study of this kind is at the mercy of its methods and constraints. The route of the pipeline itself provides one limitation. In using the results to draw conclusions about wider landscapes, the subtle biases introduced by the constraints on pipeline routes should be borne in mind. The most salient of these is the avoidance of any modern buildings, so that the late Anglo-Saxon and medieval antecedents of towns and villages are invisible to the pipeline archaeologist. The archaeology of areas of present-day woodlands and the more extreme elements of landscapes, such as hill-tops and wetlands, is also under-represented, as well as previously known archaeological sites, including avoidable sites identified by desk-based studies in the pre-construction stages of work.

As pipeline construction proceeds most efficiently on a relentless, unforgiving timetable, the programming of archaeological investigations is crucially important and the identification of significant remains at as early a stage as possible assumes a particular urgency. In the case of Easington to Ganstead, the techniques of pre-construction prospection located all of the larger sites along the route, including the Mesolithic flint site at Sproatley, only identified at this early stage because of the very clear pattern of geophysical anomalies produced by the Iron Age ditch system. The programme of work allowed for many of the sites to be investigated in 2007, the year before the pipeline was constructed, a benefit partly negated by the extreme weather of that summer. Monitoring of ground-disturbing operations during construction work in 2008 revealed the other, smaller, sites, allowing them to be excavated and recorded without unduly affecting the construction programme.

Of the excavated sites, the spread of early Mesolithic flint-working debris at Sproatley, lying at its original site of deposition, was an exciting and important find, its value only slightly compromised by the disturbance from the later pits and probably also by a degree of vertical mixing. The flintwork seems to have been deposited over a period of time, although there was little evidence of stratification, the flint assemblages from the upper and lower deposits showing no significant differences in their compositions. Other finds from Sproatley demonstrate the high archaeological potential of the relatively isolated gravel areas among the Holderness claylands.

The pipeline provided only very occasional glimpses of the Neolithic inhabitants of Holderness, but finds such as the leaf-shaped arrowhead from Fosse Hill, Skeffling contribute to a broad picture of continuing sporadic activity in the period. There is a rather more from the Bronze Age: Beaker pottery from Sproatley and Gilcross, and Biconical Urn from Churchlands, as well as diagnostic flintwork such as the two barbed and tanged arrowheads from Sproatley. A lack of datable material precluded confirmation that that the Sproatley finds were related to a funerary landscape, but the interpretation of the two large annular features as the ditches of round barrows remains credible. Overall, the findings from the Neolithic and Bronze Age are compatible with existing conceptual models of the periods.

The Iron Age sites paint a picture of a landscape of small farmsteads, each consisting of one or two roundhouses, some perhaps with smaller ancillary buildings. Of the design of the roundhouses, the results leave much room for speculation, though providing evidence for the use of wattle and daub, and possibly also turf. The apparent use of rope and daub at Burton Constable is, to say the least, unusual.

Some of the larger roundhouses, such as Structure 5 at Burton Constable may have achieved a degree of sophistication, with internal fixtures and partitioning, and possibly even upper floors or galleries, as has been suggested for the larger post-built roundhouses of southern England. But for the most part they may perhaps be better interpreted as cruder sod-built constructions. In the intensively cultivated agricultural land of modern Holderness, much of the detail of the roundhouses did not survive. Not one of the excavated examples showed any trace of an internal hearth, though they would all almost certainly have originally had one.

Taken as a whole, the most striking impression from the results is of the frequency of these sites through the landscape, at least in those parts that were clear of the wetland zone but which afforded some protection from the worst of the winter winds. Although the greater archaeological visibility of the more settled communities of the Iron Age may create, to some extent, a false impression, the pervading sense that the landscape 'filled up' during the Iron Age is a compelling one. Whether this was a result of changes in the hydrological regime, perhaps linked to climatic amelioration, or was chiefly a cultural phenomenon is open to debate, although similar observations have been made for other regions (e.g. Hill 1999) and it seems to have been equally true across lowland Britain as a whole. There is little doubt that the aspect of Holderness at the end of the Iron Age would have been very different to that at its start. While there are difficulties in determining which of the settlements would have been contemporary, their density and spacing suggests the land may have been close to its carrying capacity, with as many settlements as the contemporary economic basis would support.

Because of the quality of the cropmarks in the Wolds, there has been much study of the patterns of land division in East Yorkshire and the Easington to Ganstead results can contribute to these discussions. The Iron Age settlements, with the exception of Out Newton Road, seem not to have been enclosed, the pattern of radiating ditches at Sproatley and the early phase ditch at Patrington being the only other substantial linear features dated to the Iron Age. This situation changed towards the end of the Iron Age, or in the early post-conquest period, by which time some of the settlement sites had fallen out of use while the others evolved into something different: the surrounding land becoming sub-divided by ditched boundaries into separate plots. The weight of evidence seems to imply that the roundhouse, as the predominant style of building, had ceased to exist in this region by this time, but settlement continued on or near several of the sites into the second or third century AD.

Southern Holderness seems to reflect, on a smaller and less visible scale, the cultural changes in the wider East Yorkshire region in the later pre-Roman Iron Age. In the Wolds, square barrows and chariot burials went out of use as forms of funerary monument, while to the west, the iron industry of the Foulness Valley apparently foundered; ritual deposition of metalwork in wetlands possibly also ceased at around the same time. Systems of fields and ditched enclosures, increasingly appear across the region, including the conjoined systems of enclosures that formed the characteristic 'ladder settlements', clearly visible in cropmark sites of the Wolds. The twilight of the ring-gullied roundhouses may belong with the same suite of cultural changes.

The immediate effects of the Roman conquest may have been limited, with activity continuing at many of the Iron Age sites. This would chime with other available evidence, which implies that the extension of Roman hegemony north of the Humber was achieved by peaceable accommodation with the indigenous leadership (Millett 1990, 54). It is perhaps also the case that the Imperial project relied on the strength of the native leadership (*ibid.* 99) and that the south Holderness peninsula was sufficiently remote to be of only limited interest to either the local leadership or the Roman authorities. However,

in one locality at least, the effects of the conquest were felt directly. The Scorborough Hill finds assemblage indicates a strong military association, dating from the later first century AD, or early second. The nature of this site remains a mystery, the remains extending beyond the limits of the excavation area, but its situation suggests that it may have owed its presence to the proximity of a navigable creek through the Humber saltmarshes.

There seems to have been a more radical change around the middle or later part of the third century when most of the earlier settlements were abandoned. Activity at Old Ellerby continued, perhaps intermittently, through this period. Around the same time, occupation at Burton Constable resumed after a long hiatus, based around a group of contiguous ditched enclosures. If there is any effect of Romanisation to be seen here, it would be of a move towards aggregated settlements: small hamlets rather than isolated farmsteads. Economic factors could be invoked to account for this, but it would also have necessitated new rights of land usage, and could have been driven by changes of proprietorship.

The Burton Constable site provides an example of a recurring theme among the sites along the pipeline route, of reoccupation following a period of disuse. Once an area becomes a 'place', that sense seems to persist, possibly because the community maintains a memory of it as a site of occupation or perhaps because its abandonment and decay eventually creates a space within a landscape that is otherwise fully apportioned and utilised. Whether similar explanations can be invoked in the case of Lelley, where the period of disuse apparently lasted from the late Iron Age until post-Roman times, is more debatable, and it may be that patterns of drainage influenced by the slight ridge of land across the site were a common factor in the siting of both the Iron Age and later communities.

The excavation at Lelley has gone some way towards characterising the cropmarks previously identified with the historic site of Lund Garth. The site flourished in the twelfth and thirteen centuries, but its origins have been pushed back deep into the Anglo-Scandinavian period and perhaps beyond. Elsewhere, with the exception of the system of contiguous ditched enclosures at Winestead, for which an Anglo-Saxon date seems likely, there was no evidence of post-Roman settlement. This might be a result of the present-day pattern of settlement having already been established at this early date.

As well as examining the archaeology of the individual excavation sites, monitoring of construction work provided additional detail of a transect across most of southern Holderness. Between the sites described above, little was visible below the modern ploughsoil apart from the remains of medieval or post-medieval ridge and furrow ploughing, and modern land drains and ploughscores. These negative results provide the blank parts of the patterns of activity in earlier periods, giving a better sense of how the landscape was organised and utilised on a grander scale. The distribution of stray finds told a similar story: manuring finds from the medieval period onwards occurred throughout the pipeline route, as might be expected from this arable landscape, but earlier finds beyond the bounds of the excavation areas were very scarce.

In its potential contribution to future archaeological research, the analysis of the hand-made pottery, especially the typology of vessel forms, is an important advance for ceramic studies of the region, and is likely to be one of the abiding legacies of this project. By stressing the importance of vessel form, the analysis has directed attention to the function of vessels: not only the question of how the range of vessel forms is related to the nature of the settlements, but also of how vessels may have been perceived and classified by their makers and users. Those assemblages in which hand-made wares occur alongside datable wheel-thrown pottery provide fertile material for further study.

But as ever in archaeology, it is in the particular, the unexpected and the quirky that the past comes alive.

Evaporating salt beside the creeks of the Humber to trade along the Burstwick valley or using rope to repair their roundhouse at Burton Constable; suffering with the effects of brucellosis or tuberculosis, or, like the first-century family at Brandywell, dressing the body of their cherished child with bronze hair-rings and a precious necklace of coloured glass beads, it is with these small details that the earlier residents of this corner of Yorkshire have left us fresh insights into how they lived their lives.

Before this project started, South Holderness seemed to be very much an archaeological poor relation of the Yorkshire Wolds to the west. As a result of this and other recent projects, the 'mersshy contree' of Chaucer's Somonour (Robinson 1974, 94) has become a little more accessible: Holderness and the Wolds can begin to stand together, allowing a deeper understanding of the development of the wider region. And it is worth reiterating the words of one of the contributors to this volume: 'the quantity and quality of the data emerging from developer-funded work surely demands some degree of investment in the production of interpretative accounts of the archaeology of the region, to do justice to the significant commercial investment.'

Bibliography

Abramson, P. 1996. 'The Excavations along the Caythorpe Gas Pipeline, North Humberside'. *Yorks. Archaeol. J.* 68, 1-88

Albarella, U. 2007. 'The end of the sheep age: people and animals in the late Iron Age', in Haselgrove and Moore 2007

Allason-Jones, L. 1996. *Roman Jet in the Yorkshire Museum*, Yorkshire Museum, York

Allason-Jones, L. 2002. 'The jet industry and allied trades in Roman Britain' in Wilson and Price 2002, 125-132

Allason-Jones, L. and Miket, R. 1984. *The Catalogue of Small Finds from South Shields Roman Fort,* Society of Antiquaries of Newcastle Monograph Series 2, Newcastle upon Tyne

Allason-Jones, L. and McKay, B. 1985. *Coventina's Well, a Shrine on Hadrian's Wall*, Trustees of the Clayton Collection, Chesters Museum, Hexham

Allen, M. 2008. *Report on trial trenching of the proposed Easington to Paull natural gas pipeline*; Allen Archaeological Associates report number 2008/056, unpublished

Allen, T. 1851. *A new and complete history of the County of York*, I. T, Hinton, London

Allison, K. J. 1984. *Victoria County History: Yorkshire, East Riding*, vol. 5, OUP, Oxford

Anderson, R. 2008. *Annotated list of the non-marine Mollusca of Britain and Ireland*, Conchological Society of Great Britain and Ireland, London

ApSimon, A. M. 1972. 'Biconical Urns outside Wessex', in F. Lynch and C. Burgess (eds.), *Prehistoric Man in Wales and the West*, Adams and Dent, Bath, 141-16

Armstrong, P. and Armstrong, J. 1987. 'The clay roof tile' in P. Armstrong P and B. Ayers 'Excavations in High St and Blackfriargate', *East Riding Archaeologist 8/ Hull Old Town Report Series 5*, 234-240

Armstrong, P. 1991. 'The clay roof tile', in Armstrong, Tomlinson and Evans 1991, 201-207

Armstrong, S. 1992. 'Clay roof tile and roof furniture', in D. H. Evans and D. G. Tomlinson 1992. 'Excavations at 33-35 Eastgate, Beverley 1983-86', *Sheffield Excavation Reports 3*, 219-226

Armstrong, P., Tomlinson, D. G. and Evans, D. H. 1991. *Excavations at Lurk Lane, Beverley 1979-82*, Sheffield Excavation Rep. 1

Arnold, D. E. 1985. *Ceramic Theory and Cultural Process*, Cambridge University Press

Ashbee, P. and ApSimon, A.M. 1956. 'Barnby Howes, Barnby, East Cleveland, Yorkshire', *Yorks Archaeol J.* 39, 9-31

Atkinson, D. 1942. *Report on Excavations at Wroxeter (the Roman City of Viroconium) in the County of Salop 1923-1927*, Birmingham Archaeol. Soc., OUP, Oxford

Atkinson, D. 1999. 'Archaeological Excavations on the Easington Coastal Protection Works, Easington, East Riding of Yorkshire', *Humber Archaeology Rep. 39*, unpublished

Aufderheide, A. C. and Rodríguez-Martín, C. 1998. *The Cambridge Encyclopedia of Human Paleopathology*, CUP, Cambridge

Bamford, H. 1985. *Briar Hill: excavation 1974-1978*, Northampton Development Corporation

Bartlett, J. 1963. 'Beaker Burials from Brantingham, Melton and South Cave', Hull Museum Publication 214, 17-22

Bartlett, J. E. and Mackey, R. W. 1973 'Excavations at Walkington Wold, 1967-9', *E. Riding Archaeol.* 1, 1-93

Bayley, J., Paynter, S. and Dungworth, D. 2001. *Archaeometallurgy*, Centre for Archaeology Guidelines 2001/01, English Heritage, London

Beckett, S. 1975. *The late quaternary vegetational history of Holderness, Yorkshire*, unpublished PhD thesis, University of Hull

Beckett, S. 1981. 'Pollen Diagrams from Holderness, North Humberside', *Journal of Biogeography*, 8, 177-198

Bell, A. C, 1999 'The Romano-British Salt-making Site at Shell Bridge, Holbeach St Johns: Excavations 1983' in A. Bell *et al.* 1999

Bell, A., Gurney, D. and Healey, H. 1999. *Lincolnshire Salterns: Excavations at Helpringham, Holbeach St Johns and Bicker Haven*, East Anglian Archaeol. 89

Bell, A. and Evans, J. 2002. 'Pottery from the CFA excavations', in P. R. Wilson (ed.) 'Cataractonium: Roman Catterick and its hinterland. Excavations and research, 1958-1997', *CBA Research Rep. 128*, 352-497

Bennett, K. A. 1965. 'The etiology and genetics of wormian bones', *American Journal of Physical Anthropology* 23: 255-260

Berggren, G. 1981. *Atlas of seeds and small fruits of Northwest-European plant species with morphological descriptions*, Stockholm

Bevan, B. 1999a. 'Land-Life-Death-Regeneration: interpreting a middle Iron Age landscape in eastern Yorkshire', in Bevan 1999b, 123-148

Bevan, B. (ed.) 1999b. *Northern Exposure: interpretative devolution and the Iron Ages in Britain*, Leicester Archaeol. Monographs 4

Biddle, M. 1990. *Object and Economy in Medieval Winchester, Winchester Studies 7ii, Artefacts from Medieval Winchester*, Clarendon Press, Oxford

Bidwell, P. 2005. 'The dating of Crambeck Parchment Ware'. *Journal of Roman Pottery Studies*, 12, 15-21

Bidwell, P. T. and Croom, A. T. 1997. 'The Coarse Wares' in Wenham and Heywood 1997, 61-103

Bidwell, P. and Croom, A. 2010. 'The supply and use of pottery on Hadrian's Wall in the 4th century', in R. Collins and L. Allason-Jones, *Finds from the Frontier: Material Culture in the 4th-5th centuries*. CBA Research Rep 162, 20-36

Binford, L. 1981. *Ancient Men and Modern Myths*, Academic Press, New York

Boessneck, J. 1969. 'Osteological Differences in Sheep (*Ovis aries* L.) and Goat (*Capra hircus* L.)', in D. Brothwell and E. Higgs (eds), *Science in Archaeology*, Thames and Hudson, 331-358

Boardman, S. and Jones, G. E. M. 1990. 'Experiments on the effects of charring on cereal plant components', *J. Archaeol. Science* 17(1), 1-12

Bourdieu, P. 1992. *The logic of practice*, Polity Press, Cambridge

Boyle, A., Didsbury, P., Vince, A. and Young, J. 2011. 'The Medieval Pottery' in H. E. M Cool and M. Bell (eds.), *Excavations at St. Peters Church, Barton upon Humber*, English Heritage [internet], Available at <// archaeologydataservice.ac.uk>

Boyle, A. and Young, J. 2008. *A Fabric Type Series for Post-Roman Pottery from North Lincolnshire (5th to sixteenth centuries)*, unpublished, for North Lincs Museum

Bradley, J. and Steedman, K. 2014. 'Iron Age and Romano-British Settlement at the Aldbrough Gas Storage Facility, Aldbrough, East Yorkshire' *East Riding Archaeologist* 14, 1-64

Bradley, P. 1999. 'Worked flint', in A. Barclay and C. Halpin, *Excavations at Barrow Hills, Radley, Oxfordshire. Vol. 1: The Neolithic and Bronze Age monument complex*, Oxford Archaeology 211-227

Brigham, T., Buglass, J. and George, R. 2008. *Rapid Coastal Zone Assessment Survey Yorkshire and Lincolnshire, Bempton to Donna Nook. English Heritage Project 3729*, Humber Archaeology Rep. 235 Parts 1 and 2

Brigham, T., Buglass, J. and Steedman, K. 2008. *A Desk-Based Resource Assessment of Aggregate-Producing Landscapes in the East Riding of Yorkshire. English Heritage Project 4828*, Humber Archaeology Rep. 261 Vols 1-3

Brigham, T. and Jobling, D. 2011. *Rapid Coastal Zone Assessment Yorkshire and Lincolnshire Bempton to Donna Nook English Heritage Project 3729, Phase 2* Humber Archaeology Rep. 324

Brooks, C. M., 1987. 'Medieval and Later Pottery from Aldwark and Other Sites', in *The Archaeology of York: the pottery*, 16/3, CBA Research Rep., London

Brown, F., Howard-Davis, C., Brennand, M., Boyle, A., Evans, T., O'Connor, S., Spence, A., Heawod, R. and Lupton, A. 2007. *The archaeology of the A1(M) Darrington to Dishforth Road Scheme* Lancaster Imprints 7

Buckland, P. C., Dolby, M. J., Hayfield, C. and Magilton, J. R. 1979. 'The Medieval Pottery Industry at Hallgate, Doncaster', in *The Archaeology of Doncaster vol 2, part 1: The Medieval Town,* Doncaster Museums and Arts Services

Buckland, P. C., Magilton, J. R. and Hayfield, C. 1988. *The Archaeology of Doncaster 2; The Medieval and Later Town*, B.A.R. Brit, Ser, 202

Buckland, P., Runnacles, R. B. and Sumpter, A. B. 1990. 'The petrography of the Iron Age pottery', in S. Wrathmell and A. Nicholson (eds.), *Dalton Parlours: Iron Age settlement and Roman villa*, Yorkshire Archaeology 3, West Yorkshire Archaeology Service

Bunn, D, 2007. *Fluxgate gradiometer survey: Easington to Paull proposed gas pipeline*, Pre-Construct Geophysics, unpublished

Bunn, D, 2008 *Fluxgate gradiometer survey: Easington to Paull proposed gas pipeline, Addendum 1*, Pre-Construct Geophysics, unpublished

Bush, M. B. 1993. 'An 11 400 year paleoecological history of a British chalk grassland', *J. Vegetation Science*, 4 (1), 47-66

Bush, M. B. and Ellis, S. 1987. 'The sedimentological and vegetational history of Willow Garth', in Ellis 1987, 42-52

Butler, C. 2005. *Prehistoric flintwork*, Tempus, Stroud

Camden, W. 1701. *Britannia, abridged*, Joseph Wild, London

Cappers, R. T. J., Bekker, R. M. and Jans, J. E. A. 2006. *Digitale Zandenatlas Van Nederland*, Groningen University

Case, H. 2001. 'The Beaker Culture in Britain and Ireland: Groups, European Contacts and Chronology' in Nicolis, F. (ed.): *Bell Beakers Today: pottery people, culture, symbols in prehistoric Europe*, Servizio Beni Culturali Ufficio Beni Archeologici, Trento, 361-377

Casswell, C. and Daniel, P. 2010. *Stone was the one crop that never failed: the archaeology of a Trans-Pennine pipeline*, B.A.R. Brit. Ser. 526, Oxford

Catt, J. A. 2007.'The Pleistocene glaciations of eastern Yorkshire: a review'. *Proceedings of the Yorkshire Geological Society*, 56, 177-207

Chadwick, A. 2009. *Fields* for *Discourse. Landscape and Materialities of Being in South and West Yorkshire and Nottinghamshire during the Iron Age and Romano-British Periods*, unpublished PhD thesis, University of Wales

Challis, A. J. and Harding, D. W. 1975. *Later Prehistory from the Trent to the Tyne*, B.A.R. Brit. Ser. 156

Chapman, H., Fletcher, W., Fenwick, H., Lillie, M. and Thomas, G. 2000. 'The archaeological survey of the Hull valley', in Van de Noort, R. and Ellis, S. (eds) *Wetland Heritage of the Hull Valley, an Archaeological Survey*, 105-173, Humber Wetlands Project, University of Hull

Chowne, P. and Healey, H. 1999. 'Briquetage' in A. Bell *et al*, 16-17

Clapham, A., Tutin, T. and Moore, D. 1987. *Flora of the British Isles, 3rd edition*, CUP, Cambridge

Clark, J. G. D. 1954. *Excavations at Star Carr: An early Mesolithic site at Seamer near Scarborough, Yorkshire*, Cambridge University Press

Clark, J. and Godwin, H. 1956. 'A Maglemosian site at Brandesburton, Holderness, Yorkshire', *Proc. Prehist. Soc.*, 22, 6-22

Clark, J. G. D., Higgs, E. S. and Longworth, I. H. 1960. 'Excavations at the Neolithic site of Hurst Fen, Mildenhall, Suffolk, 1954, 1957 and 1958' *Proc. Prehist. Soc.* 26, 202-245

Clarke, D. N. 1970. *Beaker Pottery of Great Britain and Ireland*, CUP, Cambridge

Clarke, J. C. 1990. 'Miscellaneous Stone and Ceramic Artefacts (excluding structural stonework)', in S. Wrathmell and A. Nicholson, *Dalton Parlours : Iron Age settlement and Roman villa*, 120-126, West Yorkshire Archaeology Service

Clarke, J. C. 1998. 'Other artefacts of stone', in H. E. M. Cool and C. Philo, *Roman Castleford: Excavations 1974-1985, vol. 1, The Small Finds*, 253-265, West Yorkshire Archaeology Service

Clarke, J. (ed.) 1995. *The Medieval Horse and its Equipment*, Boydell, Woodbridge

Coles, B. J. 1998. 'Doggerland: a speculative survey', *Proc Prehist Soc.* 64, 45-81

Coles, J. M. 1987. *Meare Village East: the Excavations of A. Bulleid and H. St. George Gray*, Somerset Levels Papers, No. 13, Exeter

Coles, B. J., Coles, J. M. and Jørgensen, M. S. (eds.). 1999. *Bog Bodies, Sacred Sites and Wetland Archaeology*, Exeter Wetland Archaeology Research Project in B. J. Coles, J. M. Coles and M. S. Jørgensen (eds.), *Bog Bodies, Sacred Sites and Wetland Archaeology*, 69-78, Exeter Wetland Archaeology Research Project

Collis, J. R. 2003. *The Celts; origins, myths and inventions*, Tempus, Stroud

Colyer, C., Gilmour, B. J. J. and Jones, M. J. 1999. *The defences of the Lower City: Excavations at the Park and West Parade 1970-2 and a discussion of other sites excavated up to 1994*, CBA Research Rep. 114

Cool, H. E. M. 2006. *Eating and Drinking in Roman Britain*, CUP, Cambridge

Copley, I. B. 1953. *Early Iron Age remains at Gransmoor, East Yorkshire*, unpublished interim report, Centre for Continuing Education, University of Leeds

Corder, P. 1930a. *The Roman Pottery at Throlam, Spalding-on-the-Moor: East Yorkshire, Roman Malton and District Report No. 3*, Yorkshire Archaeol. Soc., Leeds

Corder, P. 1930b. *The defences of the Roman fort at Malton: Roman Malton and District Report No. 2*, Yorkshire Archaeol. Soc., Leeds

Corder, P. and Kirk, J. L. 1932. *A Roman Villa at Langton, near Malton, East Yorkshire: Roman Malton and District Report No. 4*, Yorkshire Archaeol. Soc., Leeds

Corder, P. and Birley, M. 1937. 'A pair of fourth-century Romano-British pottery kilns near Crambeck with a note on the distribution of Crambeck ware by Margaret Birley', *Antiq. J.* 17, 392-413

Cowgill, J., de Neergaard, M. and Griffiths, N. 1987. *Knives and Scabbards, Medieval Finds from London 1*, HMSO, London

Credland, A. G. 1995. *The Hull Whaling Trade: an Arctic Enterprise*, Hutton Press, Beverley

Creighton, J. 1999. 'The Pottery' in Halkon and Millett 1999, 141-164

Crummy, N. 1983. *Colchester Archaeological Report 2: The Roman Small Finds from Excavations in Colchester 1971-9*, Colchester Archaeol. Trust and DoE, Colchester

Cumberpatch, C. G. 1991. *The production and circulation of Late Iron Age slip decorated pottery in Central Europe*, unpublished PhD Thesis, University of Sheffield

Cumberpatch, C. G. 1997. 'Towards a phenomenological approach to the study of medieval pottery', in Cumberpatch and Blinkhorn, 1997

Cumberpatch, C. G. 2002. 'The Medieval and Later Pottery', in I. Roberts, *Pontefract Castle, Archaeological Excavations 1982-86*, Yorkshire Archaeology 8, Leeds

Cumberpatch, C. G. 2003. 'The transformation of tradition; the origins of the post-medieval ceramic tradition in Yorkshire', http://www.shef.ac.uk/assem/issue7/cumberpatch.html

Cumberpatch, C .G. 2007. 'Iron Age and Romano-British hand-made pottery' in: M. Lightfoot (ed.), *A165 Reighton by-pass, Reighton, North Yorkshire*, Archaeological Services WYAS Rep. 1720

Cumberpatch, C. G. 2009a. *Pre-Roman Iron Age and Romano-British hand-made pottery from sites on the course of the Easington to Ganstead (EAG) gas pipeline: an assessment*, unpublished report for Network Archaeology

Cumberpatch, C. G. 2009b. *Handmade prehistoric pottery and early Roman pottery from the Bridlington to Haisthorpe pipeline (SKP 06 and BBA 06)*, unpublished archive report for Northern Archaeological Associates

Cumberpatch, C. G. 2011 *Pottery from excavations at Sheffield Manor Lodge 2010 (SML10)* Unpublished archive report for Sheffield University

Cumberpatch, C. G. unpublished 1. *Hand-made pottery of later prehistoric and Roman date from excavations on the A165 Reighton by-pass, North Yorkshire*, unpublished archive report for Archaeological Services WYAS

Cumberpatch, C. G. unpublished 2. *Hand-made pottery from the Bridlington to Haisthorpe water improvement scheme (SKP and BBA 06)*, unpublished archive report for Northern Archaeological Associates

Cumberpatch, C. G. unpublished 3. *Prehistoric and Roman period hand-made pottery from excavations in advance of the Dishforth to Barton A1 widening scheme*, unpublished archive report for Northern Archaeological Associates

Cumberpatch, C .G. in prep. 'The organisation of pottery production in Yorkshire during the 17th and 18th centuries' in C. Cumberpatch and P.W. Blinkhorn (eds.), *The chiming of crack'd bells; Recent approaches to artefact analysis in archaeology*

Cumberpatch, C. G. and Blinkhorn, P. W. 1997. *Not so much a pot, more a way of life*, Oxbow Monograph 83, Oxbow Books

Cunliffe, B. W. 2005. *Iron Age Communities in Britain: An account of England, Scotland and Wales from the seventh century BC until the Roman Conquest (4th ed.)*, Routledge, Abingdon

Dandy, D. J. and Edwards, D. J. 1998. *Essential Orthopaedics and Trauma*, 3rd edition, Churchill Livingstone, London

Daniel, P., Casswell, C. and Moore, R. forthcoming, *Perspectives on Ancient East Yorkshire: The Archaeology of the Ganstead to Asselby pipeline*

Darling, M. J. 1981. 'Early Red-Slipped Ware from Lincoln', in A. C. Anderson and A. S. Anderson, *Roman Pottery Research in Britain and North West Europe: Papers in Honour of Graham Webster, vol. 2*, B.A.R. Int. ser. 123(*ii*), 397-415

Darling, M. J. 1984. *Roman Pottery from the Upper Defences*, Lincoln Archaeological Trust Monograph Series XVI-2

Darling, M. J. 2004. 'Guidelines for the archiving of Roman pottery', *J. Roman Pottery Studies* Vol 11, 67-75

Darling, M. J. and Wood, K. 1976. 'Washingborough Roman Tile Kiln', *Annual Report of Lincoln Archaeol Trust 4*, 22-3, Lincoln Archaeol Trust, Lincoln

Davies, B., Richardson, B and Tomber, R. 1994. *A Dated Corpus of Early Roman Pottery from the City of London*, CBA Research Rep. 98, York

Davies, P. 2008. *Snails: archaeology and landscape change*, Oxbow, Oxford

De Brisay, K. and Evans, K. A. (eds.) 1975 *Salt: The Study of an Ancient Industry*, Colchester Archaeology Group, Colchester

Defoe, D. 1727. *A Tour Thro' the Whole Island of Great Britain Divided into Circuits or Journies*, G. Strahan, London

Dent, J. S. 1983. 'A summary of the excavations carried out in Garton and Wetwang Slack 1964-80', *East Riding Archaeologist* 7, 1-14

Dent, J. S. 1995. *Aspects of Iron Age settlement in East Yorkshire*, unpublished PhD thesis, University of Sheffield

Dickson, A. and Hopkinson, G. 2011. *Holes in the Landscape. Seventeen Years of Archaeological Investigations at Nosterfield Quarry, North Yorkshire*, Archaeological Planning Consultancy report http://www.archaeologicalplanningconsultancy.co.uk/thornborough/pdf/holes_in_the_landscape.pdf

Didsbury, P. 2004. 'The Iron Age and Roman pottery' in P. A. Rahtz and L. Watts, *The north manor and north-west enclosure Wharram: A study of settlement on the Yorkshire Wolds IX*, York University Archaeological Publications 11

Didsbury, P. 2006. *An assessment of the pottery from excavations on the A165 Reighton By-Pass, North Yorkshire*, unpublished assessment report for Archaeological Services WYAS

Didsbury, P. 2009a. 'Iron Age and Roman pottery', in: I. Roberts (ed), 'An Iron Age and Romano-British settlement at High Wold, Bempton Lane Bridlington', *Yorkshire Archaeol. J.* 81, 85-101

Didsbury, P. 2009b. 'Iron Age and Roman pottery', in Fenton-Thomas 2009

Didsbury, P. 2011. 'The pottery', in Richardson 2011

Didsbury, P. unpublished. 'The pottery', in *Creyke Beck Iron Age settlement*, unpublished report, Northern Archaeological Associates

Didsbury, P. and Holbrey, R. 2009. 'Pottery Wasters from Annie Reid Road, Beverley', *East Riding Archaeologist* 12, 208-231.

Didsbury, P. and Vince, A. 2011. 'First millennium BC pottery', in C. Fenton-Thomas 2011, 184-198

Didsbury, P. and Watkins, J. G. 1992. 'The Pottery', in D. H Evans and D. G. Tomlinsin, *Excavations at 33-35 Eastgate, Beverley, 1983-1986*, Sheffield Excavation reports 3, 81-120, Sheffield

Dimbleby, G. 1985. *The palynology of archaeological sites*, Academic Press, London

Dinnin, M. 1995. 'Introduction to the palaeo-environmental survey', in Van der Noort and Ellis 1995, 27-48

Dinnin, M. and Lillie, M. 1995. 'The palaeo-environmental survey of the meres of Holderness', in Van der Noort and Ellis 1995, 49-86

Dinnin, M. and Van de Noort, R. 1999. 'Wetland habitats, their resource potential and exploitation: a case study from the Humber wetlands', in Coles *et al.* 1999, 69-78

Dobney, K. and Ervynck, A. 2007. 'To fish or not to fish? Evidence for the possible avoidance of fish consumption during the Iron Age around the North Sea', in Haselgrove and Moore 2007, 403-41

von den Driesch, A. 1976. *A Guide to the Measurement of Animal Bones from Archaeological Sites*, Peabody Museum

Dungworth, D. 1997. 'Iron Age and Roman Copper Alloys from Northern Britain', *Internet Archaeology*, http://intarch.ac.uk/journal/issue2/dungworth_index.html

Egan, G. and Pritchard, F. 1991. *Dress Accessories, Medieval Finds from Excavations in London*, HMSO, London

Ekwall, E. 1960. *The concise Oxford dictionary of English place names*, OUP, Oxford

Ellis, B. 2002. *Prick Spurs 700-1700*, Datasheet 30, Finds Research Group

Ellis, S. (ed) 1987. *East Yorkshire field guide*, Quaternary Research Association, Cambridge

Ellis, S (ed.) 1993. *Wetland Heritage: An archaeological assessment of the Humber Wetlands*, English Heritage

Ellis, S. 1995. 'Physical Background to Holderness', in Van de Noort and Ellis 1995, 9-16

Elsdon, S. 1992. 'East Midlands Scored ware', *Trans. Leicester Archaeol. and Hist. Soc.* LXVI; 83-91

Elsdon, S. 1996. *Iron Age pottery in the East Midlands: a handbook*, Department of Classics and Archaeology, University of Nottingham

Elsdon, S. 1997. *Old Sleaford revealed*, Nottingham Studies in Archaeology, Oxbow Monograph 78

English Heritage 1991. *Management of Archaeological Projects, second Edition.* English Heritage, London

Evans, D. H. and Atkinson, R. 2009. 'Recent Archaeological Work in the East Riding' *East Riding Archaeologist* 12, 258-289

Evans, D. H., and Steedman, K. 1997. 'Recent Archaeological Work in the East Riding', *East Riding Archaeologist* 9, 116-171

Evans, D. H., and Steedman, K. 2001. 'Recent Archaeological Work in the East Riding', *East Riding Archaeologist* 10, 67-156

Evans, J. 1985. Aspects of later Roman pottery assemblages in Northern England, unpublished Ph.D. Thesis, University of Bradford

Evans, J. 1988. 'All Yorkshire is divided into three parts: Social aspects of later Roman pottery distribution in Yorkshire', in: J. Price and P. R. Wilson (eds.), *Recent research in Roman Yorkshire*, B.A.R. Brit. Ser. 193; 323-337

Evans, J. 1993. 'Pottery function and finewares in the Roman north', *J. Roman Studies* 6, 95-119

Evans, J. 1995. 'Later Iron Age and 'native' pottery in the north-east', in: B. Vyner (ed), *Moorland Monuments: Studies in the archaeology of north-east Yorkshire in honour of Raymond Hayes and Don Spratt*, CBA Research Rep. 101

Evans, J. 2005. 'Late Iron Age and Romano-British pottery', in Roberts, I., 'Ferrybridge Henge: The Ritual Landscape', *Yorkshire Archaeology* 10, 130-142

Evans, J. 2006. 'The Roman Pottery', in M. Millett 2006, 126-202

Evans, J. and Creighton, J. 1999. 'The Hawling Road Ceramic series', in Halkon and Millett 1999, 200-218

Faegri, K. and Iversen, J. 1989. *Textbook of Pollen Analysis* (4th edn), John Wiley & Son. Chichester

Farey, J. 1811. *General View of the Agriculture and Minerals of Derbyshire I*, Board of Agriculture, London, 435-440

Feinman, G., Upham, S and Lightfoot, K. 1981. 'The production step measure: An ordinal index of labor input in ceramic manufacture', *American Antiquity* 46, no. 4, 871-884

Fenton-Thomas, C. 2003. Late prehistoric and early historic land-use on the Yorkshire Wolds, B.A.R. Brit Ser. 350, Oxford

Fenton-Thomas, C. 2009. *A Place by the Sea: Excavations at Sewerby Cottage Farm, Bridlington*, On-Site Archaeology Monograph 1, York

Fenton-Thomas, C. 2011. *Where Sky and Yorkshire and Water Meet: The Story of the Melton Landscape from Prehistory to the Present*, On-Site Archaeology Monograph 2, York

Finn, N. 2012. *Bronze Age Ceremonial Enclosures and Cremation Cemetery at Eye Kettleby, Leicestershire: the development of a Prehistoric Landscape*, Leicestershire Archaeol. Monograph 20, 68-76

Fletcher, W. and Van de Noort, R. 2007. 'The lake-dwellings of Holderness, East Yorkshire revisited: a journey into antiquarian and contemporary wetland archaeology', in C. Green *Archaeology from the Wetlands: Recent Perspectives*, Society of Antiquaries of Scotland, Edinburgh

Flintoft, P. 2008. *Easington to Ganstead proposed natural gas pipeline: archaeological reconnaissance, fieldwalking and geophysical survey: report on further works*, Network Archaeology rep. 545, unpublished

Flintoft, P. and Glover, G. 2010. *Easington to Ganstead natural gas pipeline: archaeological excavations and watching brief, post-excavation assessment of potential for analysis and updated project design*, Network Archaeology rep. 561, unpublished

Fraser, J. 2004. *An Archaeological Evaluation by Trial Trenching on Land Adjacent to Hull High School, Tranby Croft, Anlaby, East Riding of Yorkshire*, Humber Field Archaeology rep., unpublished

Frere, S. S. 1972. *Verulamium Excavations Volume I*, Society of Antiquaries of London, Oxford

Gaffney, V., Thomson, K. and Fitch, S. (eds) 2007. Mapping Doggerland, Archaeopress, Oxford

Gaffney, V., Fitch, S. and Smith, D. 2009. *Europe's Lost World: The Rediscovery of Doggerland*, CBA Research Rep. 160

Gibson, A. 1982. *Beaker domestic sites: a study of the domestic pottery of the late third and early second millennia BC, in the British Isles*, B.A.R. Brit. Ser. 107, Oxford

Giddens, A. 1984. *The constitution of society*, Polity Press, Cambridge

Gilbertson, D. 1984. *Late Quaternary environments and man in Holderness*, B.A.R. Brit. Ser. 134

Giles, M. 2000. *Open-weave, Close-knit: Archaeologies of Identity in the later prehistoric landscape of East Yorkshire*, unpublished PhD thesis, University of Sheffield

Giles, M. 2007. 'Making metal and forging relations: ironworking in the British Iron Age' *Oxford Journal of Archaeology* 26 (4), 395-413

Giles, M. 2012. *A Forged Glamour: Landscape, Identity and Material Culture in the Iron Age*, Oxbow, Oxford

Gillam, J. P. 1970. *Types of Roman Coarse Pottery Vessels in Northern Britain* (3rd ed.), Oriel Press, Newcastle upon Tyne

Giovas, C. M. 2009. 'The Shell Game: analytic problems in archaeological mollusc quantification', *J. Archaeol. Science* 39, 1557-1564

Grant, A, 1982. 'The Use of Tooth Wear as a Guide to the Age of Domestic Ungulates', in B Wilson *et al. Ageing and Sexing Animal Bones from Archaeological Sites*, B.A.R. Brit Ser. 109, 91-108, Oxford

Grant, A, 1989. 'Animals in Roman Britain', in M.Todd (ed.) *Research on Roman Britain: 1960-89*, Britannia Monograph 11, 135-173

Green, H. S. 1980. *The Flint Arrowheads of the British Isles*, B.A.R. Brit Ser. 75, Oxford

Green, F. J. 1982. 'Problems of interpreting differentially preserved plant remains from excavations of urban medieval sites', in A. R. Hall and H. K. Kenward (eds), *Environmental Archaeology in the Urban Context*. CBA Research Rep. 43

Gregory, T. 1992. *Excavations in Thetford 1980-1982 Fison Way, vol 1*, Norfolk Museums Service: Norfolk

Gregory, A. K. 1996. 'Romano-British Pottery', in May 1996, 513-63

Gregory, R. A., Daniel, P. and Brown, F. 2013. *Early Landscapes of West and North Yorkshire: Archaeological Investigation along the Asselby to Pannal Natural Gas Pipeline 2007-8*, OAN Lancaster Imprints, Lancaster

Grime, J., Hodgson, J. and Hunt, R. 2007. *Comparative Plant Ecology: a functional approach to common British species*, (2nd edn.), Castlepoint Press, Colvend

Guido, M, 1978. *The Glass Beads of the Prehistoric and Roman Periods in Britain and Ireland, Rep. Res. Comm. Soc. Antiq. London* 35

Guido, M. (ed Welch, M.) 1999. *The Glass Beads of Anglo-Saxon England c AD 400-700, Rep. Res. Comm. Soc. Antiq. London* 58

Gwilt, A. 2006. 'The quernstones', in Millett 2006, 106-219; 244-48

Habermehl, K. H. 1975. *Die Alterbestimmung bei haus- und Labor-tieren*, Parey, Berlin

Halkon, P. 2004. *Valley of the first iron masters: a case study in inclusion and interpretation*, B.A.R. Brit. Ser. 362

Halkon, P. 2008. *Archaeology and Environment in a Changing East Yorkshire Landscape. The Foulness Valley c. 800BC to c. AD200*, B.A.R. Brit. Ser. 472

Halkon, P. and Millett, M. 1999. *Rural settlement and Industry: Studies in the Iron Age and Roman Archaeology of Lowland East Yorkshire*. Yorkshire Archaeological Report 4, Leeds

Hall, A. 2003. *Recognition and characterisation of turves in archaeological occupation deposits by means of macrofossil plant remains*, English Heritage Centre for Archaeology Rep. 16/2003, Portsmouth

Halstead, P. 1985. 'A Study of Mandibular Teeth from Romano-British Contexts at Maxey', in F Pryor, *Archaeology and Environment in the Lower Welland Valley*, East Anglian Archaeol. Rep. 27, 219-224

Harding, D. W. 2009. *The Iron Age Round-House*, OUP, Oxford

Harding, P. 1990. 'The worked flint' in J. C. Richards, *The Stonehenge environs project*, English Heritage, London, 15-25

Hartley, K. 1995. 'Mortaria' in Phillips, D. and Heywood, B. *Excavations at York Minster*, vol. I, part 2, 'The Finds'. HMSO, London, 304-323

Haselgrove, C. and Moore, T. (eds) 2007. *The Later Iron Age in Britain and beyond*, Oxbow Books, Oxford

Hattatt, R. 1987. *Brooches of Antiquity*, Oxbow, Oxford

Havinga, A. 1964. 'Investigation into the differential corrosion susceptibility of pollen and spores' *Pollen et Spores* 6, 621-635

Havinga, A. 1967. 'Palynology and pollen preservation', *Review of Palaeobotany and Palynology* 2, 81-98

Hawkes, C. F. C. and Hull, M. R. 1947. 'Camulodunum', *Rep. Res. Comm. Soc. Antiq. London* 14, Oxford

Hayes, R. H., Hemmingway, J. E. and Spratt, D. A. 1980. 'The Distribution and Lithology of Beehive Querns in north east Yorkshire', *Journal Archaeolog. Science* 7, 297-324

Hayes, R. H. and Whitley, E. 1950.*The Roman Pottery at Norton, East Yorkshire*, Roman Malton and District report No. 7, Leeds

Hayfield, C. and Slater, T. 1984. *The Medieval Town of Hedon, Excavations 1875-1976*. Humberside Heritage Publication 7

Hayward, P. J., Wigham, G. D., and Yonow, N. 1995. 'Molluscs', in , P. J. Hayward and J. S. Ryland (eds.), *Handbook of the Marine Fauna of North-West Europe*, OUP,Oxford, 484-629

Head, R. 1995. 'The use of lithic material in prehistoric Holderness' in Van de Noort and Ellis 1995, 311-322

Healy, F. 1988. *The Anglo-Saxon cemetery at Spong Hill, North Elmham, Part VI: Occupation in the seventh to second millennia BC*. Norfolk Archaeological Unit, Gressenhall

Herrmann, B. 1970. 'Anthropologische Bearbeitung der Leichenbranden von Berlin-Rudow', *Ausgrabungen in Berlin* 1, 61-71

Heslop, D. H. 1988. 'The Study of Beehive Querns', *Scottish Archaeological Review* 5, 59-65

Heslop, D. H. 2008. *Patterns of quern production, acquisition and deposition. A Corpus of Beehive Querns from Northern Yorkshire and Southern Durham*, Yorkshire Archaeological Society, Occasional paper 5

Heslop, D. and Gaunt, G. 2009. 'Querns' in I. Roberts, 'A Late Iron Age and Romano-British Settlement at High Wold, Bempton Lane, Bridlington, East Yorkshire', *Yorkshire Archaeol. J.* 81, 105-107

Hill, J. D. 1995. *Ritual and rubbish in the Iron Age of Wessex*, B.A.R. Brit. Ser. 242

Hill, J. D. 1999. 'Settlement, landscape and regionality: Norfolk and Suffolk in the pre-Roman Iron Age of Britain and beyond', in J. A. Davies and T. Williamson (eds), *Land of the Iceni: the Iron Age in northern East*

Anglia, Studies in East Anglian History 4, Norwich, 185-207

Hingley, R. 2006. 'The deposition of iron objects in Britain during the later prehistoric and Roman periods: contextual analysis and the significance of iron', *Britannia* 37, 213-257

Hyland, L. 2009. 'The Roman archaeological evidence of Holderness' *Yorkshire Archaeol. J.* 81, 179-197

Holdsworth, J., 1987. 'Selected Pottery Groups AD 650-1780', *The Archaeology of York : the pottery, 16/1*, CBA Res Rep., London

Holgate, C. and Ralph, S. 2006. *Easington to Ganstead Proposed Gas Pipeline: a desk-based assessment*, Network Archaeology rep. 519, unpublished

Holst, M. 2010. *Osteological Analysis, Heslington East*, York Osteoarchaeology Report 1010, unpublished

HFA 2001. *TSEP Teeside to Saltend Etylene Pipeline: Assessment of the results of archaeological excavations in the East Riding of Yorkshire (Report 7)* unpublished Humber Field Archaeology report

Hurcombe, L. 2007. 'Plant processing for cordage and textiles using serrated flint edges: new chaînes operatoires suggested by ethnographic, archaeological and experimental evidence for bast fibre processing' in V. Beugnier and P. Crombé, *Plant processing from a prehistoric and ethnographic perspective/Préhistoire et ethnographie du travail des plantes: proceedings of a workshop at Ghent University, November 28, 2006*, B.A.R. Int Ser. 1718, 41-66

Inizan, M-L., Roche, H. and Tixier, J. 1992. *Technology of knapped stone*, CREP, France

Ixer, R. 2005. 'Petrographic analysis of the vessel from OVM01 Trench 15m Context 021', in: C. Cumberpatch, A. Walster, R. Ixer and E. Morris, 'Mellor: A review of the later prehistoric ceramics', in Nevell and Redhead 2005

Ixer, R. and Vince, A. 2009. 'The provenance potential of igneous glacial erratics in Anglo-Saxon ceramics from Northern England', in Quinn. P. (ed) *Interpreting Silent Artefacts. Petrographic Approaches to Archaeological Ceramics,* 11-24, Archaeopress, Oxford

Jackson, D. and Dix. B. 1986-87. 'Late Iron Age and Roman settlement at Weekley, Northants', *Northamptonshire Archaeology* 21, 41-93

Jackson R, 1990. *Camerton, Late Iron Age and Early Roman Metalwork*, British Museum Press, London

Jacobi, R. 1978. 'The Mesolithic of Sussex', in P. L. Drewett (ed.), *Archaeology in Sussex to AD 1500*, 15-22, Council for British Archaeology, CBA Research Rep. 29, York

Jacobsen, G. and Bradshaw, R. 1981. 'The selection of sites for palaeo-vegetational studies', *Quaternary research* 16, 80-96

Jacomet S. 2006. *Identification of Cereal Remains from Archaeological Sites*, unpubl. 2nd edn, Archaeology Laboratory, IPAS, Basel University

Jay, M. and Richards, M. P. 2006. 'Diet in the Iron Age cemetery population at Wetwang Slack, East Yorkshire, UK: carbon and nitrogen stable isotope evidence', *J. Archaeol. Science 33*, 653-662

Jelgersma, S. 1979. 'Sea-level changes in the North Sea basin', in E. Oele, R. T. E. Schuttenhelm and A. J. Wiggers, *Acta Universitatis Upsaliensis Symposia Universitatis: Upsaliensis Annum Quingentesimum Celebrantis 2*, 233-48

Jennings, S. 1981. *Eighteen Centuries of Pottery from Norwich*, E. Anglian Archaeol 13, The Norwich Survey, Norwich

Johnson, S. 1983. *Burgh Castle, excavations by Charles Green 1958–61*, E. Anglian Archaeol. 20

Kent, P. E., Gaunt, G. D., Wood, C. J. and Wilson, V. 1980. *British regional geology: Eastern England from the Tees to the Wash*. London, HMSO

Kenward, H. K., Hall, A. R. and Jones, A. K. G. 1986. *Environmental Evidence from a Roman Well and Anglian Pits in the Legionary Fortress*, Council for British Archaeology, York

Kerney, M. P. and Cameron, R. A. D. 1979. *A Field Guide to the Land Snails of Britain and North West Europe*, William Collins, Glasgow

Kinnes, I., Schadla-Hall, T., Chadwick, P. and Dean, P. 1983. 'Duggleby Howe reconsidered', *Archaeological Journal* 140, 83-108

Kirkham, B. 2001. Iron Age and Roman saltmaking on the Lindsey coast and marshland, in Lane and Morris 2001, 405-410

Knight, D. 1998 *Guidelines for the recording of later prehistoric pottery from the East Midlands* Trent and Peak Archaeological Trust, University of Nottingham

Knight, D. 2002 *A regional ceramic sequence: pottery of the first millennium BC between the Humber and the Nene* in A. Woodward and J.D. Hill (Eds.) *Prehistoric Britain: The ceramic basis* Prehistoric Ceramics Research Group, Occasional Publication 3, Oxbow Books

Knight, D. 2010. 'Later Bronze Age and Iron Age pottery', in T. Lane and D. Trimble (eds.) *Fluid landscapes and human adaption: Excavations on prehistoric sites on the Lincolnshire Fen Edge 1991-1994*, Lincs Archaeol. and Heritage Rep. 9

Knox, R. 1855. *Descriptions, Geological, Topographical, and Antiquarian in East Yorkshire in Eastern Yorkshire, Between the River Humber and Tees*, published by the author, London

Lane, T. and Morris, E. L. 2001. *A millennium of saltmaking: prehistoric and Romano-British salt production in the fenland*, Lincs Archaeol. and Heritage Rep Ser. 4

Lanting, J. N, and van der Waals, J. D. 1972. 'British Beakers as seen from the Continent'. *Helinium* 12, 20-46.

Leahy, K. A. 2003. *Anglo-Saxon Crafts*, Tempus, Stroud

Leary, R. S. 2006. *Tiln 05 Romano-British Pottery Report*, unpublished report for Trent and Peak Archaeology

Leary, R. S. 2009. *Tiln Grange Farm (TGF) Romano-British Pottery Romano-British Pottery Report*, unpublished report for Trent and Peak Archaeology

Leslie, K., Middleton, A. and Rigby, V. 2004. 'The petrography of the pottery', in V. Rigby, *Pots in Pits: The British Museum Yorkshire settlements project 1988-92*, East Riding Archaeologist 11

Levine, M. A. 1982. 'The Use of Crown Height Measurements and Eruption-Wear Sequences to Age Horse Teeth', in B. Wilson *et al. Ageing and Sexing Animal Bones from Archaeological Sites*, B.A.R. Brit. Ser. 109, 223-250

Lillie, M. C. and Gearey, B. R. 2000. 'The palaeo-environmental survey of the Hull Valley', in Van de Noort R. and Ellis S. (eds) *Wetland Heritage of the Hull Valley*, Hull

Lillie, M. C., Gearey, B. R. and Chapman, H. P. 2003 'Geoarchaeological evidence for Holocene landscape evolution in the Hull Valley, eastern England, UK', in A. J, Howard, M. G. Macklin and D. G. Passmore (eds.) *Alluvial Archaeology in Europe*, Balkema, Rotterdam

de Lotbiniere, S. 1977. 'The story of the English gunflint, some theories and queries', *Journal of the Arms and Armour Society* 9 (1), 18-53

de Lotbiniere, S. 1984a Gunflint Recognition. *The International Journal of Nautical Archaeology and Underwater Exploration* 13 (3), 206-209

de Lotbiniere, S. 1984b. *The manufacture of gunflints by Sydney B.J. Skertchly, F.G.S. London, 1879 with an introduction by Seymour de Lotbiniere*, Museums Restoration Service, Canada

Loughlin, N. and Miller, K. R. 1979. *A Survey of Archaeological Sites in Humberside*, Humberside Joint Archaeol. Com. Hull

Loveluck, C. 1999. 'Archaeological expressions of the transition from the late Roman to early Anglo-Saxon period in Lowland East Yorkshire', in Halkon and Millett 1999, 228-236

Lucas, V. A. and Paynter, S. 2010. *Park Farm East, Ashford, Kent: a Compositional Analysis of Crucibles from the Iron Age Settlement*, English Heritage Research Department Rep. Ser. 30/2010

Lyman, R. L. 1996. *Vertebrate Taphonomy*, Cambridge Manuals in Archaeology, CUP, Cambridge

McCarthy, M R. and Brooks, C. M. 1988. *Medieval Pottery in Britain AD900-1600*, Leicester Univ. Press, Leicester

McCoy, M. 2008. *An Archaeological Evaluation by Monitored Topsoil Strip and Targeted Trial Excavation at Catwick Quarry, East Riding of Yorkshire*, ARCUS, unpublished, rep. 2111.1(1)

MacGregor A 1985, *Bone, Antler, Ivory and Horn, the Technology of Skeletal Materials since the Roman Period*, Croom Helm, London

MacGregor, A. 2000. 'A seventh-century pectoral cross from Holderness, East Yorkshire', *Medieval Archaeology* 44, 217-222

MacGregor, A. and Bolick, E. 1993. *A Summary Catalogue of the Anglo-Saxon Collections (Non-ferrous metals)*, Ashmolean Museum and Tempus Reparatum, B.A.R. Brit Ser., 230, Oxford

MacGregor, M. 1976. *Early Celtic Art in North Britain, a Study of Decorative Metalwork from Third Century BC to the Third Century AD*, Leicester Univ. Press, Leicester

Macinnes, L. 1989. 'Baubles, bangles and beads: trade and exchange in Roman Scotland', in Barrett, J. C., Fitzpatrick, A. P. and Macinnes, L. (eds) *Barbarians and Romans in North-West Europe from the Later Republic to Late Antiquity*. B.A.R. Int Ser. 471, Oxford, 108-16

Mackenzie, R. 2010. *Archaeometallurgical assessment of production process residues*, in Flintoft and Glover 2010

Mackey, R. 1998. 'A round barrow at Easington: a summary report of the 1996 excavation', *Yorks Archaeol. Soc. Prehist, Res. Sect. Bull.* 35, 1-5

Mackey, R. 2003. 'The Iron Age in EastYorkshire: a summary of current knowledge and recommendations for future research', in Manby, Moorhouse and Ottaway 2003

McKinley, J.I. 1994. 'Bone fragment size in British cremation burials and its implications for pyre technology and ritual', *J. Archaeol. Science* 21: 339-342

Mainland, I. L. 2006. 'The Mammal and Bird Bone', in Millett 2006

Mainman, A. 1990. 'Anglo-Scandinavian Pottery from Coppergate', *The Archaeology of York: the pottery, 16/5*, CBA Research Rep, London

Mainman, A. 1997. 'The Pottery' in 'Excavations in Deanery Gardens and Low St Agnesgate, Ripon, North Yorkshire', *Yorks Archaeol. J.* 69

Manby, T. G. 1966. 'A Creswellian site at Brigham, East Yorkshire'. *Antiquaries Journal*, 46

Manby, T. G. 1980. 'Bronze Age Settlement in Eastern Yorkshire', in J. Barrett and R.Bradley (eds.), *Settlement and Society in the British Later Bronze Age*, 307-370, BAR Brit. Ser. 83, Oxford

Manby, T. G. 1988. 'The Neolithic in eastern Yorkshire' in T. G.Manby (ed.). *Archaeology in Eastern Yorkshire. Essays in honour of T. C. M. Brewster*, Sheffield, 35-88

Manby, T. G. 2004. 'Food Vessels with handles', in A. Gibson and A.Sheridan (eds), *From Sickles to circles: Britain and Ireland at the time of Stonehenge* 215-42, Tempus, Stroud

Manby, T. G. 2013. 'Easington Wetland Excavation: The Prehistoric Pottery', unpublished report for West Yorkshire Archaeological Services

Manby, T. G., King, A., and Vyner, B. E. 2003. 'The Neolithic and Bronze Age: A Time of Early Agriculture', in Manby, Moorhouse and Ottaway 2003, 35-116

Manby, T. G., Moorhouse, P. and Ottaway, P. 2003. *The Archaeology of Yorkshire: An assessment of the beginning of the 21ˢᵗ century*, Yorks Archaeol. Soc. Occasional Paper 3

Mann, R.W. and Murphy, S.P. 1990. *Regional Atlas of Bone Disease: a Guide to Pathologic and Normal Variation in the Human Skeleton*, Charles C. Thomas, Illinois

Matson, F. R. 1971. 'A study of temperatures used in firing ancient Mesopotamian pottery' in R. Brill (ed.) *Science in Archaeology*, 65-99, MIT Press, Cambridge, Mass.

May, J. 1976. *Prehistoric Lincolnshire*, History of Lincolnshire Committee, Lincoln

May, J. 1996. *Dragonby. Report on Excavations at an Iron Age and Romano-British Settlement in North Lincolnshire*, Oxbow Monograph 61

Mays, S. A. 2005. 'Paleo-pathological study of hallux valgus' *American Journal of Physical Anthropology* 130, 190-200

Mellars, P. 1976. 'Settlement patterns and industrial variability in the British Mesolithic' in G. d. G. Sieveking, I. H. Longworth, K. E. Wilson and G. Clark, *Problems in economic and social archaeology*, 375-399, Duckworth, London

Merrifield, R. 1987. *The Archaeology of Ritual and Magic*, Batsford, London

Merrony, C. 2007. *Archaeological survey at Sproatley, East Yorkshire*, unpublished report by University of Sheffield, for Sandsfield Quarries Ltd

Metcalfe, S. E., Ellis, S., Horton, B. P., Innes, J. B., McArthur, J. J., Mitlehner, A., Parkes, A., Pethick, J. S., Rees, J., Ridgway, J., Rutherford, M. M., Shennan, I. and Tooley, M. J. 2000. 'The Holocene evolution of the Humber Estuary: reconstructing change in a dynamic environment', in I. Shennan (ed.), *Holocene land-ocean interaction and environmental change around the North Sea*, Geological Society Special Publication 166, 97-118

Middleton, R. 1995. 'Landuse in Holderness', in Van de Noort and Ellis 1995, 17-26

Millett, M. 1990. *The Romanization of Britain*, Cambridge Univ. Press

Millett, M. 2006. *Shiptonthorpe, East Yorkshire: Archaeological Studies of a Romano-British Roadside Settlement*, Yorkshire Archaeological Reports 5

Monaghan, J. 1997. 'Roman pottery from York' in P. V. Addyman (ed.) The archaeology of York, fasc. 16/8, CBA, for York Archaeological Trust

Moore, D. T. 1978. 'The Petrography and Archaeology of English Honestones', *J. Archaeol. Science* 5, 61-73

Moore, P. and Webb, J. 1978. *An illustrated guide to pollen analysis*, Hodder & Stoughton, London

Moore, P., Webb, J. and Collinson, M. 1991. *Pollen Analysis*, Blackwell, Oxford

Morris, E. 1994. 'Production and distribution of pottery and salt in Iron Age Britain: a review', *Proc. Prehist. Soc.* 60; 371-393

Morris, E. 1996. 'Iron Age artefact production and exchange' in T. C. Champion and J. R. Collis (eds.),

The Iron Age in Britain and Ireland: Recent trends, 41-66, University of Sheffield

Morris, E. L. 2001. 'Briquetage' in T. Lane and E.L Morris (eds), 33-63 and 351-375

Morris, E. L., and Percival, S. 2001 'Briquetage' in Lane and Morris 2001, 323-41

Morris, E. L. 2011. 'The Briquetage' in Richardson 2011, 95-100

Mortimer, J. R. 1905. *Forty Years Researches in British and Saxon Burial Mounds of East Yorkshire*. A. Brown and Sons, London

Murphy, P. L. and Wiltshire P. E. J. 1994. 'A Proposed Scheme for Evaluating Plant Macrofossil Preservation in some Archaeological Deposits', *Circaea* 11, 1

Murray, D. and Ralston, I. 1997. 'The excavation of a square ditched barrow and other cropmarks at Boysack Mills, Inverkeilor, Angus', *Proc. Soc. Antiquaries of Scotland* 127, 359-386

NAA Heritage Consultants. http://northernarchaeologicalassociates.co.uk/profile/23-WGS.htm

Nailor, V. and Young, J. 2001. *A fabric type-series for post-Roman pottery from Nottingham City (5th to 16th centuries)*, unpublished report for Nottingham City Museum

Neave, S. 1991. *Medieval parks of East Yorkshire*, Hutton Press, Beverley

Needham, S. 1996. 'Chronology and Periodisation in the British Bronze Age', in K. Randsborg (ed.) 'Absolute Chronology: Archaeological Europe 2500-500 BC', *Acta Archaeol.* 67, 121-140, Copenhagen

Needham, S. 2005. 'Transforming Beaker Culture in North-West Europe; Processes of Fusion and Fission', *Proc. Prehist. Soc.* 71. 171-217

Needham, S. 2012. 'Case and Place for the British Chalcolithic', in M. J. Allen, J. Gardener and A. Sheridan (eds.), *Is there a British Chalcolithic?: People, place and polity in the late 3rd millennium*, Prehistoric Society Research Paper 4, Oxbow, Oxford

Nevell, M. and Redhead, N. 2005. *Mellor: Living on the edge*, Manchester Archaeological Monographs 1

North, J. J. 1963. *English Hammered Coinage*, Spink, London

Oliver, G. 1829. *The History and Antiquities of the Town and Minster of Beverley*, M. Turner: Hull

Onhuma, K. and Bergman, C. A. 1982. 'Experimental studies in the determination of flake mode', *Bull. Ins. Archaeol. London* 19, 161-171

Ortner, D. J. 2003. *Identification of Palaeopathological Disorders in Human Skeletal Remains*, Academic Press, Amsterdam

Ortner, D .J. and Putschar, W. G. J. 1985. *Identification of Pathological Conditions in Human Skeletal Remains*, Smithsonian Institute, Washington DC

Osgood, R. 1998. *Warfare in the Late Bronze Age of North Europe*, B.A.R. lnt. Ser. 694

Parker Pearson, M. 2003. 'The Roman Whetstones' in N. Field and M. Parker Pearson, *Fiskerton, An Iron Age*

Timber Causeway with Iron Age and Roman Votive Offerings: the 1981 Excavations, 120-124, Oxbow Books

Peacock, D. P. S. 1977. *Pottery and early commerce*, Seminar Press, London

Peacock, D. P. S. 1982. *Pottery in the Roman world: an ethnoarchaeological approach*. Longmans, London

Perrin, J. R. 1999. 'Roman Pottery from Excavations at and near to the Roman Small Town of Durobrivae, Water Newton, Cambridgeshire, 1956-5', *Journal of Roman Pottery Studies* 8

Perrin, J. R. and Hartley, K. F. 1996. 'The mortaria' in Mackreth, D. F. *Orton Hall Farm: a Roman and early Anglo-Saxon farmstead*, East Anglian Archaeol. 76, 191–204

Ponsford, M. W. 1992. 'A late Iron Age and Romano-British settlement at Rampton, Nottinghamshire', *Trans. Thoroton Soc.* 96, 91-121

Pope, R. 2003. *Prehistoric Dwelling: Circular Structures in North and Central Britain* c 2500 BC – AD 500, unpublished PhD thesis, University of Durham

PAS. Portable Antiquities Scheme, website. www.finds.org.uk

Poulsen, G. 1841. *The History and Antiquities of the Seigniory of Holderness*, T. Topping. London

Powlesland, D. with Haughton, C. and Hanson, J. 1986. 'Excavations at Heslerton, North Yorkshire 1978-82', *Archaeol. J.* 143, 53-173, and micro-fiche

PCRG. 2011. *The Study of Later Prehistoric Pottery: General Polices and Guidelines for Analysis and Publication*, Prehistoric Ceramics Research Group Occasional Papers 1 and 2, revised 3rd edition

Price, J. 1988. 'Romano-British glass bangles from East Yorkshire', in Price, J. and Wilson, P. R. (eds), *Recent Research in Roman Yorkshire*, B.A.R. Brit. Ser. 193, Oxford, 339-66

Prummel, W. and Frisch, H.-J. 1986. 'A Guide for the distinction of species, sex and body size in bones of sheep and goat', *J. Archaeol. Science* XIII, 567–77

Quinn, J. D., Philip, L. K. and Murphy, W. 2009. 'Understanding the recession of the Holderness Coast, East Yorkshire, UK: a new presentation of temporal and spatial patterns', *Quarterly Journal of Engineering Geology and Hydrogeology*, 42:165-178

Rackham, J. 2010. 'Environmental samples from Plot 26 flint scatters' in Flintoft and Glover 2010

Radley, J. and Mellars, P. 1964. 'A Mesolithic structure at Deepcar, Yorkshire, England, and the affinities of its associated flint industry', *Proc. Prehist. Soc.* 30, 1-24

Rees, H., Crummy, N. and Dunn, G. 2008. *Artefacts and Society in Roman and Medieval Winchester, Small Finds from the Suburbs and Defences, 1971-1986*, Winchester Museum, Winchester

Reid, C. 1913. *Submerged Forests*, Cambridge Univ. Press

Reynier, M. J. 1998. 'Early Mesolithic settlement in England and Wales: some preliminary observations' in N. Ashton, F. Healy and P. Pettitt, *Stone Age Archaeology: Essays in Honour of John Wymer*, 174-184, Oxbow Monograph 102, Oxford

Reynolds, P. J. 1979. *Iron-Age Farm: the Butser Experiment*, British Museum, London

Rhodes, M. 1986. 'Stone Objects', in T Dyson (ed), *The Roman Quay at St Magnus House, London. Excavations at New Fresh Wharf, Lower Thames Street, London 1974-78*, 240-3, Museum of London and Middlesex Archaeol. Soc.

Richardson, J. 2011. 'Bronze Age cremations, Iron Age and Roman settlement and early medieval inhumations at the Langeled Receiving Facilities, Easington, East Riding of Yorkshire', *Yorks Archaeol. J.*, 83

Rigby, V. 1980. 'Coarse pottery' in I. M. Stead (ed.), *Rudston Roman villa*, Yorkshire Archaeological Society

Rigby, V. 2004. *Pots in Pits: The British Museum Yorkshire settlements project 1988-92*, East Riding Archaeologist 11

Rigby, V. and Stead, I. M. 1976. 'Coarse Pottery', in Stead 1976, 136-190

Riley, D. N. 1957. 'Neolithic and Bronze Age Pottery from Risby Warren and other occupation sites in North Lincolnshire', *Proc. Prehist. Soc.* 23, 40-56

Robbins, G. 1999. 'Research and regionality: South Yorkshire as an example', in: Bevan 1999b, 123-148

Roberts, C. A. and Cox, M. 2003. *Health and Disease in Britain from Prehistory to the Present Day*, Sutton Publishing, Stroud

Roberts, C.A. and Manchester, K. 2005. *The Archaeology of Disease*, Sutton Publishing, Stroud

Roberts, I. 2003. *Excavations at Topham Farm, Sykehouse, South Yorkshire*, Archaeological Services WYAS Publications, Leeds

Roberts, I. (ed.) 2005. *The Iron Age settlement at Ledston: a report on the excavations of 1976 and 1996*, Archaeological Services WYAS Publications, Leeds

Roberts, I. and Cumberpatch, C. 2009. 'A Stamford Ware Pottery Kiln in Pontefract', *Medieval Archaeol.* 53, 45-50

Robinson, F. N. (ed.) 1974. *The complete works of Geoffrey Chaucer*, OUP, Oxford

Rogers, G. B. 1974. *Poteries Sigillées de la Gaule Centrale I: les motifs non figurés*, Gallia Supplement 28

Rowland, S. and Wegiel, R. 2012. *Easington to Paull Natural Gas Pipeline, East Yorkshire: Post-Excavation Assessment of Archaeological Fieldwork Results*, Oxford Archaeology North report, unpublished

Rush, P., Dickinson, B., Hartley, B. and Hartley, K. F. 2000. *Roman Castleford: Excavations 1974-85 Volume III: the Pottery*, West Yorkshire Archaeological Services, Leeds

Rye, O. 1981. *Pottery Technology:Principles and Reconstruction, Manuals in Archaeol.* 4, Taraxacum, Washington D.C.

Saville, A. 1980. 'On the measurement of struck flakes and flake tools', *Lithics* 1, 16-20

Savage, R. 2011. *Easington to Ganstead Proposed Gas Pipeline: Archaeological Trench Evaluation.* Network Archaeology rep. 538, unpublished

Savage, R. 2014. 'Salt End to Aldbrough: the archaeology of a high-voltage electricity cable route', *East Riding Archaeologist* 14, 65-104

Selling, D. 1955. *Wikingerzeitliche und Frühmittelalterliche Keramik in Schweden,* Pettersons, Stockholm

Serjeantson, D. 1996. 'The Animal Bones, in E. S. Needham and T. Spence (eds.), *Refuse and Disposal at Area 16, East Runnymede: Runnymede Bridge Research Excavations*, Vol. 2, British Museum Press, London

Shaffrey, R. 2009. 'The Other Worked Stone', in C. Howard-Davis (ed), *The Carlisle Millennium Project: Excavations in the Roman fort and medieval castle at Carlisle, 1998-2001, Vol. 2, Finds*, 873-887, Lancaster Imprints 15

Shaffrey, R. 2011. 'The Worked stone' in Daniel *et al.* forthcoming

Shaw, P. and O'Meara, D. 2010. 'An assessment of the plant macrofossils and other organic remains' in Flintoft and Glover 2010

Shepherd, W. 1972. *Flint: its origin, properties and uses,* Faber, London

Sheppard, J. A. 1956. *The Draining of the Marshlands of East Yorkshire*, PhD Thesis, Univ. of Hull

Sheppard, J. A. 1957. 'The Medieval meres of Holderness', *Transactions of the Institute of British Geographers,* 23, 75-86

Sheppard, J. A. 1966. *The Draining of the Marshlands of East Yorkshire*, East Yorks Local History Soc, Hull

Sheppard, T. 1912. *The lost towns of the Yorkshire Coast*, Brown and Sons, London and Hull

Sheppard, T. 1922. 'The Romans in East Yorkshire', *Handbook to Hull and the East Riding of Yorkshire*, Brown and Sons, London and Hull, 201-213

Silver, I. A. 1969. 'The Ageing of Domestic Animals', in D. Brothwell and E. S. Higgs, *Science in Archaeology*, Thames and Hudson, London

Sitch, B. 1989. 'A Small Roman port at Faxfleet near Broomfleet', in P.Halkon (ed.) *New Light on the Parisi: Recent discoveries in Iron Age and Roman East Yorkshire*, ERAS, Hull, 10-14

Sitch, B. and Jacobi, R. 1999. 'The Great Holderness Harpoon Controversy', *Yorks Archaeol. J.* 71

SKEALS. no date. *An Archaeological Excavation at Easington: Easington, Round Barrow* and *Neolithic Settlement (Ta 4087/180)* Spurn, Kilnsea and Easington Area Local Studies Group [online] http://www.skeals.co.uk/Articles/Archaeological%20Excavation.html [accessed 3rd August 2010]

Slowikowski, A. M., Nenk, B. and Pearce, J. 2001. *Minimum standards for the processing, recording, analysis and publication of post-Roman ceramics,*

Occasional paper 2, London: Medieval Pottery Research Group

Smith, A. H. 1995. 'A late Iron Age Settlement in the Winestead Drain (Holderness)', in *First annual report of the Humber Wetlands Survey*, Hull, Univ. of Hull

Smith, R. 1911. 'Lake-dwellings in Holderness', *Yorkshire Archaeologia* 62, 593-610

SSEW 1983. *Legend for the 1:250,000 Soil Map of England and Wales,* Soil Survey of England and Wales

Spikins, P. 1999. *Mesolithic Northern England: environment, population and settlement,* Archaeopress, London

Spratling, M. G., 1979. 'The Debris of Metalworking' in G .J. Wainwright, *Gussage All Saints: An Iron Age Settlement in Dorset*, DoE. Archaeol. Reports 10, HMSO, London

Stace, C. 2010. *New Flora of the British Isles* (3rd edn), CUP, Cambridge

Stanfield, J. A. and Simpson, G. 1958. *Central Gaulish Potters*, OUP, Oxford

Stead, I. M. 1976. *Excavations at Winterton Roman Villa and other Roman Sites in North Lincolnshire*, Department of the Environment Archaeological Report 9, HMSO, London

Stead, I. M. 1979. *The Arras Culture*, Yorkshire Philosophical Society, York

Stead, I. M. 1980. *Rudston Roman Villa*, Yorkshire Philosophical Society, York

Stead, I. M. 1981. *The Gauls: Celtic Antiquities from France*, British Museum Press, London

Stead, I. M. 1984. 'Some notes on imported metalwork in Iron Age Britain', in S. Macready and F. H. Thompson (eds), *Cross-Channel Trade between Gaul and Britain in the Pre-Roman Iron Age*, 43–66. London Society of Antiquaries of London Occasional Paper 4

Stead, I. M. 1986. 'A group of Iron Age barrows at Cowlam, North Humberside', *Yorks. Archaeol. J.* 58, 5-15

Stead, I. M. 1991. *Iron Age cemeteries in East Yorkshire*, English Heritage, London

Steedman, K. 1993. *Excavations on the route of the Leven -Brandesburton Bypass: An interim report*, Humber Archaeology Unit report, unpublished

Stevenson, J. 2012. 'Swords, Settlement and Sacred Places: The Archaeology of Brisley Farm, Ashford, Kent', *Archaeology International*, DOI: http://dx.doi.org/10.5334/ai.1507

Stoetz, C. 1997. *Ancient Landscapes of the Yorkshire Wolds, Aerial Photographic Transcription and Analysis*, RCHME, Swindon

Sugita, S. 1991. 'Pollen Representation of Vegetation in Quaternary Sediments: Theory and Method in Patchy Vegetation', *Journal of Ecology*, 82, 881-797

Sumpter, A. B. 1990. 'Iron Age pottery' and 'Pottery from Well 1', in Wrathmell and Nicholson 1990, 128-130, 235-245

Swan, V. G., 1992. 'Legio VI and its men: African legionaries in Britain', *Journal of Roman Pottery Studies* 5, 1-33

Swan, V. G. 1996. 'The dating and wider context of the pottery from kiln 5', in May 1996, 577-9

Swan, V. G. 2002. 'The Roman Pottery of Yorkshire in its Wider Historical Context', in Wilson and Price 2002, 35-79

Swan, V. G. 2009. *Ethnicity, Conquest and recruitment: two case studies from the northern military provinces*, J. Rom. Arch. Supplementary Series 72, 15-95

Symonds, R. P. and Wade, S. 1999. *Roman Pottery from Excavations in Colchester, 1971-86*, Colchester Archaeological Reports 10, Colchester

Tait, J. 1965. *Beakers from Northumberland*, Oriel Press, Newcastle-upon-Tyne

Taylor, D. 1995. *New pollen data from the Keyingham valley, southern Holderness*, in Van de Noort and Ellis 1995, 121-127

Thomas, J. 2008. *Monument, Memory, and Myth: Use and Re-use of Three Bronze Age Round Barrows at Cossington, Leicestershire*, Leicester Archaeol. Monograph 14, Leicester

Tibbles, J. 2008. 'Notes on the Romano-British Tile from the Easington to Paull', in Allen 2008, 52

Todd, M. 1968. '*Trent Valley ware*: A Roman coarse ware of the middle and lower Trent Valley', *Trans. Thoroton Soc.* 72, 38-41

Tomber, R. and Dore, J. 1998. *The National Roman Fabric Reference Collection: A Handbook*, MoLAS Monograph 2, London

Topping, P. 2011. *Introductions to Heritage Assets: Burnt Mounds*, English Heritage

Tuffreau-Libre, M. 1992. *La Céramique Commune Gallo-Romaine dans le Nord de la France*, Errance, Paris

Tyers, P. 1996. *Roman Pottery in Britain*, Batsford, London

Van de Noort, R. 2004. *The Humber Wetlands: The Archaeology of a Dynamic Landscape*, Windgather Press, Macclesfield

Van de Noort, R. and Davies, P. 1993. *Wetland Heritage, an archaeological assessment of the Humber wetlands*, in Ellis 1993

Van de Noort, R. and Ellis, S. (eds.) 1995. *Wetland Heritage of Holderness: an archaeological survey*, Humber Wetlands Project, Univ. of Hull

Vince, A. 2006. *The Roman Ceramic Building Material from Archaeological Excavations along the A16/A158 Partney By-Pass*, unpublished report AVAC 2006/7

Vince, A. and Irving, A. 2011. 'The Ceramic Building Material', in P. Cope-Faulkner, *Clampgate Road, Fishtoft: Archaeology of a Middle Saxon Island Settlement in the Lincolnshire Fens*, Lincolnshire Archaeology and Heritage Rep. Ser. 10

Vince, A. G. and Steane, K. 2005. *The Humberware Pottery from Blue Bridge Lane, Fishergate,*

York, unpublished report, online: http://www.archaeologicalplanningconsultancy.co.uk/mono/index.php, accessed 21/313

Vince, A. and Steane, K. 2006. *The Roman Ceramic Building Material from Archaeological Excavations along the A16/A158 Partney By-Pass*, unpublished report AVAC 2006/49

Vince, A. and Steane, K. 2009. 'Ceramic building material, fired clay and stone' in Flintoft and Glover 2010

Vince, A. G. and Young, J. 2007. 'The Medieval and Post-medieval pottery', in F. Brown *et al.* 2007, 254-275

Wacher, J. 1969. 'Excavations at Brough-on-Humber, 1958-61', *Res. Rep. Soc Antiq. London* 25

Wastling L. M. 2009. 'Structural fired clay or daub' in D.H. Evans and C. Loveluck, *Life and Economy at Early Medieval Flixborough c. AD 600-1000: The Artefact Evidence*, Excavations at Flixborough Vol. 2, 154-59, Oxbow, Oxford

Watkins, J. G. 1987. 'The Pottery', in P. Armstrong, and B. S. Ayres, 'Excavations in Blackfriargate and High Street', *East Riding Archaeol.* 8 (Hull Old Town Report Series 5), 1987, 53-181

Watkins, J. G., 1991. 'The pottery' in Armstrong, Tomlinson and Evans 1991, 61-103

Watkins, J. G., 1993. 'The Pottery' in Evans, D. H. (ed.), 'Excavations in Hull 1975-76', *East Riding Archaeol.* 4 (Hull Old Town Report Series 2), 75-139

Wenham, L. P. 1960. 'Seven Archaeological Discoveries in Yorkshire', *Yorks. Archaeol. J.* 40, 298-328

Wenham, L. P. and Heywood, B. 1997. *The 1968 to 1970 Excavations in the vicus at Malton, North Yorkshire*, Yorkshire Archaeological Society, Leeds

White, S. D. 2009. *Easington to Ganstead gas pipeline: Clay Pipe Assessment*, in Flintoft and Glover 2010

Williams, D. 1973 'Flotation at Sīraf', *Antiquity*, 47, 198-202

Wild, J. P. 1970. 'Button and loop fasteners in the Roman Provinces', *Britannia*, 1, 137-55

Willis, S. 2007. *Sea, Coast, Estuary, Land and Culture in Iron Age Britain*, in Haselgrove and Moore 2007, 107-129

Wilson, P. R. (ed) 1989. *The Crambeck Roman pottery industry*, Yorkshire Archaeological Soc., Leeds

Wilson, P. and Price, J (eds.) 2002. *Aspects of Industry in Roman Yorkshire and the North*, Oxbow

Wilson, T. 2006. *Easington to Ganstead Proposed Gas Pipeline: archaeological reconnaissance, fieldwalking and geophysical survey*, Network Archaeology report no. 528, unpublished

Wilson, T. 2007. *Easington to Ganstead: proposed natural gas pipeline: archaeological reconnaissance, fieldwalking and geophysical survey, vol. 2*, Network Archaeology report no. 528/1, unpublished

Wilson, V. 1948. *British Regional Geology: East Yorkshire and Lincolnshire*. HMSO, London

Woodward, A. 2002. 'Inclusions, impressions and interpretation', in: A. Woodward and J.D. Hill *Prehistoric Britain: The ceramic basis*, Prehistoric

Ceramics Research Group Occasional Publication 3, Oxbow Books

Woodward, A. 2012. 'Discussion of the early to Middle Bronze Age pottery', in Finn 2012, 73-76

Woodward, A. and Blinkhorn, P. 1997. 'Size is important: Iron Age vessel capacities in central and southern England', in Cumberpatch and Blinkhorn 1997

Woodward, A., and Marsden, P. 2012. 'Early and Middle Bronze Age Pottery', in Finn 2012, 68-73

Wrathmell, A. and Nicholson, A. (eds.) 1990. *Dalton Parlours: Iron Age settlement and Roman villa* Yorkshire Archaeology 3, West Yorkshire Archaeology Service

Wright, E. M. 1996. 'Querns', in May 1996, 365-376

Wright, E. M. 2002. 'Querns and Millstones', in P. R. Wilson, *Cataractonium: Roman Catterick and its hinterland. Excavations and Research, 1958-1997, Part II*, CBA Research Rep. 129, 267-285

Wright, E. 2004. 'Worked Stone', in P. G. E. Neal and R. Fraser, 'A Romano-British enclosed farmstead at Billingey Drive, Thurnscoe, South Yorkshire', *Yorks. Archaeol. J.* 76, 54-58

Wymer, J. J. and Bonsall, C. J. 1977. *Gazetteer of Mesolithic sites in England and Wales with a gazetteer of Upper Palaeolithic sites in England and Wales*, CBA Research Rep. 20, London

Young, J. 2009. 'The Post-Roman Pottery' in Boyer, P., Proctor, J. and Taylor-Wilson, R. 2009, *On the Boundaries of Occupation: Excavations at Burringham Road, Scunthorpe and Baldwin Avenue, Bottesford, North Lincolnshire*, Pre-Construct Archaeology Monograph 9

Young, J. 2011. *The Post-Roman Pottery for 23 Clifford Street York*, unpublished report for Field Archaeology Specialists, York

Young, J. 2012. *The Post-Roman Pottery from The Dean's Building, Monks Road, Lincoln*, unpublished report for Allen Archaeology

Young, J. and Didsbury, P. forthcoming. 'The Post-Roman Pottery from Wetherby Castle'

Young, J. and Perry, G. 2011. *The pottery from Test Pitting at Torksey, Lincolnshire*, unpublished rep. for Sheffield University

Young, J. and Perry, G. forthcoming. *Torksey Ware Revisited*

Young, J. and Vince, A. 2009. 'The Anglo-Saxon Pottery' in Evans, D. H. and Loveluck, C. *Life and Economy at Early Medieval Flixborough, c AD 600-1000: The Artefact Evidence*, Excavations at Flixborough vol. 2, Oxbow, Oxford

Young, J., Vince, A. and Nailor, V. 2005. *A Corpus of Anglo-Saxon and Medieval Pottery from Lincoln*, Lincoln Archaeological Studies 7, Oxbow, Oxford

Zienkiewicz, J. D. 1986. *The Legionary Fortress Baths at Caerleon: II the Finds*, National Museum of Wales, Cardiff